A COTTON MATHER READER

A COTTON MATHER READER

Edited and with an Introduction
by Reiner Smolinski and Kenneth P. Minkema

Yale
UNIVERSITY
PRESS
New Haven & London

Published with assistance from the Annie Burr Lewis Fund.

Yale University Press books may be purchased in quantity for educational,
business, or promotional use. For information, please e-mail sales.press@yale.edu
(U.S. office) or sales@yaleup.co.uk (U.K. office).

Set in PostScript Electra and Trajan types by Westchester Publishing Services.

.

Library of Congress Control Number: 2021940603
ISBN 978-0-300-22997-4 (hardcover)
ISBN 978-0-300-26018-2 (paper : alk. paper)

A catalogue record for this book is available from the British Library.

CONTENTS

ACKNOWLEDGMENTS

The editors would like to thank Griffin Black and Andy Juchno of Yale Divinity School for their invaluable assistance in identifying potential selections from Mather's large corpus. Harry S. Stout and Jan Stievermann provided helpful suggestions on the introduction and selections. A special note of thanks to the two anonymous reviewers of our manuscript for their valuable comments and suggestions. Cotton Mather's autobiography "Paterna" is part of the Special Collections, Tracy W. McGregor Library of American History, Albert and Shirley Small Special Collections Library, University of Virginia, Charlottesville. We wish to thank Anne Causey, reference librarian of special collections, for her extraordinary helpfulness in making images of this document available, and the University of Virginia for permission to transcribe and publish our excerpts from the holograph manuscript. Furthermore, we wish to thank Hanna Elder, Massachusetts Historical Society reproductions coordinator, for her kind help, and the Massachusetts Historical Society for permission to reproduce the first page of "Exodus, chap. 1," from Cotton Mather's *Biblia Americana* manuscript in the Mather Family Collection. The American Antiquarian Society graciously allowed us to transcribe and publish excerpts from "The Angel of Bethesda." Jennifer Banks at Yale University Press was a faithful shepherd of this book from start to finish, and Susan Laity and Margaret Hogan expertly took it through the production phase.

Note on the Text

We have made an effort here to preserve as many features as possible of Mather's unique writing style and the way it was rendered in print, including the as-yet-unsettled variations in spelling, diction, and punctuation that characterized early modern English writing. Modern readers will also notice the inordinate number of italicized, capitalized, and even boldfaced words and passages; these different sorts of type and font suggest emphasis in oral delivery and visual, thematic links in printed homiletic discourse. Mather was a linguistic genius who could speak and write in seven languages, and this skill is on display in the many quotations in Latin, Greek, and Hebrew with which his texts are studded. While these doses of classical languages may strike us today as pretentious, Mather's target audience—all college-trained theologians—was fully conversant in these "dead" languages, and for them classical citations added authenticity. If Mather does not give his translations in his text, we have supplied them in the notes. Identities of lesser-known authors and works to which Mather refers, as well as explanations of historical or biographical references, are also to be found in the notes. To enclose his own references, insertions, and asides, Mather used parentheses ( ) and square brackets [ ], which are retained. Thus, textual interpolations by the editors of this volume, usually to provide biblical references but occasionally to insert a missing word, are enclosed in braces { }. (Square brackets are used to indicate titles the editors supplied.) Ellipses (. . .) indicate an omitted passage or that a text continues where we have chosen to end an excerpt. In *Psalterium Americanum*, Mather uses double vertical lines (||) to signal the end of each verse in Psalms XXIII and CXXXVII. Finally, Mather's occasional use of the letter *ß* (like the Greek *beta*) to signal a doubled *ss* in words like *Holineß* is here regularized as *ss*. Thus, *Holiness*.

Editors' Introduction

He was perhaps the *principal Ornament* of his
Country, and the *greatest Scholar* that was ever bred in it.
—*New-England Weekly Journal*, February 19, 1728

As one of colonial America's most controversial figures, Cotton Mather (1663–1728) is well known to scholars of early American religion, history, and literature, even as popular culture is disposed to demonize him or sometimes writes him out of existence. Today, if students have heard about him at all, he is mostly associated with Salem witchcraft. Yet his life and writings helped shape one of the most powerful and influential societies in early America.

As a distinguished Puritan theologian, historian, and natural philosopher of science and medicine, Mather was a pivotal figure in the transformation of Boston from the Puritan "Theopolis Americana" into the mercantile capital of the British Empire in North America. As a self-help advocate and advisor to several governors and magistrates, he promoted the introduction of paper money when Massachusetts could no longer foot its bills with its own illegitimately minted silver coin, the Pine Tree shilling. He sponsored female education; funded a free school for Blacks and Native Americans; and persuaded Elihu Yale, a wealthy New England–born merchant and board member of the East India Company, to endow a new college in New Haven, which bears his name. When a smallpox epidemic killed Bostonians by the hundreds, Mather rose in opposition to the medical establishment and introduced a new prophylactic method of inoculation (a precursor to vaccination) that saved the lives of nearly two hundred people. He corresponded with hundreds of leading figures on three continents— even as far away as southern India. As a fervent Pietist, he sought to overcome sectarian divisions by uniting all Protestant churches in America and Europe on the basis of three doctrinal principles. More than anyone else in his circle, Cotton Mather embodied the Enlightenment philosophy of his age in which old-time religion, ecumenical relations, and religious revivals went hand in hand with scientific discoveries and the emergence of a transatlantic capitalist economy that transformed Boston, a nearly autonomous city-state, into the second most important metropolis in the British Empire in the early eighteenth century.[1]

Historians and biographers have begun to rediscover Cotton Mather as a quintessential American thinker in Britain's transatlantic empire. More than ten book-length biographies and dozens of doctoral dissertations on Mather have appeared since the end of the nineteenth century. He is the focus of hundreds of academic essays; he has made appearances in classic American fiction, poetry, and drama; and he has taken center stage in plays, comic strips, cartoons, and even made-for-cable television productions. Given Mather's wide presence in American culture and the longtime scholarly interest in him— interest that is increasing as more of his previously unpublished writings are made available—it is time to reappraise his achievement in light of his huge body of published and unpublished works. Doing so gives us the *real* Cotton Mather in his own words: the man behind the caricature his nineteenth-century critics made of him, the thinker, writer, preacher, scientist, moralist, and Christian philosopher. He was the foremost scholar and innovative thinker of his generation in New England.

A SHORT SKETCH OF COTTON MATHER'S LIFE

When young Cotton Mather, not quite sixteen, took his first degree at Harvard in 1678, college president Urian Oakes singled him out as the valedictorian of a handful of fellow graduates: "COTTONUS MATHERUS," he intoned in his Latin commencement address, "*Quantum Nomen!*" What a Name! But apologizing for his witty mistake, Oakes resumed, "*quanta Nomina!*" What Names! In young Cotton Mather, the patronymics of his grandfathers, Richard Mather (1596–1669) and John Cotton (1585–1652), coalesced, Oakes declared, and the spirit of the Bay Colony's two most distinguished architects would revive to new glory. No telling if President Oakes knew more than his well-meaning panegyric let on at the time, for in terms of clerical descendants, his forecast for the Mather dynasty and its influence came true beyond measure. The male line of Richard Mather's progeny born before the American Revolution

The Reverend Cotton Mather, D.D., F.R.S. (1663–1728), by Peter Pelham.
The Metropolitan Museum of Art, New York, bequest of
Charles Allen Munn, 1924 (www.metmuseum.org)

included no less than fourteen clergymen; his female descendants bore yet another twenty-one ministers.[2]

The most influential and distinguished members of this remarkable family are Increase Mather (1639–1723) and his son Cotton. Together, they swayed public opinion from their Boston North End pulpit for more than seventy years. Measured in terms of their combined publication record alone, father and son published more than six hundred books, dissertations, sermons, tracts, and essays on virtually every aspect of theology, history, ecclesiology, and the natural sciences. At their deaths, they left behind a cache of manuscripts equal in size and number to their printed output—enough theology to keep Boston's printers and booksellers busy for years on end.[3]

The eldest son of Reverend Increase Mather and Maria Cotton Mather (1642–1714), Cotton Mather was born in his maternal grandfather's old homestead on "Cotton Hill" in Boston on February 12, 1663, a stone's throw away from what would become the site of the Old State House. As a precocious boy fluent in Latin and Greek, and possessing the rudiments of Hebrew, he was admitted to Harvard at age twelve; took his first baccalaureate degree at fifteen, and his master's degree at eighteen, in 1681. He received an honorary doctorate in divinity from the University of Glasgow, Scotland, in 1710, and in 1713 was elected a fellow of one of the most distinguished scientific bodies in the world, the Royal Society of London. His correspondence spanned three continents and included more than one hundred intellectual movers and shakers in England, Scotland, Ireland, the Low Countries, France, Germany, the West and East Indies—even Lutheran missionaries among the Tamils in faraway Tranquebar, in southeastern India.[4]

Cotton Mather was ordained at his father's North Meeting House, the Second Church, Congregational, in 1685. For forty-two years, he served as pastor of more than 1,500 parishioners, perhaps the largest congregation in all of English America at the time. In 1686, he married Abigail Phillips (1670–1702), the fifteen-year-old daughter of a well-to-do Charlestown merchant and politician; she bore him nine children. By all accounts, their marriage was very happy. A year after her death from breast cancer, Mather married the widow Elizabeth Clark Hubbard (1675–1713); she bore him six children before a measles epidemic took her and three of her youngest children in a single week.

Mather's third wife, whom he married in 1715, was Lydia Lee George (d. 1734), the widow of an affluent Boston merchant, John George, part owner of Boston's Long Wharf. Mather's third marriage was ill-fated if not disastrous. As Lydia's new husband and co-executor of her inherited estate, he also assumed the debts of the George estate, which turned out to be substantial. In the legal wrangling that dragged on for years, Lydia and Cotton went bankrupt—forfeiting all but the apple of his eye, his prized library of more than three thousand books and manuscripts. Whether Lydia was mentally ill or merely depressed by her unforeseen loss of fortune is debatable. If Cotton Mather's diary provides objective evidence, both were deeply unhappy. Their marriage remained childless. Of his fifteen children by his first two wives, five lived to adulthood and only one survived him. They, along with their father, are interred in the Mather family tomb his congregation purchased for them on Copp's Hill Burial Ground in Boston's North End.

With so much tragedy and pain in his family, what was Cotton Mather like as a person? By all accounts, he was a loving husband and warm and generous father to his children. His son Samuel reported that he would mention every one of them by name in his prayers, take each one of his children into his study to pray with them individually, and implore God to "*guide them* by his *Counsel* and bring them *to Glory.*" From their early childhood onward, he would teach them "delightful *Stories*" from the Bible. At dinner, he engaged them with charming lessons and tales and "let fall some *Sentence* or other, that might be monitory or profitable to them." In matters of good behavior, his son fondly remembered, Mather showed them how with sweetness of temper they could win over rowdy playmates, especially by returning "*good* Offices for *Evil* ones." He instilled in them "Principles of *Reason* and *Honour*" and the love of learning as "*the noblest Thing in the World.*" Instead of rewarding them with play and diversion for things done well, he would gratify them with some curious anecdote or other. If any of his children misbehaved, he would banish them from his presence or punish them by not allowing them "*to read, or to write, or to learn*" something. In this manner, he used positive reinforcement to let them see that it is "a *Privilege to be taught.*" And to punish children "with *Raving & Kicking & Scourging*" (all too common "in *Schools* as well as *Families*," Samuel noted), Cotton absolutely abhorred and spoke out in private and public against all forms of child abuse.[5]

To his visitors and friends, Reverend Thomas Prince (1687–1758) of Boston related, Mather was a gracious host and lively conversationalist, of "*quick Apprehension*, tenacious Memory, lively Fancy, ready Invention, unwearied Industry: of vast Improvements in Knowledge; and flaming Piety." And yet, in spite of his full schedule and countless activities, "He never seemed to be in a *Hurry*"— always available to everyone who came to him even in the most unseasonable hours of the day or night. He would entertain "with Ease & Pleasure, even in his Studying Hours." He was "gentle, free and courteous in his Treatment of all" who visited him, "agreeably temper'd with a various mixture of Wit and

Chearfulness." If differences of opinions arose in his circle of friends, he would handle them in the most agreeable and inoffensive manner. He did so by indirection, "*in the Form of a pleasant* Narrative, *which he had ready at hand for all Occasions*," leaving his friends to decide the matter for themselves.[6] For another Boston minister, Benjamin Colman (1673–1747), of the Brattle Street Church, Mather's genial conversation in private meetings

> discovered the vast compass of his Knowledge and the Projects of his Piety. . . . Here he excell'd, here he shone; being exceeding communicative, and bringing out of his *Treasury* things new & old, without measure. Here it was seen how his Wit, and Fancy, his Invention, his Quickness of thought, and ready Apprehension were all consecrated to God, as well as his Heart Will and Affections; and out of his Abundance within his *lips* overflow'd, *dropt as the honey-comb, fed* all that came near him, and were as the *choice silver*, for richness and brightness, pleasure and profit.[7]

In the pulpit, Mather was a fiery preacher but also a witty one, incredibly erudite, with the ability to draw on biblical, classical, and contemporary literature for anecdotes, thereby maintaining his listeners' attention. His flock, Prince remembered, "used to see his Spirits rais'd and all on Fire. . . . What a Son of Thunder to impenitent Sinners! What a Son of Consolation to discouraged Souls! What a passionate Pleader with all to come into the Acceptance of CHRIST."[8] Before George Whitefield, before itinerant preaching and camp meetings, there was Cotton Mather. When Mather filled a pulpit for a colleague, or went on one of his annual preaching tours to Salem, Ipswich, or Dedham, large crowds would throng the meetinghouses, and he would often preach more than one sermon on the same day to satisfy their demand. Wherever he went, Mather recorded in his diary, "the *Curiosity* and *Vanity* of the people discovers itself, in their *great Flocking* to hear mee; with no little Expectation." And yet, he was all too conscious of the snares such popularity might breed. He sought to humble himself before God, crying "from the Dust unto Him, that the *fond Expectation* of the *People*" might not rebound.[9]

If his family, friends, and admirers loved him as the embodiment of everything pious and noble about a New England pastor, his foes despised him as an execrable and meddlesome Puritan priest, a superannuated effigy of whatever was hateful and wrong with a theocratic colony in which Moses and Aaron made common cause. His enemies blamed him for callously sacrificing the lives of innocent people on the Salem scaffold, Quakers charged him with hypocrisy and bloody persecution, at least one royal governor sought to arrest him for treason, a scornful dropout of his North End church named his dog Cotton Mather, frightened Bostonians tried to assassinate him for allegedly spreading smallpox, and historians looking back in anger sought a villain to whose coattails they tied a tin can and let it bang and rattle through the pages of their histories.[10]

As Mather was in his pulpit, so in his politics: a passionate critic of the abuse of power and of the government's painful disregard for the ministry—often to his own detriment. A case in point was the installment of Sir Edmund Andros (1637–1714), James II's newly appointed governor, after the revocation of the First Charter of Massachusetts in 1684. Up to this point, the Bay Colony was able to elect its own governor, selectmen, and representatives; the charter enabled them to raise their own taxes, mint their own coinage, buy and sell land without prior approval from the crown, and establish citizenship and the franchise on the basis of membership in the Congregational Church. These uncommon privileges for the colony came to an abrupt stop when the charter was annulled, and James II's Anglican governor appointed to enforce the crown's law. Tension between Boston's old-order dissenting leaders and those who favored Andros's pro-royalist and pro–Church of England policies climaxed in 1688, when a small clandestine delegation, including Increase Mather, was sent to England to redress their grievances and appeal the loss of their rights and privileges anchored in the Massachusetts Charter.[11] Left at the helm of a huge congregation, Cotton Mather, then barely twenty-five, took over from his father the leading role among Andros's political opponents. On more than one occasion, Andros issued a warrant for his arrest for sedition. The Glorious Revolution in England, which had occurred in November 1688, resulted in the deposition of James II and the accession of William and Mary as Protestant coregents. When news arrived in Boston in April 1689, the leading citizens rose up, with young Cotton Mather at their head, against Governor Andros and his proxies. They imprisoned Andros and temporarily restored the cherished old charter with Simon Bradstreet as governor. To prevent a bloodbath, Mather's first biographer tells us, "the principal Gentlemen in *Boston* met with Mr. [Cotton] MATHER to consult what was best to be done" and tasked him to draft "The Declaration of the *Gentlemen*, *Merchants*, and *Inhabitants* of BOSTON, and the Countrey Adjacent." Mather himself read it before the Old Town-House on April 18, 1689, to the cheers of tumultuous crowds ready to hang Andros and his ilk. On the fateful day, however, "Mr. MATHER appeared . . . and reasoned down the Passions of the Populace." He "set himself both *publickly* & *privately* to hinder the Peoples proceeding any further than to reserve the Criminals for the Justice of the *English* Parliament."[12]

If the overthrow of Andros's government remained bloodless, another crisis, this time deadly, soon rocked New England: the devil loosed in Salem.[13] When

Increase Mather returned to Boston on May 14, 1692, with the new charter in
hand and Sir William Phips (1691–1695), the newly appointed governor, in tow,
prisons in Boston, Salem, and neighboring towns were jam-packed with women,
men, and children—all accused of witchcraft. To be sure, witchcraft was a capital crime in Old and New England until 1735, when Parliament finally repealed James I's Witchcraft Act of 1604. The new governor acted promptly and
appointed a Court of Oyer and Terminer. On June 10, the authorities executed
the first of twenty victims by hanging. Five days later, fourteen leading ministers, with Cotton Mather as principal author and secretary, issued "The Return
of Several Ministers Consulted," advising Phips and his councilors to disallow
the court's reliance on "spectral evidence" (ghosts, demons, and witches' familiars) visible only to the afflicted accusers. The devil and his minions might
impersonate innocent individuals, the clergy warned. The court remained un-
phased. By September 22, a total of fourteen women and five men had been
hanged on Gallows Hill in Salem; one man, Corey Giles, was pressed to death
for refusing to respond to the court's charges. By the time Governor Phips dissolved the court, fifty-five of the condemned witches escaped penalty by confessing, while another fifty or more committed to prison were reprieved and
their cases eventually dismissed.[14] In mid-October, Cotton Mather published
Wonders of the Invisible World, which presented his ambidextrous defense of
the court, caveats against spectral evidence, and extracts of the court records of
five of the most "notorious" cases. It proved to be Mather's most infamous work,
and the ignominy it gained determined to a great degree his unmerited reputation as an enabler of the executions. Even after witchcraft as a capital offense
had long been repealed, and the rise of Enlightenment philosophy had made
belief in the invisible world subject to ridicule, Mather's critics—rationalist
Unitarians combating the specter of orthodox hegemony and historians looking askance at the foibles of a bygone age—found ample munitions in Mather's
old book. His "Wonder Book," as his foes dubbed it mockingly, became synony-
mous with Cotton Mather, the hateful Puritan priest.

Perhaps an unexpected consequence of the Salem crisis for Mather's North
Church was the adoption of the so-called Halfway Covenant, thirty years after
a 1662 Synod had lowered the bar to church membership. In the New England
colonies founded by Puritan Congregationalists, birth into a given parish did
not determine church membership, infant baptism, and admission to the
Lord's Supper (as was the case in the Church of England). Rather, admission
was granted only after the minister and congregation carefully examined an ap-
plicant's behavior and, in most places, their narrative of religious experience.
Until the revocation of the old charter in 1684, church membership even gov-

erned freemanship, or citizenship, the right to vote, and eligibility for public office in Massachusetts. If anxiety-ridden conversion was more common to those Puritan colonists who had experienced persecution for their faith in old England, their offspring were more hard-pressed to replicate their parents' spiritual trauma. Although baptized, the succeeding generations frequently lacked this impetus and fewer and fewer attained full status. The Halfway Covenant granted baptism to a child if at least one of the parents was a full member. Ironically, ecclesial independency permitted each congregation to determine its own governing principles; many churches refused to accept the broadening of who was a visible saint and thereby a communicant. To them, this innovation watered down the purity of God's community. In fact, many parishioners were frightened that if they were unworthy of the Lord's Supper and yet partook of it nonetheless, they would judge themselves and forfeit their eternal salvation.[15]

The Mather church was one of a few in Massachusetts to hold out against the Halfway Covenant. In spite of Richard Mather's fervent defense of its adoption and of broadening the covenant, Increase Mather and a few leading members of his congregation resisted. Significantly, Cotton Mather—though dependent on his father's superior standing in the church and its conservative group of deacons—labored hard to change their minds.[16] Cotton's *Companion for Communicants* (1690) set out to accomplish just that: instead of warning applicants against false signs of regeneration, as was the custom, he argued that fear itself and a desire to come to the Lord's Table were signs of efficacious grace, that such people were *not* unregenerate and should therefore come forward to embrace the covenant and Christ's call. If the Salem crisis signaled that the devil had breached the defensive hedge around New England's churches, then the sacraments of baptism and the Lord's Supper were the best protection against evil. When matters came to a vote in the North End, Increase Mather finally relented. By the end of 1693, more than ninety new parishioners and their baptized children were admitted to church membership.[17]

Cotton Mather's involvement in these ecclesiastical issues highlights his primary callings as a pastor and preacher, the duties of which inspired his writings. Among the trove of documents of the Mather Family Papers at the Massachusetts Historical Society in Boston is a pocket-sized calendrical booklet containing the names and dates of church admissions, deaths, censures, and excommunications—all in Mather's own hand. It provides valuable insights into the goings on in the Second Church during the ministry of father and son. This document—especially when compared to the official record book of the North Church (1662–1728)—allows for several significant inferences about the changes the congregation went through during this sixty-year period. It indicates that Increase and Cotton Mather and their successors flung open the church gates much wider than is commonly assumed. Numerous peaks in the number of new admissions can be found in the years between 1668 and 1728, often concurrent with periods of political and social upheaval, particularly after the revocation of the old charter, the adoption of the Halfway Covenant in 1690, and the Salem debacle in 1691–92; during epidemics such as yellow fever in 1693, measles (1713), and smallpox (1721–22); as well as in the wake of repeated tremors and earthquakes that shook New England in 1727 and 1728. In terms of exercising church discipline, Cotton Mather labored intensely to bring errant members back into the fold. In fact, only the most recalcitrant and unrepentant were actually excommunicated, yet nothing stood in the way of their readmission, often occurring within weeks, months, even decades later.

Closely related to fostering this group dynamic were Cotton Mather's regular pastoral visits of his flock—generally from three to five families on Thursday afternoons. Mather has been credited with setting new standards for this pastoral practice.[18] His diary reveals that he commonly singled out specific families whom, duly informed ahead of time, he would visit, sound out their spiritual needs, offer prayer and comfort, and bestow on them printed copies of some of his many homilies on issues he deemed apropos for the occasion. Thus, families with young children might receive copies of one of Mather's many homilies on *Early Piety, Exemplified* (1689), *Early Religion, Urged* (1694), *The Duty of Children* (1703), or *Good Lessons for Children* (1706); adolescents might receive *Things that Young People should Think upon* (1700), *The Young Man Spoken to* (1712), or *Youth Advised* (1719); young women, mothers, and widows might receive his ever-popular book *Ornaments for the Daughters of Zion* (1692, 1694, 1741); disorderly families might receive copies of *Help for Distressed Parents* (1695), *A Family Well-Ordered* (1699), or *Family-Religion, Excited and Assisted* (1705); pregnant women lying in, his *Elizabeth in her Holy Retirement* (1710); the elderly, *Death made Easie & Happy* (1701) or *Death Approaching* (1714); those caring for the sick and dying during epidemics, his *Wholesome Words* (1713) or *A Pastoral Letter, to Families Visited with Sickness* (1702, 1713, 1721); the distressed or bereaved, *A Comforter of the Mourners* (1704) or *Marah spoken to* (1718); sailors or ship captains, *The Religious Marriner* (1700) or *The Sailours Companion and Counsellour* (1709); householders with servants and slaves, *A Good Master well Served* (1696); serious students of theology at Harvard, *Manuductio ad Ministerium* (1726); and wealthy merchants and leaders of the community, his influential *Bonifacius. An Essay Upon the Good, that is to be Devised and Designed* (1710). In short, Mather's pastoral output on nurturing his extended flock and the community at large could easily fill a shelf or two in any of

Boston's several bookshops. So popular were his sermons, self-help manuals, theological tracts, and public addresses that many went through several editions, often paid for by grateful parishioners or by Mather himself to replenish his stock to give away during his pastoral family visits.

Cotton Mather's nineteenth- and twentieth-century biographers have frequently looked askance at his more than four hundred published works and seen in them an obsessive-compulsive personality and a vain craving for recognition. However accurate, such psychologizing fails to consider that the printing press was the best available means at the time of reaching out to an audience in and beyond his immediate parish. Mather knew it and exploited the press in ways that few others in his time did. An example of Mather's method of maximizing a sermon's impact was his popular *Family-Religion, Excited and Assisted* (1705). "I printed a thousand of them," he recorded in his diary, packed them in bundles with a letter, and requested each recipient "to find out what *prayerless Families* there may be in the Town where he lives, and to lodge these Essayes of Piety in them." In this manner, he sent "a Bundle to every Town in all these Colonies, and unto some other Places."[19] If Mather's pastoral concern accounts for a large number of his published sermons on current events, then his "itch" for publishing was as much rooted in his quest for prestige as it was in his endeavor to reach an audience beyond the purview of his own congregation. Boston's bookseller-printers, for instance, would frequently sound out parishioners' enthusiastic response to Mather's preaching and then publish his sermons to cash in on a ready market. Well-heeled church members would frequently show their gratitude by paying for the cost of publishing and distributing his sermons or public addresses.[20] As a pastoral leader concerned with communicating, Mather made effective use of the principal mass medium available at the time.

Cotton Mather demonstrated his religious and civic leadership in many other ways as well, none more prominent than during the smallpox epidemic that ravaged the Bay Colony in 1721–22. As he put it in *Parentator* (1724), his biography of his father, "The *Besome of Destruction* swept away near a Thousand People."[21] This deadly plague, it is well known, was a perennial visitor in Africa, Europe, and colonial America but perhaps nowhere more devastating than among the Indigenous populations of the New World after contact with European arrivals. When "the Destroying Angel" returned to Boston once again in 1721–22, this time on a ship from the West Indies, Mather was prepared to employ science to back him up. In a circular letter to Boston's physicians, he called for a joint response to the variola virus with the revolutionary technique of inoculation, a prophylactic method of inducing immunity by injecting the contagion from a fully recovered person.[22] He had learned about this immunological procedure from accounts of two reputable European physicians who had witnessed it in Greece and Turkey, where it was a common practice; they subsequently published their accounts in the *Proceedings of the Royal Society of London*. But Mather also was told of the practice by his slave Onesimus, who assured him that it was common in Africa. When news first got out that Boston physician Zabdiel Boylston had performed inoculation on several individuals, a firestorm of accusations and malicious invectives rained down as the city had never seen before: Boylston and Mather were spreading smallpox![23]

Swimming against the tide of popular opinion and opposing the policies of the crown earned Mather lasting reproach, even abject hatred. He vehemently disapproved of several royally appointed governors for their corruption, nepotism, trading with the enemy, or abandoning the precepts of the Congregational Church. When he voiced his objections, he was accused of meddling in affairs beyond his station. Joseph Dudley (1647–1720), erstwhile proxy of the hated Andros, censor of the press, chief justice of the Superior Court, and the crown's subsequent choice of Massachusetts governor (1702–15), was the most prominent case in point. Although of old New England stock, Dudley struck the conservative Mathers as too friendly with the Church of England, which had established a beachhead in Boston under the ousted Andros. So too Dudley opened old wounds when, for instance, he joined the Church of England and petitioned the archbishop of Canterbury to supply funds for a new church building to serve the increasing number of Anglican residents in Boston. Worse yet, Dudley was instrumental in removing Governor Sir William Phips, close friend of the Mathers and member of their church. Furthermore, Dudley's campaign against French Canada during Queen Anne's War (1702–13) ended in disaster, leading to accusations that he and his cronies had made common cause with the French enemies for alleged kickbacks by selling gunshot to the French Indians. The cancerous boil was lanced with the anonymous publications in Boston of *A Memorial Of the Present Deplorable State of New-England* (1707) and, for good measure, its sequel in London, *The Deplorable State of New-England* (1708)—both accusing Dudley and his toady councilors of what amounted to high treason. Yet the claims of maladministration, profiteering, bribery, and packing the council and assembly came to nothing. Dudley was cleared of all charges for lack of tangible evidence (and bribes in high places went a long way in England). It was widely believed that the Mathers were behind the publications, and Governor Dudley certainly knew how to hurt them the most by declaring them persona non grata during his time in office.[24]

Likewise, Dudley had the temerity (it was rumored) to encourage Harvard students to seek ordination in the Church of England and to endorse the rival

Anglican Society for the Propagation of the Gospel in New England. What may have been the final straw for Mather was the appointment of John Leverett (1662–1724), Dudley's candidate, to the Harvard presidency (1708–24). Leverett, a lawyer by training (rather than an ordained minister), serving as president of a Puritan divinity school! If anyone was the most qualified scholar to occupy this position of leadership, it was none other than Cotton Mather—so many felt, including Mather himself. But learned qualifications are one thing; temperament and personality quite another. And alienating the members of the Harvard Corporation by charging them with lax morals and inadequate preparation of the students did not help Mather's cause either.[25] No surprise, then, when the position became vacant once again upon Leverett's death in 1724, the majority of the members of the corporation added insult to injury by choosing as their next president the young and inexperienced Benjamin Wadsworth (1725–37), sidelining Mather once and for all. If Governor Dudley had banned Mather from his table at public feast days, and if the opposition to the hegemony of the Mathers waxed and waned, Boston, mercantile capital of English North America, and her powerful merchants were turning elsewhere in the new century, away from the old-order clerical leadership. They were more concerned with circumventing the Navigation Act, which restricted trade; enhancing their cash flow; and fostering transatlantic networks of supply and demand than with matters of salvation, sectarian strife, or political infighting.[26]

This does not mean that Mather sat idly by nursing his real and imagined wounds. If anything, he turned his attention—as he had done all along—to the social and moral reform of Boston's populace.[27] He established numerous neighborhood Bible studies, organized self-help groups for families in need, funded a free school for Blacks and Indians at his own expense, founded several societies for the advancement of young men (the ancestor of the YMCA), donated books to start a public library, and established a "Society of Negroes" for mutual edification. At one time, Mather related in his diary, he chaired some twenty societies that he had brought to life.[28] His brand of reformism is perhaps best seen in his *Methods and Motives for Societies to Suppress Disorders* (1703) and in *Bonifacius*, better known as *Essays to Do Good* (1710). The latter manual remains remarkably readable and went through at least fifteen editions until the end of the nineteenth century. Even Benjamin Franklin, who extolled Mather's *Bonifacius* as a work that inspired his own social activism, echoed Mather's philanthropic dictums in his autobiography. So did the self-made tycoon of the Gilded Age, Andrew Carnegie (1835–1919), in his *Gospel of Wealth* (1889): those who accumulated a fortune, Carnegie recounted in his own success story, should employ it "for public ends" and return a sizeable portion of it to the community "from which it chiefly came."[29] "I will put *Rich Men* in mind of the Opportunities to *Do Good*, with which the God, who *gives Power to Get Wealth*, has favoured and obliged and enriched them," Mather reminded Boston's affluent of the stewardship of their God-given wealth, with which the Lord had "betrusted you."[30] Whether or not the philanthropy of Elihu Yale (1649–1721) was inspired by this remarkable book, Mather did persuade his fellow New Englander, now a wealthy diamond merchant in London and representative of the East India Company, to bestow his munificence on a new college at New Haven that now bears his name. Mather had been busy raising funds for this new nursery of Puritan clergymen: "The chief good that we have in our estates lies in the good we do with them," he prompted Elihu Yale with an eye toward perpetuating the benefactor's name. "If what is forming at New Haven might wear the name of YALE COLLEGE, it would be better than *a name of sons and daughters*," better yet indeed "than an Egyptian pyramid."[31]

If Increase Mather was the last American Puritan, as his most recent biography dubs him, Cotton Mather was the first American polymath, equally at home in the wisdom of the ancients and moderns as he was in the Enlightenment debates in natural philosophy and the sciences. He died on February 13, 1728, a day after his sixty-fifth birthday, of "an hard *Cough* and a suffocating *Asthma* with a *Fever*; but he felt no great Pain." It had prostrated him since the end of December. Surrounded by friends and parishioners, his son movingly related that on his deathbed Mather "had the sweet *Composure* and *easy Departure*, for which he had entreated so often and *fervently* the sovereign Disposer of all Things."[32] When his body was laid to rest in the family tomb on February 19, an icy Monday afternoon, a long train of mourners went up Hull Street and paid their last respects. "His *Name* is like to live a great while among us in his *printed Works*," Benjamin Colman prophesied from the pulpit at Cotton Mather's memorial service several days after his funeral. "But yet *these* will not convey to Posterity, nor give to Strangers, a just Idea of the real *Worth* and great *Learning* of the *Man*."[33] Following Colman's lead, let us turn next to Mather's most significant and lasting legacy: his published and unpublished works, which help us understand this complex mind and character.

MAJOR WRITINGS AND MAJOR TOPICS

Of his many publications, it is fair to say a select few stand out as representative of Mather's achievement and his influence on American religion, history, culture, and science. We here include a brief overview of their significance as a whole because our excerpts below are arranged topically. In order of their publication date, they include *Wonders of the Invisible World* (Boston, 1693), *Magnalia Christi Americana* (London, 1702), *Bonifacius* (Boston, 1710), *Psalterium Americanum* (Boston, 1718), *The Christian Philosopher* (London, 1721), *Manuductio ad Ministerium* (Boston, 1726), *The Diary of Cotton Mather* (1911–12, 1962), *The Angel of Bethesda* (1972), *Paterna* (1976), *Triparadisus* (as *The Threefold Paradise of Cotton Mather*, 1995), and the grandest of them all, *Biblia Americana* (2010–). They range in size from a little more than 200 octavo pages to more than 10,000 quarto pages and over 3 million words. We single them out here because these works, along with several lesser-known ones discussed below, incorporate the main topics we have chosen for our *Reader*: (1) autobiography and meditations; (2) New England history and the Glorious Revolution; (3) gender, childrearing, and education; (4) natural philosophy (science); (5) medicine and the cure of diseases; (6) mercantilism and paper money; (7) biblical hermeneutics; (8) the invisible world and Salem witchcraft; (9) race, slavery, and servitude; (10) Puritans and Native Americans; (11) Pietism and world missions; and (12) the Second Coming and millennialism. The sheer scope and variety of these pivotal themes are indicative of Cotton Mather as an early American polymath for whom all knowledge was interconnected. These topics were as relevant in his time as they are germane to our own modern self-understanding; they demonstrate not only his wide reading and interests in multiple fields but also his enlightened contributions to the Republic of Letters.

Of his many books, *Magnalia Christi Americana* (1702), "the mighty works of Christ in America," is Mather's most celebrated tome. In seven books or parts, it is the first ecclesiastical history of New England from its founding in 1620 to 1698 and preserves material nowhere else extant. It sketches the settlement and history of the New England colonies (book 1); the lives of its governors and assistants (book 2); sixty biographies of its most famous ministers (book 3); the history of Harvard and of some of its most distinguished graduates (book 4); the history of New England's Congregational Church and Confession of Faith (book 5); miraculous rescues at sea, surprising conversions, remarkable judgments of God, executions of criminals, and missionary successes among Native Americans—as well as other stories of providence (book 6); and disturbances and disagreements in New England's churches, Indian captivity narratives, and disputes with Quakers (book 7). Next to his *Wonders of the Invisible World* (1693), *Magnalia Christi Americana* is his most cited work. As "America's Literary Old Testament," it is a capacious providence history of God's dealings with his American Zion written in grand Virgilian cyphers as only Cotton Mather could deliver.[34]

His next most celebrated work in terms of his social ethic is *Bonifacius* (1710), better known by its descriptive moniker *Essays to Do Good*. It is perhaps

Mather's finest and most influential volume on social responsibility and uplift of every class, station, and member of society. Doing good and imitating Christ, he believed, was the best way to glorify God. Thus, Mather pinpointed how people could best live up to their obligations: elected magistrates to the charge of their office, ministers to their flocks, schoolteachers to their students, physicians to their patients, merchants and mechanics to the rules of the marketplace, parents to their children, masters and servants to each other, the rich to the poor. Together, they could practice the old maxim, Love your neighbor as yourself. To be sure, *Bonifacius* did not purport to be a collection of well-meaning platitudes of do-gooding. Rather, it identified specific ways each member of society could contribute to the betterment of society as a whole and serve God as well.

In its day, *Bonifacius* was perhaps Mather's most civic-minded and influential work. More than fifty years after Mather's death, in a letter to Mather's son Samuel on May 12, 1784, Benjamin Franklin attributed his own social ethic to Cotton Mather and *Bonifacius*: "When I was a Boy," he wrote late in life to Samuel Mather,

> I met with a Book intitled *Essays to do Good*, which I think was written by your Father. It had been so little regarded by a former Possessor, that several Leaves of it were torn out: But the Remainder gave me such a Turn of Thinking as to have an Influence on my Conduct thrô Life, for I have always set a greater Value on the Character of a *Doer of Good*, than on any other kind of Reputation; and if I have been, as you seem to think, a useful Citizen, the Publick owes the Advantage of it to that Book.[35]

A long section on family matters and education, topical citations, and references to *Bonifacius* are included in our *Reader*, but modern reprints of Mather's *Essay to Do Good* are easily available.

Psalterium Americanum (1718) is an oft-ignored work though it has recently gained attention due to renewed interest in hymnody and sacred music.[36] Yet in its day, his more than four-hundred-page translation of the Psalms in blank verse, complete with Mather's "*Golden Keyes*" to unlock the Psalms' prophetic meaning, contributed to a major reform of Psalmody in New England's Congregational churches. Singing Psalms at home and in church was a mainstay of Puritan worship, but many parishioners disapproved of the available Psalters because translators were more concerned with "*a little Jingle at the end of the Line*" than with being faithful to the written word. In fact, translators "*leave out a vast heap of those rich things, which the Holy SPIRIT of GOD speaks in the Original Hebrew*" and thus debased the Psalter with their own interpolations merely to maintain a congenial meter and rhyme scheme, Mather protested.[37]

This dissatisfaction with interpretations of the Psalms was no minor issue in the minds of serious believers. After all, David's Psalter, Mather signified in his preface, was "*A Second Pentateuch.*" For King David in the Psalms is nothing but a prophetic type of the Messiah in the New Testament, Mather declared. "The sense which concerns the *Types*, is a piece of *Canvas*, on which the Holy Spirit has inlaid the *Mystical sense*, which concerns our SAVIOUR, as a *Golden Embroidery.*"[38] The best way to preserve this mystical sense in a new translation of the Psalms, Mather insisted, was to retain the original Hebrew meaning by rendering the Psalms in blank verse with brief annotations. And to teach parishioners indifferently able to read music, Mather adapted his Psalter to commonly available tunes. In this way, the "*Odd Noise*" coming from the galleries might turn the whole North Church into proficient harmonizers, as suggested by his sermon *The Accomplished Singer* (1721). *Psalterium Americanum*, Mather hoped, would replace *The Whole Booke of Psalmes Faithfully Translated into English Metre* (1640), better known as *The Bay Psalm Book*, which his grandfather Richard Mather, John Weld, and John Eliot had translated, and Henry Dunster, the first present of Harvard College, had "Revised and Refined" for use in New England's congregations. By Cotton's time, this collection, though venerable, was no longer considered adequate for modern tastes.[39]

Mather's *The Christian Philosopher* (1721) is a grand compendium of natural philosophy and the scientific discoveries of his age. Published under the distinguished auspices of the Royal Society of London (of which body he was an elected member), it is a teleological paean to God's creation that aims to demonstrate that natural science "is no *Enemy*, but a mighty and wondrous *Incentive* to *Religion*."[40] In thirty-two essays, Mather deploys the best available scientific theories to illuminate the wonders of the physical cosmos: fixed stars and the planets of the solar system; the natural occurrence of comets; meteorology and the causes of thunder and lightning; gravity and magnetism; the great chain of being from insects, reptiles, aquatic species, ornithology, and mammalian quadrupeds, all the way up to the crown of God's creation, humankind. His last—and longest—essay celebrates the human body as a magnificent machine endowed with an immortal soul. In doing so, Mather relies on the newest discoveries in anatomy and physiology, skeletal structure, muscles, the heart and its arteries, pulmonary organs, blood circulation, the nervous system, and more. In terms of miracles, Mather was prepared to grant that the laws of nature governed the cosmos' great mobile through the mechanics of secondary causes but that the Almighty was not bound by them and could intervene at any time because God stood above the material universe. *The Christian Philosopher* was the first textbook of natural philosophy composed by an American. It allowed

Mather to spice his pulpit oratory and essays with the wonders of God's creation. Mather was comfortably ensconced in the Enlightenment philosophy of
his day—even popularized it from his North End pulpit. He was equally at
home in the wisdom of the ancients whose books he had been reading all his
life. This comfortable middle ground between the old and the new is apparent
in all of his published and unpublished works.

As the eighth of only about forty-eight colonial Americans elected to membership in the Royal Society of London, Mather emulated the scientific achievements of his peers.[41] Nearly all of his works from the 1690s onward make reference
to new discoveries in the sciences. If Harvard's first telescope, obtained in 1672,
allowed Mather to scan the Milky Way, his own microscope aided him in the
discovery of all sorts of little animals "animalculae" in the blood and in water.[42]
To be sure, Mather was no physician in the modern sense, yet his lifelong study
of medical books furnished him with nearly as much (if not more) knowledge
of the body's microcosm as any of the medical practitioners of his day had at
their disposal.[43] Although it remained unpublished for nearly 250 years after his
death, *The Angel of Bethesda* (1972), a medical handbook on the prime diseases
and their potential cures, was circulated in his family and among friends and
neighbors as the need arose. By some accounts, Mather's *Angel* was "the only
large inclusive medical work of the entire American colonial period."[44] It was
intended as a handbook for laypeople who could not afford to buy similar reference works published abroad or to pay practicing physicians. Why it was never
published is subject to conjecture. Certainly, the expense for such a long manuscript would have required prepaid subscriptions from many individuals. Those
who could afford to contribute were more likely to consult their physicians.
Boston's medical establishment, however, saw no reason to sponsor a work (from
a meddling clergyman) that might undercut their own competitive edge.

The Angel of Bethesda consists of sixty-six chapters, treating nearly as many
diseases and maladies and offering remedies and their dosages, which he
gleaned from several hundred authorities. The text also includes traditional
herbal medicines from the local flora and fauna (or "Physick-Garden"), from
Native American medicine men, and from the time-honored pharmacopeia of
the Gallenical and Paracelsian schools. His handbook offers treatments for
everything from toothache, rheumatic fever, epilepsy, jaundice, diarrhea, and
female ailments to venereal disease, consumption, cancer, measles, and smallpox.
Significantly, he also included nostrums on how to treat "melancholy" (depres-
sion), nightmares, and stammering—all of which he experienced firsthand. To
be sure, as a physician of the soul and body, Mather did not neglect to remind
his readers of the origin of all diseases—Adam's Fall—and how sins in their

various manifestations lead to ailments of the mind and body. Above all, repentance and prayer were the one panacea that the Savior proffered to all who petitioned him in faith. In Mather, scientific and faith approaches to illness were joined, but manmade medicines could never replace prayer.

Manuductio ad Ministerium, published in 1726, was a manual for ministers to cultivate the minds and manners of young "Gentlemen." It enjoyed great popularity in its day and went through several reprints and editions in the eighteenth and nineteenth centuries; it has even made a comeback in the twenty-first century. Far from being stodgy, *Manuductio* was a practical handbook on the study of classical languages, the natural sciences, poetry and style, mathematics, history, divinity, pulpit oratory, and rules of health: cleanliness, physical exercise, balanced diet, and abstinence from sot-weed—tobacco. Most of all, Mather's young ministers were to be gentlemen pastors equally at home in church as in polite society. In each chapter, Mather listed the most important authors, books, and controversies. Significantly, "the *Living Tongues*," Mather reasoned, were as important as such classical languages as Latin, Greek, Hebrew, and Syriac. *Manuductio* ended on a hopeful wish that all Protestant churches would abandon sectarian divisions and unite into one on the basis of his trio of "Maxims of the Everlasting Gospel": One God—Father, Son, and Holy Spirit; Christ, his only begotten son, who died for the sins of immortal souls; and "do unto *Other Men*, as I must own it Reasonable for them to do unto *myself*"—all else is mere commentary.[45]

Of the works *not* intended for public consumption were the nearly 1,700-page diary, published as the *Diary of Cotton Mather, 1681–1724* (1911–12, 1964), and his 300-page spiritual autobiography *Paterna* (1976)—both didactic ledgers to instruct his son (and descendants) in the spiritual lessons of his life. The diary was one of the largest personal records of the colonial period, a Puritan memoir par excellence. When compared to other diaries of the time, Mather's stands out because he revised and edited the whole bundle of annuals beginning in 1710, throwing out what he deemed no longer serviceable. He restructured his diary as "Revised Memorials," an enormous record of the devotions, prayers, fasting, vigils, and thanksgivings of a soul struggling to subject his fallen self to the image of Christ. Yet he also included his observations on the tasks of the day, his encounters with angels, worries about his family and congregation, the social and political upheavals at home and abroad, and how they all impacted his vision of Christ's millennial kingdom looming on the horizon. At some point, he clearly tired of recording the minutia of every day, broke with his established pattern, and hereafter recorded only what he deemed the best way to glorify Christ: "Doing Good." Henceforth, he began every daily entry with "G.D." (Good Done), and recorded activities that clearly benefited his family, flock, and individuals who turned to him for help, and the community at large. From his diary we also learn why he chose to preach on specific topics, and why his occasional, doctrinal, or polemical sermons, tracts, and books were published when they were. Its deliberate selectivity notwithstanding, Mather's diary is perhaps the most important written source on his life.

Of all Mather's published and unpublished works, *Biblia Americana*, a 3-million-word commentary on all the books of the Bible composed in several phases between 1693 and 1728, is his most significant intellectual achievement. It is a gargantuan compilation of biblical, philosophical, scientific, and herme-neutic debates of the early Enlightenment that swept through Europe and chal-lenged the time-honored belief in the divine inspiration and textual inviolability of the Holy Scriptures. *Biblia* is significant in that it presents the pros and cons of Cartesian mechanism, Hobbesian materialism, Spinozist pantheism, and the argument that the Bible is not a book of science but of faith. For as Galileo Galilei put it in his letter to the Grand Duchess Christina in 1615, "The inten-tion of the Holy Spirit is to teach us how one goes to heaven and not how heaven goes."[46] Here, Mather actually agreed with the heretic Spinoza—whom father Increase, with an ethnic slur, called "that ingenious Jew"—that the Bible was not a book of natural science but a work to inspire devotion and faith in God. Cotton Mather's *Biblia* listens to all sides in the many debates, adapts what is suitable and reconcilable with conservative belief in the Holy Scrip-tures, and attempts to invalidate those arguments that he believed lead to athe-ism. Significantly, he frequently demystified miracles by providing natural explanations of what to the ancients were God's wonders. And yet, in the Penta-teuch, Mather would also defend the Flood as a worldwide event in time, rather than as a mere local inundation somewhere in Mesopotamia, as some newfan-gled philosophers had argued. Mather pointed to Native American flood stories and geological evidence—giant petrified bones and shark teeth found far in-land—as proof that the American hemisphere was *not* excluded as some skep-tics had argued, ostensibly because no one lived there at the time of Noah. For Mather, then, science was a helpmeet to explicate incomprehensible phenom-ena in the Bible with systematic tools.

More than that, in *Biblia Americana* Mather sought to justify the ways of God to humanity. He defended the Old Testament prophecies and their fulfilments in the New; explicated the Old Testament types and figures as prophetic mark-ers of Christ as the promised Messiah; corrected the chronology of the Old and the sequence of Christ's miracles in the New Testament; revised mistranslations, textual lacunae, and after-the-fact interpolations that had crept into the Holy Scriptures; cited proof from pagan histories that the mythologies of the ancients were derived from the Hebrew scriptures, and much, much more. Mather labored on *Biblia Americana* for more than thirty years—to the end of his life. By that time, his folio manuscript had become such a colossal tome that no American press could handle it, and London publishers would not touch it unless a whole slew of sponsors and subscribers would underwrite the expense. Nearly three hundred years have elapsed, but Mather's dream of publishing *Biblia Americana* is finally coming true.

UNPUBLISHED WRITINGS

Besides his considerable body of printed works, Cotton Mather left behind a trove of unpublished manuscripts that are grouped with those of his father, grandfather, and other family members. The documents, under the title of the Mather Family Papers, are in the collections of the Massachusetts Historical Society (MHS) and the American Antiquarian Society (AAS).[47] While we cannot here describe all of Cotton Mather's unpublished manuscripts, the following deserve attention for the scope of what remains to be done in Mather scholarship:

(1) First and foremost, "Curiosa Americana" (1712–24), his rich collection of eighty-two epistolary essays, his companion to *The Christian Philosopher* on natural phenomena and scientific discussions sent to the Royal Society of London. Topics range from American plants, birds, rattlesnakes, passenger pigeons, the American moose, terrestrial and marine fossils, and insects to such phenomena as monstrous births, parhelia, eclipses, earthquakes, and hurricanes, along with such significant contributions to science as his essays on variola and smallpox inoculation, nidification of pigeons, aurora borealis, marine volcanoes, and more.

(2) Correspondence, consisting of more than six hundred extant manuscript letters, dating from 1690 to 1724, some of which have been edited in Kenneth Silverman's edition of *Selected Letters* (1971). This archive preserves Mather's communications with figures on both sides of the Atlantic.

(3) His "Quotidiana," a commonplace book of sorts consisting of a huge collection of quotations (in English, Latin, Greek, Hebrew, French, and Spanish) from books Mather read throughout his life.

(4) Sermons: Mather's substantial collection of sermon outlines and sermon notes, dating from 1676 to 1720, including notes on sermons (indexed) preached by his father and colleagues in the Bay Colony. Most of these manuscript materials are preserved at the MHS; the AAS; Andover-Harvard Library, Cambridge; Boston Public Library; University of Virginia Library, Charlottesville; Congregational Library and Archives, Boston; Yale University's Beinecke Library, New Haven, Connecticut; Huntington Library, San Marino, California; and the Royal Society of London.

(5) Mather's personal booklet containing the names and dates of church admissions, deaths, censures, and excommunications, as described in the introduction, and the record book of the North Church (1662–1728), containing entries by Increase and Cotton Mather, both at the MHS.

(6) In addition to this collection of unpublished materials, there are countless separate items on a vast variety of issues too numerous to be itemized here. They are widely dispersed in the repositories named above.

MATHER'S REPUTATION AND INTERPRETATION

Cotton Mather died in 1728, a day after his sixty-fifth birthday, "as merry as one bound for heaven." He was given a massive funeral, and eulogists held him up as the star preacher and minister of New England, praising him for his learning and for his personal qualities. His son "Sammy" noted his father's many international connections, among whom Cotton stood as a representative of America: "*He alone* was able to support the Character of *this* Country abroad."[48]

The period immediately following was no time to speak ill of Cotton Mather, but that time eventually came. In the century and a half after his death, Mather the polymath, natural scientist, physico-theologian, Christian philosopher and scholar, linguist, and ecumenist was largely forgotten. *Bonifacius*, the *Essays to Do Good*, was his most oft-reprinted work, while his treatises on church polity were parochial resources for New England Congregationalists as disestablishment loomed in the early nineteenth century. By the 1860s, however, it was Mather the supporter of the Salem witch trials that dominated, and would continue to do so for the next century and half or more. He was conveniently pigeon-holed as pompous, undemocratic, superstitious, a representative of a repressive Puritan tradition that had no place in a modern United States of the Progressive Era and Jazz Age. As biographer Kenneth Silverman puts it, Mather became, and has remained to a great degree, the "national gargoyle." Reflecting on the "abridgement" of Mather, historian of religion E. Brooks Holifield aptly observes, "Cotton Mather was trapped in Salem."[49]

It is safe to say that this estimation of Mather still prevails in most circles. However, beginning about half a century ago, there were signs of renewed interest in Mather, with first printings and reprintings of his works not dealing with witchcraft or devils. In the 1970s, David Levin's portrait of Mather as a young man and Richard F. Lovelace's study of Pietism's influence on Mather in some ways marked a turning point. These were followed in the 1980s by Mitchell R. Breitwieser's comparison of Mather and Benjamin Franklin, by Robert Middlekauff's important study of the Mather family of ministers, and by Kenneth Silverman's prize-winning biography of Cotton Mather. With the tercentenary of the Salem witch trials in the early 1990s came reassessments of the causes, participants, and effects. The new millennium has seen work on Mather, both textual and interpretive, take off in an unprecedented manner, especially the publication of the multivolume "Biblia Americana" and new scholarship stemming from that project, led by Reiner Smolinski and Jan Stievermann. As Stievermann has pointed out, a turning away from national narratives among historians has led to a reconsideration of Mather for his roles in the Christian Enlightenment in the Atlantic world; in ecumenism, missions, and reform movements; and in the formation of modern evangelicalism and revivalism.

If certain persistent stereotypes of Mather have discouraged fuller study of him, another factor might be the incredible attention that has been given to another colonial Puritan luminary, Jonathan Edwards. Both were giants of the eighteenth century, but Edwards has come out much better, and perhaps fault is to be laid in part at the feet of scholars such as Perry Miller and Samuel Eliot Morison, who belittled Mather even as they genuflected before Edwards, thereby prejudicing subsequent generations. Perhaps too the sheer volume of Mather's publications is a deterrent in comparison to those of Edwards. In any case, Mather's reputation has suffered as Edwards's has ascended, but hopefully future scholarship will achieve a more balanced appreciation of Mather and so repatriate him.

To make sense of the important transitions that took place in early New England and in American religious history generally, we must look to Cotton Mather, for he lived through, reflected, and even directed those changes. He truly is a pivotal figure through whose activities and writings we can view the society in which he worked. His was a society that became radically different over the course of his life, but he exercised significant influence in bringing about those changes.

By virtue of his wide-ranging involvements and writings, Cotton Mather is at once a unique voice and an invaluable window onto nearly every aspect of the colonial experience. He identified himself, somewhat facetiously, as "American"—at the time a belittling term, signifying an uncouth barbarian—yet also saw himself as part of a global community, the church, broadly conceived. There are definitely aspects of Mather that make him of a different time and place. But if the phrase "Think globally, act locally" describes anyone, it is Cotton Mather. While involving himself intricately in the concerns of his congregation, his city, and his colony, he embodied an international spirit of cooperation and inquiry that speaks to global sensibilities and realities today.

A COTTON MATHER READER

AUTOBIOGRAPHY AND MEDITATIONS

Cotton Mather's life writings and meditations furnish a glimpse of his complex personality: his Job-like wrestling with his God, his spirituality, and the self-representation of his heart, mind, and soul. To be sure, the term "autobiography" was not coined until the early nineteenth century, and Mather's "Paterna" might best be described as a memoir or didactic ledger of his spiritual life. It is important to remember that until the nineteenth century, publishing one's own autobiography, memoir, letters, or diaries during one's lifetime violated the conventions of propriety. At the most, such manuscripts were "scribally published," that is, shared with immediate family members or close friends after the death of the author for personal instruction. The sixty biographies in Mather's *Magnalia Christi Americana* (1702) testify to the fact that such private documents were made available to authors who commemorated the lives of their friends and colleagues.

Culled from the pages of Mather's diary is "Paterna," his spiritual autobiography or memoir, left in manuscript until 1976. Perhaps punning on the concepts of "pattern" and "pater" (Latin for "father"), Mather's "Paterna" set out to do just that: to provide an exemplary pattern for his Christian Everyman.[1] To achieve this goal, Mather hid his identity and deliberately elided any possible reference to himself, his family, or relatives whose identities might reveal his authorship. His secretiveness should not come as a surprise. To be sure, Mather's memoir bears little if any resemblance to Benjamin Franklin's famous autobiography,

3

though both are conventionally addressed to *"My Son."* If Franklin provided detailed information about his ancestors and made every effort to tell a good story about his life's achievements, Mather did nothing of the sort. "Paterna" was deliberately opaque and impervious to anyone looking for biographical specifics, precisely because he aimed to create the persona of a spiritual "Exemplar" patterned after Christ. Consequently, individuality and uniqueness—qualities in high esteem in our times—were at cross-purposes with his sought-after exemplariness and therefore needed to be erased. But "Paterna" was also an astonishing, even heartrending, self-analysis of a Puritan who scrutinized virtually every impulse and motion of his mind and heart, ceaselessly questing for absolution and assurance of his election, even as he strove to emulate Christ's suffering. "My Life," Mather wrote in his diary in December 1713, "is almost a constant Conversation with Heaven."[2] His struggle for evidence of his conversion and assurance in the realm of feeling was not a single event in time but a lifelong endeavor intermittently measured by his rigorous self-abasement and intense prayers to be found worthy of Christ. In this manner, he devised two narrators: a younger one ceaselessly swimming against the tide of temptation and corruption, and an older and wiser one who looks over the younger's shoulders, calmly noting the blunders of his ways.

What emerges from this back and forth is a spiritual journal that might startle modern readers not used to tallying their own shortcomings. One of his innumerable unspecified recollections reserved for his son's contemplations begins, "Some of my Bitterest Confessions and Confusions this Day before the Lord, were, That a vast Variety of successive *Temptations* has Assaulted me." At another point, Mather bared his breast: "I not only kept many *Dayes of Humiliation*, but I also composed a Writing of several Pages, entitled, THE TRUE PICTURE OF—myself. Herein I did, with *Black*, but yett with too *True*, Characters, describe my own Vileness at such a rate, that it cannot be look'd upon, without Horrour of Soul; but I Resolved, often to look upon it."[3] Keeping track of one's heart of darkness, depravity, and self-loathing—shocking as it might appear to our standards of a healthy mind—served dual purposes: on the one hand, it reminded the meditating soul of his dire want of grace and utter dependence on Christ;

on the other, it gauged a person's state of regeneration. The more sins he found, the more he felt assured his soul was filled with regenerating grace that enabled him to uncover and bewail his hidden sins. And yet, pouring over the black characters of "THE TRUE PICTURE OF—myself" allowed him to initiate his frame of mind into states of self-abnegation during secret fasts from which he could but rise victoriously with his faith restored in Christ's pardon.

Opaque revelations about the nature of one's sins were perfectly intelligible to those with whom Mather shared a religious culture. And ritualistic meditation, coupled with fasting and prayer, was the means to root out depravity. At other moments, when his soul emerged from the dark night of self-analysis, his emotions could reach heights of ravishing ecstasy. When undertaking one of hundreds of "*Secret Fasts*" recorded in his diary and "Paterna," his joy could mount to a stunning trance: "*Oh, I feel! I feel! I feel! I love the Lord Jesus Christ; I love Him dearly, I love Him greatly, Yea, I love Him above all. And What? Will God love me? . . . Oh, Joy unspeakable & full of Glory!—Oh, what Love, what Love, what Love is This! That I, who have been so Polluted and so Unworthy, should be loved by the Great God! Now, oh, that I could Praise thy Name, and Love thee again!*"[4] For many readers today, such terms of self-abasement culminating in mystical ecstasy are, perhaps, best consumed in small doses, else their seeming repetitiveness loses vivacity and comes across as scripted without being any less sincere. Mather's diary and autobiography, then, manifest a deep soul in constant want of approval from his heavenly father, from whose path he could never stray very far without rushing back for absolution. Mather's very essence depended on the peace and joy that came from feeling reconciled with his God.

Our second selection to illustrate the preoccupations of an early American religious believer is *Christianus per Ignem* (1702), a captivating manual for meditation to raise the mind from transient objects in the here and now to thoughts of everlasting bliss in Heaven. The ancient practice of meditation is more than a mere pondering of one's deeds or surroundings. It is a cognitive exercise to extract spiritual lessons from even the most pedestrian objects that reveal God's hidden glory. Its purpose is to sharpen the faculty powers of memory (the storehouse of past experience) and understanding (assessment of what *is* versus what *ought to be*) in order to raise the affections (fear of punishment versus love and gratitude) and shape volition (the will to act) in order to embrace what is good or to resist what is evil. Mather demonstrated the lessons of this divine art, for example, in his *Winter-Meditations* (1693) as well as in *Christianus per Ignem* (1702). In the latter work, excerpted below, he invoked René Descartes's famous dictum "Cogito, ergo sum," or, as Mather rendered it, "*I think, therefore I am*," though reminding his readers that "it is no *New Divinity* to teach, that *As Men Think, so they are*."[5] In playing on Descartes's phrase, Mather cautions readers that the right way of thinking is to stimulate the love of God, not to probe the limits of true knowledge. The origin of his *Christian by the Fire*, the English title of this meditation, amounts to a wager (so he claims) with several of his friends sitting by his fireside that "*as dry a Subject*" as the fire before them could yield a whole collection of beneficial thoughts. His book of two hundred pages and forty meditations certainly did not turn out to be "*dry*" at all but filled with dry wit and acumen as only Mather knew how.

"PATERNA"

TO MY SON

God, who hath given you to *me*, requires and expects, my Endeavours, that on the most peculiar Accounts, you may be *His*.

What have been my *Prayers* for you, both before and after my Receiving of you from the Lord, and what *Hopes* I have had concerning you, perhaps you may somewhat inform your self, if you should Live to Read, the Passages of my *Life*, Recorded from time to time, as they occurr'd, in *Reserved Memorials*, which I leave behind me.[6]

From those *Memorials*, I am now going to *Extract* certain Passages, that may be *Particularly Instructive* to *you*; because to do so, I thought, would be one Reasonable *Essay*, That all my *Prayers*, and *Hopes* about you, may not be defeated.

The *Instruction* of a *Father*, carries much of Authority and Efficacy with it; It seems intimated in the Divine Oracles, That if the Servants of God *WILL command their Children, they SHALL keep the Way of the Lord*: And some famous Orators going to write Advice unto *Young* Persons, have Ingeniously introduced, with a most Agreeable *Fiction*, the *Dead Parents* of those Persons, as thus Advising of them. Tho' I shall quickly be *Dead*, yett I am still *Alive*; and because the *Exemple* of a *Father* added unto his *Instruction*, may render it Singularly Efficacious, I have chosen to give you, without the least *Fiction* in the World, a Number of those *Experiences* and *Contrivances*, which I have had, in my own poor *Walk with God*. . . .

The First Part

§   Being desirous to Discover myself unto None, but *You*, My SON, I must here leave unmentioned, *When* and *Where* (as well as, *of Whom*) I was born, lest the mention thereof should afford some Light unto the Discovery, against which I would be cautious.

Wherefore, I Begin by observing to you, That I desire to bewayl unto the very *End* of my Life, the early Ebullitions of *Original Sin*, which appeared at the very *Beginning* of it. Indeed, your Grandfather,[7] tho' he were a Wise and Strict Parent, would from the Observation of some Dispositions in me, comfort himself with an Opinion of my being *Sanctified by the Holy Spirit of God, in my very Infancy* {Rom. 15:16}. But he knew not how Vile I was; he saw not the Instances of my *going astray*, even while I was yett an *Infant*.

§   However, there were *some Good things* in my *Childhood*, in which I wish you, *My Child*, may *do better than I*. I began to *Pray*, even when I began to *Speak*. I learn'd myself to *Write*, before my going to School for it. I used *Secret Prayer*, not confining myself to *Forms* in it: And yett I composed *Forms* of *Prayer*, for my School-mates, (I suppose, when I was about Seven or Eight Years old) and obliged them to *Pray*. Before I could *Write Sermons*, in the public Assemblies, I commonly *Wrote* what I Remembred, when I came home. I Read the Scripture, with so much Ardour, that for one while nothing less than *Fifteen Chapters* a Day, Divided into three Exercises, for Morning and Noon, and Night, would suffice me. I Rebuked my Play-mates, for their Wicked *Words* and *Wayes*; and sometimes I suffered from them, the Persecution of not only *Scoffs*, but *Blowes* also, for my Rebukes: which, when some-body told your Grandfather, I remember, he seem'd very *Glad*, yea, almost *Proud*, of my Affronts; and I then wondred at it, tho' afterwards, I better understood this Heavenly Principle.

§   One Special Fault of my Childhood, (against which, I would have you, *My Son*, be caution'd,) was, *Idleness*. And one thing that occasion'd me much *Idle Time*, was the Distance of my Fathers Habitation from the *School*; which caused him, out of Compassion unto my Tender and Weakly Constitution, to keep me at home in the *Winter*. However, I then much employ'd myself in *Church-History*: And when *Summer* arrived, I so plied my Business, that thro' the Blessing of God upon my Endeavours, at the Age of little more than *Eleven Years*, I had composed many *Latin* Exercises, both in *Prose* and *Verse*, and could speak *Latin* so readily, that I could write Notes of Sermons after the English Preacher, in it. I had conversed with *Cato, Corderius, Terence, Tully, Ovid,* and *Virgil.* I had made *Epistles,* and *Themes;* presenting my First Theme to my Master,[8] without his requiring or expecting as yett any such thing of me; whereupon he complemented me, *Laudabilis Diligentia tua!*[9] I had gone thro' a great Part of the New Testament in *Greek:* I had read considerably in *Isocrates* and *Homer;* and I had made some Entrance in my Hebrew Grammar. And I was upon a Strict Examination of the Praesident & Fellowes, Admitted into a Colledge, the Name whereof need not here be mentioned.[10] And, I think, before I came to *Fourteen*, I composed *Hebrew* Exercises, and *Ran* thro' the other Sciences, that *Academical Studies* ordinarily fall upon. I composed *Systems*, both of *Logick*, and *Physick*, in Catechisms of my own, which have since been used by many others. I went over the Use of the *Globes*, and proceeded in *Arithmetic*, as far as was ordinary. I made *Theses* and *Antitheses*, and also disputed upon the main *Quaestions* that lay before us. For my *Declamations*, I ordinarily took some Article of *Natural Philosophy*, for my *Subject*, by which Contrivance I did kill Two Birds with One Stone. Hundreds of Books I read over; & I kept a *Diary* of my Studies.

   My Son, I would not have mentioned these things, but that I may provoke *Your* Emulation.

§   Before I was quite arrived unto this Age, I *Apostatised* from God, in diverse Miscarriages, which made me suspect, that I had never yett experienced any more than some *Common* Works of His Holy Spirit, and I was yett but a *Refined Hypocrite*. At length, upon Occasion of *Bodily Indisposition*, which I fear'd would End in Death, my Suspicion of my Interior & Eternal State, was terribly Awakened. I Trembled, when I thought, that after I had *Hop'd Well* of myself, & many Servants of God had *Spoke Well* of me, I should be a *Castaway* after all; and I remember, God sett home that Consideration upon me, with a very particular Pungency, *How shall I be able to look my own Father in the Face, at the Day of Judgment?* While I was under my Distresses, I heard some Sermons, on Luk. 7.47. *Her Sins, which were many, are Forgiven;* and on Rev. 22.17, *Whosoever will, let him take of the Water of Life freely.* The Grace of God in the Lord Jesus Christ, and the Gracious Offer of the Lord Jesus Christ, wonderfully affected me; my Heart was exceedingly Broken & Melted at it; and it embolden'd me to Come, and Lay Hold upon Him, who is able to *Save unto the uttermost all that come unto Him* {Heb. 7:25}. I had Frequent Returns of *Doubts* and *Fears;* but I frequently Renewed my Closures with the Lord Jesus Christ, as my only Releef against them. Once Laboring & even Languishing, under a Sense of my own horrible Vileness, and thinking, *Will the Lord Jesus Christ Accept of a Vile Wretch, that hath been & hath done, as I have!* I had some Discourse with your Grandfather about it. He told me, *That as for that Matter, there was no Returning Sinner, but the Lord Jesus Christ would most freely Accept of him: For* (said he) *observe it even among Men: There's a vile Sinner, an Holy Man Beholds him and Abhors him: Yett if this vile Sinner ever comes to be converted, the same Holy Person, can & will, notwithstanding his former loathsome Vileness, embrace him in his very Bosome; and This* (he said) *is an Emblem & Effect of the Spirit of the Lord Jesus Christ.* I shall never *forgett,* how much these Words did *Quicken* me! In my Addresses to Heaven under the Exercises of my Mind, about my *Reconciliation* to God, I now sometimes received Strange, and Strong, and Sweet Intimations, That I was Accepted of the Lord. Once especially, having heard a Sermon, on Isa. 44.3. *I will pour my Spirit on thy Seed, & my Blessing on thy Offspring;* I pleaded that Promise before the Lord, and in my Pleading of it, the *Spirit* of the Lord, wonderfully dissolved my Heart, with Assurances, That it should be fulfilled upon me. . . .

§ Moreover, I may mention it unto you, That when I was about this Age, I fell under the Power of *Melancholy,*[11] to such a Degree, that I exceedingly wonder, it had no worse Effects upon me. And studying *Physick* at this time, I was unhappily led away with *Fancies,* that I was myself Troubled, with almost every *Distemper* that I read of, in my Studies: which caused me sometimes, not only *Needlessly,* but also *Hurtfully* to use *Medicines* upon myself, that I might Cure my *Imaginary Maladies.* But the Troubles of *Sin* accompanied these my Confusions, which horribly overwhelmed me: Until once Crying to the Lord in Prayer, and Casting my *Burdens* on the Care of the Lord Jesus Christ, I sensibly felt an unaccountable *Cloud* and *Load* go off my Spirit, and from that Minute I was as much altered, by a New *Light,* and *Life,* and *Ease* arriving to me, as the *Sunrise* does change the World, from the Condition of *Midnight.*

§ I will further inform you, *My Son;* That one singular Advantage to me while I was thus a Lad, was my Acquaintance with, and Relation to, a *Society of Young Men* in our Town, who mett every *Evening* after the *Lords-day,* for the Services of Religion. There we constantly *Pray'd,* both before and after the Repetition of a *Sermon;* and Sang a *Psalm;* taking our *Turns* in such Devotions. We then had a Devout *Quaestion,* proposed a Week before; whereto any one present gave what *Answer* he pleased; and I still concluded the *Answer.* As the Lord made poor *me,* to be a little useful unto these (and other) Meetings of *Young People,* in my *Youth,* so He made these Meetings very useful unto me. Their *Loves* to me, and their *Prayers* for me, and my *Probationary Essays* among them, had a more than ordinary Influence upon my *After-Improvements.* . . .

DIARY (MARCH 1681)[12]

[Mather's "Infirmity"]

Another thing that much exercised mee was, that I might not bee left without necessary Supplies of *Speech* for my Ministry. God was pleased so far to lett my *Infirmity* remain, that altho' by a careful *Deliberation* my *public Services* were freed from any Blemish by it, yett I was, by His Wisdome, kept in continual *Prayer*, and *Fear*, and *Faith*, concerning it. How many Thousands of sollicitous Thoughts I underwent concerning it, is best known to Him, who by those Thoughts *drove* mee and kept me *nearer* to Himself.

SAMUEL MATHER, *LIFE* (1729)

[Mather Is Given a Way to Minimize His Stutter]

2. WHILE he was full of Concern for Relief from this troublesome Infirmity, that good old Schoolmaster Mr. CORLET[13] gave him a Visit on purpose to advise Him; *Sir*, said he, *I should be glad if you would oblige your self to a* dilated *Deliberation in speaking; for as in* Singing *there is no one who* Stammers, *so by prolonging your* Pronunciation *you will get an Habit of speaking without Haesitation.*

3. HERE I must inform my Reader, that because of his *Stammering*, he had almost, for some Time, laid aside the Tho'ts of being a *Minister*, and had with great Application studied *Physic*: But, upon prosecuting Mr. CORLET's Advice, and having procured with Divine Help an *happy Delivery*, he was perswaded by his Friends to desert the Calling of a *Physician*; He did so: And after having studied *Theology* rationally and without Prejudice, he prepared for *public Appearance*: And because of the Calling he had relinquished, he did in his first Sermon consider our Blessed SAVIOUR as the glorious *Physician of Souls*; chusing those words for his first Text in Luke IV.18. *He hath sent me to heal the brokenhearted.*[14] . . .

§ When I was come to be Eighteen Years of Age my Mind was exceedingly taken up, with the great Action, of, A *Closing with the Lord Jesus Christ.* In the Prosecution of this Action, I may say, t'was the *Spirit* of God, that was my *Teacher*; no *Man*, or *Book*, show'd me the Way of managing this Action; but I was by the *Spirit* of God, led on to a most explicit Procedure in it. One Day, I used such Words as these, among others, before my Lord-Redeemer.

"Oh, my dear Lord; Thy *Father* ha's committed my Soul into thy Hands: There is a *Covenant of Redemption*, wherein I am concerned: I know my *Election* by my *Vocation*, and my Concernment in that *Covenant*, by my being made Willing to Come under the Shadow of thy Wings in the *Covenant of Grace*. Now in that ancient *Covenant*, the *Father* said unto the *Son*, *Such an Elect Soul there is, that I will bring into thy Fold, and thou shalt undertake for that Soul, as a Sufficient and an Eternal Saviour.* Wherefore I am now in thy Hands, O my Lord: Thy Father ha's putt me there, and I have putt myself there; O Save me, O Heal me, O Work for me, Work in me the good Pleasure of thy Goodness." . . .

Two things I will observe unto you, *My Son*, concerning this matter.

One thing is This; When I Renewed, (as I often did, and with great Variety of Expression,) this Action of, *Coming to the Lord Jesus Christ*, I frequently sett apart Whole Dayes, for *Prayer* with *Fasting* in my Study; and in those Dayes, I usually underwent, first of all, grievous Conflicts, and Sorrows, and Horrors of Mind, and horrible Amazements about the Condition of my Soul. These *Agonies* came upon me, without my Calling for them; and they were accompanied with an inexpressible Bitterness, which made me dread the Repetition of them. When my Want of a *Christ*, and the Worth of a *Christ*, was hereby powerfully sett home upon me, I still with unutterable Fervency struggled, until I found myself assisted from on High, to Lay Hold on the Lord Jesus Christ, in all His *Offices*; and then a Sweet Satisfaction of Mind succeeded. Thus I was (while an Ignorant Youth) strangely led on by the *Spirit* of the Most High, to go the whole *Work of Conversion* often over & over again. And, tho' at the Beginning of a Day sett apart for such Devotions, I should even tremble in the Thoughts of the *Travail* that I foresaw, I should pass thro', yet I comforted myself, that my frequent *Renewing* of this Action, would be my *Assuring* of it. . . .

§   I had, from my Childhood, employ'd at least a *Tenth*, of what Money I gott, in *Pious Uses*; and now I had a considerable Quantity of Money annually coming in, I employ'd much more than a *Tenth* on such Uses. *My Son*, Do you alwayes Devote a *Tenth* of your Gains, unto the Special Service of our Great *Melchisedeck*, the Lord JESUS CHRIST. I Earnestly Exhort you, and Advise you: And you shall be no Loser by it, I Assure you.

But what I have here to note, is, That one of the First Contrivances, for the Glorifying of the Lord, which I Recorded, was, *To Spend much in Buying of Good* BOOKS, *to give away.*

How many *Hundreds*, yea, how many *Thousands*, of *Good Books*, I have thus given away, I cannot reckon. I suppose, I have given away near a *Thousand*, in One Year.

But I will observe Two Things unto you, *My Son*, upon it.

One Observable is This. While I gave away *Small Books* unto others, God gave *Great Books* unto me. I mean, That I had a secret, & a wondrous Blessing of God upon my *Library*. A *Good Library* was a thing, I much Desired & Valued, and by the Surprising Providence of God, it came to pass, That my *Library*, without my Pillaging of your Grandfathers, did by cheap, and strange Accessions, grow to have I know not how many more than *Thirty Hundred* Books in it; and I lived so near your Grand-fathers, that *his*, which was not much less than Mine, was also in a Manner *Mine*. This was much for a *Non-Conformist* Minister.

Another Observable is This. While I was giving away *Good Books* written by *Other Men*, I had all along a Secret Perswasion, That a Time would come, when I should have many *Books* written by *myself* likewise to give away. And I have lived since to see this Perswasion most Remarkably Accomplished. I shall too far Discover myself, if I should *Particularly* relate, how Remarkably. All I will say, is, That no *Non-Conformist* Minister now surviving in the Nation hath had so many. . . .

§　*My Son*; I lately mentioned unto you, a Contrivance, to carry on *Ejaculatory Prayers*, while I walk'd in the *Street*, or satt in a *Room* (with my Mind otherwise unemploy'd;) by contriving of some suitable *Blessing* for such Persons, as I should have before me, & then Directing it in the form of an *Ejaculation* unto Heaven for them, unobserved by any but Heaven, in the doing of it. In the *Twenty first* Year of my Age, I carried on this Exercise of *Religion* and *Charity*, to more of Exactness, and it hath ever since been with me, a frequent Exercise, and as *pleasant* as it has been *frequent*.

The Lord only knowes, how many Thousands of *Ejaculatory Prayers*, I have thus made for my Neighbours. But that you, *My Son*, may be Assisted in your Imitation, I will only Recite a *few* such *Ejaculatory Prayers*, from whence you may conjecture, how *I* did, and *You* may, use to shape such Devotions.

At a *Table*, where I being the Youngest of the Company, it was not proper for *me*, to Discourse at all, & the Discourses of others were too trivial to be worthy of my Attention.

Looking on the Gentlewoman that carved for us,
Lord, *Carve of thy Grace and Comforts, a rich Portion to that Person.*
A Gentlewoman stricken in Years.
Lord, *Adorn that Person with the Vertues, which thou praescribest unto Aged Women, and praepare her for her Dissolution.*
A Gentlewoman lately Married.

Lord, *Espouse & Marry the Soul of that Person to thyself, in a Covenant never to be forgotten.*

A Gentlewoman very Beautiful.

Lord, *Give that Person an Humble Mind, and Lett her Mind be most concern'd for those Ornaments, that are of Great Price in thy Sight.*

One of our Magistrates.

Lord, *Inspire that Person, with Wisdome, Courage, & Goodness, to seek the Welfare of thy People.*

One of our Ministers.

Lord, *Incline & Assist that Person to be a faithful Steward in thy House.*

One unhappy in his Children.

Lord, *Convert the Children of that Person, and Lett him have the Joy to see them walking in thy Truth.*

One Crazy and Sickly.

Lord, *Lett the Sun of Righteousness arise unto that Person, with Healing in His Wings.*

A Physician.

Lord, *Lett that Person be successful in his Practice, & Lett him successfully carry the Distempers of his own Soul, unto the Lord, his Healer.*

One that had mett, with great Losses.

Lord, *Give to that Person, the Good Part, which cannot be taken away.*

A Servant giving Attendance.

Lord, *Make that Person a Servant of Jesus Christ, & one of thy Children.*

In like Manner, when I have been sitting in a Room full of People, at a *Funeral*, where they take not much Liberty for *Talk*, and where much Time is most unreasonably lost, I have usually sett my poor Witts a Work, to contrive *Agreeable Benedictions*, for each Person in the Company.

And thus, in passing along the *Street*, I have sett myself to *Bless* Thousands of Persons, who never knew that I did it; with *Secret Wishes* after this Manner sent unto Heaven for them. . . .

§ Many of my Neighbours were now often proposing to me, a MARRIED STATE OF LIFE. But I thought it necessary to Address Heaven with more than ordinary *Prayer*, and *Fasting*, before I took a Step in an Affayr of such Importance. I kept many *Dayes* on this Occasion, in such Devotions.

On one of those Dayes, I find this Record of my Proceedings.

"I acknowledge unto the Lord, my own Unworthiness of any Good Thing; especially of That *Good Thing*, which is found by them that *obtain Favour of the Lord*. I Professed, That I would Study to do nothing hereabout, that should be Displeasing unto Him. I Declared, That I desired nothing in this World, which might prejudice my Glorifying of Himself. I Said, That if He Saw any thing would *Hinder* me from *Honouring* of Him, I should be glad if *He* would *Hinder* me from *Having* of *That*, whatever my misguided Appetites, might plead unto the Contrary. I Said, That if He would have me to embrace a *Caelibacy*, I would evermore take a Contentment in it, as that which would capacitate me, to Serve my *Parents*, & His *People*, to whom I owe my All. Nevertheless, to This I Subjoined, That since my Inclinations and Invitations did now seem to Recommend a married Estate unto me, I begg'd of the Lord, That He would *Lead me in the Way wherein I should Go* {Ps. 32:8}. And I made a *Vow*, That if the Lord would prevent all Obstructions of my Desireable Settlement, in a Marriage with one, who should be a Blessing to me, in Evangelical Services, *I will Twice at least, every Year, join with her, in keeping a Day of Thanksgiving*, privately unto Himself;—Except His Providence at any time, give a sufficient Cause for the Omission of it."

On another of these Dayes, I thus Recorded, what occurred.

"This Day, with Anguish of Soul, in the Sense of my own Sinfulness and Filthiness, I cast myself prostrate on my *Study-floor*, with my Mouth in the Dust. Here I Lamented unto the Lord, my *Follies*, which might have an Influence to deprive me of the *Blessings* which I was now pursuing. I Judged, I Loathed, I Hated Myself, because of those *Accursed Things*, & besought the *Forgiveness* thereof, thro' the *Blood of the Covenant*. I then Begg'd of the Most High, That He would, notwithstanding all my Miscarriages, bestow upon me, *A Companion for my Life*, by whose Prudence, Vertue, Good Nature, I might, while I am alive in this World, be Assisted in the Service of my Master, and who might accompany me to the Heaven of the Blessed forever. I pleaded, That *Marriage* was His *Ordinance*; and that He had promised, *No Good Thing shall be witheld from me*. I said unto Him, That I *Cast* the whole *Burden* of the *Care* about this Affayr, upon *Him: Expecting*, That He would mercifully divert my *Inclinations* from this Matter, if it would prove Displeasing to Him, or Disadvantageous to my Opportunities of Serving Him: *Entreating*, That if it may be best for me to proceed, He would please to Direct my *Choice*, & Order my *Way*, & Over-rule the Hearts of my Friends, and of *Her* unto whom I may make my Addresses, to favour what I prosecute: And in His due Time, to settle me, as to give me Rich Demonstrations of His Loving-kindnesses: *Engaging* herewithal, That I would more than Ever glorify Him, and spend my Time, in making of Blessed *Matches*, between the Son of God, and the Souls of Men."

Having taken these *Methods* to obtain the Blessing of God, on this weighty Concern, I may now tell you, *My Son*, I was wonderfully Blessed in it. When I was Entring the Twenty Fourth Year of my Age, I was by the wonderful Favour of Heaven brought into an Acquaintance with a Lovely and Worthy young Gentlewoman, whom God made a Consort, & a Blessing to me.[15] . . .

§ On a certain Day of *Prayer* with *Fasting*, which I kept in the Thirty-first Year of my Age, my *Special Errand* unto the Lord was, *This*: That whereas His *Good Angels* did by *His Order*, many *Good Offices* for His People, He would please to grant unto me, the Enjoyment of those *Angelical* Kindnesses and Benefits, which use to be done by *His Order*, for His *Chosen Servants*. I Requested only those Kindnesses, which the *Written Word* of God mentioned, as belonging to the *Heirs of Salvation*; but I Requested, that I might Receive those Benefits, in a Manner and Measure, more *Transcendent*, than what the great *Corruptions* in the Generality of *Good Men*, permitted them to be made Partakers of. . . .

In the close of these Proceedings, I wrote these Words;

I do now Beleeve, That some Great Things are to be done for me, by the ANGELS of God.

And now, *My Son*, It is *not lawful for me to utter*, the marvellous and amazing Favours, which I have since received from the Blessed ANGELS. I have seen, and felt, most wonderful Effects of their *Ministry*, Directing my Studies, Assisting my Labours, Preventing of Wrong Steps which I have been just ready to take; Supplying my Wants, and Comforting me under & against my Temptations. Yea, their *Ministry* hath proceeded so far, that I must here bear this *Testimony*, against the *Sadducism* of this Generation, That I have as infallible Demonstration of the Existence and Agency of those *Heavenly Spirits*, as I have to prove any Matter of *Sense* in the World. It is possible I may leave to you, *My Son*, a particular History by itself, of *Angelical Operations*, and of *Matters of Fact*, relating to things done by Good and Bad *Angels*, whereof I have been myself the Attentive *Witness*: Tho' I must not Forgett my Promise of *Concealing* such Things as are not proper to be exposed.[16] . . .

Another is This: There fell out in my Neighbourhood, not many Months after the *Day of Prayer* above said, an astonishing Thing, which I am well satisfied, is true; It were unreasonable for me, to desire a greater Satisfaction, than I had for the Truth of it. I will insert it, as I chose then for some Reasons, to insert it, in the Language, which I thought most proper for it.

Res Mirabilis, et Memorabilis. Post fusas, Maximis cum Ardoribus Jejunijsque Preces, apparuit Angelus, *qui Vultum habuit solis instar Meridiani Micantem, caetera Humanum, at prorsus Imberbem; Caput Magnificà Tiarâ obvolutum; In Humeris, Alas; Vestes deinceps Candidas et Splendidas; Togam nempè Talarem, et Zonam circà Lumbos, Orientalium cingulis non absimilem.*

Dixitque hic Angelus, à Domino JESU se missum, ut Responsa cujusdam Juvenis precibus articulatim afferat.

Quam plurima retulit hic Angelus, quae hic scribere non fas est. Verum inter alia Memoratu digna, futurum hujusce Juvenis Fatum, optimè posse exprimi asseruit, in illis Vatis Ezekielis *Verbis.*[17]

EZEK. 31. 3, 4, 5, 7, 8, 9.

Behold, He was a Cedar in Lebanon, with fair Branches, and with a Shadowing Shrowd, & of an High Stature, and his Top was among the Thick Boughs.

The Waters made him great, the Deep sett him up on high, with her Rivers running about his Plants.

His Heighth was exalted above all the Trees of the Field, and his Boughs were multiplied, and his Branches became long, because of the Multitude of Waters, when they shott forth.

Thus was he fair in his Greatness, in the Length of his Branches, for his Root was by the great Waters.

Nor was any Tree in the Garden of God, like unto him, in his Beauty.

I have made him fair by, the Multitude of his Branches; so that all the Trees of Eden, that were in the Garden of God, envied him.

Atque particulariter Clausulas, de Ramis ejus extendendis, exposuit hic Angelus, de Libris ab hoc Juvene componendis, et [non tantum in America, sed etiam in Europa,] *publicandis.*[18] *Addiditque peculiares quasdam Praedictiones,* [et pro Tali ac Tanto peccatore, valde Mirabiles] *de Operibus Insignibus, quae pro Ecclesiâ Christi, in Revolutionibus jam appropinquantibus, hic Juvenis olim facturus est.*

Domini JESU! Quid sibi vult haec res tam Extraordinaria? A Diabolicis Illusionibus, obsecro te, Servum tuum Indignissimum, ut Liberes ac defendes.[19]

At another Time, and in another Place, tis possible, *My Son,* I may tell you *more.* All that I will here say, is; Be sure to Beleeve, That there are *Holy Angels,* and Behave yourself so Holily that the *Good Angels* may take Pleasure to do you Good; But keep close to the *Written Word of God,* in your whole Conduct, and affect not *Extraordinary Dispensations,* lest you run into Delusions and Confusions, of the worst Consequence imaginable. Your sinful Father, has more than ordinary Cause, to Bless the Lord, for his own Praeservation from them. . . .

§ This Year, my little and only Bird, was taken so dangerously sick, that small Hope of her *Life*, was left unto us.[20] In my Distress, when I saw the Lord thus *Quenching the Coal that was left* unto me {2 Sam. 14:7}, and rending out of my Bosom, one that had lived so long with me, as to steal a *Room* there, and a *Lamb* that was indeed unto me *as a Daughter*, I cast myself at the Feet of His Holy Sovereignty. When I was going to Resign the Dying Child, in a *Prayer* for that Purpose over it, I took the *Bible* into my Hand, Resolving to Seek and Read first, some agreeable Portion of the *Scripture*. The *First* Place, that accidentally fell under my View, was, the Story of our Lords Raising the *Little Daughter* of the *Ruler of the Synagogue*, in the Eighth Chapter of *Luke*. Amazed at the Pertinency of the Place, I readd it with *Tears*; and then, with more *Tears* I turned it into a *Prayer*; wherein I freely gave up this Child unto the Lord; Assured, That it should be a *Vessel* of His *Glory* forever. But I also begg'd for the Life of the Child in this World; promising to the Lord, with His Help, That I would bring her up for *Him*, and that I would likewise assay to do some Special Service quickly for the Young People of my Neighbourhood. Immediately, the Child fell into a Critical and Plentiful *Bleeding*, and Recovered from that Hour, unto the Admiration of all. However, *This Day* to prepare my own Heart for all Events, and express what should be in the Heart of others, I preached a Sermon on those Words, *The Lord is able to give thee much more than this* {2 Chron. 25:9}. . . .

§ Being Invited unto a more than ordinary Action of Publick Service,[21] for the Lord, and for His People, I thought myself concerned in a more than ordinary Manner, to Abase myself before the Lord. And that I might keep myself under a Lasting Abasement, I not only kept many *Dayes of Humiliation*, but I also composed a Writing of several Pages, entitled, THE TRUE PICTURE OF— myself. Herein I did, with *Black*, but yett with too *True*, Characters, describe my own Vileness at such a rate, that it cannot be look'd upon, without Horrour of Soul; but I Resolved, often to look upon it.[22] . . .

My Son, it was not until after *Seven Lustres*[23] of my Life were expired, that God bestow'd upon me, a Son that lived unto an Age to Read what I write.[24]

The Day before he was born, I spent in Praying and Fasting before the Lord, and Crying to Heaven, for the Welfare of my Consort, and of her expected Offspring. A Son had been foretold me, in an Extraordinary Way, some Years before; and in the Evening of the Day, which I had now kept, I entertained my Family, before our Evening-Prayers, with a Meditation on Joh. 16.21. *A Woman, when shee is in Travail, hath Sorrow because her Hour is come; but as soon as she is delivered, of the Child, she remembreth no more the Anguish, for Joy that a Man is born into the World.*

After I had commended my Consort unto the Lord, I laid me down to Sleep (after Midnight,) that I might be fitt for the Services of the Day ensuing, which was the *Lords-Day*; and in a Chamber by myself, because of her Expecting at this Time her Travail. But after One a Clock in the Morning, I Awoke, with a great Concern upon my Spirit, which obliged me to Arise, and Retire into my Study. There I cast myself on my Knees before the Lord, confessing my Sins that rendred me unworthy of His Mercy, but imploring His Mercy to my Consort, in the Distress now upon her.

While my Faith was pleading, that the Saviour, who was *Born of a Woman*, would send His Good *Angel* to Releeve my Consort, the People ran to my Study-Door, with the Acceptable Tidings, *That a Son was born unto me!*

In the Forenoon following, I preached unto our Great Congregation, on that Scripture, Psal. 90.16. *Lett thy Work appear unto thy Servants, and thy Glory unto their Children*; managing this Doctrine; *That the Enjoyment of the Precious Christ, who is the Glorious Work, of God, is the Great Blessedness desired by Good Men, both for Themselves and for their Children.*

But tho' this were a Son of Great *Hopes*, and one who had Thousands & Thousands of *Prayers* . . . employ'd for him; yett after all, a Sovereign GOD would not Accept of him. He was Buried in the *Atlantic* Ocean. And you, my only Son,[25] Surviving, are the Person for whom these Memorials are intended & reserved.

And now, because I may upon my looking back, meet with several Passages yett unmentioned, that may be as Instructive to you, as those whereof I have already made mention; and others are occurring, in that Part of your Fathers Life, which is now running; I shall proceed without any *Method* at all, to sett before you what I may think proper & useful for you. And it may be, the less of *Method* there is in this Work, it will be but the more *Natural*, and *Beautiful*, and it may carry the more of a *Parental Authority* upon it. . . .

§   Finding, that whenever I go abroad into other Towns, the *Curiosity* and *Vanity* of the People discovers itself, in their *Great Flocking* to hear me, with I know not what *Expectations*: This hath still caused me aforehand exceedingly to *Humble* myself before the Lord, (even with *Fasting* and *Prayer* oftentimes) that the fond *Expectations* of the *People*, may not be chastised upon *myself*, in His Leaving of *me* to any Inconvenience. By this Method, I not only am in a comfortable Measure kept from the foolish *Taste* of *Popular Applause* in my own

Heart, but also from the *Humbling Dispensations* of Heaven, whereto the Fondness of the People might otherwise expose me.

My Son, you may live to make some Use of this Hint.

§ Keeping a Day of Secret THANKSGIVING, my Soul was raised unto more than ordinary *Delights* and *Raptures*. The Holy Lord even dealt *Familiarly* with me; I went into the very *Suburbs* of *Heaven*; the *Spirit* of my *Lord* carried Me thither, and made known unto me Glorious Things; Yea, *Heaven* came near unto me, & fill'd me with *Joy unspeakable and full of Glory*. I cannot, I may not, *Utter* the Communications of Heaven, whereto I was this Day admitted. All that I shall observe to you, *My Son*, is, That within a few Hours, I was *Buffeted* with some things in my Neighbourhood, that had a more than ordinary Measure of Temptation, & Vexation in them. And lett my *Experience* confirm unto you this *Observation*, That immediately after extraordinary *Communion* with *Heaven*, you shall ordinarily meet with some *Accident* on Earth, which will mortify you with some special *Affliction* and *Abasement*. . . .

§ On a Day of *Prayer* with *Fasting*, which I kept, under Sore *Temptations*, I find I have entred this Record.

"It was a Day full of astonishing Enjoyments; a Day filled with Resignations and Satisfactions, and Heavenly Astonishments. *Heaven* has been opened unto me this Day. Never did I so long to Dy, and fly away into Heaven! I have seen and felt *unutterable Things*. I have *Tasted that the Lord is Gracious* {Ps. 8:34}. I can by no means Relate, the Communications with Heaven, whereto I have been this Day admitted. I am now sure, That the Great GOD is *my God*; that I stand before God in the *Righteousness* of my Lord JESUS CHRIST; that no *Good Thing shall be witheld from me* {Ps. 84:11}; that God will make an amazing use of me, to glorify Him; and that I shall be an Object, for the everlasting Triumphs of Sovereign & Infinite *Grace*."

"I was not able to bear the *Extasies* of Divine *Love*, into which I was Raptured; They exhausted my Spirits; they made me Faint, & Sick; they were Insupportable; I was forced, even to withdraw from them, lest I should have Swoon'd away under the Raptures."

But, I can tell you, *My Son*; there soon followed a *Storm* of Great Reproaches & Confusions upon me. Gett Good by what I tell you! . . .

§ If I hear that any Person has done me *wrong* in Word or Deed, I find, it is *Often*, (perhaps, not *Alwayes*,) the best way in the World, *Not to lett them know*, *that I have any Knowledge of it.* The best way is, to Forgive and Forgett the Wrong, and bury it in *Silence.* For, besides the Consideration due to the Internal Advantage, reap'd by such Christianity, there is *this* to be considered: Such is the Malignity in the most of Men, that they will *Hate* you, only because *you know* that they have *wrong'd* you. They will, as far as they can, *Justify* the *Wrong* they have done; and because their Wicked Hearts Imagine that you must needs bear a *Spite* unto them, for the *Wrong* you have received from them, they will bear a *Confirmed Spite* unto you, on that vile Account. Whereas, I have often found, That my *Concocting* with Patience and Silence, a *Sleight,* or an *Hurt* that has been offered unto me, has been *Followed* (and *Rewarded* by God) with this Consequence; That the *very Persons* who have *wrong'd* me, have afterwards been made Instruments of *Signal Service* unto me.

§   When any *Remarkable Affliction* befalls me, I sett myself to consider, *what Advantage I may contrive to my Flock, and to the People of God, out of this Affliction?* The *Affliction* awakens me to *Preach,* and perhaps to *Write,* those things, which may be of *General Advantage.* I think with myself, It may be the Lord intends now to make me bear some *Special Fruits* for His Glory and Service in His Churches, which else would never have been found upon me. And I can truly say, That tho' *Affliction be not Joyous but Grievous* {Heb. 12:11}, yett the very *Prospect* of this *Effect,* while I have been but *Entring* into the *Darkness,* which I saw coming upon me, and while I have been yett in the *Dark,* as to the particular Benefits & Revenues, for the Service of Religion, which could arise from it; It has caused my Spirit exceedingly to *Triumph over Troubles*; I have, with a Triumphant Satisfaction Rejoiced in it, that the Lord would please to send *Sorrowes,* with such admirable *Designs* upon me. . . .

§   I have all this while omitted the Mention of the various Intentions and Contrivances, with which the Dispensation of the *Alms,* that have even filled my Life, have been carried on. The Reason of the Omission has been; Because I thought an *Eternal Concealment* most proper for them; a Concealment even from a *Son,* that is to be as my very Hand unto me.

But, inasmuch as the Design of these Memorials, is to instruct you, *My Son,* in the Methods of *Godliness* and *Fruitfulness,* I will rescue from the Midst of that *Concealment,* at least one way to *Devise Good,* which ha's been sometimes practiced with me.

I have several times, taken little Parcels of *Money,* (*Seven* perhaps at a time,) containing about Half a Peece of Eight in a Paper;[26] These Parcels of *Money,* I have accompanied, with so many *Books of Piety.* I have sent *Packets* unto *Ministers* abroad, in such Towns as I have thought convenient; and sometimes, (that

Grace might herein have the more Triumphant Exercise,) I have sent them to such Ministers, as have treated me, not so well as they might have done. I have Directed a *Nameless Letter* unto them, in such a way, as they might not know, that I was the Person with whom they were now concerned. I have desired them, to find out so many *Poor* and *Bad* People, in their Flock, & bestow these *Alms*, and *Books*, in their *own Names*, (if they pleased) upon them; with their own Holy Counsils and Warnings unto them, to lay hold on Eternal Life. In this way, I proposed, not only to *Do Good* unto the Elect of God, but also to awaken the *Ministers* themselves, unto a more flaming Zeal to *Do Good*. But that I may more exactly Describe, what I would be at, I will Transcribe, one of the Letters, which I sent, (copied by a *Female* Hand, for my being the better under *Covert*,) on these Occasions.

"Syr. From an Unknown Hand, there is a small Trouble now impos'd upon you. A little *Silver* is, with the Propriety thereof, devolved into your Hand. It is now no longer any Mans else, but *Yours*; nor is any other Name now to be used on this Occasion, but *Yours*. But it is desired, That you would find out as many Persons in your Flock, who are in very *poor* Circumstances, both on Temporal and Spiritual Accounts as you find the Summ divided into Parcels; and Distribute the Parcels unto them. At the same time, it is desired, That you would bestow your Holy Counsils and Warnings upon them; and not leave them, until they have Resolved upon the Practice of Serious Piety. If then you lodge with them the little *Books*, with which you are now also for that Purpose furnished, your Advice will be Remembred the better with them. Who can tell, but under an *Angelical Conduct*, you may now find out some of the *Elect* of God, among the *Poor*, who thus *have the Gospel preached unto them*? {Matt. 11:5} Your own Ministry will also be rendred very acceptable, among a People, to whom you make such *Pastoral Visits*.[27] Lett not a Word be spoken, about the Original of this Action: For there is but one Man in the World, who knowes any thing of it, or is like to know. A glorious CHRIST be with you!——"

§   I have had my Mind strangely and strongly *buffeted*, with *Temptations* of this Importance.

I have now for many, and weary Years, been leading a *Laborious Life*, in the Wayes of Religion. I have lived in a *Continual Flame*. The Care to carry on Ordinary and Extraordinary *Devotions*, & to have my Heart filled with perpetual Thoughts of a Devout Character, & Tendency; and Suppress and Destroy all the Corrupt Inclinations of my Soul; and my Watchful, Various, Numberless *Contrivances* to *Do Good*, unto all that I converse withal, and abroad in the World; and my perpetual *Warfare* with successive *Temptations*; whereof my

Course of Living ever now and then Renewes a *Tempest* upon me: All these things together, fill my Life with *Labours* and *Sorrowes*. I gett nothing of *this World* by these Labours; There is no worldly Profit of them. I miss many Advantages to come at worldly Riches, by reason of them. If there be any *One Point*, wherein above the rest, I may pretend unto any Shadow of a *Vertue*, it is ordered, that in *that* very Point, I am singularly misunderstood & calumniated. My *Serviceableness* does but expose me to *Malignity*. My very *Essayes* to be *Serviceable*,[28] are made my *Blemishes* and *Reproaches*. The *Blessedness* of the *Future State*, who can tell, what it is? And it may be, tis *uncertain*, whether I shall arrive to any such *Blessedness*. Why then should not my weary Mind, abate of this *Flame*? I don't propose to turn a *Profane* & a *Debauch't* sort of a Divel; But why may I not leave off the *Labours* of my *Flights* in Piety and Usefulness? Why may I not suffer myself, to *sink down*, into the Low, Dull, Slothful Measures, of the *Common* and *Barren* Christianity? Why may not I content myself, to Jog on, as the Christians of the *Lowest Form*, who, if they can but just *Creep* along, in some *Formalities*, and keep clear of *Grosser Scandals*, do not seem to care for any more: How *easy* should I make myself by such a Conduct! Why should I be an Enemy to such a *Grateful Easiness*? To what Purpose will be my Perseverance?

But now, to these *Hellish Temptations*, I have still my Answer, from the Oracle of Heaven: 1. Cor. 15.58. *Be yee stedfast & unmoveable, alwayes abounding in the Work of the Lord: forasmuch as yee know, that your Labour is not in vain in the Lord.*

And looking up to the Lord, for the Aids of His Grace, I have then found my *Resolutions* fixed more than ever in my Life, to live unto Christ, & *bring forth much Fruit* unto Him, & never to *be weary of well-doing*. . . .

§ *My Son*, There is a Disposition and an Experiment, which your Father is able thus to declare unto you.

I am not unable, with a little Study to write in *Seven Languages*; I have written and printed in them.[29] I feast myself with the Sweets of all the *Sciences*, which the more Polite Part of Mankind ordinarily pretend unto. I am entertained with all kinds of *Histories* Ancient and Modern. I am no Stranger to the *Curiosities*, which by all Sons of Learning are brought unto the Curious. These *Intellectual* Pleasures, are beyond any *Sensual* Ones. Nevertheless, All this affords me not so much Delight, as it does, to Releeve the Distresses of any one Poor, Mean, and *Miserable Neighbour*; and much more, to do any extensive Service for the Redress of those *Epidemical Miseries*, under which *Mankind* in general is languishing, and to advance the *Kingdome* of GOD in the World.[30] . . .

§ I think,

If I were fastened unto a CROSS, *and under all the Circumstances of a* Crucifixion, *what would be My Dispositions, what My Exercises?*

I should look on my approaching *Death*, as unavoidable; and the Approaches of it would now be welcome to me, not having any Prospect of being any other Way delivered from Numberless Uneasinesses.

I should look on all the *Delights* and *Riches* and *Honours* of the World from which I am departing, as things of no *Use* and no *Worth* unto me.

I should have done Expecting of *Satisfaction* from any thing of *This World*; and no more propose a *Portion* in any thing that is done under the Sun. . . .

Tho' I should have done with This World, yett I should express a Concern for the *Relatives* which I leave behind me, in a Land of *Pitts* & of *Droughts*, & *fiery flying Serpents* {Isa. 14:29}. . . .

I should, with continual *Acts of Resignation*, committ my *Spirit* into the Hands of my FATHER {Luke 23:46}, and my SAVIOUR; with Assurance of my Speedy Reception into a *Paradise*, where I shall be *Comforted*.

I should endeavour to Look into the *Heavenly World*; and Rejoice in the View of the *Joy Sett before me* {Heb. 12:2} there, and count *the Light Afflictions here which are but for a Moment*, abundantly compensated in that *far more Exceeding & Eternal Weight of Glory* {2 Cor. 4:17}.

In these Things I should propound a *Conformity* to my *Crucified* JESUS.

Thus *Dying, Behold, I Live!* {2 Cor. 6:9}

And finding myself brought into these *Dispositions* and these *Exercises*, the Faith of what must most certainly follow hereupon fills me with *Joy Unspeakable & full of Glory* {1 Pet. 1:8}. . . .

This is *the Way that I take.* And in this way of *Living by Faith of the SON of GOD*, I keep *Looking for His Mercy to me in Eternal Life* {Jude 1:28}.

CHRISTIANUS PER IGNEM (1702)

[MEDITATIONS ON FIRE]

THE INTRODUCTION.[31]

One of the *Best* Things, that can be done for other men, by any man, who would make it his Business to Do *Good* unto all, is to suggest and supply **Good Thoughts** unto them. Tho' it may be disputed, whether this be the *First Proposition*, whereof any man can be certain, as a New *Philosophy* has taught us, *I think, therefore I am;*[32] yet it is no *New Divinity* to teach, that *As Men Think, so* *they are.* That Noble Faculty of *Thinking,* wherewith a man is enabled, and enobled above the *Beasts of the Field,* being well or ill employ'd, will either turn men into *Fellows* for *Angels,* or make men worse *than the Beasts that perish.* The Infinite *Perfections* of **God,** the Wonderful *Mysteries* of the Lord **Jesus Christ,** the amazing *Circumstances* of the **Future State,** the various *Preparations* of men in this world, and other *Circumstances* referring to that *State;* the Illustrious *Operations* of the Almighty both in **Creation,** and in **Government;** and His various *Dispensations* towards **our selves** in particular; such things as these, are most proper, and worthy, and useful for a Rational and a Renewed Soul to *Think* upon. And a man full of *Good,* and *Wise,* and *Right Thoughts* upon these *Great Themes,* will be a *Good man,* and furnished for the Doing of much *Good* unto many others.

Meditation is therefore a Duty of so much Evidence and Consequence in *Christianity,* that they can be no *Christians,* nor acquainted in the least measure with the Divine Oracles, who do not confess their Obligations unto it: And yet it must be confessed, That one grand cause why *Christianity* so much Languishes, is because that so few *Christians* duly practice it. Our Bible very frequently commends unto us, **Consideration,** and a *Meditating* on *God,* and on His *Laws:* And thro' the want of this *Meditation* it is that all the *Ordinances* and all the *Providences* of God, are so ineffectual unto the most of men, and they continue so much without *Life,* and *Light,* and *Peace* all their dayes, and at last perish among those who do not *Consider their Latter End.* . . .

The *Method* of proceeding in our **Occasional Reflections,** needs not be tied up unto many strict *Rules* about it. I remember, *Hugo de Sancto Victore* tells us, That there is a *Threefold Voice* of all the *Creatures* unto us, *Accipe, Redde, Fuge.*[33] All *Creatures* may put us in mind, first of something that we do **Receive** of God, in them; next, of something that we should **Return** to God for them; and thirdly, of something that we should **Avoid,** both of *Transgression* in them, and so of *Punishment* from them. And it were a very suitable *Method of Thinking,* to touch upon each of those *Three Heads* in our **Occasional Reflections.** Or at least, we may do well to oblige our selves unto the forming of a Certain *Triangle* in them, with first, **Going forth** to observe the *properties* of the *Creatures* themselves; then **Coming back,** to Advise our selves, with *Instructions* brought from them; and Lastly, **Darting up** to Him that Sitteth in the Heavens, our *Petitions,* for such Compassion and Assistance, as we now see we need.

Behold, Reader, a Book of **Occasional Reflections,** all made upon one of those *Creatures,* that we have daily before us: And if *one* of them, could afford so many *Good Thoughts,* unto one of so *dull,* and so *vain* a mind, as that which the Author of this Book, has to complain of (and yet *he himself* now finds, it might have easily afforded him as *many more!*) What an Immense Treasure of *Good*

Thoughts might we find in all the rest? The Reason, why the Author singled out the **Fire**, for his *Chymistry* to *Work upon*, (the very thing that other *Chymistry* does principally *Work withal*,) was, partly because one day perswading some of his Intimate Friends, to try their skill at **Occasional Reflections**, he accidentally let fall this Encouragement; *He would give them a Demonstration, that as dry a Subject, as for instance, that of the Fire then before us, would yield a Christian a whole Book full of Meditations;* And he was obliged then to give the *Demonstrations*. . . .

Meditation I.

On the Fire *proving it self to be indeed the* Fire.

I see the *Fire* before me; But how do I know, that it is the *Fire?* The Philosopher long ago answered, *Qui tam Stulte quaerunt, Ignem tangant.*[34] Truly, the *proof* of it, is better *Felt*, than *Spoke*. I *feel* that it is the *Fire;* I have a *Sense* of it, that I can't easily describe in Words, unto another man; I need no *Arguments* to convince me of it; and if there were *Arguments* to the contrary, shap'd with never such unanswerable *Sophistry*, I should think it Answer enough unto them, I *know 'tis otherwise!*

This Meditation carries me to consider, *How do I know the Scriptures of the Old and New Testament to be the Word of God!* And that which makes the Consideration more agreeable, is, That this *Word*, is called, Jer. 20.9. A *Burning Fire.* It is a Thing of more than ordinary consequence unto every Christian, to be well established in this point, *How may a Christian indeed know, That our Bible is the Word of God, or, a Book of Truth, and a Rule of Life, given by Inspiration from Heaven?* For, the influence of the *Bible*, on our whole *Behaviour* here, and *Blessedness* hereafter, depends on our *Faith* of this point; & our grand Enemy labours nothing more, than to keep our *Faith* hereof as Feeble as ever he can. To confirm our *Faith* of our *Bibles* being the *Word of God*, we are not unfurnished with moral *Arguments* enough to silence *the contradiction of Sinners.* It is infinitely reasonable to Believe, That the most High God has committed unto Writing, some where or other, what He would have us *Think*, and to *Do*, in order to our *Glorifying* of Him. Now, if our *Bible*, be not the *Writing*, wherein the Will of God is to be found, it is no where to be found at all; for there is none that can stand in competition with it: there is no where else to be met withal, any *Scheme* of the way for our coming to the Enjoyment of God, that can give any tolerable satisfaction to a Reasonable mind. And who else but God, could be the Author of it? *Ill men*, and *Ill Angels*, would never have connived a *System* of such an Holy and Heavenly Tenour, and so opposite, yea so Torturous, unto their own vicious Inclinations. *Good men,* and *Good Angels* would not have *Lyed* for God, and have imposed their own Inventions upon their Maker. And indeed, the Remarkable Providence of God, in preserving our *Bible*, so uncorrupt for so many Ages, notwithstanding the horrible plots of Earth and Hell, to have utterly extinguished it, (which can't be said of any other Composure). This proclaims, That it is dear to *God*, yea, that *God* Himself espouses it, as being the Author of it. . . .

But as the *Fire* passes from one *Billet* unto another, so let my *Thoughts* here, in passing along, at least glance upon one Subject more.

There are certain Enjoyments with which the Spirit of God favours the Souls of His Faithful People; and especially the perswasions of a *particular Faith*, which they sometimes Enjoy, in their *Prayers*, for this or that particular *Smile* of God on their Affayrs. This *particular Faith*, is not so much the *Duty*, as the *Dignity*, and *Priviledge*, of the Faithful, and not granted unto *all*, but here and there, according to the Sovereign pleasure of Heaven, gloriously irradiating their minds, and with a certain powerful, Heart melting, Heavenly *Afflatus*, assuring of them, *That God hath granted the Thing, which they have asked of Him.* Well, tho' this *particular Faith*, has a counterfeit, wherein many have been deceived; yet such a Thing there is, that is a special *Operation of the Spirit of God*, and perhaps of His Holy Angels, on the minds of His Holy *Children.* The Question is, *How do I know this Operation from a counterfeit?* My Answer is, That no words of mine can Answer the Question; I *know* it, as I know the *Fire* to be the *Fire*; I *feel* it, but no words of mine can express, how it *feels*. . . .

Meditation III.

On the Light *cast by the* Fire *upon the* Objects *about it.*

All the *Objects* here capable of having *direct Rays* from the *Fire* shot upon them, how *Lightsome* are they? All clothed with *Garments of Light!* The side of the *Chimney*, the Wall of the *Chamber*, the Iron *Back*, the Brazen *Tongs*, and their *Fellow-Servants*, are now distinguished, with an agreeable *Brightness.* They entertain the Beams of *Light*, which the *Fire* darts upon them, and by entertaining thereof, they have a particular *Brightness*, and Beauty upon them.

When I see the *Reflection* of the *Light*, on the Objects about the *Fire*, me-thinks, I am furnished with *Light* enough, to make a *Reflection* of my own upon it. This *Light* leads me unto that *Glory*, that shall be Enjoy'd by the Saints in the Heavenly World; and unto the very *Fountain* of all their *Glory.* If unto the *Fire*, I should Resemble the Glorious Lord JESUS CHRIST, who shall one day appear in *Flaming Fire* {2 Thess. 1:8}, the Resemblance, might with many Good Thoughts be prosecuted. It is enough, that our Lord, the *Sun of Righteousness*, is compared unto the *Sun*, which is an *Ocean of Fire*; and that Caelestial and

Wonderful *Fire ball*, corresponding with the little Flashes on my Hearth, in the property of *Luminositie*, the comparison that is now to be made, will be sufficiently vindicated. Nor will it be unserviceable unto this purpose, to remark, that in some Languages (particularly the *Syriac* and *Chaldee*) the same word that is used for *Fire*, is used also for *Light*. The Splendor of my *Fire*, tho' so sparkling and so dazzling, that the most lively Limner can't paint it out unto the Life, is but a *black Shadow*, of the *Glory*, which the Disciples in the *Holy Mountain*, saw resting on the Transfigured *Lord of Glory* {Matt. 17:1–2}. . . .

Some *Right Thoughts*, not unfit for a Child of *Jacob*, take hold on the *Heel* of those that have hitherto Entertained me: and my *Fire* has Enkindled in me some further *Desires*, and *Wishes*. I see, that when there Intervenes any thing between the *glowing Coals* in my *Fire*, and the *Brightned Walls* of my *Room*, a *Darkness* arises then so far thereupon. The *Fire shines* not upon an adjacent Object, if there be any thing between *That* and the Object. And am I not now informed, what is the Reason of the *Darkness* upon the Minds of men? Whatsoever does Interrupt the Communion between the Lord JESUS CHRIST and my Soul, brings thereby a *Darkness* upon me. In the *Light* of *Life* Enjoy'd by the Saints above, there is no *Darkness*; Why? because there is nothing to intercept the most Intimate Communion between the *Lamb*, who is the *Light of the City of God*, and the Saints who *Walk in the Light of that City* {Rev. 21:24}. But in the *Darkness of this World*, a Christian has frequent occasions, with the Philosopher, to ingeminate his cry of, *Darkness, Darkness*; and the occasions will continue, till he arrive where the *Dark Shadows flee away* {Song of Sol. 2:17}. Alas, The *Darkness*, which attends me, is like that on *Egypt*; it may be *Felt*: I feel it in a woful *Ignorance*, and grievous *Disorder*, and lamentable *Confusion* and *Sottishness*, and Horror of *Guilt* upon my Spirit. And now, by *Fire-light* I see the *Cause* of it! I would I could say, I have half a *Cure*, now I know the *Cause*. It lies here; something there lies between *me*, and my Lord JESUS CHRIST, who would *Enlighten* me. The Truth is, The very drawing of the *Curtains* of my *Earthly Tabernacle* about me, has this Influence upon me, That I am experimentally taught the meaning of those words, *Present in the Body, and Absent from the Lord* {2 Cor. 5:6}: The *Flesh* is between Him and me: Oh, Why do I no more say, I *desire to be dissolved, that I may be with my Lord* {Phil. 1:23}. But that which is yet worse is, That my *Corruptions* do send up that ugly *Smoke*, which hinders the *Shine* of my Lord JESUS CHRIST from comforting of me; And sometimes I lay too many *Logs* on the *Fire*, verifying the old Observation, *In multitudine Negotiorum periclitatur pietas.*[35] I take too many *Diverting Businesses* upon me, by which I Restrain those *Emanations* from the Fountain of *Light*, wherewith I might otherwise, be Irradiated. *Be advised, O my Soul; be well advised!* . . .

Meditation VI.

On the Fire *of* Hell.

Descendamus viventes, et non descendamus morientes. Chrys.[36]

In some Countreys 'tis a Custome, when a *Light* is brought into the Room, to wish [*Deus det vobis Lucem Æternam,*] *God grant you Everlasting Light:* But when I come to a *Fire* in a Room, it shall be my wish, *God save me from Everlasting Fire!* {Matt. 25:41}. I find my self unable to bear the *Fire:* if the *Fire* on my Hearth were to touch my *Flesh,* I should soon cry out of it; the Torture of being scorch'd in the *Fire* would be intolerable; perhaps there is no other Torment more intolerable, than that which the *Fire* gives to our Nerves, when it seizes on them. And yet I am led now to think, of something that is more intolerable than the *Fire,* and that on the score of its being so, is called the *Fire.* . . .

It is asserted in *Scripture,* it is affirmed by *Reason;* the Demonstrations of it are *Irrefragable,* That there is another World, wherein a *due punishment* is *reserved* by the *Wrath* of God, for all His *Enemies.* This *punishment,* as it is called, *Hell,* so it is called, *Fire,* and from the Temper of the *Fire* now before me, I may Learn, that the *Fire* of *Hell,* will be *intolerable.* If there were nothing else to prove it, but This, here would be proof enough. There are *Impious* men, who have taken *Innocent* men, yea, very *Vertuous* ones, and have *Rosted* them to Death in the *Fire,* with lingring and horrid Agonies, and Exercised a thousand other exquisite Cruelties upon them. Now these Monsters of Impiety, never did receive any Recompence of their Cruelties in this World, any more than *Alva,* or *Bonner.*[37] It followeth then, that in another World, there must be *Miseries* intended for these *Humane Devils,* at least, as Exquisite, as being Rosted to Death in the *Fire.* This must follow, if you confess a *God,* and confess the *Justice* of God. But which yet more evidently proclaims the *punishment* of the *Damned* in the *Fire* of *Hell* to be *intolerable,* is, the *Nature,* and *Author,* of the *punishment.* Now the *principal punishment* in the *Fire* of *Hell,* is the *Wrath* of the Infinite GOD, immediately smiting of the *Soul.* The *Conscience* of a Sinner, which is a Faculty by his Creator put into him, to be a special Instrument of Him that Created it, *This* being set on *Fire,* by immediate Impressions, from the Wrath of God upon it, will fill the Sinner with terrible Dolour, and Horror, and Anguish throughout Eternal Ages. . . .

But if the *Fire* or *Hell,* be so *Intolerable,* what an unaccountable Madness will it be, for a man by Sin, to throw himself into that *Fire?* It is a proverb for the greatest Aversation imaginable; *I have no more mind unto such a thing, than to run my Hand into the Fire.* Alas, If any Sin, be so dear unto me, that I can part with it no more than my *Right-Hand,* not my *Hand* only, but my *whole Body will be cast into the Fire of Hell* {Matt. 5:30}. One that was Tempted unto Lewdness, did thus very significantly resist and repel the Tempter, *Hold your Hand one Quarter of an Hour in the Fire on the Hearth before you, or else don't Expect, that I will for your sake burn in the Fire of Hell for ever.* Truly, To Sin is to run into the most *Formidable Fire: Sin* is therefore worse than a *Brutish Folly;* in *Sin* a man does worse than play the *Bruit.* O my Soul, when I am sollicited unto any Sin, Let me set the *Fire* of *Hell* before my Eyes, and realize the hideous Condition of them that are burning in that *Intolerable Fire;* and Resolve, like one who had no *Faith* of this *Fire* in him, and yet having a price of *Unchastity* proposed unto him, said, *No, I will not buy Repentance at so dear a rate!* . . .

Meditation XI.
On throwing a piece of Leather *into the* Fire.

One casting into the *Fire,* a bit of *Leather,* its moving, its wriggling, its twisting one way and another, carried some show of *Sense* with it: It seemed as if it had the same *sense* in it, which there would have been in the Creature to which it once belonged; One is ready to expect a *Cry* from it. A thing wholly *Insensible,* does in the *Fire* I see, put on a Semblance of mighty *Sensibility.*

An *Hypocrite* is one without a principle of *Life:* He is one altogether destitute of that *Life,* wherein God is Known, and Serv'd, and Glorified. He has no *Living Sense* of Spiritual and Eternal Objects. But when an *Hypocrite* is cast into the *Fire* of some *Affliction,* he seems as if he had some *Life* in him: his *Prayers,* and his *Vows,* and his *Devout Resolutions,* and various *Devotions,* look very *Sensibly,* when some Grief or Fear is *Afflicting* of him. One would think, who but a *Child of God,* could be so serious, and so *Sensible,* as we see this *Afflicted Hypocrite?* Oh, There's no Relying on the *Showes,* that men make in their *Affliction.* I will mention but one Observation to confirm it. I have often been concerned with Criminals under the Sentence of *Death,* having their Souls in a *Fire* of Agony. In this *Fire,* and *Fright,* Oh, the sorrow for *Sin,* and hatred of it, Oh, the hope in Christ, and love to God, and resolutions never to Sin on any Terms any more, which these Wretches have now *Show'd* unto me. I could scarce imagine it possible for any but Regenerate Souls to speak so sensibly well; many of these have been *Reprieved,* and *Pardoned* by the Government; but of them all I never knew two, but what proved afterwards meer *Devils Incarnate.* All I will add is This; If men be not Religious in *Prosperity,* as well as in *Adversity,* there is no true *Life* of Religion in them. They that never *stir,* but in the *Fire,* let them then *stir* never so promisingly, are yet *alienated from the Life of God.* O my Soul, Read, Psal. 78. 34, 36. . . .

Meditation XVIII.
On the Coals.

I know not, whether there are more *Coals* at this Time, in my *Fire,* than there are *Thoughts,* in my mind, which may take *Fire* from them. *Lord, Graciously and Mercifully Touch my Pen with a Coal from thine Altar, that so it may in an Holy strain write some of those Things, which a polluted Sinner, that yet serves at thine Altar, is now for that Service Meditating* {Isa. 6:6–7}.

And now, first, Methinks, I should be as loth to commit a *Sin,* as to handle a *Coal.* If I should go to take up a *Coal* in my Hand, it would both *Smutt* me, and *Scorch* me. I am certain, a *Sin* taken into my Heart, would have the like, and worse effects upon me. Every *Sin* is of a *Filthy* consequence, and by it, even the *Conscience is defiled.* And *Sin* admitted, and allowed, will scald the *Conscience,* at last into as much anguish, as ever the bloody hand of *Ravilliac,* burning with his Knife in it, suffered at his Execution.[38] Oh, that I were now as much afraid of every *Sin,* and all the *Works of the Flesh,* as of a *Coal* to be clapt upon my *Flesh.* The Purest *Nazarites,* once contaminated with *Sins* against the Holy Laws of God, may have that *Lamentation* made upon them, Lam. 4.8. *Their Visage is now blacker than a Coal.* Wherefore, Let me take heed, lest I Blacken my self by the *Coals,* and not *Abhorring that which is Evil* Rom. 12:9]. It is the Wise mans Disswasive, relating to the particular Sins of *Unchastity,* Prov. 6. 27, 28. *Can a man take Fire in his Bosom, and his Cloaths not be burnt? Can one go upon hot Coals, and his Feet not be burnt? So,*—Now let me by this Consideration, be Disswaded and Affrighted from all other *Sins. They are so many Coals; why should I meddle with them!* . . .

While I am in this Meditation, I call to mind, the parable, by which the Sins of *Dishonesty,* have been sometimes painted out unto us. To carry *Burning Coals into his Nest,* was in the issue, no Advantage to the *Thievish Bird of Prey.* Should I convey an Handful of these *Burning Coals,* into the Boxes, where ly my Papers, and the best of my other Treasures, what mad work should I make! Truly, those men, that add unto their Estates, by Fraudulence, by Oppression, by any *Dishonesty,* do but convey *Burning Coals* among all their Treasures; and what, may we foresee, will be the Issue? *He gets Riches, and not by Right, He shall leave them in the midst of his Days, and at his End shall be a Fool* {Jer. 17:11}.

And yet, there is a sort of *Coals,* that we may become free withal. 'Tis required, Prov. 25. 21, 22, [And repeated, Rom. 12. 20.] *If thine Enemy be Hungry, give him Bread to eat; and if he be Thirsty, give him Water to Drink; for thou shalt heap Coals of Fire on his Head, and the Lord shall Reward thee.* The Lord help his poor Servant, ever to avoid all *Revenge* upon *Personal Enemies;* but rather to Wish them, and Do them, all the *Good* that is possible for their *Evil.* It were a very lamentable Thing, for a Christian who hath suffered any *Injuries,* and *Reproaches,* to manifest his Forgiving of his *Personal Enemies,* by making those very *Injuries,* to be the occasions of his *Praying* by Name for *them,* for whom it may be, he never so pray'd before. And Christianity will be further Exemplified, if we don't *Shun*, but rather *Watch*, all opportunities to show *Kindnesses* unto them, that have been most *Unkind* unto us. But how will this, *Heap Coals of Fire on the Heads of* my Adversaries? {Prov. 25:22}. If I should Answer, That then the *Righteous God*, will take my Adversaries into His Hand, and *Revenge* the wrongs done to me, with Judgments that shall fall as *Burning Coals* upon them that have wronged me, the Answer would be true; but I must have a care of having this Intention, in my silence, my patience, my forbearing to *Retaliate*. Wherefore, I will rather put a sweeter sense upon it. My *Gentleness* towards my Adversaries, will perhaps *melt* their *Hearts*, as much as if *Coals of Fire* were thrown upon them; and the *Envy* and *Malice*, with which they treat me, will become as uneasy to themselves as if *Coals of Fire* were Lying on their *Heads*, and the Torment which a Reflection on their own past *Baseness* towards me, will give unto them, will be as bad as if *Coals of Fire* were vexing of them. All I shall add, is, That it is an hard Lesson, which is now prescribed unto me; & therefore, even with the ardour of *Coals of Fire*, I would pray, as the Disciples of our Lord once did, on the Hearing of this Lesson, *Lord, Increase my Faith* {Luke 17:5}.

Meditation. XIX.
Upon some Dead Coals.

Though the *Dead Coals* on the *Hearth*, will not *Warm* ones *Exteriour*, I will try whether my *Interiour* can't fetch as much *Warmth* from them, as from the *Living* ones. I am therefore from these *Dead Coals*, to receive some *Living Admonitions*.

A *Dead Coal*, would first most naturally put one in mind, of a *Dead man*. The *Extinction* of a *Coal*, does (at least as with a Coal) draw a Picture of *Mortality*. And she that had but one Son, being afraid of his *Death*, Expressed her Fear, 2 *Sam*. 14. 7. of *Quenching the Coal that was left*. Now, when I see how much longer some *Coals* do last, than others, it invites me to think, how *Long Lived* some, in comparison of others, are. Since the unaccountable *Abbreviation* of Humane Life, unto the Term, at which it hath stood for near Four Thousand years, we see, That while some *Coals* are put out by thousands of Accidents, *before their Time*, there are men who not only Live to the Term of *Threescore years and Ten*, but also keep some Light and Heat, unto a much Greater Age; yea, and this although they never took such a *Temperate & Accurate* way of Living, as did the famous *Cornaro*, to *prolong their Lives*.[39] . . .

But seeing a *Dead Coal*, I enquire, what made it so? And this *Enkindles* another Thought. If the *Dead Coal* were lying among the *Living* ones, it would be no longer so *Dead*. *Lively Christians* in like manner (say I) keep one another

Alive, by being *Together*. The *Company* and the *Conference* of *Lively Christians*, has a mighty Tendency to keep Christianity *Alive* among them. A *Dead*, Stupid, Formal Frame of Spirit, is the usual Effect of keeping at a Distance from the Society of *Lively Christians*. It has been particularly found, that *Religious Meetings* wisely managed, have had a more than ordinary tendency to preserve the *Life* of *Religion* among a People. Wherefore, let those *Pastors*, that would approve themselves Faithful unto the Interests of *Religion* in their Flocks, Countenance and Encourage *Religious Meetings*, for *Prayers*, and *Repeting of Sermons*, and for *Discoursing* on the Things of God. And let them very peculiarly direct and Excite their **Young People**, to the maintaining of such *Meetings*.[40] It will be found that the *Life* and *Power* of *Godliness* will be marvellously maintained by such Things. And it will be found, That where persons withdraw from the Fellowship of *Lively Christians*, and *Forsake the Assembling of themselves together*, it won't be long before the *Coals goe out*. May I value and enjoy the *Fellowship* of *Lively Christians* {Heb. 10:25}; and may I, by Serious and Modest, and Fruitful *Speeches* in their Fellowship, both have and give those things, upon which it shall be said, *While we spake, did not our Hearts burn within us!* {Luke 24:32} . . .

Meditation XXIX.
On the Sap *of the* Wood, *forced out by the* Fire.

When I see the *Sap* forced out of the *Wood*, by the *Fire*, I sometimes think on the *Tears* of a *Forced Repentance*. The Sacred Scriptures report unto us, the Instances both of *Persons* and *Peoples*, from whom the *Fiery Judgments* of God have sometimes fetch'd Expressions of Sorrow and Remorse for their Sins against Him. And we see it in our daily experience, That Sinners under grievous *Affliction*, have seem'd very penitent, and with *Tears* have profess'd their penitence. But the *Liquor* which drops out at the end of the Consuming *Wood*, is not more loathsome, or Despis'd by any of us, that look upon it, than the *Tears* of a *Repentance*, produced by the meer Torture of the *Divine Judgments* upon us, are to the God who *Weighs our Spirits*. The *Tears* of Wretches under punishment, shed only because they feel themselves punished, are none of them any more in the *Bottel* of God, than that wretched *Water* which runs from our *Brands Ends*, is thought worthy to be preserved by us, in any of our *Vials*. One *Tear* proceeding from a genuine, and gracious principle, of Trouble and Anger at our selves for having offended the Holy God, and of Admiration at His Goodness, in providing for us, revealing to us, and Inviting us into the Methods of *Reconciliation* to himself, is of more account, than a River of those that are the Fruit of meer *Vexation* at our own uneasy circumstances. . . .

Meditation XXXI
On the Wood *Lying* too close.

We know, That *Air* is necessary to *Flame*. And our knowledge of it, is notably confirmed, by the Experiment of the *Air Pump*,[41] where *Gunpowder* it self, cast upon *Hot Iron*, will only *melt* and not *flash* in the Exhausted *Receiver*. And possibly to this may be owing the Experiment mentioned by my Lord *Bacon*,[42] That if you hold an Arrow in the Flame for ten pulses, you shall find those parts of the Arrow which were on the *Out side* of the Flame far more burned and blacked, when that *in the midst* of the *Flame*, will be as if the *Fire* had hardly touched it. Yea, the Divine Oracles, [for such is the *Fulness* of them!] do seem to take notice of this Experiment, in Ezek. 15: 4. Where, first, *Both Ends of the Vine stalk are devour'd and then the midst of it is burnt.* But without those Experiments, we have enough of it every day, when our *Fire* will not burn, because the *Wood lies too close*. The *Fire* will be smothered and obstructed, if the *Air* have not Access unto it.

This thought invites me, in the first place, to consider the Necessity of *Air* to *Life* in our selves: For, tho' I am not such a *Psychopyrist* as to call the *Soul,* a *Fire,* yet, I see not why *Life* may not be called so; and without *Air,* we see (howbeit there have been some rare Instances of persons that have *Lived Breathless* for many days together; it may be, *Sal Ammoniack*[43] has revived the *Flame;*) that it will be soon extinguished. I would therefore give Thanks to the Good God, who by His *Air* does *uphold my Soul in Life;* and I would look upon it, as a very signal point of *Health* for me to be cautious, what *Air* I choose to be much conversant in; and not look to survive any long while, because none of my caution can secure me from the unseen *Miasmata* of the *Air,* which will damp all before them.

Dismissing of this Thought, I presently fall into another; Namely, That *Smothered Griefs,* are worse things than *Smothered Fires,* and not so likely to go out. If a man have any *Griefs,* or *Fears,* or *Cares* upon his mind, let them have *Air,* and they will the sooner evaporate. All will be the more *Lightsome* with us, if we don't let them *Ly too close* upon our mind. He that has any Remarkable Guilt, lying with distress upon his Conscience, let him single out some *Faithful Pastor,* to whom what he confesses will be as it were but confessed unto the Lord. The *Reveling* of the matter, and his ensuing *Prayers,* and Counsils, and Cordials, will be of a blessed consequence unto *an Heart that will be Hot, thro' a Fire burning in it, until it hath spoken with the Tongue* {Ps. 39:3}. And let him that has any other Anguish, afford *Vent* and *Air* unto it, by some Agreeable Expressions of it: The *Air* will be a kindness to the *Fire* in the Soul; and all things will be the Better, and the Brighter for an Anguish not *Lying too close* upon it. . . .

Meditation XXXIV.
On the quick passage of the Fire, *from one Object unto another.*

The *Fire*, I see, nimbly passes, from one *Stick* to another: Yea, there are several sorts of combustible Materials lying together; but the *Fire* swiftly takes hold, first on one, then on another, and uses no great formality in the *Transition*. This puts me in mind of a Thing very observable in the Prophetical Writings, and which being well observed, would be a good *Key* to the meaning of them; and that is the sudden and obscure *Transition* of the Prophets from one Subject unto another. The Holy Spirit suggested unto their minds, first the Thoughts of Writing on such or such a Subject, and then assisted them as far as was requisite in the composition. But then at once the Holy Spirit carries them, like a *Spreading Flame*, into new, and rare, and rich thoughts, and surprizing *Idea's*, of the *Messiah* and His Kingdom; and what began in a sort of *Inspired Reasoning* proceeds unaccountably to an *Extatic Revelation*. The *First Subject* is in a manner Deserted, and upon a *New Hint*, the Prophets perhaps without fully understanding, or comprehending the *Transition* themselves, are transported into predictions of the *Messiah*, and characters of His Person, and Office, and Actions. Many parts of the Bible will be the better Interpreted, if we do behold them, in the *Fire Light* of this Observation. . . .

Meditation XXXVII.
On the Ashes.

My *Hearth* has now an heap of *Ashes* upon it. But can my *Heart* Read nothing there? Methinks, I can Read several Admonitions written in the *Ashes*, though no one has formed any distinct characters on them. To find *Salt* in the *Ashes*, would be no difficulty: to fetch *Grace* from the *Ashes*, (that Heavenly *Salt!*) would be a greater and a better Action. . . .

And first, *I* remember, the famous *Quercetanus*,[44] together with other *Labourers in the Fire*, have told us, That they can take a *plant* in its more vigorous consistence, and after a due *Maceration, Fermentation*, and *Separation*, Extract the *Salt* of that *plant*, which, as it were, in a *Chaos*, invisibly reserves the Form of the whole, with its vital principle; and that keeping the *Salt* in a *glass* Hermetically Sealed, they can, by applying a *Soft Fire* to the *glass*, make the *Vegetable* rise by little and little out of its *Ashes*, to surprize the Spectators. I am not sure, That this Report is to be Relied upon, and much less am I sure, of what they further tell us, That the *Essential Salt* of *Animals* being thus prepared and preserved, an ingenious man might raise the shape of them, at his pleasure. What I would Remark, is This. If *Plants* could be Revived out of their *Ashes*, or if the *Oak*, and *Ash*, and *Walnut*, would grow, from the Scattered *Ashes*, which I have now before me, it would unavoidably Lead our Meditations to the *Resurrection of the Dead.* Yea, Whatever may be done by Nature, on and from the *Ashes* of my *Wood,* I am very sure, That I shall one day Rise out of my own *Ashes. Resurrectio mortuorum Fiducia Christianorum.*[45] He that is, *The Life,* and, *The Resurrection to Life,* has assured me, That after I am *Dead,* He will give my Incinerated Body a *Resurrection to Life.* We see a parcel of *Quick silver* may put off its Form, and put on that of a *Vapour;* and from a *Vapour* be transformed into an insipid *Water;* and from a *Water* be transmuted into a White, or a Red, or a Yellow *Powder;* and from this *Powder* be made a *Salt;* and from that *Salt* a malleable *Metal;* and yet a skilful Chymist, will reduce it, out of all those various Contextures, into its old Natural Form, of plain, shining, running *Mercury.* How much more, can an Omnipresent, Omnipotent, Omniscient God, bring back the *Ashes* of my *Dead Body,* into the Figure that it shall receive at the *Resurrection of the Dead?* . . .

Another thing observable to me in the *Ashes,* is, That tho' the *Wood* was of several sorts, *distinguishable* one from another, yea, *preferrible* one to another, yet now they are all in *Ashes,* there is no sensible *Distinction* of them, they ly together *undistinguished.* Behold, O my Soul, Behold the Effect of *Mortality. Death* is the grand *Leveller.* One Tree must be made *Ashes* as well as another: and when once we are made *Ashes,* What will be the Difference between *Solomon* and *Diglus Petargus,* between *Croesus* and *Irus,* between the Richest *Emperour,* and the Poorest *Beggar!*[46] All *Skulls* are of equal Dignity in the *Charnel house;* and as *Herbert* Elegantly,

> *The Brags of Life are but a nine days wonder;*
> *And after Death, the Fumes that spring*
> *From private Bodies make as big a Thunder,*
> *As those which rise from a huge King.*[47]

Indeed, I have Read concerning a *Difference* in *Dust;* namely, the powder of *Diamonds,* or princely Dust: *Gold Dust,* or the Remains of Noblemen; *Pin Dust,* or the Remains of Trades men; *Saw Dust;* or the Remains of Mechanicks; and *Common Dust,* or the Remains of the more unobserved sort of people. Yet even here 'tis confest, All is *Dust.* But in *Ashes* there is not so much Difference to be discerned. All that we can allow, is, That our Lord Jesus Christ, at the *Resurrection of the Just,* will distinguish the *Ashes* of the Saints, which are United unto Himself, from those of other men; more Effectually, than a *Load stone* would any Filings of *Steel,* mixed with the common *Ashes.* Were I all this while seeking satisfaction, in Creatures, I should be doing what the Oracles of God most expressively call, *Feeding on Ashes* {Isa. 44:20}. But while we are thus *Thinking on Ashes,* and learning the Instructions of Piety from them, I hope we are not *Feeding on Ashes.* . . .

While we have been bringing of *Lessons* from the *Ashes*, we have been as good as making of *Glasses* from them, for all those Uses. My *Ashes* undergo an happy and useful *Vitrification*, when they yield these *Lessons* unto us.

But I will, in one word, give the sum of all the *Lessons*: It happens, (and it is a meer *Hap*,) to be a *Wednesday*, wherein I write these things. I have before I am aware, made it, an *Ash Wednesday*. And tho' I don't keep the day, yet I'l write the word for the Day, *Memento, Homo, quod Cinis es.*[48] . . .

I wish our Meditations then may not be *like unto Ashes.* . . .

Meditation XXXIX.
On the Fire's *going out.*

The Wood on my *Fire*, was in a mighty *Blaze*, that seemed as if it would have been a lasting one, at its first Blowing up: Nevertheless, the *Bellows* giving over to *Blow*, the *Fire* gave over to *Burn* immediately. Methoughts, I now saw an Emblem of that *Apostasy*, which often attends *Good Beginnings* in Religion, where the Grace of the Lord Jesus Christ (that Heavenly *Fire*) never took yet an *Effectual Hold* upon the Soul. Many *Beginners*, in Religion, and *Professors* of it, seem very forward for the Services of Christianity, and make a mighty *Blaze* of Profession; but it is not a Lasting one: *It goeth away.* May the God of all Grace, make all our Young People, exceedingly apprehensive of, *The Apostates Doom*, and afraid of *Turning aside unto crooked ways* {Ps. 125:5}, thro' the Influences of *Evil Company*, or any other Temptation, after they have made *Good Beginnings* in Religion, lest they have that awful word fulfill'd upon them, *If any man draw back, my Soul shall have no pleasure in him* {Heb. 10:38}.

Hereupon Resuming the *Bellows* for a *Second Blast*, I Renewed and Revived the *Fire*, until it so arrested the *Wood*, as to carry all before it. And this put me in mind of an Astonishing Favour, which I had *my self* Received from Heaven, and which *many more* of the Elect have likewise Received. It is very commonly so, That the *Elect* of God, which enjoy a Religious Education, have by the Spirit of God excited in them, very *Fervent* Inclinations to piety, while they are in their *Childhood*: But when they advance into more of *Youth*, Temptation so prevails upon them, that for a while, all seems to be *Gone out*, and their former Inclinations are hardly to be discerned: Nevertheless the Spirit of God will not let their *Youth* proceed very far, before He, who had been *Grieved* and *Quenched* by their Vanities, [*Lord, can I write this, and not mingle my Tears with my Ink!* (Psal. 102:9)] does again *Blow* upon their Souls. A *Fire* is then Recovered, that shall never be extinguished! . . .

At last, While I was minding other matters, the *Fire* on my *Hearth*, was upon the point of Expiring, meerly because the *Fuel* was all spent, that should have supported it. I have been told, that *Vulcan* was of old feigned *Lame* for this reason; The *Wood* on the *Fire*, is the *Staff* which he is always calling for. I now Thought of several Things, that Need *Recruits*, if we would keep them from Expiration; But I thought of one among the rest, which I wish'd might never be Recruited. Sinful *Contention* is a sort of a *Fire*; and it is said of a *Contentious* man, (which, *Lord*, Let me neither Be, or Bear!) *He is an Ungodly man who diggeth up Evil and in his Lips there is, as a burning Fire* {Prov. 16:27}. And it is said, *As Coals are to Burning Coals, so is a Contentious man to kindle Strife* {Prov. 26:21}. Now 'tis among the Observations of Wisdom, in Prov. 26. 20, 21. *Where no Wood is, there the Fire goeth out; So where there is no Tale bearer, the Strife ceaseth.* Wherefore, as coming at length to hear the *Couvrefeu Bell,*[49] if any *Contention* do arise, where I am concerned, I would use all the care imaginable, That (while I may *Contend earnestly for the Faith*, or Order, *Delivered unto the Saints*,) I may avoid bringing any Sinful *Fuel* to the *Contention*, by any *Tale bearing*, any *Whispering*, any *Slandering*, or any *Railing Accusations*. Let me rather cast such things, even where *Constantine* cast the *Contentious Papers*; That is, Into the *Fire*.[50]

If a *Quarrelsome Disposition* be mischievous any where, tis in the *Married Life*, in the *Conjugal-State*. And upon the mention of This, I call to mind a Rabbinical Fancy: *Isch* signifies, A *Man; Ischah* signifies, A *Woman;* Hence they Note, In the Name of the *Man*, there is *Jod*, which is not in the Name of the *Woman;* In the Name of the *Woman*, is *He*, which is not in the Name of the *Man;* These two Letters make *Jah*, which is the Name of God; and these being taken away, there is nothing but *Esch*, in both Names; and that signifies *Fire;* This is to shew (they say) that as long as Man & Wife agree, *God is with them;* when God is not with them, and when they disagree, there is nothing but *Fire* in the House. But surely, the *Coldest Wigwam* were better than such an House! . . .

Meditation XL
On throwing my Pen *into the* Fire. Dec. 31. 1700.

Thus at length, in the *Thirty Eighth* year of my Age, I have Resumed and Finished the Reflections which I had begun, (and written many of them,) and then thrown by, many years ago. And having made an End of Writing my Reflections on the *Fire*, the old and worn *Pen*, with which I wrote the last of them, shall be thrown into the *Fire*. But before it goes, it shall enter for me a very Solemn *Admonition*.

There are *Men*, (as well as *Pens*,) who have written many, Good Things, & thereby done considerable Service for the Churches of the Lord; but have been cast into the *Fire* after all: God has cast them into the *Fire that never shall be*

Quenched {Mark 9:43}. Many Learned, yea, many Devout, Writers have been *Cast-aways*: because they have contented themselves with a meer *Pen-and-Paper Piety*: and going down to the *Unquenchable* and *Everlasting Fire* have had cause to say, *Surgunt indocti et rapiunt coelum; nos, cum nostra Doctrina, mergimur in Infernum.*[51] Some writers have the Fancy to place their *Pictures* before the Title page of their Books; but they that write of *Piety*, should have their Books themselves to be their *Pictures:* They have no other way to prevent being thrown into the *Fire.*

I do therefore, with an Humble and a Trembling Supplication, beseech of thee, *O my God, in my Lord Jesus Christ!* That I may not only *Write* Good Things, but also *Do* what I *Write*, lest my *Writings* be made but the Fuel of the *Fire* that would be the just punishment of my *Hypocrisy. Lord*, Help me to *Transcribe* my Writings into my *Life*, lest I be all this while writing my own *Condemnation to Death:* and let thy Grace Help me not only to *Write well*, but also to *Live well*; that so instead of being thrown into the *Fire*, I may have a place in the *Wings* of the *Heavenly Armies.*

NEW ENGLAND HISTORY AND THE GLORIOUS REVOLUTION

ather's *Magnalia Christi Americana* stands as one of the great works of colonial American writing, and even as one of the first in a distinctly American world literary tradition. First published in London in 1702, it contains seven books that chronicle and illustrate, as the subtitle announces, "The Ecclesiastical History of New England from Its First Plantings in 1620." Mather's subject was the establishment and development of the churches, and specifically the English Congregational churches, whose principles, growing out of the Protestant Reformation and Puritanism, were transplanted in America.

The *Magnalia* has been interpreted from many angles, but we can here only touch on a few prominent characterizations. Perry Miller, an influential twentieth-century Harvard historian, regarded the work as one great "jeremiad." A jeremiad, a term taken from the biblical prophet Jeremiah, is an oration or piece of literature that laments a people's decline and recalls them to recommit to their unity around their original values. Late seventeenth-century New England preachers, including to no small degree the Mathers, perfected the jeremiad as a way of getting their fellow colonists to rekindle what they presented as the founders' "errand" into the wilderness: to build a "Bible commonwealth" that would serve as a model for the warring nations and churches of Europe. By the time Mather began *Magnalia*, however, the dream of a holy society had faded after Puritanism as a political experiment ended and New England began to reflect the diversity, pursuits, and tastes of the mother country. Sacvan Bercovitch, a later Harvard literary historian, observed that Mather wrote his history from the perspectives both of memory and of anticipation: memory in the form of presenting a history and vindication of the theocracy and its major players, and anticipation in the form of the impending millennium, when the work of the church would come to fruition. For Karen Halttunen, Mather found meaning in the suffering and trials that the founders of New England endured, undergoing, in their parts as instruments in the cosmic conflict between God and Satan, persecution, deprivation, and sacrifice. However, their descendants, by Mather's lights, were rejecting and abandoning their ancestors. And Jan Stievermann has observed that Mather's often ridiculed but inimitable "baroque" style, so much on display in *Magnalia*—studded with foreign-language quotations, biblical citations, literary allusions, poetry, and even seemingly random italicization and capitalization—reflected his adherence to a specific stylistic ideal that had at its core the unity of all knowledge.[1]

The selection below reproduces the "General Introduction" to *Magnalia*, with its famous opening line adapted from seventeenth-century English poet George Herbert, proclaiming the westward course of empire: "I WRITE the *Wonders* of the CHRISTIAN RELIGION, flying from the Depravations of *Europe*, to the *American Strand*." Mather's introduction has been called the "most animated apologia for the Puritan errand" in colonial American literature.[2] Here, Mather was the first to use the term "American" to designate a person of European descent born in the Western Hemisphere. It was in America, the "New World" (though not new to the Indigenous peoples who had lived there for thousands of years), that many Europeans believed their corrupt bodies and souls could be purified in a New Eden.[3]

And it was to America, providentially, that God had led his persecuted followers to establish true, "evangelical" churches and thereby complete the work begun in the Protestant Reformation. Mather's focus was not just on Protestant religion but specifically on "Reformed" churches, which Mather likened to the churches in "*First Ages* of Christianity," as related in the New Testament. "In short," Mather wrote, "The *First Age* was the *Golden Age*: To return unto *That*, will make a Man a *Protestant,* and I may add, a *Puritan.*" Resisting this histori-cal and epoch-making effort to restore the purity of Christianity in accordance with the Bible were the forces in league with the devil, including the Antichrist, the biblical figure that early modern Protestants equated with the Catholic Church, its popes and clergy, and with Catholic political leaders, such as the kings and queens of Spain and France. To tell this story, Mather gave a history of the colonies and principal "Actors"; the challenges overcome; "Memorable Occurrences," including Salem witchcraft and Indian captivities; and even a his-tory of Harvard College.

Section 4 of Mather's General Introduction begins, "But whether *New-England* may *Live* any where else or no, it must *Live* in our *History!*" Although Europe may not have recognized and learned from the *"Golden Candlesticks"* set up by God in the wilderness, Mather would preserve the annals of their er-rand. This determination elicited from our author a consideration of the nature of history and of history writing. For Mather, church history was the highest form of historiography, because God made the world for the church, and therefore was the most worthy object of the historian's interest. In pursuit of that goal, Mather affirmed that he had followed the criteria of the best historians down through time. The "truth" of his history he had verified with facts; his approach, he declared, was nonpartisan and objective. However much Mather's assertion that the *"Congregational"* was the true church discipline belied his claims of impartiality, and however much he expected his work to be met with harsh re-views by the enemies of what he considered true religion, he rested in the hope that *Magnalia* would have a ripple effect throughout the Christian world.

In *Magnalia,* Mather provided a series of biographical sketches of key form-ers of the New England Way. Arguably the most famous of these sketches was that of John Winthrop (1588–1649), who served as governor of Massachusetts Bay a number of times, and also in many other roles, from its founding in 1630. More recent classic biographies have presented Winthrop as the person who, in Ed-mund Morgan's apt term, lived the "Puritan dilemma": how to live righteously in an unrighteous world. For historian Francis Bremer, Winthrop is America's "forgotten founding father." For Stievermann, Mather's biographies, particularly that of Winthrop, constitute a "genuine expression of New World experience in the form of representative American (auto)biography."[4]

But for Mather, Winthrop was "Nehemias Americanus," an American Nehemiah. The biblical book of Nehemiah tells the story of a leader of the Israelites in Persian captivity who returns to Jerusalem and oversees the rebuilding of the city's walls, which he accomplishes despite much local opposition and hard toil. For authors such as Mather, steeped in the scriptures, the biblical world found both types and antitypes, extensions and parallels in the New World. As a latter-day Nehemiah, Winthrop, a lawyer and politician, ensured that the people obeyed the laws of God. In Mather's hands, Winthrop was the godly judge and leader who brought the *"Behaviour of a Christian"* to his public duties. In his role as governor, **"Moderation"** and *"Lenity"* were guiding principles—though he could also render swift and certain judgment, as in his banishment of Anne Hutchinson for heretical principles. In his role as neighbor, Winthrop helped fellow colonists in public and in private; he was a model of frugality, humility, and charity. He conquered envy of others, Mather wrote, "by being free from it himself." This was the character of the godly ruler to which Mather was calling leaders of his day.[5]

With the collapse of the Puritan interregnum and the restoration of the monarchy, Charles II assumed the English throne in 1660. Upon Charles's death in 1685, James VII of Scotland became James II of England. James was a Catholic sympathizer, a direct threat to the Protestant interest in the country and in many of the colonies. One of James II's policies was to exert more direct royal control over his colonies. In 1684, the English government nullified Massachusetts Bay's charter; two years later, a royally appointed governor, Edmund Andros (1637–1714), arrived in Boston, along with "several Companies of *Red Coats*," to take control of the newly created "Dominion of New England," which brought the northeastern British American colonies together under one administrative jurisdiction.[6] These momentous events created among New Englanders a conviction that there was an "Infandous Plot" to destroy pure religion and subjugate the colonies where such religion had found a haven. In the midst of rumor and uncertainty, Increase Mather left clandestinely for England to plead for relief and to negotiate a new charter, leaving Cotton in charge of their congregation for the first time.

Meanwhile, larger plots were afoot. Resentful of the prospect of a Roman Catholic succession, English religious and political leaders were negotiating with William III, prince of Orange (1650–1702), and his wife, Mary, James II's daughter and the next in line to the English crown. Both were Protestants. In June 1688, the queen of England gave birth to a son who was to be raised a Catholic. This moved James's opponents to action. They issued a formal invitation to William and Mary to assume the throne, and his army landed in early November, with William pledging to uphold English liberties and secure Protestantism. James's support quickly faded; he was forced to abdicate and left for France. In a virtually bloodless coup, which came to be called the "Glorious Revolution," the monarchy changed hands.

Such momentous events had ripple effects across the Atlantic, including in the colonies of New York, Maryland, and Massachusetts, where changes in government took place by force. In Boston and other parts of the Dominion, the abuses and missteps of Andros—which included calling a day of thanksgiving for the birth of James's son—solidified opposition to him and his policies well before news of the ascension of William and Mary to the English throne arrived in April 1689.[7] Andros tried to quash any dissemination of the report, but in vain. On April 18, the people of Boston and environs armed themselves and rose up. Andros and his associates were imprisoned, and the Dominion ceased to exist.

Mather was part of a group of Boston-area leaders, many of them ministers, who planned the coup. A warrant was even issued for Mather's arrest, but friends in the government suppressed it. Instead, it was Andros who was under arrest. On that busy day, *The Declaration, of the Gentlemen, Merchants, and Inhabitants of Boston, and the Countrey Adjacent* was read, in all likelihood by Mather, to a crowd assembled at the Old Town-House. Mather had co-authored the address, written in anticipation of just this occasion.

Like the Declaration of Independence nearly a century later, this *Declaration* laid out the principles of the actors and their grievances. In twelve articles, it describes a conspiracy by Andros and his cronies to enrich themselves and humiliate the Dominion's inhabitants. Not only had a royally appointed governor and council been forced on them, but this had been accompanied by the threat of coercion in the form of companies of British regulars, the first time such a thing had been done in Massachusetts. Andros had used his power to negate all land titles, effectively declaring void all colonial deeds. He suspended the requirement that an accused person be brought before a judge, and in spite of long-held Puritan beliefs against taking oaths, required jury members to swear on the Bible. He denied that colonists had "the Priviledges of *English* men," because they were not born in England. He also embroiled them in a questionable war with Native tribes to the northeast, in which colonial volunteers were placed under Catholic commanders. In light of all these insults, the *Declaration* states with a mixture of aggression and submission, "We do therefore seize upon the persons of those few *Ill men* which have been (next to our sins) the grand authors of our miseries." Eventually, Andros was packed off to England to stand trial.

The *Declaration* was an important document because it sought to justify the overthrow of legal (and therefore God-ordained) authorities—admittedly, a task rendered somewhat easier by a more momentous coup in the mother country. Furthermore, rather than using theological or providential arguments, the *Declaration's* reasonings are constitutional and legal. Couched in the provincial identity of "God's chosen people," it claims English rights for colonists, including consent, or a say in their own rule, especially the legitimacy of town meetings and the election of deputies, which Andros had suspended. These were important precedents for later generations. As Mather biographer Kenneth Silverman observes, the overthrow of Andros, in which Mather played so signal a role, launched "a New England revolutionary tradition that would culminate in 1776."[8] In recognition of his leadership in the event, the restored authorities placed Mather on an advisory council that declared its loyalty to the new monarchs and reinstated—at least for the time being—the old charter.

MAGNALIA CHRISTI AMERICANA (1702)

A GENERAL INTRODUCTION

§. 1.

I WRITE the *Wonders* of the CHRISTIAN RELIGION, flying from the De-pravations of *Europe*, to the *American Strand*:[9] And, assisted by the Holy Author of that *Religion*, I do, with all Conscience of *Truth*, required therein by Him, who is the *Truth* it self, Report the *Wonderful Displays* of His Infinite Power, Wisdom, Goodness, and Faithfulness, wherewith His Divine Providence hath *Irradiated* an *Indian Wilderness*.

I Relate the *Considerable Matters*, that produced and attended the First Settlement of COLONIES, which have been Renowned for the Degree of REFORMATION, Professed and Attained by *Evangelical Churches*, erected in those *Ends of the Earth*: And a *Field* being thus prepared, I proceed unto a Re-lation of the *Considerable Matters* which have been acted thereupon.

I first introduce the *Actors*, that have, in a more exemplary manner served those *Colonies*; and give *Remarkable Occurrences*, in the exemplary LIVES of many *Magistrates*, and of more *Ministers*, who so *Lived*, as to leave unto Poster-ity, *Examples* worthy of *Everlasting Remembrance*.

I add hereunto, the *Notables* worthy of the only *Protestant University*,[10] that ever *shone* in that Hemisphere of the *New World*; with particular Instances of *Criolians*,[11] in our *Biography*, provoking the *whole World*, with virtuous Objects of Emulation.

I introduce then, the *Actions* of a more Eminent Importance, that have sig-nalized those *Colonies*; Whether the *Establishments*, directed by their *Synods*; with a Rich Variety of *Synodical* and *Ecclesiastical* Determinations; or, the *Dis-turbances*, with which they have been from all sorts of *Temptations* and *Ene-mies* Tempestuated; and the *Methods* by which they have still weathered out each *Horrible Tempest*.

And into the midst of the *Actions*, I interpose an entire *Book*, wherein there is, with all possible Veracity, a *Collection* made, of *Memorable Occurrences*, and amazing *Judgments* and *Mercies*, befalling many *particular Persons* among the People of *New-England*.

Let my Readers expect all that I have promised them, in this *Bill of Fare*; and it may be they will find themselves entertained with yet many other Passages, above and beyond their Expectation, deserving likewise a room in *History*: In all which, there will be nothing, but the *Author's* too mean way of preparing so great Entertainments, to Reproach the Invitation.

Magnalia Christi Americana:

OR, THE

Ecclesiastical History

OF

NEVV-ENGLAND,

FROM

Its Firſt Planting in the Year 1620. unto the Year
of our LORD, 1698.

In Seven BOOKS.

I. Antiquities: In Seven Chapters. With an Appendix.

II. Containing the Lives of the Governours, and Names of the Magiſtrates of *New-England :* In Thirteen Chapters. With an Appendix.

III. The Lives of Sixty Famous Divines, by whoſe Miniſtry the Churches of *New-England* have been Planted and Continued.

IV. An Account of the Univerſity of *Cambridge* in *New-England*; in Two Parts. The Firſt contains the Laws, the Benefactors, and Viciſſitudes of *Harvard College*; with Remarks upon it. The Second Part contains the Lives of ſome Eminent Perſons Educated in it.

V. Acts and Monuments of the Faith and Order in the Churches of *New-England*, paſſed in their Synods; with Hiſtorical Remarks upon thoſe Venerable Aſſemblies; and a great Variety of Church-Caſes occurring, and reſolved by the Synods of thoſe Churches: In Four Parts.

VI. A Faithful Record of many Illuſtrious, Wonderful Providences, both of Mercies and Judgments, on divers Perſons in *New-England :* In Eight Chapters.

VII. *The Wars of the Lord.* Being an Hiſtory of the Manifold Afflictions and Diſturbances of the Churches in *New-England*, from their Various Adverſaries, and the Wonderful Methods and Mercies of God in their Deliverance: In Six Chapters: To which is ſubjoined, An Appendix of Remarkable Occurrences which *New-England* had in the Wars with the *Indian* Salvages, from the Year 1688, to the Year 1698.

By the Reverend and Learned *COTTON MATHER*, M. A.
And Paſtor of the North Church in *Boſton, New-England.*

LONDON:

Printed for *Thomas Parkhurſt*, at the *Bible* and *Three
Crowns* in *Cheapſide.* MDCCII.

Magnalia Christi Americana (London, 1702), title page

§. 2. The Reader will doubtless desire to know, what it was that

> ————tot Volvere casus
> *Insignes Pietate Viros, tot adire Labores,*
> *Impulerit.*[12]

And our *History* shall, on many fit Occasions which will be therein offered, endeavour, with all *Historical* Fidelity and *Simplicity*, and with as little Offence as may be, to satisfie him. The Sum of the Matter is, That from the very Beginning of the REFORMATION in the *English Nation*, there hath always been a Generation of *Godly Men*, desirous to pursue the *Reformation of Religion, according to the Word of God, and the Example of the best Reformed Churches*; and answering the Character of *Good Men*, given by *Josephus*, in his Paraphrase on the words of *Samuel* to *Saul*, μηδὲν ἄλλο πραγθήσεσθαι καλῶς ὑφ᾽ ἑαυτῶν νομίζοντες ἢ ὅτι ἂν ποιήσωσι τοῦ θεοῦ κεκελευκότος.[13] *They think they do nothing Right in the Service of God, but what they do according to the Command of God.* And there hath been another Generation of Men, who have still employed the *Power* which they have generally still had in their Hands, not only to stop the Progress of the Desired *Reformation*, but also, with Innumerable Vexations, to Persecute those that most Heartily wished well unto it. There were many of the *Reformers*, who joined with the Reverend JOHN FOX, in the *Complaints* which he then entred in his *Martyrology*, about the *Baits of Popery* yet left in the Church, and in his *Wishes, God take them away, or ease us from them, for God knows, they be the Cause of much Blindness and Strife amongst Men!*[14] They Zealously decreed[15] the *Policy* of complying always with the *Ignorance* and *Vanity* of the *People*; and cried out earnestly for *Purer Administrations* in the House of God, and more *Conformity* to the *Law of Christ*, and *Primitive Christianity:* While others would not hear of going any further than the *First Essay of Reformation.* 'Tis very certain, that the *First Reformers* never intended, that what *They* did, should be the *Absolute Boundary* of *Reformation*, so that it should be a Sin to proceed no further; as, by their own going beyond *Wicklift*,[16] and *Changing* and *Growing* in their own *Models* also, and the Confessions of *Cranmer*, with the *Scripta Anglicana* of *Bucer*, and a thousand other things, was abundantly demonstrated.[17] But after a Fruitless Expectation, wherein the truest Friends of the *Reformation* long waited, for to have that which *Heylin*[18] himself owns to have been the *Design* of the *First Reformers*, followed as it should have been, a Party very unjustly arrogating to themselves, the Venerable Name of, *The Church of* England, by Numberless Oppressions, grievously *Smote those their Fellow-Servants.* Then 'twas that, as our Great OWEN hath expressed it, *Multitudes of Pious, Peaceable Protestants, were driven, by their Severities, to leave their Native*

Country, and seek a Refuge for their Lives and Liberties, with Freedom, for the Worship of God, in a Wilderness, in the Ends of the Earth.[19]

§. 3. It is the History of the PROTESTANTS, that is here attempted: PROTESTANTS that highly honoured and affected *The Church of* ENGLAND, and humbly Petition to be a *Part* of it: But by the *Mistake* of a few powerful *Brethren*, driven to seek a place for the Exercise of the *Protestant Religion*, according to the Light of their Consciences, in the Desarts of *America*. And in this Attempt I have proposed, not only to preserve and secure the Interest of *Religion*, in the Churches of that little Country NEW-ENGLAND, so far as the Lord Jesus Christ may please to Bless it for that End, but also to offer unto the Churches of the *Reformation*, abroad in the World, some small *Memorials*, that may be serviceable unto the Design of *Reformation*, whereto, I believe, they are quickly to be awakened. I am far from any such Boast, concerning these Churches, *That they have Need of Nothing*, I wish their *Works* were more *perfect before God*. Indeed, that which *Austin* called *The Perfection of Christians*, is like to be, until the Term for the *Antichristian Apostasie* be expired. *The Perfection of Churches* too; *Ut Agnoscant se nunquam esse perfectas.*[20] Nevertheless, I perswade my self, that *so far as they have attained*, they have given *Great Examples* of the *Methods* and *Measures*, wherein an *Evangelical Reformation* is to be prosecuted, and of the *Qualifications* requisite in the Instruments that are to prosecute it, and of the *Difficulties* which may be most likely to obstruct it, and the most likely *Directions* and *Remedies* for those Obstructions. It may be, 'tis not possible for me to do a greater Service unto the Churches on the *Best Island* of the Universe, than to give a distinct Relation of those *Great Examples* which have been occurring among Churches in *Exiles*, that were driven out of that *Island*, into an horrible *Wilderness*, meerly for their being Well-willers unto the *Reformation*. When that Blessed Martyr *Constantine* was carried,[21] with other Martyrs, in a *Dung-Cart*, unto the place of Execution, he pleasantly said, *Well, yet we are a precious Odour to God in Christ* {2 Cor. 2:15}. Tho' the *Reformed Churches* in the *American Regions*, have, by very Injurious Representations of their Brethren (all which they desire to Forget and Forgive!) been many times thrown into a *Dung-Cart*; yet, as they have been a *precious Odour to God in Christ*, so, I hope, they will be a *precious Odour* unto *His People*; and not only *Precious*, but *Useful* also, when the *History* of them shall come to be considered. A *Reformation of the Church* is coming on, and I cannot but thereupon say, with the Dying *Cyrus* to his Children in *Xenophon*, Ἐκ τῶν προγεγενημένων μανθάνετε, αὐτὴ γὰρ ἀρίστη διδασκαλία.[22] *Learn from the things that have been done already, for this is the best way of Learning.* The Reader hath here an Account of *The Things that have been done already. Bernard* upon the Clause in the *Canticles,* [*O thou fairest among Women*] has this ingenious Gloss, *Pulchram, non omnimode qui-dem, sed pulchram inter mulieres eam dicit, videlicet cum Distinctione, quatenus et ex hoc amplius reprimatur, & sciat quid desit sibi.*[23] Thus I do not say, That the Churches of *New-England* are the most *Regular* that can be; yet I do say, and am sure, That they are very like unto those that were in the *First Ages* of Christianity. . . . In short, The *First Age* was the *Golden Age:* To return unto *That,* will make a Man a *Protestant,* and I may add, a *Puritan.* Tis possible, That our Lord Jesus Christ carried some Thousands of *Reformers* into the Retirements of an *American Desart,* on purpose, that, with an opportunity granted unto many of his Faithful Servants, to enjoy the precious *Liberty* of their *Ministry,* tho' in the midst of many *Temptations* all their days, He might there, *To* them first, and then *By* them, give a *Specimen* of many Good Things, which He would have His Churches elsewhere aspire and arise unto: And *This* being done, He knows not whether there be not *All done,* that *New-England* was planted for; and whether the Plantation may not, soon after this, *Come to Nothing.* Upon that Expression in the Sacred Scripture, *Cast the unprofitable Servant into Outer Darkness* {Matt. 25.30}, it hath been imagined by some, That the *Regiones Ex-terae* of America, are the *Tenebrae Exteriores,* which the *Unprofitable* are there condemned unto.[24] No doubt, the Authors of those Ecclesiastical Impositions and Severities, which drove the English Christians into the *Dark Regions* of America, esteemed those *Christians* to be a very *unprofitable* sort of Creatures. But behold, ye *European* Churches, There are *Golden Candlesticks* [more than *twice Seven times seven!*] in the midst of this *Outer Darkness;* Unto the *upright* Children of *Abraham,* here hath arisen *Light in Darkness.* And let us humbly speak it, it shall be *Profitable* for you to consider the *Light,* which from the midst of this *Outer Darkness,* is now to be Darted over unto the other side of the At-lantick Ocean. But we must therewithal ask your Prayers, that these *Golden Can-dlesticks* may not *quickly* be *Removed out of their place!*

§. 4. But whether *New-England* may *Live* any where else or no, it must *Live* in our *History!*

HISTORY, in general, hath had so many and mighty Commendations from the Pens of those Numberless Authors, who, from *Herodotus* to *Howel,* have been the professed Writers of it, that a tenth part of them Transcribed, would be a Furniture for a *Polyanthea in Folio.*[25] . . . But of all *History* it must be confessed, that the *Palm* is to be given to *Church History;* wherein the *Dignity,* the *Suavity,* and the *Utility* of the *Subject* is transcendent.[26] I observe, that for the Descrip-tion of the *whole World* in the Book of *Genesis,* that *First-born of all Historians,* the great *Moses,* employs[27] but *one* or *two* Chapters, whereas he implies, it may be *seven times* as many Chapters, in describing that one little *Pavilion, The*

Tabernacle. And when I am thinking, what may be the Reason of this *Differ-ence,* methinks it intimates unto us, That the *Church* wherein the Service of God is performed, is much more Precious than the *World,* which was indeed created for the Sake and Use of the *Church.* . . . The *Atchievements* of one *Paul* particularly, which that Evangelist hath *Emblazon'd,* have more *True Glory* in them, than all the Acts of those Execrable *Plunderers* and *Murderers,* and irre-sistible *Banditti* of the World, which have been dignified with the Name of *Conquerors. Tacitus* counted *Ingentia bella, Expugnationes urbium, fusos cap-tosque Reges,* the Ravages of *War,* and the glorious *Violences,* whereof great War-riors make wretched Ostentation, to be the *Noblest Matter* for an *Historian.*[28] But there is a *Nobler,* I humbly conceive, in the planting and forming of *Evan-gelical Churches,* and the *Temptations,* the *Corruptions,* the *Afflictions,* which assault them, and their *Salvations* from those Assaults, and the Exemplary *Lives* of those that Heaven employs to be Patterns of *Holiness* and *Usefulness* upon Earth: And unto such it is, that I now invite my Readers; Things in comparison whereof, the Subject of many other Histories, are of as little weight, as the Ques-tions about Z, the last Letter of our Alphabet, and whether H is to be pronounced with an Aspiration, where about whole Volumes have been written, and of no more Account, than the Composure of *Didymus.*[29] But for the *manner* of my treating this *Matter,* I must now give some account unto him.

§. 5. *Reader!* I have done the part of an *Impartial Historian,* albeit not without all occasions perhaps, for the Rule which a worthy Writer, in his *Historica,* gives to every Reader, *Historici Legantus cum Moderatione & venia, & cogitetur fieri non posse ut in omnibus circumstantiis sint Lyncei.*[30] *Polybius* complains of those *Historians,* who always made either the *Carthaginians* brave, and the *Romans* base, or *è contra,* in all their Actions, as their Affection for their own *Party* led them.[31] I have endeavoured, with all *good Conscience,* to decline this writing meerly for a *Party,* or doing like the Dealer in History, whom *Lucian* derides, for always calling the Captain of his own Party an *Achilles,* but of the adverse Party a *Thersites:*[32] . . . I have not *Commended* any Person, but when I have really judg'd, not only *That* he *Deserved* it, but also that it would be a Benefit unto Posterity to know, Wherein he deserved it: And my Judgment of *Desert,* hath not been *Biassed,* by Persons being of my own particular Judgment in matters of *Disputation,* among the Churches of God. I have been as willing to wear the Name of *Simplicius Verinus,*[33] throughout my whole undertaking, as he that, be-fore me, hath assumed it: Nor am I like Pope *Zachary,*[34] impatient so much as to hear of any *Antipodes.* The Spirit of a *Schlusselbergius,*[35] who falls foul with Fury and Reproach on all who differ from him; The Spirit of an *Heylin,* who seems to count no Obloquy too hard for a *Reformer;* and the Spirit of those (*Folio-*

writers there are, some of them, in the English Nation!) whom a Noble Historian Stigmatizes, as, *Those Hot-headed, Passionate Bigots, from whom, 'tis enough, if you be of a Religion contrary unto theirs, to be defamed, condemned and pursued with a thousand Calumnies.* I thank Heaven I Hate it with all my Heart. But how can the *Lives* of the *Commendable* be written without *Commending* them? Or, is that Law of *History* given in one of the eminentest pieces of *Antiquity* we now have in our hands, wholly antiquated, *Maxime proprium est Historiae, Laudem rerum egregie gestarum persequi?*[36] Nor have I, on the other side, forbore to mention many *Censurable* things, even in the Best of my Friends, when the things, in my opinion, were *not Good;* or so bore away for *Placentia,* in the course of our Story, as to pass by *Verona;*[37] but been mindful of the Direction which *Polybius* gives to the Historian, *It becomes him that writes an History, sometimes to extol Enemies in his Praises, when their praise-worthy Actions bespeak it, and at the same time to reprove the best Friends, when their Deeds appear worthy of a reproof; in-as much as History is good for nothing, if Truth (which is the very Eye of the Animal) be not in it.*[38] Indeed I have thought it my duty upon all accounts, (and if it have proceeded unto the degree of a *Fault,* there is, it may be, something in my *Temper* and *Nature,* that has betray'd me therein) to be more sparing and easie, in thus mentioning of *Censurable* things, than in my *other Liberty:* A writer of *Church-History,* should, I know, be like the *builder of the Temple,* one of the *Tribe* of *Naphthali;* and for this I will also plead my *Polybius* in my Excuse; *It is not the Work of an Historian, to commemorate the Vices and Villainies of Men, so much as their just, their fair, their honest Actions: And the Readers of History get more good by the Objects of their Emulation, than of their Indignation.*[39] Nor do I deny, that tho' I cannot approve the Conduct of *Josephus,* (whom *Jerom* not unjustly nor ineptly calls, *The Greek Livy*) when he left out of his *Antiquities,* the Story of the *Golden Calf,* and I don't wonder to find *Chamier,* and *Rivet,*[40] and others, taxing him for his *Partiality* towards his Country-men; yet I have left unmentioned some *Censurable Occurrences* in the *Story* of our *Colonies,* as things no less *Unuseful* than *Improper* to be raised out of the Grave, wherein *Oblivion* hath now buried them; lest I should have incurred the *Pasquil* bestowed upon Pope *Urban,*[41] who employing a *Committee* to Rip up the *Old Errors* of his Predecessors, one clap'd a pair of Spurs upon the heels of the Statue of St. *Peter;* and a *Label* from the *Statue* of St. *Paul* opposite thereunto, upon the Bridge, ask'd him, *Wither he was bound?* St. *Peter* answered, *I apprehend some Danger in staying here; I fear they'll call me in Question for denying my Master.* And St. *Paul* replied, *Nay, then I had best be gone too, for they'll question me also, for Persecuting the Christians before my Conversion.* Briefly, My Pen shall Reproach none, that can give a Good Word unto any

Good Man that is not of their *own Faction*, and shall *Fall out* with none, but those that can *Agree* with no body else, except those of their own *Schism*. . . . But altho' I thus challenge, as my due, the Character of an *Impartial*, I doubt I may not challenge *That* of an *Elegant Historian*. I cannot say, whether the *Style*, wherein this *Church-History* is written, will please the Modern *Criticks*: But if I seem to have used ἁπλουστάτῃ συντάξει γραφῆς,[42] a Simple, Submiss, Humble *Style*, 'tis the same that *Eusebius* affirms to have been used by *Hegesippus*, who, as far as we understand, was the first Author (after *Luke*) that ever composed an entire Body of *Ecclesiastical History*, which he divided into *Five Books*, and Entitled, ὑπομνήματα των ἐκκλησιαστικῶν πράξεων.[43] Whereas *others*, it may be, will reckon the *Style* Embellished with too much of *Ornament*, by the multiplied References to other and former Concerns, closely couch'd, for the Observation of the *Attentive*, in almost every Paragraph; but I must confess, that I am of his mind who said, *Sicuti sal modice cibis aspersus Condit, & gratiam saporis addit, ita si paulum Antiquitatis admiscueris, Oratio fit venustior.*[44] And I have seldom seen that Way of Writing faulted, but by those, who, for a certain odd Reason, sometimes find fault, *That the Grapes are not ripe*. . . . Now, of all the Churches under Heaven, there are none that expect so much *Variety* of Service from their Pastors, as those of *New-England*; and of all the *Churches* in *New-England*, there are none that require more, than those in *Boston*, the Metropolis of the English *America*; whereof *one* is, by the Lord Jesus Christ, committed unto the Care of the unworthy Hand, by which this *History* is compiled. Reader, Give me leave humbly to mention, with him in *Tully, Antequam de Re, Pauca de Me!*[45] Constant *Sermons*, usually more than once, and perhaps three of four Times, in a Week, and all the other Duties of a *Pastoral Watchfulness*, a very *large Flock* has all this while demanded of me; wherein, if I had been furnished with as many *Heads* as a *Typheus*, as many *Eyes* as an *Argos*, and as many *Hands* as a *Briareus*,[46] I might have had Work enough to have employ'd them all; nor hath my *Station* left me free from Obligations to spend very much time in the *Evangelical Service* of *others also*. It would have been a great *Sin* in me, to have *Omitted*, or *Abated*, my Just Cares, to *fulfil my Ministry in these things*, and in a manner *Give my self wholly to them*. All the time I have had for my *Church-History*, hath been perhaps only, or chiefly, that, which I might have taken else for less profitable Recreations; and it hath all been done by *Snatches*. My Reader will not find me the Person intended in his *Littany*, when he says, *Libera me ab homine unius Negotis:*[47] Nor have I spent *Thirty Years* in shaping this my *History*, as *Diodorus Siculus* did for his, [and yet both *Bodinus* and *Sigonius* complain of the Ζφαλματα attending it.][48] But I wish I could have enjoy'd entirely for this Work, one quarter of the little more than *Two Years* which have roll'd away since I began it; whereas I have been forced sometimes wholly to throw by the Work whole Months together, and then resume it, but by a stolen hour or two in a day, not without some hazard of incurring the *Title* which *Coryat* put upon his History of his Travels, *Crudities hastily gobbled up in five Months.*[49] *Protogenes* being seven Years in drawing a Picture, *Apelles* upon the sight of it, said, *The Grace of the Work was much allay'd by the length of the Time.*[50] Whatever else there may have been to take off the *Grace of The Work*, now in the Readers hands, (whereof the *Pictures* of Great and Good Men make a considerable part) I am sure there hath not been the *length of the Time* to do it. Our English Martyrologer, counted it a sufficient *Apology*, for what Meanness might be found in the first Edition of his *Acts and Monuments*, that it was *hastily rashed up in about fourteen Months:*[51] And I may Apologize for this collection of our *Acts and Monuments*, that I should have been glad, in the little more than *Two Years* which have ran out, since I enter'd upon it, if I could have had one half of *About fourteen Months* to have entirely devoted thereunto. But besides the *Time*, which the *Daily Services* of *my own* first, and then many *other* Churches, have necessarily call'd for, I have lost abundance of precious *Time*, thro' the feeble and broken State of my *Health*, which hath unfitted me for *Hardy Study*; I can do nothing to purpose at *Lucubrations.*[52] And yet, in this *Time* also of the two or three Years last past, I have not been excused from the further Diversion of *Publishing* (tho' not so many as they say *Mercurius Trismegistus* did,)[53] yet more than a *Score* of other *Books*, upon a copious Variety of other Subjects, besides the composing of several more, that are not yet published. . . .

Reader, I also expect nothing but *Scourges* from that Generation, to whom the *Mass-book* is dearer than the *Bible*. But I have now likewise confessed another Expectation, that shall be my Consolation under all. They tell us, That on the highest of the *Caspian* Mountains in *Spain*, there is a Lake, whereinto if you throw a Stone, there presently ascends a Smoke, which forms a dense Cloud, from whence issues a Tempest of Rain, Hail, and horrid Thunder-claps, for a good quarter of an hour. Our Church-History will be like a Stone cast into that Lake, for the furious Tempest which it will raise among some, whose Ecclesiastical Dignities have set them, as on the top of Spanish Mountains. The Catholick Spirit of Communion wherewith 'tis written, and the Liberty which I have taken, to tax the Schismatical Impositions and Persecutions of a Party, who have always been as real Enemies to the English Nation, as to the Christian and Protestant Interest, will certainly bring upon the whole Composure, the quick Censures of that Party, at the first cast of their look upon it. . . .

But since an Undertaking of this Nature, must thus encounter so much Envy, from those who are under the Power of the *Spirit that works in the Children of*

Unperswadeableness {Eph. 2:2}, methinks I might perswade my self, that it will
find another sort of Entertainment from those Good Men who have a better
Spirit in them: For, as the Apostle *James* hath noted, (so with Monsieur *Claude*[54]
I read it) *The Spirit that is in us, lusteth against Envy* {James 4:5}; and yet even
in *us* also, there will be the *Flesh*, among whose Works, one is *Envy*, which will
be *Lusting* against the *Spirit*. All Good Men will not be satisfied with every thing
that is here set before them. In my own Country, besides a considerable number of loose and vain Inhabitants risen up, to whom the Congregational Church-
Discipline, which cannot Live well, where the Power of Godliness dyes, is
become distastful for the Purity of it; there is also a number of eminently Godly
Persons, who are for a Larger way, and unto these my Church-History will give
distast, by the things which it may happen to utter, in favour of that Church-
Discipline on some few occasions; and the Discoveries which I may happen to
make of my Apprehensions, that *Scripture*, and *Reason*, and *Antiquity* is for it;
and that it is not far from a glorious Resurrection. But that, as the Famous
Mr. *Baxter*,[55] after Thirty or Forty Years hard Study, about the true Instituted
Church-Discipline, at last, not only own'd, but also invincibly prov'd, That it is
The Congregational; so, The further that the *Unprejudiced Studies* of Learned
Men proceed in this Matter, the more generally the *Congregational Church-
Discipline* will be pronounced for. On the other side, There are some among
us, who very strictly profess the *Congregational Church-Discipline*, but at the
same time they have an unhappy Narrowness of Soul, by which they confine
their value and Kindness too much unto their own Party; and unto those my
Church History will be offensive, because my Regard unto our own declared
Principles, does not hinder me from giving the Right hand of Fellowship unto
the valuable Servants of the Lord Jesus Christ, who find not our Church-
Discipline as yet agreeable unto their present Understandings and Illuminations. If it be thus in my own Country, it cannot be otherwise in That whereto
I send this account of my own.[56] . . .

However, All these things, and an hundred more such things which I think
of, are very small Discouragements for such a Service as I have here endeavoured. I foresee a Recompence, which will abundantly swallow up all Discouragements! It may be *Strato* the Philosopher counted himself well recompensed
for his Labours, when *Ptolomy* bestow'd fourscore Talents on him.[57] It may be
Archimelus the Poet counted himself well recompensed, when *Hiero* sent him a
thousand Bushels of Wheat for one little Epigram: And *Saleius* the Poet might
count himself well recompensed, when *Vespasian* sent him twelve thousand and
five hundred *Philippicks*; and *Oppian* the Poet might count himself well recompensed, when *Caracalla* sent him a piece of Gold for every Line that he had

inscribed unto him.[58] As I live in a Country where such Recompences never were in fashion; it hath no Preferments for me, and I shall count that I am well Rewarded in it, if I can escape without being heavily Reproached, Censured and Condemned, for what I have done: So I thank the Lord, I should exceedingly Scorn all such mean Considerations, I seek not out for Benefactors, to whom these Labours may be Dedicated: There is ONE to whom all is due! From Him I shall have a Recompence: And what Recompence? The Recompence, whereof I do, with inexpressible Joy, assure my self, is this; *That these my poor Labours will certainly serve the Churches and Interests of the Lord Jesus Christ.* And I think I may say, That I ask to live no longer, than I count a Service unto the Lord Jesus Christ, and his Churches, to be it self a glorious Recompence for the doing of it. When *David* was contriving to build the House of God, there was that order given from Heaven concerning him, *Go tell* David, *my Servant* {2 Sam. 7:5}. The adding of *that* more than *Royal Title* unto the Name of *David*, was a sufficient Recompence for all his Contrivance about the House of God. In our whole *Church-History*, we have been at work for the House of the Lord Jesus Christ, [Even that *Man* who is the *Lord God*, and whose *Form* seems on that occasion represented unto His *David*] And herein 'tis Recompence enough, that I have been a *Servant* unto that heavenly Lord. The greatest *Honour*, and the sweetest *Pleasure*, out of *Heaven*, is to Serve our Illustrious Lord JESUS CHRIST, who hath *loved us, and given himself for us* {Eph. 5:2}; and unto whom it is infinitely reasonable that we should *give our selves*, and all that we *have* and *Are*: And it may be the *Angels* in *Heaven* too, aspire not after an higher Felicity.

NEHEMIAS AMERICANUS: THE LIFE OF JOHN WINTHROP, ESQ.

§. 1. LET *Greece* boast of her patient *Lycurgus*, the *Lawgiver*, by whom *Diligence, Temperance, Fortitude* and *Wit* were made the *Fashions* of a therefore Longlasting and Renowned Commonwealth: Let *Rome* tell of her Devout *Numa*, the *Lawgiver*, by whom the most Famous Commonwealth saw *Peace* Triumphing over extinguished *War*; and cruel *Plunders*, and *Murders* giving place to the more mollifying Exercises of his *Religion*.[59] Our *New-England* shall tell and boast of her **Winthrop**,[60] a *Lawgiver*, as patient as *Lycurgus*, but not admitting any of *his* Criminal Disorders; as Devout as *Numa*, but not liable to any of *his* Heathenish Madnesses; a *Governour* in whom the Excellencies of *Christianity* made a most improving Addition unto the *Virtues*, wherein even without *those* he would have made a *Parallel* for the Great Men of *Greece*, or of *Rome*, which the Pen of a *Plutarch* has Eternized.[61]

§. 2. A stock of *Heroes* by right should afford nothing but what is *Heroical;* and nothing but an extream Degeneracy would make any thing less to be expected from a Stock of *Winthrops.* Mr. *Adam Winthrop,* the Son of a Worthy Gentleman wearing the same Name, was himself a Worthy, a Discreet, and a Learned Gentleman, particularly Eminent for *Skill* in the *Law,* not without Remark for *Love* to the *Gospel,* under the Reign of King *Henry* VIII. And Brother to a Memorable *Favourer* of the *Reformed Religion* in the Days of Queen *Mary,* into whose Hands the Famous Martyr *Philpot* committed his *Papers,* which afterwards made no Inconsiderable part of our *Martyr-Books.*[62] This Mr. *Adam Winthrop* had a Son of the same Name also, and of the same Endowments and Imployments with his Father; and this Third *Adam Winthrop* was the Father of that Renowned *John Winthrop,* who was the Father of *New-England,* and the Founder *of a Colony,* which upon many Accounts, like *him* that Founded it, may challenge the *First Place* among the *English* Glories of *America.* Our **John Winthrop** thus Born at the Mansion-House of his Ancestors, at *Groton* in *Suffolk,* on *June* 12. 1587. enjoyed afterwards an agreeable Education. But though he would rather have Devoted himself unto the Study of Mr. *John Calvin,* than of Sir *Edward Cook;*[63] nevertheless, the Accomplishments of a *Lawyer,* were those wherewith Heaven made his chief Opportunities to be Serviceable.

§. 3. Being made, at the unusually early Age of *Eighteen,* a *Justice of Peace,* his Virtues began to fall under a more general Observation; and he not only so *Bound himself to the Behaviour* of a *Christian,* as to become Exemplary for a Conformity to the *Laws* of *Christianity* in his own Conversation, but also discovered a more than ordinary Measure of those Qualities, which adorn an *Officer of Humane Society.* His *Justice* was Impartial, and used the *Ballance* to weigh not the *Cash,* but the *Case* of those who were before him: *Prosopolatria,*[64] he reckoned as bad as *Idololatria:* His *Wisdom* did exquisitely Temper things according to the *Art of Governing,* which is a Business of more Contrivance than the *Seven Arts* of the *Schools:*[65] *Oyer* still went before *Terminer*[66] in all his Administrations: His *Courage* made him *Dare to do right,* and fitted him to stand among the *Lions,* that have sometimes been the *Supporters* of the Throne: All which Virtues he rendred the more Illustrious, by *Emblazoning* them with the Constant *Liberality* and *Hospitality* of a *Gentleman.* This made him the *Terror* of the Wicked, and the *Delight* of the Sober, the *Envy* of the many, but the *Hope* of those who had any *Hopeful Design* in Hand for the Common Good of the Nation, and the Interests of Religion.

§. 4. Accordingly when the *Noble Design* of carrying a Colony of *Chosen People* into an *American* Wilderness, was by *some* Eminent Persons undertaken, *This* Eminent Person was, by the Consent of all, *Chosen* for the *Moses,* who must be the Leader of so great an Undertaking: And indeed nothing but a *Mosaic Spirit* could have carried him through the *Temptations*, to which either his *Farewel* to his *own Land*, or his *Travel* in a *Strange Land*, must needs expose a Gentleman of his *Education*. Wherefore having Sold a fair Estate of Six or Seven Hundred a Year, he Transported himself with the Effects of it into *New-England* in the Year 1630, where he spent it upon the Service of a famous Plantation founded and formed for the Seat of the most *Reformed Christianity*: And continued there, conflicting with *Temptations* of all sorts, as many Years as the *Nodes* of the *Moon* take to dispatch a Revolution.[67] Those Persons were never concerned in a *New-Plantation*, who know not that the unavoidable Difficulties of such a thing, will call for all the *Prudence* and *Patience* of a Mortal Man to Encounter therewithal; and they must be very insensible of the Influence, which the *Just Wrath* of Heaven has permitted the *Devils* to have upon *this* World, if they do not think that the Difficulties of a *New-Plantation*, devoted unto the *Evangelical Worship* of our Lord Jesus Christ, must be yet more than Ordinary. How *Prudently*, how *Patiently*, and with how much Resignation to our Lord Jesus Christ, our brave *Winthrop* waded through these *Difficulties*, let Posterity Consider with Admiration. And know, that as the *Picture* of this their *Governour*, was, after his *Death*, hung up with Honour in the *State-House* of his Country, so the *Wisdom, Courage,* and Holy *Zeal* of his *Life*, were an Example well-worthy to be Copied by all that shall succeed in *Government*.

§. 5. Were he now to be consider'd only as a *Christian*, we might therein propose him as greatly Imitable. He was a very *Religious* Man; and as he strictly kept his *Heart*, so he kept his *House*, under the Laws of *Piety; there* he was every Day constant in Holy Duties, both Morning and Evening, and on the *Lord's Days*, and *Lectures;* though he *wrote* not after the Preacher,[68] yet such was his *Attention*, and such his *Retention* in *Hearing*, that he repeated unto his *Family* the *Sermons* which he had heard in the Congregation. But it is chiefly as a *Governour* that he is now to be consider'd. Being the *Governour* over the considerablest Part of *New-England*, he maintain'd the Figure and Honour of his Place with the Spirit of a true *Gentleman;* but yet with such obliging *Condescention* to the Circumstances of the Colony, that when a certain troublesome and malicious Calumniator, well known in those Times, printed his Libellous *Nick-Names* upon the chief Persons here, the worst *Nick-Name* he could find for the Governour, was *John Temper-well;*[69] and when Calumnies of that ill Man caused the Arch-Bishop to Summon one Mr. *Cleaves* before the King, in hopes to get some Accusation from him against the Country, Mr. *Cleaves*[70] gave such an Account of the Governour's laudable Carriage in all Respects, and the serious Devotion wherewith Prayers were both publickly and privately made for His

Majesty, that the King expressed himself most highly *Pleased* therewithal, only *Sorry* that so Worthy a Person should be no better Accommodated than with the Hardships of *America*. He was, indeed, a *Governour*, who had most exactly studied that Book, which pretending to Teach *Politicks*, did only contain *Three Leaves*, and but *One Word* in each of those Leaves, which Word was, **Moderation**. Hence, though he were a Zealous Enemy to a *Vice*, yet his *Practice* was according to his *Judgment* thus expressed; *In the Infancy of Plantations, Justice should be administred with more Lenity than in a settled State; because People are more apt then to Transgress; partly out of Ignorance of new Laws and Orders, partly out of Oppression of Business, and other Straits.* [**Lento Gradu**][71] *was the old Rule; and if the Strings of a new Instrument be wound up unto their heighth, they will quickly crack.* But when some Leading and Learned Men took Offence at his Conduct in this Matter, and upon a *Conference* gave it in as their Opinion, *That a stricter Discipline was to be used in the beginning of a Plantation, than after its being with more Age established and confirmed,*[72] the Governour being readier to see *his own* Errors than *other Mens*, professed his Purpose to endeavour their Satisfaction with less of *Lenity* in his Administrations. At that *Conference* there were drawn up several other *Articles* to be observed between the Governour and the rest of the Magistrates, which were of this Import: *That* the *Magistrates*, as far as might be, should aforehand ripen their *Consultations*, to produce that *Unanimity* in their *Publick Votes*, which might make them liker to the *Voice of God; that* if *Differences* fell out among them in their Publick Meetings, they should speak only to the *Case*, without any Reflection, with all due *Modesty*, and but by way of *Question;* or Desire the deferring of the *Cause* to further time; and after *Sentence* to imitate privately no *Dislike; that* they should be more *Familiar*, Friendly and Open unto each other, and more frequent in their *Visitations*, and not any way expose each other's *Infirmities*, but seek the *Honour* of each other, and all the Court; *that* One Magistrate shall not *cross* the Proceedings of another, without first advising with him; and *that* they should in all their Appearances abroad, be so circumstanced as to prevent all Contempt of Authority; and *that* they should Support and Strengthen all *Under Officers*. All of which *Articles* were observed by no Man more than by the *Governour* himself.[73]

§. 6. But whilst he thus did as our *New-English Nehemiah*, the part of a *Ruler* in Managing the Publick Affairs of our *American Jerusalem*, when there were *Tobijahs* and *Sanballats* enough to vex him,[74] and give him the Experiment of *Luther's* Observation, *Omnis qui regit, est tanquam signum, in quod omnia Jacula, Satan & Mundus dirigunt;*[75] he made himself still an exacter *Parallel* unto that Governour of *Israel*, by doing the part of a *Neighbour* among the distressed People of the *New-Plantation*. To teach them the *Frugality* necessary for those times, he abridged himself of a Thousand comfortable things, which he had allow'd himself elsewhere: His *Habit* was not that *soft Raiment*, which would have been disagreeable to a *Wilderness*; his *Table* was not covered with the *Superfluities* that would have invited unto *Sensualities*: *Water* was commonly his *own Drink*, though he gave Wine to *others*. But at the same time his *Liberality* unto the Needy was even beyond measure Generous; and therein he was continually causing *The Blessing of him that was ready to Perish to come upon him, and the Heart of the Widow and the Orphan to sing for Joy* {Job 29:13}: But none more than those of Decease'd *Ministers*, whom he always treated with a very singular Compassion; among the Instances whereof we still enjoy with us the Worthy and now Aged Son of that Reverend *Higginson*, whose Death left his Family in a wide World soon after his arrival here, publickly acknowledging the Charitable *Winthrop* for his *Foster-Father*.[76] It was oftentimes no small Trial unto his *Faith*, to think, *How a Table for the People should be furnished when they first came into the Wilderness!* And for very many of the People, his *own good Works* were needful, and accordingly employed for the answering of his *Faith*. Indeed, for a while the Governour was the *Joseph*, unto whom the whole Body of the People repaired when their *Corn* failed them {Gen. 41:35, 36}: and he continued Relieving of them with his *open-handed Bounties*, as long as he had any Stock to do it with; and a lively *Faith* to *see* the return of the *Bread after many Days*, and not *Starve* in the Days that were to pass till that *return* should be *seen*, carried him chearfully through those Expences. . . .'Twas his Custom also to send some of his Family upon Errands, unto the Houses of the Poor about their *Meal time*, on purpose to *spy* whether they *wanted*; and if it were found that they *wanted*, he would make *that* the Opportunity of sending Supplies unto them. And there was one Passage of his *Charity* that was perhaps a little *unusual*: In an hard and long Winter, when *Wood* was very scarce at *Boston*, a Man gave him a private *Information*, that a needy Person in the Neighbourhood stole *Wood* sometimes from *his* Pile; whereupon the Governour in a seeming Anger did reply, *Does he so? I'll take a Course with him; go, call that Man to me, I'll warrant you I'll cure him of Stealing!* When the Man came, the Governour considering that if he had *Stoln*, it was more out of *Necessity* than *Disposition*, said unto him, *Friend, It is a severe Winter, and I doubt you are but meanly provided for Wood; wherefore I would have you supply your self at my Wood-Pile till this cold Season be over.* And he then Merrily asked his Friends, *Whether he had not effectually cured this Man of Stealing his Wood?*

§. 7. One would have imagined that so *good* a Man could have had no *Enemies*; if we had not had a daily and woful Experience to Convince us, that *Goodness* it self will *make* Enemies. It is a wonderful Speech of *Plato*, (in one of his

Books, *De Republica* [Bk. II]) *For the trial of true Vertue, 'tis necessary that a good Man* μηδὲν {γὰρ} ἀδικῶν, δόξαν ἐχέτω τὴν μεγίστην ἀδικίας.[77] *Tho' he do no unjust thing, should suffer the Infamy of the greatest Injustice.* The Governour had by his unspotted *Integrity,* procured himself a great Reputation among the *People;* and then the Crime of *Popularity* was laid unto his Charge by such, who were willing to deliver him from the Danger of having *all Men speak well of him.* Yea, there were Persons eminent both for Figure and for Number, unto whom it was almost *Essential* to *dislike* every thing that came from *him;* and yet *he* always maintained an Amiable Correspondence with them; as believing that they acted according to their Judgment and Conscience, or that their Eyes were held by some *Temptation* in the worst of all their Oppositions. Indeed, his *right Works* were so many, that they exposed him unto the *Envy* of his Neighbours; and of such *Power* was that *Envy,* that sometimes he could not *stand before it;* but it was by *not standing* that he most effectually *withstood* it all. All Great Attempts were sometimes made among the *Freemen,* to get him left out from his Place in the *Government* upon little Pretences, lest by the too *frequent Choice* of One Man,[78] the *Government* should cease to be by *Choice;* and with a particular aim at *him,* Sermons were Preached at the Anniversary Court of *Election,* to disswade the *Freemen* from chusing *One Man* Twice together. This was the Reward of his *extraordinary Serviceableness!* But when these Attempts *did* succeed, as they sometimes *did,* his Profound *Humility* appeared in that *Equality of Mind,* wherewith he applied himself cheerfully to serve the Country in whatever Station their *Votes* had allotted for him. And one Year when the *Votes* came to be Numbered, there were found Six less for Mr. *Winthrop,* than for another Gentleman who then stood in Competition: But several other Persons regularly Tendring their *Votes* before the *Election* was published, were, upon a very frivolous Objection, refused by some of the Magistrates, that were afraid lest the *Election* should at last fall upon Mr. *Winthrop:* Which though it was well perceived, yet such was the *Self-denial* of this *Patriot,* that he would not permit any Notice to be taken of the Injury. But these *Trials* were nothing in Comparison of those harsher and harder *Treats,* which he sometimes had from the *Frowardness* of not a few in the Days of their *Paroxisms;* and from the *Faction* of some against him, not much unlike that of the *Piazzi* in *Florence* against the Family of the *Medices:*[79] All of which he at last Conquered by Conforming to the Famous *Judges* Motto, *Prudens qui Patiens.*[80] The Oracles of God have said, *Envy is rottenness to the Bones* {Pro. 14:30}; and *Gulielmus Parisiensis* applies it unto Rulers, who are as it were the *Bones* of the Societies which they belong unto: *Envy,* says he, *is often found among them, and it is rottenness unto them.*[81] Our *Winthrop* Encountred this *Envy* from others, but Conquered it, by being free from it himself.

§. 8. Were it not for the sake of introducing the Exemplary Skill of this Wise Man, *at giving soft Answers*, one would not chuse to Relate those Instances of *Wrath*, which he had sometimes to Encounter with; but he was for his *Gentleness*, his *Forbearance*, and his *Longanimity*, a Pattern so worthy to be Written *after*, that something must here be Written *of* it. He seemed indeed never to speak any other Language than that of *Theodosius*,[82] *If any Man speak evil of the Governour, if it be thro' Lightness, 'tis to be contemned; if it be thro' Madness, 'tis to be pitied; if it {be} thro' Injury, 'tis to be remitted.* Behold, Reader, the *Meekness of Wisdom* notably exemplified! . . . {T}here was a time when the Suppression of an *Antinomian* and *Familistical* Faction,[83] which extreamly threatned the Ruin of the Country, was generally thought much owing unto this Renowned Man; and therefore when the Friends of that Faction could not wreak their Displeasure on him with any *Politick* Vexations, they set themselves to do it by *Ecclesiastical* ones. Accordingly when a Sentence of *Banishment* was passed on the Ringleaders of those Disturbances, who

—*Maria & Terras, Caelumque profundum,*
Quippe ferant, Rapidi, secum, vertantque per Auras;[84]

many at the Church of *Boston*, who were then that way too much inclined, most earnestly solicited the Elders of that Church, whereof the Governour was a *Member*, to call him forth as an *Offender* for passing of that Sentence. The *Elders* were unwilling to do any such thing; but the Governour understanding the *Ferment* among the *People*, took that occasion to make a Speech in the Congregation to this Effect.[85] "*Brethren*, Understanding that some of you have desired that I should Answer for an *Offence* lately taken among you; had I been called upon so to do, I would, *First*, Have advised with the Ministers of the Country, whether the *Church* had Power to call in Question the *Civil Court*; and I would, *Secondly*, Have advised with the rest of the *Court*, whether I might discover their Counsels unto the *Church*. But though I know that the Reverend *Elders* of this Church, and some others, do very well apprehend that the *Church* cannot enquire into the Proceedings of the *Court*; yet for the Satisfaction of the weaker who do not apprehend it, I will declare my Mind concerning it. If the *Church* have any such Power, they have it from the Lord Jesus Christ; but the Lord Jesus Christ hath disclaimed it, not only by *Practice*, but also by *Precept*, which we have in his Gospel, *Mat.* 20. 25, 26. It is true indeed, that *Magistrates*, as they are *Church-Members*, are accountable unto the *Church* for their Failings; but that is when they are out of their Calling. When *Uzziah* would go offer Incense in the *Temple*, the Officers of the *Church* called him to an account, and withstood him [2 Chr. 26.18]; but when *Asa* put the Prophet in Prison, the Officers of the *Church* did not call *him* to an account for *that* {2 Chr. 16:10}. If the *Magistrate* shall in a *private way* wrong any Man, the *Church* may call him to an Account for it; but if he be in Pursuance of a Course of *Justice*, though the thing that he does be *unjust*, yet he is not accountable for it before the *Church*. As for myself I did nothing in the Causes of any of the *Brethren*, but by the Advice of the *Elders* of the *Church*. Moreover, in the *Oath* which I have taken there is this Clause, *In all Causes wherein you are to give your Vote, you shall do as in your Judgment and Conscience you shall see to be Just, and for the publick Good.* And I am satisfied, it is most for the Glory of God, and the *publick Good*, that there has been such a *Sentence* passed; yea, those *Brethren* are so divided from the *rest* of the Country in their Opinions and Practices, that it cannot stand with the *publick Peace* for them to continue with us; *Abraham* saw that *Hagar* and *Ishmael* must be sent away" {Gen. 21:14}. By such a Speech he marvellously convinced, satisfied and mollified the *uneasie Brethren* of the Church; *Sic cunctus Pelagi cecidit Fragor—*.[86] And after a little patient waiting, the *differences* all so wore away, that the Church, meerly as a Token of Respect unto the Governour, when he had newly met with some *Losses* in his Estate, sent him a Present of several *Hundreds* of Pounds. Once more there was a time, when some active Spirits among the *Deputies* of the Colony, by their endeavours not only to make themselves a *Court of Judicature*, but also to take away the *Negative* by which the *Magistrates* might check their *Votes*, had like by over-driving to have run the whole Government into something too *Democratical*. And if there were a Town in *Spain* undermined by *Coneys*, another Town in *Thrace* destroyed by *Moles*, a Third in *Greece* ranversed by *Frogs*,[87] a Fourth in *Germany* subverted by *Rats*; I must on this Occasion add, that there was a Country in *America* like to be confounded by a *Swine*.[88] A certain *stray Sow* being found, was claimed by Two several Persons with a Claim so equally maintained on both sides, that after Six or Seven Years *Hunting* the Business, from one Court unto another, it was brought at last into the *General Court*, where the final Determination was, *that it was impossible to proceed unto any Judgment in the Case.* However in the debate of this Matter, the *Negative* of the *Upper-House* upon the *Lower* in that Court was brought upon the Stage; and agitated with so hot a Zeal, that a *little more and all had been in the Fire.* In these Agitations the Governour was informed that an offence had been taken by some eminent Persons, at certain Passages in a Discourse by him written thereabout; whereupon with his usual *Condescendency*, when he next came into the General Court, he made a Speech of this Import.[89] "I understand, that some have *taken* Offence at something that I have lately written; which *Offence* I desire to remove now, and begin this Year in a reconciled State with you all. As for the *Matter* of my Writing, I had the

Concurrence of my *Brethren*; it is Point of *Judgment* which is not at my own dis-
posing. I have examined it over and over again, by such *Light* as God has given
me, from the Rules of *Religion, Reason* and *Custom*; and I see no cause to Re-
tract any thing of it: Wherefore I must enjoy my *Liberty* in *that*, as *you* do your
selves. But for the *Manner, this*, and all that was blame-worthy in it, was wholly
my own; and whatsoever I might alledge for my own Justification therein before
Men, I waive it, as now setting my self before another *Judgment-Seat*. However,
what I wrote was upon *great Provocation*, and to vindicate my self and others
from great Aspersion; yet that was no sufficient Warrant for me to allow any *Distemper of Spirit* in my self; and I doubt I have been too prodigal of my *Brethren's
Reputation*; I might have maintained my Cause without casting any Blemish
upon others, when I made that my Conclusion, *And now let Religion and sound
Reason give Judgment in the Case*; it look'd as if I arrogated too much unto *my
self*, and too little to *others*. And when I made that Profession, *That I would maintain what I wrote before all the World*, though such Words might modestly be
spoken, yet I perceive an unbeseeming *Pride* of my own Heart breathing in them.
For these Failings I ask Pardon both of God and Man."

> *Sic ait, & dicto citius Tumida Æquora placat,*
> *Collectasque fugat Nubes, Solemque reducit.*[90]

This *acknowledging Disposition* in the Governour, made them all *acknowledge*,
that he was truly *a Man of an excellent Spirit*. In fine, the *Victories* of an *Alexander*,
an *Hannibal*, or a *Caesar* over *other Men*, were not so Glorious, as the *Victories* of
this great Man over *himself*, which also at last prov'd *Victories* over *other Men*. . . .

§. 12. He that had been for his Attainments, as they said of the blessed *Macarius*,[91] a Παιδαριογέρων, *An old Man, while a young One*, and that had in his
young Days met with many of those *Ill Days*, whereof he could say, he had *little
Pleasure in them*; now found *old Age* in its Infirmities advancing *Earlier* upon
him, than it came upon his much longer lived Progenitors. While he was yet
Seven Years off of that which we call *the great Climacterical*,[92] he felt the Approaches of his *Dissolution*; and finding he could say,

> *Non Habitus, non ipse Color non Gressus Euntis,*
> *Non Species Eadem, quae fuit ante, manet.*[93]

he then wrote this account of himself, *Age now comes upon me, and Infirmities
therewithal, which makes me apprehend, that the time of my departure out of this
World is not far off. However our times are all in the Lord's Hand, so as we need
not trouble our Thoughts how long or short they may be, but how we may be found
Faithful when we are called for.* But at last when *that Year* came, he took a *Cold*

which turned into a *Feaver*, whereof he lay *Sick* about a Month, and in that *Sickness*, as it hath been observed, that there was allowed unto the *Serpent* the *bruising of the Heel* {Gen. 3:15}; and accordingly at the *Heel* or the *Close* of our Lives the *old Serpent* will be Nibbling more than ever in our Lives before; and when the Devil sees that we shall shortly be, *where the wicked cease from troubling* {Job 3:17}, that *wicked One* will *trouble* us more than ever; so this eminent Saint now underwent sharp Conflicts with the *Tempter*, whose *Wrath* grew *Great*, as the *Time* to exert it grew *Short*; and he was Buffetted with the Disconsolate Thoughts of Black and Sore *Desertions*, wherein he could use that sad Representation of his own Condition.

> *Nuper Eram Judex; Jam Judicor; Ante Tribunal,*
> *Subsistens paveo, Judicor ipse modo.*[94]

But it was not long before those *Clouds* were Dispelled, and he enjoyed in his Holy Soul the *Great Consolations of God!* {Philem. 7}. While he thus lay *Ripening* for Heaven, he did out of Obedience unto the *Ordinance* of our Lord, send for the *Elders of the Church* to *Pray* with him; yea, they and the whole Church *Fasted* as well as *Prayed* for him; and in that *Fast* the venerable Cotton[95] Preached on *Psal.* 35. 13, 14. *When they were Sick, I humbled my self with Fasting; I behaved my self as though he had been my Friend or Brother; I bowed down heavily, as one that Mourned for his Mother:* From whence I find him raising that Observation, *The Sickness of one that is to us as a Friend, a Brother, a Mother, is a just occasion of deep humbling our Souls with Fasting and Prayer;* and making this Application, "Upon this Occasion we are now to attend this Duty for a *Governour,* who has been to us a *Friend* in his *Counsel* for all things, and *Help* for our *Bodies* by *Physick,* for our *Estates* by *Law,* and of whom there was no fear of his becoming an *Enemy,* like the *Friends* of *David:* A *Governour* who has been unto us as a *Brother;* not usurping *Authority* over the Church; often speaking his *Advice,* and often contradicted, even by Young Men, and some of low degree; yet not replying, but offering Satisfaction also when any supposed Offences have arisen; a *Governour* who has been unto us as a *Mother,* Parentlike distributing his *Goods* to Brethren and Neighbours at his first coming; and *gently* bearing our *Infirmities* without taking notice of them."[96]

Such a *Governour* after he had been more than *Ten* several times by the People chosen their *Governour,* was *New-England* now to lose; who having, like *Jacob,* first left his *Council* and *Blessing* with his Children gathered about his Bed side; and, like *David, served his Generation by the Will of God* {Acts 13:36}, he *gave up the Ghost,* and *fell asleep on March* 26, 1649. Having, like the dying Emperour *Valentinian*, this above all his other *Victories* for his Triumphs, *His overcoming of himself.*

The Words of *Josephus* about *Nehemiah*, the Governour of *Israel*, we will now use upon this Governour of *New-England*, as his

EPITAPH.

Ἀνὴρ ἐγένετο χρηστὸς τὴν φύσιν, καὶ δίκαιος,
Καὶ περὶ τοὺς ὁμοεθνεῖς φιλοτιμότατος·
Μνημεῖον αἰώνιον αὐτῳ καταλιπὼν τὰ τῶν
Ἱεροσολύμων τείχη·

VIR FUIT INDOLE BONUS, AC JUSTUS:
ET POPULARIUM GLORIÆ AMANTISSIMUS:
QUIBUS ETERNUM RELIQUIT MONUMENTUM,
Novanglorum MOENIA.[97]

THE DECLARATION, OF THE GENTLEMEN, MERCHANTS, AND INHABITANTS OF BOSTON, AND THE COUNTREY ADJACENT (1689)

§ I. Wee have seen more than a decad of years rolled away, since the *English* World had the Discovery of an horrid *Popish Plot*;[98] wherein the bloody *Devoto's* of *Rome* had in their Design and Prospect no less than the execution of the *Protestant Religion*: which mighty Work they called *the utter subduing of a Pestilent Heresie*: wherein (they said) there never were such hopes of Success since the Death of Queen *Mary*[99] as now in our dayes. And we were of all Men the most insensible, if we should apprehend a Countrey so remarkable for the true Profession and pure Exercise of the Protestant Religion as *New-England* is, wholly unconcerned in the Infandous Plot; to crush and break a Countrey so intirely and signally made up of *Reformed Churches*, and at length to involve it in the miseries of an utter Extirpation: must needs carry even a Supererogation of merit with it, among such as were intoxicated with a Bigotry inspired into them by the great *Scarlet Whore*.[100]

§ II. To get us within the reach of the desolation desired for us, it was no improper thing that we should first have our *Charter* Vacated and the hedge which kept us from the wild Beasts of the field effectually broken down. The accomplishment of this was hastned by the unwearied solicitations and slanderous accusations of a man for his *Malice* and *Fals-hood* well known unto us all.

Our *Charter* was with a most injurious pretence (& scarce *that*) of Law, Condemned before it was possible for us to appear at *Westminster* in the legal defence of it: and without a fair leave to answer for our selves concerning the crimes falsly laid to our charge, we were put under a *President* and *Councill*, without any liberty for an Assembly which the other *American Plantations* have, by a Commission from his *Majesty*.

§ III. The Commission was as *Illegal* for the forme of it, as the way of obtaining it was *Malicious* and *unreasonable:* yet we made no resistance thereunto as wee could easily have done; but chose to give all *Man-kind* a demonstration of our being a people sufficiently dutifull and loyall to our King: and this with yet more Satisfaction because wee took pains to make our selves believe as much as ever we could of the Whedle then offer'd unto us; That his *Majestys* desire was no other then the happy encrease & advance of these *Provinces* by their more immediate dependance on the *Crown* of *England*. And we were convinced of it by the courses immediately taken to damp and spoyl our *trade;* wherof decayes and complaints presently filled all the Countrey; while in the mean times neither the Honour nor the Treasure of the King was at all advanced by this new Model of our Affairs, but a considerable Charge added unto the Crown.

§. IV. In little more than half a Year we saw this Commission superseded by another, yet more Absolute and Arbitrary, with which Sr. *Edmond Andross* arrived as our Governour: who besides his Power, with the Advice and Consent of his Council, to make Laws and raise Taxes as he pleased; had also Authority by himself to Muster and Imploy all Persons residing in the Territory as occasion shall serve; and to transfer such Forces to any English Plantation in *America*, as occasion shall require. And several Companies of *Red Coats* were now brought from *Europe*, to support what was to be Imposed upon us, not without repeated Menaces that some hundreds more were intended for us.

§ V. The Government was no sooner in these Hands, but care was taken to load Preferments principally upon such Men as were strangers to, and haters of the People: and every ones Observation hath noted, what Qualifications recommended a Man to publick Offices and Employments, only here and there a *good man* was used, where others could not easily be had; the Governour himself with assertions now and then falling from him made us jealous that it would be thought for his Majesties Interest, if this People were removed and another succeed in their room: And his far fetched Instruments that were growing Rich among us, would gravely inform us, that it was not for His Majesties Interest that we should thrive. But of all our oppressors we were cheifly *Squeezed* by a crew of abject Persons fetched, from *New-York* to be the tools of the adversary standing at our right hand; by these were extraordinary and intollerable fees extorted from every one upon all occasions, without any Rules but those of their own insatiable avarice and beggary; and even the probate of a will must now cost as many *Pounds* perhaps as it did *Shillings* heretofore; nor could a small Volume contain the other Illegalities done by these *Horse-leaches* in the two or three years that they have been sucking of us; and what Laws they made it was as impossible for us to know, as dangerous for us to break; but we shall leave the men of *Ipswich* and of *Plimouth* (among others) to tell the Story of the kindness which has been shown 'em upon this account. Doubtless a land so Ruled as once *New-England* was, has not without many fears and sighs beheld the wicked walking on every side and the vilest men exalted.

§ VI. It was now plainly affirmed both by some in open Council and by the same in private converse, that the people in *New-England* were all *Slaves* and the only difference between them and *Slaves* is their not being bought and sold; and it was a maxim delivered in open Court unto us by one of the Council, that we must not think the Priviledges of *English* men would follow us to the end of the world: Accordingly we have been treated with multiplied contradictions to *Magna Charta*, the rights of which we laid claim unto. Persons who did but peaceably object against the raising of Taxes without an Assembly have bene for it Fined, some twenty, some thirty, and others fifty Pounds. Packt and pickt Juries have been very common things among us, when under a pretended form of Law the trouble of some perhaps honest and worthy Men has been aimed at: but when some of this Gang have been brought upon the State, for the most detestable Enormities that ever the Sun beheld, all Men have with Admiration seen what methods have been taken that they might not be treated according to their Crimes. Without a Verdict, yea, without a Jury sometimes have People been fined most unrighteously; and some not of the meanest quality have been kept in long and close Imprisonment without any the least Information appearing against them, or an *Habeas Corpus* allowed unto them. In short, when our Millstones have been a little out of Money, 'twas but pretending some Offence to be enquired into, and the most innocent of Men were continually put into no small expence to answer the Demands of the Officers, who must have Money of them, or a Prison for them: though none could accuse them of any Misdemeanour.

§ VII. To plunge the poor People every where into deeper Incapacities, there was one very comprehensive abuse given to us; multitudes of Pious and Sober Men through the Land scrupled the mode of Swearing on the Book, desiring that they might Swear with an uplifted hand, agreeable to the ancient custome of the Colony; and though we think we can prove that the Common Law amongst us (as well as in some other places under the *English Crown*) not only indulges, but even commands and enjoyns the rite of lifting the hand in *Swearing*; yet they that had this doubt were still put by from serving on any Juryes; and many of them were most unaccountably Fined and Imprisoned. Thus one grievance is a *Trojan Horse*, in the Belly of which it is not easy to recount how many insufferable Vexations have been contained.

§ VIII. Because these things could not make us miserable fast enough, there was a notable Discovery made, of, we know not what *flaw* in all our *Titles to our Lands*; and, though *besides* our purchase of them from the Natives, and, *besides* our actual peaceable unquestioned Possession of them, for near threescore years, and besides the Promise of K. *Charles II.* In his Proclamation sent over to us, in the Year 1683, that *no man here shall receive any Prejudice in his Free-hold or Estate:* we had the Grant of our Lands, under the Seal of the *Council* of *Plymouth*, which Grant was Renewed and Confirmed unto us by King *Charles I.* Under the great Seal of *England;* and the *General Court* which consisted of the Pattentees and their Associates, had made particular Grants hereof to the several *Towns* (though 'twas now deny'd by the Governour, that there was any such Thing as a *Town*) among us; to all which Grants the *General Court* annexed for the further securing of them, A *General Act* Published under the Seal of the Colony, in the Year 1684. Yet we were every day told, *That no man was owner of a Foot of Land in all the Colony.* Accordingly, *Writs of Intrusion* began every where to be served on People; that after all their sweat and their cost under their formerly purchased lands, thought themselves *Free-holders* of what they had. And the Governour caused the Lands pertaining to these and those *particular men,* to be measured out, for his Creatures to take possession of; and the *Right Owners,* for pulling up the Stakes, have passed through Molestations enough to tire all the patience in the world. They are more than a few, that were by Terrors driven to take *Pattents* for their Lands at excessive rates, to save them from the next that might Petition for them: and we fear that the forcing of the people at the *Eastward* hereunto gave too much Rise to the late unhappy Invasion made by the *Indians* on them. *Blanck Pattents* were got ready for the rest of us, to be Sold at a Price, that all the Money and Moveables in the Territory could scarce have paid. And several *Towns* in the Country, had their *Commons* beg'd by Persons (even by some of the Council themselves) who have been privately encouraged thereunto, by those that sought for occasions to impoverish a Land already *Peeled, Meeted out and Trodden down.*

§ IX. All the Council were not ingaged in these Ill actions but those of them which were true Lovers of *their Country*, were seldom admitted to, and seldomer consulted at the Debates which Produced these unrighteous things: Care was taken to keep them under disadvantages; and the Governour with five or six more did what they would. We bore all these, and many more such things, without making any attempt for any Relief; only *Mr.* {Increase} *Mather* purely out of Respect unto the good of his Affected Country, undertook a Voyage into *England*; which, when these men suspected him to be preparing for, they used all manner of Craft and Rage, not only to interrupt his *Voyage*, but to ruine his *Person* too. God having through many Difficulties given him to arrive at *White-Hall*, the King more than once or twice Promised him a certain *Magna Charta* for a speedy redress of many things which we were groaning under: and in the mean time, said, *That our Governour should be written unto, to forbear the measures that he was upon.* However, after this, we were injured in those very things, which were complained of; and besides what wrong hath been done in our civil Concerns, we suppose the *Ministers,* and the *Churches* every where have seen our Sacred Concerns a pace going after them: How they have been Discountenanced, has had a room in the reflections of every man, that is not a stranger *in our Israel.*

§ X. And yet that our Calamity, might not be terminated here, we are again Briar'd in the Perplexities of another *Indian War*;[101] how, or why; is a mystery too deep for us to unfold. And tho' 'tis judged, there are not *one hundred* of our enemies, yet an Army of *one thousand* English hath been raised for the Conquering of them; which Army of our poor Friends and Brethren now under *Popish Commanders* (for in the Army as well as in the Council Papists are in Commission) Has been under such a conduct that not one *Indian* hath been kill'd, but more English are supposed to have died through sickness, and hardship, and in a way little satisfactory to their Friends, then we have adversaries there alive; and the whole War hath been so managed, that we can't but suspect in it, a branch of a Plot, *to bring us Low*; which we propound further to be in due time enquired into.

§ XI. We did nothing against these Proceedings, but only cry to our God; they *have caused the cry of the Poor to come unto him, and he hears the cry of the Afflicted* {Job 34:28}. We have been quiet hitherto; and so still we should have been, had not the Great God at this time laid us under a *double engagement* to do something for our security: besides, what we have in the strangely unanimous inclination, Which our Countrymen by extreamest necessities are driven unto. For first, we are Informed that the rest of the English *America* is Alarmed with just and great fears, that they may be attaqu'd by the *French,* who have lately ('tis said) already treated many of the English with worse then *Turkish* Crueltys; and while we are in equal danger of being surprised by them, it is high time we should be better guarded, then we are like to be while the Government remains in the hands by which it hath been held of late. Moreover, we have understood, (though the *Governour* has taken all imaginable care to keep us all ignorant thereof) that the Almighty God hath been pleased to prosper the noble undertaking of the Prince of *Orange*, to preserve the three Kingdoms from the horrible brinks of Popery and Slavery,[102] and to bring to a Condign punishment those *worst of men*, by whom *English Liberties* have been destroy'd; in compliance with which Glorious Action, we ought surely to follow the Patterns which the Nobility, Gentry and Commonalty in several parts of the Kingdom have set before us, though *they* therein have chiefly proposed to prevent what *we* already endure.

§ XII. We do therefore seize upon the persons of those few *Ill men* which have been (next to our sins) the grand authors of our miseries: Resolving to secure them, for what Justice, Orders from his Highness with the *Parliament* shall direct, lest ere we are aware we *find* (what we may *fear*, being on all sides in danger) our selves to be by them given away to a Forreign *Power*, before such orders can reach unto us; for which Orders we now Humbly wait. In the mean time firmly believing: that wee have endeavoured nothing but what meer Duty to God and our *Country* calls for at our Hands, we commit our *Enterprise* unto the Blessing of Him, *who hears, the cry of the Oppressed* {Job 34:28}; and advise all our Neighbours for whom we have thus ventured our selves to joyn with us in Prayers and all just Actions for the Prosperity of the Land.

GENDER, CHILDREARING, AND EDUCATION

Colonial New England Puritans compared the extended family to a "little commonwealth," a microcosm of the larger society. All members acted on behalf of the "common weal," or collective good. For this to be possible, in societies large and small, members had to live in a hierarchy—part of the "great chain of being"—in which everyone had an assigned position. Men and husbands were at the top, acting as patriarchs and directing all below them. Women and wives were on the next rung down, operating in deference to their husbands but also as "deputy husbands," assuming specific, defined responsibilities and obligations within the domestic sphere. Below these family heads, in descending order of authority and with ascending degrees of required obedience, were children, servants and slaves, and then animals.

Mather's depictions of women are especially revealing as expressions of an idealized view of womanhood meant to achieve social morality and harmony through holiness, and thereby bring down God's blessings. Reality was often far removed from such ideals, and the actual sufferings and advances of women varied widely. With regard to gender roles, Mather was both a "guardian of orthodoxy and an innovator."[1] In a time when writers (who just happened to be males) assumed women were more subject to passions and less intellectually capable than men, Mather argued that women were as thoroughly rational as men and that the race's mother, Eve, exercised reason as strongly as Adam. Far from being inherently weak, women were more spiritual and more apt to be converted than men, and were deserving of access to higher education. Mather saw in women a future as writers for the church and society. Indeed, Cotton Mather virtually invented the genre of female eulogy in late seventeenth-century New England: funeral sermons of women that held up their subjects as models of piety and learning.

Ornaments for the Daughters of Zion was published in 1692, right before tumultuous events in Salem would strain, if not redefine, assumptions about gender, the body, and religious experience in New England. But the work encapsulated contemporary views of women in their different roles through the lifecycle, as "maids," wives, mothers, and widows, while revealing some ways in which Mather pushed the bounds of prescribed female roles.

Young, unmarried women were to have their characters ornamented with devotion, modesty, industry, discretion, and obedience. They were to exhibit these virtues as models to their peers but ultimately to attract the attention of a potential husband, since that was the perceived God-ordained place for women in premodern societies. Once married, a wife was to show unstinting love for her husband, never displease him, preserve peace with him, and be thrifty and faithful. Mather wrote these injunctions more than two decades before he married his third wife, the contentious and self-assertive Lydia Lee George. Their marriage was often combative and in some ways miserable, so Mather's assumptions must have been put to the test.[2] Even so, in a time when corporal punishment of wives was, sadly, legal and all too typical, Mather nonetheless declared the practice a "Sacriledge"; men who beat their wives were "Monsters." All the same, he enjoined wives who were beaten to "bear it" with the sure knowledge of "*Rewards* hereafter." As in so many spheres of earthly life, suffering was to be seen as temporary and as preparation for heights of happiness in the spiritual realm. However much modern readers may not agree with this idea of deferring happiness to another world, understanding it is vital to achieving empathy with someone like Cotton Mather and with those who shared his assumptions.

A woman who was to be a mother was to pray to God that her child might be a "*Holy Thing*," an elect vessel. A mother preparing to give birth was to give herself up to God and have faith that she and her child would be safely delivered, rather than die from complications—an all-too-common occurrence at that time, as Mather emphasized in his tract *Elizabeth* (1710) and in "Retired Elizabeth," part of his medical handbook *The Angel of Bethesda* (not to be confused with his 1722 sermon by that title). He did direct that a mother was to offer praise to God on a safe delivery. Commenting on what appears to have been a growing practice to put out one's children to wet nurses, Mather insisted that a mother nurse her own children. No one, he admonished, should consider herself too high a lady to suckle her own children. Mothers too were to be instrumental in bringing up offspring in the *"Nurture and Admonition of the Lord."* If disasters or ill providences befell one's progeny, mothers were to turn them into benefits, teaching that good came out of evil.

Widows similarly had duties inherent to their place and experience. Curiously, a widow was to give her deceased husband a decent burial, though not one *"above her Estate"* or station—advice that joined an awareness of maintaining social place with a distaste for ostentation. Mourning was certainly appropriate, but too profusive and prolonged grieving was considered indecent because it revealed an attachment higher than one's commitment to God and the concerns of one's spirit. Instead, the widow was now to consider God as her husband. Even so, she was to act both as father and mother to her children. She should not be eager to remarry, but if she did, she was to be a good stepmother to her husband's children. In all things, she was to model holy, prudent, and wise behavior, as a "mother in Israel" (Judg. 5:7).

Whether as maids, wives, mothers, or widows, women were, within the family structure, members of a network of mutual relationships. Although this web of obligations extended to wider kinship, it was particularly important in the nuclear family, consisting of spouses and children. Mather treated this theme, among others, in *Bonifacius. An Essay Upon the Good.* Published in 1710 and presenting pithy advice on how to live a life of serviceable charity—"Do Good"—it is arguably Mather's most popular work, whose influence Benjamin Franklin professed.

In section 11 of *Bonifacius*, a portion of which is presented below, Mather considered how the *"Useful Man"* can do good for his family and near relations.[3]

"One Great way to prove our selves *Really Good*," Mather jovially quipped, "is to be *Relatively Good*." "*Domestick Relations*," for Mather, began with the "**Conjugal**," that is, between husband and wife. First and foremost, spouses should constantly think about how they could be blessings to each other, benefiting each other not only materially but spiritually. They could even be the means of each other's conversion. In all things, they were to emulate in their behavior toward each other the kindness of Jesus.

But it was the duties of parents toward their children that most concerned Mather here. In the role of the male head of the family, as was typical of the time, he enumerated a score of particulars about how he would raise children, many of which no doubt reflected his actual practices. First, parents should solemnly "give up" or devote their children to God in baptism. As the child grew, she was to be reminded of her "*Baptismal Engagements*" to love God and others. Fathers and mothers were to offer fervent daily prayers on behalf of their offspring, mentioning each one by name to God every day; likewise, they were to teach children to pray themselves. The Bible contained "*Delightfull* Stories" and lessons with which to entertain and form children. Alongside inculcating scripture, parents were to have their sons and daughters learn the catechism—the Shorter Westminster Catechism was a favorite in colonial New England—drawing out "proofs" from each of the questions and answers that composed it. Instilling a "*Temper of Benignity*," a spirit of charitableness and helpfulness, was another parental obligation. Teaching progeny to read and to write in "a Fair Hand" was a basic skill for a life of doing good, but equally if not more important was the passing on principles of reason and honor, which parents could model by how they treated their children: giving advice, avoiding punishment, and behaving in such a way as to make children love to be in their parents' company. Such principles were so many steps to "*Higher Principles*": loving God and being sensible of God's parental eye on them at all times. As spiritual counselors, fathers and mothers were to inquire regularly into the state of their offspring's souls, monitor the company they kept, encourage them in the development of particular skills, have children remember the main "end" for which they live (glorifying God), and examine every act to ensure that they would not regret it "on a deathbed."[4]

Within Puritan and post-Puritan cultures, children were seen as the sinful progeny of Adam, whose wills had to be broken early and redirected from self to God. Childhood was a vital stage in life for forming a child's character, not to mention maximizing its chances for redemption. Mather was brought up in this milieu, and while he perpetuated its norms in his own child-rearing advice and practices, he anticipated modern attitudes and methods.[5] In this part of *Bonifacius*, Mather was much less particular with his advice to children than to parents, but neither did he forget them. Just as spouses were to be blessings to each other, so sons and daughters were to be blessings to their parents, instruments of good and comfort to them.

As detailed in the "Sketch" of Mather's life in the introduction to this volume, his history with his own marriages and children was tragic. Two of his wives died, and his third marriage was, to say the least, tumultuous. Only one of his fifteen children outlived him: Samuel, or "Sammy," who became, like his forebears, a minister. A particular source of grief to Cotton was his eldest son, Increase, or "Creasy," a black sheep of the family who led an epicurean life, fathered a child out of wedlock, and died at sea as a common sailor in 1724. For all that Creasy vexed his father, or perhaps because of it, he was the favorite whose rebellious ways and early death were always on Cotton's heart, not least because Cotton doubted that Creasy had died a saint.

ORNAMENTS FOR THE DAUGHTERS OF ZION (1692)

THE VERTUOUS MAID

Tis the Wish of the Psalmist, in Psal. 144.12. *That our Daughters may be as Corner Stones, Polished after the Similitude of a Palace.* The Name of *Pernel* [or *Petronella*] which Signifies, *A Pritty Little Stone,* has been sometimes put upon a *Daughter.* And now behold, *A Vertuous Daughter* is here styled, *A Polished Corner Stone,* by the Spirit of God; She is indeed a *Margaret,* that is to say, *A precious one.* It seems, tis a thing that more than a little sets off the Happiness of a

People, When the *Young Women* among them, have Accomplishments which render them, like the Tall, Fine, Costly *Pillars,* that are usually at the Gates of *Palaces.* The most *Christian Jew* in his Translation of that Place, makes the Wish to run, *That our Daughters may be—the Building of the Temple.* And indeed it is no small Happiness unto a People, when the *Young Women* among them, do *Build* the *Temple* of God, and become *Stones* fit for a Room in that *Building.* It ha's doubtless been a most Encouraging thing unto some one Gather'd *Church* of the Lord Jesus, To see about Thirty or Forty Gracious *Young women,* in two or three Years time (as perhaps there have been seen) Addressing them for their Sacred Communion at the Table of the Lord.[6] Now tis by, *The Fear of God,* that a Maid may become one of these Happy *Daughters.* A *Vertuous Maid,* will not count her self too Young to be Concerned about, *The Fear of God,* but she Ob-eyes that Call, *Remember thy Creator in the Dayes of thy Youth* {Eccl. 12:1}; She beleeves that Word, *Behold, Now is the Accepted Time, Behold, Now is the Day of Salvation!* {2 Cor. 6:2}. And let us now see what her Carriage is.

I. Such is her *Devotion,* that while she *Prudently* avoids the Reading of *Romances,* which do no less Naturally than Generally Inspire the minds of Young People with *Humours,* that are as *Vicious* as they are *Foolish;* on the other side, she *Piously* Reads the Bible Every Day, and she thence fetches those Humble and Holy, and serious *Prayers* which do obtain for her, all manner of *Grace to help in a Time of Need.* The Name of *Agatha,* or, *A Good One,* is that which for this cause Pertains unto her; and She is an *Anna,* or an *Hannah,* which is to say, *A Gracious One.*

II. Such is her *Purity,* that while she will not suffer the least *Behaviour* or *Expression* to proceed from her, which may Savour of Obscaenity; so neither will she *Permit,* much less *Invite,* the Dalliances of any Wanton Creatures which may design any thing besides what is *Honourable* on her; nor will she *Endure* to hear any Talk that shall not sound Innocently, without bestowing the Rebuke of at least *that* which for her sake we stile, *A Maiden Blush,* upon it. She is an *Agnes,* that is, *A Chast One.* The Name of a *Catharine,* that is, a *Puritan,* agrees well unto her; and she had rather have it, though with a scornful Nick name, than go with out it.

III. Such is her *Modesty,* that she Chooses to be *Seen* rather than *Heard* wher-ever she comes: and instead of that *Confidence* in *Repartees* and *Railleries* which passes for Good Breeding with a Debauched Generation, or instead of being like those who (as one says) *More Bridle in their Chins, than their Tongues,* she Counts *Tace,*[7] which in English is, *Hold* your *Peace,* a Name sometimes worn by some of her Sex, to be a Rule alwayes to be heeded by her self. But if she be Constrained, at all to speak, she still is, an *Eulalia,* or, a *Well Spoken One;* and though she will not be, *As an Hind let loose,* yet she will ever, *Give Goodly Words.*

IV. Such is her *Industry*, that she betimes applies her self to Learn all the Affairs of *Housewifry*, and besides a good skill at her *Needle*, as well as in the *Kitchen*, she acquaints her self with *Arithmetick* and *Accomptantship*, [perhaps also Chirurgery] and such other Arts relating to *Business*, as may Enable her to do the *Man* whom she may hereafter have, *Good and not Evil all the Days of her Life*. If she have any Time after this to Learn *Musick* and *Language* she will not Loose her *Time*, and yet she will not be proud of her *Skill*, though the Name of *Lora*, that is, *Learning*, (which the *Saxons* had in use among them for their Women) should justly belong unto her. She would with all good Accomplishments be a *Ruth*; which is to say, *A Filled One*.

V. Such is her *Discretion*, that while 'tis too absurdly counted a *Great Curse* to be an *Old Maid*, she makes her *Single* State a *Blessed* One by Improving her *Liesure* from the Encumbrances of a Family, in *Caring for the Things of the Lord, that she may be Holy both in Body and in Spirit*: and when she sees what Liberty she thereby has, *To serve the Lord without Distraction*, she calls her self a *Beatrice*, that is, *A Blessed Woman*. She does not *Vow* a perpetual Virginity, lest her *Vow* should happen to Expose her; while there are *Devils* as well as *Angels*, which do *not Marry, nor are given in Marriage* {Matt. 22:30}. But yet instead of using any Hasty Method to get into the *Married Row*, and instead of taking a *Bad* Husband meerly to avoid the little Reproach of having *None*, she do's by her Gravity and Holiness, convince all the World, that her present circumstances are of *Choice* rather than *Force*; and the Longer she is in them, the more she do's *Consecrate* her self unto the Lord.

VI. Such is her *Obedience*, that as 'twas none of her manner to seek a Match for her self, by putting her self into a *Flaunting Dress*, knowing that such a Dress would make a *Wiseman* afraid of her, and it were better to have no *Husband*, than to have such a *Buzzard* as could be caught by any *Cassandra's* [or Women that *set men on fire*] in the Snares of an Extravagant Gaiety and Bravery; so when a Match do's offer himself unto her, she wisely leaves it unto the Reasonable Judgment of her Parents, or Guardians, whether he be indeed a *Match* for her, or no; nor will she dispose of her self without their Consent, Conduct, and Blessing in it. Indeed, she reckons this is a proper *Test*, by which a Real and a Worthy *Lover* may be try'd; *Let my Superiours, that have the Disposal of me, know your Mind!* so doth she make her self an *Abigail*, or her *Fathers Joy*: and not a *Dinah*, that is a *Judgment* unto him.

THIS is a Vertuous MAID! And those *Virgins* which were so *Sacred* among the Ancient Romans, as to be made the *Sanctuaries* of the greatest Reverence, did not more deserve all Respect and Honour, than the *Virgins* which thus manifest, *The Fear of God*. But we hope it will not be long before she becomes a

WIFE; which will render her a *Mary,* that is, an *Exalted* One; and let us now
see, what a *Vertuous* One.

THE VERTUOUS WIFE

. . . It was a great abuse which the Ancients who doted upon *Virginity,* put
upon those words of the Apostle, in Rom. 8.8. *Those that are in the Flesh, cannot please God;* when they supposed all *Married Persons* to be *Those* intended.
A *Vertuous wife* is one that *pleaseth God,* as much as if she were cloistered up in
the strictest and closest *Nunnery;* and there *with* yea, there *in* she pleases a *Vertuous Husband* also; she studies to render her self a true *Mabel,* or *amiable* Person, in his Eyes; and a Right *Evodias,*[8] or, one *of a Good Savour* to him. You
shall now hear her Qualities.

I. As for her *Love* to her Husband, I may say, *'Tis even strong as Death, many
Waters cannot quench it, neither can the Floods drown it* {Cant. 8:6, 7}. She can
like, *Sarah, Rebeckah, Rachel,* freely leave all the Friends in the World for *his*
company; and she looks upon that charge of God unto His Ministers, *Teach the
Young Women to Love their Husbands* {Tit. 2:4}, as no less profitable, than highly
Reasonable. When she Reads, That Prince *Edward* in his Wars against the *Turks,*
being stabbed with a poisoned Knife, his Princess did suck the Poison out of his
Wounds, with her own Royal *Mouth,* she finds in her own *Heart* a principle dis-
posing her to show her own Husband as great a *Love.*[9] When she Reads of a
Woman called *Herpine,* who having her Husband Apoplex'd in all his Limbs,
bore him on her Back a thousand and three Hundred *English* Miles to a Bath,
for his Recovery, she finds her self not altogether unwilling to have done the Like.
When she Reads of those famous Women, who after a hot Siege in the Castle
of *Winsberg,* having obtained this Liberty from their Enraged Enemies, *That
they might themselves go out, and also take any one thing that they could carry
with them,* very bravely took up each one her Husband, and so delivered them;[10]
she *Applauds* the Example and would *Follow* it. And, when she Reads of that
Generous Young Woman, *Clara Cerventa,* who having for her Husband, one
Valdaura, that prov'd full of most loathsome *Diseases,* yet she tended him with
all the care and cost imaginable, and Sold her Jewels to maintain him; and at
his Death, after ten long years of Languishment, she Reply'd unto her Friends
who would rather have Congratulated her Deliverance, *That she would freely
lose the best of her Enjoyments, to purchase her Dear* Valdaura *again!* She resolves the *Imitation* of such a Carriage, while she bestows an *Admiration* on it.
Her *Affections* were not at first founded on the *Estate* or *Beauty* of her Husband;
and therefore if *These* happen to be Consumed, *Those* do out-live their Funeral.

'Tis Her *Piety* towards the Commandment and Ordinance of God, that Inspires her Affections; and so they do not grow Cold like a Smith's red hot *Bar of Iron*, when taken out from the *Fire* of a misplaced *Lust*. When she addresses him, with such a Compellation, as, LOVE, her *Heart* goes with her *Lip*, and she *means* what she *speaks*.

II. But her *Love* to her Husband, will also admit, yea, and Produce the *Fear* of, *A Cautious Diligence never to Displease him*. T'was this which the Apostle *Peter* meant, when he Recommends unto the Women, *A Chast Conversation Coupled with Fear* {1 Pet. 3:2}; and *Paul*, when he requires of the woman, *To Reverence her Husband* {Eph. 5:33}. While she looks upon him as, *Her Guide*, by the Constitution of God, she will not Scruple with *Sarah*, to call him, *Her Lord*; and though she do's not *Fear* his *Blowes*, yet she do's *Fear* his *Frowns*, being Loth in any way to Grieve him, or cause an *Head-ake* in the Family by Offending him. She would have that famous *Decree of the Persians* mentioned in the Sacred Bible, *That all the Wives give to their Husbands Honour both to Great and Small* {Esth. 1:20}, to be as a *Law of the Persians*, altogether, *Unalterable*. In every *Lawful* thing, she submits her *Will* and *Sense* to his, where she cannot with Calm *Reasons* Convince him of, *Inexpediencies*; and instead of Grudging or Captious *Contradiction*, she acts as if there were but *One Mind* in *Two Bodies*. If her *Abraham* give order, *Make Ready quickly three Measures of Meal*, or the like, 'tis as *quickly* done; If her *Jacob* say to her, *I must have you go with me*, she most readily yeelds unto him. When she is for Obeying him, *In Omnibus Licitis* [*i.e.* in every Lawful thing] she do's not English it, as once the Gentlewoman did, *as far as my List is*. If his *Unreasonable Humours* happen to be such, that she must give some Diversion to them, she Remembers that Rule, *In her Tongue is the Law of Kindness* {Pro. 31:26}; 'tis by the *Kindness*, the Sweetness, the Goodness of her Expressions, that she gives *Law* unto him. . . .

III. But her *Fear* of Displeasing her Husband, most remarkably appears in the *Peace* that she preserves with him; and her *Antipathy* to all *Contention*, unless it be *That* of, *Provoking one another to Love and Good Works*. A *Susan* she is, that is, *A Lilly*; but never, *A Briar*, to him; nor will she give him cause to call her, *Barbara*. She will have no such *Passion* towards her Husband as may make her worthy to be call'd, *A Fury*; but if he be himself in a *Passion*, she strives with the *Soft Answers* of Meekness, to Mollify it first, and so to Overcome it: She is a true *Rachel*, that is to say, *A Sheep* under the greatest Exasperations. A Reverend Person seeing once a Couple that were very Cholerick, yet live most lovingly and peaceably together, demanded of them, *Whence it was?* and the man made him this Answer, *Sir, When my Wife is in a Passion I yield unto her; and when I am in a Passion, she yields unto me; so that we never are in our passionate*

Fits together! The Good Woman will make it her Endeavour to attend the *last part* of this Contrivance, and will give small or no Occasion for the *First.* The Marriners count it *Bodes well* to see *Two Fire-Balls* appearing in a *Ship* together; but our Good Woman counts *Two Fire Balls* in an *House* together to *Bode Ill* as the worst of Omens; nor will she be a party to maintain a *Civil War* within the Walls of her Dwelling. She thinks that if there be nothing but *Fire! Fire!* in the House, 'tis a sign that God, Who is, *The God of Peace,* is not graciously present there; as the Jewish Rabbins have noted upon the Hebrew Names of *Ish,* an Hus-band, and *Ishah,* a Wife; out of which if you take the Two Letters which make the Name of *Jah,* there will remain only *Esh, Esh,* that is, *Fire! Fire!* The old Heathen took the *Gall* from the Nuptial Sacrifices, and threw it behind the Al-tar, to intimate, That all *Bitterness* is to be thrown away by all Married People; *Mercury,* or Good Language, is to stand by *Venus.* And this Woman accordingly, puts away, all *Bitterness, Anger, Clamour,* and *Evil-Speaking;* She is a Right *Re-bekah,* which carries, *The Blunting or Hindring of Contention,* in the significa-tion of it; and a Right *Shelomith,* which is to say, A *Peaceable One.*

IV. But she is for *Plenty* as well as *Peace* in her Houshold; and by her *Thrifti-ness* makes an Effectual and Sufficient Reply unto her Husband, when he *do's* ask her, as he *must, Whether he shall Thrive or no?* She is a *Deborah,* that is, A *Bee,* for her Diligence and Industry in her *Hive.* As on the one side she will have none in her House to *Want,* so on the other side, she will have all of them to *Work;* or as the Holy Spirit of God Expresses it, *She Looks well to the Ways of her Houshold, and Eats not the Bread of Idleness* {Pro. 31:27}. Her Husbands *Gains* are so managed by her Houswifry and Providence, that he finds it his Advan-tage to let her keep the *Keys* of all; and she will so Regulate all the Domestick Expences, that he shall not complain of, *Any Thing Embezzled.* Her very *Fore-cast* is as useful as much of her Husbands *Business;* and the Pennyes that she *Saves* do add unto the heaps of the Pounds that are *Got* by him. He has a rich *Portion* with her, meerly in her *Prudence;* that is it which renders *her* a true *Je-rusha,* or an *Inheritance* unto him. She is particularly careful, that she do not bear such a Sail of *Gallantry,* either in her *Table,* or her *Apparel,* or her *Furni-ture,* as may sink her Husband; nor will she be one of those Women, who (as one says) are *now such Skilful Chymists, that they quickly turn their Husbands Earth into Gold; only they pursue the Experiment too far, making that Gold too Volatile, and let it all Vapour away in Insignificant, tho' Gaudy Trifles.* That Woman deserves the Name of *Dalilah,* that is, *Poverty;* [unless you will venture upon so hard a Name as *Jezabel,* that is, A *Wo to the House;*] Whose *Discretion* shall not be better than a *Dowry,* to her Owner.

V. And this *Thriftiness* is accompany'd with such a *Fidelity* to her Husband, as that she will not give a *Lodging* to the least straggling or wandring *Thought* of Disloyalty to his *Bed*; lest by her parlying with wicked *Thoughts*, the Devil should insensibly Decoy her to the *Deeds* which *God will Judge*. She is a *Dove*, that will sooner Dy than leave her *Mate*; and her Husband is to her, *The Covering of her Eyes* {Gen. 20:16}, at such a rate, that she sees a *Desirableness* in him, which she will not allow her self to behold or suppose in *any other*; neither will she look upon *Another*, any more than the Wife of *Tigranes*,[11] who after the Wedding of *Cyrus*, whom every one did commend as the Rarest Person in all the Company, being by her Husband asked, *What she Thought of him?* answered roundly, *In truth I look'd at no Body there, but you, my Husband.* A Wanton had as good *eat Fire*, as go to Enkindle any *False Fire*, or *Fools Fire* in her holy Breast; she accounts *Adultery* to be as the Law of *Moses* adjudged it, *A Capital Crime*; and if the *Egyptians* of old, cut off the Nose of the *Adulteress*, Or, if the *Athenians* tore her in pieces with wild Horses, rather had she undergo the *Pain* of such things than Commit the *Crime*. She is a *Gertrude*, or *All true*, in the Marriage Covenant. Yea, She will even *Abstain from all Appearance of Evil*; and as 'tis abominable unto her to Entertain the least groundless and causeless *Jealousie* of her Husband, or to Torture and Expose her own Soul by the uneasy Frenzy of uncharitable Surmizes concerning him, so she will not give *him* the least opportunity to Think hardly of her self. She will not therefore be too much *from Home*, upon Concerns, that perhaps to *him* are *Unaccountable*: but if the Angels do Enquire, where she is, her Husband may Reply, as once *Abraham* did, *My Wife is in the Tent* {Gen. 18:9}. Altho her Husband be not such an *Egyptian* as to deny her *Shoes*; yet her usage of them is, as if like a *Scythian*, she had the *Axle-tree* of the Charriot which carried her Home after her Wedding, burned at the Door; and she is willing to be painted as the Wives of the Ancients were, with a *Snail* under her Feet. She affects to be an *Esther*, that is, *An Hidden One*. But if a foolish and froward Husband will wrong her, with unjust suspicion of her *Honesty*, she will thence make a Devout Reflexion upon her *Disloyalty* to God; but at the same time very patiently vindicate her *Innocency* to man; and the more *patiently* because the *Water of Jealousie* procured greater Blessings to those that have it Unrighteously and Abusively Imposed upon them. . . .

THIS is a Vertuous WIFE! And such an One she will be although her Husband should be very Disobliging to her; She Considers, *Tis to the Lord*. I Confess the Difficulties that some *Unhappy Wives* do meet withal, are such, that if they be not very *Vertuous Wives*, they cannot possibly Conform to these Directions; but this I would say, Their being *Vertuous* is the most Likely way to provide against their being *Unhappy.* But if the Case of any such Wise should be so Remarkably Hard, That her *Husband* proceeds to abuse her with a *Cudgel,* [an *Hard Case* indeed! that a *Bride-bash* ever should have any *Cudgels* growing in it!] I know not what further Advice to give her; Only THIS; Let the Candidness of her Behaviour be her *Charm* against the Assaults of such a *Divel;* and *if That* would further Help to lay such a *Fiend,* I am Content she should read unto him, Not only the *Laws* of God and Man against that Barbarity, or the Opinion of Old *Cato,* That *for a man to Beat his Wife was as bad as any Sacriledge;* but also the Emphatical Words of the Blessed Ancients in the Church of God, Loudly Thundering against this Inhumanity; and Particularly Those of the Renowned *Chrysostom,* which are to this Purpose; (if you will allow *me,* the Translating, of them) "It is the Highest *Ignominy,* not of the *Wife,* but of the *Man,* for a *Man* to beat his *Wife.* But if thou hast an Husband that will do so, bear it patiently; and know thou shalt have *Rewards* hereafter for it, as well as *Praises* here. As for You, *Man,* Let me admonish you, that there is no Fault so great, as may compel you to beat your *Wives.* Your *Wives* did I say? 'Tis a Dishonour for a *Man* to bestow Blows upon his *Maid;* and much more upon his *Wife*—We might learn this from the *Law-givers* among the *Gentiles,* who take a *Wife* away from the *Man* that has beaten her, for indeed he is a *Man* unworthy of a *Wife.* Such a *Man,* if he may be call'd a *Man,* and not rather a *Beast,* is to be counted as a Murderer of his *Father* or his *Mother.* If a Man must leave his *Father* and *Mother* for the sake of his *Wife,* by the Ordinance of God; what a mad Wretch is he that shall abuse *her* for whom his very *Parents* were to be forsaken? Indeed there is not a simple *Frenzy* in this thing; an *Intollerable Disgrace* do's also accompany it. At the Sighs and Cries of the Abused *Wife,* all the Neighbourhood run to the Base Fellow's House, as for the Rescue of a Prey fallen into the Talons of a *Wild Beast* that had broken in. And such a Rascal were better *Buried alive,* than show his Head among his Neighbours any more." See *Homil.* 26 *in* 1 *Ep. ad Corinth.*[12]

But wishing all Good Women, a Deliverance from such Monsters of Husbands, we will suppose our *Vertuous Wife,* now grown a *Mother;* and see how she acquits her self.

THE VERTUOUS MOTHER

The Apostle Wills, *That the Younger Women, Marry, and Bear Children* {1 Tim. 5:14}; and as 'tis too soon for them to *Bear Children* till they *Marry,* so tis Ordinarily Expected, that they will *Bear Children* when they *Marry.* If a *Vertuous Wife* be Deny'd the Blessing of *Children* her *Not Bearing* is not a Trial that she can *not Bear.* She humbly, addresses the God of Heaven, like *Hannah,* for that Gracious and Powerful *Word* of His which makes Fruitful, as Remembring, That *Children are an Heritage of the Lord, and the Fruitful Womb is His Reward* {Psa. 127:3}; But she will not Impatiently long like *Rachel, Give me Children or else I Die* {Gen. 30:1}, Lest she Dy by her having of those *Children*. Much less, will she have so Little Wit as to suspect her own *Eternal Happiness*, because of her *Natural Barrenness*, like those mistaken little Women who have thus argued from that Scripture, *She shall be saved in Child-bearing* {1 Tim. 2:15}; Very fine indeed! as if *Child-bearing* were no less a Condition in the Covenant of Grace, than *Repenting* and *Believing!* But her *Natural Barrenness* is rather improv'd by her as an Occasion of her *Eternal Happiness*, by the *Spiritual Fruitfulness* whereto she is thereby Excited and Assisted; it causes her to be more *Fruitful* in all the good Works of *Piety* and *Charity*; more *Fruitful* in her Endeavours otherwise to *Serve her Generation after the Will of God*; more *Fruitful* in all those things whereby, *The Heavenly Father may be Glorified*: and she will Consider with her self *What Service for God, and His People, and my own Soul, have I now a Liesure for?*

NEVERTHELESS if our *Vertuous Woman* become a Parent, we shall see what a *Vertuous Mother*, she will approve her self.

I. She is no sooner sensible, that she has *Conceiv'd*, but she Presently and Solemnly, and Perhaps with *Fasting* as well as *Prayer*, applyes her self to the God of Heaven, That *He* would with *His* own Holy Spirit *Fill* and *Shape* what is in her; and that what is to be born of her, may be, *An Holy Thing*. She accounts the *Treasure* now Lodged in her, to be of more Account than all the Riches of a Thousand *India's*; inasmuch as tis a Never-dying SOUL, by which the Almighty God may be forever Glorify'd. And as therefore she carefully avoids all that may prejudice the Formation of the *Infant* in her, so she layes in aforehand with a due *Earliness*, and *Earnestness*, that the *Infant* may be, *Sanctify'd in the womb*. She is not Inordinately set upon having an Infant of *One Sex*, more than another; but her great Concern is that which a *Big bellied* Woman once recorded in a Legacy left Written as her Desire for her Unborn Infant, *That she may be a Mother to one of Gods Children!* Suppose it be a *Daughter*, which usually (and perhaps needlessly) is less long'd for; yet if it may be a *Bethiah*, that is, *A Daughter of the Lord*, or, a *Diana*, that is, *A Daughter of God*, she has her Choice; and she, is freely willing that God should have the *Proportioning* of Sexes in the World. . . .

III. When she is well Delivered, she is a true *Judith*, or a *Praysing* One; O how is that Thankful Question immediately Working in her Breast, *What shall I Render to the Lord for all His Benefits!* {Psa. 116:12}. When she finds her self strong Enough to Hear and Think, she makes, *The Hundred and Sixteenth Psalm*, to be Read unto her; and when she Contemplates what a Million of Mercies there are in the Birth of one *Perfect Child*, she would, if it were *Proper*, Name every One, *Mehetabel*, that is, *How Good is God!* However, She now Devotes her Child unto God, saying with *Hannah*, *I have lent it unto the Lord as long as it Lives* {1 Sam. 1:28}; even, every Daughter shall be a *Bathsheba*, that is, *A Daughter of an Oath*, to God, that so she may be a *Bathsheba*, that is, *A Daughter of Salvation* from the Lord. And she desires the *Baptism* of it, not as the Formality of putting a *Name* upon it, nor as an Opportunity for *Dressing* and *Showing* of it, but that thus *Coming into the Bond of the Covenant*, it may *Pass under* the Lords Tything *Rod*, as a *Lamb* set a part for Him. And how ardent are her *Groans*, as if she were even *Travelling*[13] *in Birth again*, That her Child may be washed in the *Laver* of the *New-Birth* betimes!

IV. Her Care for the *Bodies* of her Children showes it self in her *Nursing* of them her self, if God have made her *Able* for it, and it *Easy* for her. She is not a *Dame* that shall Scorn to Nourish in the *World*, the Children whom she ha's already Nourish'd in her *Womb:* if like *Sarah*, she be a *Lady*, yet she counts it not below her to be a *Nurse*. If God have granted her Bottles of *Milk* on her Breast, she thinks that her Children have a Claim unto them. It shall not be her *Niceness*, but her *Necessity* and *Calamity*, if she do not Suckle her own Off-Spring; and she will not from *Sloth* and *Pride*, be so Unnatural as to give Cause for that Exclamation. *The Sea-Monsters, draw out the Breast, they give suck to their Young ones; But the Daughter of my People, is become Cruel, like the Ostrich in the Wilderness, who is hardened against her Young ones, as though they were not hers* {Lam. 4:3}. Now having Nurs'd her Young ones, tis her next care, that they be well provided, as with such *Conveniences* as belong to their present state, so with such *Callings* and *Portions* as may hereafter make them Serviceable in their Generation; and when they are grown *Marriageable*, her Discretion and her Tenderness is yet more Eminently seen in her *Matching* of them.

V. But her *Zeal* for the *Spirits* of her Children, is that which does most *Eat her up*; O how concerned she is, that they may be *Brought up in the Nurture and Admonition of the Lord!* {Eph. 6:4}. When She first Received her Children, she Imagined the Immortal God committing them to her charge, as the Princess of *Egypt* unto the Mother of *Moses*, *Here, Take this Child, Nurse it for me, and I'll give thee thy Wages* {Ex. 2:9}. Wherefore she becomes a *Martha*, that is, A *Teacher*, to them all. She begins with them while they are upon her *Knees*, and instructs them how to fall down in *Prayer* upon their own. She will not put them upon *Revenge*, by asking them To give her a *Blow* that she may *Beat* any thing that vexes them; but she fears they will soon Learn *That*, and every other Vice, without a *Teacher*. The *First Liquors* that she puts into those *Little Vessels* are Histories and Sentences fetch'd from the Oracles of God, and Institutions, *How to Pray in Secret unto their Heavenly Father*. She then proceeds to make 'em Expert in some *Orthodox Catechisms*, and will have 'em Learn to *Read* and *Write*, as fast as ever they can take it; and so she passes to the other parts of an *Ingenious Education* with them. She is, like another *Bathsheba*, always instilling into their Children, something that is *Wise* and *Good*; and she keeps up that *Authority* over them that they *Fear* as well as *Love* her; and they dare not *Refuse* what she shall *Command*. Unto her *Instruction* she also joyns an *Inspection* of them; so that she is very gravely *Inquisitive* into their Employments, their Companies, their Experiences: nor will she spare *Corrections*, where their Miscarriages do call for the *Rod*; and she will not *overlay* them with her Sinful Fondness, lest God make them *Crosses* to her, for her being afraid of *Crossing* them in their Exorbitancies. And besides the *Exemple* of all Vertue that she sets before them, she is frequently Praying *with* them, as well as *for* them, *That they may be Saved*. She pursues the Lord with such Cries for her Children as the *Canaanitess* used, *Lord, Heal my Child, that is annoy'd by a Devil!* {Mat. 15:22} and such as *Monica* used for *Austin*,[14] upon which a great Person said unto her, *'Tis impossible that a Child of so many Tears should ever perish!* And she will carry 'em one after another alone into her Closet with her, where she do's wrestle with God for them all, professing, *I will not let thee go, except thou Bless them* {Gen. 32:25}. Her Children being thus well *brought up*, she will do as the Lady *Cornelia* did unto the Ladies who expected she would show *them* her *Jewels*, as they had shown her *Theirs*; even *Bring forth her well Educated Children as her Jewels*.[15]

VI. If she meets with any *Disasters* in her Children, by her *Patience* and her *Piety* she turns them into *Benefits*. 'Tis possible, her *Children* may *Sin*; but this causes her presently to reflect upon the Errors of her own *Heart* and *Life*, and especially upon any Defect in her Conduct unto *them*. So she is put upon, *The Repentance which is not to be Repented of!* {2 Cor. 7:10}. 'Tis also possible, her *Children* may *Dy*; but she is not then like the overwhelmed Women of *Bethlehem, Weeping for their Children, and not willing to be Comforted, because they are not* {Jer. 31:15}. Instead of saying like *Jacob, All these things are against me* {Gen. 42:36}, she rather says, like *Joseph, God may mean it unto Good* {Gen. 50:20}. She do's not Roar like a Beast, and Howl, *I cannot bear it*; but she rather says, *I can take any thing well at the Hands of God*. She follows them to the Grave, as a very moderate Mourner, with *Hopes*, That God is carrying on the Everlasting Designs of *his Grace* in *her Soul* by these Dispensations; and with

Hopes, That *their Souls* are gone to be, *With Christ, which is by far the Best of all.* She look'd upon her Children as meer *Loans* from God, which He may call for, when He please; and she quietly submits, if God say, *Give them up, you have had them long enough!* . . .

THIS is the Vertuous MOTHER! And she is One that also counts her *Servants* to be after a Sort her *Children* too; She, *Guides the House,* according to her Office prescribed by the Apostle; So, that with a *Motherly* Deportment, unto them, with an Obliging, but yet Reserved Carriage towards them, and with a Charitable Regard unto the Everlasting Welfare of their Souls, You may see her acquitting her self evermore as a *Vertuous Mistress* likewise in the Family. But there is Danger lest she become a *Widow* before she dy; if she do, let us now take notice of her Frame and Mein, in the Sorrowful Condition that is now come upon her.

THE VERTUOUS WIDOW

The Vast Numbers of Poor *Widows* in Every Neighbourhood, make it very Suspicious, that our *Vertuous Mother* may at some time or other, tast the Sad, Sowre, Tear-ful *Cup* of *Widow-hood.* If This be the *Portion of her Cup,* We must suppose that she gives her Husband a *Decent Burial;* that is, as on the One side, a Funeral that shall not be *below* his Figure, so on the other side, a Funeral that shall not be *above* her Estate; and while she Dislikes the Expensive Humors of *Poland,* where two or three Funerals coming One upon another, are so Extravagantly Chargeable as to Ruine a whole Family; She nevertheless will give as Honourable an *Interment* as ever she can to the *Forsaken Mansion* of the *Soul* which was dearer to her than the World.

CONCEIVING our *Vertuous Woman* to have her *Widows* Vail upon her, we may behold her demeaning her self as a most *Vertuous* Person in it.

I. Her *Grief* on the Death of her Husband, is *Great* and yet *Wise,* and as *wisely Great* as *Greatly Wise.* Her Mourning is more like a still *Rain,* than a loud *Storm;* and instead of *Bellowing Passions* which usually Moulder a way into a Total and the Coldest Forgetfulness, faster than the Corpse of the Husband in the Grave, she ha's a *Silent* but a *Lasting* sorrow; and yet that sorrow Moderated by a Filial Submission to the Hard of that Glorious God, before whom she *Opens not her Mouth* any more than Humbly to say, *Lord, Thou didst it* {Psa. 39:9}. She will not by Intemperate *Vexations* and *Afflictions* of her self, make her self, like the Frantick Women in the *East-Indies,* which burn themselves to Death, in the Fire wherein they consume the Dead Bodies of their Husbands; but yet she calls her self, *Marah,* saying, *The Lord ha's dealt bitterly with me!*

II. It is now her main study and solace to have an interest in that Promise, {Isa. 54:5}. *Thy Maker is thy Husband.* And therefore, like her whom the Apostle calls, *A Widow indeed* {1 Tim. 5:3}; she, *Trusteth in God, and Continueth in Supplications and Prayers, Night and Day.* She Considers her self as now more than ever belonging to, *The Family of God;* with a perswasion that He will Certainly and Faithfully Provide for her. Hence also, The Time that she formerly spent in *Conversation* with her Husband, she now spends in *Supplication* to, and *Meditation* on, her God; and by an Extraordinary *Devotion,* she seeks to find all that in the Alsufficient JESUS, which may Repair the Absence of the best Husband upon Earth. She is an *Elizabeth,* or one to whom the *Fulness of God,* in the *Promise of God* is enough. . . .

III. She reckons that she must now be *Father* as well as *Mother* to the *Orphans* with whom she is Left Entrusted; and their *Fathers* Beloved Image on them, do's farther Augment, yea, Double her Care concerning them. While her Husband was *Alive,* she still acted as a *Deputy Husband,* for the maintaining of all good Orders in the House, when he was out of the way. And now her Husband is *Deceas'd,* she thinks that upon the Setting of the *Sun,* the *Moon* is to Govern, and there shall not be one *Prayer* the less performed, or one *Fault* the more Indulged, among her poor Lambs, because he is gone. The *Kindred,* of her Expired Husband are also still Welcome and Grateful to her, upon *his* Account. But she is now particularly more Sollicitous than ever to Teach her *Children how* to obtain that Favour of God, *When my Father is gone, the Lord shall take me up* {Psa.27:10}. Some Women have the Names of Men, a little altered, as *Jaquet* (from *Jacoba*) *Joanna, Joan, Jane, Jennet,* (all from *John*) *Thomasin, Philippa, Frances, Henrietta, Antonia, Julian, Dionysia,* and the like; But all our Widows are put upon thus doing the *Works* of Men; may their God help them!

IV. She is not Forward and Hasty now to *Take* the Liberty, which the Scripture does *Give* unto *Younger Widows;* that is, *to Marry.* While she has one Eye *Weeping* for her Departed Husband, she has not the other *open* to see, *Who comes next?* nor will she think an *Ephesian Matron,* a fit Copy for her. She counts it no hard Law, which even the Ancient *Pagans* kept with great Severity, *That no Widow should Marry within Ten or Twelve Months after the Death of her Husband;* and she wonders that any *Christians* ordinarily can, *Marry sooner.* If she had a *Good* Husband, his *Memory* has been so Embalmed with her, that she cannot presently make a Room in her Affections for another. If she had a *Bad* Husband, the Cross felt so heavy, that she will be *Slow* to be *Sure,* that it been't Renew'd upon her. But if after a convenient stay she do *Marry,* it shall be, *Only in the Lord,* Unto a Man that shall be neither *Heretical* in his principles, nor *Exorbitant* in his practices; and unto one that may be *proper* for her. Wherefore also if she be very *Old*, She will not without special Causes, marry one that is very *Young*; suspecting that such a pretended Lover may Count *Hers* more than *Her*, and that if there be too much (as perhaps a score of Years) Inequality in *Age*, it may otherwise *Prove* as Temptatious, as it *Looks* indecent. Indeed *Jerom* tells us,[16] of an Old man at *Rome*, who had Buried Twenty Wives, which he took one after the Death of t'other; and that he then took the Twenty first, who also had Buried Nineteen Husbands; but methinks, They were an, *Ugly Couple*. And the Woman whereof *Buxtorf* relates in his *Talmudic Lexicon*,[17] that she Buried *Eleven Husbands*, and had then an Epitaph of *Eleven Verses* bestowed upon her self, deserved sure the last stroke of her Epitaph, which was to this purpose, *A Woman fit to have No Bed but a Cold Grave*.

V. When she is *Match'd* unto a *Second Husband*, whom she will never twit with any Reflecting and Uncomely Remembrances of her *First*; She is more than Ordinarily Sollicitous to be, *A Good Mother in Law*, if she must be One at all; and so do her part for the Removing of those *Imputations*, which *Mothers in Law* have generally Laboured under. She knowes that the way for her to have the Blessing of Heaven upon *Her* Children, is for her to make her self a Blessing to *His*; and Unkindnesses to the *Motherless* Little Birds which now call her, *Their Dam*, will Certainly be Repay'd by the Just Revenges of God. She is therefore so far from the partiality of that *Mother-in law*, who when her own Child hurt a Child of her Husbands by Throwing of a Stone, *Whipped the Child that felt the Stone for standing in the Way of the Child, that flung it*; that she makes no Observable Difference between *his* Children and *hers*; unless it be *This*, That She Corrects *hers* her self, and refers *his* to *Him*; and yet for her at any Time to inform her Husband of any Ill Manners in *his* Children, is a thing whereto she has an *Aversion* so Extream, that she will never do it, unless upon Extream *Necessity*. Indeed she Essayes to be such a Wife unto him, that she may not merit the Name which the *Second Wife* of *Lamech* had; Namely, *Zillah*, or, but, *A Shadow*, of a Wife: much less would she be as the *First* of them was called, an *Anah*, that is, *An Afflicter*, to him.

VI. At Length *Old Age* comes upon her; and *Prisca* or *Priscilla*, that is, *An Old Woman*, is her Title; but by an, *Hoary Head found in the Way of Righteousness* {Pro. 16:31}, it is, that she now Challenges the Honour of, *A Saint*, even from those Abusive Tongues, which use to traduce for, *A Witch*, Every *Old Woman*, whose Temper with her Visage is not eminently Good. She thoroughly studies Every Particle of the Apostolical Charge, *That the Aged Women, be in Behaviour, as becometh Holiness; not make-bates*,[18] *not given to much Wine, Teachers of Good Things* {Tit. 2:3}; *That they may Teach the Young Women*; and the nearer she comes to her *End*, the more Acquainted she is with, *Him that is from the Beginning.* She is not Impatient of being Esteemed, *Old;* and styled, *Bilhah,* that is, *Fading;* nor do's it Offend her, as once an English Queen, to be told, *That Age hath Sprinkled its Meal upon her Head.* But she keeps longing for the Day, when the Lord Jesus will send His Angels to fetch her unto the Regions of Everlasting Light and Life, and keeps Wishing, *Oh Come, Lord Jesus!* till she Arrive to be, *Forever with the Lord.*

THIS is a Vertuous WIDOW. God Grant that our *widows* may not be *Multiply'd;* but for them that *are,* GOD Grant that they may be thus *Vertuous! That* is it which will render them all, *Jochobeds,* which is, *Most Glorious Ones.*

BONIFACIUS. AN ESSAY UPON THE GOOD (1710)

[HUSBAND, WIFE, PARENTS, AND CHILDREN]

§ 11.[19]   The *Useful Man* may now with a very good Grace, Extend and Enlarge the *Sphere* of his consideration. My next PROPOSAL now shall be; Let every Man consider the **Relation,** wherein the Soveraign God has placed him, and let him *Devise what Good he may do,* that may render his *Relatives,* the Better for him. One Great way to prove our selves *Really Good,* is to be *Relatively Good.* By This, more than by any thing in the World, it is, that we *Adorn the Doctrine of God our Saviour.* It would be an *Excellent Wisdom* in a man, to make the *Interest* he has in the Good Opinion and Affection of *any One,* an *Advantage* to do Good Service for God upon them: He that *has a Friend* will show himself indeed *Friendly,* if he think, *Such an One Loves me, and will hearken to me; what Good shall I take advantage hence to perswade him to?*

This will take place more particularly, where the Endearing Ties of *Natural Religion* do give us an *Interest.* Let us call over our several *Relations,* and let us have *Devices* of Something that may be called *Heroical Goodness,* in our Discharging of them. Why should we not, at least Once or Twice in a *Week,* make this *Relational Goodness,* the Subject of our *Enquiries,* and our *Purposes?* Particularly, Let us begin with our *Domestick Relations;* and *Provide for those of our House;* Lest we *Deny* some Glorious Rules and Hopes of our Christian *Faith,* in our Negligence.

First; In the **Conjugal Relation,** how agreeably may the *Consorts* think of those Words; *What knowest thou, O Wife, whether thou shalt Save thy Husband? Or, How knowest thou, O man, whether thou shalt Save thy Wife?*

The **Husband** will do well to think; *What shall I do, that my Wife may have cause for ever to Bless God, for bringing her unto me?* And, *What shall I do that in my Carriage towards my Wife, the Kindness of the Blesses* JESUS *towards His*

Church, may be followed and resembled? That this Question may be the more perfectly answered, Sir, Sometimes ask her to help you in the Answer; Ask her to tell you, what she would have you to do.

But then, the **Wife** also will do well to think; *Wherein may I be to my Husband, a Wife of that Character;* She will do him Good, and not Evil, all the Dayes of his Life?

With my *Married People,* I will particularly leave a Good Note, which I find in the Memorials of *Gervase Disney* Esq.[20] *Family-Passions, cloud Faith, disturb Duty, darken Comfort.* You'l do the more Good unto one another, the more this Note is thought upon. When the *Husband* and *Wife* are alwayes contriving to be *Blessings* unto one another, I will say with *Tertullian, Unde Sufficiam ad Enarrandam faelicitatem Ejus Matrimonii!*[21] O Happy Marriage!

Parents, Oh! How much ought you to be continually *Devising,* and even *Travailing,* for the *Good* of your *Children.* Often *Devise;* How to make them *Wise Children;* How to carry on a Desireable *Education* for them; an *Education* that shall render them Desireable; How to render them Lovely, and Polite Creatures, and *Serviceable* in their Generation. Often *Devise,* How to Enrich their Minds with Valuable *Knowledge;* How to Instill Generous, and Gracious, and Heavenly *Principles* into their Minds; How to Restrain and Rescue them from the *Pathes of the Destroyer,* and fortify them against their *Special Temptations.* There is a World of *Good,* that you have to Do for them. You are without *Bowels,* Oh! be not such *Monsters!* if you are not in continual Agony to do for them all the *Good* that ever you can. It was no mistake of *Pacatus Drepanius* in his Panegyric to *Theodosius; Instituente Natura Plus fere Filios quam nosmet ipsos diligimus.*[22]

I will Prosecute this Matter, by Transcribing a Copy of PARENTAL RESOLUTIONS, which I have some-where met withal.

I. 'At the Birth of my Children, I would use all *Explicit Solemnity* in the *Baptismal* Dedication and Consecration of them unto the LORD. I would present them to the BAPTISM of the Lord, not as a meer Formality; but wondring at the Grace of the Infinite GOD, who will accept *my* Children, as *His,* I would Resolve to do all I can that they may be *His.* I would now actually Give them up unto GOD; Entreating, that the Child may be a *Child* of God the *Father,* a *Subject* of God the *Son,* a Temple of God the *Spirit,* and be rescued from the Condition of a *Child of Wrath,* and be Possessed and Employed by the Lord as an Everlasting Instrument of His Glory.

II. 'My Children are no sooner grown capable of Minding the Admonitions, but I would often, often Admonish them to be sensible of their *Baptismal Engagements* to be the Lords. Often tell them, of their *Baptism,* and of what binds 'em to: Oftner far, and more times than there were *Drops of water,* that were cast on the Infant, upon that occasion!

'Often say to them, *Child, You have been Baptised; You were washed in the Name of the Great God; Now you must not Sin against Him; To Sin is to do a Dirty, a Filthy thing.* Say, *Child, You must every Day cry to God that He would be your Father, and your Saviour, and your Leader; In your Baptism He Promised that He would be so, if you Sought unto Him.* . . . Tell the Child; *What is your Name; you must sooner Forget this Name, that was given you in your Baptism, than forget that you are a Servant of a Glorious Christ whose Name was put upon you in your Baptism.*

III. 'Let my *Prayers* for my *Children* be Daily, with Constancy, with Fervency, with Agony; Yea, *By Name* let me mention each One of them, every Day before the Lord. I would Importunately Beg for all Suitable Blessings to be bestow'd upon them; That God would *Give them Grace, and give them Glory, and withold no Good Thing from them;* That God would *Smile on their Education, and give His Good Angels the charge over them, and keep them from Evil, that it may not grieve them;* That when *their Father and Mother shall forsake them, the Lord may take them up.* With Importunity I would please that Promise on their behalf; *The Heavenly Father will give the Holy Spirit unto them that Ask Him.* Oh! Happy Children, If by *Asking* I may obtain the *Holy Spirit* for them!

IV. 'I would betimes entertain the Children, with Delightful *Stories* out of the Bible. In the Talk of the *Table,* I would go thro' the *Bible,* when the *Olive-Plants about my Table* are capable of being so *Watered.* But I would always conclude the *Stories* with some *Lessons* of Piety, to be inferred from them. . . .

VI. 'I would betimes cause my Children to Learn the *Catechism.* In *Catechising* of them, I would break the Answer into many Lesser and Proper *Quaestions;* and by their Answer to them, Observe and Quicken their *Understandings.* I would bring every *Truth,* into some *Duty* and *Practice,* and Expect them to *Confess* it, and *Consent* unto it, and *Resolve* upon it. As we go on in our *Catechising,* they shall, when they are able, Turn to the *Proofs,* and *Read* them, and say to me, *What* they prove, and *How.* Then, I will take my times, to put nicer and harder *Questions* to them; and improve the Times of Conversation with my Family, (which every man ordinarily has or may have), for conferences on matters of Religion.

VII. 'Restless would I be, till I may be able to Say of my *Children, Behold, They Pray!* I would therefore Teach them to *Pray.* But after they have Learnt a *Form of Prayer,* I will press them, to proceed unto Points which are not in their *Form.* I will show them the *State of their own Souls;* and on every Stroke Enquire

of them, *What they think ought now to be their Prayer.* I will direct them, that
very Morning they shall take one Text or Two out of the *Sacred Scripture,* and
Shape it into a *Desire,* which they shall add unto their *Usual Prayer.* When they
have heard a *Sermon,* I will mention to them over again the main Subject of it,
and ask them thereupon, *What they have now to Pray for.* I will charge them, with
all possible cogency, to *Pray in Secret;* And often call upon them, *Child, I hope,
You don't forget my charge to you, about Secret Prayer: Your crime is very great, if
you do!*

VIII. 'I would betimes do what I can, to beget a *Temper of Benignity* in my
Children, both towards one another, and towards all other People. I will instruct
them how Ready they should be to *Communicate unto others,* a part of what
they have; and they shall see, my Encouragements, when they discover a *Loving,* a *Courteous,* an *Helpful* Disposition. I will give them now and then a piece
of Money, for them with their own Little Hands to dispense unto the Poor.
Yea, if any one has *hurt* them, or *vex'd* them, I will not only forbid them all
Revenge, but also oblige them to do a *Kindness* as soon as may be to the *Vexatious* Person. All *Coarseness* of *Language* or *Carriage* in them, I will discountenance it.

IX. 'I would be Sollicitous to have my *Children* Expert, not only at *Reading*
handsomely, but also at *Writing* a fair Hand. I will then assign them such *Books*
to *Read,* as I may judge most agreeable and profitable; obliging them to give me
some Account of what they *Read;* but keep a Strict Eye upon them, that they
don't Stumble on *the Devils Library,* and poison themselves with foolish *Romances,* or *Novels,* or *Playes,* or *Songs,* or *Jests that are not convenient.* I will set
them also, to *Write* out such things, as may be of the greatest Benefit unto them;
and they shall have their Blank Books, neatly kept on purpose, to Enter such
Passages as I advise them to. I will particularly require them now and then, to
Write a *Prayer* of their own Composing, and bring it unto me; that so I may discern, what sense they have of their own Everlasting Interests.

X. 'I Wish that my *Children* may as soon as may be, feel the Principles of *Reason* and *Honour,* working in them, and that I may carry on their Education,
very much upon Principles. Therefore, first, I will wholly avoid, that harsh, fierce,
crabbed usage of the Children, that would make them Tremble, and Abhor to
come into my Presence. I will so use them, that they shall *fear* to offend me,
and yet mightily *Love* to see me, and be glad of my coming home, if I have been
abroad at any time. I would have it Look'd upon as a Severe and Awful *Punishment* for a crime in the Family, To be *forbidden for a while to come into my Presence.* I would raise in them, an High Opinion of their Fathers *Love* to them,
and of his being *better able* to Judge what is Good for them, than they are for

themselves. I would bring them to Believe, *Tis best for them to be and do as I would have them.* Hereupon I would continually Magnify the matter to them, What a brave thing 'tis to *Know* the things that are Excellent; and more brave to *Do* the things that are Vertuous. I would have them to propose it as a *Reward* of their Well-doing at any time, *I will now go to my Father, and he will teach me something that I was never taught before.* I would have them afraid of doing any *Base* Thing, from an horrour of the *Baseness* in it. My first Animadversion on a Lesser Fault in them, shall be a *Surprise*, a *Wonder*, vehemently Express'd before them, that ever they should be guilty of doing so foolishly; a vehement *Belief*, that they will never do the like again; a Weeping Resolution in them, that they will not. I will never dispense a *Blow*, except it be for an atrocious Crime, or for a lesser Fault Obstinately persisted in; either for an Enormity, or for an *Obstinacy.* I would ever *Proportion* chastisements unto Miscarriages; not Smite bitterly for a very small piece of *Childishness*, and only frown a little for some real *Wickedness.* Nor shall my *Chastisements* ever be dispensed in a *Passion* and a *Fury*; but with them, I will first show them the Command of GOD, by Transgressing whereof they have displeased me. The Slavish, Raving, Fighting way of Education too Commonly used, I look upon it, as a considerable Article in the Wrath and Curse of God, upon a miserable World.

XI. 'As soon as we can, wee'l get up to yet *Higher Principles.* I will often tell the *Children*, What cause they have to *Love* a Glorious CHRIST, who has *Dy'd* for them. And, How much He will be *Well-pleased* with their *Well-doing.* And, what a Noble Thing, 'tis to follow His *Example*; which *Example* I will describe unto them. I will often tell them, That the *Eye of God* is upon them; the Great GOD Knowes all they do, and Hears all they Speak. I will often tell them, That there will be a Time, when they must appear before the *Judgment-Seat* of the Holy LORD; and they must *Now* do nothing, that may *Then* be a Grief & Shame unto them. I will Set before them, The Delights of that *Heaven* that is prepar'd for Pious Children; and the Torments of that *Hell* that is prepared of old, for naughty ones. I will inform them, Of the *Good Offices* which the *Good Angels* do for *Little Ones* that have the Fear of God, and are afraid of Sin. And, how the *Devils* tempt them to do Ill Things; how they hearken to the *Devils*, and are like *them*, when they do such things; and what mischiefs the *Devils* may get leave to do them in this World, and what a Sad thing t'wil be, to be among the *Devils* in the *Place of Dragons* {Ps. 44:19}. I will cry to God, That He *will make them feel the Power of these Principles.*

XII. 'When the *Children* are of a Fit Age for it, I will sometimes *Closet* them; have them with me *Alone*; Talk with them about the State of their Souls; their *Experiences*, their *Proficiencies*, their *Temptations*; obtain their Declared Consent

unto every Stroke in the *Covenant of Grace*; and then Pray with them, and
Weep unto the Lord for His *Grace*, to be bestow'd upon them, and make them
Witnesses of the Agony with which I am *Travailing* to see the Image of CHRIST
formed in them. Certainly, They'l never forget such Actions!

XIII. 'I would be very Watchful and Cautious, about the *Companions* of my
Children. I will be very Inquisitive, what *Company* they keep; If they are in hazard
of being Ensnared by any *Vicious Company*, I will earnestly pull them out of it,
as *Brands out of the Burning.* I will find out, and procure, *Laudable Companions* for them. . . .

XVII. 'I incline, that among all the Points of a Polite Education which I would
endeavour for my *Children*, they may each of them, the *Daughters* as well as the
Sons, have so much Insight into some *Skill*, which lies in the way of *Gain*, (the
Limners, or *Scriveners*, or the *Apothecaries*, or Some other *Mystery*, to which their
own Inclination may most carry them,) that they may be able to Subsist themselves, and get something of a Livelihood, in case the Providence of God should
bring them into Necessities. Why not they as well as, *Paul the Tent-Maker!* The
Children of the best Fashion, may have occasion to bless the Parents, that make
such a Provision for them! The Jews have a saying; Tis worth my Remembring
it. *Quicunque Filium suum non docet opificium, perinde est ac si eum doceret
Latrocinium.*[23]

XVIII. 'As soon as ever I can, I would make my Children apprehensive of the
main END, for which they are to *Live*; that so they may as may be, *begin to Live*;
and their *Youth* not be nothing but *Vanity.* I would show them, that their main
END must be, *To Acknowledge the Great* GOD, *and His Glorious* CHRIST; *and
bring Others to Acknowledge Him:* And that they are never *Wise* nor *Well*, but
when they are doing so. I would show them, what the *Acknowledgments* are, and
how they are to be made. I would make them able to Answer the Grand Question, *Why they Live; and what is the End of the Actions that fill their Lives?* Teach
them, How their *Creator* and *Redeemer* is to be Obey'd in every thing; and, How
every thing is to be done in *Obedience* to Him; Teach them, How even their
Diversions, and their *Ornaments*, and the *Tasks* of their Education, must all be
to fit them for the *further Service* of Him, to whom I have devoted them; and
how in these also, His Commandments must be the Rule of all they do. I would
sometimes therefore Surprize them with an Enquiry, *Child, What is this for?
Give me a Good Account, Why you do it?* How comfortably shall I see them *Walking in the Light*, if I may bring them *Wisely* to answering this Enquiry; and
what *Children of the Light?*

XIX. 'I would oblige the *Children*, to Retire sometimes, and Ponder on that
Question; *What shall I wish to have done, if I were not a dying?* And Report unto

me, their *own Answer* to the Question; Of which I would then take Advantage, to inculcate the *Lessons of Godliness* upon them. I would also Direct them and Oblige them, at a proper Time for it, Seriously to Realize, their own Appearance before the awful *Judgment-Seat* of the Lord JESUS CHRIST, and Consider, *What they have to Plead, that they may not be sent away into Everlasting Punishment? What they have to Plead, that they may be Admitted into the Holy City?* I would instruct them, What *Plea* to prepare; First, Show them, how to get a part in the *Righteousness* of Him that is to be their *Judge*; by Receiving it with a Thankful *Faith*, as the *Gift* of infinite Grace unto the Distressed and Unworthy Sinner: Then, Show them how to prove that their *Faith* is not a counterfeit, by their continual Endeavour to please Him in all things, who is to be their *Judge*, and to Serve His Kingdom and Interest in the World. And I would have them, to make this preparation.

XX. 'If I Live to see the Children *Marriageable*, I would, before I consult with Heaven and Earth for their best Accommodation in the *Married State*, Endeavour the *Espousal* of their Souls unto their only *Saviour*. I would as plainly, and as fully as I can, propose unto them, the Terms on which the Glorious Redeemer would *Espouse* them to Himself, *in Righteousness and Judgment, and Favour, and Mercies for ever*; and Sollicit their Consent unto His Proposals and Overtures. Then would I go on, to do what may be Expected from a Tender Parent for them, in their *Temporal Circumstances*.'

From these *Parental Resolutions*, how *Naturally*, how *Reasonably* may we pass on to Say?

Children, The *Fifth Commandment* confirms all your other Numberless and Powerful Obligations, often to *Devise, Wherein may I be a Blessing to my Parents? Ingenuity* would make this the very Top of your *Ambition*; To be a *Credit*, and a *Comfort* of your *Parents*; to *Sweeten*, and if it may be, to *Lengthen* the *Lives* of those, from whom, under God, you have received *your Lives*. And *God the Rewarder* usually gives it, even *in this Life*, as most observable Recompence. But it is possible, you may be the Happy Instruments of more than a little *Good* unto the *Souls* of your *Parents*; [will you Think, *How!*] Yea, tho' they should be Pious Parents, you may by some Exquisite Methods, be the Instruments of their Growth in Piety, and in Preparation for the Heavenly World. *O Thrice and Four times Happy Children!* Among the Arabians, a Father sometimes takes his Name from an Eminent SON, as well as a Son from his Reputed Father. A Man is called with an *Abu*, as well as an *Ebn*. Verily, A Son may be such a Blessing to his Father; that the best Sir-name for the glad Father would be, *The Father of such an One*.

NATURAL PHILOSOPHY (SCIENCE)

I n Mather's lifetime, the old Ptolemaic cosmology depicting the earth as God's footstool at the center of the universe (geocentrism) was still very much ensconced in the minds of the people, even if Harvard's graduates would have learned about the Copernican Revolution (heliocentrism) from Charles Morton's *Compendium Physicae* (chap. 4), circulated in manuscript (1686), or from one of the popular almanacs of the period, like Zechariah Brigden's *An Almanack of the Coelestial Motions* (Cambridge, Mass., 1659). Yet not even learned elites like Judge Samuel Sewall would necessarily welcome the introduction of the Copernican heliocentric system in homiletic discourse. It did not belong there, or so he felt: "Dr. C. Mather preaches excellently from Ps. 37. Trust in the Lord &c. only spake of the Sun being in the centre of our System," Sewall grumbled in his diary on December 23, 1714. "I think it inconvenient to assert such Problems."[1]

By the time Cotton Mather's *Christian Philosopher* was published by the Royal Society of London (1721), he was fully engaged in disseminating the new philosophy from his North Church pulpit. *Christian Philosopher* is one of those timely works of early Enlightenment philosophy in which the "Handmaiden of Theology" (natural philosophy) had begun to displace the "Queen of Science" (theology). Although he would deny it vehemently, Mather's choice of vocabulary was virtually indistinguishable from that of the "despised" Deists who appeared to celebrate the almighty as a Great First Cause and Nature as an independent automaton to the exclusion of all else: "The Great God has contrived a mighty *Engine*, of an Extent that cannot be measured," he sang as a hymn of praise in the twenty-seventh essay of his *Christian Philosopher*, "and there is in it a Contrivance of wondrous *Motions* that cannot be *numbred*. He [God] is infinitely gratified with the View of this *Engine* in all its *Motions*, infinitely grateful to Him [for] so glorious a Spectacle!"[2] At least his choice of language bespeaks Mather's immersion in the ideology of Deism. To be sure, Mather's deity was never the remote God of the Deists, whose mighty machine unerringly followed the laws of nature. If miracles might yet offset the laws of nature, Mather believed, they were embedded with foresight in God's eternal plan from the beginning of time. God's telos, or reason for which God created the universe, was still the time-honored mode of justifying the ways of God to man, and it drove Mather to pore over the publications of his European peers and cull from them whatever seemed most suitable to his own purposes.

Our first selection in this section is Mather's essay "*Of the* LIGHT." It begins with a synopsis of Sir Isaac Newton's laws of motion as mediated by the English scientist George Cheyne, on whose *Philosophical Principles of Natural and Revealed Religion* (1705) Mather here relies. He sheds light on the matter by turning to the source that makes everything visible to the inner and outer eyes of the mind. Light consists of translucent, vibrating particles of so fine a substance and traveling at such high velocity ("9000 Miles" per second) that it can penetrate the pores of other bodies, Mather delights to tell. Because of its vibration, light causes heat when it shines on a body, and when its rays are refracted or pass through a prism or drop of water, they display their spectral colors as seen in the rainbow. Most astounding to Mather is the speed of light, which is "about six hundred thousand times more swift than *Sound*. Amazing Velocity!" And yet, lest he forget the real purpose of his numerical data, Mather reminds his readers that all the wisdom they have gained from the study of nature and its benefits points to a loving creator and his Christ, to whom their adoration should fly as swiftly as light itself. His emerging views on comets, certainly informed by his father's Κομητογραφια; *or, A Discourse Concerning Comets* (Boston, 1683), is yet another litmus test of sorts by which we can gauge just how far Mather had turned his back on the hoary belief in comets as portents of ill omen. As late as the 1680s, faith in prodigies as signs of God's wrath was as common and widespread as ever. However, by the time young Cotton Mather published his Thanksgiving sermon *Wonderful Works of God Commemorated* (1690), the superstitious views of blazing stars had become suspect to anyone who had read recent works that explained the natural causes of seeming portents.[3] Thirty years later, when he offered his *Christian Philosopher* to the Royal Society of London, Mather's tune had changed. He now invoked Newton and his peers on the Continent to emphasize a comet's natural composition, function, orbit, gravitational pull, and regular appearance in the solar system.

So too Mather's twenty-first essay, "Of GRAVITY," exhibits all the telltale signs of an enlightened gentleman divine who was as comfortably at home in theology as in the scientific theories of his day. He took for granted that gravity was a centripetal force which pulled heavy matter toward the center of the earth, just as much as the centrifugal force of the earth's rotation pushed lighter matter away from the center to the surface—even into outer space—if it were not kept in place by its opposite force. As Mather puts it, if the motion caused by the earth's revolution did not exist, our globe would either be crushed by its own weight or "be soon dissipated, and spirtled [whirled] into the circumambient Space." Likewise, he accepted Newton's well-known definition that the gravitational pull between two objects is proportional to their masses, and that gravity, the force of attraction, increased or diminished reciprocally at the rate of the square of the distance between them. Yet as tidy as this definition of gravity may appear, Mather interjected, it does not explain what caused this force to operate in the first place. Rejecting mechanistic or materialistic explanations, he agreed with the famous mathematician Edmond Halley (1656–1742) in asserting that gravity "must be religiously resolv'd into the *immediate Will* of our most wise CREATOR, who, by appointing this *Law*, throughout the material World, keeps all Bodies in their proper Places and Stations, which without it would soon fall to pieces, and be utterly destroy'd." Gravity, then, was nothing but the Divine Being whose force penetrated everything: "I cannot stir *forward* or *backward*," Mather sang, "but I *perceive* Him in the *Weight* of every *Matter*; on the *Left-hand* and on the *Right* I see Him *at work*." Even so, it is God as the prime mover who holds in His hand "the *Springs* of this immense *Machine,* and all the several Parts of it." Without God's constant influence, all would fall to pieces: "Yet besides this, He has reserved to Himself the power of *dispensing* with these *Laws,* whenever He pleases." God was above nature, not bound by it.

Mather's encomium at the end of his *Christian Philosopher* celebrated the grandeur of the almighty. The creator's natural laws and the operations of the universe, Mather stated, echoing Gottfried Wilhelm Leibniz's famous dictum, were so finely tuned that they could not possibly have been made any better. They proved that atheism was now to be "chased and hissed out of the World."

THE CHRISTIAN PHILOSOPHER (1721)

The Works of the Glorious GOD in the *Creation* of the World, are what I now propose to exhibit; in brief *Essays* to enumerate *some of them,* that He may be glorified in them: And indeed my *Essays* may pretend unto no more than *some of them;* for, *Theophilus* writing, *of the Creation,* to his Friend *Autolycus,* might very justly say, That if he should have a *Thousand Tongues,* and live a *Thousand Years,* yet he were not able to describe the admirable Order of the Creation, διὰ τὸ ὑπερβάλλον μέγεθος καὶ τὸν πλοῦτον σοφίας τοῦ Θεοῦ.[4] *Such a Transcendent Greatness of God, and the Riches of his Wisdom appearing in it!*

Chrysostom, I remember, mentions a *Twofold Book* of GOD; the Book of the *Creatures,* and the Book of the *Scriptures:* GOD having taught first of all us διὰ πραγμάτων, by his *Works,* did it afterwards διὰ γραμμάτων, by his *Words.*[5] We will now for a while read the *Former* of these *Books,* 'twill help us in reading the *Latter:* They will admirably assist one another. The Philosopher being asked, What his *Books* were; answered, *Totius Entis Naturalis Universitas.*[6] All Men are accommodated with that *Publick Library. Reader,* walk with me into it, and see what we shall find so legible there, *that he that runs may read it.* Behold, a Book, whereof we may agreeably enough use the words of honest *Ægardus; Lectu hic omnibus facilis, etsi nunquam legere didicerint, & communis est omnibus, omniumque oculis expositus.*[7]

ESSAY I: OF THE LIGHT

Would it not be proper, in the first place, to lay down those *Laws of Nature,* by which the *Material World* is governed, and which, when we come to consider, we have in the Rank of *Second Causes,* no further to go? All *Mechanical*

THE
Christian Philosopher:
A
COLLECTION
OF THE
Best Discoveries in Nature,
WITH
Religious Improvements.

By COTTON MATHER *D. D.*
And Fellow of the ROYAL SOCIETY.

LONDON;
Printed for EMAN. MATTHEWS, *at the* Bible *in* Pater-Noster-Row. **M. DCC. XXI.**

The Christian Philosopher (London, 1721), title page

Accounts are at an end; we step into the Glorious GOD *Immediately*: The very *next Thing* we have to do, is to Acknowledge Him, who is the *First Cause* of all: and the CHRISTIAN PHILOSOPHER will on all Invitations make the *Acknowledgements*. The acute Pen of Dr. *Cheyne* has thus delivered them.[8]

I. All *Bodies* persevere in the same State of *Rest*, or of *Moving* forwards in a *strait Line*, unless forced out of that State, by some *Violence* outwardly impressed upon them.

II. The *Changes* made in the *Motions* of *Bodies*, are always proportional to the *Impressed Force* that move them; and are produced in the same *Direction* with that of the Moving Force.

III. The *same Force* with which one *Body* strikes another, is *returned* upon the first by that other; but these Forces are impressed by *contrary Directions*.

IV. *Every Part* of every Body *attracts* or *gravitates* towards *every Part* of every other Body: But the *Force* by which one Part attracts another, in different Distances from it, is reciprocally as the *Squares* of those Distances; and at the same Distance, the *Force* of the Attraction or Gravitation of one Part towards divers others, is as the Quantity of Matter they contain.[9]

These are *Laws* of the Great GOD, *who formed all things*. GOD is ever to be seen in these *Everlasting Ordinances*. But now, in proceeding to *magnify that Work of God which Men behold*, it seems proper to begin with *that* by which it is that we *Behold* the rest.

The LIGHT calls first for our Contemplation. A most marvellous Creature, whereof the Great GOD is the *Father*:

Illic incipit DEUM nosse.[10]

The *Verus Christianismus* of the pious *John Arndt* very well does insist upon that Strain of Piety; GOD and His LOVE exhibited in the *Light*.[11]

It was demanded, *In what Place is the Light contained? By what Way is the Light divided?*

Aristotle's Definition of *Light*; Φῶς ἐστιν ἡ ἐνέργεια τοῦ διαφανοῦς, *Light is in the Inworking of a Diaphanous Body*; is worth an attentive Consideration.[12]

Light is undoubtedly produced, as Dr. *Hook* judges, by a *Motion*, quick and vibrative.[13]

It is proved by Mr. *Molyneux*, That *Light* is a *Body*.[14] Its *Refraction*, in passing thro a *Diaphanous Body*, shews that it finds a *different Resistance*; *Resistance* must proceed from a Contact of *two Bodies*. Moreover, it requires *Time* to pass from one place to another, tho it has indeed the quickest of all Motions. Finally, it cannot by any means be *increased* or *diminished*. If you *increase* it, it is by robbing it of some other part of the Medium which it would have occupied, or by bringing the *Light*, that should naturally have been diffused thro some other Place, into that which is now more enlightened.

Sir *Isaac Newton* judges, 'Tis probable, that *Bodies* and *Light* act mutually on one another. *Bodies* upon *Light*, in emitting it, and reflecting it, and refracting it, and inflecting it: *Light* upon *Bodies*, by *heating* them, and putting their Parts into a *Vibrating Motion*.[15]

All *Hypotheses* of *Light* are too *dark*, which try to explain the *Phaenomena* by *New Modifications* of *Rays*; they depend not on any such *Modifications*, but on some *Congenite* and *Unchangeable* Properties, essentially inherent in the Rays.

The *Rays of Light* are certainly little Particles, actually emitted from the *Lucent Body*, and refracted by some *Attraction*, by which *Light*, and the *Bodies* on which it falls, do mutually act upon one another. It is evident, That as Rays pass by the Edges of Bodies, they are *incurvated* by the Action of these *Bodies*, as they pass by them.

And it is now perceived, That *Bodies* draw *Light*, and this *Light* puts Bodies into *Heat*: And that the Motion of *Light* is therefore swifter in *Bodies*, than *in vacuo*, because of this Attraction; and slower after its being *reflected*, than in its Incidence.

Irradiated by the Discoveries of the Great Sir *Isaac Newton*, we now understand, That every *Ray* of *Light* is endowed with its own *Colour*, and its different Degree of *Refrangibility* and *Reflexibility*. One Ray is *Violet*, another *Indigo*, a third *Blue*, a fourth *Green*, a fifth *Yellow*, a sixth *Orange*, and the last *Red*. All these are *Original Colours*, and from the Mixture of these, all the intermediate ones proceed; and *White* from an equable Mixture of the whole; *Black*, on the contrary, from the small Quantity of any of them reflected, or all of them in a great measure suffocated. It is not *Bodies* that are *coloured*, but the *Light* that falls upon them; and their *Colours* arise from the *Aptitude* in them, to *reflect* Rays of one Colour, and to *transmit* all those of another. 'Tis now decided, *No Colour in the dark!*

Tho *Light* be certainly a *Body*, it is almost impossible to conceive how *small* the Corpuscles of it are. Dr. *Cheyne* illustrates it with an Experiment, That it may be propagated from innumerable different Luminous Bodies, without any considerable Opposition to one another. Their several *Streams of Light* will be together transmitted into a dark Place, thro the least Orifice in the World. Suppose a Plate of Metal, having at the top the smallest Hole that can be made, were erected *perpendicularly* upon an *Horizontal Plane*, and about it were set numberless luminous Objects of about the same Height with the Plate, at an ordinary Distance from it; the *Light* proceeding from every one of these Objects, will be propagated thro this Hole, without interfering.

Mr. *Romer*, from his accurate Observations of the *Eclipses* on the *Satellits* of *Jupiter*, their Immersions and *Emersions*, thinks he has demonstrated, That *Light* requires one Second of Time to move 9000 Miles. He shews, that the Rays of *Light* require ten Minutes of Time to pass from the *Sun* to us. And yet Mr. *Hugens* hath shewn, That a Bullet from a Cannon, without abating its first Velocity, would be 25 Years passing from us to the *Sun*. So that the Motion of *Light* is above a million times swifter than that of a Cannon-Ball; yea, we may carry the Matter further than so.[16]

We suppose the Distance of the *Sun* from the *Earth* to be 12000 Diameters of the *Earth*, or suppose 10000, the *Light* then runs 1000 Diameters in a Minute; which is at least 130,000 Miles in a Second. Dr. *Cheyne* shews, That *Light* is about six hundred thousand times more swift than *Sound*. Amazing Velocity!

To chequer the Surprize at so *swift* a Motion, I may propound one that shall be as very surprizingly *slow*. *Dee* affirms, that he and *Cardan* together saw an Instrument,[17] in which there was one Wheel constantly moving with the rest, and yet would not finish its Revolution under the space of seven thousand Years. 'Tis easy to conceive with *Stevinus*,[18] an Engine with twelve Wheels, and the Handle of such an Engine to be turned about 4000 times in an Hour, (which is as often as a Man's Pulse does beat) yet in ten Years time the Weight at the Bottom would not move near so much as an Hair's Breadth: And as *Mersennus* notes, it would not pass an Inch in 1,000,000 Years;[19] although it be all this while in Motion, and have not stood still one Moment: for 'tis a Mistake of *Cardan*, *Motus valde tardi, necessario quietes habent intermedias*.[20] . . . .

The *Jews* have a good Saying, *Opera Creationis externae habent in se Imaginem Creationis internae*.[21] It will well enough become a *Christian Philosopher*, to allow for that *Image* in his Contemplations, and with devout Thoughts now and then reflect upon it.

Before I go any further, I confess myself unable to *resist* the Invitation, which, I think, that I have, to insert an *Observation* of *Hugo de Sancto-Victore*; That every Creature does address a *Treble Voice* unto us: ACCIPE, REDDE, FUGE;[22] indeed, *there is no Speech nor Language where their Voice is not heard* {Ps. 19:3}. It is an Exercise highly becoming the *Christian Philosopher*, to fetch *Lessons of Piety* from the whole Creation of GOD, and hear what *Maxims of Piety* all the Creatures would, in the way of *Reflection* and *Similitude*, mind us of. In the Prosecution of these *Meleteticks*,[23] what better can be considered, than this *Treble Voice*, from all these Thousands of *Powerful Preachers*, whom we have continually surrounding of us? First, *Accipe Beneficium*:[24] Consider, *What is the Benefit which a Good GOD has, in this Creature, bestowed upon us?* Secondly, *Redde Servitium*:[25] Consider, *What is the Service which I owe to a Gracious GOD, in the Enjoyment of such a Creature?* Lastly, *Fuge Supplicium:*[26] Consider, *What is the Sorrow which a Righteous GOD may inflict upon me by such a Creature, if I persist in Disobedience to Him?* Even a Pagan *Plutarch* will put the Christian *Philosopher* in mind of this,[27] That the World is no other than the *Temple* of GOD; and all the *Creatures* are the *Glasses,* in which we may see the *Skill* of Him that is the Maker of all. And his Brother *Cicero* has minded us, *Deum ex Operibus cognoscimus.*[28] 'Tis no wonder then that a *Bernard* should *see* this; *Verus Dei Amator, quocunque se vertit, familiarem Admonitionem sui Creatoris habet.*[29] The famous Hermite's Book, of those three Leaves, the *Heaven,* the *Water,* and the *Earth,* well studied, how nobly would it fill the *Chambers* of the Soul with the most *precious and pleasant Riches? Clemens* of *Alexandria* calls the World, *A Scripture of those three Leaves;* and the Creatures therein speaking to us, have been justly called *Concionatores Reales,*[30] by those who have best understood them:

> *Obvia dum picti lustro Miracula Mundi,*
> *Naturae intueor dum parientis Opus:*
> *Emicat ex ipsis Divina Potentia Rebus;*
> *Et levis est Cespes qui probat esse Deum.*[31]

But the *Light* now calls for me.

¶. How *Glorious* a Body! "But how infinitely, and beyond all Comprehension *Glorious* then, the Infinite GOD, who has challenged it as His Glory! Isa. xlv.7. *I form the Light.* The GOD of whom we have that *Sublime Stroke,* in the History of the Creation; he said, *Let there be Light, and there was Light!.* . . .

"And, O my Soul, why art thou *slow* in thy Contemplations of GOD, and CHRIST, and HEAVEN; fly thou thither, with a Swiftness beyond that of the *Light,* [for so thou canst] upon all Occasions."

ESSAY XXI: OF GRAVITY

To our Globe there is one Property so exceedingly and so generally subservient, that a very great Notice is due it; that is, GRAVITY, or the Tendency of Bodies to the *Center.*

A most notable Contrivance (as Mr. *Derham*[32] observes) to keep the several Globes of the Universe from shattering to pieces, as they would else evidently do in a little Time, thro their swift Rotation round their own *Axes.* Our *Globe* in particular, which revolves at the rate of above a thousand Miles an Hour, would, by the centrifugal Force of that Motion, be soon dissipated, and spirtled into the circumambient Space, were it not kept well together by this wondrous Contrivance of the Creator, *Gravity,* or the *Power of Attraction.* By this

Power also all the Parts of the *Globe* are kept in their proper Place and Order; all Bodies gravitating thereto do unite themselves with, and preserve the Bulk of them entire; and the fleeting Waters are kept in their constant Æquipoise, remaining in the *Place with God has founded for them, a Bound which He hath set, that they may not pass, that they turn not again to cover the Earth* {Ps. 104:8–9}. It is by the virtue of this glorious Contrivance of the *great God, who formed all Things*, that the Observation of the Psalmist is perpetually fulfilled: *Thou rulest the raging of the Sea; when the Waves thereof arise, thou stillest them* {Ps. 89:9}.

Very various have been the Sentiments of the Curious, what *Cause* there should be assign'd for this great and catholick Affection of Matter, the *Vis Centripeta*:[33] I shall wave them all, and *bury* them in the *Place of Silence*, with the *Materia Striata* of *Descartes*,[34] which our *Keil*[35] has very sufficiently brought to *nothing*; and perhaps the *Fluid* of Dr. *Hook*[36] must go the same way. 'Tis enough to me what that incomparable Mathematician Dr. *Halley*,[37] has declar'd upon it: That, after all, *Gravity* is an Effect insolvable by any *philosophical Hypothesis*; it must be religiously resolv'd into the *immediate Will* of our most wise CREATOR, who, by appointing this *Law*, throughout the material World, keeps all Bodies in their proper Places and Stations, which without it would soon fall to pieces, and be utterly destroy'd.

All Bodies descend still towards a Point, which either is, or lies near to, the *Center* of the *Globe*. Should our Almighty GOD change that *Center* but the two thousandth part of the *Radius* of our Globe, the Tops of our highest Mountains would be soon laid under Water.

In all Places equi-distant from the *Center* of our Globe, the Force of Gravity is nearly equal.

Indeed, as it has been proved by Sir *Isaac Newton*, the *Equatorial* Parts are something higher than the *Polar* Parts; the difference between the Earth's *Diameter* and *Axis* being about thirty-four *English* Miles.

Gravity does equally affect all *Bodies*. The *absolute Gravity* of all is the same. Abstracting the resistance of the Medium, the most *compact* and the most *diffuse*, the *greatest* and the *smallest*, would descend an equal Space in an equal Time. In an exhausted Receiver a *Feather* will descend as fast as a *Pound of Lead*. But this resistance of the *Medium* has produc'd a *comparative* Gravity. And upon the difference of *specifick* Gravity in many Bodies, the Observations of our Philosophers have been very curious.

According to the exquisite *Halley* and *Huygens*, the *Descent of heavy Bodies* is after the rate of about *sixteen Foot* in *one Second* of Time.

Nevertheless this Power *increases* as you descend to, *decreases* as you ascend from the *Center* of the Globe, and that in proportion to the Squares of the

Distances therefrom reciprocally; so as, for instance, at a double distance to have but a quarter of the Force. A *Ton* Weight on the Surface of the Earth, raised Heaven-wards unto the height of one Semidiameter of the Earth from hence, would weigh but one quarter of a *Ton*. At three Semidiameters from the Surface of the Earth, it would be as easy for a Man to carry a *Ton*, as here to carry little more than an hundred Pounds. At the distance of the *Moon*, which suppose to be sixty Semidiameters of the Earth, 3600 Pounds weigh *one Pound*; and the Fall of Bodies is but sixteen Foot in a whole Minute.

I remember I have somewhere met with such a devout Improvement of this Observation: "The Further you fly towards *Heaven*, the more (if I may use the *Falconers* Word) you must *lessen*. There is great reason why it should be so. *Defamations* particularly will be Things by which you must be *lessen'd:* you must meet with *heavy* Things; *Defamations* are in a singular manner such; they are not easy to *carry*; 'tis not easy to carry it well under them; some of them are a *Ton* Weight. But, *my Friend*, if you were as near *Heaven* as you ought to be, you would make *light* of them; you would bear them wonderfully!"

The *acute Borelli* has demonstrated that there is no such thing as *positive Levity*, and that *Levity* is only a lesser degree of *Gravity*. But how useful is this, not only to divers Tribes of *Animals*, but also to the raising up of the many *Vapours*, which are to be convey'd about the World? The Evaporations, which, according to Mr. *Sedileau*'s Observations,[38] and others are the fewest in the Winter, and greatest in the Summer, the most of all in windy Weather, and considerably exceed what falls in *Rain*, many being tumbled about and spent by the Winds, and many falling down in Dews.

The ingenious *Halley* has yet a suspicion that there may be some certain Matter, which may have a *Conatus*[39] directly contrary to that of *Gravity*; as in *Vegetation* the Sprouts directly tend against the *Perpendicular*.

Dr. *Gregory*[40] demonstrates, that the antient Astronomers were not ignorant of the heavenly Bodies *gravitating* towards one another, and being preserv'd in their Orbits by the Force of Gravity.

Mr. *Keil* shews, that the Force of *Gravity* to the *centrifugal Force*, in a Body placed at the Equator of our Globe, is as 289 to 1; so that by the *centrifugal Force* arising from the Earth's Rotation, any Body placed in the Equator loses a 289th part of the Weight it would have if the Globe were at rest. And since there is no *centrifugal Force* at the *Poles*, a Body there weighs 289 Pounds, which at the Equator would weigh but 288. On our Globe the decrease of *Gravity*, in going from the Poles towards the *Equator*, is always *as the Square of the Cosine of the Latitude.*—*Quod facit Natura* (to use *Tully*'s Words) *per omnem Mundum, omnia Mente & Ratione conficiens.*[41]

Mr. *Samuel Clark*[42] observes, 'Tis now evident that the most universal Principle of *Gravitation*, the Spring of almost all the great and regular inanimate Motions in the World, answering not at all to the *Surfaces* of Bodies, by which alone they can act one upon another, but entirely to their *solid Content*; cannot possibly be the result of any *Motion* originally impressed on *Matter*, but must of necessity be caused by something which penetrates the very Substance off all Bodies, and continually *puts forth in them* a *Force* or *Power* entirely different from that by which *Matter* acts on *Matter*. This (he adds) is *an evident Demonstration, not only of the World's being made originally by a supreme intelligent Cause, but moreover that it depends every moment on some superior Being, for the Preservation of its Frame, and that all the great Motions in it are caused by some immaterial Power, not having originally impressed a certain Quantity of Motion upon Matter, but perpetually and actually exerting itself every Moment in every Part of the World: which preserving and governing Power gives a very noble Idea of* PROVIDENCE.[43]

Dr. *Cheyne* demonstrates, That *Gravity*, or the *Attraction* of Bodies towards one another, cannot be mechanically accounted for. The *Planets* themselves cannot continue their Motions in their Orbs without it. It is not a Result from the *Nature* of *Matter*, because the Efficacy of *Matter* is communicated by *immediate Contact*, and it can by no means act at a distance. Whereas this Power of *Gravitation* acts at all Distances, without any *Medium* or Instrument for the Conveyance of it, and passes as far as the Limits of the Universe. *Matter* is indeed entirely *passive*, and can't either *tend* or *draw*, with regard unto other Bodies, no more than it can *move itself.* And what is essential to *Matter* cannot be intended or be remitted; but *Gravity* increases or diminishes reciprocally, as the Squares of the Distances are increased or diminished. 'Tis plain this universal Force of *Gravitation* is the Effect of the *Divine Power* and *Virtue*, by which the Operations of all *material Agents* are preserved. They that press for a *mechanical Account* of *Gravity*, advance a Notion of a *subtile Fluid*, unto the Motion whereof they would ascribe it. But then still those Parts of Matter must be destitute of *Gravity*, which were very unlikely! And this *Hypothesis* would still remove us but one Step further from *immechanical Principles*; for the Cause of the Motion of your *subtile Fluid*, this, *Gentlemen*, you must own to be *immechanical*. Since you must admit a *first Cause*, you had as good be sensible of it in this place. 'Tis *He* who does immediately impress on *Matter* this Property. There never was yet afforded unto the World (as my Doctor observes) a *System of Natural Philosophy* which did not require *Postulates*, that are not *mechanically* to be accounted for. The fewest any one pretends to, are, *the Existence of Matter*, and *the Impression of rectilinear Motions*, and *the Preservation of the Faculties of natural Agents*.

No Man has pretended to fetch from the Principles of *Mechanism* an Account for these. The *Impression of an attractive Faculty upon Matter,* is no harder a *Postulate* than the rest. It is a *Matter of Fact,* that *Matter* is in possession of this Quality. And it can be referred unto nothing, but the Influence of that Glorious ONE, who is the *first Cause* of all Things.

"Behold, a continual Opportunity for a considerate and religious Man, to have a *Sense* of a Glorious GOD awaken'd in him! And what is a *Walk with God,* but that *Sense* kept alive in every Step of our *Walk?* I am continually entertain'd with *weighty Body,* or *Matter* tending to the *Center of Gravity;* I feel it in *my own.* The *Cause* of this *Tendency,* 'tis the Glorious GOD. *Great GOD, Thou givest this Matter such a Tendency, and thou keepest it in its Operation.* There is no other Cause but the *Will* and *Work* of the Glorious GOD. I am now effectually convinc'd of that antient Confession, and must with Affection make it, *He is not far from every one of us* {Acts 17:27}. When I see any thing moving or settling that way that its *heavy Nature* carries it, I may very justly think, and I would often form the Thought, *it is the Glorious GOD, who now carries this Matter such a way!* When *Matter* sinks *downward,* my Spirit shall even *therefore* mount *upward,* in acknowledgment of the God who orders it. I will no longer complain, *Behold, I go forward, but He is not there, and backward, but I cannot perceive Him; on the Left-hand, where He doth work, but I cannot behold Him; He hideth himself on the Right-hand, that I cannot see Him* {Job 23:8–9}. No, I am now taught where to meet with Him, even at *every turn. He knows the way that I take* {Job 23:10}. I cannot stir *forward* or *backward,* but I *perceive* Him in the *Weight* of every *Matter;* on the *Left-hand* and on the *Right* I see Him *at work.* My *way* shall be to improve this as a *weighty* Argument for the Being of a God. I will argue from it, *Behold, there is a God, whom I ought for ever to love, and serve, and glorify.* Yea, and if I am *tempted* to the doing of any wicked thing, I may reflect, that it cannot be done without some Action, wherein the *Weight of Matter* operates. But then I may carry on the Reflection, *How near am I to that Glorious GOD, whose Commands I am going to violate! Matter keeps his Laws; but, O my Soul, wilt thou break 'em! How shall I do this Wickedness, and therein deny the God, who not only is above, but also is most sensibly now exerting His Power in the very Matter, upon which I make my criminal Misapplications!*"

¶. Before we go any further, it appears high time to introduce an Assertion or two of that excellent Philosopher Dr. *Cheyne,* in his *Philosophical Principles of natural Religion.* He asserts, and with Demonstration, (for truly without *that* he asserts nothing!) that there is no such thing as an *universal Soul,* animating the vast System of the World, according to *Plato;*[44] nor any *substantial Forms,* according to *Aristotle;*[45] nor any omniscient *radical Heat,* according to *Hippocrates;*[46] nor any *plastick Virtue,* according to *Scaliger;*[47] nor any *hylarchick Principle,* according to *More*.[48] These are mere *allegorical* Terms, coined on purpose to conceal the Ignorance of the Authors, and keep up their Credit with the credulous Part of Mankind. These *unintelligible Beings* are derogatory from the Wisdom and Power of the Great GOD, who can easily *govern* the Machine He could *create*, by more direct Methods than employing such subservient *Divinities*; and indeed these Beings will not serve the Design for which we invent them, unless we endow them with Faculties above the Dignity of *secondary Agents*. It is now plain from the most *evident Principles*, that the Great GOD not only has the *Springs* of this immense *Machine*, and all the several Parts of it, in his own Hand, and is the *first Mover*; but that without His *continual Influence* the whole Movement would soon fall to pieces. Yet besides this, He has reserved to Himself the power of *dispensing* with these *Laws*, whenever He pleases.

My Doctor[49] has made it evident, That it is not essential to *Matter* to be either in *Rest* or in *Motion*: But tho there is in *Matter* a *Vis inertiae*,[50] by which all Bodies resist, to the utmost of their power, any *Change* of their State, whether of *Rest* or *Motion*; yet this *Vis* is not essential to *Matter*, but a *positive Faculty* implanted therein by the Author of Nature. It is therefore evident that the Preservation of a *Body* in *Rest* or in *Motion* (after the first Instant) absolutely depends on the Almighty GOD, as the Cause. No part of *Matter* can move itself, nor when put into *motion*, is this *Motion* absolutely essential to its Being, nor does depend upon itself; and therefore the *Preservation* of this *Motion* must have its Dependance on some other Cause. But there is no other Cause assignable besides the *omnipotent Cause*, who preserves the Being and Faculties of all natural Agents.

Great GOD, on the Behalf of all thy Creatures, I acknowledge in Thee we move and have our Being!

CONCLUSION

¶. *Hear now the Conclusion of the Matter* {Eccles. 12:13}. To enkindle the *Dispositions* and the *Resolutions* of PIETY in my Brethren, is the *Intention* of all my ESSAYS, and must be the *Conclusion* of them.

Atheism is now for ever chased and hissed out of the World, every thing in the World concurs to a Sentence of *Banishment* upon it. *Fly, thou Monster, and hide, and let not the darkest Recesses of Africa itself be able to cherish thee; never dare to shew thyself in a World where every thing stands ready to overwhelm thee!* A BEING that must be *superior* to *Matter*, even the *Creator* and *Governor* of all *Matter*, is every where so conspicuous, that there can be nothing more *monstrous* than *to deny the God that is above* {Job 31:28}. No *System* of *Atheism* has ever yet been offered among the Children of Men, but what may presently be convinced of such *Inconsistences*, that a Man must ridiculously believe *nothing certain* before he can imagine them; it must be a *System* of *Things which cannot stand together!* A Bundle of *Contradictions* to themselves, and to all *common Sense*. I doubt it has been an *inconsiderable* thing to pay so much of a Compliment to *Atheism*, as to bestow solemn *Treatises* full of learned *Arguments* for the Refutation of a *delirious Phrenzy*, which ought rather to be put out of countenance with the most *contemptuous Indignation*. And I fear such Writers as have been at the pains to put the *Objections* of *Atheism* into the most plausible Terms, that they may have the honour of *laying a Devil when they have raised him,*[51] have therein done too *unadvisedly*. However, to so much notice of the raving *Atheist* we may condescend while we go along, as to tell him, that for a Man to question the *Being* of a GOD, who requires from us an *Homage* of *Affection*, and *Wonderment*, and *Obedience* to Himself, and a perpetual Concern for the Welfare of the *Human Society*, for which He has in our *Formation* evidently *suited* us, would be an *exalted Folly*, which undergoes especially two Condemnations; it is first condemned by this, that every Part of the *Universe* is continually *pouring in* something for the *confuting* of it; there is not a Corner of the whole World but what supplies a *Stone* towards the Infliction of such a *Death* upon the *Blasphemy* as justly belong to it: and it has also this condemning of it, that Men would soon become *Canibals* to one another by embracing it; Men being utterly destitute of any Principle to keep them *honest in the Dark*, there would be no *Integrity* left in the World, but they would be as the *Fishes of the Sea to one another*, and worse than *the creeping Things, that have no Ruler over them* {Hab. 1:14}. Indeed from every thing in the World there is the Voice more audible than the loudest Thunder to us; *God hath spoken, and these two things have I heard!* First, *Believe and adore a glorious GOD, who has made all these Things, and know thou that He will bring thee into Judgment!* And then *be careful to do nothing but what shall be for the Good of the Community which the Glorious GOD has made thee a Member of* {Jer. 14:22; Eccles. 11:9; 1 Cor. 12:12–27}. Were what God *hath spoken* duly regarded, and were these *two things* duly complied with, the World would be soon revived into a desirable *Garden of God*, and Mankind would be fetch'd up into very comfortable Circumstances; till *then* the World continues in a wretched Condition, *full of doleful Creatures*, with *wild Beasts crying* in its *desolate Houses, Dragons* in its most *pleasant Palaces* {Isa. 13:21–22}. And now declare, *O every thing that is reasonable*, declare and pronounce upon it whether it be possible that *Maxims* absolutely *necessary* to the *Subsistence* and *Happiness* of Mankind, can be *Falsities?* There is no possibility for this, that *Cheats* and *Lyes* be so *necessary*, that the *Ends* which alone are worthy of a glorious GOD, cannot be attain'd without having *them* imposed upon us!

Medicine and the Cure of Diseases

I
n early modern Anglo-American cultures, medicinal remedies and healing practices were still largely the province of local women, often midwives,
whose knowledge and techniques had origins deep in folkways. That, however, was beginning to change. Over the course of the eighteenth century,
a professional, university-trained class of medical practitioners came to domi-
nate the field, a process by which male doctors slowly replaced female healers.
An exception to this, especially in rural areas, was the village minister, who, perhaps because of an interest in medicine or out of necessity on the part of his
congregation, often doubled as what at the time was called a "chirurgeon," or
physician (the supplemental income could have been an incentive as well).
Because "natural philosophy" involved the study of many interrelated disciplines,
anatomy, chemistry, herbology, and similar knowledge could become part of a
college student's pursuits, or be imparted by an older minister or practitioner.[1]

Although Cotton Mather did not engage in the regular treatment of his congregants, he was a prime example of the clergyman-physician. As in other areas
of learning, he read widely in medical texts of the day. Characteristically, he even
wrote his own treatise, the only full-length medical work from colonial New
England, his "The Angel of Bethesda," which remained unpublished during his
lifetime and for long after. This work blended science, medical prescriptions,
and exhortations to temperance and moderation with pious reflections. While
many proposed remedies partake of the esoteric and even (to the modern reader

anyway) the bizarre, "Angel" considered some very modern topics. In a time when water was still considered suspect, he recommended regular bathing and hygiene. He affirmed the most current trends by advocating chemical and toxicological treatments for illnesses. Himself a stutterer, Mather included the first treatise on this condition. As a young person whose speech impediment threatened his ability to preach, Mather initially turned to studying medicine. One of the most effective ways to control stammering was suggested to him by a local schoolteacher: speak very deliberately, in a *"Drawling* that shall be little short of *Singing"*—a method still used by speech therapists today.[2]

In the excerpt from "The Angel of Bethesda" included below, Mather drew on his reading in treatises by experts such as London physician Benjamin Marten and botanist and horticulturalist Richard Bradley, summarizing their findings and hypotheses about the origins of diseases. Then, Mather himself synthesized his own theory by describing the causes of diseases as the incursion of "animalcula," or microscopic insects, into the skin, vessels, and bodily organs. Incredibly, as historian Kenneth Silverman observes, it may be that Mather "stumbled unaided on the momentous germ theory of disease."[3] Ever a clinician of the soul, Mather concludes with *"Sentiments of PIETY,"* reflecting on how all life lies at the mercy of God, and that a human is a "poor Thing," susceptible to a *"Worm* inconceivably less than the *Light Dust of the Balance."* What is needed, Mather concludes, is a "Potent *Worm-killer"*—what we today would call a vaccine.

Mather's drive to find and suggest the best remedies not only for the soul but also for the body had its origins in his social-mindedness, in his desire to do good. But it no doubt also arose from the suffering he observed and experienced in his own family, and from the wave after wave of deadly epidemics that swept through New England on a regular basis in the late seventeenth and early eighteenth centuries. In 1713 and 1714, for instance, measles killed several hundred people in Boston alone, including Mather's second wife and three of his children. From his tragic experience, Mather published *A Letter About a Good Management under the Distemper of the Measles* (1713), his own treatise on how to treat the illness.[4]

In order to understand the way in which illness was perceived in Mather's time and place, it is important to step back and consider its theological and religious meanings. The inhabitants operated within a worldview in which everything had spiritual import. God, as the sovereign disposer of all things, could work his will through miracles certainly, but usually did so more mundanely through secondary causes, such as natural or human-made events. In other words, nothing happened for nothing; everything had a meaning, and it was up to the subjects of particular events—drought, famine, military defeat—to reflect on God's message in those events. They used the term "providence" to describe these phenomena that were outside human ken and control, and so they had a providential view of causation and history: all things were ordered by God to fulfill God's ultimate plans. It was up to the people who were under these providences—whether an individual, a community, or a people—to discern and submit to God's sovereign will.

Illness fell within this spectrum of assumptions. If one became ill, one tried to understand God's intent in bringing this illness upon them. On the one hand, God could be punishing an individual or a people for unrepented sins; on the other, God could be "trying," or testing, their faith, using illness as a way of strengthening their belief. The issue, again, was submission to divine fiat.

Against this backdrop, we can turn to Mather's life in May 1721, when town officials detected smallpox in Boston. The pestilence had arrived with the crew of a ship docked in the harbor and gradually spread to the inhabitants. Efforts were made by the city's doctors—most of them not professionally trained—to combat the disease using traditional methods. At the time, a "humoral" conception of the body still prevailed, that is, that the body had four "humors" and the prevalence of any one of them created an imbalance, and thereby an illness. The procedures for treating illnesses included bleeding, blistering, and purging, which could often be more debilitating than the disease itself.

In the case of pestilence, the best course was quarantining and monitoring. Beyond that, there was little that could be done. Nearly half of the town's population became infected, and in the end nearly a thousand people died. From the start, Mather sprang into action to minimize its impact. His proposal was revolutionary: unaffected individuals should be inoculated. In his diary he wrote, "G[ood] D[one]. The grievous Calamity of the *Small-Pox* has now entered the Town. The Practice of conveying and suffering the *Small-Pox* by Inoculation, has never been used in *America*, nor indeed in our Nation. But how many Lives might be saved by it, if it were practised? I will procure a Consult of our Physicians, and lay the matter before them."[5]

An Account of the Method and Success of Inoculating the Small-Pox is Mather's letter, addressed September 7, 1721, to colonial agent and Yale College benefactor Jeremiah Dummer (1681–1739), published in London the following year. From the start of the epidemic, Mather had encouraged Boston physician Zabdiel Boylston (1679–1766) to implement inoculation, which he did, starting with his own son, his slaves, and subsequently Mather's youngest son Samuel.

If the politicizing of the Covid-19 pandemic in 2020 seemed to be a new thing to those who went through it, the reactions of Bostonians to the smallpox three centuries earlier teach us otherwise. Despite Boylston's marked success, the practice brought down a firestorm of misinformation, vitriol, and fear. The population, newspapers, pamphleteers, and doctors were mostly against inoculation, though most of Mather's fellow clergy seemed to favor it. Religious objections to this form of preventive medicine abounded. It was, some argued, a sin to introduce disease into oneself, not only because one could do harm to oneself but because thwarting the progress of disease was coopting God's prerogative and sovereign will in affairs, including the span of life. With a rhetorical roll of his eyes, Mather commented that, however sincere such objectors were, their "*Hearts* are better than their *Heads*." A newspaper, the *New-England Courant*, was founded by Benjamin Franklin's brother specifically to serve as a mouthpiece for those opposing inoculation. Town doctors were bitterly critical of Boylston's methods, protesting that they were untried and potentially disastrous. They likened infusing one's system with a dose of smallpox, according to Mather, to injecting "the Venom of *Serpents*, or the Oil of *Tobacco*" into one's veins. A pamphlet war ensued in which anonymous authors presented arguments for and against the procedure.

In his letter to Dummer, Mather presented his case for inoculation. First, to show that this was by no means a new, unknown, and untried thing, he cited learned figures from as far away as Constantinople and Smyrna who had observed the very positive effects of inoculation. For his part, Mather pointed out that before he had read anything by these scientists, he actually learned of the process from his slave Onesimus, who declared that the members of his tribe back in Africa had used inoculation for a long time, describing the usual effects and recovery time.

After appealing to learned experts, Mather then brought in practical observation. In answer to the many ill-informed criticisms, he replied, "And of what Significancy are most of our *Speculations?* EXPERIENCE! EXPERIENCE! 'tis to THEE that the Matter must be referr'd after all." And so, he detailed the procedure from Boylston's experiments, tracking how patients reacted, and eventually recovered, usually after only a secondary, mild sickness. In the end, Mather took the view that it was God who made available new knowledge, such as *"preventing Physick,"* or preventive and prophylactic measures, through human efforts, and it was therefore the duty of believers to accept and use this knowledge. Science, for Mather, was in the service of religion. As Boylston himself queried of this "Remedy" that God has "taught us": "Whether a Christian may not employ this *Medicine,* (let the *Matter* of it be what it will) and humbly give Thanks to God for his *good Providence,* in discovering it to a miserable World; and humbly look up to his *good Providence* (as we do in the Use of any other *Medicine*) for the Success of it?" His answer, as well as Mather's, was an emphatic "yes."

Despite all of his efforts—or perhaps because of them, by which he may have appeared interfering and sanctimonious—Mather became an object of resentment yet again. The measure of that resentment was made palpable on the night of November 14, 1721, when a "fired Granado," a grenade, was thrown through the first-floor window of a room in his house. Because the bomb was apparently amateurishly made, it did not explode, otherwise it is likely the entire house would have been destroyed, with all inside. But the dud provided an opportunity to read the vicious note attached: "COTTON MATHER, *You Dog, Dam you; I'l inoculate you with this, with a Pox to you.*"

"THE ANGEL OF BETHESDA" (c. 1693)

CAP. VII: *CONJECTURALES*

Or, Some Touches upon, A *New Theory* of many *Diseases*.
Faelix qui potuit Rerum cognoscere causas![6]

OF a *Distemper* we commonly say, *To know the Cause, is Half the Cure.* But, alas, how little Progress is there yett made in the *Knowledge! Physicians* talk about the *Causes* of *Diseases.* But their Talk is very *Conjectural,* very *Uncertain,* very *Ambiguous;* oftentimes a meer *Jargon;* and in it, they are full of *Contradiction* to one another. It may be, one of the truest Maxims ever yett advanced by any of the Gentlemen, has been That; *Ventriculus malis Effectus est Origo omnium Morborum.* A *distempered Stomach* is the Origin of all *Diseases.* I am sure Tis as useful a Caution as ever they gave; & it is the very Sum of all *Prophylactic Physick.* But, Syrs, whence is It, that the *Stomach* is *distempered?*—

—Since we are upon *Conjectures,* I pray, Lett us allow some room, to those of Dr. *Marten* and Company.[7]

Every Part of Matter is *Peopled.* Every *Green Leaf* swarms with *Inhabitants.* The Surfaces of *Animals* are covered with other *Animals.* Yea, the most Solid *Bodies,* even *Marble* itself, have innumerable Cells, which are crouded with imperceptible Inmates. As there are Infinite Numbers of these, which the *Micro-scopes* bring to our View, so there may be inconceivable Myriads yett Smaller than these, which no Glasses have yett reach'd unto. The *Animals* that are much *more* than Thousands of times *Less* than the finest Grain of Sand, have their *Motions;* and so, their Muscles, their Tendons, their Fibres, their Blood, and the *Eggs* wherein their Propagation is carried on. The Eggs of these Insects (and why not the *living Insects* too?) may insinuate themselves by the *Air,* and with our *Aliments,* yea, thro' the Pores of our Skin; and soon gett into the Juices of our Bodies. They may be convey'd into our Fluids, with the Nourishment which we received, even before we were born; and may ly dormant until the Vessels are grown more capable of bringing them into their Figure & Vigour for Operations. Thus may Diseases be convey'd from the Parents unto their Children, before they are born into the World. As the *Eggs* whereof *Cheese-mites* are produced, were either in the *Milk* before it came from the Cow, or at least the *Run-net* with which the Cheese was coagulated. If they meet with a *Proper Nest* in any of our Numberless Vessels, they soon multiply prodigiously; and may have a *greater Share in producing many of our Diseases than is commonly imagined.* Being brought into Life, then either by their spontaneous Run, or by their Disagreeable Shape, they may destroy the Texture of the Blood, and other Juices: or they may gnaw and wound the Tender Vessels. It may be so, that one Species of these Animals may offend in one Way, and another in another; and the *Various* Parts may be *Variously* offended: From whence may flow a *Variety* of Diseases. And Vast Numbers of these Animals keeping together, may at once make such Invasions, as to render Diseases *Epidemical;* which those particularly are, that are called, *Pestilential. Epidemical* and almost universal *Coughs,* may by this *Theory* be also accounted for.

Strange *Murrains* on Cattle seem to have been sometimes of this Original. Dr. *Slare* observes, of the famous one that passed from *Switzerland* thro' *Germany* to *Poland,* that in its Progress, it spred still Two *German* Miles in Twenty four Hours; and he sais, *"It were worth Considering,* whether this Infection is not carried on by some *Volatil Insect,* that is able to make only such short Flights as may amount to such Computations."[8]

As for the Distempers in Humane Bodies, *Kircher* and *Hauptman* assert, that *Malignant Fevers* never proceed from any other Cause than *Little Animals. Blancard* affirms, That the *Microscope* discovers the *Blood* in *Fevers* to be full of *Animals.*[9]

Ettmuller sais, unwonted Swarms of *Insects* resorting to a Countrey, foretell a *Plague* impending.[10]

And thus we may conceive, how Diseases are convey'd from distant Countreys or Climates; By the *Animalcula,* or their *Eggs,* deposited in the Bodies or Cloathes or Goods of Travellers.

Tis generally supposed, that *Europe* is endebted unto *America* for the *Lues Venerea.*[11] If so, *Europe* has paid its Debt unto *America,* by making unto it a Present of the *Small-Pox,* in Lieu of the *Great* one.

Dr. *Lister* having observed, That the *Plague* is properly a Disease of *Asia,* and still comes from thence; he adds, That the *Small-Pox* is an Exotic Disease of the Oriental People, and was not known to *Europe,* or even to the Lesser *Asia,* or to *Africa,* till a Spice-trade was opened by the latter Princes of *Egypt,* unto the remoter Parts of the *East-Indies;* from whence it originally came, and where at this Day it rages more cruelly than with us. Dr. *Oliver* likewise gives it as his Opinion, That we received *Small-Pox* and *Measles* from *Arabia;* and that *Europe* was wholly unacquainted with them, until by the frequent Incursions of the *Arabians* into *Africa,* and afterwards into *Spain,* the Venom came to be spread as now it is.[12]

The Essential Cause of the *Itch,* appears to be a vast Number of *Minute Animals,* that make Furrows under the Scarf-skin, and stimulate the Nervous Fibres; as may be demonstrated by a *Microscope,* examining the Humour in the little Bladders rising between the Fingers. The Insects contained in a very small Part of the Humour, fixed upon the Skin of a Sound Person, either by shaking

Hands with the Mangy, or using a Towel or a Glove after him; these do soon insinuate into the Pores, and then quickly multiply enough to occupy almost all the Surface of the Body. Hence, if the Cure be not so closely followed, as not only to check, but also to kill, all the Animals, they soon increase, & become as Troublesome as they were before. In the like Manner is a yett more Filthy Disease communicated. Thus tis that *GOD Judges you, O Ye Whore-mongers and Adulterers!*

M. *Hartsoecker* does not scruple to say, *I beleeve that Insects occasion most of the Diseases which Mankind is attack'd withal.*[13]

Dr. *Marten* suspects, that there is possibly no *Ulcer*, or ulcerated Matter, but what may be stocked with *Animals*, which being of different Species, the Ulcerations may be more or less violent according to them.

The learned *Borellus* assures us, That several times he hath seen *Animals* upon *Plaisters* taken from *Fistulous Ulcers;* and he adds, *Thus we are held of many Diseases which come from Invisible Animals, or such as can only be perceived by Microscopes.*[14]

The famous *Mayern* also observed a *Cancerous Breast*, full of these *Animals.*[15]

Dr. *Andry* found, *That* the *Pustles* of the *Small-Pox* are full of them; and so is the Blood and Urine of them that have it: *That* in the *Venereal Distemper*, there is hardly any Part of the Body that is not gnaw'd by them; *That* in the *Fistula Lacrymalis* the Water that comes from the Eyes is full of them; *That* our *Cancers* are horribly replenished with them, which gnaw upon all the Sieves of the Glands with prodigious Consequences: And, *That* as these *Animals* grow old, they assume *New Forms*, which would be very Terrible unto People, if they could but see the Terrible Spectacles.[16]

Dr. *Marten* is not without Suspicion, That a *Consumption* may often be of this Original; and that these *Animals* or their Seed, may sometimes be by Parents Haereditarily conveyed unto their Offspring; or communicated by Sick Persons to Sound Ones, that are too conversant with them. He also supposes, That tho' great Quantities of these *Animals*, or of their *Eggs*, may be lodged in our Blood & Juices, yea, and in our Vessels find a Nest which may bring them into Life; yett while our Secretions are duely performed, or usual Evacuations continued, the *Animals* may be cast out of their Bodies as fast as they are bred there; and their own very Motion may contribute unto it. But when the Emunctories, thro' Cold or any other Cause are obstructed, or any usual Evacuations are stopped; this prevents their passing off, and many Mischiefs ensue upon it.

While I was thus entertaining myself with the Speculations of Dr. *Marten*, and his Auxiliaries, upon this *New Theory of Diseases*, I litt on Mr. *Bradly's* New *Improvements of Planting & Gardening;*[17] who maintains, That the *Blights* upon the *Vegetable World* are owing to *Insects;* whereof he discovered some (a thousand times less than the least Grain of Sand) which found the *Cold* so agreeable an Element unto them, that at a Yards Distance from a slow Fire the Heat would burn them to Death. But those Insects he thought overgrown Monsters, to those which have been discovered by M. *Lieuenhoek* (and other Ey-witnesses) whereof above Eight Million may be found in one drop of Water: And Mr. *Hook* proceeded so far as to demonstrate Millions of Millions contained in such a mighty Ocean. A very gentle Air may carry these from one Place to another, and so our Plants become infested with them.[18]

On this Occasion I find his Friend Mr. *Ball,* modestly but very learnedly offering his Apprehensions, That our *Pestilential Diseases* may be of the like Original.[19] In *Europe,* the *Plagues* are brought by Long, Dry, *Easterly Winds,* which Mr. *Ball* thinks, may bring infinite Swarms of these Destroyers; and that most probably they come from *Tartary:* For he has never heard of properly *Pestilential Distempers* any where in the World, but where the *Tartarian Winds* have reached them. When the *Plague* raged in *London,* those Places which had Scents that probably kill'd or chas'd away these *Animals,* were kept from the Infection.

This Conjecture about the *Origin of Disease,* may be as good as many that have been more confidently Obtruded and more generally Received.

But what *Remarks* are to be made upon it; what *Sentiments of PIETY* to be produced?

"How much does our *Life* ly at the Mercy of our GOD! How much do we walk thro' *unseen Armies* of Numberless Living Things, ready to sieze and prey upon us! A *Walk,* like the *Running* of the *Deadly Garloup,* which was of old called, *A Passing thro' the Brick-kiln!* What *Unknown Armies* has the Holy One, wherewith to Chastise, and even Destroy, the Rebellious Children of Men? Millions of Billions of Trillions of Invisible *Velites!*[20] Of sinful Men *they* say, *Our Father, Shall We Smite them?* On *His* Order, they do it Immediately; they do it Effectually."

"What a poor Thing is *Man;* That a *Worm* inconceivably less than the *Light Dust of the Balance,* is too hard for him!" {Isa. 40:15}.

"How much is it our Interest and our Prudence, to *keep resolves in the Love of GOD!*"

But, O Ye Sons of Erudition, and, Ye *Wise Men of Enquiry;* Lett this *Enquiry* come into a due Consideration with you; How far a Potent *Worm-killer,* that may be safely administered, would go further than any Remedy yett found out, for the Cure of many Diseases!

Mercury; We know thee: But we are afraid, Thou wilt kill *us* too, if we employ thee to kill *them* that kill us.

And yett, for the Cleansing of the small *Blood-Vessels*, and making Way for the free Circulation of the Blood and Lymph, & so to serve the greatest Purposes of Medicine, there is nothing like *Mercurial Deobstruents*;[21] of which, the *Cinnabar* of *Antimony*, *Æthiops Mineral*, and the Antihectic of *Poterius*, may be reckoned the Principal.[22] But after all, tis time to have done with the *Metaphysical Jargon*, which for a long Time has passed for the *Rationale* of Medicine; How much would the *Art of Medicine* be improved, if our Physicians more generally had the *Mathematical* Skill of a Dr. *Mead* or a Dr. *Morgan*, and would go his Way to Work, *Mathematically*, and by the *Laws* of *Matter* and *Motion* to find out the *Cause* and *Cure* of *Diseases*?[23]

The Words of one of them are worth reciting: "Since the Animal Body is a *Machine*, and Diseases are nothing else but its Particular Irregularities, Defects, and Disorders, a *Blind* Man might as well pretend to Regulate a Piece of *Clockwork*, or a *Deaf* Man to tune an *Organ*, as a Person ignorant of *Mathematicks* and *Mechanism*, to cure Diseases, without understanding the Natural Organization, Structure, & Operations of the *Machine*, which he undertakes to regulate."

AN ACCOUNT OF THE METHOD AND SUCCESS OF INOCULATING THE SMALL-POX (1722)

SIR,[24]

A Gentleman[25] well known in the City of *Boston*, had a *Garamantee* Servant,[26] who first gave him an Account, of a Method frequently used in *Africa*, and which had been practis'd on himself, to procure an *easy Small-Pox*, and a perpetual Security of neither *dying* by it, nor being again infected with it.

Afterwards he successively met with a Number of *Africans*; who all, in *their* plain Way, without any Combination, or Correspondence, agreed in *one Story*, *viz.* that in their Country (where they use to die like *Rotten Sheep*, when the *Small-Pox* gets among them) it is now become a *common Thing* to cut a Place or two in their Skin, sometimes one Place, and sometimes another, and put in a little of the Matter of the *Small-Pox*; after which, they, in a few Days, grow a *little Sick*, and a few *Small-Pox* break out, and by and by they dry away; and that no Body ever dy'd of doing this, nor ever had the *Small-Pox* after it: Which last Point is confirm'd by their constant Attendance on the Sick in our Families, without receiving the Infection; and, so considerable is the Number of these in our Neighbourhood, that he had as evident Proof of the *Practice, Safety*, and *Success* of this Operation, as we have that there are *Lions* in *Africa*.

After this, he heard it affirm'd, That it is no unusual Thing for our Ships on the Coast of *Guinea*,[27] when they ship their Slaves, to find out by Enquiry which of the Slaves have not yet had the *Small-Pox*; and so carry them ashore, in this Way to give it to them, that the poor Creatures may sell for a better Price; where they are often (inhumanly enough) to be dispos'd of.

Some Years after he had receiv'd his first *African* Informations, he found publish'd in our *Philosophical Transactions*,[28] divers Communications from the *Levant*, which, to our Surprize, agreed with what he had from *Africa*.

First, That very valuable Person, Dr. *Emanuel Timonius*, writes from *Constantinople*,[29] in *December* 1713, That the Practice of procuring the *Small-Pox*, by a Sort of *Inoculation*, had been introduc'd among the *Constantinopolitans*, from the more Eastern and Northern *Asiaticks*, for about forty Years.[30] At the first (he says) People were cautious and afraid; but the *happy Success* on Thousands of Persons, for (then) eight Years past, had put it *out of all Suspicion*. His Account is, That they who have the *Inoculation* practis'd upon them, are subject to very *slight Symptoms*, and sensible of but very little Sickness; nor do what *Small-Pox* they have, ever leave any *Scars* or *Pits* behind them. They make Choice of as healthy a young Person as they can find, that has the *Small-Pox* of the best Sort upon him; on the *Twelfth* or *Thirteenth* Day of his *Decumbiture*, with a *Needle* they prick some of the larger *Pustules*, and press out the Matter coming from them into some *convenient Vessel*, which is to be stopt *close*, and kept *warm*, in the Bosom of the Person that carries it to the intended Patient. This *Person* ought rather to be some *other*, than he who visited the *sick Chamber* for it; lest he should carry the Infection in the *common Way*, which might prove dangerous. The Patient is to have several *small Wounds* made with a *Needle*, or *Lancet*, in two or more Places of the *Skin*, (the best Places are the Muscles of the *Arm*) and immediately let there be dropt out a *Drop* of the Matter in the Glass on each of the Places, and mix'd with the Blood that is issuing out. The Wound should be cover'd with some little *Concave Vessel*, and bound over, that the Matter may not be rubb'd off by the Garments, for a few Hours. And now, let the Patient (having *Fillets* on the Wounds) keep House, and be careful of his *Diet*. The Custom at *Constantinople*, is to abstain from *Flesh* and *Broth* for twenty Days, or more; and they chuse to perform the Operation, either in the Beginning of the *Winter*, or the *Spring*: The *Small-Pox* begins to appear sooner in some than in others; and with lesser Symptoms in some than in others; but *with happy Success in all*.

Commonly ten or twenty *Pustules* break out; here and there one has no more than two or three, few have an *Hundred*: There are some in whom no *Pustules* rise, but in the Places where the *Incision* was made: And here the Tubercules will be purulent; yet even these have never had the *Small-Pox* afterwards, tho' they have cohabited with Persons that had it on them. No small Quantity of Matter will run, for several Days, from the Places of the *Incision*; but the *Peeks* arising from the Operation, are dry'd up in a little while, and fall of, partly in thin Skins, and partly vanishing by an insensible Wasting: The Matter being hardly so thick a *Pus* as in the common *Small-Pox*; tho,' at the Places of the *Incision*, 'tis more of the common Sort; and there the *Scars* will always remain, as Remembrancers of it. If an *Apostem* should break out in any, (which is more frequent in *Infants*) yet there is no Fear; for 'tis healed safely by Suppuration:[31] In fine, this learned Person assures us, that he never yet observ'd any *bad Consequence* of the Practice, which now so many come into.

After this, we find an honourable Person, whose Name is *Jacobus Pylarinus*, the *Venetian* Consul at *Smyrna*, (who was, I suppose, wholly a Stranger to what had been written by the former) publishing what is entituled, Nova, ac Tuta Variolas Excitandi per Transplantationem Methodus.[32]

This Gentleman observes, that this *wonderful Invention*, was first, *à plebeia rudique Gente, in Humani Generis adjumentum & in saevissimi Morbi solamen detecta*, found out, not by the learned Sons of *Erudition*, but by a mean, coarse, rude Sort of People, for the *Succour of Mankind*, under and against one of the most cruel Diseases in the World. It was rarely, if ever used among the People of *Quality*, till after the Beginning of the present Century. A *noble Grecian* happening then to try it with happy Success upon four little Sons of his own Family. *Mirum quam multas Nobiliorum Familias ad Imitationem traxit.* It was wonderful to see how many *People of Fashion* presently follow'd the Example; so that at this Day (he says) every one does, *without any Hesitation*, and with all the Security imaginable, practice the *Transplantation*, except here and there a few *Cowards*, that are afraid of their *Shadows*. Indeed, the *Turks* who ascribe all Events to *Fate*, for that Reason come but slowly into it.

The Instructions given by *Pylarinus* about the Operation, differ little from those of *Timonius*, and so there is no Need of repeating them.

He adds, That some do the Business with no more than *one Incision*.

The Ferment comes into Action sooner in some than in others; usually 'tis on the *seventh* Day, sometimes on the *first*.

The *Symptoms* prove *remis*, or *intense*, according to the various Constitutions of the Bodies.

The *Small-Pox* proves of the *distinct Sort*, and there are but few of them.

In some few, the *Incision* has produc'd no *Small-Pox* at all; but the Persons have afterwards been taken in the *common Way*, and handled with it like other People.

The *Wounds* made for the *Incision*, prove often very sore; and with some they degenerate into *Apostems*; nay they swell sometimes, and rise and fall, and rise again. There has also happen'd on this Occasion, an *Abscess* with Suppuration, in some Emunctory of the Body; but this is a rare Occurrence.

In fine, *Pylarinus* affirms, it was hardly ever known, that there was any *ill Consequence* of this Transplantation. *Quinimò ritè rectéque tractata, & in Corporibus per peritum Medicum aptè praeparatis, certissimam promittit Salutem.* The Business being well, and wisely manag'd, and the Body being, by a skilful Physician, well prepar'd, you may depend upon it. (He says) in an ordinary Way, there can be *nothing but a good Issue* of it.

After these Communications, and the Thing *establish'd in the Mouths of two such Witnesses*, we met with some ingenious Travellers, who knew so much of the Matter, as very much to confirm the Ideas we had entertain'd of it.

Were one of an ordinary Capacity (for no better is he that is now writing) willing to try a little how far *Philosophy* might countenance the Matter: One might think, the venomous *Miasms* of the *Small-Pox*, entering into the Body, in the Way of *Inspiration*, are immediately taken into the Blood of the *Lungs*; and, I pray, how many *Pulses* pass, before the very *Heart* is pierc'd with them? And within how many more they are convey'd into all the *Bowels*, is easily apprehended, by all who know any Thing how the *Circulation of the Blood* is carry'd on; at the same Time the *Bowels* themselves are infeebled,[33] and their Tone impair'd, by the *Venom* that is thus insinuated. Behold the Enemy at once got into the very *Center* of the Citadel; and the invaded Party must be very strong indeed, if it can struggle with him, and after all entirely expel and conquer him: Wheras the *Miasms* of the *Small-Pox*, being admitted in the Way of *Inoculation*, their Approaches are made only by the *Out Works* of the *Citadel*, and at a considerable Distance from it. The Enemy, 'tis true, gets in so far, as to make some *Spoil*; even so much as to satisfy him, and leave no *prey* in the Body of the Patient, for him ever afterwards to seize upon: but the *vital Powers* are kept so clear from his Assaults, that they can manage the *Combat* bravely; and tho' not without a *Surrender* of those Humours in the *Blood*, which the Invader makes a Seizure on, they oblige him to *march out the same Way he came in,* and are sure of never being troubled with him any more. If the *Vermicular Hypothesis* of the *Small-Pox* be receiv'd with us, (and it be, as many now think, an *animaculated Business*) there is less of *Metaphor* in our Account, than may be at first imagin'd.

But to what Purpose is all this *Jargon?* And of what Significancy are most of our *Speculations?* EXPERIENCE! EXPERIENCE! 'tis to THEE that the Matter must be referr'd after all: a few *Empericks* here, are worth all our *Dogmatists*.

About three Months ago [May 1721], the *Small-Pox* broke in upon the City of
Boston, where it very much appeared with the *Terrors of Death* to the Inhabitants. On this Occasion, there was address'd a Letter to the *Physicians* of the City,
with an Account of the Communications from the illustrious *Timonius*, and *Pylarinus*, entreating them to meet for a *Consultation* upon it, *Whether the new
Practice might be introduc'd and countenanc'd among us?*[34] The Writer was perswaded, that herein he did but his Duty, and express'd no other than the *Charity of a Christian*, and a proper Concernment and Compassion for his poor
Neighbours, whom he saw likely to die by Hundreds about him. His Address
found (for what Reasons I know not, or am not willing to know) an *indecent Reception* with our Physitians; all the Return he had, was a Story which they
spread about the Town and Country, that he had given an *unfaithful Account* of
the Matter to them, tho' they had it in the printed *Philosophical Transactions* before their Eyes to justify it. Then the Story was turn'd, that either Dr. *Halley*[35] had
suppress'd Part of the true Account, or *Timonius* and *Pylarinus* were themselves
fallacious: Nevertheless, one who had been a more *successful Practitioner* than
most of them, and had with a singular Dexterity in his Practice, perform'd Things
not attempted by any of them, (namely, Mr. *Zabdiel Boylston*) was prompted,[36]
by his enterprising Genius, to begin the Operation. He thought it most generous to make his first Beginning upon his *own Family*; and here, to make not
only two *Slaves*, but a beloved *Son* of his own, (about five or six Years of Age) the
Subjects of it: He made the *Transplantation* into them with two or three *Incisions* a-piece, taking the *Leg* as well as the *Arm*, (and in one of them the *Neck*)
for the Places of them: He did not use the *Precaution* of sending for the ferment-
ing *Pus* by a third Person: He staid not for what some would have thought more
proper Seasons; but he did it in the very *Heat* of *Midsummer*; which, with us,
is hot enough: He did nothing at all to *prepare* their Bodies; and he chose to
leave them to the *Liberties*, which Persons infected with the *Small-Pox* in the
common Way, do generally take, before their *Decumbiture*, without any Detriment to them.

Under all these Disadvantages, did this Gentleman make his Experiments;
but *they succeeded to Admiration*. About the seventh Day the Patients began to
grow Feverish, and out of Order; on the third and fourth Day from their falling
ill, his Child's Fever grew to an Heighth, beyond his Expectation, which (from
the *Novelty* of the Business) did, for a few Hours, considerably terrify him: He
had Recourse to the common Remedies of Blisters, and gave the Child a *Vomit*,
and presently all the Fright was over: The *Eruption* began; and from the Time
of its doing so with the *Child*, and with the two *Slaves*, there was no Occasion
for any *other Medicine*; they were easy from this Time; their *Pustules* (which

where, tho' not many, yet somewhat more for Number, than what is usual in the *Levant*) grew, and fell off, as they do in the *Levant;* and their *Sores*, which had an agreeable Discharge at them, seasonably dry'd up of themselves; and they all presently became as hail and strong as ever they were in their Lives.

It is incredible, what a *Storm* was rais'd, and very much of it principally owing to some of our enrag'd *Physicians*, on this Occasion.

The Gentleman was threaten'd with an *Indictment* for *Felony;* (tho,' in your Country, they talk of no such Thing, for them who carry their Children into *infected Chambers*, on Purpose to make them take the *Infection* after the common Way in their Minority) and Words were given out, which had a Tendency to raise the *Mob* upon him.

The *select Men* (an Order of Men, who are the *Overseers* and *Managers* of the *Town-Affairs*) associating with some of the *Justices*, order'd him to appear before them, and severally reprimanded him for spreading the *Small-Pox;* (which was already spreading in the *common* Way) and with high Menaces warned him against proceeding with his Practice any farther. At the same Time, the *Practitioners* of the Town publish'd a Declaration, "That the *Inoculation* of the *Small-Pox* had prov'd the Death of many Persons, soon after the Operation; and brought Distempers on many others, which have, in the End, prov'd fatal to them; which (they said) appear'd by numerous Instances: *That* the natural Tendency of infusing such malignant Filth in the Mass of Blood, is to corrupt and putrify it; and lay a Foundation for many dangerous Diseases: *That* the Operation tends to spread and continue the Infection in a Place, longer than it might otherwise be; and *that* the continuing of the Operation among us, is likely to prove of most dangerous Consequences." . . .

At the same Time, there was publish'd in our *News-Letter*, a bitter Satyr upon Dr. *Boylston* for his late Action;[37] and his *putting this far fetch'd*, and (it was pleas'd to say) *not well vouch'd Method, into Practice.* They compar'd it to the Infusion of the Venom of *Serpents*, or the Oil of *Tobacco*, by Injection, immediately into the Mass of *Blood;* and affirm'd, that it would produce only an *eruptive Fever:* but *nothing Analogous to the* Small-Pox; (tho' they inveigh'd against the Gentleman for spreading the *Small-Pox* in what he did) and that the Sufferers might, notwithstanding, receive the *Small-Pox* afterwards in the ordinary Way: They also asserted, that the Thing had been among the Learned universally known in *England*, above *twenty* Years; (and more than twice seven Years before, the Secretary of the ROYAL SOCIETY first recommended it as a *new Thing*, inviting the Thoughts of the Curious in the *English* Nation upon it) but it had never been practis'd, because it was deem'd *wicked* and *felonious;* and then they referr'd the CASE to the *Divines*, which was express'd in these emphatical Terms:

How the trusting more the groundless Machinations *of Men, than to our Preserver in the ordinary Course of Nature, may be consistent with that Devotion and Subjection we owe to the All-wise Providence of God Almighty.* Six of our Ministers thought themselves bound in Duty to bestow a *publick Rebuke* upon this indecent Satyr; and answer'd the CASE not much to the Satisfaction of some that offer'd it. But the Rage of the People, was, with a very powerful *Pharmacy,* boil'd up to a very great Extremity; and for the more effectual enraging of them, there was a strange Use made of a Passage, that one must have had the *Sense of three Men* in him, to have made such a Construction of it. *Pylarinus* had said, *That sometimes an Abscess happen'd in some Emunctory of the Body;*[38] *which yet* (he said) *was a rare Occurrence.* Now, tho' our Gentlemen knew, that this is a Thing which *daily occurs,* among the People recovering from the *Small-Pox* in the *ordinary Way;* (and we had never seen any Thing of it in our *incisious Way*) yet they rais'd a horribly Cry of *Raw-Head* and *Bloody-Bones,* that the *Inoculation* of the *Small-Pox* would bring in the *Plague* among us. It must needs be so, because *Plague Sores* were often in some *Emunctory of the Body;* and so *Boston* was going at once to be another *Marseilles;* and they had the *Plague* at *Constantinople,* since *Inoculation* had been admitted there. Our People were scar'd (I cannot say) *out of their Wits.* But the Gentleman having succeeded so well in his first *Experiments,* and being perswaded, that if God would please to make him the happy Instrument of saving the precious *Lives* of his poor Neighbours, it would make amends for all the Obloquies which his *envious Brethren* might raise upon him: He took *little Notice* of the *Inhibition* that had been given him. Divers pious and worthy People consider'd how dreadfully the *Small-Pox* handled many of their Neighbours, and how much the *sixth Commandment* order'd them the Use of Means to preserve and prolong their Lives. They consider'd also, that by managing and governing the Approach of the *Small-Pox,* in the Way of *Inoculation,* they had a Method of securing their *Lives* from the Dangers of it; and that there never arriv'd unto us a *Medicine* of so great a *Recommendation;* it having been used upon so many *Thousands,* and never *one* known to have miscarry'd under it. They therefore apply'd themselves to Dr. *Boylston,* with Desires to come under the Operation; and he charitably gratify'd them in the Thing desir'd; tho' the Objects were most of them, either so *Old,* or so *Weak,* that they would have been the *last* that one would have chosen for it; and one would apprehended no little Hazard of the *Event:* But they all got *well* and *soon* through it, and so much beyond their Expectation, that they zealously gave Thanks to God, for leading them into it; and seriously profess'd to their Neighbours, that they had rather suffer the Operation *twice* every Year, than *once* to undergo the *Small-Pox*, as it is most *commonly suffer'd*, tho' they should be sure of surviving it.

The *Fever* in these also, was, for a few Hours before the Eruption, more Intense, and the *Pustules* after it, were more numerous, than what is usual in the *Levant*; but in a few Days, and much sooner than what is commonly done, where they have the *Small-Pox* the common Way, they recover'd their entire Strength, and were, on all Accounts, as well as they were before; and the *Sores* of the *Incision* also heal'd of themselves, rather sooner than they wish'd for. Whereupon, they publish'd a *Declaration* in our *Gazette*, that they might stop *false Reports*, and satisfy the Minds of sober People, in the Midsts of the *Ephesian* Clamours now prevailing; for truly, while these Things were doing, the Town was fill'd with Iniquity, to a Degree which good Men could not observe, without being more than a little *griev'd* at it.

I must say it, I never saw the Devil so *let loose* upon any Occasion. A *lying Spirit* was *gone forth* at such a Rate, that there was no believing any Thing one heard. If the *inoculated Patients* were a little *sickish*, or had a *Vomit* given them, it was immediately reported, That they were at the *point of Death*, or *actually dead*. While the Patients lay blessing and praising Almighty God, for shewing them this *easy Way to escape* a formidable Enemy, it was confidently reported, *That they bitterly repented of what had been done upon them, and would not, upon any Terms, be brought into it, if it were to do again*. When the Patients had their *incisious Places*, either actually and perfectly heal'd in some, or within a Day or two of it in others, it was confidently reported, *That they were perishing under terrible Ulcers, and had their Arms or Legs rotting off*.

These, and the like Things, were asserted with such impudent Confidence, even by such as liv'd in the nearest Neighbourhood, that one was almost ready to fear a Beating, if they durst offer to question them. Then the People would assert, that here were Persons on the very Spot, who underwent the *Inoculation* in *England* a great many Years ago; but afterwards had the *Small-Pox* in the common Way; and, they said, they would *bring these Persons to us*. A few Minutes after, they would assert, that it was never practis'd in England; but there was an *Act of Parliament* which made it *Felony*; and, they said, they would produce the Act to us. But never any Patient had so many *Pustules* of the *Small-Pox*, as there were *Lies* now daily told, and spread among our deluded People.

That which much added to the Misery, was, that the People who made the *loudest Cry*, (who most commonly were what we may not improperly call *of the confluent Sort*, and such also as were past the Dangers of the *Small-Pox* themselves) had a very *Satanic Fury* acting them.

They were like the *possess'd People* in the Gospel, *exceeding fierce*; insomuch, that *one could scarce pass by the Way* where they were to be met withal. Their common Way was to rail and rave, and wish *Death*, or other Mischiefs, to them that practis'd, or favour'd this *devilish Invention*. To inflame them in their Transports, and harden them in their Violences and Exclamations, they pretended *Religion* on their Side; and charg'd all that were not so, with denying and renouncing the *divine Providence*, and I know not how many more *Abominations*; yea, with *going to the Devil*, and the *God of Ekron*.[39] And how strangely they treated the most meritorious Ministers of the Gospel, who did not come into their *Frenzies*, I leave unmention'd. *Father forgive them.*

The View of these Things caus'd some considerate Persons to think, whether the *Angel of Death* promising himself a great *Feast* in this miserable City, *it might not put him that had the Power of Death, that is, the Devil*, into a great *Rage*, to see coming in among us, a *Method* of rescuing many *Morsels* from him. They were sure, the *Lying*, and the *Malice*, and the *Outrage*, that manag'd, and carry'd on the Opposition to it, must needs be of a *Satanic Original*; there could be nothing more contrary to the Spirit of a *meek* JESUS.

But the *Opposers* could not hinder the *Proselytes* from increasing. Dr. *Boylston* has his Patients multiplying; and, instead of any one miscarrying, they come off easier, with less *Fever*, and fewer *Pustules*, than those that *led the Van* in his Experiments. He grows more *expert* every Day; and many of the most vehement Opponents, daily come over to an Approbation of the Practice; and People that see their Neighbours, either dying in a tragical Manner about them every Day, or, at best, having their *Loins fill'd with a loathsome Disease*, won't permit themselves to be *talk'd out of their Lives*, by pitiful Impertinencies.

Of what my ingenious Friend hitherto *does*, and *finds*, you will now accept this brief Account.

He makes usually *two Incisions*, (tho' sometimes but one) in the two *Arms* (or an *Arm*, or a *Leg*) of his Patients; and then he puts into them a little Bit of *Lint*, which he has dipp'd into the Quitter, that he had newly fetch'd in a little *Bottle*, warm from the Pustules of one who has the *Small-Pox* of a good Sort, now turning upon him. This he covers with a little Plaister of *Diachylon*, to keep it close for two or three Days in its Operation there.

In his first Practice, upon his removing the little *Pledget*, the *Sores* of the *Incision* would sometimes *heal up*, and anon swell and break forth of themselves, when the *Fever* came to be over: But he thought afterwards, that by keeping the Sores *constantly open*, in the Way we do an ordinary *Issue*, the *Fever*, and other Symptoms, presently to come on, are sensibly *moderated*. He allows the Patients, for a while, to go *abroad* about their Business, if the *Weather* be good, and be no Danger of getting any Cold; but he directs them to regulate their *Diet*, and, particularly to retrench a little their *Carnivorous* Inclinations: And yet he does little this Way, because he finds no great Advantage by thus enfeebling of them.

About the *seventh* Day, (and sometimes a little before, and sometimes a little after) the Patients grow dull, and feel a *feverish* Disposition, and grumbling Pains of the *Head* and *Back*, as in the Invasions of the *Small-Pox* 'tis usual. In some, the *Symptoms* are very *Remiss*, in others they are more *Intense*. But the Doctor governs the *Fever* at his Pleasure, in the Ways that every Body now treats a common putrid *Fever*.

Sometimes on the third or fourth Day, the *Fever* seems, for a few Hours, a little rampant; but then he gives a gentle *Vomit*, and afterward a *Blister*, and the *Eruption* begins without fail immediately.

If you expect now a *long Story* about the Managements in the *Progress* of the Distemper, I shall disappoint you; for *here's the End on't*; there's *no more* to be done; there's no farther *Illness*; no farther *Trouble*; the *Storm* is over; there is not one Atom of that *second Fever*, which, in the *Small-Pox*, is what People generally die of. The Patients have no more to do, but be *still*, and keep *warm*, and entertain their Friends, and study how to glorify the God of their Lives.

The *Pustules* in some, have been very few, perhaps twenty, or thirty, or so; in others, they have risen to *several Hundreds*; yea, few have come off without *several Hundreds*: In this Point, that is to say, the Number of the *Pustules*, we differ from the *Levant* considerably; and are yet at a Loss for a Reason of it; but in a few Days, as those of the ordinary *distinct Small-Pox*, they are gone.

The *Sores* continue running somewhat longer, (and longer in some than in others) even some Days after their going abroad again. But they dry up of themselves, *Tutò, Citò, ac Jucundè.*[40]

None of the *inoculated* Patients have yet had any of those *Boils*, which People, recover'd of the *Small-Pox* in the *ordinary way*, are commonly vexed withal. If there had been one Instance of them, our Practitioners would have taught the People to cry, *the Plague! the Plague!* upon it.

Thus Dr. *Boylston* goes on with his Practice *hitherto* successfully. There is one Difficulty, indeed, which very much incumbers him. He has employ'd the *Inoculation* upon one Person, who, having been just before tending two *Patients* that were under it, had very strongly receiv'd the Infection in the *common Way*: The Person was in a few Hours taken down, and prov'd very full of the *Small-Pox*, of the *confluent Sort*, and very narrowly escap'd with Life; to the Preservation whereof, it was yet thought, that the running of the *incisious Sores* might a little contribute.

The Miscarriage of this Person would have been, by the *Mob* as aforesaid, improv'd as a sufficient Subject for their Exclamations. 'Tis therefore no little Distress to the *Doctor*, how they that are *already strongly infected*, may be easily distinguish'd *from those* who are not so, in a Place where the Distemper is become *Epidemical*; for the Condition of every one, will not always allow them to perform the *Quarentine* that would be necessary for it. How he will get over this Difficulty, 'tis yet such *early Days* with us, that I cannot inform you.

Our Practitioners, and the People under their Influences, having had their *other Prejudices* confuted by the happy *Experience* of the Neighbourhood, now chiefly insist upon this, *Well, two or three Years hence you will see the dreadful Effects of this wicked Practice; you'll see what happens to the People that are under it.* And the sad Things that were to happen, when the *Lark-time* arrives, are now to terrify us. They are so unreasonable, that one had as good speak *Reason* to a *Post*, or argue with a *Whirlwind.* Were a *Rorarius* alive again, what would he say to such *unreasonable Persons.*[41] A Crazy old Man, that is near *Seventy*, having lately enjoy'd the Benefit of *Inoculation*, 'tis thought, that if he should happen to die one Minute before *Ninety*, these People (if not come to their Wits before) will say, *This Inoculation kill'd him.*

It may, perhaps, a little divert you, to see the Humour on't.

A *Negro*, who pretends he can just remember, that he was *inoculated*, when he was a *Pickaninny*, in his own Country, perhaps thirty Years ago, (and was here under Cure for the *French Pox*, a little while ago) lately grew indispos'd, and was laid in a Room where another *Negro* lay, full of the *Small-Pox* upon him. At first it was confidently affirm'd, that this Fellow had also the *Small-Pox* broke out full upon him; and tho,' till *now*, the mention of a *Negro* (or of any Thing from *Africa*) was hiss'd at, yet *now*, all on a sudden, a *Negro* was become good Authority, and poor *Inoculation* was like to be knock'd on the Head.

But after the Fellow's lying many Days in the infected Chamber, it is impossible to produce the least Eruption of the *Small-Pox* upon him. What is now to be done? Why, they find something of a *Swelling* under his Arm; and some of our D——s cry out, that this is the *Small-Pox*, in the Form, you must Note, of a large *Tumour*; and this *pestilential Form* is also owing to his *Inoculation* in his Infancy.

But among all the *Oppressions*, under which this *new Practice* is a Sufferer among us, the chief comes from a *Scruple of Conscience*, which no doubt, in many People, whose *Hearts* are better than their *Heads*, may be sincere and serious.[42]

They plead, That *the Whole have no Need of a Physician*; and that it is not lawful for me to *make myself sick, when I am well*; and bring a *Sickness* on myself; no, tho' it be to *prevent* a *greater Sickness*. 'Tis to no Purpose to tell them, that they cavil against the Use of all *preventing Physick*; and that they confute themselves as often as they take a *Vomit*, or use a *Blister*; and much more, if they undergo *Salivation* (a Thing a thousand Times worse than the *Dispumation*[43] which is now in Controversy) to prevent a Malady which may be fear'd, but is not actually come upon them; and that they are not *the whole*, while they have the Fuel of the *Small-Pox* lodg'd in them; or are in that *Anxiety of Mind* about it, which is, indeed, an *evil Disease*.

They plead, *That what is now done, is a Thing learnt from the* Heathens; *and it is not lawful for* Christians *to learn the Way of the* Heathen. 'Tis to no Purpose to tell them, that *Hippocrates*, and *Galen* were *Heathen*; and that the Gentleman who invented the blundering (but strangely useful) Composition, call'd *Venice-Treacle*,[44] was an *Heathen*, who was Physician to no better a Man than a *Nero*: And from whom is it that we have our *Mithridate?*[45] And how many noble *Specificks* have we *learnt* from our *Indians?* And from whom did they *learn* to smoak *Tobacco*; or drink *Tea* and *Coffee?*

In fine, (tho' there is *no End* of their Follies) while they have been taught the Clamour, *That we take up this new Thing from the* Turks; [A Mistake; for it comes not from *such*, but from the *Greeks*] Their main Cavil against it, were more fit for the Mouths of *Turks*, and is the very thing that keeps the *Turks* from coming much into it: That God has *decreed when*, and *how* we shall *dye*, and for us to pretend a Remedy that won't fail to *safe our Lives*, and secure us from *Death* by the *Small-Pox*, is to take the *Work of God* out of his Hands. And how do we know, that God will send the *Small-Pox* upon us at all, since there will be some that will escape it, where-ever it comes? 'Tis to no Purpose to attempt their *Instruction*; for if one does, they will quickly, in express Terms, tell him, *You shall never convince me*. But that they may *convince us*, that it is *Religion* which inclines and fixes them, 'tis well if we don't hear them fall to *wishing of Miseries* to them that shall try this *new Practice*, and *railing bitterly* against the most venerable Servants of God in the Land, and giving all the Signs of a *Satanic Energy* upon them. Alas! *Pudet haec opprobria*.[46]

To quiet the Minds of People that would *think soberly*, the Doctor stated *the Case of Conscience* in these Terms,

"Almighty God, in his great Mercy to Mankind, has taught us a *Remedy* to be used, when the Dangers of the *Small-Pox* distress us; upon the Use of which *Medicine*, they shall, in an ordinary Way, be sure to have it not so severely as in the other Way, and consequently, not to be in such Danger of *dying* by this dreadful Distemper; as also to be deliver'd from the *terrible Circumstances* which many of them, who recover of this Distemper, do suffer from it. Whether a Christian may not employ this *Medicine*, (let the *Matter* of it be what it will) and humbly give Thanks to God for his *good Providence*, in discovering it to a miserable World; and humbly look up to his *good Providence* (as we do in the Use of any other *Medicine*) for the Success of it?"

And he thought it Answer enough to say upon it, *It may seem strange, that any Wise Christian cannot answer it.*

Sir, The Reason of my thus giving you the Story of the way to *save the Lives* of People, and *keep them easy too*, from one of the most *formidable Diseases* in the World, thus far practis'd and prosper'd among us, is, because I imagine so considerate and charitable a Mind as yours, may do something to bring it into Consideration, *How far the Thing may be encourag'd in our Nation*, where this Distemper sometimes makes terrible Ravages, and where there are so many Persons of great *Ranks* and *Hopes*, that would be very thankful for some *Assurance of their Lives*, in a Point wherein they will always be *hanging in doubt*, till the *Small-Pox* be over with them.

And then, the Reason of my also giving you the Story of the *Opposition* which the Thing has here met withal, and reporting such *foolish Things* as might be better bury'd in Oblivion, which yet I do without exposing the *Name* of any Person, as if I had been vindictively inclin'd, I might have done; 'tis because it's a thousand to one, that the Thing may meet with the same *Opposition* (for the *Corruptions* and *Weaknesses* of People are the same) on your Side of the Water; and the Knowledge of what has occurr'd, may be of some *Service* to arm you against many of your *Discouragements*. But I shall write a *Treatise*, rather than a *Letter*, if I do not here break off.

I do it with my hearty Wishes, that you may be a great Blessing to the World, and that a World of People may fare the better for you. What better can be wish'd you? By,

S I R,

Boston, in *New-England,*
Sept. 7, 1721.   *Your hearty Friend,*
                                   and Servant.

DIARY (NOVEMBER 14, 1721)

[ASSASSINATION ATTEMPT ON COTTON MATHER]

Towards three a Clock in the Night, as it grew towards Morning of this Day, some unknown Hands, threw a fired *Granado* into the Chamber where my Kinsman lay, and which used to be my Lodging-Room. The Weight of the Iron Ball alone, had it fallen upon his Head, would have been enough to have done Part of the Business designed. But the *Granado* was charged, the upper part with dried Powder, the lower Part with a Mixture of Oil of Turpentine and Powder and what else I know not, in such a Manner, that upon its going off, it must have splitt, and have probably killed the Persons in the Room, and certainly fired the Chamber, and speedily laid the House in Ashes. But, *this Night there stood by me an Angel of the GOD, whose I am and whom I serve;* and the merciful Providence of GOD my SAVIOUR, so ordered, it that the Granado passing thro' the Window, had by the Iron in the Middle of the Casement, such a Turn given to it, that in falling on the Floor, the fired Wild-fire in the Fuse was violently shaken out upon the Floor, without firing the Granado. When the *Granado* was taken up, there was found a Paper so tied with String about the Fuse, that it might out-Live the breaking of the Shell, which had these words in it; COTTON MATHER, *You Dog, Dam you; I'l inoculate you with this, with a Pox to you.*

MERCANTILISM AND PAPER MONEY

B y the time the Massachusetts Bay Colony lost its old charter (1684), Boston had transformed from a City on a Hill, the center of Puritan New England's covenanted society, into the mercantile capital of English North America, tied into a transatlantic network of trading routes and modes of financial exchange that linked countinghouses and their bills of credit with those of foreign merchants across the hemispheres. Anyone strolling down King's Street to the Long Wharf or south on Ship Street to Clarke's Wharf in Boston Harbor would have encountered English navy ships alongside flotillas of merchant vessels from the Caribbean, the Canaries, the Azores, Portugal, Spain, France, the Low Countries, the Baltic, and even the Ottoman Empire, Madagascar, and as far away as India. Exotic merchandise piling up in Boston's warehouses and displayed in shops became a sight as common as the mariners in foreign dress, speaking unfamiliar tongues, cooped up for weeks on board ship, eagerly seeking to release their pent-up vigor in Boston's taverns and shanties of ill repute. Almost overnight, the Golden Calf in the guise of old mammon seemed to command as much attention as the triune deity who had led the exodus of the patriarchs out of their English Egypt, and yet the leeks and fleshpots of Egypt seemed more alluring than the deserts of their New English Canaan. The Boston of John Cotton and John Winthrop was no more.[1]

Such drastic changes in the economic and moral makeup of Boston's marketplace left neither the clergy nor the metaphors of their public addresses unaffected. The language of commerce easily mingled with the moral allegories of the New Testament that likened the kingdom of heaven to "a merchant man, seeking goodly pearls" (Matt. 13:45). It is fair to argue that Cotton Mather took the gospel of the marketplace one step farther: when the public treasury of the Bay Colony was empty in the wake of Captain William Phips's disastrous campaign against the French enemy in Quebec in October 1690, Mather promoted the introduction of paper money as legal tender during the War of the Grand Alliance (1688–97), also known as King William's War. Demoralized soldiers and sailors demanded their pay, threatening mutiny—and not so much as a single Spanish silver dollar (pieces of eight), or the colony's own Pine Tree shilling, in the state coffers! "There being *Forty Thousand pounds*, more or less, now to be paid," Cotton Mather remembered in his *Pietas in Patriam*, his biography of Sir William Phips, "and not a Penny in the Treasury to pay it withal."[2]

No English colony was allowed to mint its own coinage or print its own paper money—these being jealously guarded prerogatives of the crown. Spanish silver dollars, universally accepted as instruments of exchange, were only used for transatlantic payments, and Massachusetts's illegal minting of its own Pine Tree shilling (1652–86) had been shut down under Andros's administration. What made matters worse, the Glorious Revolution further hampered the flow of money within and outside the colony until such time as William III would grant a new charter (1691) and restore the colonists' titles to the land that Andros had declared null and void. Thus, when Phips's unhappy troops arrived in Boston in late 1690 and demanded their pay, the temporary government under old Simon Bradstreet had nothing to offer them but promissory paper notes, IOUs, to supply their immediate wants. But which merchant would accept such notes backed by the mere promise of an interim government that had neither mandate nor clear legitimacy?

Something drastically new had to be devised to redress this problem. "The *General Assembly*," Mather recounted, "first pass'd an *Act*, for the Levying of such a sum of *Money* as was wanted" (Tax-Act), printed paper bills from "*Copper-Plates*" that could not be counterfeited, and ordered that these bills of credit henceforth "be Accepted by the Treasurer" and subordinate officers "in all

A View of Part of the Town of Boston in New-England . . . 1768 ([1770]), engraving by Paul Revere. (The Mather church is the third church building from the right.) Courtesy of the Norman B. Leventhal Map & Education Center at the Boston Public Library

ND ANDER TISH SHIPS OF WAR LANDING THEIR TROOPS! 1768

Is the Earl of
Hillsborough, His
Majesties Sec'y of State for
America. This VIEW of
the only well-Plan'd
EXPEDITION, formed for
supporting y'e dignity
of BRITAIN
& chastising y'e insolence
of AMERICA, is humbly
scrib'd.

...ups the Harbour and Anchored round the TOWN; their Cannon loaded | A Long Wharf
... the fourteenth & twenty-ninth Regiments, a detachment from the 59th Reg't | B Hancock's Wharf
... their Formed and Marched with insolent Parade, Drums beating & Fifes | C North Battery
...ounds of Powder and Ball.

ENGRAVED PRINTED & SOLD by PAUL REVERE, BOSTON!

publick Payments, at Five *per cent.* more than the Value expressed in them."[3]
This ruse was readily accepted, especially because it allowed holders of these
bills of credit to pay their biennial taxes at a discount. With the value of each
bill set at 5 percent above the amount printed on the bill, the recipient would
gain a shilling on every pound—an outright bargain, if it proved not to be a hollow promise. To sweeten the deal even more, the General Assembly further
stipulated that taxes paid in grain or barley ("country-pay"), the most common
form of tax payment in farming communities, would henceforth be worth
5 percent *less* than if paid with any other specie of monetary value, a double
incentive no doubt for anyone willing to accept paper bills.[4] "And so the *Sailors*
and *Souldiers* put off their *Bills*, instead of *Money*, to those, with whom they
had any Dealings, and they *Circulated* through all the Hands of the Colony,
pretty Comfortably," Mather remembered. Those who were still reluctant to
accept the General Assembly's IOUs as pay or in exchange for goods, especially in light of Whitehall's pending settlement of the new government, were
reassured when some well-heeled Bostonians, most notably the self-made man
Sir William Phips, "cheerfully laid down a Considerable Quantity of *ready Money*
[Spanish pieces of eight] for an equivalent parcel of them" in paper bills. "And
thus in a little time, the Country waded through the Terrible *Debts* which it
was fallen into," Mather related in his biography of Phips, published nine years
after the financial crisis of 1690–91 had been warded off.[5]

At the height of the crisis, however, things did not look as propitious. *Some
Considerations on the Bills of Credit Now passing in New-England* (Boston, 1691),
the next selection, evinces Cotton Mather's public (albeit anonymous) intervention in the dire debt crisis of the day. "*Mr. Treasurer,*" he publicly addressed
Colonel John Phillips, a wealthy Charlestown merchant, magistrate, and treasurer of Massachusetts, who just happened to be Mather's own father-in-law by
his first wife, Abigail Phillips Mather. "You know Sir you and *I* have had some
former Discourse about the *Nature of Mony* That (as such) it is but a *Counter* or
Measure of mens Properties, and Instituted *mean* of permutation." So Mather
entered the fray over bills of credit by theorizing the value and meaning of money.

"As *metal* indeed it is a commodity, Like all other things, that are Merchant-able," he continued. "But as *Mony* it is no more than" the value embossed on it. Yet what should be done if neither silver nor country pay could cover their debts? Thus, "what remains but *Accounts, Bills,* or such like *Paper-pay?* and certainly this necessity may (if *I* mistake not) bring to the whole Country no small advantage." What follows in *Some Considerations* is Mather's enumeration of the benefits for issuing government-backed bills of credit and circulating them as "*Running Cash*" in the colony.

Closely related to the public debt of the Bay Colony was the corruption of the marketplace, the inevitable byproduct of an emerging capitalist market economy in which the ends were justified by the means, the profits of the market by sharp dealings. True, many New England merchants, by no means any more honest than their peers abroad, did resort to cheating, inflated prices, selling inferior quality goods, using false weights and measures, or failing to pay their debts in whole and on time while living beyond their means. Over a twenty-year period, Mather published a number of jeremiads to redress these evils. Most notable among them are *Lex Mercatoria* (Boston, 1705); *Fair Dealing between Debtor & Creditor* (Boston, 1716); and *Theopolis Americana. An Essay on the Golden Street Of the Holy City: Publishing, A Testimony against the Corruptions of the Market-Place* (Boston, 1710).

Excerpted below is *Theopolis Americana,* that is, *The City of God in America,* one of his most imaginative homilies on the pitfalls of the marketplace. Mather preached this sermon to the General Assembly on November 3, 1709, a great honor afforded only to the most distinguished clergymen of Massachusetts. "I fill'd the Sermon with Testimonies for God and Right, and against the Sins of Dishonesty, and the Snares of Intemperance; and added my Hopes for a City of God, yett to be seen in *America*," he remembered in his diary. His homily attracted sufficient attention after publication that *Theopolis Americana* was dispersed "into every Town of all these Colonies; and into some other Parts of *America*."[6] Even his friend Samuel Sewall, with whom Mather shared a mutual interest in millennialism and to whom Mather dedicated his

Theopolis Americana, took the trouble to get a set of unbound sheets from the printer: "I stich'd me up a Book, and sent the Revd Author one to compleat his."[7] What made this work so appealing to Mather's contemporaries?

As in John Bunyan's famous allegory *Pilgrim's Progress* (London, 1678), Mather seemingly guided his Christian Mercator from Vanity Fair to the Celestial City, the millennial New Jerusalem (Rev. 21), which Mather saw manifesting in the chronometry of the Second Coming: "*GLORIOUS Things are Spoken of thee, O thou City of God!* The STREET be in Thee O New-England; *The Interpretation of it*, be unto you, O *American* Colonies." This was how Mather opened his dreamlike vision of America's place during the halcyon days of the millennium. Lest anyone misread his intention, as some modern critics have done who claimed that Boston would be *the* New Jerusalem of John's Revelation, he made sure to point out that "the **Street** here means, and so it may be translated, *The* **Market-Place**; the Place where the Affairs of Trade bring together a Concourse of People."[8] The business of the marketplace, Mather emphasized, must be conducted with integrity, "without *Corruption*" or "*Base* Dealing." For the "Street" of the New Jerusalem is as "*Transparent Glass*" and made of "**Pure Gold**," so that all the godly "shall be willing to have their very Hearts *Look'd into*."

No jeremiad came without a list of grievances threatening punishment, and no tongue-lashing without comforting hope to regain God's blessings. And like Jeremiah of old, Mather addressed the elected representatives of the colony, magistrates, wealthy merchants, Governor Joseph Dudley, and all the movers and shakers of the colony: "I have a Commission that Ennables me, and Emboldens me, to say among you; **Wo, Wo, Wo,** to you Professors, and **Hypocrites**, who can make a Show of this and that Piety and *Purity*; but can *Cheat*, and *Cousen* [i.e., "cozen," or deceive], and *Oppress*, and *Wrong* other People in your Dealing with them!" Stark words these, no doubt, as Mather devoted the better part of fifty printed pages to bewail Ichabod, for the glory had departed from their great experiment in the wilderness. And yet, true to the ancient prophets, Mather could not but strike a more hopeful tone toward the end of his discourse: "There are many Arguments to perswade us, That our Glorious LORD, will have an **Holy City in AMERICA**; a *City*, the **Street** whereof will be *Pure* **Gold**."

SOME CONSIDERATIONS ON THE BILLS OF CREDIT (1691)

Mr. Treasurer,[9]

I Am told, and am apt to believe it, That the Exchequer in *Silver* Runs very Low; Nor can *I* think that the Country in General is much better furnished. 'Twas an honest and good method you took, to pay by *Bonds* what you could not by *Ready Cash.* I therefore cannot a little wonder at the great indiscretion of our Countrymen who Refuse to accept that, which they call *Paper-mony,* as pay of equal value with the best *Spanish* Silver. What? is the word *Paper* a scandal to them? Is a *Bond* or *Bill-of-Exchange* for 1000*l*,[10] other than *Paper?* and yet is it not as valuable as so much Silver or Gold, supposing the Security of payment be sufficient? If the Countries *Debts* must be paid (as I believe they must, and *I* am sure in justice they ought) whatever change of Government shall come, then the *Country* must make good the *Credit,* or *more Taxes* must be still Raised, till the publick Debts be Answered. *I* say, the Country, and not the *Gentlemen* who *Administer* the Government, who are but the *Countries Agents* in this Affair. *All the Inhabitants* of the Land, taken as one Body are the *Principals,* who Reap the *Benefits,* and must bear the *Burden,* and are the Security in their *Publick Bonds.* What do the Gentlemen get, but their labour for their pains, and perhaps not a little Obloquie into the bargain? can all their *Estates* (with all their *Gains,* if there were any) bear the *Charge of Government* for the whole Land? no, no, it cannot be supposed. If any murmur at their management as ill, and that they have needlesly drawn the Charges upon us; pray tell them, as long as they enjoy the *Choice of Administrators,* they must bear what's *past,* and right themselves for the *future,* by chusing better next, if they know where to find them. So Merchants do with their Factors, and 'tis their only Remedy.

You know Sir you and *I* have had some former Discourse about the *Nature of Mony* That (as such) it is but a *Counter* or *Measure* of mens Properties, and Instituted *mean* of permutation. As *metal* indeed it is a commodity, Like all other things, that are Merchantable. But as *Mony* it is no more than what was said, And had it's *Original* from a general ignorance of Writing and Arithmetick; But now these Arts being commonly known may well Discharge *many* from the conceited Necessity thereof in Humane Traffick. Is not *Discount* in Accounts current good pay? Do not *Bills* Transmit to Remote Parts, vast summs without the intervention of *Silver?* Are not *Taxes* paid and received by *mutual Credit* between the Government requiring the Country to give them Credit where-with to pay the Countries Debts, and then again receive the same Credit of the Country as good pay? 'Tis strange that in the mean-while; between the *Governments* paying the People, and the *Peoples* paying the Government: The Governments (or rather the *Countries*) *Bills* should not pass between *Man and Man.* 'Tis strange that one Gentlemans Bills at *Port-Royal* for divers years, and that among For-reigners; or another Gentlemans *Bills* in the Western Parts for as many or more years should gain so much Credit as to be current pay, among the Traders in those places; yea, That the Bill (as *I* have heard) of any *one Magistrate* in the *Western English Plantation,* shall buy any Commodities of any of the Planters; and yet our people (in this pure air) be so sottish as to deny Credit to the Government, when 'tis of their own *Chusing:* Had the *single Gentlemen* (above named) as good bottom for their Credit in their *Ware-houses,* and are not the whole *Estates* of the *Massachusets* as good? Is the Security of one Plantation-Magistrate, better than that of *All* the *Massachusets Representatives?* can that one *Magistrate* give force to the Contracts, and cannot *All our Government* do the same.

Certainly Sir were not peoples Heads Idly bewhizled with Conceits that we have no *Magistrates,* no *Government,* And by Consequence, that we have no *Security* for any thing which we call our own (a *Consequence*) they will be Loth to allow, though they cannot help it, If once we are Reduced to *Hobs* his state of *Nature,*[11] which (says he) is a *state of War,* and then the *strongest* must *take all*) I say if such foolish conceits were not Entertained, there would not be the least Scruple in accepting your Bills as Currant Pay.

If you should require the Country to pay their *Taxes in Silver,* that so you might be enabled to bear the Charges of the Government by Silver, when such quantity of it as is needful for that purpose cannot be had in the Country, or at least not in any proportion to be procured, unless men (according to the Proverb) should *Buy Gold too Dear,* and so Ruinously undervalue the fruits of their Labours; and their Lands. This were to require men to *Make Bricks without Straw.* . . .

If neither *Silver* can be had, nor *Corn* brought in without loss both to the Government and People, what remains but *Accounts, Bills,* or such like *Paper-pay?* and certainly this necessity may (if *I* mistake not) bring to the whole Country no small advantage; for

1. Is there not hereby 40000*l Running Cash* in the Country more than *ever was,* If mens folly hinder not its Currency? yea and more than they are *ever like* to have, so long as they cannot keep Silver in the Country, which they will never do while the *Europaean Trade* continues, and that is like to be as long as we are a people. *Silver* in *New-England* is like the water of a *swift Running River,* always coming, and as fast going away; one (in its passage) dips a Bucket-full, another a Dish or Cup-full for his occasions; but if the *Influx* of plate from the *West-Indies* be stopt but for a little while, and the *Efflux* in Returns for *England*

continue; will not the Mill-pond be quickly drained, so as neither Bucket nor Cup can dip its fill? Whereas on the contrary,

2. This our *Running* Cash is an *abiding Cash*: for no man will carry it to another Country, where it will not pass; but rather use it here, where it will (or at least) *ought*: and then only the *Growths of the Country* will be carried off, and that will be no Damage but rather an Advantage to us.

3. If this be made Currant, the *Credit* of the Colony will *rise* to the utmost height of its ability on all Extraordinary Emergencies; whereas otherwise you may be quickly Distressed; for if the Soldiers cannot put off their Pay to Supply their necessities, who will hereafter serve the Country in their greatest Dangers, and if the Merchants cannot Buy as well as Sell for Credit, how shall they carry on their Trades? and how shall they lend upon great occasions if the Countries Bill lie dead on their hands? surely they'l no more trust the Country, whatever suddain need we should have, unless on the bare consideration of their own Security. . . .

A better way (in my opinion) to make the *Credit passable* without Interruption, is,

1. To Raise the Rates of those above the *common Standard*, whom you catch Tardy in Debasing the Credit of your bills either by purchasing them with little mony; or selling commodities for them at Excessive dearer Rates:

2. Let all refusers to receive them have forthwith their *Taxes* demanded in *Silver*, nor let them have the benefit of paying *them*, who will not also Receive them. And in the like manner several such, as shall at any time reproach them as a *Grand Cheat*. Who is but *They*, that makes 'em so.

3. What if the *General Court* Declare by a Law, that if any man tender these Bills for payment of his Debts, to be accepted at their full value, which the Country has put upon them; If any private person will not receive them so, That then the Government will not concern themselves for the recovery of those Debts, till all the *Publick Debts* are discharged. It is a known Maxim of Law in *England* (and I think in all other Countrys) that *of Debts, The Kings must be first paid*. And great reason for it; for why shall the Government secure *others Debts* by Law; and not *their own*? now if these refusers stay for their Debts till the Country be first serv'd they may stay till they are weary. And if hereafter they resolve to make no more *Debts* (for fear of this Law) I believe their Trading will be very dull. Whereas (on the Contrary) If they shall accept the *Bills*, 'tis probable their Debts will come in apace; their Trading will revive, and the Countries Credit become Currant. . . .

These are my present thoughts, which you may communicate as you see cause; mean while please to accept them as Really intended for the Publick good. By a well *wisher* to *New-England* & your *Humble Servant*. &c.

THEOPOLIS AMERICANA (1710)

Pure Gold in the Market-Place.[12]
Rev. XXI. 21.
The Street of the City was Pure Gold.

GLORIOUS *Things are Spoken of thee, O thou City of God!* The STREET be in Thee, O New-England; *The Interpretation of it,* be unto you, O *American* Colonies.

The Invitation, sounds Angelically; But my Hearers must have it now given them; *Come hither, and I will show you,* an admirable Spectacle! 'Tis an Heavenly CITY, *descending out of Heaven,* from GOD. There is an Heavenly CITY, which the Great GOD, has *Prepared* for them, to whom *He will be a God:* A CITY to be inhabited by an *Innumerable Company of Angels,* and by the *Spirits of Just Men made Perfect* by a Resurrection from the Dead, with JESUS *the Mediator of the New Covenant* shining upon them: A CITY; where *God shall dwell with men, God Himself shall be with them,* and we shall *Inherit all things.* There will be a Time, when that *Holy City,* will be nearer to this *Earth,* than it is at this Day; and the *Saved Nations* of the *Earth* shall after a wonderful manner *Walk in the Light* thereof. . . .

But shall we not imagine, that there will be then to be seen on the *Earth,* some sweet Reflections of the *Light,* which the *City of Glorified Saints* will shed down upon it? Yes; Tis not ill done by those Interpreters [*Provided always,* they do not Exclude the *Principal Intention,* which they are too apt to do!] I say, Tis not Ill done by them, who in the Vision that is now before us, look to find the **State of the Church on Earth**, after the Approaching Fall of Antichrist. . . . There will be a Time, when *Jerusalem* shall be Literally Rebuilt, and People *all over the World* shall be under the Influences of that Holy *City.—Orbis erit.*[13] The CHURCH of God, *all over the World,* shall in some sort be the *City.*

One incomparable Glory of the **City**, is now singled out for our present Meditation. **The Street of the City is Pure Gold.** I concur with *Peganius,*[14] and conceive, That the **Street** here means, and so it may be translated, *The* **Market-Place**; the Place where the Affairs of Trade bring together a Concourse of People. The meaning it, The *Business* of the CITY, shall be managed by the *Golden* Rule. The Things that use to be done in the *Market-Place,* shall be done without *Corruption.* There shall be no *Base* Dealing in it. It is added, It is *as it were Transparent Glass:* That is, The Dealing shall be so *Honest,* that it shall bear to be *Look'd* into; it shall be so *Sincere,* that men shall be willing to have their very Hearts *Look'd into.* There shall be no *False-Dealing:* All shall be done with all possible *Integrity.* . . .

The Thing which I am to *Observe*, is, That in a CITY of GOD, the **Street** will be **Pure Gold.** The *Business* transacted in the **Market-Place** of an *Holy City*, will have a *Golden*, that is to say, a *Gracious* Character upon it. *Golden* Proceedings, that is to say, *Godly* ones, will be found in the **Market-Place** of a CITY, which the Son of God, has favour for.

My **Doctrine** is Written on the *Conscience* of all People, *as with a Pen of Iron.* I Preach no other *Doctrine*, than what will be defended by many more than a Thousand *Preachers* at this Instant in the Congregation. The *Conscience* in every one of the Hearers, will Oblige him to Consent unto it. CON-SCIENCE, Do thou thine Office; *Run thou to and fro, thro' the Street* of our City, and make men to Know, If *Judgment* and *Truth* do not Reign in the **Market-Place**, the Holy SON of GOD, will not Favour it, or *Pardon* it! If a *Scripture* must be quoted on the occasion, take that One instead of a Thousand; Jer. 31. 23. *They shall use this speech in the Land of Judah, and in the Cities thereof, The Lord Bless thee, O Habitation of Righteousness, and Mountain of Holiness.* The *Blessed* CITY, is that, in the **Street** whereof, *Righteousness* and *Holiness* has an *Habitation*; a **Market-Place** of *Righteousness*, a *Mountain* of *Holiness.* Oh! May such a *Speech be used* in this our Land! *Grant it, Oh! Grant it, Thou God of our Salvation!*—But the Lord calls upon us; *Get thee up!* Do thy part, that it may be so.

The Thing which I am then to *Enquire*, is;

> *What is to be done, that the* **Street** *of our City, may be Pure* **Gold?** And, What have we to do in our **Market-Place**, that so our Great SAVIOUR, may *Espouse* us for, *A City of God*, and become our *Saviour*?

The Enquiry shall be answered with *Faithful Sayings.* Oh! Let them find *All Acceptation.*

I. Oh! That the **Street** may be full of *Good Men!* Full of *Righteous & Holy* Ones. It is but an Easy *Metonymie*, to make the **Street**, signify the *Men* that fill the *Street.* Our **Street** will be Pure **Gold**, when they that walk in it, are those that may be called, *The Precious Sons of Zion, Comparable to fine Gold.* There is a Work of GRACE, which is wrought by the Holy Spirit of God, in the Minds of His Chosen People. Tis in one word, the Glorious *Image of God* revived in the Soul. A *Good Work in the Soul*, is the Name, which the Sacred Oracles put upon it. This **Grace** of God is called, Rev. 3. 18. *Gold tried in the Fire.* Yea, *Grace* is better than *Gold.* . . .

O Lovely Work! O Matchless Work! A *Work*, which for ever changes into *Gold*, the Metal which it is wro't upon! There are some, who often *Examine* themselves, Whether such a *Work* be produced in them. Oh! Let every one of us do so! My Friend, Thou art yet a Stranger to the *Work*, if thou do it not. But the Issue and Result of the *Examination* sometimes is that; Job. 23. 10. *When He hath Tried me, I shall come forth as Gold.*

And now; the **Street** of the CITY, is *Pure* **Gold**, when the *Street* is filled with *Regenerate Christians*; with men that have the **Grace** of GOD, shining in them. O *Golden City*; where the Angels of God may look down on the **Market-Place**, and say, *There is a Glorious Work of GOD on the Souls of the People that are walking there.* The *Neapolitan Poet* sings of his Beautiful City *Naples*, It was *doubtless dropt down from Heaven!* The Inclinations of the Citizens, in so near a Neighbourhood of the flaming *Vesuvio* too; would make one fear, lest it ere long *drop down into Hell!* But how much rather may the Elegy of an *Heavenly Original* be ascribed, where the Citizens are generally *Bound for Heaven! Oh! Holy SPIRIT of God and Grace; Make thy Sanctifying Work very frequent among us! Thou, Thou art He, who Leadest into a Land of Rectitude!* Oh! Let our People generally breathe after this Work; Do so; Seek it; Get it; *O all ye People; Every one of you!* . . .

II. The **Street** must have no *Dirty Ways* of *Dishonesty* in it. I beseech you, Sirs; Let there be none but *Just* and *Fair* Dealings in the **Market-Place.** Let all the Actions of the **Market-Place** be carried on with a *Golden* Equity and Honesty regulating of them.

I should be very unworthy to stand here, if I should be *Afraid of Dealing Plainly* with you. God and Men demand, that *Plain Dealing* be used, when *Fair-Dealing* is to be insisted on.

Sirs, NEW-ENGLAND is a Countrey, that has made a more than ordinary *Profession* of Religion. Our *Profession* is *Weigh'd* in the *Balances* of GOD. If there be any thing Defective, in the *Honesty* of our Dealing with one another, our *Profession* will have a woful MENE TEKEL Written upon it. Let a man be never such a Professor and Pretender of *Religion*, if he be not a *Fair-Dealer.* **That Mans Religion is Vain.** A Noise about *Faith & Repentance*, among them that forget **Moral Honesty**, tis but an Empty Noise. The men are utter Strangers to *Faith* and *Repentance;* God will *Reject all their Confidences*, of their being, **The People of God,** and they shall *not Prosper in them.* I have a Commission that Ennables me, and Emboldens me, to say among you; **Wo, Wo, Wo,** to you Professors, and **Hypocrites**, who can make a Show of this and that Piety and *Purity;* but can *Cheat*, and *Cousen*, and *Oppress*, and *Wrong* other People in your Dealing with them!

It is true, I must believe, that *New-England* is not worse than other Places; There is more *Ill-Dealing*, I believe, in most other Places. Men will say so, that speak Unpassionately and Impartially, and that knows this *Wicked World.* But,

O NEW-ENGLAND; There are a *Thousand* Reasons, why thou shouldest be Better than *Other Places*; A more Glorious *Land of Uprightness!* And it must be Acknowledged, That there have been Instances of *Ill-Dealing* among us, which have given horrid *Scandal;* Never, Never can the *Ill People* make a Reparation to their Countrey, for the *Scandal* and Censure and Reproach, they have brought upon it. O All you *Lovers of Truth;* Join with me this Day, in a Detestation of their *Evil Doings;* And as the Servant of God, *rent his Garments,* and *fell upon his Knees,* and *spread out his Hands* before the Lord his God, when he was told of some *Evil Doings* among His People; say with him; Ezra. 9. 6. *O my God, I am ashamed, and I blush to lift up my Face unto thee, my God.* If any *Professors* of Religion have done *Ill Things,* yet RELIGION, What has *that* done? RELI-GION shall wash her Fair Hands, and *Abhor* your Doings. Be it Proclaimed unto All the World, **Ill-Dealings** are not at all Countenanced; no, they are vehemently Disallowed, by the **Religion** of NEW-ENGLAND. We do PROTEST against them, with a transporting Vehemency, and behold with Agony the *Blood,* and the *Grace,* of our Great SAVIOUR, abused in them, with most aggravated Violations.

But I have certain MOTIONS to make; and I assure my self, that all the Good Men in the Countrey will concur to the making of them.

The **First** Thing, for which I move, is, That the **Golden Rule of Charity** may Operate, in all the *Dealings* of the **Market-Place.** Then will the **Street** be *Pure Gold,* when every thing is done in it, with an Eye to the *Golden Rule* of *Charity.* I am not versed in the Niceties and Mysteries of the **Market-Place.** But I am acquainted with a **Golden Rule,** which, I am sure, would mightily Rectify all our *Dealings* there. Tis that; Mat. 7. 12. *All things whatsoever ye would, that men should do to you, do ye even so to them.* A Rule own'd among *Pagans* as well as *Christians;* A Rule, by *Nature* Engraven on the mind of Man, and as readily confessed as any Principle of the *Mathematicks:* A Rule, which well attended, would soon turn this forlorn World, from an *Aceldama*[15] into a *Paradise.* *Christians,* Tis a *Rule* for you in all your *Dealings,* To think, *Should my Neighbour deal with me as I now deal with him, would I not think my self hardly dealt withal.* Don't sleight this *Rule;* Don't throw it by as an Useless one; You forfeit the Name of, **Christians,** if you do. I can tell the Name of a *Roman Emperor,* who would on such a Provocation have ordered, that you should not be called, **Christians,** any more.

That this *Rule* may have its *Perfect work of Charity,* Remember that Application of it; 1 Cor. 10. 24. *Let no man seek* (only) *his own, but every man anothers Wealth.* *Charitably* aim at the Benefit of *Other men,* as well as *Your own,* in your *Dealings* with them. Sir, Be willing that your *Neighbour* should be Benefited, and Encouraged, as well as *Your self.* Yea, *Desire* that he may; *Contrive* that he may. I cam certain, they will do so in the **Street** of the CITY of GOD! . . .

This were *Pure* **Gold!** Were this **Golden Rule** generally regarded, there would need no *Laws* to force men to be *Honest*; the *Courts* would have but few *Causes* brought unto them. The *Christians* which often, often *Reflect* upon this RULE, and always *Conform* unto it, verily, They are **Golden** Ones; God increase the Number of them.

The **Second** Thing for which I move, is, That all **Frauds** in our *Dealings* of all sorts, may be the *Abomination* of all that have any thing to do in the **Market-Place.** All such Things as by the Irregular & Inordinate *Love of Gold*, men are too often betray'd into! Of the various Methods, wherein men *Deal Dishonestly* with one another, in the **Market-Place**, and particularly, **False Weights and Measures**, we read, Deut. 25. 16. *All that do such things, and all that do Unrighteously, are an abomination unto the Lord thy God.* May they *Likewise*, and *Therefore*, be an *Abomination* unto you, O People of the LORD.

As now;

For men to **Lye** to one another, in Dealing with one another; *Tis an Abomination!* It was required; Lev. 19. 11. *Ye shall not Steal, neither deal Falsly, neither Lye to one another.*

For men to putt off *Adulterated* or *Counterfeited* Wares; or, for men to work up their Wares *Deceitfully*; When the **Fish** is naught; the **Tar** has undue mixtures; there is Dirt & Stone instead of **Turpentine**; there are thick Layes of **Salt** instead of other things that should be there; the **Cheese** is not made as tis affirm'd to be; the **Liquor** is not for Quantity or Quality such as was agreed for; the **Wood** is not of the Dimensions that are promised unto the Purchaser; or perhaps, there was a *Trespass* in the place of Cutting it; the **Hay** does not hold out Weight by abundance; the **Lumber** has a false Number upon it; or, the *Bundles* are not as Good *Within* as they are *Without*; Tis an *Abomination!*

For men to *Over-reach* others, because they find them *Ignorant*, or Scrue grievously upon them, only because they are Poor and Low, and in great *Necessities*; to keep up the *Necessaries* of Humane Life, (I say, the *Necessaries*, which I always distinguish from the *Superfluities*,) at an *Immoderate Price*, meerly because other People want them, when we can more easily spare them; *Tis an Abomination!*

For men to *Employ* others, and not *Reward* them according to *Contract*; [A Crime, not at all the less, because the *Minister* is not seldom the *Sufferer* from it!] Or, to with-hold from the *Labourer* his *Wages*, till his *Cry* reach up to Heaven; or break their Faith with their *Creditors*, and keep them out of their *Dues!* *Tis an Abomination!*

To Rob the *Publick Treasury*, by *False Musters*, or any other Articles of Charge falsely given in; or, to Abett the Robbers, by any Assistence or Connivance at such things in *Auditing* their Accompts; This also is a thing to be *Repented* of, where any have been Guilty of it.

I hope, I speak to none, but those that can say; *These are Abominable Things: the Soul of the Lord hates them; And, O my Soul, Do thou also hate them.* I wish, All my People had such a sense of some *Other things*, which I am now going to mention.

But in my way to those *Other Things*, methinks, I am stopped by something like a Dead *Amasa*,[16] lying in the *midst of the High-way* before me.

I hope, the *Merchant*, uses all possible Caution, as well as the Lesser Dealers, to keep clear of that Blemish, Hos. 12. 7. *He is a Merchant, the Balances of Deceit are in his hand; he Loves to Oppress.*

And so well, Sirs, do I wish to your Voyages, that I would Entreat you, that for the *Manning of your Vessels* in this Evil Time, there may be no such *Unfair Methods* used, as may Entail Disasters upon them.

There is one sort of *Trade* also, about which my way of Addressing you, shall be by Reciting the words of the Excellent BAXTER. They are these; [His *Christian Directory*. Part II. Chap. 14.]

"To go as *Pirates*, and Catch up poor *Negroes*, or People of another Land, that have never forfeited Life, or Liberty, and to make them *Slaves*, and Sell them, is One of the worst kinds of Thievery in the World; and such Persons are to be taken for the common Enemies of Mankind; and they that buy them, and use them as *Beasts*, for their meer Commodity, and betray, or destroy, or neglect their Souls, are fitter to be called, *Incarnate Devils*, than *Christians*, tho' they be no *Christians* whom they so Abuse."[17]

I will go on to say; When we have *Slaves* in our Houses, we are to treat them with *Humanity*; we are so to treat them that their *Slavery* may really be their *Happiness*; Yea, in our treating of them, there must be nothing but what the Law of CHRIST will Justify. Above all, we are to do all we can to *Christianize* them. I will again give you the Words of my Honoured BAXTER.

"So use them, as to preserve Christs Right and Interest in them. Those that keep their *Negro's* and Slaves, from Hearing of Gods Word, and from becoming Christians, because, they shall then lose part of their Service, do openly profess Rebellion against God, and contempt of Christ the Redeemer of Souls, and a contempt of the Souls of Men, and indeed, they declare, that their Worldly profit, is their Treasure and their God."[18]

Fidelity to the cause of *Righteousness*, obliges me, to take Notice of One thing more.

If there be any *English* People, who are concerned with our *Christianized Indians*, but then take advantage of their *Ignorance*, or their *Indigence*, or their
unchristian *Love of the Bottel*;[19] and then use Indi-
rect and Oppressive ways, to Exact an *Unreasonable Satisfaction* from them, and
Sell them for Servants, or *Send* them out of their own Country; This Trade, will
be a Reproach to our *Christianity*, and I am sure, it will be *Bitterness in the Latter End*. Certainly, our *Justices* will concern themselves to Rebuke and Prevent
such Doings, lest the Guilt become so *Publick*, as to provoke the Justice of Heaven
to Revenge it, by *Indian* Depredations.

The **Third** Thing for which I move, is; That there may not be so much as
any **Tendency** to any thing *Oppressive* or *Injurious*, in the *Dealings* of the **Market-
Place**. The thing for which I bring a very pressing Exhortation, is that; 1 Thes.
5. 22. *Abstain from all Appearance of Evil*. If any thing *Approach* to a thing, that
Appears an *Evil*; Sirs, Beware of it! There are Some *Ill Things*, too frequently
done among those who would count themselves greatly *Wrong'd*, if they be not
thought *Good People*. But they are things which anon, I am sure, prove a notorious *Wrong* to many others, that really are *Good People*.

I will be free with you. There are *Crooked Things* that cannot be *Numbred*; I
wish, they could be *Streightned*.

I conceive, There are some of them, in certain *Extortions*, used by some of
them, who let out *Money* upon *Interest*. I mean, when they make People pay
Interest, for a Sum, that really never was in their Hands; As it is, when the Usu-
rer immediately takes into his own, the whole first years *Interest*, at the Instant
of his Letting out the Money.

I will go on to say. 'Tis a Thing of an *Evil Tendency*, for People to Live *beyond
themselves*, or to take it for granted, that they must brave it out with such a *Table*,
or with such an *Habit*, tho' they have not wherewithal to bear the Expences of
it; They won't take in a *Reef* of their *Sails*, tho' they are on the point of Suffering *Ship-wreck*; tho' they must borrow, and defraud, and Whiffle, and hurt other
People, to Support their Vanity. How contrary, How contrary, is this, to that *Poverty of Spirit*, which must be found in all, that would have a claim to a part in
the *Golden City*!

'Tis a thing of an *Evil Tendency*, for People to Run into *Debt*, when they know,
they can't Run *out of it*, as well and as fast, as they Run *into it*; so they Spend
what is none of *their Own*; They Forget that Precept, *Owe nothing to any man,
but to Love one another*.[20]

'Tis a thing of an *Evil Tendency*, for People to go from year to year, without
Settling their Accounts; to Jog on in a blind Confusion, and not know how much
they may be *gone back-ward*, or whether they have any thing, they may call, *Their*

Own, or no. If they would have done like *Honest Men*, their *Insolvency* should have been ingenuously Confessed some years ago!

And then, sometimes People that *Break*, deal not so fairly, so truly, so justly with their *Injured Creditors*, as they ought to do. Perhaps there are *Indirect Wayes* taken, to *Cover* from other Men, what justly belongs unto them. . . .

I have been Surprised at the Reading of a Passage in a Pagan Writer, who flourished more than Fifteen Hundred years ago. Tis *Ælian*,[21] a Grecian Writer, who sayes, That in Times long preceding his, there was a Tradition, that *Europe* and *Asia* and *Africa*, were encompassed by the Ocean; But without and beyond the Ocean, there was a *great Island*, as big as *They*. And in that Other World, there was an huge CITY, called, Ευσεβης. **The Godly City.** In that **City**, Says he, they enjoy all Possible *Peace* and *Health*, and *Plenty*: And, he Says, *They are without Controversy a very Righteous People*; So *Righteous*, that they have God marvellously coming down among them. I know not what well to make of a Tradition so very *Ancient*, and yet having such an *American* Face upon it. All I will say, is thus much. There are many Arguments to perswade us, That our Glorious LORD, will have an **Holy City in AMERICA**; a *City*, the **Street** whereof will be *Pure* **Gold.** [We cannot imagine, that the brave Countries and Gardens which fill the *American Hemisphere*, were made for nothing but a *Place for Dragons*.][22] We may not imagine, That when the *Kingdom* of God is *come*, and His *Will is done on Earth as it is done in Heaven*, which we had never been taught to Pray for, if it must not one day be accomplished, a *Ballancing Half of the Globe*, shall remain in the Hands of the *Devil*, who is then to be *Chained up* from *deceiving the Nations*. Has it not been promised unto our Great Saviour? Psal. 2. *I will give thee the uttermost parts of the Earth for thy Possession.* And, Psal. 86. 9. *All Nations whom thou hast made, shall come and worship before thee, O Lord, and shall glorify thy Name.* And, has it not been promised? Mal. 1. 11. *From the Rising of the Sun even unto the going down of the same, my Name shall be great among the Gentiles.* AMERICA is Legible in these Promises.

BIBLICAL HERMENEUTICS

Cotton Mather's interpretation of the scriptures, including his late translation of the psalter, must be framed by his commitment to new ways of understanding God's word in light of the philosophical and scientific challenges emerging in Europe. Mather welcomed state-of-the-art directions in biblical scholarship and tried to square them in ways that would add to, or at least not jeopardize, the old. His employment of fresh ideas is particularly apparent in his *Psalterium Americanum* (1718) and, most of all, in his *Biblia Americana*, his massive commentary on all books of the Bible.

Metrical Psalm- and hymn-singing occupied an important place in New England's homes, schoolhouses, and congregations from the arrival of the Pilgrims in 1620 to the late eighteenth century, when more polite European church music at last eclipsed such old mainstays as Thomas Sternhold and John Hopkins's *The Whole Booke of Psalmes* (London, 1562); Henry Ainsworth's *The Book of Psalmes* (Amsterdam, 1612); and, most of all, *The Whole Booke of Psalmes* (Cambridge, Mass., 1640)—the first book printed in the Bay Colony. Better known by its moniker *The Bay Psalm Book*, this psalter was translated into common meter by a committee of revered clergymen and soon replaced all other psalters in use in New England. It had gone through at least fifty editions by the middle of the eighteenth century.[1] Yet impeccably translating Hebrew poetry into idiomatic English without compromising the original metaphors, meter, and rhythm is a high art few people could muster, then as now. The translators of

The Bay Psalm Book acknowledged the near impossibility of their task and opted for accuracy rather than harmony: "If therefore the verses are not alwayes so smooth and elegant as some may desire or expect," they averred, "let them consider that Gods Altar needs not our pollishings."[2]

Singing the Lord's song in a strange land according to divine will (and human ability) may have satisfied the needs of the early settlers. But by the time Cotton Mather offered his own translation of the Psalms in blank verse, his *Psalterium Americanum*, New England's congregations were feuding over whether singing according to musical notes should be taught in church, especially to the younger generation, or whether the old version of the founders was still good enough and more comforting to the older members of the flock. A clear division between the citified elites, with exposure to the art of caroling to the tunes of stylish music, and the conservative countryside, unwilling to hang their harps upon the willows, engulfed the choristers in a cacophonous give-and-take that elicited a small handful of pamphlets on either side.[3]

For his part, Cotton Mather was clearly dissatisfied with the low performance skill of psalmody in his own family and among his flock; in fact, he frequently felt the need to omit it altogether.[4] His nephew Reverend Thomas Walter of Roxbury, Massachusetts, was more outspoken and complained in his *The Grounds and Rules of Music* (Boston, 1721) that "Our Tunes are, for want of a Standard to appeal to in all our Singing, left to the Mercy of every unskilful Throat to chop and alter, twist and change according to the infinitely diverse and no less odd Humours and Fancies" of the congregants.[5] Walter's pamphlet, accompanied by sample musical notations, was endorsed by no less than fifteen prominent Boston ministers, merchants, and magistrates, ostensibly to underscore the urgency of the reform.

Even a cursory perusal of Mather's introduction to his *Psalterium Americanum* clearly demonstrates that "regular singing" according to notes was not the sole purpose of improving psalmody. Much more important to him was what he called *"The Affectual way"* of singing the psalter, for the metrical rhythm of the Psalms, coupled with the sonorous chanting of the tune, was to have the singers feel the Holy Spirit's *"Impressions* on the *Affections"* of King David, who composed his songs when filled with a divine afflatus. This goal, Mather felt, could best be accomplished in a blank-verse translation without the *"little Jingle at the end of the Line."* To his thinking, most previous translators who preferred a rhymed version *"left out* much of that which the Holy SPIRIT has provided for us, and *put in* much more that is none of His Provision."[6]

Reading the Bible resolutely and unceasingly was central to the faithful in Mather's day but especially to young students who wished to embrace the ministry. His *Manuductio ad Ministerium* (1726), a popular handbook for the education of young divinity students, offered hands-on advice in all matters of theoretical and practical education. The brief selection included here shows Mather's abiding concern with what he called the *"Porismatic Way"* of reading, that is, dwelling on each grammatical unit and inferring the spiritual impulse behind the meaning that God is to have intended when He inspired His prophets to write it down. To be sure, the historical, contextual, and lexical meanings of a sentence or paragraph were not the primary goals; they were merely the scaffolding on which the pious were to raise their affections and to let their *"Heartstrings"* resound to the music of the spheres. More than mere rational understanding by itself, affective reading—that is, the emotional absorption of the mystical spirit—was to sway the faculties of the will and action.

Biblia Americana (1693–1728) is Cotton Mather's grandest and most significant work among both his published and his unpublished writings. Composed over a period of more than thirty years but not published until the early twenty-first century, it is the Western Hemisphere's first synoptic commentary on the entire Bible. Yet unlike the expositions of his more famous European peers, *Biblia Americana* united in one gigantic organon the best of the scientific, philosophical, and hermeneutical debates that impacted traditional biblical interpretation in the seventeenth and early eighteenth centuries. Mather accomplished his task by synthesizing the new theories of his day and harmonizing them with conservative explanations in lengthy essays attached to the cruxes of each book, chapter, and verse. It is no exaggeration to call *Biblia Americana* America's first encyclopedic commentary on the entire Bible and related texts.

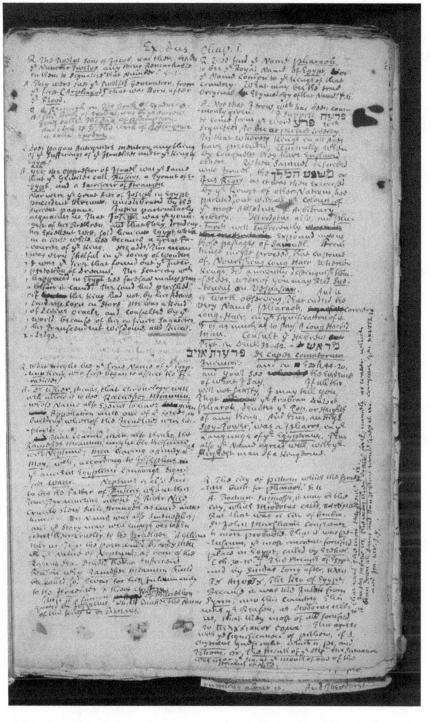

Biblia Americana, holograph manuscript (1693–1728), Exodus, chap. 1. Collection
of the Massachusetts Historical Society, Boston

Our first selection from *Biblia Americana* is an unusual explication of the Mosaic hexameron in terms of ancient Greek atomism, the materialist theory devised by Democritus and Leucippus, propagated by Epicurus and Lucretius, and revived in the Renaissance, that all matter consists of indivisible particles. Through the rediscovery of Lucretius's lost poem *De Rerum Natura* (first century BCE) in a German monastery in 1417, atomism, the theory that all matter in the universe consists of minute indivisible building blocks or particles (atoms), and of divisible corpuscles (molecules), became a foundational concept in the works of such seventeenth-century philosophers as René Descartes, Thomas Hobbes, Pierre Gassendi, Robert Boyle, Sir Isaac Newton, and many others. Cotton Mather in faraway America was no exception, except that he argued, with assistance from an English colleague, that the divine lawgiver Moses—if rightly understood—was the first atomist from whom the Greeks had stolen their philosophy. The Creator God had taught atomism to Adam in paradise, so the argument went, whose descendants dispersed this ancient knowledge, the *prisca theologia,* or pristine theology, in the religions of all peoples, albeit in corrupted form. Moses restored this knowledge to its original state. Thus, the terminology used in Moses's creation account—if properly translated—was nothing else but atomism writ large. With *Physica Vetus & Vera* (London, 1702) at his side, a huge Latin tome by the English alchemist Edmund Dickinson, M.D. (1624–1707), Mather rewrote the Mosaic story in atomist terms for each of the six consecutive days.

The creator instructed our progenitors in paradise in the principles of the corpuscular philosophy, Mather asserted, and taught them that miniscule corpuscles, or atoms, were the building blocks of all matter and the keys of nature. Although invisible to the naked eye, these atoms were neither *"Absolutely Indivisible"* nor all of the same shape or size. When God formed universal matter out of nothing, these particles at first were totally disordered, unformed, and separated by "empty Spaces" between them. God's spirit imprinted on these particles a concourse of motion, "that *Force* which we call *Nature,*" and directed atoms of the same agreeable size and figure "to join, and stick together, in *Bodies.*" They gradually cohered into a vast mass of molecules. Through the centrifugal motion that separated the atoms and corpuscles of diverging shape from one another, God allowed these *"Pilulae"* (little pills), *"Globuli"* (globules), *"Bracteo-lae"* (leaflike parts shaped like sticks), and "a Fourth sort, of a grosser Consistence," to form the four elements of fire, water, air, and earth. Fire and light came into existence when the *pilulae* (small, round, subtle, and swiftly flying) separated from the other corpuscles; water was formed when the *globuli* (less subtle and larger in size) separated from the grosser molecules of different contours; air took shape when the *bracteolae* were allowed to move freely with plenty of space between them; finally, the element earth, by its very constitution denser, heavier, and amorphous, was distinguished from all the others. From these elements compounded into different molecules God shaped the whole universe.

But how come these building blocks were not mentioned in the Mosaic hexameron? The word "atom" was known by different names to different peoples, Mather argued. For what the Greek philosopher Democritus called "atoms," some called "waters," "sand," "dust," or "particles." What the Greek philosopher Thales called "water," Pherecydes called "earth," and so forth. What about the original among the Hebrews? "If we should particularly instance in, *Hyle* [matter, chaos], as the *Egyptians* called it, or, *Ile*, as the *Phoenicians*," we do not find exactly the same term in Genesis, nor should we expect to find "all the *Terms of Art*" used in the same way. "And yett it is very probable, That *Hyle*, or *Ile*," which signifies earth, clay, or sand, "may be found in the Hebrew /חול/ *Hhiul*," signifying whirling particles and *"The Sand."* "How agreeably indeed, are *Atoms* called *Sands*, as well for their *Exility*, as for their *Fluidity?*" So too it is also called "*Waters*," Mather applauded. The ancient Hebrews, on the other hand, called these particles *"Dust"*—no doubt a fitting "Name for any *Multitude!*"[7] All things considered, Mather (via Dickinson) not only asserted that the pagan philosophers derived their atomist philosophy from the Hebrews—a prevalent claim in Mather's time—but that philologists could reconcile terminological differences with the vocabulary used by Moses, if done correctly.

The miracles of the Exodus saga demythologized, the next selection, illustrates Mather's approach to explicating biblical queries in light of the best available scientific information of his day. His exegesis of Exodus 16:33 in *Biblia*

Americana sought to explain why the manna that miraculously fed the Israel-ites in the wilderness bred worms and stank if kept till the next morning. In Mather's time, this question was still subject to debate because of the belief in abiogenesis, the theory that insects, flies, maggots, and worms sprang spontane-ously from the slime of the earth. Of course, today we know that insects propa-gate by laying fertilized eggs, which hatch in time and feed on whatever nutrients are available to them. This natural phenomenon was not well understood in the seventeenth century. If natural science demystified the Bible, it did not under-mine the miracle of God's creation. In short, Mather went out of his way to sup-ply the best research of his day to elucidate unsolved questions posed in the Bible.

Mather's annotation on Joshua 10:12, the miraculous arrest of the sun, dem-onstrated that he wanted to have his cake and eat it too. With John Locke, Mather viewed a miracle as an event in nature whose causes were unknown or not un-derstood. Thus, if the causes were discovered, such an event should cease to be a miracle, right? Yes, but there might have been other circumstances that re-sisted demystification, as the case of Joshua's stopping the sun proved. To be sure, the Copernican Revolution, which knocked the old Ptolemaic or geocentric sys-tem off its pedestal and replaced it with heliocentrism was still hotly debated by ministers and yeomen alike; it was not part of Harvard's curriculum until the 1670s and did not find wide acceptance until decades later.[8] Perhaps this bibli-cal conundrum might be solved more elegantly, as Mather did in another vol-ume of *Biblia Americana*. The sun standing still in Joshua's day was possibly nothing but a linguistic metaphor for the longest day in summer—as the Jewish philosopher Maimonides explained in his *Guide of the Perplexed*.[9]

In the next example, Mather examined the tragic story of Jephthah's hapless daughter (Judg. 11:30–40), who was sacrificed in fulfillment of her father's vow to God, for its similarity to that of Iphigenia, Agamemnon's daughter, in Greek mythology. This story was well known to the college-educated few, and Mather was no exception. Today, modern mythologists might argue that both Greeks and Hebrews drew on a single, more ancient Ur-text, as was the case of the fa-mous flood stories of Noah, the Greek Deucalion, and Akkadian Gilgamesh.

In Mather's time, however, parallels between Israelite, Egyptian, Phoenician, Greek, or Latin literature signified that the stories and heroes of the pagans were derived, though corrupted, from the Hebrew Bible, the original source of them all.[10]

Typology, the art of discovering predictive parallels between the Hebrew and Christian scriptures, remained a cherished technique of hermeneutics among some in Mather's day, such as his uncle Samuel Mather, who wrote the popular *Figures or Types of the Old Testament* (1683). For instance, such Old Testament characters as the prelapsarian Adam, Noah, Moses, David, and Solomon could all be read as lesser types foreshadowing Christ as the larger antitype in the New Testament. Similarly, Noah's flood in the Old Testament might typify the great conflagration in the New; Noah's Ark, the Christian church; and the brazen serpent on a pole in the camp of the Israelites, the savior on the cross. Mather welcomed this time-honored technique of stitching together the Old and New Testaments by hiding the sutures behind typical characters and events that unified both Hebrew and Christian scriptures.

Then as now, the book of Psalms was highly esteemed by people of faith. In fact, the Psalms was one of Mather's favorites, as we have seen in his *Psalterium Americanum*, his own translation of the Psalter adapted for singing at home and in church. The excerpt from *Biblia Americana* included here demonstrates he had a particular interest in rabbinic annotations and commentaries on the Psalms, which Mather drew on mostly in Latin translations.

Mather's annotations on Isaiah, otherwise known among commentators as the most Christian of Hebrew books, demonstrate how up to date he was on the interpretative disputes of his day. He was not afraid to engage his European peers when he disagreed with them. One such melee started when the English theologian and crypto-Arian William Whiston (1667–1752) launched a controversy in 1708 that cast serious doubt on the traditional, Christological interpretation of Isaiah's famous prophecy, "Behold, a virgin shall conceive, and bear a son, and shall call his name Immanuel" (Isa. 7:14). To make matters worse, Whiston followed up with his *Essay Towards the Restoring the True Text of the Old Testament* (1722), where he pointed to numerous and deeply troubling verbal discrepancies between the messianic prophecies in the Old Testament and the wording used by the apostles in the New. To solve this disagreement, Whiston proposed to restore textual accuracy and literal correspondences by putting the apostles' inspired wording back into the Old Testament, precisely in those places where they had been deliberately falsified by post-exilic rabbis, or so he claimed. Mather was deeply shocked by the direction this debate was taking, for it played into the hands of those who rejected Christ's divine origin and the Trinity. Mather joined the joust in his *Threefold Paradise* and tried to redress the problem in *Biblia Americana*. The excerpt included below reproduces a slice of Mather's contribution to this debate.

The next group of selections addresses the perennially important Pauline question of whether the old covenant of works given to the first Adam was completely supplanted through the incarnation by a new covenant of faith given by Christ, the second Adam. Mather's annotation, excerpted below, clearly demonstrates his orthodoxy on this issue. Believers were saved by faith in Christ, and yet they manifested their gracious faith through good works, which, as they were but the fruit of grace, were not meritorious in themselves. Mather also addresses these points at greater length in *Free Grace Maintained* (1706) and *Grace Defended* (1712).

In his glosses on Ephesians 5:32 and 5:22–32, the final two selections, Mather supplied typological parallels among the love of Adam and Eve, Solomon's love of the Shulamite, and Christ's love of his bride, the church. Literally and typologically, husband and wife were married to one another, just as Jesus Christ was married to the church of the elect. As evidence of this spiritual allegory, Mather drew from the mystical writings of the Jewish Kabbalah and other writings to underscore that, just as Eve was taken from Adam's side, so Christ's bride, the church, was made from Christ's dying on the cross.

All told, these brief topical extracts from *Biblia Americana* provide a mere taste of Mather's enlightened position on numerous issues. They illustrate how he responded to the challenges of his time and how he harmonized them with reformed theology and evangelical piety. Unlike lesser lights who frequently ignored uncomfortable issues, resorted to name-calling, or engaged in outright condemnation, Mather gave fair quarter to a range of opinions, old and new, and provided a platform for their debate. Indeed, *Biblia Americana* is an immense resource for students, scholars, and pastors interested in early modern religious and intellectual history.

PSALTERIUM AMERICANUM (1718)

INTRODUCTION[11]

§. 1. THERE have appeared in the World some *Humane Composures*, which have been so *favoured*, and perhaps *flattered* by Mankind, as to have it asserted concerning them, *That no Mans Reproach could lessen, and no Mans Applause could heighten, the Reputation which belong'd unto them.* The Assertion may be made without Controversy concerning the *Divinely Inspired Book of* PSALMS; than which the Church of GOD is enriched with nothing more Glorious, among all its Incomparable Writings. . . .

§. 3. OUR Poetry has attempted many Versions of the PSALMS, in such *Numbers* and *Measures*, as might render them capable of being *Sung*, in those grave *Tunes*, which have been prepared and received for our *Christian Psalmody*. But of all the more than twice Seven Versions[12] which I have seen, it must be affirmed, That they *leave out* a vast heap of those rich things, which the Holy SPIRIT of GOD speaks of in the Original Hebrew; and that they *put in* as large an Heap of poor Things, which are intirely *their own.* All this has been meerly for the sake of preserving the *Clink* of the *Rhime:* Which after all, is of small consequence unto a Generous *Poem;* and of none at all unto the Melody of *Singing;* but of how little then, in *Singing unto the LORD!* Some famous pieces of Poetry, which this Refining Age has been treated withal, have been offered us in **Blank Verse**. And in **Blank Verse** we now have the Glorious Book of PSALMS presented unto us: The PSALMS fitted unto the *Tunes* commonly used in the Assemblies of our *Zion:* But so fitted, that the *Christian Singer* has his Devotions now supplied, with ALL that the Holy SPIRIT of GOD has dictated, in this Illustrious and Caelestial Bestowment upon His Church in the World; There is NOTHING BESIDES the pure Dictates of that Holy SPIRIT imposed on him. Now, True PIETY, Thou shalt be Judge, whether such a *Divine matter* for thy *Songs* thus disencumbered from every thing that may give them any *Humane Debasements*, be not really to be preferred before any Compositions thou hast ever yet been entertain'd withal. . . .

§. 4. FOR the *New Translation* of the PSALMS, which is here endeavoured, an *Appeal* may be with much Assurance made, unto all that are Masters of the **Hebrew Tongue**, whether it be not much more agreeable to the *Original*, than the *Old* one, or than any that has yet been offered unto the World. Perhaps there

is more Liberty taken here in Translating the *First Verse* of the *Psalter*, than almost any Verse in the whole Book beside. It keeps close to the *Original*; and
even when a *word of supply* is introduced, it is usually a needless Complement
unto the *care of exactness*, to distinguish it at all, as we have done, with an *Italica-
Character*; for it is really in the Intention and Emphasis of the *Original*. Yea,
the just *Laws of Translation* had not been at all violated, if a much greater Liberty had been taken, for the beating out of the Golden and Massy *Hebrew* into
a more *Extended English*. . . . We have tied our selves to *Hebraisms*, more scru-
pulously, than there is real occasion for. . . .

BRIEFLY, Upon *Difference* in this, from the former and common Translation, if the most Learned Reader will please to Examine the *Original*, there will
be no Fear of its being Justified. But then, this Translation may deserve some
Thanks for the Religious part of Mankind, for having tendred a plain, clear, fair
sense of many Passages, which have hitherto been so Translated, that People
could scarce tell how well to understand them: In which regard, this very *Translation* alone, without any of the *Notes* that wait upon it, may be esteemed a
Commentary.

§. 5. MOST certainly, our Translation of the PSALMS, without the Fetters of
Rhime upon it, can be justly esteemed no *prejudice* to the Character of *Poetry*
in the performance. For indeed, however it is now appropriated, according to
the true sense of the Term, to *Rhythme* it self a *Similis Desinentia*, or, a *likeness
of sound* in the last Syllables of the Verse, is not essential. . . . Be that as the
Critics on the Term shall please, our *Translation* is all in *Metre*; and really more
tied unto *Measure*, than the *Original* appears to have been, by all the Examinations that have as yet been employ'd upon it. For, however it might be with the
Song of *Moses* in *Deuteronomy*, and, with the Book of *Job*, and of the *Proverbs*;
My incomparable Master *Alsted* allows me to say, That in the PSALMS, *Nul-
lum canticum sit metricis legibus astrictum, sed mera soluta sit oratio, charactere
Poetico animata.*[13] . . .

§. 8. AND *yet I shew unto you a more Excellent way.* Go on, O People of GOD,
in *His Way*, and in the *Path of the Just* which is now becoming plain before you;
And proceed unto the *Reading* of the *Psalter*, and of the *Bible*, in that which we
will call, *The Affectual way*, according to a PROPOSAL which is now to be seriously thought upon.

WE are to consider, That the *Holy Men of GOD*, who wrote the SCRIPTURE,
were *moved by His Holy Spirit*, in and for the Writing of it; and the *Spirit of Holiness* at the Time of the Inspiration made suitable *Impressions* on the *Affections*
of His Faithful Servants. The Good Men had their *Hearts* Holily, Graciously,
Divinely, and suitably *Affected* with the *Matter*, which the Spirit of GOD
employ'd their Pens to leave upon their Parchments. . . .

Now, *Christian*, Discover which of these *Affections* may be most obvious and evident, in the *Sentence*, which may be now under thy consideration: And make a *Pause!*—But *Restles* until thou find the same *Affections* beginning to stir in thy own Soul, and marvellously to Harmonize & Sympathize, with what the Holy SPIRIT of GOD raised in His *Amanuensis*, at the moment of His Writing it. Be not at *Rest* until thou feel *thy* Heart-strings quaver, at the Touch upon the Heart of the *Sacred Writer*, as being brought into an *Unison* with it, and the *Two Souls* go up in a Flame together.

AN ADMONITION CONCERNING THE TUNES

OUR VERSION is fitted unto all the Common TUNES, the Notes whereof are *Eight* and *Six*.

BUT some of them are accommodated for a well-known *Longer Metre*, by putting in Two Syllables of the **Black Letter**, which are, without any Damage to the Truth of the Translation, found enclosed between Two such Crotchets as these, [ ] And which being left out, the Metre, with the Sense yet remaining entire, is again restored unto the usual, *Eight & Six*.[14]

AND some of them are so contrived, that by leaving out what is the **Black Letter**, between the Two Crotchets, [ ] which may be done without any manner of Damage, they are accommodated unto a well-known *Shorter Metre*.

THE Director of the Psalmody, need only to say, *Sing with the* **Black Letter**, or, *Sing without the* **Black Letter**, and the *Tune* will be sufficiently directed.[15]

IN the *Addition* of the CANTIONAL, the Singer will find, That besides what is done for the *Tune*, which uses to go by the Name of, *CXLVIII Psalm-Tune*, or, the *Hallelujatic Tune*; by Taking or Dropping the Two Syllables of **Black Letter**, between the Crotchets, [ ] a Variety of *Other Tunes* is provided for.

PSALM XXIII

A Psalm of David.

MY Shepherd is th' ETERNAL God; ‖ I shall not be in [**any**] want: ‖

2 In pastures of a tender grass ‖ He [**ever**] makes me to lie down: ‖ To waters of tranquillities ‖ He gently carries me, [**along.**] ‖

3 My *feeble and my wandring* Soul ‖ He [**kindly**] does fetch back again; ‖ In the plain paths of righteousness ‖ He does lead [**and guide**] me along, ‖ because of the regard He has ‖ [**ever**] unto His *Glorious* Name. ‖

4 Yea, when I shall walk in the Vale ‖ of the dark [**dismal**] shade of Death, ‖ I'll of no evil be afraid, ‖ because thou [**ever**] art with me. ‖ Thy rod and thy staff, these are what ‖ yield [**constant**] comfort unto me. ‖

5 A Table thou dost furnish out ‖ richly [**for me**] before my face. ‖ 'Tis in view of mine Enemies; ‖ [**And then**] my head thou dost anoint ‖ with fatning and perfuming Oil: ‖ my cup it [**ever**] overflows. ‖

6 Most certainly the thing that is ‖ Good, with [**most kind**] Benignity, ‖ *This* all the days that I do live ‖ shall [**still and**] ever follow me; ‖ Yea, I shall dwell, and Sabbatize, ‖ even to [**unknown**] length of days, ‖ *Lodg'd* in the House which does belong ‖ to [**Him who's**] the ETERNAL God. ‖

PSALM CXXXVII

WE by the Rivers which do run ‖ thro' Babylon, sat there; ‖ yea, we pour'd out our Tears when we ‖ remembred Zion *there.* ‖

2 Upon the Willows in the midst ‖ thereof we hung our Harps. ‖

3 For they that Captiv'd us did there ‖ demand of us *to Sing* ‖ words of a Song, and they who laid ‖ us in our ruinous heaps, ‖ *demanded* mirth, Sing us, *said they,* ‖ a Song of Zion, *Sing!* ‖

4 *Our Answer was,* How can we do ‖ to Sing a Song that is ‖ for the ETERNAL God, in the ‖ Land of a stranger here? ‖

5 O *dear* Jerusalem, If I ‖ of thee forgetful grow! ‖ As soon shall my Right-hand forget ‖ *what it is us'd unto!* ‖

6 My Tongue shall to my Palate cleave, ‖ when thee I do not mind! ‖ If I don't set Jerus'lem at ‖ the top of all my Joy. ‖

7 Remember, O ETERNAL God, ‖ the Sons of Edom, who ‖ said in Jerus'lems day, Rase, Rase, ‖ to its foundation bare. ‖

8 Daughter of Babylon, who art ‖ to be made desolate, ‖ Happy, who shall repay to thee ‖ the pay thou'st paid to us! ‖

9 O the great blessedness of him ‖ who shall lay hold upon, ‖ and who against the solid Rock ‖ shall dash thy little ones! ‖

MANUDUCTIO AD MINISTERIUM (1726)

[READING THE SACRED SCRIPTURES]

§. 14. Can a Man be a Thorough *Divine* without *Reading* the SACRED SCRIPTURES? No, Verily; Not so much as a Common *Christian. Read* them, *Child;* I say, *Read* them, with an Uncommon Assiduity. To *Dig* in these Rich Mines, make it your *Daily Exercise.* Hold on doing so, until you are, I will not say, *Bonus Textuarius,*[16] but until you are, *An Eloquent Man, and Mighty in the Scriptures.*

To this Purpose, My Advice to you is, That it be your Practice, to *Read* the *Sacred Scriptures* in the *Porismatic Way;*[17] Or, with a Labour to observe and educe, the *Doctrine of Godliness*, which this inexhaustible *Store House of Truth*, will yield unto them that are seeking after it. Make a *Pause* upon every *Verse*, and see what *Lessons of Piety* are to be learnt from every *Clause*. Turn the *Lessons* into *Prayers*, and send up the *Prayers* unto the GOD, who is now Teaching of you: *As Arrows from the Hand of a mighty Man* {Ps. 127:4}, send them up with *Lively Ejaculations* unto the Heavens. What Exercise can be more Enlightening, more Sanctifying, more Comfortable, than such an *Intercourse*, of GOD uttering His *Voice*, and, *Lo, a mighty Voice!* —unto you, and your Holy Returning of it, unto Him, in such *Echo's of Devotion!* I will say this for your Encouragement. In your *Searching of the Scriptures* {Acts 17:10–11}, you will forever have *something that is New* to entertain you. They are a *Treasury*, which (beyond that at *Venice*) you cannot reach to the *Bottom* of. *Austin* in his Epistle to *Volusi[an]us* has not said a Thousandth Part of what may be said,[18] about fetching still every Day *fresh Entertainments* and Advantages from them, after one has already Spent an Age in the Study of them. The Jews have *Reason* on their Side, when they say of the Scripture, *Versa eam, et Versa eam, nam omnia sunt in ea.*[19] . . . Now, Do you lay One Sentence, and then Another, and so a third, of your *Bible* before you. Find out, which of these *Affections* is Obvious and Evident, in the *Sentence* under Consideration. Try, Strive, Do your Best, that the same *Affections* may Stir, yea, Flame in your Soul. Be Restless, till you find your Soul Harmonizing and Symphonizing, with what the Holy SPIRIT of GOD raised in his *Amanuensis* at the time of His Writings. Be not at Rest, until you find your *Heart-strings quaver* at the *Touch* upon the Heart of the Writing, as being brought into an *Unison* with it, and the *Two Souls* go up in a Flame together. Consider what *Affections of* PIETY are plainly discernible in the *Word* that is before you; and then, with a Soul turning unto the Lord, assay to utter the Language of the like Affections. E're you are aware, you will be *caught up to Paradise* {2 Cor. 12:4}; you will *mount up as with the Wings of Eagles!* {Isa. 40:31} . . .

BIBLIA AMERICANA (1693–1728)

[ENTRY ON GENESIS 1:31 (ATOMIST EXPLANATION
OF THE MOSAIC CREATION ACCOUNT)]

Genesis 1:31.
And God saw every thing that he had made, and, behold, it was very good. And the evening and the morning were the sixth day.

Q. The *Theories* of the *Creation*, (particularly what I last offered you,)[20] invented by our Modern Philosophers, do certainly make too bold with the *Mosaic*, and *Inspired* History thereof. It were a Noble, and a Worthy Work; to Illustrate that History, and rescue it from the praesumptuous Glosses, that many *Neotericks* have made upon it. v. 31.

A.   It is notably done, by the most ingenious Dr. *Dickinson* in his, *Physica Vetus et Vera.*[21] That Gentleman who near Fifty Years ago, obliged the World with the Curiosities of his *Delphi Phoenicissantes,* ha's now in this present Year, 1702. presented us, with a curious Treatise of above three hundred Pages in *Quarto,* in which he proves, *In Historia Creationis, tum generationis universae methodum atque modum, tum verae philosophiae principia, strictim atque breviter à Mose tradi.*[22] To this Treatise I shall now be beholden, for the Illustration upon the *Mosaic Hexaemeron,*[23] with which I am now going to entertain you. . . .

Now, inasmuch as all the *Ancient Philosophy,* which was the Daughter of the *Mosaic,* pretended unto an Account of nothing less, than the *whole Creation,* tis highly probable that *Moses* would give no less in his *Cosmology.* But being thus praepared, Lett us view the *Six Dayes* of the *Creation,* and what was done in each of them.

The First Day.

In the Beginning was *Universal Matter* by God first created of nothing; a wondrous *Congeries* of all sorts of *Particles,* unform'd, and unmov'd, and every where separated from one another with empty Spaces. This *Universal Matter* was putt into *Motion,* by the *Spirit of God,* and not left unto a fortuitous *Motion* and *Concourse.* Thus was there given unto *Matter,* that *Force* which we call *Nature;* for, *Nature* is nothing but that *Motion* which the *Spirit of God* ha's imprinted upon *Matter,* and which He perpetually governs with His infinite Wisdome. The *Atoms* of this *Universal Matter,* must not be supposed *Absolutely Indivisible;* tis enough, that they were very *Minute Particles.* And the *Motion* at first given to the *Atoms* we may suppose to have been *Twofold.* The *first Motion,* may be called, A *Motion of Praeparation.* This might be *Transverse,* or, *Across;* in which the various Meetings of the *Atoms* one with another, gave an Opportunity for such whose Figures were agreeable unto one another, to join, and stick together, in *Bodies,* that from this *First Concretion,* would soon grow into *Elements.* The *Second Motion* may be called, A *Motion of Separation.* This might be *circular.* And the first Essay of it, might be the Producing of *Fire* or *Light.* The *Atoms* are of diverse Figures; according to which they may be some of them called, *Pilulae,* others, *Globuli,* others, *Bracteolae,*[24] and a Fourth sort, of a grosser Consistence, and of so many Forms, that it is not easy to assign a fitt Name for them. It may be, the *Fire* is composed of the First Sort, the *Water* of the Second, the *Air* of the Third, and the *Earth,* of the Last. And there may be a *Fifth Sort,* smaller than any of these; broken off perhaps from the rest in their Circumgyration; and subservient especially to Matters in the *Firmament.* The

Motion where into the *Universal Matter* was now putt, no doubt carried off the *Pilulae,* into that vast Collection of them, which we call the *Empyraean Heaven,*[25] (or the *Sphaere,* whereof see Prov. 8.22, and Job. 22.14.) And this *Fire,* is implied in that *Light,* whereof we find it so early spoken, *Lett there be Light* {Gen. 1:3}; and whereof *Hippocrates* takes Notice, That the ancients called it, *Æther.*[26] Had the Word, *Ur,* been so translated, some Scoffers at *Moses* had been silenced. But when *Fire* was produced, *Light* was also produced; which is no other than *Ignis Effluxio.*[27] It was not amiss in *Empedocles,* to call this *Light,* ἤλιον ἀρχέτυπον, *Solem Originalem et Primigenium.*[28] The First *Day* and *Night* were distinguished, by the Rotation of that *Matter,* so elevated and congregated, and carryed about with such a Glare, that if there had then been a *Prae-adamite,*[29] he might by the Shine of it, have seen the rest of the *Abyss.* The *Lucid Particles* of that *Matter,* may be the *Morning Stars,* that *sang together,* when the *Angels shouted for* Joy, at the Laying of *Foundations of the Earth.* But it must be re-membred, that the *Motion* which thus carried off the *Pilulae,* did carry off, & carry up, vast Numbers of the *Globuli* too: by which Means we find Real and Natural *Waters,* as well as *Fire,* in the Highest *Heavens:* As in a Distillation we see, that in a Pound of *Spirit of Wine,* so inflammable a thing! there are carried over, several Ounces of *Water* with it. The very Name /שמים/ *Shamajim,* seems composed of /אש/ *Fire,* and /מים/ *Water.* This was the Philosophy of the Ancient *Hebrewes.* [Compare Psal. 148.4. and Psal. 104.3.] These *Waters* may be of un-known Uses, in those Heavens; To Temper the *Heat,* of the Heavenly Bodies; and Augment their *Light,* as Chrystals about them; and convey subtile Influ-ences from thence to the *Inferior Orbs.*

The Second Day.

The whirling Motion of the *Abyss,* or *Universal Matter* yett continuing, the *Atoms* of a more *Bracteal* Figure, now possessed themselves of that vast Space, which *Moses* calls, *The Firmament.* But probably, the Mixture of them, near the Surface of our Globe, was yett so thick and so dark, that the *Light* could hardly yett make its Passage hither; And this may be the Cause, why God would not call it, *Good:* The Figure of these *Atoms,* would not allow them so swift a Flight, towards the *Selvidge*[30] of the World, as those which gott the Start of them. The *Atoms,* of the whole *Expanse,* and of the *Air,* may be the same; except, that near the Surface of our Globe, there are added such Vapours, as to distinguish that Region, which we call *Our Atmosphaere.* The Name /רקיע/ *Rakiah,* used by Mo-ses, (*cui semper placuere compendia*)[31] for this *Expanse,* is admirably suited, to express the Nature of the Particles that compose it; It signifying, both to *Expand,* and also to *Constringe,* or *Compress.* They spread themselves, and chase away all others from themselves, and at the same time, they do firmly as far as they can compel together, those that are within their Embraces. Tis by the Efficacy of these, that God, [Job. 26.7.] *hangs our Globe upon nothing*; and [Psal. 104.5.] He *layes Foundations*, not only for the *Earth*, but for the *Stars* too, that *shall not be removed forever.*

The Third Day.

The *Conatus Dispansivus*,[32] of those *Atoms*, to whom the Creator ha's assign'd so large a Province in His Creation, now accomplished, *That the Waters under the Heaven, were gathered together into one Place, and the Dry Land appeared.* It protruded the Particles of Grosser Matter, down toward the Center; where they need no other *Cement*, than their *Agreement in Figure*, to produce their firm *Cohaerence*. But from their various Distribution, and perhaps from some other Varieties, arose the *Inaequality* of the Surface of the *Earth*. And a considerable Portion of the *Globular Atoms* being left here, behold, the *Waters*, whose Figure disposes them to run and fill all the Cavities provided for them. Nor is it amiss to repraesent all the *Seas*, as *one*, in this Collection of *Waters*, inasmuch as they have (like the *Caspian* with the *Mediterranean*,) their *Subterraneous* Communications with one another. And tho' the *Earth* have the Name of *Dry Land* given unto it, yett it is not so Dried, as to be left wholly destitute of that *Humour*, which must accompany all *Seeds*, to carry on the several Generations in the World. But the *Vapour* and *Humour* so sent forth continually, supposes a *Central Fire* in the Bowels of the *Earth*; which probably is a vast Congregation of *Pilular Atoms*, by the Wisdome of God, so placed at first in the Center of the *Abyss*, that being hedged about with such a Number of Gross Particles, when God gave to *Matter* its first *Motion*, they could not make their Way thorough, with their Companions, up unto the *Æther*; and they putt on the more *Fiery Appearance*, because they are cramm'd so close together. The *Mist* whereof we read, *That it watered the whole Face of the Earth, before God had caused it yett to Rain upon the Earth* {Gen. 2:5–6}, seems to have been a *Vapour* of *Watry Particles* boil'd forth, by that *Central Fire*. We may add, That the unaequal Descent of the *Terrestrial Particles*, at the first Settlement, produced not only the vast Basons, wherein the *Sea's* are lodged, but also the *Channels*, wherein the *Rivers* flow about the World, like the *Veins* and *Arteries*, in an Humane Body. But, that the *Central Fire*, may not be, thro' Length of Time, and long Evaporation, wasted, it seems, that Heaven affords it a Nourishment, in a continual Descent of *Sulphureous Particles*, which being absorb'd by the Sea, sink to the bottom, until they find their Way in proper Channels, to that awful Receptacle. By the warm Aspirations of the *Central Fire*, the Generation of *Plants*, on the *Third Day*, was forwarded; of *Seed* made by the Immediate Hand of God. There might be something peculiar in the Season, for a vigorous Effort of Nature, as well as a Display of the Divine Power & Energy, in the Acceleration of such a Generation. The *Succus Nutritius*[33] requisite unto this Generation, is not *Water*, but a certain, special, *Viscous Matter*, which lies in *Water*, and which cannot well permeate the Pores of the *Vegetables*, unless there be *Water* to attenuate it.

The Fourth Day.

A vast Multitude of *Igneous Particles* were left all this while scattered throughout the whole *Expanse*. The Great Creator of the World therefore, collected them into that one Globe, which we call, *The Sun*, & which *Empedocles* call'd, πυρὸς ἄθροισμα μέγα, *A Great Heap of Fire*. The *Solar Matter* thus collected, keeps continually whirling about, with great *Inaequalities* in the *Surface* of it; and is more *changeable* than the very *Moon* itself: which alone, might be enough to lead Reasonable Men, from the Worship of *That*, unto the Worship of that glorious *Father of Lights*, who is *without Variableness or Shadow of Turning*. The *Sun* being always upon a vast Expence of itself, God ha's both encompass'd it, with a Transparent Sort of a *Covering Shell*, or *Hedge*; and the *Atoms* of the *Expanse* are also of such a Figure, as to leave Channels, thro' which there is a continual Recourse of a Nourishment unto it, and unto that *Covering* from all Parts of the Creation. But yett such is the Contexture of that *Covering* upon the *Sun*, that sometimes tis thick enough, to check the Passage of the *Sun-beams*; from whence arise the *Maculae Solares*;[34] yea, the Countenance of the *Sun* sometimes is paler than ordinary, for a whole Month together; and *Pliny* tells the Time, when the Sun, *Totius Anni ferè Spacio palluit*.[35] Thus hath the Almighty sett *Bars* about the *Sun*, (as well as about the *Sea*) and said, *Here, shall thy Fiery Waves be staid!* This Heavenly *Carbuncle*, thus formed by God, seems designed, not only to impart *Light* and *Heat* unto the rest of the Creation, but also to have in it the most subtil *Sulphur of Nature*, by the Steams whereof it produces most eximious Effects in the other Creatures, and particularly in the *Bodies*, (and by Consequence, in the *Spirits*,) of Men. That rich *Sulphur of Nature*, (which *Moses* may mean, by, *The precious Things putt forth by the Sun & Moon, the precious Things of the lasting Hills* {Deut. 33:14–15},) may have certain fine Particles of the *Coelestial Waters*, as well as *Fires*, to constitute it. An agreeable *Motion* is therefore ordered for the *Sun*; which Motion, we find celebrated by *Abraham*, the most Renouned Astronomer of the Ancients. . . . But then, that the scalding Influences of the *Sun* might be conveniently Tempered, God created, that other *Planet*, the *Moon*; of a wat'ry and moister Texture, to dispense unto the *Earth*, which cannot bear to be scorch'd, a certain *Fatt Liquor*, which is wondrously agreeable to the *Humidum Radicale*[36] of things

generated on this *Terraqueous Globe*. . . . All we will add, shall be, That probably the *Moon* shone before the *Sun*, on that *Haemisphere* where *Moses* lived;
and this may be a Reason for his putting the *Evening* before the *Morning*, in his
History of the Creation. The *Expanse* was now *Good*; that is to say, *Perfect*; nor
was it called *Good*, until it was thus admirably furnished.

The Fifth Day.

Moses proceeds now, to the *Animated Parts* of the Creation. The *Water* and
the *Earth* were the *Elements*, (and the fittest ones,) to be employ'd in producing
of them. And yett, all that they could pretend, was, to carry the *Seeds* thereof in
their Bowels, and afford that warm and moist Matter unto them, which might
be their Nourishment. God immediately creating the *Souls* of *Animals*, probably lodg'd them in a *Seminal Matter*, which carried the Figure of an *Egg*. For
which Cause, the Ancient Philosophy, both *Egyptian* and *Graecian*, discoursed
much of the *Egg*, at the Mouth of God, and the Ὠὸν πρωτόγονον, *Ovum Primigenium*,[37] from whence all things had their Original. In that *Egg*, with the
Souls of the *Animals*, there were also the *Shapes* of them, formed by the Finger
of God; or the *Pores* of them so disposed, as to entertain the *Nutritious Juice*,
which does increase their *Bodies*, into what at last they come to. For these *Corporeal Idaeas*, our sacred Philosopher uses the Word, מין/ *Min*, which we render, *Their Kind* {Gen. 1:21}. God gave to the *Seeds* of *Animals*, the faculty of
admitting from the circumambient Slime, a *Nutritious Juice*, into all the Parts
of them; and so to dispose thereof, as to augment, & perfect, and specificate the
Animals. The *Souls* of *Animals*, which God produced indeed from the *Earth*,
(but no Doubt sublimed into a very fine *Essence*, by His own Omnipotent Hand,)
were of a most *Subtil*, and *Active* Nature; and the *Seeds*, whereto God united
them, were admirably suited, for their *Animal*-Functions; and that *Fatt Clay*,
wherein the Almighty *Potter*, putt them, yeelded *Liquors* very agreeable for their
Concretion and Accretion; and the *Vapour* which ascended, before the Lord had
caused it as yett to *Rain upon the Earth*, was doubtless a very *Digesting* sort of a
Thing. Old *Archelaus* was not altogether ignorant of this Proceeding, when he
said, γεννᾶσθαι τὰ ζῶα ἐκ θερμῆς τῆς γῆς, καὶ ἰλὺν παραπλησίαν γάλακτι, οἷον
τροφὴν ἀνιείσης; *Genita fuisse Animalia Terrae calore, limum lacti similem in
alimentum liquante.*[38] And the Generation of the *Aquatils*, was carried on like
that of the *Terrestrials*. But after this Day, (such is the Order of God,) the Generation must be carried on, by a Conjunction of *Male* and *Female*; in the *Seed*
whereof lies hid, that fine *Spirit*, much more fine than the *Æther* itself, which
is the *Soul* of the *Animal*; and yett that *Soul* being but *Sublimed Earth*, is *Corporeal*, and at length returns to the *Earth*: but that fine *Spirit*, when enkindled,

finds in the *Seed*, the *Idaea* of an *Organic* Body, of a most wonderful Structure, which it manages accordingly.

The Sixth Day.

At last, MAN, the Lord and King, of the other Creatures is introduced, into the Palace, thus Erected and Furnished for him. The *Soul* of Man is a most Noble Thing; and called, Gen. 2.7. *A Breath of Lives*, in the Plural Number; because by it a Man does not only *live* the present *Life*, which is Frail, and Earthly and Mortal, but also *breathe* after, & at length come to live, a *Life Eternal* in the Heavens, *aequal to the Angels*. It is said to be *Breathed* by God *into his Nostrils*, (or Hebr. *Into his Face*,) because, God both made his *Body*, [see Job. 10.8. and Psal. 119.73. and Isa. 64.8.] and then so infused the *Soul*, that from the action of *Breathing* and other *Senses* appearing in the *Face*, it appear'd, that he was indeed *Alive*. The Lodging provided for this Noble Thing, the *Soul*, was not immediately made of the *Common Earth*, (tho' it had before been such *Dust*) but of *Adamah*, a Red, Rich, Rosie, and *Shining* Sort of Earth, by an unknown Fermentation, advanced now into a Sort of a *Quintessence*; and, no doubt, the *Body* of *Adam*, did by his Fall, unhappily lose much of the *Primitive Glory*, wherein it shone like the *Ruby*. The *Body* of Man was perhaps, the most Illustrious Thing in the whole Visible Creation, and the most precious Treasures of the *Stars* themselves, not excepting the very *Sun*, were in the Composition of it. The fitter Habitation it was, for the Heavenly *Soul*, which *Moses* chooses to call by the Name of /נשמה/ *Neshamah*,[39] wherein he alludes to the Word, /שמים/ *Shamajim*, for this Cause, because it came from thence. . . . A *Seed*, formed by the exquisite Workmanship of Heaven, was now putt into the *Body* of Man, a fitt Instrument for the *Soul*, in carrying on the succeeding Generations. It is the *Soul*, that Begins and Perfects every *Generation*: and Excites the united *Seed* of the Parents, and cherishes that purer *Seed*, the *Bullula*,[40] and digests that thicker *Seed*, in the Χόριον, and by its *aethereal* and *plastick* Warmth manages the whole affair, except the first Delineation of the Parts, which it finds lodged there by the peculiar Work of God. The *Seed* would be altogether Torpid, & and not bring anything to Effect, if it were not for the *Formative Power*, which God, the great γενεσιουργος,[41] hath implanted in the *Soul*. *Harvey*'s History of *Generation*[42] makes it evident, that the *Soul* in the *Seed*, carries on all, without any Assistence from the Mother, for at least the First *Three Months*, in all which Time, the *Embryo* remains, not fastned unto the Mother, by any *Ligaments*. In what Part of the *Body* soever, the *Soul* may have its principal Seat, which is variously disputed, it is most certainly no other than a *Foreigner* and a *Sojourner* here, and placed by God in this earthly Tabernacle, for a certain *Term*; upon the Expiration of which Term, it should go back, to its *heavenly Countrey;* even the Countrey, which *Plato* acknowledged, when he called it, ὑπερουράνιον τόπον, *The Super-Coelestial Place;*[43] and *Pythagoras,* when he called it, ἐλεύθερον ἀιθέρα, *Liberum Æthera,* where he taught that the *Souls* of *Hero's,* after they left their *Bodies,* remained, ἀθανάτους καὶ ἀμβρότους, *Immortales et Incorruptibiles.*[44] But since the *Souls* of Men come from Heaven, and are not generated by our Parents, it may justly be enquired, How it could be said unto Mankind, *Increase and Multiply.* Tis very sure, That the *Souls* of Men, are in our Sacred Bible, repraesented as, the *Sons* of God. And the ancient Philosophy of the Gentiles called them, *The Offspring of God,* and called God, *Their Father.* Whereas our *Bodies* are called, *Branches;* which intimates their Derivation from the *Seed* of our *First Parents;* wherein there is yett also, a very Divine Workmanship. The Wisdome of the Ancients, looks upon the Humane *Seed,* as of a very sublime Nature; and not only akin, τῷ τῶν ἄστρων στοιχείῳ, *To the Element of the Stars,*[45] (as *Aristotle* expresses it,) but also peculiarly stamp'd with a very Divine Character. This little Portion of the *Humane Body,* whereby a thing of so vast Consequence, as the Propagation of Mankind, was to be carried on, was framed with a most astonishing Artifice, & made capable of being multiplied; but the True & Pure *Seed,* which is but a little Portion of that Mass, which we call so, is a most *refined Essence,* capable of an inexpressible *Mixture* (as one may call it,) with the very *Soul* itself, so that the Affections of the very *Soul* of the Parents, may by it, as by an agreeable Vehicle, be transferr'd unto their Children. . . .

This is the Scheme, & the Summ, of the *Philosophy,* which our *Dickinson* supposes constantly praeserved among the *Patriarchs,* down unto the Dayes of *Moses.* Nor is it likely, that the *Israelites* were Strangers to this *Philosophy,* even while they were in *Egypt.* They were an Ingenious Nation, and probably the *Egyptians* themselves among whom they lived, were not in the Dayes of *Joseph,* sunk into that *Idolatry,* to which they afterwards degenerated; but worshipped the same True God, with the *Israelites,* and according to the Instructions of *Joseph,* who *taught their Senators Wisdome.* . . . But for *Moses* himself, the whole World could not show a Man, that was more Accomplished. His Education in the Court of *Egypt;* His Fellowship in the Colledge of *Diospolis;*[46] His Expedition into *Æthiopia;* His Conversation with the wisest Men of *Arabia,* and *Idumaea,* and, perhaps *Phoenicia,* during his long Exile; But above all, His Intimate Communion with Heaven; All conspire to Invite our Expectations, of great Things from him. Among his other Excellencies, it seems likely that his *Chymistry* enabled him to do such things, as the Philosophers in our Age, are Strangers unto.

Exod. 16:33.

And Moses said, Let no man leave of it [manna] *till the morning. Notwithstand-*
ing they hearkened not unto Moses; but some of them left of it until the morning,
and it bred worms and stank: and Moses was wroth with them

Q.   The Manna *unduely* Reserved, *Bred Worms & Stank:* It may be, some philosophical Disquisitions about the Generation of Insects, on this Occasion, may
bee serviceable to the Illustration of the Scriptures, & particularly affect our
True Apprehensions of the *Creation* therein described? v. 33 [20].

A.   Know, in general, That no Animal ever did proceed aequivocally from
Putrefaction,[47] but all, even the most contemptible Insects, are generated, by Parents of their own kind, *Male* and *Female.* This is a Discovery of great Importance, that, a learned Person saises, *perhaps few Inventions of this Age can pre-*
tend unto aequal Usefulness & Merit, & it were sufficient alone, to exterminate
rank Atheism out of the World.[48] For if all Animals bee propagated by Generation, from Parents of their own Species, and there bee no Instance in Nature of
so much as a Gnat, or a Mite, spontaneously *de novo* produced, how came there
to bee such Animals in Being, & whence could they proceed?

Lett us appeal unto Experiment. It ha's been the general Tradition and Opinion, that *Maggots, Worms,* and *Flies,* breed in putrified Carcases; *Bees* from
Oxen, *Hornets* from Horses, & *Scorpions,* from Crabfish; and the like. But it is
all Fable and Mistake. The Sagacious *Francisco Redi,*[49] made Innumerable Trials
of all sorts, on Beasts, on Fowls, on Fishes, on Serpents, on corrupted Cheese,
on Herbs, on Fruits, and even on Insects themselves; and hee constantly found,
that all those Kinds of *Putrefaction,* did only afford a Nest and Food, for the Eggs
and Young, of these Insects, that hee admitted thereunto; but produced no Animal of themselves, by a Spontaneous Formation; when hee suffered those
things to putrefy, in Hermetically Sealed Glasses, and Vessels close covered with
Paper, Yea, and, lest the Exclusion of the Air might bee supposed an Hindrance
to the Experiment, in Vessels covered with Fine Lawn,[50] so as to Admitt the *Air,*
& Keep out the *Insects,* no living thing was ever produced there, tho' hee expos'd
them to the Action of the Sun, in the Warm Climate of *Florence,* & at the most
kind Season of the Year. Even *Flies* mortified and corrupted, when inclosed in
such Vessels, did never procreate a *New Flie.* But when the *Vessels* were open,
& the Insects had free Access unto the Aliment in them, hee diligently observed,
That no other Sort were produced, but of such as hee saw go in to deposit their
Eggs there; which they would readily do in all Putrefaction; even in a Mucilage

of bruised *Spiders*, where Worms were soon hatch'd out of Eggs, and quickly *chang'd* into *Flies* of the same Kind with their Parents.

As to the Worms bred in the *Intestines*, and other Internal Parts of living Creatures, the happy Curiosity of *Malpighi*,[51] and others, hath informed us, That each of those *Tumors* of Plants, out of which there generally issues a *Worm*, or a *Flie*, are first made by such Insects, which wound the Tender Buds, with a long hollow Trunk, and lay an Egg in the Hole, with a sharp corroding Liquor, which causes a Swelling in the Leaf, & so closes the Orifice: and within this Tumour, the Worm is hatch't, & receives its Aliment, until it hath eaten its Way through. Neither need wee recur to an aequivocal Production of Vermin, in the *Phthiriasis*, and in *Herods* Disease, who was, σκωληκόβρωτος, *Eaten of Maggots*.[52] Those horrible Distempers, are alwayes accompanied with putrefying Ulcers; & it hath been observed by *Lewenhoeck*,[53] that Lice and Flies, which have a most wonderful Acuteness of Sense, to find out convenient Places for the nourishment of their Young do mightily endeavour to lay their *Eggs* upon *Sores*; and that one laies above an Hundred, which may naturally increase to some Hundreds of Thousands, in a quarter of a Year; which may give a satisfactory Account of the *Phaenomena*, in those Diseases. And whereas it is here said, That some of the *Israelites left of the Manna, until the Morning, & it bred Worms & stank*; it is to bee understood no otherwise, than that it was *Fly-blown*. It was then the Month of *October*, which in that Southern Climate, after the Autumnal Rains, doth afford a fitt Season, & a full Repast, for infinite Swarms of Insects. It was rather a Miracle, that all the rest of the *Manna* was kept untainted, than that this *Bred Worms*. If any one rigidly urge the literal Expression of *Breeding*, tis to bee answered, that in the common affayrs of Life, the Language of the Vulgar is to bee used.

If wee consult the Accurate Observations of *Swammerdam*,[54] wee shall find, that the supposed Change of *Worms* into *Flies*, is but supposed: for the most of those Members, which at last become visible to the Eye, are existent, in the Beginning, artificially complicated in one another, & covered with Membranes, & with *Tunicles*,[55] which are afterwards laid aside; and all the rest of the Process, is no more surprising, than the Eruption of *Horns* in Bruits, or of *Teeth* and *Beard* in Men, at certain Periods of Age. No, nor indeed can the meanest *Plant* bee raised without *Seed*, by any Formative Power, that is Residing in the *Seed* which may bee gathered. First, for the *Known Seeds* of all Vegetables, one or two only excepted, that are left unto future Discovery; which Seeds, by the Help of *Microscopes*, are all found Real and Perfect *Plants*, with the Trunk, & its Leaves, curiously enclosed in the *Cortex*: Nay, one single Grain of *Wheat*, *Rye*, or *Barly*, shall contain four or five distinct Plants, under one common Covering:

A convincing Argument of the wonderful Providence of God, that those Vegetables, which were to bee the chief Sustenance of Mankind, should have that
multiplied faecundity above others: And, secondly, by that famous Experiment
of *Malpighi*, who a long Time enclosed a Quantity of Earth in a Vessel, secured
by a fine Clothe, from the Small Imperceptible Seeds of Plants, that are blown
about with the Winds, & had that Success of the Curiosity, to discover this noble Truth; That no Species of *Plants* can bee produced out of the Earth *de novo*,
without a praeexistent Seed; and consequently, they were all created, at the Beginning of things, by God the Almighty Gardener. See Mr. *Bentleys* Confutation of Atheism.[56]

[ENTRY ON JOSHUA 10:12 (ON THE SUN STANDING STILL)]

Joshua 10:12.
*Then spake Joshua to the Lord in the day when the Lord delivered up the
Amorites before the children of Israel, and he said in the sight of Israel, Sun,
stand thou still upon Gibeon; and thou, Moon, in the valley of Ajalon.*
Q. But you know, That it is now the Received Opinion, that the *Sun* is the
Center of the *System*, and that the *Earth* moves about the *Sun*; and therefore,
why should the *Sun* be bidden to *Stand Still?* It seems a Command fitter to be
directed unto the *Earth*, than unto the *Sun?* v. 12.
A. *Loquendum cum Vulgo.*[57] Wee consider, That the Motion of the *Earth*,
may be argued, even from this very Speech of *Joshua*. For *Joshua* had no Occasion for any Service from the *Moon*; Why did he command the *Moon* to *Stand
still*, as well as the *Sun?* Why, A Stop given to the *Diurnal Motion* of the *Earth*,
unavoidably produces the *Phaenomena*, of the *Moon Standing still*, as well as the
Sun. And besides all this; Lett the *Cartesian* Cavils[58] be heard: According to
them, The *Earths Motion* depends on the Motion of the *Sun* about its own *Axis*,
which Course it finishes in *Twenty Six* Dayes. Now there was Occasion to bid
the *Sun stand Still*, on this account, in order to the Stopping of the Motion of
the *Earth*.

[ENTRY ON JUDGES 11:38 (THE SACRIFICE OF JEPHTHAH'S DAUGHTER)]

Judges 11:38.
*And he said, Go. And he sent her away for two months: and she went with her
companions, and bewailed her virginity upon the mountains.*
Q. The Sacrifice of *Jephtahs Daughter*, does Pagan Antiquitie Remember it,
or Imitate it? v. 38.

A. Twas doubtless from hence, that the Greek Poets made the Story of *Iphigenia's* being sacrificed by her Father *Agamemnon.*[59]

The Chronology of *Jephtah* and *Agamemnon* is the same. For tho' wee dare not say with *Chrysostom,*[60] that there was no *Trojan War* at all, but that the whole Tale, was a fiction, derived from the History of *Jephtahs* warring with the *Ammonites,* and *Ephraimites*; yett this wee say, The *Trojan War* was contemporaneous with the Government of *Jephtah.*[61]

Moreover, *Jephtah* and *Agamemnon,* agree in the same Character, of *great Captains.* And their Daughters, were both of them, *only Daughters*: and both *Virgins*: and both, Devoted by their Fathers, when Warring against their Enemies: and both had a Reprieve after their Destination to Sacrifice; the one *wandred up & down the Mountains* with her *Companions,* the other, turned into an Hinde by *Diana,*[62] to range in the *Woods & Mountains.*

Lastly, what is the very Name of *Iphigenia,* but *Iphthigenia,* or, *Iephthigenia*; that is, the Daughter of *Jephtha?*

Upon the whole, either the Daughter of *Agamemnon,* was no other than the Daughter of *Jephtah*; whereof the *Phoenicians* coming to, & planting in, *Greece,* made famous Reports; which Posteritie thus Disguised in their Histories: or else, which might happen in other Cases, the Divel might among the *Gentiles* choose to Ape still, those Methods, and those Actions, which the good Spirit of God had produced among the *Jewes*: And hence, by the way, *Humane Sacrifices* might grow so Commendable and Fashionable, as they did, among the Heathen, by the Instigation of Satan, in Imitation of such great Exemples as that of *Jephtah.*

But which way soever you take it; still the sacred Story, was the *Original.*

[ENTRY ON 2 CHRONICLES 1:1 (SOLOMON A TYPE OF CHRIST)]

2 Chronicles 1:1.
And Solomon the son of David was strengthened in his kingdom, and
the Lord his God was with him, and magnified him exceedingly.

Q. Wherein may wee reckon *Solomon,* a *Type* of our Lord Jesus Christ? v. 1.
A. *A Greater than Solomon is Hee!* But,

Solomon was the Son of *David.* And so was our Lord Jesus Christ: the Apostle to the *Hebrewes* proves it [Heb. 11]; and the Afflicted Suppliants that addressed Him sometimes, did own it.

But more than so. The Almighty God said concerning *Solomon, I will bee his Father, and hee shall bee my Son* {1 Chron. 17:13}. Whereas, if *Solomon* were a

Son, of God by *Adoption,* so was our Lord by *Generation;* what *Solomon* was by *Favour,* our Lord was by *Nature.*

[Consider Psal. 89.26, 27.]

Solomon, was a *Preacher in Jerusalem.* From whence, wee need not quaestion, Whether hee Repented of his former Apostacies & Miscarriages. Indeed, a King may without any Degradation, become an *Ambassadour,* for the *King of Kings.* *Joseph* of *Arimathaea,* was a Counsellour of State {Mark 15:43}. *Ambrose* was a Consul of *Millain. Chrysostom,* was a Nobleman of *Antioch. John a Lasco* was a Nobleman of *Poland. George,* the Prince of *Anhalt* is well-known.[63] Yea, And our Lord Jesus Christ also, was a *Preacher in Jerusalem:* a Preacher that *Sought out acceptable Words,* that *Spoke so as never Man Spake.* I have heard it so expressed, *The God of Heaven had but one Son, & Hee made a Minister of Him.*

Solomon signifies, *The Peaceable,* or, *The Peace-maker.* [See 1. Chron. 22.9.] Tis our Lord Jesus Christ, that is the great *Giver of Peace,* to all under His Blessed *Government.* [Consider, Isa. 9.6. and Eph. 2.14. and Mic. 5.5. and Luc. 2.14.]

The *Wisdome of Solomon,* was Incomparable. [1. King. 4.29, 30.] Hee had a most comprehensive Intellect, fraught with Rare Notions, beyond all Number. But, hee is infinitely exceeded by our Lord Jesus Christ. [Col. 2.3.] I Beleeve, all the *Works* of God, yea, all His *Decrees,* are known to that *Man,* who is God as well as Man.

Pharaohs Daughter became *Solomons* Wife; and shee seems a *Proselyte,* whom hee might lawfully espouse. Hee sinned, in his other outlandish Marriages; but I suppose, not in *This.* And hence, I conceive, this *Match,* never became a *Snare* unto him; I find no *Egyptian* Idols, in all the False-Worship, that hee tolerated. This was *Typical;* as the forty fifth Psalm does intimate. Well; *Egyptians,* or, Foreigners; namely, wee poor Gentiles, are married unto our Lord Jesus Christ; our Lord ha's betrothed unto Himself, *Aliens from the Commonwealth of Israel* {Eph. 2:12}.

Finally, The Throne of *Solomon,* admirably represents unto us, the *Throne* of the Lord Jesus Christ. [It is described, in 1. King. 10.18.—]

This *Throne,* is made of *Ivory;* there is not one *Black Spot* of Injustice on it; it is called, *A Great White Throne* {2 Chron. 9:17}.

This *Throne,* tis many Stairs *High;* our Lord that sitts upon it, is *Ascended* and *Exalted,* above all Creatures whatsoever.

This *Throne,* ha's Two *Pillars* to bear it up; the Two *Pillars* of Recompence for the Good, & Punishment for the Wicked.

This *Throne,* ha's *Lions* that stand about it; & those no *Painted* ones: the Angels are like so many Rampant *Lions,* to execute the Orders of the Lord.

What shall I say more? *This Throne has None like unto it.*

[ENTRY ON THE PSALMS (A JEWISH CURIOSITY ABOUT THE PSALMS)]

The Psalms

Q. Can you mention any Jewish Curiosity about the *Psalms*, that may discover the *Subtilty* of Satan, & the *Sinfulness* of Men, to Abuse the Holy Word of God?

A. Yes. But that I may not lay a Snare before ordinary Readers, Who are easily decoy'd into those wicked *Sorceries*, by which they pay an Homage to the *Divel*, and give the *Divel* a Command over themselves, I will forbear Translating, what I read in *Amamas Antibarbarus Biblicus*.[64] Nevertheless it shall be Transcribed, for the Entertainment of those Ingenious and Religious Readers, who will with a due Abhorrence Look upon it.

Possideo Psalterium, quod Aditum est Savionetae 1556. *Ad Eius calcem additus est Libellus hoc Titulo* / שמוש תהלים / *id est* Usus Psalmorum. *In Eo singulis Psalmis suus assignatur usus. Dabo gustum.*[65]

Psal. 2. *Ut Libereris ex Tempestate Maris recita hunc Psalmum et inscribe eum testae et projice illam in mare et consilescet.*

Si cui caput dolebit, scribe hunc Psalmum usque ad illa, confringes eos virga ferrea, et suspende illam Chartam de Capite eius.[66]

Psalm. 3. *Si quis humerum et caput dolebit, pronuntiet hunc Psalmum super oleo olivarum et inungat eo partes affectas.*[67]

Psal. 7. *Utilis est iste Psalmus ne homines tibi possint nocere, et ut in fugam vertas inimicum tuum, qui te persequitur.*

Accipe pulverem ex terrâ et recita super eo hunc Psalmum et sparge Pulverum istum coram inimico tuo, qui te persequitur et retrocedet.

Porro, si quis habeat inimicum, accipiat Ahenum novum et impleat illud ex fonte Aquarum et recitet hunc Psalmum quater à / קומה יהוה / *usque ad finem, et effunde illam aquam in loco inimici tui et prevalebis ei.*[68]

Psal. 120. *Cum vides serpentem aut scorpionem, recita eum septies.*[69]

Psal. 123. *Contrà servum fugitivum. Inscribe laminae plumbi duo illa nomina* / אדון / *Dominus, et* / עבד / *Servus, et revertitur.*[70]

Psal. 126. *Utilis est mulieri cujus liberi moriuntur: scribe eum in pergameno, et adscribe haec* / שנוי סנסנוי סמנגלף / *in postremâ lineâ, et pones illud in quatuor angulis domus.*[71]

Psal. 130. *Quando vigiles circumeunt urbem si velis invisibilis transire coram illis, mussa eum versus quatuor plagas mundi, et obruet eos sopor. Taedet plura adscribere.*[72]

T'wil be an *Ornament* unto a learned Man to *know* such things. For any Man to *use* them, would be a Damnable Wickedness. Lett no Reader now serve me, so wickedly, as a Scholar of *Hemingius* did him, upon his reciting certain Superstitions.[73]

[ENTRY ON ISAIAH 7:14 (ISAIAH'S PROPHECY ON A VIRGIN CONCEIVING)]

Isaiah 7:14.

Therefore the Lord himself shall give you a sign; Behold, a virgin shall conceive, and bear a son, and shall call his name Immanuel.

Q. A Fresh Operation on that famous Prophecy; *Behold, A Virgin shall conceive?* v. 14.

A. A Gentleman, whose Name is Mr. *John Green*,[74] in some Letters published, 1726. has argued well upon it.

It may be owned, that the Infant *Shearjashub*, whom the Prophet by the Order of Heaven took with him, when he was to meet *Ahaz*, was a *Sign* to *Ahaz*, that *Isaiah* was really a Prophet of the Lord; and that the Projects of the Enemies to *Judah*, would according to his Praediction, be confounded. His Name signifying, *The Remnant shall return*, given him just about the Time when the Two Kings had invaded *Judaea*, & carried great Multitudes into Captivity, was a Token, that some of them should be sent home again; which came to pass accordingly. [2. Chron. XXVIII.5, 16.] And the Sight of *this Child* might be a proper *Sign* for this Purpose.

But when the *Word* of *Isaiah*, and the *Sign* in his hand, was disregarded, GOD offers to *Ahaz* any *Sign*, (or *Miracle*) he should make his Choice of. And this gracious Offer being refused, *Ahaz* has no further *Sign* for this Purpose given him. Had any *Sign* been given him, he was a Wretch that would not have spent one Thought upon it. The *Hypocrite* pretended a Fear of Transgressing the Divine Command, *Ye shall not Tempt the Lord your GOD* {Deut. 6:16}: But in Reality, he paid more of Respect unto *Baalim*, than unto the True GOD; and instead of waiting on the GOD of *Israel*, he was resolved on flying to the King of *Assyria* for Assistance.

And if it had been the Intent of the Holy One, to have given *Ahaz* a *Sign*, certainly He would have done it *at first*, and not have given him Opportunity to *Sleight* it and *then* even *Force* it upon him. Yea, from the Dreadful Judgments which are threatened in the very Breath in which this Prophecy is delivered, it is plain, that GOD had no Design any further to comfort *Ahaz*, with an Assurance that the Plotts of his Enemies would be in a little time defeated. The Threatening is, *The Lord shall bring upon thee, & upon thy Fathers House, Days that have not come, from the Day that Ephraim departed from Judah; even the King of Assyria* {Isa. 7:17}. And the rest of the Chapter foretells the Depopulating of the Countrey by him. We know accordingly what was done to *Ahaz,* by *Tiglath-Pilneser;*[75] a great Monarch, that was a greater Plague to him, than the Two petty Princes he had now to deal withal: and how from this Time the Jews were excluded from all their Traffic into the *Southern Sea,* which they had ow'd most of their Wealth unto.

In short; The Prophet leaves *Ahaz,* as a Person on whom he despaired of doing any Good; and except the Prophesy of the *Messiah,* to be *Born of a Virgin,* dropt for the Comfort of the Religious among the Jews, and the Benefit of the Church in after-ages, you hear nothing besides terrible Comminations.

The *Birth* of a Son from a *young Woman,* foretold as a *Sign,* that the *Enemies* now feared, should be defeated, would have signified but very little. For their Enemies had now taken the Field, yea, probably were on their full March to *Jerusalem.* Their Armies were Numerous, and Well-appointed; and flush'd with former Victories; and the Jews but ill-praepared for opposing them. Yea, they expected within a very Few Months to be swallowed up. They wanted Comfort under their *present* Anxiety & Perplexity. Now, how useless a *Sign,* would such a *Remote Matter* have been to them, under their *present Anguish.*

As to *Maher-shalal-hashbaz,* all that we can collect with Certainty is, That the Prophet was ordered first of all to write those *Words* on a *Roll* before Witnesses, without any Intimation of a *Son* to be born unto him. Some time after this, the Prophetess having been delivered of a *Son,* he was commanded for to putt all the *Words* into his Name, as a Prophecy of the speedy Ruine to come on the *Syrians* and the *Israelites.*

Briefly; This Prophecy, cannot in any Sense at all relate unto a young Woman in the Days of *Ahaz.* But *Matthews* Interpretation of it, is *literal,* and *obvious,* and indeed the *only* one that can be given {Matt. 1:21–23}. This makes the Prophecy serve to a considerable End; conspicuously distinguishing the *Messiah* from all other Persons: An End, worthy of the solemn Introduction: *Behold!* None but JESUS ever was born of a *Virgin:* And none but He could be called, *Immanuel;* And of none but Him could it be said, *His Name shall be called, The mighty GOD* {Isa. 9:6}. All too high for a *Maher-shalal-hashbaz,* or for an *Hezekiah,* or for any meer Man in the World.

Here are evidently Two distinct Praedictions. The first, That a *Virgin* should conceive & bear a Son. The second, That the Land of the Enemies to *Judah* should be forsaken of its Kings, before *Shearjashub* should know to Refuse the Evil & Chuse the Good. The one of these Praedictions is made a *Sign* of the other, and was to be fulfilled, in Token, that the other should also come to pass in the Season of it. GOD here assures the House of *David,* That a *Virgin* should bring forth a Son, who should be an *Immanuel*. And since many of them were *staggering* at the *Promise thro' Unbeleef*, that the *Messiah* should be born to the House of *David*, then in such melancholy Circumstances; and since this was a Thing that has never been heard of before, and yett more Incredible, *That He should be born of a Virgin*, GOD kindly tells them, That He would give *This* as the *Sign* of His Giving a most certain Accomplishment unto that glorious Prophecy; The *Land* of their Enemies, would be *forsaken of their Kings*, before *Shearjashub*, [whom we may suppose the Prophet then pointing at] *should know, to refuse the Evil & chuse the Good*; tho' he should *eat Butter & Honey* [and have a Plenty of the Food suitable to his Age,] *that he might be in a Capacity of doing it assoon as possible*. Thus we have a *Sign*, soon coming to pass, of a Thing to be performed above seven hundred Years afterwards.

Mr. *Green* gives us this Paraphrase. *"Therefore*, or, *Notwithstanding*, tho' *Ahaz* & such as join'd with him, have carried it in so provoking a Manner, *the Lord Himself* out of His abundant Grace and Mercy *will give you a Sign*; a *Sign* to another Purpose, than that which was before offered unto *Ahaz*, and suddenly refused; a *Sign* of a much more wonderful thing than the Delivering of you from your Enemies. *Behold*, Take particular Notice of what I say; A pure and undefiled *Virgin, shall conceive & bear a Son, and shall* with Reason, *call His Name* IMMANUEL*;* for such shall He be, *GOD with us*; JESUS *the Saviour: The promised* MESSIAH. This is the *Praediction* to be confirm'd by the *Sign* the Lord will give you; and the *Sign* that I am speaking of, is this. You see, here is this little Child *Shearjashub: Butter & Honey shall he eat, that he may know to refuse the Evil & chuse the Good*; or attain to Years of Discretion; *for, or, but, before the Child shall know to Refuse the Evil & Chuse the Good, the Land that thou abhorrest*, the Land of *Syria*, and the Land of *Israel, shall be forsaken of both her Kings."*[76]

Thus, How does GOD *in Wrath remember Mercy?* And how admirably does *He* provide for the Few Beleevers now among His People? Were they fearful, that their Enemies pursuant unto their League, would sett up the Son of *Tabeal* for their King & frustrate the grand Promise of the *Messiah? Behold*, That grand Promise is Renewed; The Manner of it is declared; and a *Sign* is given of its Performance; a *Sign* that was not long to be waited for; and a *Sign* that fixed their Eyes on one, whose prophetical Name, *Shearjashub*, gave them Reason to receive *Isaiah*, as a Prophet of the Lord! *Behold*, How the *Messiah* is at the same time, distinguished; and a Provision made against the *False Christs* that might arise, by foretelling that the *Messiah* should be *born of a Virgin!*

[ENTRY ON ISAIAH 7:16 (THE APPLICABILITY
OF ISAIAH'S PROPHECY TO CHRIST)]

Isaiah 7:16

Q. A little further, upon this Prophecy. [*For before the child will know to refuse the evil, and choose the good, the land that thou abhorrest shall be forsaken of both her kings.*] *v.* 16.

A. There ha's been a Controversy of late managed particularly between Mr. *Whiston,* and Dr. *Clagget.*[77]

The former[78] maintains, That the Language & Intent of the Prophets, is ever *Single:* and that their Prophecies are not capable of a Double Sense, & of such Typical Interpretations, as many Christian Expositors putt upon them. The latter[79] gives us a Collection of Twenty Five Prophecies, which he allowes to be meant only of the *Messiah,* & applicable to no other. But then he maintains, That there are Prophecies of the *Messiah,* which carry a *Double Sense* in them: & that it is fitt there should be so. One of those, he supposes to be that which is now before us. He observes, The *Sign* of Deliverance given to *Ahaz,* is a Prophecy of *the Holy Child,* and of *Another Child.* A Prophecy of a *Child,* that should be born in *Isaiah's,* and *Ahaz's* Time, & of a *Child* that should not be born till some Hundred Years after. A Prophecy, that within the Time, that a *Virgin* should marry, & conceive, & bring forth, & the Child should be grown to distinguish between Good and Evil, *Ahaz* should be delivered from the Two Kings he feared. And a Prophecy that a *Virgin,* while a *Virgin,* should conceive, & bring forth, a Son for the Deliverance of Mankind. Here is a Prophecy of a Child, that should be called, *Immanuel;* as token of the Presence of God, with the House of *David.* And a Prophecy of a *wonderful Child,* who should be called, *Immanuel,* because he should be God Incarnate. The former, to have another Name of Distinction; even *Maher-shalal-hashbaz.* The latter to be distinguished by the Name of JESUS. If the Child, that should eat *butter and honey,* & before whose Knowing to *Refuse* the Evil, and *Chuse the Good,* the Land which *Ahaz* abhorred, should be *forsaken of both her Kings,* be the Child *Immanuel,* then tis plain, the Sense is double; because the Prophecy of *Immanuel* is most certainly a Prophecy of the *Messiah.* And as there is a *double Sense* in the Prophecy, so it gave a *Double Sign* of the Deliverance for the House of *David;* & a *Double Security* against their Destruction by *Rezin* or *Pekah.* The Promise of *Maher-shalal-hashbaz,* the Son of the Prophetess, assured *Ahaz,* he should be delivered of his Oppressors in two or three Years. The Promise of the *Messiah,* assured him, that the Tribe of *Judah,* and Family of *David,* must be yett preserved for seven Centuries.

[ENTRY ON ROMANS 3:31 (ON A SINNER'S JUSTIFICATION)]

Romans 3.31.
Do we then make void the law through faith? God forbid: yea,
we establish the law.

Q.   The Doctrine of A *Sinners Justification*, taught in the Epistle to the *Romans?* v. 31.

A.   O Church of *Rome*, In that Article, *How a Sinner may be Justified*, lies very much of that *Apostasy*, which the *Spirit of Prophecy* foresaw coming upon thee. Our God commanding us, *Come out of her, My People*, an Epistle to that Church, admirably furnishes us in our *Coming out*; and fortifies us for the Required *Reformation*. It is a Remark which we may make by the way, That there is no Fear of a *Relapse into Popery*, by those, whose Hearts once have the Doctrine of, A *Sinners Justification*, as it is taught in this Epistle, imparted on them.

The Thing proved by the Inspired Scribe of Heaven is, That the Sinful Children of Men, be they who or where they will, can do no other than Despair of being *Justified by the Works of the Law*; or, by their own Obedience to that *Law*, which God ha's given to Man, as the *Everlasting Rule* of Living unto Him. We are, by this Confession, unavoidably shutt up unto the *Faith of the Gospel*. We now can expect *Justification*, only thro' a lively *Faith*, in the Satisfaction, which the glorious JESUS ha's given to the Demands of the *Law* for us. An Admirable Saviour and Surety, entring into a *Covenant* with His eternal Father for that Purpose, ha's then undergone the *Penalty*, which the *Law* threatened unto the Sinner; and ha's yielded an exact and perfect Obedience to the *Praecept* of it, in the Room of His People, for whom His eternal Father allow'd Him to become Responsible. By *Faith* we are to plead this with God; renouncing all other Plea's and Hopes for our *Justification*: And so, the sovereign *Grace* of God Imputes to us, and Reckons to our Account, this *Justifying Righteousness* of our great Redeemer. None of our *good* Works are sett down in the Register of God, as a *Balance*, for the *Debts* contracted by our Sins. It is the *compleat Righteousness* of the Son of God, fully answering His *Law*, which is offered by the *Grace* of God unto us for that Purpose, and Received, and Applied by the *Faith*, which His *Grace* works in us; It is *This* that becomes the *Propitiation* for us. This is the *Pauline* Doctrine of *Justification*. . . .

The *Moderns* will more generally come into such Sentiments, when they take a Course, which an excellent Friend of Mine, [Mr. *Isaac Watts*][80] ha's in an Essay of his, from his own Experience commended unto us. His Words are worth transcribing. "If I might acquaint the World with my own Experience; After some Years spent in the Perusal of controversial Authors, & finding them insufficient to settle my Judgment and Conscience, in some great Points of Religion, I resolved to seek a Determination of my Thoughts, from the Epistles of *Paul*; and especially in that weighty Doctrine of *Justification*. I perused his Letter to the *Romans* in the Original, with the most fixed Meditation, laborious Study, and Importunate Requests to God, for several Months together. First, without consulting any Commentator; and afterwards calling in the Assistance of the best Criticks & Interpreters. I most heartily bless the Divine Goodness, that at last established my Judgment and Conscience in that Glorious and Forsaken Doctrine, of, *The Justification of a Sinner in the Sight of God, by the Imputation of a perfect Righteousness, which is not originally his own.*"[81]

But now, Our Apostle supposes an Objection against this Doctrine. *Then Good Works are not Necessary; Then a Care of Piety may be laid aside; Then we may live at a loose End; and yett we may enjoy the Consolations and Expectations of the Justified.* It is by the way, well observed, by one of the Acutest Men that have ever handled the Pen of the Writer, namely M. *Basnage*; That this is an Objection, which could never arise from such *Systems*, as are by some fathered on our Apostle.[82] If the *Sacrifices* and the *Ceremonies* of the *Law*, had been the *only* Things excluded from the Matter of our *Justification*, & not also all the *Good Works* of our *Piety*, it follows not by any Shadow of Consequence, that *Piety* is to be neglected. But then, if our Obedience to the *Moral Law* be excluded, this gives unto wicked Men, some Handle for a Cavil, That the Love of *Good Works* is now stifled; and since we are not *Justified* by *Good Works*, they are no longer to be insisted on. And, *as was the Master so was the Scholar*, in this important Matter. *Clemens Romanus* too, was afraid, some would conclude, *That Good Works may be neglected.*[83] And that Servant of God thus went on to answer it; *What shall we do, Brethren? Shall we now leave off doing of Good, & neglect Charity? God forbid, On the contrary, lett us make Haste, to produce those Good Actions, with Zeal & Eagerness.* But, of what use can these *Good Actions* be, if they have no Share in our *Justification*? They shall not be lost, saies our *Clemens Romanus*; For, *God will take Delight in them.* And so, our Apostle here, extinguishes the Objection, against the Necessity of *Good Works* drawn from our *Justification* another way, with a, *God forbid!* And with a Declaration, That the *Law*, which requires our *Good Works*, is indeed so far from *evacuated*, that it is *established*, by the *Faith* of the *Gospel*, which retires to the *Righteousness* of our Blessed JESUS, & expects to be *Justified* only by that; *Making mention of thy Righteousness, O Lord, even of Thine only, O our Saviour!*

I have repeted these Thoughts, in my poor Treatise; *Adversus Libertinos.*[84]

[ENTRY ON EPHESIANS 5:32 (THE MYSTERY IN THE MARRIAGE
OF ADAM AND EVE)]

Ephesians 5:32.
*So ought men to love their wives as their own bodies. He that loveth
his wife loveth himself.*

Q.   The *Mystery* in the Marriage of *Adam* and *Eve?* v. 32.

A.   Dr. *Alix*[85] notes, That as the first Mark between *Adam* and *Eve*, was a Type
of that between *Christ* and His *Church*; So, in this, the Apostle had the Jewish
Notion to concur with him; For the *Jewes* tell us, according to *Voisin*, *And the
Mystery of Adam, is the Mystery of the Messiah*, who is the Bridegroom of the
Church.[86] It was the Observation of *Munster*, That *the Creation of the Woman
from the Rib of the Man, was made by the Jewes, to signify the Marriage of the
caelestial Man, who is blessed,* (or, of the Messiah) *with the Church.*[87] Hence the
Apostle applies the very Words, which *Adam* uttered, concerning *Eve*, his
Spouse, unto those Christians, who are the Spouse of Christ; *We are Members
of His Body, & of His Flesh, & of His Bones.*

[ENTRY ON EPHESIANS 5:22–32 (MARRIAGE AS A TYPE OF UNION
BETWEEN CHRIST AND THE CHURCH)]

Ephesians 5:22–32

Q.   Why should Persons in a *Married Estate,* consider so Attentively, as the
Apostle doth advise them, the *Union* between the Lord Jesus Christ, and His
Church, as a Mystery instructive to them in their Marriage? v. 22.—32.

A.   Tis a true and a deep Speculation of the *Platonists*, Τὰ αἰσθητα τῶν νοητῶν
μιμήματα,[88] *Material* Things are but *Ectypal* Resemblances and Imitations of
Spiritual Things, which are the Archetypal, Original, and Primitive Beings of
all.[89] Nor is there any thing more obvious to a wise Contemplator, than that
of *Reuchlin, Deum solere uno Sigillo Varias Materias signare.*[90] There are *parallel
Signatures* imprinted by the God of Heaven, upon several Subjects, which render them not meer *Similitudes* of one another, as the *Kingdome of Heaven,* may
bee likened unto a *Grain of Mustard-seed;* but are, as my Lord *Verulam* expresses
it, *Una eademque Naturae Vestigia, diversis Materijs et Subjectis Impressa.*[91]

Here lies the sounder Part of the Jewish *Cabala;* and hence an Hebrew Doctor, tells us, *The several Worlds were printed with the same Print, and sealed with
the same Seal; and that which receiveth the Sigillation here below, is like to the
Shape & Form of those things above, which did stamp the Signature upon them.*

In *Heaven*, there is according to those Observers, *The World of Emanation*; and in the visible Creation, there are the Marks of things flowing from that World.

So say those *Poets*; And, THIS WITNESS IS TRUE.—

Well then; I say, That the Lord Jesus Christ, and His Church, are, *Sponsus et Sponsa Archetypi*;[92] a Man and his Wife, are, *Sponsus et Sponsa Ectypi*.[93]

God from all Eternity purposed and promised, a *Church* unto the Lord *Jesus Christ*. As well in this Eternal *Idaea*, as in the Actual *Fulfilment*, the Lord Jesus Christ, Loves, Pitties, and Supplies His Church; the Church, Loves, Honours, and Obeyes the Lord Jesus Christ; and the *Union* between them is most gloriously Intimate, they are most nearly concerned in one anothers Interests. Now, in the right Order of things, pursuant unto, and consequent upon, the Establishment of this Design, a *Man* and a *Woman* is made; and they are given unto each other with a particular Instruction, that in their Affection, Relation, & Behaviour towards each other, they consider the *Union* between the Lord Jesus Christ, and His Church, as the grand *Exemplar*, whereto they are to conform themselves.

The Marriage between *Tipheret* and *Malcuth* [in English, *The (male) Beauty*, and, *The (female) Kingdome*] ha's been very notably handled by the Israelitish Doctors, who have handled, the Mysteries of the *Sephiroth* [or, Emanations of Light] in the *Messiah*. And it was their Opinion, That in the *Canticle of Solomon, Sponsum Tipheret et Sponsam Malcuth, introducit ad invicem loquentes*.[94]

I will at this time carry you, no further, lest I confound you. But you shall now learn from hence, why the Notion of *Man* and *Wife*, the whole Bible over, is employ'd, to describe the *Union* between the Lord Jesus Christ, and His Church; and so, why *False Worship* is described as a *Fornication*. Our Lord led, an otherwise *unmarried* Life; but you see, to whom Hee is truly *married*. And indeed, as *Eve* was fetched out of the Side of sleeping *Adam*, so *Jerom* tells us, *Eva in Typo Ecclesiae, de costâ Viri aedificata est*.[95] Yea, the dull School Men, at last hitt upon it, *Ecclesia facta est de Latere Christi dormientis in cruce*.[96]

The Invisible World and Salem
Witchcraft

The Salem witchcraft trials (1692–93) have become a permanent fixture in our national mythology, yet many questions remain unanswered: Was witchcraft really practiced among God-fearing New England Puritans at the time? How did the Salem debacle get started, who was involved, and what was the outcome? What was the role of the clergy during the proceedings? Could the accused have saved their lives? Were the executions of the witches a miscarriage of justice? Although a minor event in the annals of our country, the enigma of the Salem witch hunt has long been a cultural bugbear and pointed weapon for numerous social, religious, and political groups over the past three hundred years. It is fair to argue that the events of 1692–93 constituted a cornerstone in the foundation of American literature and culture. The selections in this section shed light on Cotton Mather's place in and contribution to the ongoing debate.

In our postmodern, post-Christian world, many individuals believe in and practice the manipulation of natural and even supernatural forces—what was known and roundly condemned in Mather's day as "witchcraft." But it is perhaps unfathomable for some modern readers that people once believed in the existence and supernatural power of devils and demons, and the culpability of those accused of practicing witchcraft. "Thou shalt not suffer a witch to live" (Exod. 22:18) was a well-known biblical maxim, and there were many women, men, and even children who unjustifiably lost their lives in the enforcement of this law in the Old and New Worlds. Closer to Mather's own time, King James I's Witchcraft Act of 1604 decreed witchcraft a capital crime in England, Scotland, Ireland, and the English colonies in America. It was repealed under King George II in 1735—more than forty years after the Salem debacle. What complicated matters was that our modern concept of the presumption of innocence of an accused did not become firmly anchored in British law until the late eighteenth century. Put in a different way, the accused were assumed guilty until proven innocent, and torture was permissible when voluntary confessions were not forthcoming. At pretrial hearings or during the trials themselves, the defendants had neither benefit of counsel nor witnesses to speak up for the accused. The appointed judges and magistrates, with little or no experience in matters of criminal prosecution for witchcraft, based their verdict on common-law precedent in England that most closely resembled their own case at hand.[1] Irony of ironies, *dis*believing in witches and the power of their demonic minions was similarly blameworthy, for unbelief or skepticism was tantamount to atheism, a felony equally punishable. No devils, no witches, ergo no God, no angels: so the logic went at the time. And no one in his or her right mind would dare to question the existence of the invisible world or laugh it off as superstition—not even skeptics such as Robert Calef (1648–1719), a Boston cloth merchant who in 1700 laid the blame for the death of the executed squarely at the feet of Mather and his fellow ministers.

Seven years after the main actors in the Salem tragedy had been laid to rest, Calef, Mather's old nemesis, published *More Wonders of the Invisible World* (1700), the title satirically alluding to Mather's 1693 *Wonders of the Invisible World*. Calef portrayed Mather as singularly gullible and cruel and singled him out as "the most active and forward of any Minister in the Country in those matters . . . [that] threatned the devouring this Country."[2] One point in Calef's smear campaign was representative of the whole of Calef's *More Wonders*: Mather's alleged cruelty at the execution of Reverend George Burroughs (c. 1650–1692). Calef's account proved so convincing to subsequent generations of historians that they adapted and embellished the story for their own rhetorical ends. When Burroughs "was upon the Ladder" with the noose about his neck, Calef related, he addressed the crowd of spectators in such heart-melting words and concluding with the Lord's Prayer so composedly and with "such (at least seeming) fervency of Spirit" that "he drew Tears from many (so that it seemed to some, that the Spectators would hinder the Execution)[;] the accusers said the black Man stood and dictated to him; as soon as he was turned off, Mr. *Cotton Mather*, being mounted upon a Horse, addressed himself to the People, partly to declare, that he [Burroughs] was no ordained Minister, and partly to possess the People of his guilt; saying, That the Devil has often been transformed into an Angel of Light; and this did somewhat appease the People, and the Executions went on." To add insult to injury, Calef continued, Burroughs's corpse was "dragged by the Halter to a Hole, or Grave, between the Rocks, about two Foot deep, his Shirt and Breeches being pulled off, and an old pair of Trousers of one Executed, put on his lower parts, he was so put in, together with *Willard* and *Carryer*, one of his Hands and his Chin, and a Foot of one [of] them being left uncovered."[3] Such is the gruesome tale of Cotton Mather on horseback working the crowd to keep the mob from interfering in Burroughs's execution. And it was this vivid legend that had Mather riding on horseback through our histories and schoolbooks until the late twentieth century.

Calef's anecdote appears in his *More Wonders*, published eight years after the fact.[4] It is corroborated by none of his contemporaries. Neither Judge Samuel Sewall (1652–1730), an eyewitness who addressed the incident in his *Diary*, nor Thomas Brattle (1658–1713), Harvard treasurer and affluent merchant, agrees with Calef's description of the events.[5] Certainly no friend of the Mathers, Brattle related the episode in terms quite the reverse of Calef's accusation. In his "Letter, Giving a Full and Candid Account," written on October 8, 1692, less than two months after Burroughs's execution, Brattle relates that the condemned "protested their innocency as in the presence of the great God, whom forthwith they were to appear before. . . . With great affection they intreated Mr. C[otton] M[ather] to pray with them: they prayed that God would discover what witchcrafts were among us; they forgave their accusers; they spake without reflection on Jury and Judges, for bringing them in guilty, and condemning them."[6] There is no word in the entire letter of Mather working the mob. As to the victims about to be hanged, they sought Mather as their spiritual counselor—hardly what they would have done if he had been the vile and heartless witch-doctor that Calef made him out to be.

It is a question, then, whether Mather's small handful of publications on the invisible world (which constitutes less than 2 percent of his nearly 400 published works) really stoked the fire of the Salem trials as Calef's accusation implies. Modern historians still agree to disagree, even as popular culture has willingly embraced Mather's effigy as America's own bogeyman. Perhaps David Levin, the distinguished historian and biographer of Mather, says it best: "The problem for the modern biographer is not how to defend Mather. Answering such distortions tend to perpetuate the effigy both by repeating the memorable rhetoric and by casting the discussion or the characterization in the rigid mold of prosecution or defense."[7] That said, we invite readers to form their own opinions on the matter by perusing representative excerpts from Mather's vast oeuvre. Only a wide review of his works can help us attain a more balanced viewpoint.

Cotton Mather's *Memorable Providences* (1689), the first selection, was no exception. It was a case-study of the bewitchment or possession, starting in 1688, of four of John Goodwin's children, ranging in age from five to thirteen. As Mather related the story, an altercation between Martha, Goodwin's eldest daughter, and Ann Glover, an Irish Roman Catholic who worked as a laundress in their Charlestown neighborhood, started the episode. When Martha accused Goodwife Glover of having purloined some linens, Glover retaliated by bestowing a mighty curse on the thirteen-year-old girl. Nowadays, we might shrug off curses and respond in kind, but back then curses and imprecations were potent maledictions, especially if they invoked the devil. People believed in their efficacy and in the power of words. The same night, Martha and three of her younger siblings developed strange fits, intermingled with episodes of catatonia; contortions of their necks, backs, and limbs; and hideous screams.[8] The symptoms persisted over several days, yet none of the local doctors could diagnose any physical ailment and concluded that the symptoms were diabolical in origin. Glover was hauled before a judge, interrogated, and ultimately convicted of sorcery, especially after witchcraft paraphernalia—"poppets"—were found in the cellar of her house. Her summary execution, however, did nothing to ease the suffering of the Goodwin children. To study these seemingly supernatural phenomena, Cotton Mather recommended that the children be separated and taken to different homes for closer observation, and thus to prevent further accusations. He invited young Martha to stay in his home and employed a regimen of prayer, fasting, and spiritual conversation to save her from her affliction. In this way, Mather and his fellow clergymen could study her possession firsthand.

Four years later, suspicions followed by growing accusations of witchcraft abounded in Salem and in Essex County, Massachusetts, until hundreds had been named and arrested. Mather drew up "The Return of Several Ministers Consulted," on June 15, 1692, as an official clerical recommendation to Governor William Phips and the Court of Oyer and Terminer on how to proceed in the sprawling cases of witchcraft. The document was sent to the governor after the execution of Bridget Bishop on June 10, 1692, the first of nineteen victims hanged on Gallows Hill in Salem. "The Return" recommended guidelines by English Puritan divines and warned against reliance on "spectral evidence" in the conviction of the accused. As nearly everyone believed at the time, witches had covenanted with the devil by selling their souls in exchange for supernatural powers to cast spells, afflict people and their livestock with disease or death, choke them at night by invisibly sitting on their chests, and cause untold harm with their malefic magic.[9] The problem was that only the afflicted people were able to "see" the "specters," or shapes, of the accused witches and their "familiars," a kind of totem animal, such as a cat, dog, or bird, that carried out the bidding of the witches. These familiars suckled on the witches' teats, moles, or other physical protuberances of their bodies—hence physical examinations were a standard regimen of the ordeal. It is at this point that "The Return" became a crucial document. Mather specifically warned the judges against convicting an accused person on the sole basis of spectral evidence, for the devil might assume the shape of an innocent person. Some of the judges heeded the warnings; most did not. The extant trial records reveal that spectral evidence constituted a major part of the evidence in at least one hundred cases. Growing criticisms of the trials and the arrival of the new governor halted the proceedings, gradually bringing an end to the tragedy, but not before about two dozen people had lost their lives at the gallows, in prison, or (in one case) through heavy rocks piled on his chest.

The next selection, an excerpt from Mather's diary, provides a glimpse of his private feelings and reflections on the Salem debacle. Although dated "May, 1692," internal references clearly indicate that Mather either did not record his reflections until several months after his *Wonders of the Invisible World* had appeared in print, or that he revised his original thoughts of May 1692 when he reworked his journal into his "Revised Memorials," perhaps even as late as 1709.[10] Marginal insertions in the manuscript further indicate several such revisions and afterthoughts. The excerpts included here reveal his deep anxiety about the upheaval of the day, his dismay at being blamed for his alleged part in the matter, and his almost ritualistic approach to countering the devil's machinations. Notable too is his deep respect for the judges, some of whom were personal friends of his family and members of the Mather church. As junior pastor and assistant to his father, the younger Mather was clearly caught between compassion for the victims and the accused on one side and the deference he was expected to pay to his seniors and superiors on the other. Nonetheless, the agony and ecstasy of his prayers are worth remembering, especially in light of the fact that he never attended any of the court sessions—and more telling yet, that his repeated offers to take up to six of the afflicted into his home and restore them through a regimen of fasting and prayer, as he had done in the case of Martha Goodwin, were ignored.[11]

Historians, perhaps justifiably, have singled out Judge Samuel Sewall for his public recantation and apology for his role as a judge in the witch hunt. Courageous and praiseworthy as Sewall's confession may strike us, the context of his diary entry perhaps illuminates his reasons for doing so: "the reiterated strokes of God upon himself and his family"—particularly, the deaths of his young daughter and newborn son. In light of Sewall's act of humility, Mather's acts of self-abasement, described by himself below, do not compare unfavorably.[12]

The next selection included here, Cotton Mather's "Letter to John Foster" of August 17, 1692, further demonstrates Mather's public and private stance on the

Salem executions. John Foster (1648–1711), a wealthy Boston merchant, deacon of Mather's church, and member of the General Court, had asked Mather for advice on the Salem trials. Again, Mather pointed out that spectral evidence was insufficient to convict, let alone execute, an accused witch, for the devil might assume the shape of anyone. Likewise, he spoke out against the use of a "touch" test—that is, forcing an accused witch to touch their supposed victim, causing the bewitchment to return to its source—to establish guilt. If no trustworthy evidence could be established beyond reasonable doubt, Mather recommended the court reprieve the accused, release them on bail, or exile them, rather than have one innocent person suffer. Regrettably, the General Court in Boston did not heed his advice, but neither did Mather force the issue.

At last, we come to the work for which Cotton Mather is most (in)famous: *The Wonders of the Invisible World*, published in late October 1692 but postdated 1693. It proved so popular that over the next three hundred years it was reprinted, excerpted, and anthologized more often than any of Mather's other works. To be sure, *Wonders* was not one book but several. It consisted of a collection of preliminaries, sermons, judicial guides to examining witches, excerpts from witchcraft cases in England and Sweden, court records, manifestations of walking ghosts, accounts of executions, and a discourse on the machinations of the devil, all woven into a tapestry of eschatological explanations for why the devil's time to seduce people was running out. If it seems disorganized by our standards, *Wonders* was really a work in progress and mirrored the muddle of 1692: Mather was putting the various pieces together while he was waiting for transcripts of the Salem court records to come in. He added bits and pieces of related matter as he went along, especially several of the sermons he preached at the height of the Salem crisis in August. This *omnium gatherum* was intended to calm the waves, squelch rumors, and still the pain of those who had lost loved ones. And, being published not only in Boston but in London, it was intended to stop the mouths of English critics who demanded to know what was going on in their far-flung North American colony.

Wonders of the Invisible World appeared in print just a week or two before Increase Mather's *Cases of Conscience*, which roundly condemned the court's sole reliance on spectral evidence in some of the capital cases.[13] Increase's *Cases* was signed by fourteen ministers, yet his son's signature was notably missing. It was not that Cotton disagreed with them on condemning the court's flimsy methods; rather, he felt that *Cases of Conscience* by itself would only exacerbate the mob's rising discontent with the judges, and his own *Wonders* would thus present a more balanced, if not favorable, account of the court's procedures.[14] He hoped to calm the waves by exonerating the judges on the one hand while offering the most incriminating evidence of witchcraft perpetrated by those who had been executed. "I did with all ye modesty I could use, decline, setting my hand unto ye Book [Increase's *Cases of Conscience*]," Cotton Mather confessed to his uncle in Plymouth, because "I had already a Book in ye Press [*Wonders*], which would sufficiently declare my opinion."[15] It is fair to argue that the Mathers and their colleagues did not backstab the Salem judges but coordinated their efforts with them to pour oil on the troubled waters. Too much was at stake. Cotton Mather's September 2 letter to Chief Justice William Stoughton is a case in point. Mather offered to write a defense of the court so as "to flatten that fury" against the judges, in exchange for Stoughton's summary approbation: "I shall think myself highly favored," Mather petitioned the presiding judge, "if you do but let me see that you approve my cares to sanctify the terrible hand of God, which is now upon us."[16] Stoughton was only too happy to oblige. He praised Mather for his "Elaborate and most seasonable Discourse"; for the "Good News of, *The Shortness of the Devils Time*"; and for his ability "to *Lift up a Standard* against the Infernal Enemy, that hath been *Coming in like a Flood upon us*."[17] Visions of the devil's time running out provided for Mather's book of wonders a credible framework, a cosmological rationale, for what was happening in Salem and for the measures the clergy and judges were taking to thwart the devil and his minions.

The excerpt below begins with Mather's rationale for why the devil had come down in Massachusetts, especially since the long-anticipated Second Coming was imminent and might occur as early as 1697, so Mather conjectured.[18] The devil's attack on New England was not some minor event for Mather: it was no less than the prelude to the last battle looming on the horizon. "I have indeed set my self to Countermine the whole PLOT of the Devil, against *New-England*, in every branch of it," Mather reassured his anxious readers early on.[19] The wily serpent had ensnared a knot of witches with promises of rewards to carry out his bidding and pester God-fearing Christians into signing the devil's book, so Mather rehearsed the well-known tale familiar to every child and adult.[20]

Three-quarters through compiling the book, Mather finally received what he had been waiting for: the trial records of five of the most notorious witchcraft cases. Included in the selections below are two, the most famous one on Reverend George Burroughs, the former pastor of Salem Village, where the accusations began after Reverend Samuel Parris (1653–1720) had succeeded him, and the trial of Susanna Martin. In many respects, Burroughs's character is most intriguing, for it garnered Mather's abject detestation. A minister of God turned wizard! Mather could not even bring himself to spell out his full name, lest *Wonders* become a memorial to Burroughs. From our viewpoint, the sensational depositions of eyewitnesses embedded here were shocking for their flimsiness. These testimonies included accounts of the spectral winding sheets of Burroughs's dead wives, seen by gossips who bore him grudges; a brother-in-law who related that Burroughs could render himself invisible and listen in on private conversations; Burroughs's superhuman strength, though a puny man; and apparitions of the dead appearing in court, crying for vengeance. Deeply troubled by the minister's alleged part in the Salem mayhem, Mather maintained anything but an objective distance to the charges he found in the court records.

Susanna Martin pleaded not guilty, though she could have saved her life with a lie by confessing to the charges of witchcraft. This is one of the ironies of Salem that is hard to fathom: false confessions did save lives in New England. Real witches would never voluntarily confess to having covenanted with the devil; the devil would never allow them to expose him in this manner, so the judges believed. But if an indicted witch somehow did plead guilty and repented, she—and the majority of accused and executed were women—might join the chorus of accusers as proof she had broken the chains of her master. She might get off with a lighter punishment, perhaps lose whatever property she or her family might possess, but she would indeed save her life—her earthly life, that is—by forfeiting her life in heaven. Hitherto, any confessing witch would be executed. But at Salem, that logic was reversed: confessed witches were spared. The trial record of Martin spoke loudly, for it demonstrated how the magistrate's cross-examination sometimes entangled the accused in contradictions and inadvertent admissions of guilt. And, of course, there were also the depositions of her vengeful village neighbors who were eager to pay her back for some supposed past offenses such as bewitching their cattle or causing the wheel of an overloaded wagon to break. If that was not enough to find her guilty, the young women performed their possession before the court, throwing themselves on the ground and crying out, to the amazement of all bystanders, which sealed Martin's fate. On July 12, 1692, Lieutenant Governor and Chief Judge William Stoughton signed her death warrant, along with those of Sarah Good, Elizabeth How, Sarah Wildes, and Rebecca Nurse. Seven days later, they were all hanged on Gallows Hill, in Salem.[21] (Contrary to popular conceptions, no witches were burned at Salem— that was a European practice.) *The Wonders of the Invisible World* stands as a testimonial to the delusions of a bygone age and as a warning to us all.

MEMORABLE PROVIDENCES, RELATING TO WITCHCRAFTS AND POSSESSIONS (1689)

WITCHCRAFTS AND POSSESSIONS

The *First* EXEMPLE.

SECTION I. There[22] dwells at this time, in the *south* part of *Boston*, a sober & pious man, whose Name is *John Goodwin*, whose *Trade* is that of a *Mason*, and whose *Wife* (to which a *Good Report* gives a share with him in all the Characters of *Vertue*) has made him the Father of *six* (now living) *Children*. Of these Children, all but the Eldest, who works with his Father at his Calling, and the *Youngest*, who lives yet upon the Breast of its mother, have laboured under the direful effects of a (no less *palpable* than) stupendous WITCHCRAFT. Indeed that exempted *Son* had also, as was thought, some lighter *touches* of *it*, in unaccountable stabbs and pains now & then upon him; as indeed every person in the Family at some time or other had, except the *godly Father*, and the *sucking Infant*, who never felt any impressions of it. But these *Four* Children mentioned, were handled in so sad & *strange* a manner, as has given matter of *Discourse* and *Wonder* to all the Countrey, and of *History* not unworthy to be considered by more than all the *serious* of the *curious* Readers in this *New-English* World. . . .

SECT. *III.* About *Midsummer,* in the year 1688. the *Eldest* of these Children, who is a *Daughter,* saw cause to examine their Washer woman,[23] upon their missing of some *Linnen,* which twas fear'd she had stollen from them; and of what use this *linnen* might bee to serve the *Witchcraft* intended, *the Theef's Tempter knows.* This *Laundress* was the Daughter of an ignorant and scandalous old Woman in the Neighbourhood; whose miserable Husband before he died, had sometimes complained of her, that she was undoubtedly a *Witch,* and that whenever his Head was laid, she would quickly arrive unto the punishments due to such an one. This Woman in her daughters Defence bestow'd very bad Language upon the *Girl* that put her to the Question; immediately upon which, the poor child became variously indisposed in her health, and visited with *strange Fits,* beyond those that attend an *Epilepsy,* or a *Catalepsy,* or those that they call *the Diseases of Astonishment.*

SECT. *IV.* It was not long before *one* of her Sisters, and *two* of her Brothers, were seized, in Order one after another, with *Affects* like those that molested *her.* Within a few weeks they were all *four* tortured every where in a manner so very grievous, that it would have broke an heart of stone to have seen their Agonies. Skilful Physicians were consulted for their Help, and particularly our worthy and prudent Friend Dr. *Thomas Oakes,*[24] who found himself so affronted by the Distempers of the children, that he concluded nothing but an hellish *Witchcraft* could be the Original of these Maladies. And that which yet more confirmed such Apprehension was, That for one good while, the children were tormented just in the *same part* of their bodies all at the *same time* together; and tho' they saw and heard not one anothers complaints, tho' likewise their pains and sprains were swift like Lightening, yet when (suppose) the *Neck,* or the *Hand,* or the *Back* of *one* was Rack't, so it was at that instant with t'*other* too.

SECT. *V.* The variety of their tortures increased continually; and tho' about Nine or Ten at Night they alwaies had a Release from their miseries, and *ate & slept* all night for the most part indifferently well, yet in the *day* time they were handled with so many *sorts* of Ails, that it would require of us almost as much time to *Relate* them all, as it did of them to *Endure* them. Sometimes they would be *Deaf,* sometimes *Dumb,* and sometimes *Blind,* and often, *all this* at once. One while their *Tongues* would be drawn down their Throats; another while they would be pull'd out upon their *Chins,* to a prodigious length. They would have their *Mouths* opened unto such a Wideness, that their *Jaws* went out of joint; and anon they would clap together again with a Force like that of a strong *Spring-Lock.* The same would happen to their *Shoulder-Blades,* and their *Elbows,*

and *Hand-wrists,* and several of their joints. They would at times ly in a be-
nummed condition; and be drawn together as those that are ty'd *Neck & Heels;*
and presently be *stretched out,* yea, drawn *Backwards,* to such a degree that it
was fear'd the very skin of their Bellies would have crack'd. They would make
most pitteous out-cries, that they were cut with *Knives,* and struck with *Blows*
that they could not bear. Their *Necks* would be broken, so that their *Neck-bone*
would seem dissolved unto them that felt after it; and yet on the sudden, it would
become again so *stiff* that there was no stirring of their *Heads;* yea, their Heads
would be twisted almost *round;* and if main Force at any time obstructed a dangerous motion which they seem'd to be upon, they would roar exceedingly.
Thus they lay some weeks most pittiful Spectacles; and this while as a further
Demonstration of *Witchcraft* in these horrid Effects, when I went to *Prayer* by
one of them, that was very desirous to hear what I said, the Child utterly *lost* her
Hearing till our *Prayer* was over. . . .

SECT. *VII.* The Report of the Calamities of the Family for which we were
thus concerned, arrived now unto the ears of the *Magistrates,* who presently and
prudently apply'd themselves, with a just vigour, to enquire into the story. The
Father of the Children complained of his Neighbour, the suspected ill woman,
whose name was *Glover;* and she being sent for by the Justices, gave such a
wretched Account of her self, that they saw cause to commit her unto the Goal-
ers Custody. *Goodwin* had no proof that could have done her any Hurt but the
Hag had not power to deny her interest in the Enchantment of the Children;
and when she was asked, *Whether she believed there was a God?* her Answer was
too blasphemous and horrible for any Pen of mine to mention. An experiment
was made, *Whether she could recite the Lords Prayer;* and it was found, that tho'
clause after clause was most carefully repeated unto her, yet when she said it
after them that prompted her, she could not possibly avoid making *Nonsense* of
it, with some ridiculous Depravations. This Experiment I had the curiosity since
to see made upon *two more,* and it had the same Event. Upon the Commitment
of this *extraordinary* Woman, all the Children had some present ease; until one
(related unto *her*) accidentally meeting one or two of them, entertain'd them
with her *Blessing,* that is, *Railing;* upon which *Three* of them fell ill again, as
they were before.

SECT. *VIII.* It was not long before the *Witch* thus in the Trap, was brought
upon her *Tryal;* at which, thro' the Efficacy of a *Charm,* I suppose, used upon
her, by *one* or *some* of her *Crue,*[25] the Court could receive Answers from her in
none but the *Irish,* which was her *Native* Language; altho' she understood the
English very well, and had accustomed her whole Family to none but *that* Language in her former Conversation; and therefore the Communication between

the *Bench* and the *Bar*, was now cheefly convey'd by two honest and faithful men that were *Interpreters*. It was long before she could with any direct Answers plead unto her *Indictment*; and when she *did* plead, it was with *Confession* rather than *Denial* of her Guilt. Order was given to search the old womans house, from whence there were brought into the Court, several small *Images*, or *Puppets*, or *Babies*, made of Raggs, and stufft with *Goats hair*, and other such Ingredients. When these were produced, the vile Woman acknowledged, that her way to torment the Objects of her malice, was by wetting of her *Finger* with her *Spittle*, and stroaking of those little *Images*. The abused Children were then present, and the Woman still kept stooping and shrinking as one that was almost prest to Death with a mighty Weight upon her. But one of the *Images* being brought unto her, immediately she started up after an odd manner, and took it into her hand; but she had no sooner taken *it*, than *one* of the Children fell into sad *Fits* before the *whole Assembly*. This the Judges had their just Apprehensions at; and carefully causing the Repetition of the Experiment, found again the same event of it. They asked her, *Whether she had any to stand by her:* She replied, *She had*; and looking very pertly in the *Air*, she added, *No, He's gone*. And she then confessed, that she had *One*, who was her *Prince*, with whom she maintained, I know not what Communion. For which cause, the night after, she was heard expostulating with a *Devil*, for his thus deserting her; telling him that *Because he had served her so basely and falsly, she had confessed all*. However to make all clear, The Court appointed five or six *Physicians*, one evening to examine her very strictly, whether she were not craz'd in her *Intellectuals*, and had not procured to her self by *Folly* and *Madness* the Reputation of a *Witch*. Diverse hours did they spend with her; and in all that while no Discourse came from her, but what was pertinent & agreeable: particularly, when they asked her, What she thought would become of her soul? she reply'd *You ask me a very solemn Question, and I cannot well tell what to say to it*. She own'd her self a *Roman Catholick*; and could recite her *Pater Noster* in Latin very readily; but there was one Clause or two alwaies too hard for her, whereof she said, *She could not repeat it, if she might have all the world*. In the up-shot, the Doctors returned her *Compos Mentis*;[26] and Sentence of Death was passed upon her.

SECT. IX. Diverse dayes were passed between her being *Arraigned* and *Condemned*. In this time one of her Neighbours had been giving in her Testimony of what another of her Neighbours had upon her Death related concerning her. It seems one *Howen* about *Six years* before, had been cruelly bewitched to Death; but before she died, she called one *Hughes* unto her, Telling her that she laid her Death to the charge of *Glover*; That she had seen *Glover* sometimes come down her Chimney; That she should remember *this*, for within this *Six years* she might have Occasion to declare it. This *Hughes* now preparing her Testimony, immediately one of her children, a fine boy, well grown towards Youth, was taken ill, just in the same woful and surprising manner that *Goodwins* children were. One night particularly, The Boy said he saw a *Black thing* with a *Blue Cap* in the Room, Tormenting of him; and he complained most bitterly of a *Hand* put into the Bed, to pull out his Bowels. The next day the mother of the boy went unto *Glover,* in the Prison, and asked her, *Why she tortured her poor lad at such a wicked rate?* This Witch replied, that she did it because of wrong done to her self & her daughter. *Hughes* denied (as well she might) that she had *done her any wrong. Well then,* sayes *Glover, Let me see your child and he shall be well again. Glover* went on, and told her of her own accord, *I was at your house last night.* Sayes *Hughes, In what shape?* Sayes *Glover, As a black thing with a blue Cap.* Sayes *Hughes, What do you do there?* Sayes *Glover, with my hand in the Bed I tryed to pull out the boyes Bowels, but I could not.* They parted; but the next day *Hughes* appearing at *Court,* had her Boy with her; and *Glover* passing by the Boy expressed her good wishes for him; tho' I suppose, his Parent had no design of any mighty Respect unto the *Hag,* by having him with her there. But the Boy had no more Indispositions after the Condemnation of the Woman.

SECT. X. While the miserable old Woman was under Condemnation, I did my self twice give a visit unto her. She never denied the guilt of the *Witchcraft* charg'd upon her; but she confessed very little about the *Circumstances* of her Confederacies with the *Devils* only, she said, That she us'd to be at meetings, which her *Prince* and *Four* more were present at. As for those *Four,* She told *who* they were; and for her *Prince,* her account plainly was; that he was the *Devil.* She entertained me with nothing but *Irish,* which Language I had not Learning enough to understand without an Interpreter; only one time, when I was representing unto her *That* and *How* her Prince had cheated her, as her self would quickly find; she reply'd I think in *English,* and with, *passion* too, *If it be so, I am sorry for that!* I offer'd many Questions unto her, unto which, after long silence, she told me, *She would fain give me a full Answer, but they would not give her leave.* It was demanded, *They? Who is that* THEY? and she return'd that *They* were her *Spirits,* or her *Saints.* [for, they say, the same Word in *Irish* signifies both.] And at another time, she included her *two Mistresses,* as she call'd them in that [*They,*] but when it was enquired, Who those *two* were, she fell into a Rage, and would be no more urged.

I Sett before her, the *Necessity* and *Equity* of her breaking her *Covenant* with *Hell,* and giving her self to the Lord Jesus Christ, by an everlasting Covenant; To which her Answer was, that *I spoke a very Reasonable thing, but she could not do it.* I asked her whether she would *consent* or *desire* to be *pray'd* for; To *that* she said, *If Prayer would do her any good, shee could pray for her self.* And when it was again propounded, she said, *She could not unless her spirits* [or angels] *would give her leave.* However, against her will I pray'd with her, which if it were a Fault it was in *excess of Pitty.* When I had done, shee thank'd me with many good Words; but I was no sooner out of her sight, than she took a *stone,* a long and *slender stone,* and with her *Finger* and *Spittle* fell to tormenting it; though *whom* or *what* she meant, I had the mercy never to understand.

SECT. XI. When this *Witch* was going to her Execution, she said, the Children should not be relieved by her Death, for others had a hand in it as well as *she*; and she named *one* among the rest, *whom* it might have been thought Natural Affection would have advised the Concealing of. It came to pass accordingly, That the *Three children* continued in their *Furnace* as before, and it grew rather *Seven times hotter* than it *was.* All their *former* Ails pursued them *still,* with an *addition* of (tis not easy to tell how many) *more,* but *such* as gave more sensible Demonstrations of an *Enchantment* growing very far *towards* a POSSESSION by *Evil spirits.*

SECT. XII. The Children in their Fits would still cry out upon, [*They*] and [*Them*] as the Authors of all their Harm; but *who* that [*They*] and [*Them*] were, they were not able to declare. At last, the *Boy* obtain'd at *some times,* a sight of *some shapes* in the room. There were Three or Four of 'em, the Names of *which* the child would pretend at certain seasons to tell; only the Name of *One,* who was counted a *Sager Hag* than the rest, he still so stammered at, that he was put upon some *Periphrasis* in describing her. A Blow at the place where the *Boy* beheld the *Spectre* was alwaies felt by the Boy himself in the part of his Body that answered what might be stricken at; and this tho' his *Back* were turn'd; which was once and again so exactly tried, that there could be no Collusion in the Business. But as a Blow at the Apparition always *hurt* him, so it alwaies *help't* him too; for after the Agonies, which a *Push* or *Stab* of *That* had put him to, were over, (as in a minute or 2 they would be) the Boy would have a respite from his Fits a considerable while, and the *Hobgoblins* disappear. It is very *credibly* reported that a *wound* was this way given to an Obnoxious *woman* in the *town*; whose *name* I will not *expose*: for we should be tender in such Relations, lest we *wrong* the Reputation of the *Innocent,* by stories not enough enquired into.

SECT. XIII. The Fits of the Children yet more arriv'd unto such *Motions* as were beyond the Efficacy of any *natural Distemper* in the world. They would bark at one another like *Dogs,* and again purr like so many *Cats.* They would sometimes complain, that they were in a *Red-hot Oven,* sweating and panting at the same time unreasonably: Anon they would say, *Cold water* was thrown upon them, at which they would *shiver* very much. They would cry out of dismal *Blowes* with great *Cudgels* laid upon them; and tho' *we* saw no *cudgels* nor *blowes*, yet we could see the *Marks* left by them in *Red Streaks* upon their bodies afterward. And one of them would be roasted on an invisible *Spit*, run into his *Mouth*, and out at his *Foot*, he lying, and rolling, and groaning as if it had been so in the most sensible manner in the world; and then he would shriek, that *Knives* were cutting of him. Sometimes also he would have his head so forcibly, tho' not *visibly*, nail'd unto the Floor, that it was as much as a strong man could do to pull it up. One while they would all be so *Limber*, that it was judg'd every *Bone* of them could be *bent*. Another while they would be so *stiff*, that not a joint of them could be *stir'd*. They would sometimes be as though they were *mad*, and then they would climb over *high Fences*, beyond the Imagination of them that look'd after them. Yea, They would *fly* like *Geese*; and be carried with an incredible *Swiftness* thro' the *air*, having but just their *Toes* now and then upon the ground, and their *Arms* waved like the Wings of a *Bird*. One of them, in the House of a kind Neighbour and Gentleman (Mr. Willis) *flew* the length of the Room, about 20 foot, and flew just into an Infants high armed Chair; (as tis affirmed) none seeing her feet all the way touch the floor. . . .

SECT. *XVI*. But nothing in the World would so discompose them as a *Religious Exercise*. If there were any Discourse of God, or Christ, or any of the things *which are not seen & are eternal*, they would be cast into intolerable Anguishes. Once, those two Worthy Ministers Mr. *Fisk* and Mr. *Thatcher*,[27] bestowing some gracious Counsils on the Boy, whom they then found at a Neighbours house, he immediately lost his Hearing, so that he heard not *one word*, but just the *last word* of all they said. Much more, All *Praying* to *God*, & *Reading* of His *word*, would occasion a very terrible Vexation to them: they would then stop their *own Ears* with their *own Hands*; and roar, and shriek; and holla, to drown the Voice of the *Devotion*. Yea, if any one in the Room took up a *Bible* to look into it, the Children could see nothing of it, as being in a croud of Spectators, or having their Faces *another way*, yet would they be in *wonderful* Miseries, till the *Bible* were laid aside. In short, *No good thing* must then be endured near *those* Children, Which (*while* they are *themselves*) do love *every* good thing in a measure that proclaims in them the Fear of God.

SECT. *XVII*. My Employments were such, that I could not visit this afflicted Family so often as I *would*; Wherefore that I might show them what kindness I could, as also that I might have a full opportunity to observe the extraordinary *Circumstances* of the Children, and that I might be furnished with *Evidence* and *Argument* as a Critical Eye-Witness to confute the Saducism[28] of this debauched Age; I took the Eldest[29] of them home to my House. The young Woman continued well at our house, for diverse dayes, and apply'd her self to such Actions not only of *Industry*, but of *Piety*, as she had been no stranger to. But on the *Twentieth* of *November* in the *Fore-noon*, she cry'd out, *Ah [They] have found me out! I thought it would be so!* and immediately she fell into her fits again. I shall *now* confine my Story cheefly to *Her*, from *whose* Case the Reader may shape some Conjecture at the Accidents of the Rest.

SECT. *XVIII*. Variety of *Tortures* now siez'd upon the Girl; in which besides the fore-mentioned Ails returning upon her, she often would cough up a *Ball* as big as a small Egg into the side of her Wind-pipe, that would near choak her, till by Stroking and by Drinking it was carried down again. At the beginning of her Fits usually she kept odly Looking up the *Chimney*, but could not say *what* she *saw*. When I bade her *Cry* to the Lord Jesus for Help, her *Teeth* were instantly sett; upon *which* I added; *Yet, child, Look unto Him*, and then her Eyes were presently pulled into her head, so farr, that one might have fear'd she should never have us'd them more. When I prayed in the Room, first her Arms were with a *strong*, tho' not *seen* force clapt upon her ears; and when her hands, were with violence pull'd away, she cryed out, *[They] make such a noise, I cannot hear a word!* She likewise complain'd, that Goody *Glover's*, Chain was upon her Leg, and when she essay'd to go, her postures were exactly such as the *chained* Witch had before she died. But the manner still was, that her *Tortures* in a small while would pass over, and *Frolicks* succeed; in which she would continue many hours, nay, *whole days*, talking perhaps never *wickedly*, but always wittily beyond her self; and at certain provocations, her *Tortures* would renew upon her, till we had left off to give them. But she frequently told us, that *if she might but steal, or be drunk, she should be well immediately*.

SECT. *XIX*. In her *ludicrous* Fits, one *while* she would be for *Flying*; and she would be carried hither and thither, tho not *long* from the ground, yet *so long* as to exceed the *ordinary power* of Nature, in our Opinion of it: . . . Moreover,

There was one very singular passion that frequently attended her. An *Invisible Chain* would be clapt about her, and shee, in much pain and Fear, cry out, When *[They]* began to put it on. Once I did *with my own hand* knock it off, as it began to be fastned about her. But ordinarily, When it was *on*, shee'd be pull'd out of her seat with such violence *towards the Fire*, that it has been as much as *one* or *two* of us could do to keep her out. Her *Eyes* were not brought to be perpendicular to her feet, when she rose out of her Seat, as the Mechanism of a Humane Body requires in them that rise, but she was once dragg'd *wholly by other Hands*: and once, When I gave a stamp on the Hearth, just between her and the Fire, she scream'd out, (tho' I think she *saw* me *not*) *that I Jarr'd the Chain, and hurt her Back*.

SECT. XX. While she was in her *Frolicks* I was willing to try, Whether she could *read* or no; and I found, not only That *If she went to read the* Bible *her* Eyes *would be strangely twisted & blinded, and her* Neck *presently broken, but also that if any one* else *did read the* Bible *in the Room, tho it were wholly out of her sight, and without the least voice or noise of it, she would be cast into very terrible Agonies.* Yet once, Falling into her Maladies a little time after she had read the 59*th Psalm,* I said unto the standers-by, *Poor child! she can't now read the Psalm she readd a little while ago,* she listened *her self* unto something that none of us could hear, and made us be silent for some few Seconds of a minute. Whereupon she said, *But I* can *read it, they say I shall!* So I show'd her the *Psalm,* and she readd it all over to us. Then said I, *Child, say* Amen *to it:* but that she could not do. I added, *Read the next:* but no where else in the Bible could she read a word. I brought her a *Quakers Book;* and *That* she could quickly read *whole* pages of; only the Name of GOD and CHRIST she still skipt over, being unable to pronounce it, except sometimes with *stammering* a minute or *two* or more upon it. When we urged her to tell what the *Word* was that she missed, shee'd say, *I must not speak it; They say I must not, you know what it is* G *and* O *and* D; so shee'd *spell* the Name unto us. I brought her again, one that I thought was a *Good Book;* and presently she was handled *with intolerable Torments.* But when I show'd her a *Jest-Book,* as, *The Oxford Jests;* or the *Cambridge Jests,* she could read them *without any Disturbance,* & have *witty* Descants upon them too. I entertain'd her with a *Book*[30] that pretends to prove, *That there are no Witches;* and *that* she could read *very well,* only the Name *Devils,* and *Witches,* could not be uttered by her without extraordinary Difficulty. I produced a Book to her that *proves, That there* are *Witches,*[31] and *that* she had not *power* to read. When I readd in the Room, the Story of *Ann Cole,* in my Fathers *Remarkable Providences,*[32] and came to the Exclamation which the Narrative saies the *Demons* made upon her, [*Ah she runs to the Book!*] it cast her into inexpressible *Agonies;* and shee'd fall into them whenever I had the Expression of, *Running to the Rock,* afterwards. *A popish Book* also she could endure *very well;* but it would kill her to look into any Book, that (in my Opinion) it might have bin profitable & *edifying* for her to be reading of. These Experiments were often enough *repeated,* and still *with the same Success,* before Witnesses *not a few.* The *good Books* that were found so mortal to her were cheefly such as lay ever at hand in the Room. One was the *Guid to Heaven from the Word,*[33] which I had given her. Another of them was Mr. *Willard's* little (but precious) Treatise *of Justification.*[34] Diverse *Books* published by my Father I also tried upon her; particularly, his *Mystery of Christ;* and another small Book of his about *Faith* and *Repentance,* and *the day of Judgement.*[35]

Once being very merrily talking by a Table that had this *last Book* upon it, she just opened the Book, and *was immediately struck backwards* as dead upon the floor. I hope I have not spoil'd the credit of the *Books*, By telling how much the *Devils* hated them. I shall therefore add, That my Grandfather *Cottons* Catechism called *Milk for Babes*, and *The Assemblies Catechism*,[36] would bring hideous *Convulsions* on the Child if she *look't* into them; tho' she had once learn't them with all the love that could be. . . .

SECT. XXIII. One of the Spectators once ask'd her, *Whether she could nor ride up* stairs; unto *which* her Answer was, *That she believe'd she could, for* her [invisible] Horse *could do very notable things*. Accordingly, when her *Horse* came to her again, to our Admiration she *Rode* (that is, was *tossed* as one that *rode* up the stairs: here then stood, open the *Study* of one belonging to the Family,[37] onto *which* entring, she stood immediately upon her Feet, and cry'd out, *They are gone; they are gone! They say, that they cannot,—God won't let 'em come here!* She also added a Reason for it, which the *Owner of the Study* thought more *kind* than *true*. And she presently and perfectly came to her self, so that her *whole Discourse* & Carriage was altered unto the greatest measure of *Sobriety*, and she satt Reading of the *Bible* and *Good Books*, for a good part of the Afternoon. Her Affairs calling her anon to go down again, the *Demons* were in a quarter of a minute as bad upon her as before, and her *Horse* was Waiting for her. I understanding of it, *immediately* would have her up to the *study* of the young man[38] where she had been at ease before; meerly to try Whether there had not been a Fallacy in what had newly happened: but she was now so *twisted*, and *writhen*, that it gave me much trouble to get her into my Arms, and much more to drag her up the stairs. She was pulled out of my hands, and when I recovered my Hold, she was thrust so hard upon me, that I had almost fallen backwards, and her own breast was sore afterwards, by their Compressions to detain her; she seem'd heavier indeed than three of her self. With incredible Forcing (tho *she* kept Screaming, *They say I must not go in!*) at length we pull'd her in; *where* she was no sooner come, but she could stand on her Feet, and with an *altered tone*, could thank me, saying, *now I am well*. At first shee'd be somewhat faint, and say, *She felt something go out of her;* but in a *minute* or *two*, she could attend any Devotion, or Business as well as ever in her Life; and both *spoke* and *did* as became a person of good Discretion.

I was loth to make a *Charm of* the Room; yet some strangers that came to visit us, the Week after, desiring to see the *Experiment* made, I permitted more than *two* or *three* Repetitions of it; and it still succeeded as I have declared. Once when I was assisting 'em in carrying of her up, she was torn out of all our hands; & to my self, she cry'd out, Mr. *M,—One of them is going to push you down the stairs, have a care.* I remember not that I *felt* any Thrust or *Blow;* but I think I was unaccountably made to *step down backward two or three stairs,* and within a *few* hours she told me by *whom* it was.

SECT. *XXIV.* . . . She had that day been diverse times warning us, that *they* [demons] had been contriving to do some harm to my *Wife,* by a *Fall* or a *Blow,* or the *like;* and when she came out of her mysterious Journeys, she would still be careful concerning *Her.* Accordingly she now calls to *her Company* again, *Hark you, One thing more before we part! What hurt is it you will do to Mrs.* Mather? *will you do her any hurt?* Here she list'ned some time; and then clapping her hands cry'd out, *O, I am glad on't, they can do* Mrs. Mather *no hurt: they* try, *but they say they can't.* So she returns and at once, Dismissing her Horse, and opening her eyes, she call'd me to her, *Now Sir,* (said she) *I'll tell you all. I have learn'd who they are that are the cause of my trouble, there's three of them,* (and she named *who) if they were out of the way, I should be well.* They *say, they can tell now how long I shall be* troubled, *But they won't. Only they seem to think, their power will be* broke *this Week,* They *seem also to say, that I shall be very ill* To morrow, *but they are themselves terribly* afraid *of to morrow;* They *fear, that to morrow we shall be delivered.* They *say too, that they can't hurt* Mrs. Mather, *which I am glad of. But they said, they would kill me to night, if I went to bed before ten a clock, if I told a word.* And other things did she say, not now to be recited.

SECT. *XXV.* The Day following, which was, I think about the twenty seventh of *November,* Mr. *Morton* of Charlestown, and Mr. *Allen,* Mr. *Moody,* Mr. *Willard,* and my self, of *Boston,* with some devout Neighbours, kept another *Day of Prayer,* at *John Goodwin's* house;[39] and we had all the Children present with us there. The children were miserably tortured, while we laboured in our *Prayers;* but our good God was nigh unto us, in what we call'd upon Him for. From this day the power of the Enemy was broken; and the children, though Assaults after this were made upon them, yet were not so cruelly handled as before. The *Liberty* of the Children encreased daily more and more, and their *Vexation* abated by degrees; till within a little while they arrived to *Perfect Ease,* which for some *weeks* or *months* they *cheerfully* enjoyed. Thus *Good it is for us to draw near to God.*

SECT. *XXVI.* Within a day or *two* after the *Fast,* the young Woman had two remarkable Attempts made upon her, by her invisible Adversaries. Once, *they were Dragging her in to the Oven that was then heating,* while there was none in the Room to help her. She clap't her hands on the *Mantle-tree* to save her self; but they were beaten off; and she had been burned, if at her Out-cryes one had not come in from abroad for her Relief. Another time, *they* putt an unseen *Rope* with a cruel *Noose* about her Neck, Whereby she was choaked, until she was black in the Face; and though it was taken off before it had kill'd her, yet there were the red Marks of *it*, and of a *Finger* & a *Thumb* near *it*, remaining to be seen for a while afterwards.

SECT. XXVII. This was the last Molestation that *they* gave her for a While; and she dwelt at my house the rest of the Winter, having by an obliging and vertuous Conversation, made herself enough Welcome to the Family. But within about a Fortnight, she was visited with *two dayes* of as Extraordinary Obsessions, as any we had been the Spectators of. I thought it, convenient for me to entertain my Congregation with a *Sermon* upon the *memorable Providences* which these Children had been concerned in. When I had begun to study my Sermon, her *Tormentors* again seiz'd upon her; and all *Fryday* & *Saturday*, did *they* manage her with a special Design, as was plain, to disturb me in what I was about. In the worst of her extravagancies formerly, she was more dutiful to my self, than I had reason to Expect, but *now* her *whole* carriage to me, was with a Sauciness that I had not been us'd to be treated with. She would knock at my Study *Door*, affirming, *That some below would be glad to see me;* when there was none that ask't for me. She would call to me with multiplyed Impertinencies, and throw small things at me wherewith she could not give me any hurt. Shee'd Hector me at a strange rate for the *work* I was at, and threaten me with *I know not what* mischief for it. She got a *History* that I had Written of this *Witchcraft*, and tho she had before this, readd it over and over, yet now she could not read (I believe) one entire Sentence of it; but she made of it the most ridiculous *Travesty* in the World, with such a Patness and excess of Fancy, to supply the sense that she put upon it, as I was amazed at. And she particularly told me, That *I should quickly come to disgrace by that History.*

SECT. XXVIII. But there were many other Wonders beheld by us before these two dayes were out. Few *tortures* attended her, but such as were *provoked;* her *Frolicks* being the things that had most possession of her. I was in *Latin* telling some young Gentlemen of the *Colledge*, That if I should bid her *Look* to God, her *Eyes* would be put out, upon *which* her eyes were presently served so. I was in some surprize, When I saw that her *Troublers* understood *Latin*, and it made me willing to try a little more of *their* Capacity. We continually found, that if an *English Bible* were in any part of the *Room* seriously look'd into, though she *saw* and *heard* nothing of it, she would immediately be in very dismal *Agonies*. We now made a Tryal more than once or twice, of the *Greek* New-Testament, and the *Hebrew* Old Testament; and We still found, That if one should go to read in it never so secretly and silently, it would procure her that Anguish, Which there was no enduring of. But, I thought, at length, I fell upon one *inferior* Language[40] which the *Daemons* did not seem, *so well* to understand. . . .

SECT. XXX. After this, we had no more such entertainments. The *Demons* it may be would once or twice in a Week, trouble her for a few minutes with perhaps a *twisting* & a *twinkling* of her eyes, or a certain *Cough*, which did seem to be more than ordinary. Moreover, Both she at my house, and her Sister at *home*, at the time which they call *Christmas*,[41] were by the *Daemons* made very *drunk*, though they had no *strong* Drink (as we are fully sure) to make them so. When she began to feel her self thus *drunk*, she complain'd, *O they say they will have me to keep* Christmas *with them! They will disgrace me when they can do nothing else!* And immediately the Ridiculous Behaviours of one *drunk*, were with a wonderful exactness represented in her Speaking, and Reeling, and Spewing, and anon Sleeping, till she was well again. But the Vexations of the Children otherwise abated continually.

They first came to be alwaies Quiet, unless upon *Provocations*. Then they got Liberty to *work*, but *not* to *read*: then further on, to read but not *aloud*, at last they were *wholly* delivered; and for many Weeks remained so.

SECT. XXXI. I was not unsensible, that it might be an easie thing to be *too bold*, and go *too far*, in making of Experiments: Nor was I so *unphilosophical* as not to discern many opportunityes of *Giving* and *Solving* many *Problemes* which the *pneumatic Discipline*[42] is concerned in. I confess I have *Learn't* much more than *I sought*, and I have bin informed of some things relating to the *invisible World*, which as I did not think it *lawful* to *ask*, so I do not think it *proper* to *tell*; yet I will give a Touch upon one *Problem* commonly Discoursed of; that is,

Whether the Devils know our Thoughts, or no?

I will not give the Reader my *Opinion* of it, but only my *Experiment*. That they *do not*, was conjectured from *this:* We could *cheat* them when we *spoke* one thing, and *mean't* another. This was found when the Children *were to be undressed*. The *Devils* would still in wayes beyond the Force of any Imposture, wonderfully *twist* the part that was to be *undress't*, so that there was no coming at it. But, if we said, *untye his neckckloth*, and the parties bidden, at the same time, understood our intent to be, *unty his Shooe!* The *Neckcloth*, and *not* the *shooe*, has been made strangely inaccessible. But on the other side, That they *do*, may be conjectured from This. I called the young Woman at my House by her Name, intending to mention unto her some *Religious Expedient* whereby she might, as I thought much relieve her self; presently her Neck was *broke*, and I continued watching my Opportunity to say what I designed. I could not get her to come out of her Fit, until I had laid aside my purpose of speaking what I thought, and then she reviv'd immediately. Moreover a young Gentleman visiting of me at my Study to ask my advice about curing the *Atheism & Blasphemy* which he complained, his *Thoughts* were more than ordinarily then infested *with;* after some Discourse I carried him down to see this Girl who was then molested with her unseen *Fiends;* but when he came, she treated him very coursly and rudely, asking him *What he came to the house for?* and seemed very angry at his being there, urging him to be gone with a very impetuous Importunity. Perhaps all *Devils* are not alike sagacious.

SECT. XXXII. The *Last Fit* that the young Woman had, was very peculiar. The *Daemons* having once again seiz'd her, they made her pretend to be *Dying;* and Dying truly we fear'd at last she *was:* She lay, she tossed, she pull'd just like one *Dying,* and urged hard for some one to dy *with* her, seeming loth to *dy alone.* She argued concerning *Death,* in strains that quite amazed us; and concluded, That though she was *loth to dy,* yet if God said she must, *she must;* adding something about the state of the Countrey, which we *wondred* at. Anon, the Fit went over; and as I guessed it would be, it was the *last* Fit she had at our House. But all my Library never afforded me any Commentary on those Paragraphs of the *Gospels,* which speak of *Demoniacs,* equal to that which the passions of this Child have given me.

SECT. XXXIII. This is the Story of *Goodwins* Children, a Story all made up of *Wonders!* I have related nothing but what I judge to be true. I was my self an *Eye-witness* to a large part of what I tell; and I hope my neighbours have long thought, That I have otherwise *learned Christ,* than to *ly* unto the World. Yea, there is, I believe scarce any one particular, in this Narrative, which more than one credible Witness will not be ready to make Oath unto. The things of most Concernment in it, were before many Critical Observers; and the *Whole* happened in the *Metropolis* of the *English America,* unto a religious and industrious Family which was visited by all sorts of Persons, that had a mind to *satisfy* themselves. I do now likewise publish the History, While the thing is yet fresh and *New;* and I challenge all men to detect so much as one designed *Falshood,* yea, or so much as one important *Mistake,* from the *Egg* to the *Apple* of it, I have Writ as *plainly* as becomes an Historian, as *truly* as becomes a Christian, tho perhaps not so *profitably* as became a Divine. But I am resolv'd after this, never to use but just one grain of patience with any man that shall go to impose upon me, a Denial of *Devils,* or of *Witches.* I shall count that man *Ignorant* who shall *suspect,* but I shall count him down-right *Impudent* if he *Assert* the Non-Existence of things which we have had such palpable Convictions of. I am sure he cannot be a *Civil,* (and some will question whether he can be an *honest* man) that shall go to *deride* the *Being* of things which a whole Countrey has now beheld an house of pious people suffering not a *few* Vexations by. But if the *Sadducee,* or the *Atheist,* have no right Impressions by these *Memorable Providences* made upon his mind; yet I hope, those that know what it is *to be sober,* will not repent any pains that they may have taken in perusing what Records of these *Witchcrafts & Possessions*, I thus leave unto Posterity.

"THE RETURN OF SEVERAL MINISTERS CONSULTED BY HIS EXCELLENCY, AND THE HONOURABLE COUNCIL, UPON THE PRESENT WITCHCRAFTS IN SALEM VILLAGE" (JUNE 15, 1692)

Boston, June 15. 1692.[43]

I. *The Afflicted State of our poor Neighbours, that are now Suffering by Molestations from the Invisible World, we apprehend so deplorable, that we think their Condition calls for the utmost Help of all persons in their* several Capacities. II. *We cannot but with all Thankfulness Acknowledge,* the Success *which the Merciful God has given unto the Sedulous and Assiduous Endeavors of our Honourable Rulers, to detect the Abominable* Witchcrafts *which have been committed in the Country; Humbly praying that the Discovery of those Mysterious and Mischievous Wickednesses, may be perfected.* III. *We judge that in the prosecution of these, and all such Witchcrafts, there is need of a very critical and Exquisite* Caution, *lest by too much* Credulity *for Things, received only upon the Devils* Authority, *there be a* Door *opened for a long Train of miserable Consequences; and* Satan *get an Advantage over us, for we should not be* Ignorant *of his Devices.* IV. *As in Complaints upon Witchcrafts, there may be matters of* Enquiry, *which do not amount unto Matters of* Praesumption, *and there may be matters of* Praesumption *which yet may not be reckoned Matters of* Conviction, *so 'tis necessary that all Proceedings thereabout, be managed with an exceeding Tenderness towards those that may be complained of; especially if they have been persons formerly of an unblemished Reputation.* V. *When the first* Enquiry *is made into the Circumstances of such as may ly under any just* Suspicion *of Witchcrafts, we could wish that there may be Admitted as little as is possible, of such Noise, Company, and Openness, as may too hastily expose them that are Examined: and that there may nothing be used as a Test, for the Trial of the Suspected, the Lawfulness whereof may be doubted among the People of God; but that the Directions given by such Judicious Writers, as* Perkins and Bernard,[44] *be consulted in such a Case.* VI. *Presumptions whereupon persons may be* Committed, *and much more,* Convictions, *whereupon persons may be* Condemned *as Guilty of* Witchcrafts, *ought certainly to be more considerable, than barely the Accused Persons being Represented by a* Spectre *unto the Afflicted; inasmuch as 'tis an undoubted and a Notorious Thing, That a* Daemon *may, by Gods Permission, appear even to Ill purposes, in the Shape of an Innocent, yea, and a vertuous man. Nor can we es-*

teem Alterations made in the Sufferers, by a Look *or* Touch *of the Accused to be an Infallible Evidence of Guilt; but frequently Liable to be abused by the Devil's* Legerdemains.[45] VII. *We know not, whether some Remarkable* Affronts *given to the Devils, by our Disbelieving of those* Testimonies, *whose whole Force, and Strength is from Them alone, may not put a period, unto the progress of the dreadful* Calamity *begun upon us, in the Accusation of so many persons, whereof we hope, some are yet clear from the* Great Transgression, *laid unto their Charge.* VIII. *Nevertheless, We cannot but humbly Recommend unto the Government, the speedy and vigorous Prosecution of such as have rendred themselves obnoxious, according to the Direction given in the Laws of God, and the wholesome Statutes of the* English *Nation, for the Detection of Witchcrafts.*[46]

DIARY (MAY–DECEMBER 1692)

[ACCOUNT OF ACTIVITIES DURING THE WITCH HUNT]

In my public Ministry, I now largely handled, the Description of the *Day of Judgment,* in the twenty-fifth Chapter of *Matthew.*

In the Spring of this Year, I preached, on the Lecture, to the Countrey, a Sermon upon *Temptations;* and now, behold, my poor Countrey entred quickly *into Temptation.*

The Rest of the Summer, was a very doleful Time, unto the whole Countrey.

The *Divels,* after a most praeternatural Manner, by the dreadful Judgment of Heaven took a *bodily Possession,* of many People, in *Salem,* and the adjacent places; and the Houses of the poor People, began to bee filled with the horrid Cries of Persons tormented by *evil Spirits.* There seem'd an execrable *Witchcraft,* in the Foundation of this wonderful Affliction, and many Persons, of diverse Characters, were accused, apprehended, persecuted, upon the *Visions* of the Afflicted.

For my own part, I was alwayes afraid of proceeding to convict and condemn any Person, as *Confoederate* with afflicting *Daemons,* upon so feeble an Evidence, as a *spectral Representation.*[47] Accordingly, I ever testified against it, both publickly and *privately;* and in my *Letters* to the Judges,[48] I particularly, besought them, that they would by no means admitt it; and when a considerable *Assembly* of *Minsters* gave in their *Advice* about that Matter, I not only concurred with their Advice, but it was *I* who drew it up.[49]

Nevertheless, on the other side, I saw in most of the *Judges,* a most charming Instance of *Prudence* and *Patience,* and I knew their exemplary *Pietie,* and the *Agony* of Soul with which they sought the Direction of Heaven; above most other People, whom I generally saw enchanted into a raging, railing, scandalous and unreasonable Disposition, as the Distress increased upon us: For this Cause tho' I could not allow the *Principles*, that some of the Judges had espoused, yett I could not but speak honourably of their *Persons*, on all Occasions; and my *Compassion*, upon the Sight of their *Difficulties*, raised by my Journeyes to *Salem*, the chief Seat of these diabolical Vexations, cause mee yett more to do so. And meerly, as far as I can learn for this Reason, the mad people thro' the Countrey, under a fascination on their *Spirits*, aequal to what our *Energumens*[50] had on their *Bodies*, reviled mee, as if I had been the Doer of all the hard Things, that were done, in the Prosecution of the *Witchcraft*.

In this *Evil-Time*, I offered, at the beginning, that if the *possessed* People, might bee scattered far asunder, I would singly provide for six of them;[51] and wee would see whether without more bitter methods, *Prayer* with *Fasting* would not putt an End unto these heavy Trials: But my offer (which none of my Revilers, would have been so courageous or so charitable, as to have made) was not accepted.

However, for a great part of the Summer, I did every *Week*, (mostly) spend a Day by myself, in the Exercises of a sacred FAST, before the Lord. On these Dayes (whereof I have kept no Record) I cried unto the Lord, not only for my own Preservation, from the Malice and Power of the *evil Angels*, but also, for a *good Issue* of the Calamities wherein Hee had permitted the *evil Angels* to ensnare this miserable Countrey.

I besought the Lord, that Hee would please accept mee, direct, mee, prosper mee, in publishing such *Testimonies* for Him, as were proper, and would bee serviceable unto His Interests, on this occasion.

Moreover, the *Prison* being filled with Persons committed on Suspicion of *Witchcraft, I went and preached unto the Persons in Prison*, (on Act. 24.25.) with a special Help from the *Spirit* of the Lord.

That a right Use, might bee made, of the stupendous and prodigious Things, which had been happening among us, I now composed and published my Book, entituled, THE WONDERS OF THE INVISIBLE WORLD:[52] in the Preface whereof, I could say, "None but the *Father who sees in secret*, knows the heart-breaking Exercises, wherewith I have composed, what is now going to bee exposed; lest I should, in any *one Thing*, miss of doing my designed Service for His Glory, and for His People: But I am now somewhat comfortably assured of *His* favourable Acceptance; and *I will not fear; what can a Satan do unto mee.*"

When this book was printed, many besotted People would not imagine any other, but that my Father's *Cases of Conscience, about Witchcraft*,[53] which came abroad just after it, were in opposition to it; which causes him, in the Postscript of his *Cases*, to say,

"Some have taken up a Notion, that the Book newly published by my *Son*, is contradictory to this of *mine*. Tis strange, that such Imaginations should enter into the Minds of Men; I perused, and approved, *that Book*, before it was printed, and nothing but my Relation to him, hindred mee, from recommending it unto the world."[54]

Tis not proper for mee to recite on this occasion, what encouraging Letters I received from some reverend Persons, about that reviled Book; and how one Sais, *I think never Book came out more seasonably; and I give Thanks to our gracious God, for His Assistence of you, both in Matter and Manner;* and how another sais, *I solemnly profess, without the least Adulation, I never mett with an humane Author in my Life, that spake more solidly and thoroughly to the Subject hee handled; and if ever one that reads it do not close with it, I shall fear gross Ignorance, inveterate Prejudice, or a paenal Stroke of God, the Cause thereof.* The Shield given by the Lieut. Governour, of the Province, under which, that Book, is walk'd abroad, is enough, and, I confess, too much.[55]

I mention, these vindicating Passages, only for some Ease of my Mind, under the many *buffeting Temptations*, which attended the Publication of that Book.

(Upon the severest Examination, and the solemnest Supplication, I still think, that for the main, I have, *written Right*.)[56] . . .

I had filled my Countrey, with little BOOKS, in several whereof, I had with a Variety of Entertainment, offered the *New-Covenant* formally drawn up, unto my Neighbours: hoping to engage them eternally unto the Lord, by their subscribing with *Heart* and *Hand*, unto the Covenant. Now in the late horrid *Witchcraft*, the manner of the *Spectres* was to tender BOOKS unto the afflicted People; solliciting of them to subscribe unto a *League* with the *Divel* therein exhibited, and so become the *Servants* of the Divel forever; which when they refused, the *Spectres* would proceed then to wound them with Scalding, Burning, Pinching, Pricking, Twisting, Choaking, and a thousand praeternatural Vexations.

Before I made any such Reflection myself, I heard this Reflection made by *others*, who were more considerate; That this Assault of the *evil Angels* upon the Countrey, was intended by *Hell*, as a particular Defiance, unto *my* poor Endeavours, to bring the Souls of men unto *Heaven*. When I more attentively considered this matter, it enflamed my Endeavours this Winter [Dec. 1692] to do yett more, in a direct *opposition* unto the Divel. Wherefore I composed and published, a little Book, entituled, AWAKENING FOR THE UNREGENERATE.[57] Wherein, I sett the *Covenant of Grace*, yett more evangelically and explicitly before the Children of Men, and besought them, to *sign* it, in order to their everlasting Happiness. And, as a further *Opposition* unto the *Divel*, besides, diverse other Discourses about the Concerns of *Regeneration*, in that Book, I added a Discourse, about, *A Name written in the Book of Life*. Promising, that, for the two Years, next ensuing, if I lived, I would of those *Books*, buy from the *Bookseller*, after the rate of *two* a Week; and scatter them, in Places, where I might Judge, most of Good would bee done by them.

Remember mee, O God, concerning this also, and spare mee according to the Greatness of thy Mercy!

(After, the *evil Angels* in a possessed young woman had reproched mee, for having never preached on that in Rev. 13.8. I, to oppose them and yett not follow them, chose to preach, on Rev. 20.15.)

MEMORANDUM.

I observed That in the horrible Assaults made by the *Invisible World*, upon some scores of people, in the Enchantments and Possessions, which amazed the Countrey, the matter still urged upon the poor *Energumens*, with a thousand praeternatural Torments, was, *to sign* (sett their Names and Hands) *unto a Book, by a Daemon presented unto them.*[58]

Hereupon, I reckoned that it would bee a convenient Contradiction unto this method of the *Divels*, for mee to subscribe unto GODS BOOK.

Wherefore, I took the BIBLES, which I most commonly used, and I wrote,
In ONE, at the Top of the first Leaf,
RECEIVED AS THE BOOK OF GOD AND OF LIFE, BY
Cotton Mather.
At the End of the last Leaf,
EMBRACED AS THE WORD OF CHRIST AND SALVATION.
Cotton Mather.

"LETTER TO JOHN FOSTER" (AUGUST 17, 1692)

S^r,[59]

You would know whether I still retain my opinion about ye horrible Witchcrafts among us, and I acknowledge that I do. I do still Think That when there is no further Evidence against a person but only This, That a Spectre in their Shape does afflict a neighbour, that Evidence is not enough to convict y^e [accused] of Witchcraft.

That the Divels have a natural power wch makes them capable of exhibiting what shape they please I suppose no body doubts, and I have no absolute promise of God that they shall not exhibit mine.

It is the opinion generally of all protestant writers that yᵉ Divel may thus abuse yᵉ innocent, yea, tis yᵉ confession of some popish ones. And oʳ Honorable Judges are so eminent for their Justice, Wisdom, and Goodness that whatever their own particular sense may bee, yett they will not proceed capitally against any, upon a principle contested with great odds on yᵉ other side in yᵉ Learned and Godly world.

Nevertheless, a very great use is to bee made of yᵉ spectral impressions upon yᵉ sufferers. They Justly Introduce, and Determine, an Enquiry into yᵉ circumstances of ye person accused; and they strengthen other presumptions.

When so much use is made of those Things, I believe yᵉ use for wᶜʰ yᵉ Great God intends yᵐ is made. And accordingly you see that yᵉ Excellent Judges have had such an Encouraging presence of God with them, as that scarce any, if at all any, have been Tried before them, against whom God has not strangely sent in other, and more Humane and most convincing Testimonies.

If any persons have been condemned, about whom any of yᵉ Judges, are not easy in their minds, that yᵉ Evidence against them, has been satisfactory, it would certainly bee for yᵉ glory of the whole Transaction to give that person a Reprieve.

It would make all matters easier if at least Bail were taken for people Accused only by ye invisible tormentors of yᵉ poor sufferers and not Blemished by any further Grounds of suspicion against them. The odd Effects produced upon the sufferers by yᵉ look or touch of the accused are things wherein yᵉ Divels may as much Impose upon some Harmless people as by the Representacôn of their shapes.

My notion of these matters is this. A Suspected and unlawfull coñunion with a Familiar Spirit, is the Thing enquired after. The communion on the Divels part may bee proved, while, for ought I can say, The man may bee Innocent; the Divel may impudently Impose his coñunion upon some that care not for his company. But if the coñunion on ye man's part bee proved, then the Business is done.

I am suspicious Lest yᵉ Divel may at some time or other, serve us a trick by his constancy for a long while in one way of Dealing. Wee may find the Divel using one constant course in Nineteen several Actions, and yett hee bee too hard for us at last, if wee thence make a Rule to form an Infallible Judgment of a Twentieth. It is oʳ singular Happiness That wee are blessed with Judges who are Aware of this Danger.

For my own part if the Holy God should permitt such a Terrible calamity to befal myself as that a Spectre in my Shape should so molest my neighbourhood, as that they can have no quiet, altho' there should be no other Evidence against me, I should very patiently submit unto a Judgment of *Transportation*, and all reasonable men would count o^r Judges to Act, as they are like ye Fathers of ye public, in such a Judgment. What if such a Thing should be ordered for those whose Guilt is more Dubious, and uncertain, whose presence y^s perpetuates ye miseries of o^r sufferers? They would cleanse ye Land of Witchcrafts, and yett also prevent ye shedding of Innocent Blood, whereof some are so apprehensive of Hazard. If o^r Judges want any Good Bottom, to act thus upon, You know, that besides ye usual power of Governors, to Relax many Judgments of Death, o^r General Court can soon provide a law.

S^r, You see ye Incoherency of my Thoughts but I hope, you will also some Reasonableness in those Thoughts.

In the year 1645, a Vast Number of persons in ye county of Suffolk were apprehended, as Guilty of Witchcraft; whereof, some confessed. The parlament granted a special commission of Oyer and Terminer for ye Trial of those Witches; in wch commission, there were a famous Divine or two, Mr Fairclough[60] particularly inserted. That Excellent man did preach two sermons to ye Court, before his first sitting on ye Bench: Wherein having first proved the Existence of Witches, hee afterwards showed ye Evil of Endeavouring ye Conviction of any upon Defective Evidence. The Sermon had the Effect that none were Condemned, who could bee saved wth^{out} an Express Breach of ye Law; and then tho' t'was possible some Guilty did Escape, yett the troubles of those places, were, I think Extinguished.

O^r case is Extraordinary. And so, you and others will pardon ye Extraordinary Liberty I take to address You on this occasion. But after all, I Entreat you, that whatever you do, you Strengthen ye Hands of o^r Honourable Judges in ye Great work before y^m. They are persons, for whom no man living has a greater veneration, than

> S^r,
> Your Servant,
> C. MATHER.

THE WONDERS OF THE INVISIBLE WORLD (1693)

ENCHANTMENTS ENCOUNTRED

S II. The *New-Englanders*, are a People of God settled in those, which were once the *Devils* Territories; and it may easily be supposed that the *Devil* was Exceedingly disturbed, when he perceived such a people here accomplishing the Promise of old made unto our Blessed Jesus *That He should have the Utmost parts of the Earth for His Possession* {Ps. 2:8}. There was not a greater Uproar among the *Ephesians*, when the Gospel was first brought among them, than there was among, *The Powers of the Air* (after whom those *Ephesians* walked) when first the *Silver Trumpets* of the Gospel here made the *Joyful Sound*. The Devil thus Irritated, immediately try'd all sorts of Methods to overturn this poor Plantation: and so much of the Church as was *Fled into this Wilderness* {Rev. 12:6}, immediately found, *The Serpent cast out of his Mouth, a Flood for the carrying of it away* {Rev. 12:15}. I believe, that never were more *Satanical Devices* used for the Unsettling of any People under the Sun, than what have been Employ'd for the Extirpation of the *Vine* which God has here *Planted, Casting out the Heathen, and Preparing a Room before it, and causing it to take deep Root, and fill the Land; so that it sent its Boughs unto the* Atlantic *Sea* Eastward, *and its Branches unto the* Connecticut *River* Westward, *and the Hills were covered with the Shadows thereof* {Ps. 80:8–11}. But, All those Attempts of Hell, have hitherto been Abortive, many an *Ebenezer* has been Erected unto the Praise of God, by His Poor People here; and, *Having obtained Help from God, we continue to this Day* {Acts 26:22}. Wherefore the Devil is now making one Attempt more upon us; an Attempt more Difficult, more Surprizing, more snarl'd with unintelligible Circumstances than any that we have hitherto Encountred; an Attempt, so *Critical*, that if we get well through, we shall soon Enjoy *Halcyon* Days with all the *Vultures* of Hell, *Trodden under our Feet* {Heb. 10:29}. He has wanted his *Incarnate Legions*, to Persecute us, as the People of God, have in the other Hemisphere been Persecuted: he has therefore drawn forth his more *Spiritual* ones to make an Attacque upon us. We have been advised, by some Credible Christians yet alive, that a Malefactor, accused of *Witchcraft* as well as *Murder*, and Executed in this place more than Forty Years ago, did then give Notice, of, *An Horrible PLOT against the Country, by* WITCHCRAFT, *and a Foundation of* WITCHCRAFT *then Laid, which if it were not seasonably Discovered, would probably Blow up, and pull down all the Churches in the Country*.[61] And we have now with Horror seen the *Discovery* of such a *Witchcraft!* An Army of *Devils* is horribly broke in, upon the place which is the *Center* and after a sort, the *First-born* of our English Settlements: and the Houses of the Good People there, are fill'd with the doleful Shrieks of their Children and Servants, Tormented by Invisible Hands, with Tortures altogether preternatural.[62] After the Mischiefs there Endeavoured, and since in part Conquered, the terrible Plague, of, *Evil Angels*, hath made its progress into some other places, where other persons have been in like manner Diabolically handled. These our poor Afflicted Neighbours, quickly after they became *Infected* and *Infested* with these *Daemons*, arrive to a Capacity of Discerning those which they conceive the *Shapes* of their Troublers; and notwithstanding the Great and Just Suspicion, that the *Daemons* might Impose the *Shapes* of Innocent Persons in their *Spectral*

Exhibitions upon the Sufferers, (which may perhaps prove no small part of the *Witch-Plot* in the issue) yet many of the persons thus Represented, being Examined, several of them have been Convicted of a very Damnable *Witchcraft*: yea, more than One *Twenty* have *Confessed*, that they have Signed unto a *Book*, which the Devil show'd them, and Engaged in his Hellish Design of *Bewitching*, and *Ruining* our Land. We know not, at least *I* know not, how far the *Delusions* of Satan may be Interwoven into some Circumstances of the *Confessions*; but one would think, all the Rules of Understanding Humane Affayrs are at an end, if after so many most Voluntary Harmonious *Confessions*, made by Intelligent persons of all Ages, in sundry Towns, at several Times, we must not Believe the *main strokes* wherein those *Confessions* all agree: especially when we have a thousand preternatural Things every day before our eyes, wherein the *Confessors* do acknowledge their Concernment, and give Demonstration of their being so Concerned. If the Devils now can strike the minds of men, with any *Poisons* of so fine a Composition and Operation, that scores of Innocent People shall Unite, in *Confessions* of a Crime, which we see actually committed, it is a thing prodigious, beyond the Wonders of the former Ages, and it threatens no less than a sort of a Dissolution upon the World. Now, by these *Confessions* 'tis Agreed, *That* the Devil has made a dreadful Knot of *Witches* in the Country, and by the help of *Witches* has dreadfully Encreased that Knot: *That* these *Witches* have driven a Trade of Commissioning their *Confederate Spirits*, to do all sorts of Mischiefs to the Neighbours, whereupon there have Ensued such Mischievous consequences upon the Bodies, and Estates of the Neighbourhood, as could not otherwise be accounted for: yea, *That* at prodigious *Witch-Meetings*, the Wretches have proceeded so far, as to Concert and Consult the Methods of Rooting out the Christian Religion from this Country, and setting up instead of it, perhaps a more gross *Diabolism*, than ever the World saw before. And yet it will be a thing little short of *Miracle*, if in so *spread* a Business, as this, the Devil should not get in some of his *Juggles*, to confound the Discovery of all the rest.

S. 3. Doubtless, the Thoughts of many will receive a Great Scandal against *New-England*, from the Number of Persons that have been Accused, or Suspected, for *Witchcraft*, in this Country: But it were easy to offer many things, that may Answer and Abate the Scandal. If the Holy God should any where permit the Devils to hook two or three wicked *Scholars*, into *Witchcraft*, and then by their Assistance to Range with their *Poisonous Insinuations*, among Ignorant, Envious, Discontented People, till they have cunningly decoy'd them into some sudden *Act*, whereby the *Toyls* of Hell shall be perhaps inextricably cast over them: what Country in the World, would not afford *Witches*, numerous to a

Prodigy? Accordingly, The Kingdoms of *Sweden*, *Denmark*, *Scotland*, yea, and *England* it self, as well as the Province of *New-England*, have had their Storms of *Witchcrafts* breaking upon them, which have made most Lamentable Devastations:[63] which also I wish, may be, *The Last*. And it is not uneasy to be imagined, That God ha's not brought out all the *Witchcrafts* in many other Lands, with such a speedy, dreadful, destroying *Jealousy*, as burns forth upon such *High Treasons* committed here in, *A Land of Uprightness*: Transgressors, may more quickly here, than else where become a prey to the Vengeance of Him, *Who ha's Eyes like a Flame of Fire* {Rev. 19:12}, and, *who walks in the midst of the Golden Candlesticks* {Rev. 2:1}. Moreover, There are many parts of the World, who if they do upon this Occasion insult over this People of God, need only to be told the Story of what happened at *Loim*, in the Dutchy of *Gulic*,[64] where, a Popish Curate, having ineffectually try'd many Charms, to Eject the Devil out of a Damsel there possessed, he Passionately bid the Devil to come out of her, into himself; but the Devil answered him, *Quid mihi Opus est eum tentare, quem Novissimo Die, Jure Optimo sum Possessurus?* that is, *What need I meddle with one, whom I am sure to have and hold at the Last Day, as my own forever!*

But besides all this, give me Leave to add; it is to be hoped, That among the persons represented by the *Spectres* which now afflict our Neighbours, there will be found *some* that never explicitly contracted with any of the *Evil Angels*. The Witches have not only intimated, but some of them acknowledge, That they have plotted the Representations of *Innocent Persons*, to cover and shelter themselves in their Witchcrafts; now, altho' our good God has hitherto generally preserved us, from the Abuse therein Design'd by the Devils for us, yet who of us can Exactly State, *How far our God may for our Chastisement permit the Devil to proceed in such an Abuse?* It was the Result of a Discourse, lately held at a Meeting of some very Pious, and Learned, Ministers among us, *That the Devils may sometimes have a permission to Represent an Innocent Person, as Tormenting such as are under Diabolical Molestations: But that such Things are Rare and Extraordinary; especially, when such Matters come before Civil Judicature.*[65] The Opinion Expressed with so much Caution and Judgment, seems to be the prevailing Sense of many others, who are men Eminently Cautious and Judicious; and have both *Argument* and *History* to Countenance them in it. It is *Rare and Extraordinary*, for an Honest *Naboth* to have his Life it self Sworn away, by two *Children of Belial*, and yet no Infringement hereby made on the Rectoral Righteousness of our Eternal Sovereign, whose *Judgments are a Great Deep*, and who *gives none Account of His matters*. Thus, although, the Appearance of Innocent Persons, in *Spectral Exhibitions* afflicting the Neighbourhood, be a thing *Rare and Extraordinary*; yet who can be sure, that the great *Belial* of Hell must needs be always *Yoked* up, from this Piece of Mischief? The best man that ever lived has been called a *Witch*: and why may not this too usual and unhappy Symptom of, A *Witch*, even a Spectral Representation, befall a person that shall be none of the worst? Is it not possible? the *Laplanders* will tell us 'tis possible for Persons to be unwittingly attended with officious *Daemons*, bequeathed unto them, and impos'd upon them, by Relations that have been *Witches*. *Quaere*,[66] also, Whether at a Time, when the Devils with his Witches are engag'd in an actual *War* upon a people, some certain steps of ours, in such a *War*, may not be follow'd with our appearing so and so for a while among them in the Visions of our af-flicted *Forlorns!* And, Who can certainly say, what other Degrees, & Methods of sinning, besides that of a *Diabolical Compact*, may give the Devils advan-tage, to act in the Shape of them that have miscarried? Besides what may hap-pen for a while, to try the *Patience* of the Virtuous. May not some that have been ready upon feeble grounds uncharitably to Censure and Reproach other people, be punished for it by *Spectres* for a while exposing them to Censure and Re-proach? And furthermore, I pray, that it may be considered, Whether a World of Magical Tricks often used in the World, may not insensibly oblige *Devils* to wait upon the Superstitious Users of them. A Witty Writer against *Sadducism*, has this Observation, That persons, who never made any Express Contract with *Apostate Spirits*, yet may Act strange Things by *Diabolick Aids*, which they pro-cure by the use of those wicked *Forms* and *Arts*, that the Devil first Imparted unto his Confederates.[67] And he adds, *We know not, but the Laws of the Dark Kingdom, may Enjoyn a particular Attendence upon all those that practise their Mysteries, whether they know them to be theirs or no.* Some of them that have been Cry'd out upon, as *Employing Evil Spirits* to Hurt our Land, have been known to be most bloody *Fortune-Tellers*; and some of them have Confessed, That when they told *Fortunes*, they would pretend the Rules of *Chiromancy*[68] and the like Ignorant Sciences, but indeed, they had no Rule (they said) but this, *The Things were then Darted into their Minds. Darted!* Ye Wretches; By whom, I pray. Surely, by none but the *Devils*; who, tho' perhaps they did not exactly *Foreknow* all the thus Predicted Contingencies; yet having once *Foretold* them, they stood bound in Honour now, to use their Interest, which alas, in *This World*, is very great, for the Accomplishment of their own Predictions. There are others, that have used most wicked *Sorceries* to gratify their unlawful Curiosities, or to prevent Inconveniencies in Man and Beast; *Sorceries*; which I will not *Name*, lest I should by Naming, *Teach* them. Now, some *Devil* is evermore Invited into the Service of the Person that shall practise these *Witchcrafts*; and if they have gone on Impenitently in these Communions with any *Devil*, the *Devil* may per-haps become at last a *Familiar* to them, and so assume their *Livery*, that they cannot shake him off in any way, but that One, which *I* would most heartily pre-scribe unto them, Namely, That of a deep and long *Repentance.* Should these *Impieties,* have been committed in such a place as *New-England,* for my part I should not wonder, if when *Devils* are Exposing the *Grosser* Witches among us, God permit them, to bring in these *Lesser* ones with the rest, for their perpet-ual Humiliation. In the Issue therefore, may it not be found, that *New-England* is not so Stock'd with *Rattle Snakes,* as was imagined?

S 4. But *I* do not believe, that the progress of *Witchcraft* among us, is all the Plot, which the Devil is managing in the *Witchcraft* now upon us. It is Judg'd, That the Devil Rais'd the Storm, whereof we read in the Eighth Chapter of *Mat-thew,* on purpose to oversett the little Vessel, wherein the Disciples of Our Lord, were Embarqued with Him. And it may be fear'd, that in the *Horrible Tempest,* which is now upon ourselves, the design of the Devil is to sink that Happy settlement of Government, wherewith Almighty, God, has graciously en-clined their Majesties to favour us. We are blessed with a GOVERNOUR,[69] than whom no man can be more willing to serve their Majesties or this their Province: He is continually venturing his *All* to do it: and were not the Interests of His Prince, dearer to him, than his own, he could not but soon be weary of the *Helm,* whereat he sits. We are under the Influence of a LIEVTENANT GOVERNOUR,[70] who not only by being admirably accomplished both with Natural and Acquired Endowments, is fitted for the Service of Their Majesties, but also with an unspotted Fidelity, applys himself to that Service. Our COUN-CELLOURS, are some of our most Eminent persons, and as Loyal Subjects to the Crown, as hearty lovers of their Countrey. Our Constitution also is attended with singular Priviledges; All which Things are by the Devil exceedingly *Envy'd* unto us. And the Devil will doubtless take this occasion, for the Raising of such complaints and clamours, as may be of pernicious consequence, unto some part of our present Settlement, if he can so far *Impose.* But that which most of all Threatenes us, in our present Circumstances, is the *Misunderstandings,* and so the *Animosity,* whereinto the *Witchcraft* now Raging, has Enchanted us. The Embroiling, first, of our *Spirits,* and then of our *Affayrs,* is evidently, as consid-erable a Branch of the Hellish Intreague, which now vexes us, as any one Thing whatever. The Devil has made us like a *Troubled Sea;* and the *Mire* and *Mud,* begins now also to heave up apace. Even, Good and Wise Men, suffer them-selves to fall into their *Paroxysms;* and the Shake which the Devil is now giving us, fetches up the *Dirt* which before lay still, at the Bottom of our sinful Hearts. If we allow the *Mad Dogs* of Hell to poison us by Biting us, we shall imagine that we see nothing but *such Things* about us, and like *such Things* fly upon all that we see. Were it not for what is IN US, for my part, I should not fear a Thousand

Legions of Devils; 'tis by our *Quarrels* that we spoil our *Prayers*; and if our Humble, Zealous, and United, *Prayers*, are once *Hindred*, alas, the *Philistines* of Hell have cut our Locks for us {Judg. 16:19}; they will then blind us, mock us, ruine us. In Truth, I cannot altogether blame it, If people are a little Transported, when they conceive all the Secular Interests of Themselves and their Families, at the Stake; and yet, at the sight of these Heart-Burnings, I cannot forbear the Exclamation of the Sweet-spirited *Austin,* in his Pacificatory Epistle, to *Jerom* on his Contest with *Ruffin, O misera et miseranda Conditio!*[71] O Condition, truly *miserable!* But what shall be done to cure these Distractions? It is wonderfully necessary, that some *Healing Attempts,* be made at this time; and *I* must needs confess, if I may speak so much, like *Nazianzen,*[72] I am so desirous of a share in them, that if, *Being thrown Over-board,* were needful to allay the *Storm,* I should think, *Dying,* a Trifle to be undergone, for so great a Blessedness.

S 5. . . . Have there been any *Disputed* Methods used, in Discovering the *Works of Darkness?* It may be none, but what have had *great Precedents* in other parts of the world: which may, tho' not altogether *Justify,* yet much *Alleviate* a mistake in us, if there should happen to be found any such mistake, in so *Dark* a matter. They have done, what they have done, with multiply'd *Addresses* to God, for his guidance, and have not been Insensible how much they have exposed themselves in what they have done. Yea, they would gladly contrive, and receive, an expedient, how the Shedding of Blood, might be spared, by the Recovery of *Witches,* not gone beyond the reach of Pardon. And after all, They invite all Good men, in Terms to this purpose, *Being amazed, at the Number, and Quality of those Accused, of Late, we do not know, but Satan, by his Wiles, may have Enwrapped some Innocent persons, and therefore should Earnestly and Humbly desire, the most Critical Enquiry upon the place, to find out the* Fallacy; *that there may be none of the Servants of the Lord, with the Worshippers of* Baal. I may also add, That whereas, if once a *Witch* do ingeniously confess among us, no more *Spectres* do in their Shapes after this, Trouble the Vicinage; if any Guilty Creatures will accordingly to so good purpose Confess their Crime to any Minister of God, and get out of the Snare of the Devil, as no Minister will discover such a *Conscientious Confession,* so I believe none in the Authority, will press him to Discover it; but Rejoyce in *A Soul sav'd from Death.* On the other *Side* [if I must again use the word, *Side,* which yet I hope, to Live, to blot out] there are very worthy men, who are not a Little Dissatisfy'd at the Proceedings in the Prosecution of this *Witchcraft.* And why? Not because they would have any such *Abominable Thing* Defended from the Strokes of Impartial Justice. No, those Reverend Persons who gave in this Advice unto the Honourable Council, "That *Presumptions,* whereupon Persons may be *Committed,* and much more *Convic-*

tions, whereupon Persons may be *Condemned,* as Guilty of *Witchcraft,* ought certainly to be more Considerable, than barely the Accused Persons being represented by a *Spectre,* unto the Afflicted; Nor are Alterations made in the Sufferers, by a *Look* or *Touch* of the Accused, to be esteemed an Infallible Evidence of Guilt; but frequently Liable to be Abused by the Devils *Legerdemains:* I say, Those very men of God, most Conscientiously Subjoined this Article, to that Advice,—*Nevertheless, we cannot but Humbly Recommend unto the Government, The speech and Vigorous Prosecution of such, as have rendred themselves Obnoxious; according to the best Directions given in the Laws of God, and the wholsome Statutes of the English Nation, for the Detection of Witchcraft.*"[73] Only, Tis a most Commendable Cautiousness, in those Gracious men, to be very Shye lest the Devil get so far into our *Faith,* as that for the sake of many *Truths* which we find he tells us, we came at length, to believe any *Lies,* wherewith he may abuse us: whereupon, what a Desolation of *Names* would soon ensue, besides a thousand other Pernicious Consequences? and lest there should be any such *Principles* taken up, as when put into Practice must unavoidably cause the *Righteous to Perish with the Wicked* {Gen. 18:25}; or procure the Bloodshed of any Persons, like the *Gibeonites,* whom some Learned men suppose to be under a false Notion of *Witches,* by *Saul* Exterminated. They would have all Due steps taken for the Extinction of *Witches;* but they would fain have them to be *Sure* ones: nor is it from any thing, but the Real and Hearty *Goodness* of such men, that they are Loth to surmise *Ill* of other men, till there be the fullest Evidence, for the surmises. As for the Honourable *Judges,*[74] that have been hitherto in the Commission, they are *Above* my Consideration: wherefore, I will only say thus much of them, That such of them as I have the Honour of a Personal Acquaintance with, are *Men of an Excellent Spirit;* and as at first they went about the work for which they were Commission'd, with a very great Aversion, so they have still been under Heart-breaking Sollicitudes, how they might therein best serve, both God and Man. In fine, Have there been Faults on any *Side* fallen into? Surely, They have at worst been but the Faults of a *well-meaning Ignorance.* On every *Side* then, Why should not we Endeavour with Amicable Correspondencies, to help one another out of the *Snares,* wherein the Devil would Involve us? To *Wrangle the Devil,* out of the Country, will be truly a New Experiment! Alas, we are not Aware of the *Devil,* if we do not think, that he aims at Enflaming us one against another; & shall we suffer our selves to be *Devil-Ridden?* Or, by any *Unadviseableness,* contribute unto the Widening of our Breaches? To say no more, There is a Published and a Credible Relation, which affirms, That very lately, in a part of *England,* where some of the Neighbourhood were Quarrelling, a RAVEN, from the Top of a Tree very Articulately and Unaccountably cry'd out, *Read the Third to the Colossians, and the Fifteenth!*[75] Were I my self to chuse what sort of *Bird* I would be transformed into, I would say, *O that I had wings like a Dove!* {Ps. 55:6} Nevertheless, I will for once do the Office, which as it seems, Heaven sent that *Raven* upon; even to beg, *That the Peace of God may Rule in our Hearts* {Col. 3:15}. . . .

We will now proceed unto several of the like Trials among our selves.

THE TRYAL OF G[EORGE] B[URROUGHS]

At a Court of Oyer and Terminer,
Held in *Salem*. 1692.[76]

Glad should I have been, if I had never known the Name of this man; or never had this occasion to mention so much as the first Letters of his Name. But the Government requiring some Account, of his Trial, to be Inserted in this Book, it becomes me with all Obedience, to submit unto the Order.

I. This *G. B.* was Indicted for *Witchcraft*; and in the Prosecution of the Charge against him, he was Accused by five or six of the Bewitched, as the Author of their Miseries; he was Accused by eight of the Confessing Witches, as being an Head Actor at some of their Hellish Randezvouzes, and one who had the promise of being a *King* in Satans Kingdom, now going to be erected; he was Accused by nine persons, for extraordinary Lifting, and such Feats of Strength, could not be done without a Diabolical Assistance. And for other such Things he was Accused, until about Thirty Testimonies were brought in against him; nor were these, judg'd the half of what might have been considered, for his Conviction: however they were enough to fix the Character of a *Witch* upon him, according to the Rules of Reasoning, by the Judicious *Gaule*,[77] in that Case directed.

II. The Court being sensible, that the *Testimonies of the Parties Bewitched*, use to have a Room among the *Suspicions*, or *Presumptions*,[78] brought in against one Indicted for Witchcraft, there were now heard the Testimonies of several Persons, who were most notoriously Bewitched, and every day Tortured by Invisible Hands, and these now all charged the Spectres of *G. B.* to have a share in their Torments. At the Examination of this *G. B.* the Bewitched People were grievously harassed, with Preternatural Mischiefs, which could not possibly be Dissembled; and they still ascribed it unto the Endeavours of *G. B.* to kill them. And now upon his Trial, one of the Bewitched Persons testify'd, That in her Agonies, a little Black-hair'd man came to her, saying his Name was *B.* and bidding her set her hand unto a Book which he show'd unto her; and bragging that he was a *Conjurer*, above the ordinary Rank of Witches; That he often persecuted her, with the offer of that Book, saying, *She should be well, and need fear no body, if she would but Sign it*:[79] but he inflicted cruel Pains and Hurts upon her, because of her Denying so to do. The Testimonies of the other Sufferers concurred with these; and it was Remarkable, that whereas *Biting*, was one of the ways which the Witches used, for the vexing of the Sufferers, when they cry'd out of G. B. biting them, the print of the Teeth, would be seen on the Flesh of the Complainers; and just such a sett of *Teeth*, as G. B's would then appear upon them, which could be distinguished from those of some other mens. Others of them testify'd, That in their Torments, G. B. tempted them, to go unto a Sacrament, unto which they perceived him with a sound of Trumpet Summoning of other Witches; who quickly after the Sound would come from all Quarters unto the Rendezvouz. One of them falling into a kind of Trance, afterwards affirmed, That G. B. had carried her into a very high Mountain, where he show'd her mighty and glorious Kingdoms, and said, *He would give them all to her, if she would write in his Book*; {Matt. 4:8; Luke 4:5} but she told him, *They were none of his to give*;[80] and refused the motions; enduring of much misery for that Refusal.

It cost the Court a wonderful deal of Trouble, to hear the Testimonies of the Sufferers; for when they were going to give in their Depositions, they would for a long while be taken with fitts, that made them uncapable of saying any thing. The Chief Judge asked the prisoner, who he thought hindred these witnesses from giving their testimonies? and he answered, *He supposed, it was the Divel?* That Honourable person, then reply'd *How comes the Divel so loathe to have any Testimony born against you?* Which cast him into very great confusion.

III. It has been a frequent thing for the Bewitched people, to be entertained with Apparitions of *Ghosts* of murdered people, at the same time, that the *Spectres* of the witches trouble them. These Ghosts do always affright the Beholders, more than all the other spectral Representations; and when they exhibit themselves, they cry out, of being Murdered by the witchcrafts or other violences of the persons who are then in spectre present. It is further considerable, that once or twice, these *Apparitions* have been seen by others at the very same time that they have shown them selves to the Bewitched; & seldom have these been these *Apparitions* but when something unusual & suspected had attended the Death of the party thus Appearing. Some that have bin accused by these *Apparitions*, accosting of the Bewitched People, who had never heard a word of any such persons, ever being in the world, have upon a fair examination freely, and fully, confessed the murders of those very persons, altho' these also did not know how the *Apparitions* had complained of them. Accordingly several of the Bewitched, had given in their Testimony, that they had been troubled with the *Apparitions* of two women, who said, that they were G. Bs. two wives; and that he had been the Death of them; and that the Magistrates must be told of it, before whom if B. upon his trial deny'd it, they did not know but that they should appear again in the Court. Now, G. B. had been infamous for the Barbarous usage of his two successive *wives*, all the Country over. Moreover; It was testify'd, the spectre of G. B. threatning of the sufferers told them, he had killed (besides others) Mrs. *Lawson* and her Daughter *Ann*.[81] And it was noted, That these were the vertuous wife and Daughter, of one at whom this G. B. might have a prejudice for his being serviceable at *Salem-village*, from whence himself had in Ill Terms removed some years before: & that when they dy'd, which was long since, there were some odd circumstances about them, which made some of the Attendents there suspect something of witchcraft, tho' none Imagined from what Quarter it should come.

Well, G. B. being now upon his Triall, one of the Bewitched persons was cast into Horror at the Ghosts of B's. two deceased wives,[82] then appearing before him, and crying for, *Vengeance*, against him. Hereupon several of the Bewitched persons were successively called in, who all not knowing what the former had seen and said, concurred in their Horror, of the Apparition, which they affirmed, that he had before him. But he, tho' much appalled, utterly deny'd that he discerned any thing of it; nor was it any part of his *Conviction*.

IV. Judicious Writers, have assigned it a great place, in the Conviction of *witches, when persons are Impeached by other Notorious witches, to be as Ill as themselves; especially, if the persons have been much noted for neglecting the Worship of God*. Now, as there might have been Testimonies Enough of G. B's. Antipathy to *Prayer* and the other Ordinances of God, tho' by his profession singularly obliged thereunto; so, there now came in against the prisoner, the Testimonies of several persons, who confessed their own having been Horrible *Witches*, and ever since their confessions had been themselves terribly Tortured by the Devils and other Witches, even like the other Sufferers; and therein undergone the pains of many *Deaths* for their Confessions.

These now Testify'd, that G. B. had been at Witch-Meetings with them; and that he was the Person who had Seduced, and Compelled them into the snares of Witchcraft: That he promised them *Fine Cloaths*, for doing it; that he brought Poppets to them, and thorns to stick into those Poppets, for the afflicting of other People: And that he exhorted them, with the rest of the Crue, to bewitch all *Salem-Village*, but be sure to do it Gradually, if they would prevail in what they did.

When the *Lancashire Witches*[83] were condemn'd, I don't Remember that there was any considerable further Evidence, than that of the Bewitched, and then that of some that confessed. We see so much already against G. B. But this being indeed not *Enough*, there were, other things to render what had been already produced *credible*.

V. A famous Divine, recites this among the Convictions of a Witch; *The Testimony of the Party Bewitched, whether Pining or Dying; together with the Joint Oathes of Sufficient Persons, that have seen certain Prodigious Pranks or Feats, wrought by the party Accused.*[84] Now God had been pleased so to leave this G. B. that he had ensnared himself, by several Instances which he had formerly given of a Preternatural strength, and which were now produced against him. He was a very Puny man; yet he had often done things beyond the strength of a Giant. A Gun of about seven foot barrel, and so Heavy that strong men could not steadily hold it out, with both hands; there were several Testimonies, given in by Persons of Credit and Honour, that he made nothing of taking up such a Gun behind the Lock, with but one hand, and holding it out like a Pistol, at Arms-end.[85] G. B. in his Vindication was so foolish as to say, *That an Indian was there, and held it out at the same time:* Whereas, none of the Spectators ever saw any such *Indian*; but they suppos'd the *Black man* (as the Witches call the *Devil*; and they generally say he resembles an *Indian*) might give him that Assistence. There was Evidence, likewise, brought in, that he made nothing of Taking up whole Barrels fill'd with *Molasses*, or *Cider*, in very Disadvantagious Postures, and Carrying of them through the Difficultest Places, out of a Canoo to the Shore.

[Yea, there were Two Testimonies, that G. B. with only putting the Fore-Finger of his Right hand, into the Muzzel of an heavy Gun, a Fowling-piece, of about six or seven foot Barrel, did Lift up the gun, and hold it out at Arms end; a Gun which the Deponents, though strong men, could not with both hands Lift up, and hold out, at the Butt end, as is usual.[86] Indeed one of these Witnesses, was over perswaded by some persons, to be out of the way, upon G. B.'s Trial; but he came afterwards, with sorrow for his withdraw, and gave in his Testimony: Nor were either of these Witnesses made use of as evidences in the Trial.]

VI. There came in several Testimonies, relating to the Domestick Affayrs of G. B. which had a very hard Aspect upon him; and not only prov'd him a very ill man; but also confirmed the Belief of the Character, which had been already fastned on him. e. g.

T'was testifyed, That keeping his two Successive Wives in a strange kind of Slavery, he would when he came home from abroad, pretend to tell the Talk which any had with them: That he ha's brought them to the point of Death, by his Harsh Dealings with his Wives, and then made the People about him to promise that in Case Death should happen, they would say nothing of it. That he used all means to make his Wives, Write, Sign, Seal, and Swear a Covenant, never to Reveal any of his Secrets. That his Wives had privately complained unto the Neighbours about frightful Apparitions of Evil Spirits, with which their House was sometimes infested; and that many such things have been Whispered among the Neighbourhood. There were also some other Testimonies, relating to the Death of People, whereby the Consciences of an Impartial Jury, were convinced, that *G. B.* had Bewitched the persons mentioned in the Complaints. But I am forced to omit several such passages, in this, as well as in all the succeeding *Trials*, because the Scribes who took Notice of them, have not Supplyed me.

VII. One Mr. *Ruck*,[87] Brother-in-Law to this *G. B.* Testify'd, that *G. B.* and he himself, and his Sister, who was *G. B.'s* Wife, going out for Two or three Miles, to gather Straw-Berries, *Ruck*, with his Sister the Wife of G. B. Rode home very Softly, with G. B. on Foot in their Company, G. B. stept aside a little into the Bushes; Whereupon they Halted and Halloo'd for him. He not answering, they went away homewards, with a Quickened pace; without any expectation of seeing him in a considerable while: and yet when they were got near home, to their Astonishment they found him on foot, with them, having a Basket of Straw-Berries. G. B. immediately, then fell to chiding his Wife, on the account of what she had been speaking to her Brother, of him, on the Road: which when they wondred at, he said, *He knew their thoughts. Ruck* being startled at that, made some Reply, intimating that the Devil himself did not know so far; but G. B. answered, *My God, makes known your Thoughts unto me.* The prisoner now at the Barr had nothing to answer, unto what was thus Witnessed against him, that was worth considering. Only he said, *Ruck, and his Wife left a man with him, when they left him.* Which *Ruck* now affirm'd to be false; and when the Court asked G. B. *What the Man's Name was?* his countenance was much altered; nor could he say, who 'twas.[88] But the Court began to think, that he then step'd aside, only that by the assistance of the *Black Man*, he might put on his *Invisibility*, and in that *Fascinating Mist*, gratify his own Jealous humour, to hear what they said of him. Which trick of rendring themselves *Invisible*, our Witches do in their confessions pretend that they sometimes are Masters of; and it is the more credible, because there is Demonstration that they often render many other things utterly *Invisible*.

VIII. *Faltring, Faulty, unconstant, and contrary Answers upon Judicial and deliberate examination*, are counted some unlucky symptoms of guilt, in all crimes; Especially in Witchcrafts.[89] Now there never was a prisoner more Eminent for them, than G. B. both at his Examination and on his Trial. His *Tergiversations, Contradictions,* and *Falsehoods*, were very sensible: he had little to say, but that he had heard some things that he could not prove, Respecting upon the Reputation of some of the witnesses. Only he gave in a paper, to the Jury; wherein, altho' he had many times before, granted, not only that there are *Witches*, but also that the present suffering of the Countrey are the Effect of horrible *Witchcrafts*, yet he now goes to, evince it, *That there neither are, nor ever were, Witches that having made a compact with the Divel, Can send a Divel to Torment other people at a distance.* This paper was Transcribed out of *Ady;*[90] which the Court presently knew, as soon as they heard it. But he said, he had taken none of it out of any Book; for which his evasion afterwards was, that a Gentleman gave him the discourse, in a manuscript, from whence he Transcribed it.

IX. The Jury brought him in *guilty;* But when he came to Dy, he utterly deny'd the Fact, whereof he had been thus convicted.

THE TRYAL OF SUSANNA MARTIN

At the Court of Oyer and Terminer:
Held by Adjournment at *Salem. June* 29, 1692.

I. *Susanna Martin,* pleading, *Not Guilty,* to the Indictment of *Witchcrafts* brought in against her, there were produced the evidences of many persons very sensibly and grievously Bewitched; who all complaned of the prisoner at the Bar, as the person whom they Believed the cause of their Miseries. And now, as well as in the other Trials, there was an extraordinary endeavour by *witchcrafts,* with Cruel and Frequent Fits, to hinder the poor sufferers, from giving in their complaints; which the Court was forced with much patience to obtain, by much waiting and watching for it.

II. There was now also an Account given, of what passed at her first examination before the Magistrates. The cast of her *eye,* then striking the Afflicted People to the ground, whether they saw that Cast or no; there were these among other passages, between the Magistrates, and the Examinate.[91]

Magistrate. Pray, what ails these People?

Martin. I don't know.

Magistrate. But, what do you think ails them?

Martin. I don't desire to spend my Judgment upon it.

Magistrate. Don't you think they are Bewitch'd?

Martin. No, I do not think they are.

Magistrate. Tell us your thoughts about them then.

Martin. No, my thoughts are my own when they are in, but when they are out, they are anothers. Their Master.—

Magistrate. Their Master? Who do you think, is their Master;

Martin. If they be dealing in the Black Art, you may know as well as I.

Magistrate. Well, what have you done towards this?

Martin. Nothing at all.

Magistrate. Why, 'tis you or your Appearance.

Martin. I cannot help it.

Magistrate. Is it nor *Your* Master? How comes your Appearance to hurt these?

Martin. How do I know? He that appear'd in the shape of *Samuel*, a Glorify'd Saint, may Appear in any ones shape.

It was then also noted in her, as in others like her, that if the Afflicted went to approach her, they were flung down to the Ground. And, when she was asked the Reason of it, she said, *I cannot tell; it may be, the Devil bears me more Malice than another.*[92]

III. The Court accounted themselves Alarum'd by these things, to Enquire further into the Conversation of the Prisoner; and see what there might occur, to render these Accusations further credible. Whereupon, *John Allen*, of *Salisbury*,[93] testify'd, that he refusing, because of the weakness of his Oxen, to cart some Staves, at the request of this *Martin*, she was displeased at it, and said, *It had been as good that he had; for his Oxen should never do him much more Service.* Whereupon, this Deponent said, *Dost thou threaten me, thou old Witch: I'l throw thee into the Brook:* Which to avoid, she flew over the Bridge, and escaped. But, as he was going home, one of his Oxen Tired, so that he was forced to Unyoke him, that he might get him home. He then put his Oxen, with many more, upon *Salisbury* Beach, where Cattle did use to get *Flesh.* In a few days, all the Oxen upon the Beach were found by their Tracks, to have run unto the mouth of *Merrimack-River,* and not returned; but the next day they were found come ashore upon *Plum-Island.* They that sought them, used all imaginable gentleness, but they would still run away with a violence that seemed wholly Diabolical, till they came near the mouth of *Merrimack-River;* when they ran right into the Sea, swimming as far as they could be seen. One of them then swam back again, with a swiftness, amazing to the Beholders, who stood ready to receive him, and help up his Tired Carcase: but the beast ran furiously up into the Island, and from thence, thorough the Marishes, up into *Newbury* Town, and so up into the Woods; and there after a while found near *Amesbury.* So that, of Fourteen good Oxen, there was only this saved: the Rest were all cast up, some in one place, and some in another, Drowned.

IV. *John Atkinson*[94] Testify'd, That he Exchanged a Cow, with a Son of *Susanna Martins,* whereat she muttered, and was unwilling he should have it. Going to Receive this Cow, tho' he Hamstring'd her, and Halter'd her, she of a

Tame Creature grew so mad, that they could scarce get her along. She broke all the Ropes that were fastned unto her, and though she were Ty'd fast unto a Tree, yet she made her Escape, and gave them such further Trouble, as they could ascribe to no cause but Witchcraft.

V. *Bernard Peache* testify'd, That being in Bed, on a Lords day Night, he heard a scrabbling at the Window, whereat he then saw, *Susanna Martin* come in, and jump down upon the Floor. She took hold of this Deponents Feet, and drawing his Body up into an Heap, she lay upon him, near Two Hours; in all which time he could neither speak nor stirr. At length, when he could begin to move, he laid hold on her Hand, and pulling it up to his mouth, he bit three of her Fingers, as he judged, unto the Bone. Whereupon she went from the Chamber, down the Stairs, out at the Door. This Deponent thereupon called unto the people of the House, to advise them, of what passed; and he himself did follow her. The people saw her not; but there being a Bucket at the Left-hand of the Door, there was a drop of Blood found on it; and several more drops of Blood upon the Snow newly fallen abroad. There was likewise the print of her two Feet just without the Threshold; but no more sign of any Footing further off.

At another time this Deponent was desired by the Prisoner, to come unto an Husking of Corn, at her House; and she said, *If he did not come, it were better that he did!* He went not; but the Night following, *Susanna Martin*, as he judged, and another came towards him. One of them said, *Here he is!* but he having a Quarter-staff, made a Blow at them. The Roof of the Barn broke his Blow; but following them to the Window, he made another Blow at them, and struck them down; yet they got up, and got out, and he saw no more of them.

About this time, there was a Rumour about the Town, that *Martin* had a Broken Head; but the Deponent could say nothing to that.

The said *Peache*[95] also testify'd, the Bewitching of Cattle to Death, upon *Martins* Discontents.

VI. *Robert Downer*[96] testifyed, That this Prisoner being some years ago prosecuted at Court for a Witch, he then said unto her, *He believed she was a Witch.* Whereat she being Dissatisfied, Said, *That some Shee-Devil would Shortly fetch him away!* Which words were heard by others, as well as himself. The Night following, as he lay in his Bed, there came in at the Window, the likeness of a *Cat*, which Flew upon him, took fast hold of his Throat, lay on him a considerable while, and almost killed him. At length he remembred, what *Susanna Martin*, had threatned the Day before; and with much striving he cryed out, *Avoid, thou Shee-Devil! In the Name of God the Father, the Son, and the Holy Ghost, Avoid!* Whereupon it left him, leap'd on the Floor, and Flew out at the Window.

And there also came in several Testimonies, that before ever *Downer* spoke a word of this Accident, *Susanna Martin* and her Family, had related, *How this* Downer *had been Handled!*

VII. *John Kembal,*[97] testifyed, that *Susanna Martin*, upon a Causeless Disgust, had threatened him, about a certain Cow of his, *That she should never do him any more Good*: and it came to pass accordingly. For soon after the Cow was found stark Dead on the dry Ground; without any Distemper to be discerned upon her. Upon which he was followed with a strange Death upon more of his Cattle, whereof he lost in One Spring to the value of Thirty Pounds. But the said *John Kembal* had a further Testimony to give in against the Prisoner which was truly admirable.

Being desirous to furnish himself with a Dog, he applyed himself to buy one of this *Martin*, who had a Bitch with Whelps in her House. But she not letting him have his Choice, he said, he would supply himself then at one *Blezdels*. Having mark'd a puppy, which he lik'd at *Blezdels*,[98] he met *George Martin*, the Husband of the prisoner, going by, who asked him, *Whether he would not have one of his Wives Puppies*; and he answered, *No*. The same Day, one *Edmund Eliot*, being at *Martins House*, heard *George Martin* relate, where this *Kembal* had been, and what he had said. Whereupon *Susanna Martin* replyed, *If I live, I'll give him Puppies enough!* Within a few dayes after, this *Kembal* coming out of the Woods, there arose a little Black Cloud, in the N. W. and *Kembal* immediately felt a Force upon him, which made him not able to avoid running upon the stumps of Trees, that were before him, albeit, he had a broad, plain Cart-way, before him; but tho' he had his Ax also on his Shoulder to endanger him in his Falls, he could not forbear going out of his way to tumble over them. When he came below the Meeting-House, there appeared unto him, a little thing like a *Puppy*, of a Darkish Colour; and it shot Backwards and forwards between his Leggs. He had the Courage to use all possible Endeavours of Cutting it, with his Ax; but he could not Hit it; the Puppy gave a jump from him, and went, as to him, it seem'd into the Ground. Going a little further, there appeared unto him a Black Puppy, somewhat bigger than the first; but as Black as a Cole. Its motions were quicker than those of his Ax; it Flew at his Belly and away; then at his Throat; so, over his Shoulder one way, and then over his Shoulder another way. His heart now began to fail him, and he thought the Dog would have Tore his Throat out. But he recovered himself, and called upon God in his Distress; and Naming the Name of JESUS CHRIST, it Vanished away at once. The Deponent Spoke not one Word of these Accidents, for fear of affrighting his wife. But the next Morning, *Edmund Eliot*, going into *Martins* house, this woman asked him were *Kembal* was? He Replyed, *At home, a bed, for ought he knew.*

She returned, *They say, he was frighted last Night.* Eliot asked *With what?* She answered, *With Puppies.* Eliot asked, *where she heard of it, for he had heard nothing of it!* She rejoined, *About the Town.* Altho' *Kembal* had mentioned the Matter to no Creature Living.[99]

VIII. *William Brown*[100] testify'd, that Heaven haveing blessed him with a most Pious and prudent wife,[101] this wife of his, one day mett with *Susanna Martin;* but when she approch'd just unto her *Martin,* vanished out of sight, and left her extremely affrighted. After which time, the said *Martin,* often appear'd unto her, giving her no little trouble; & when she did come, she was visited with Birds that sorely peck't and Prick'd her; and sometimes, a Bunch, like a pullets egg would Rise in her throat, ready to Choak her, till she cry'd out, *Witch, you shan't Choak me!* While this good Woman was in this Extremity, the Church appointed a Day of Prayer, on her behalf; whereupon her Trouble ceas'd; she saw not *Martin* as formerly; and the Church, instead of their Fast, gave Thanks for her Deliverance. But a considerable while after, she being Summoned to give in some Evidence at the Court, against this *Martin,* quickly thereupon, this *Martin* came behind her, while she was milking her Cow, and said unto her, *For thy defaming me at Court, I'l make thee the miserablest Creature in the World.* Soon after which, she fell into a strange kind of Distemper, and became horribly Frantick, and uncapable of any Reasonable Action; the Physicians declaring, that her Distemper was preternatural, and that some Devil had certainly Bewitched her; and in that Condition she now remained.

IX. *Sarah Atkinson*[102] testify'd, That *Susanna Martin* came from *Amesbury,* to their House at *Newbury,* in an extraordinary Season, when it was not fit for any one to Travel. She came (as she said, unto *Atkinson,*) all that long way on Foot. She brag'd, and show'd, how dry she was; nor could it be perceived that so much as the Soles of her Shoes were wet. *Atkinson* was amazed at it; and professed, that she should her self have been wet up to the knees, if she had then came so far; but *Martin* reply'd, *She scorn'd to be Drabbled!* It was noted, that this Testimony upon her Trial, cast her into a very singular Confusion.

X. *John Pressy,*[103] testify'd, That being one Evening very unaccountably Bewildred, near a field of *Martins,* and several times, as one under an Enchantment, returning to the place he had left, at length he saw a marvellous Light, about the Bigness of an Half-Bushel, near two Rod, out of the way. He went, and struck at it with a Stick, and laid it on with all his might. He gave it near forty blows; and felt it a palpable substance. But going from it, his Heels were struck up, and he was laid with his Back on the Ground: Sliding as he thought, into a Pit; from whence he recover'd, by taking hold on the Bush; altho' afterwards he could find no such Pit in the place. Having after his Recovery, gone five or six Rod, he saw *Susanna Martin* standing on his Left-hand, as the Light had done before; but they changed no words with one another. He could scarce find his House in his Return; but at length he got home, extreamly affrighted. The next day, it was upon Enquiry understood, that *Martin* was in a miserable condition by pains and hurts that were upon her.

It was further testify'd by this Deponent, That after he had given in some Evidence against *Susanna Martin*, many years ago, she gave him foul words about it; and said, *He should never prosper more*; particularly, *That he should never have more than two Cows; that tho' he were never so likely to have more, yet he should never have them.*[104] And that from that very Day to this; namely for Twenty Years together, he could never exceed that Number; but some strange thing or other still prevented his having of any more.

XI. *Jarvis Ring*,[105] testifyed, that about seven years ago, he was oftentimes and grievously Oppressed in the Night; but saw not who Troubled him, until at last he Lying perfectly Awake, plainly saw *Susanna Martin* approach him. She came to him, and forceably Bit him by the Finger; so that the Print of the Bite is now so long after to be seen upon him.

XII. But besides all of these Evidences, there was a most wonderful Account of one *Joseph Ring*,[106] produced on this Occasion.

This man has been strangely carried about by *Daemons*, from one *Witch-Meeting* to another, for near two years together; and for one Quarter of this Time, they have made him, and kept him Dumb, tho' he is now again able to speak. There was one *T. H.* who having as tis judged, a Design of engaging this *Joseph Ring*, in a Snare of Devillism, contrived a wile, to bring this *Ring* two Shillings in Debt unto him.

Afterwards, this poor man would be visited with unknown shapes, and this T. H.[107] sometimes among them; which would force him away with them, unto unknown Places, where he saw meetings, Feastings, Dancings; and after his Return, wherein they hurried him along thro' the Air, he gave Demonstrations to the Neighbours, that he had indeed been so transported. When he was brought unto these Hellish meetings, one of the First things they still did unto him, was to give him a knock on the Back, whereupon he was ever as if Bound with Chains, uncapable of Stirring out of the place, till they should Release him. He related, that there often came to him a man, who presented him a *Book*, whereunto he would have him set his Hand; promising to him, that he should then have even what he would; and presenting him with all the delectable Things, persons, and places, that he could imagine. But he refusing to subscribe, the business would end with dreadful Shapes, Noises and Screeches, which almost scared him out of his witts. Once with the Book, there was a Pen offered him, and an Inkhorn, with Liquor in it, that seemed like Blood: but he never toucht it.

This man did now affirm, that he saw the Prisoner, at several of those Hellish Randezvouzes.

Note, This Woman was one of the most Impudent, Scurrilous, wicked creatures in the world; & she did now throughout her whole Trial, discover her self to be such an one. Yet when she was asked, what she had to say for her self, her Cheef Plea, was, *That she had Led a most virtuous and Holy Life.*

RACE, SLAVERY, AND SERVITUDE

Cotton Mather lived at a time when slavery, of one kind or another, was practiced nearly everywhere in the world and was a condition that had been in existence since ancient times. Within the British North American colonies during the late seventeenth and early eighteenth centuries, indentured white servitude was giving way to chattel slavery as the pool of impoverished English willing to become indentured was declining, creating a need for a large, inexpensively obtained labor force that would produce the cash crops grown in the colonies—tobacco, sugar cane, wheat and other grains, indigo, and later cotton—which were in increasingly high demand in Europe. Africans were identified as an important source of that labor force. They had been shipped to the Americas since the early seventeenth century, mostly from the African west coast, taken forcibly by members of rival tribes and kingdoms or by white slave traders and sold into bondage.

Around the turn of the eighteenth century, the number of Africans being transported into the Americas was still relatively small, but Mather's last years coincided with the period in which the number of enslaved Africans was beginning to increase exponentially. During that century, it is estimated that Anglo-Americans brought over and enslaved more than 2 million Africans. While the majority of them ended up in the southern colonies, it was in the holds of New England ships that many were involuntarily, illegally, and inhumanely transported, through which means inhabitants of northern colonies, including Massachusetts, could procure slaves of their own.

Mather was one of these growing numbers of New England slaveowners, obtained either through personal purchase or as a gift from his congregation. Upper-class individuals such as himself sought to procure slaves as markers of their social standing, as unpaid workers in the home and fields, and as sources of income that could be rented out to neighbors. During his lifetime, the Mather household, typically, had a series of servants and enslaved persons, indentured and bond, white, Black, and Native, usually two or three at any given time. Furthermore, because of his strict biblicism, Mather conceded that slavery as an institution was practiced in biblical times. But he did not consider it a sin— in fact, *the* sin of the land—as reformers would consider it later in the century.

At the same time, Mather held views and initiated measures that complicate any simplistic categorization of him on the issues of race and slavery. Unusually, he manumitted two of his enslaved persons during his lifetime and a third in his will, and, contrary to the prevailing practice, he educated the enslaved persons in his household and allowed them to marry. In a time when racial identities were crystallizing so that blackness was identified with slavery, Mather refused to go along, pointing out that the Bible made no such distinctions and in fact taught the oneness of the human race. Further, he sought an end to the slave trade—that is, the practice of taking free people from their own countries— because it violated the biblical prohibitions against "manstealing." In his *Biblia Americana* entry on Genesis 47:22–23, he agreed, though not without hesitation, that the biblical patriarch Joseph, who rose from slavery to become a leader in Egypt, in turn unjustly enslaved the free people of that country. During a seven-year period of starvation, he stripped them of their natural rights and forced their relocation, a violation of the "Rules of Goodness" for which God punished Joseph. This patriarch "seems to have *destroy'd the Freedom of the Nation, &* to have committed an horrid Rape on their Liberties and Properties," Mather censured Joseph, blaming him for setting a bad example for others: "*Josephs Attempt* upon *Egypt,* was one of the First Specimens of Tyranny and Slavery given to the

World; and that other Princes in other Nations learnt the Way of it, from this very scandalous Exemple."[1] Although Mather could not get around the scriptural justifications for enslavement under certain conditions, he roundly criticized slavery as it was found in America, especially the ways that enslaved persons were brutally treated and denied knowledge of Christianity.

Expositors, both pro- and antislavery, wielded the Bible to defend their positions. As a voluminous commentator himself, Mather filled manuscripts such as *Biblia Americana* with revealing observations on some of the key polemic texts. Genesis 9, for example, contains Noah's cursing of his son Cham's posterity to perpetual bondage to one of his other son's descendants. In his comment on the text, Mather denied that this justified "our Enslaving the *Negro's*, wherever we can find them," not merely because the sentence pertained only to the youngest of Cham's sons, Canaan, but because, Mather flatly stated, "The *Negroes* are not the Posterity of *Canaan.*" Noah's curse was not for Mather an argument for the subjugation of people of color, and further, the "*Blackness* of the *Ethiopians*" was not a mark of Noah's curse but simply the result of their living in a land with a "*Hott Sun.*" In his reflections on Genesis 10:20, which begins a description of the genealogy of Cham, Mather refuted ethnogenesis—the theory that there were separate, inferior races of humanity created before Adam— and asserted monogenesis, that is, that all humanity is descended from one progenitor, and that skin color did not carry any moral or spiritual significance but was the result of long-term biological and environmental accommodations— in modern terms, evolution. The Bible, for Mather as later for liberators such as Frederick Douglass, was color blind; all humans were made by God and equal candidates for grace.

While Mather did not vigorously question the existence and expansion of African slavery in the English nation and colonies, he did commit himself personally to improving, in ways that he knew how, the condition of the "Servants among us." His ways of assisting them were by offering education and charity and encouraging conversion. In his diary for late 1693, Mather described how a company of enslaved people had approached him to establish a regular meeting. He quickly agreed, not only preaching to and praying with them but also drawing up a set of *Rules for the Society of Negroes*, couched as a covenant or even manifesto that set forth a meeting schedule. The subscribers—"Children of *Adam*, and of *Noah*"—pledged to avoid wicked company, drunkenness, and fornication; to have only English speakers lead their meetings; to refuse help to runaways; and to learn the catechism. In other words, the society, which met at Mather's home on occasion, was at once a means of mutual uplift and of monitoring behavior that enlisted the members themselves.

Colonial ministers sometimes found it useful or necessary to preach sermons that prescribed the obligations of masters and enslaved persons to each other. Mather was no exception. In *A Good Master Well Served* (1696), he set forth the dynamics of a "**Herile Society**," that is, the relationship between master and servant, which he viewed as established by God as part of the family structure. Within that little commonwealth, each had relative duties and capacities, but they had in common a spiritualized liberty, in which each had freedom, within their stations, in their obedience to God. Painting no doubt an overly rosy picture of the earliest days of Christianity, Mather wrote that then "there were Christianized **Masters**, who had much adoe to lay aside, the fierce, harsh, bruitish and bloody Usage of their *Servants*." There were likewise "Christianized **Servants**, who on the other side had much ado to maintain a due Respect unto their *Masters*, after they were by Regeneration advanced unto the priviledges of the Gospel, and made the *Sons* and *Heirs* of God." This was Mather's answer to maintaining not only a decent and civil relationship but also a spiritually significant one: both were to be devoted servants of Jesus. But the onus, at least here, was on enslaved persons, who had to renounce the "**Invisible Masters**" of the world— their sins and temptations—and be submissive and not run away. Enslaved persons were to let their service be such that it glorified Jesus, and in reverencing and obeying their masters, reverence and obey Christ. As in the *Rules for the Society of Negroes*, enslaved persons were also to avoid misspending time, idling in evil company—even, curiously, reading "**Idle Romances**."

Masters, on the other hand, were to treat their slaves as fellow human beings created by God who had "*Reasonable Souls*." In *The Negro Christianized* (1706), Mather laid out the principles and motivations of a Christian slaveowner. He espoused an ethic of "Christian slavery" that he shared with later evangelicals and was a critique of the inhumane ways in which enslaved persons were treated. In this ideal of the pious Christian master, any enslaved persons who came into his possession were to be viewed as objects of charity and as converts to true religion. Indeed, *"to Convert one Soul unto God"* from a "dark State of Ignorance and Wickedness" was the highest achievement of the slaveowner. Here, Mather approved the common argument that enslavement, especially of Africans or those from other "heathen" places, was legitimate if it were a means of spreading the gospel and saving souls. So, Mather exhorted owners to Christianize their slaves, to care for their slaves' souls as they would any other member of their family. Even if unsuccessful, God would still notice and reward these efforts. However, Mather condemned in no uncertain terms those who used their slaves "worse than their *Horses*," and he criticized those who held that Africans' darkness was an argument for doing nothing for them, and that whiteness was a sign of natural superiority. Mather cringed at the claims equating whiteness with true Christianity.

We see, then, that Mather embodied many of the contradictions, ambivalences, and rationalizations of his time when it came to issues of race and the institution of slavery. But he also departed from many of the common attitudes that justified slavery and racial prejudice in all their aspects and circumstances. Mather is a fascinating case study in the evolution of colonizers' thoughts and practices about the peculiar institution. In the end, however, for all his acuity, he could not rise above the assumptions of the age and place in which he lived. That task awaited activists Black and white of later generations.

BIBLIA AMERICANA (1693–1728)

[ENTRY ON GENESIS 9:27 (THE CURSE OF CHAM)]

Gen. 9.27. *God shall enlarge Japheth, and he shall dwell in the tens of Shem; and Canaan shall be his servant.*

Q. The *Curse* upon *Cham*, does it not Justify our Enslaving the *Negro's*, wherever we can find them? v. 27.

A. The whole Family of *Cham* was not concern'd in that *Curse*. None but *Canaan*, the youngest Son of *Cham*, is mentioned; and he is Thrice mentioned.

The *Negroes* are not the Posterity of *Canaan.* The Imprecation of the *Patriarch,* seems to be little more than a Prophecy, of the *Canaanites* Overthrow & Reduction, under the Power of the *Israelites,* who were the Posterity of *Shem.* And, as one observes, the Recording hereof by *Moses,* doth seem especially to *Justify,* or at least *Encourage,* the *Israelites,* in Dispossessing them.

Q. What Remarkable is there, in the Effects of *Noahs* Blessing and Cursing his Offspring? v. 27.
A. Mr. *Mede* hath an Observation, That there hath never yett been a Son of *Cham,* that hath shaken a Scepter over the Head of *Japhet. Shem* hath subdued *Japhet,* and *Japhet* hath subdued *Shem;* But *Cham* never subdued either. This made *Annibal,* a Child of *Canaan,* cry out with Amazement of Soul, *Agnosco fatum Carthaginis;* I acknowledge the Fate of *Carthàge.* [Livy. L. XXVII *in fine.*][2]

[ENTRY ON GENESIS 9:20–27 (THE PROPHECY OF NOAH)]

Q. *Austin* thinks it enough to bespeak the Title of a *Prophet,* for the Patriarch *Noah,* that the *Ark* which he made, *Prophetia nostrorum temporum fuit.* But he may be further entituled unto it, from his marvellous *Prophecy,* about his *Posterity;* which now calls for some Illustration? v. 20–27.[3]
A. We will again consult our learned *Heidegger;* and principally employ his Lucubrations, to furnish our Illustrations on this noble Subject.

We find the Patriarch overtaken with *Wine,* after his coming out of the *Ark,* into his *New World.* The *Hebrewes* and the *Fathers* do generally agree, That he was wholly a Stranger to the Nature of *Wine,* and that the *Inebriating Power* of it, was utterly unknown to him; or, that it was, as *Chrysostom* expresses the Matter, δια το μη ειδεναι της μεταληψεως τα μετρα εις μεθην εξεκυλισδη, *Quòd ignoraret modum hauriendi Vini, Ebrietati succubuisse.*[4] But our *Heidegger* looks on this, as an uncertain and an ungrounded Opinion; and will not be perswaded, That the Use of *Wine* had been all this while unknown unto the World; when *Vines* were so common, & the *Long Lives* of the People gave them Opportunity enough to find out what Use they might be putt unto; And our Saviour makes *Drunkenness* one prevailing Sin among the *Antediluvians.*[5] That Expression, *And Noah began to be an Husbandman;* will not imply, That there was no *Husbandry* before the Flood. It only implies, That *Noah* sett himself to restore the *Artes* βιωτικαι· which had formerly been practised.[6] Yea, and the Word ought rather to be rendred, as *Onkelos* and *Jonathan* have done it; *Et permansit.* The Great *Calvin* at last leaves the Matter so; *Ego hoc in medio relinquens, potius ex ebrietate Noë discendum esse arbitror, quàm fœda et detestabilis sit ebrietas.*[7]

The Conjectures and the Traditions of the *Jewish Expositors,* How *Noah* came to know, what had befallen him, relating to his *Denudation,* in his *Drunkenness,* are not worth a Recitation. Tis enough, that we say, with *Chrysostom,* He learn'd it by Enquiries of his Two Sons, of *Shem* and *Japhet.*

The Prophecy that followes, is *Tripartite.* The First Article, is, a *Malediction* upon *Cham;* who had been so horribly Abusive unto his Father. But it seems wonderful, that *Canaan* the Son of *Cham,* should be the Object mentioned; and a State of *Servitude* be assigned unto him. The *Hebrewes,* and *Theodoret,* and *Procopius Gazaeus,* and *Lyranus,* and *Abulensis,* and others from them, tell us, That *Canaan* was the first who saw his exposed Grandfather, and impudently and petulantly play'd upon him; and that his Father *Cham,* was by his Informations call'd into the Mockery.[8] But this is not a Thing *Declared* in the Scriptures; and therefore the Conjecture is as easily *Rejected,* as *Received. Chrysostom* therefore tells us, It was, δια τινα λογον εγκεκρυμμενον· *Ob Rationem occultam.* But the most solid Answer of all, is that given by *Austin;* [Quaest. 17. *in Genesin.*] *Quaeritur, Quarè cum Peccans Cham in Patris offensâ, non in se ipso, sed in Filio suo Canaan Maledicitur? Nisi prophetatum est, Terram Canaan, ejectis Canaanaeis indè, et debellatis, accepturos esse filios Israel, qui venient de semine Shem.*[9] *Theodoret* speaks to the like Purpose, and makes the Words of *Noah,* rather a *Praediction,* than an *Imprecation;* a *Prophecy* that the Posterity of *Canaan* should one day be ousted by the *Israelites,* who descend from *Shem,* & should possess themselves of *Palaestine;* δεδιττομενος δε τους υστερον εσομενους μη πλημμελειν εις γενεας· *Deterrens autem posteros, ne peccent in parentes.*[10] The *unsearchable Judgments* of God, visit the Sins of *Parents,* on the *Children;* but *Canaan* only is mentioned here, lest the Judgments threatned should seem to belong unto all the Children of *Cham.* And *Moses* would raise the Hopes of the *Israelites,* about the Success of the great Expedition, which was yett before them. The *Divine Sovereignty* is display'd in this Matter. And it is a Mistake in any to imagine, That the *Blackness* of the *Ethiopians* & other Children of *Cham,* arises from the Curse of *Noah* upon him. The True Cause of their *Blackness* may be this. They were made very *Brown,* by the *Hott Sun* striking upon them. They disliked this *Colour.* With proper *Juices* and *Unguents,* it was their Custome, to change their *Brown* into *Black;* and, *Versa est posteà Ars in Naturam: Nature* itself by Degrees conform'd, unto what had been by *Art* a long while Introducing. *Vossius* observes, That the Figure of the *Noses,* among the *Moors,* and other Nations, was by Degrees at length confirmed from *Artificial* into what is now *Natural* among them.[11]

The Blessing of *Japhet* is; *God shall enlarge Japhet, and he shall dwell in the Tents of Shem; and Canaan shall be his Servant.* The First Article of the Blessing is, That in the Division of the Earth, the largest Portion by far should fall to the Posterity of *Japhet*. The Next Article of the Blessing, is, The Dwelling of *Japhet* in the *Tents of Shem*. Some refer this *Dwelling in the Tents of Shem*, not unto *Japhet*, but unto *God*, who had afterwards His *Tabernacle*, and His *Temple*, and His *People*, among the *Israelites*. Thus *Philo*, and *Onkelos*, and *Theodoret*, and *Lyranus*, and *Abulensis* and others; who to this Purpose bring that Passage; Psal. 132.13.[12] *The Lord hath chosen Zion, He hath desired it for His Habitation.* N. *Fuller* largely prosecutes this Interpretation; and Interprets and Considers the Text, as pointing to the *Messiah*, who took among the Jewes, that Humanity, which He made His *Tabernacle*. Our *Heidegger* still argues for *Japhet*.[13] He finds the Promise of the *Messiah*, in that of the *Lords* being *the God of Shem*; so he thinks, there was no need of Repeating it. And the next Clause, *Canaan shall be his Servant*; this doubtless refers to *Japhet*. The *Tents of Shem* then are the *Church* of God; which continued a long while among the *Sons of Shem*. There must be a Time, when the Posterity of *Japhet*, shall be brought into the Communion of the Church; and acknowledge the *God of Shem* for their God, renouncing all their *Idols*. The *Vocation of the Gentiles*, which was to follow upon the Death of our Saviour, was understood by the Ancients, by *Chrysostom*, and *Jerom*, and *Austin*, in this Prophecy. The last Article of the Blessing, is; That, as the Land of *Canaan* must once be conquered by the Children of *Shem*, so afterwards there should be a Conquest made of it, by the Children of *Japhet*. A shrowd Intimation of what the *Jewes* have suffered from the *Gentiles*, by the hand of God upon them, for their Unbeleef.

These few Words of *Noah*, deserve to be esteemed, as, *Canon prophetiae, et omnium ferè subsequentium prophetiarum epitome.*[14]

All Christians do with Admiration behold the Accomplishment of this Prophecy.

In the Division of the World, *Shem* getts only a Part of *Asia Major*. *Cham* getts, with *Africa*, a very little Part of *Asia*. But *Japhet* shares all *Europe*; All *Asia Minor*; A very great Part of *Asia Major*; And probably, all *America* over and above.

The Church of God was for diverse Ages, remarkably maintained, and confined, among the *Sons of Shem*. A *Partition-wall* excluded the *Chamites* and the *Japhetites*.

The Land of *Canaan* was vanquished and possessed, by the *Sons of Shem*, under the Conduct of *Moses* and *Joshua*.

Here the *Messiah* was born, and came to *Tabernacle* among us.

Then the *Romans*, the Sons of *Cittim*, descended from *Japhet*, siezed upon the Land of *Canaan*.

The *Sons of Shem* are cast out of the *Tents of Shem,* and the *Sons of Japhet* are called in. All the Epistles of our Apostle *Paul,* except one, are directed unto the *Sons of Japhet.*

But are we to have no *Sons of Cham* gathered into the Communion of the Church. *Egypt* and all *Africa,* ha's once had *Christianity* in it. And many who are called *Christians* are there still to be mett withal. There is now to be no Distinction. [see Col. 3.11.] The *Sons of Cham,* are not in the *Noetic Prophecy,* excluded from the *Tents of Shem.* And yett, inasmuch as they are not *mentioned,* we may suppose the *Japhetites* to have a peculiar Prerogative in the *Church* of the *Gentiles.* We have seen it surprizingly exemplified. The Church in *Africa,* is horribly buried in Haeresy and Apostasy; Betimes it became so. The Church in *Europe* ha's had more of Evangelical Purity; The Light of the Gospel hath shone there, much more gloriously. *Antichrist* indeed ha's appeared there. But still he has been Resisted and Opposed, by a Number of the Faithful. And anon, mighty Nations & Peoples, have shaken off their Obedience unto him. The Liberty & Purity of the Christian Religion, *Longè Latius et Laetius per Dei Gratiam, inter Japheti posteros emicat, quàm unquam inter Semi et Chami posteros effloruerit:* It has most flourished among the Sons of *Japhet.*[15]

[ENTRY ON GENESIS 10:20 (THE NATIONS DESCENDED FROM ONE MAN)]

Gen. 10.20. *These are the sons of Ham, after their families,*
after their tongues, in their countries, and in their nations.

Q. According to the *Mosaic* Account, We find all Nations of Men here descended from One Man; and the Account is unquaestionably True. Yett, you know, some have doubted, how tis possible for *Blacks,* and *Whites,* to be the Children of One Man. A little Philosophy upon it, may be serviceable? v. 20.

A. And you shall have Dr. *Grewes:*

Tis true, Living and Breeding within the *Torrid Zone,* or without it, is not enough alone, to produce this Difference. For the *Ethiopians,* and the *Malabars,* tho' in Part aequally distant from the Line, yett these are no more than *Duskish,* those are *Cole-black.* And it is said, That all over *America,* there are no Blacks, but only at *Quaveca.*[16] Yett this hinders not, but that the Climate may co-operate with the *Native Causes;* which seem to be chiefly these *Three.* First, *The Distribution of the Capillary Arteries more numerously into the outer Part of the Skin.* Secondly, *A less Proportion of Capillary Veins, to return the Blood from thence.* Thirdly, *The extream Thinness of the Cuticle.* Hereby some smaller Part of the Blood becoming stagnant there, it, like any other Blood when it is Dry, or upon a Bruise, turneth *Black*. And therefore, even among the *Ethiopians*, there is a Sort of Breed, which is neither Black, nor White, nor Tawny; but, as tis likely from the Make of their Skin, of a *Pale*, and a *Dead*, Complexion. In *Blacks* themselves, the Palms of their *Hands*, and the Soles of their *Feet*, where the *Cuticle* is much Thicker, and into which the Capillary Arteries do shoot more sparingly, are of a *Whitish Red*. Where these then, and it may be some other, Native Causes, meet with a suitable Climate, we may suppose they never fail to produce a Black Breed. So, in Part of the Province of *Quantung* in *China*, the People who are near the *Torrid Zone*, are Black; but in that of *Peking*, the most Northerly, they are *White*. And some Climates may be fitter to breed *Blacks*, than others; which, tho' of the same Latitude, yett may not be so Hott; or, the Heavens or the Earth, may be different on some other Accounts. Every *Florist* can tell, how great an Alteration, the Transplanting of some Flowers, only from the Field, into a Garden, will make in their Colours. And every good *Herbalist*, can tell, the Difference in Plants of the same Kind, growing in several Parts of the World, yea, tho' in the same Latitude. Nor is the *Woolly Hair* of the Blacks, any stranger, than for a Naked Dog, when brought from an Hott to a Cold Climate, to become Hairy. If we must have one *Adam* for *Whites*, and another for *Blacks*, must we not have a Third for *Tawnies*? If one for White, & another for Black *Skins*, why not one for White, and another for Black *Hair*? and another for *Red*? Properties, which in a Breed of Parents, alwayes in the same Climate, & both of the same Colour, would be as constant in the *Hair*, as in the *Skin*. And were it not as necessary to have original Standards of Dimensions, as well as of Colours? One for the gigantic Breed of *Asia*, and another for the Dwarfs of *Lapland*?

To this Purpose, our Dr. *Grew*, in his, *Cosmologia Sacra*.[17]

DIARY (OCTOBER–DECEMBER 1693)

[ESTABLISHING A "SOCIETY OF NEGROES"]

Besides the other praying and pious Meetings, which I have been continually serving, in our Neighbourhood; a little after this Time, a company of poor *Negroes*, of their own Accord, addressed mee, for my Countenance, to a Design which they had, of erecting such a *Meeting* for the Welfare of their miserable Nation that were Servants among us. I allowed their Design and went one Evening and pray'd and preach'd (on Ps. 68.31: "Princes shall come out of Egypt; Ethiopia shall soon stretch out her hands unto God") with them; and gave them the following Orders, which I insert only for Curiositie of the Occasion.

RULES FOR THE SOCIETY OF NEGROES (1693)

WE the Miserable Children of *Adam*, and of *Noah*, thankfully Admiring and Accepting the Free-Grace of GOD, that Offers to Save us from our Miseries, by the Lord Jesus Christ, freely Resolve, with His Help, to become the Servants of the Glorious LORD.

And that we may be Assisted in the Service of our *Heavenly Master*, we now Join together in a SOCIETY, wherein the following RULES are to be observed.

    I. It shall be our Endeavour, to Meet in the *Evening* after the *Sabbath*; and *Pray* together by Turns, one to Begin, and another to Conclude the Meeting; And between the two *Prayers*, a *Psalm* shall be Sung, and a *Sermon* Repeated.

    II. Our coming to the Meeting, shall never be without the *Leave* of such as have Power over us: And we will be Careful, that our Meeting may Begin and Conclude between the hours of *Seven* and *Nine*; and that we may not be *unseasonably* Absent from the Families whereto we pertain.

    III. As we will, with the Help of God, at all Times avoid all *Wicked Company*, so we will Receive none into our Meeting, but such as have sensibly *Reformed* their Lives from all manner of Wickedness. And therefore, None shall be Admitted, without the Knowledge and Consent of the Minister of God in this Place; unto whom we will also carry every Person, that seeks for *Admission* among us; to be by Him Examined, Instructed and Exhorted.

    IV. We will, as often as may be, Obtain some Wise and Good Man, of the *English* in the Neighbourhood, and especially the Officers of the Church, to look in upon us, and by their Presence and Counsil, do what they think fitting for us.

    V. If any of our Number, fall into the Sin of *Drunkenness*, or *Swearing*, or *Cursing*, or *Lying*, or *Stealing*, or notorious *Disobedience* or *Unfaithfulness* unto their Masters, we will *Admonish* him of his Miscarriage, and Forbid his coming to the Meeting, for at least *one Fortnight*; And except he then come with great Signs and Hopes of his *Repentance*, we will utterly Exclude him, with Blotting his *Name* out of our List.

    VI. If any of our Society, Defile himself with *Fornication*, we will give him our *Admonition*; and so, debar him from the Meeting, at least *half a Year*: Nor shall he Return to it, ever any more, without Exemplary Testimonies of his becoming a *New Creature*.

RULES
For the Society of
NEGROES. 1693.

W E the Miferable Children of *Adam*, and of *Noah*, thankfully Admiring and Accepting the Free-Grace of GOD, that Offers to Save us from our Miferies, by the Lord Jefus Chrift, freely Refolve, with His Help, to become the Servants of that Glorious LORD.

And that we may be Affifted in the Service of our *Heavenly Mafter*, we now Join together in a SOCIETY, wherein the fallowing RULES are to be obferved.

I. It fhall be our Endeavour, to Meet in the *Evening* after the *Sabbath*; and *Pray* together by Turns, one to Begin, and another to Conclude the Meeting; And between the two *Prayers*, a *Pfalm* fhall be Sung, and a *Sermon* Repeated.

II. Our coming to the Meeting, fhall never be without the *Leave* of fuch as have Power over us: And we will be Careful, that our Meeting may Begin and Conclude between the Hours of *Seven* and *Nine*; and that we may not be *unfeafonably Abfent* from the Families whereto we pertain.

III. As we will, with the Help of God, at all Times avoid all *Wicked Company*, fo we will Receive none into our Meeting, but fuch as have fenfibly *Reformed* their Lives from all manner of Wickednefs. And therefore, None fhall be Admitted, without the Knowledge and Confent of the *Minifter* of God in this Place; unto whom we will alfo carry every Perfon, that feeks for *Admiffion* among us; to be by Him Examined, Inftructed and Exhorted.

IV. We will, as often as may be, Obtain fome Wife and Good Man, of the *Englifh* in the Neighbourhood, and efpecially the Officers of the Church, to look in upon us, and by their Prefence and Counfil, do what they think fitting for us.

V. If any of our Number, fall into the Sin of *Drunkennefs*, or *Swearing*, or *Curfing*, or *Lying*, or *Stealing*, or notorious *Difobedience* or *Unfaithfulnefs* unto their Mafters, we will *Admonifh* him of his Mifcarriage, and Forbid his coming to the Meeting, for at leaft *one Fortnight*; And except he then come with great Signs and Hopes of his *Repentance*, we will utterly Exclude him, with Blotting his *Name* out of our Lift.

VI. If any of our Society Defile himfelf with *Fornication*, we will give him our *Admonition*; and fo, debar him from the Meeting, at leaft *half a Year*: Nor fhall he Return to it, ever any more, without Exemplary Teftimonies of his becoming a *New Creature*.

VII. We will, as we have Opportunity, fet our felves to do all the Good we can, to the other *Negro-Servants* in the Town; And if any of them fhould, at unfit Hours, be *Abroad*, much more, if any of them fhould *Run away* from their Mafters, we will afford them *no Shelter*: But we will do what in us lies, that they may be difcovered, and punifhed. And if any *of us*, are found Faulty, in this Matter, they fhall be no longer *of us*.

VIII. None of our Society fhall be *Abfent* from our Meeting, without giving a *Reafon* of the Abfence; And if it be found, that any have pretended unto their *Owners*, that they came unto the *Meeting*, when they were otherwife and elfewhere Employ'd, we will faithfully *Inform* their Owners, and alfo do what we can to Reclaim fuch Perfon from all fuch Evil Courfes for the Future.

IX. It fhall be expected from every one in the Society, that he learn the *Catechifm*; And therefore, it fhall be one of our ufual Exercifes, for one of us, to ask the *Queftions*, and for all the reft in their Order, to fay the *Anfwers* in the *Catechifm*; Either, The *New-Englifh* Catechifm, or the *Affemblies* Catechifm, or the Catechifin in the *Negro Chriftianized*.

Rules for the Society of Negroes. 1693 (Boston, c. 1706–13), title page

VII. We will, as we have Opportunity, set our selves to do all the Good
we can, to the other *Negro-Servants* in the Town; And if any of them
should, at unfit Hours, be *Abroad*, much more, if any of them should
Run away from their Masters, we will afford them *no Shelter:* But
we will do what in us lies, that they may be discovered, and punished.
And if any *of us*, are found Faulty, in this Matter, they shall be no
longer *of us*.

VIII. None of our Society shall be *Absent* from our Meeting, without giving a *Reason* of the Absence; And if it be found, that any have pretended unto their *Owners*, that they came unto the *Meeting*, when
they were otherwise and elsewhere Employ'd, we will faithfully *Inform* their Owners, and also do what we can to Reclaim such Person
from all such Evil Courses for the Future.

IX. It shall be expected from every one in the Society, that he learn the
Catechism; And therefore, it shall be one of our usual Exercises, for
one of us, to ask the *Questions*, and for all the rest in their Order, to
say the *Answers* in the *Catechism;* Either, The *New-English* Catechism, or the *Assemblies* Catechism, or the Catechism in the *Negro
Christianized*.

A GOOD MASTER WELL SERVED (1696)

THE *Great God who Formed all things*, and who particularly, *Formed the
Spirit of man within him*, hath *Formed* Us with a *Sociable* Disposition; which
Disposition to **Society**, Planted by God in our *Nature*, hath *Positive Rules* given
by our God in His Word, for the Regulation of it.

The *First Society*, which Mankind falls, and indeed *Naturally* falls into, is *Domestical;* the *Society*, that makes a **Family**. Now, by the Demands of *Nature* it
self, 'tis come to pass, that in such a *Society* there must be a *Superiority*, and
an *Inferiority;* there must be some who are to *Command*, and there must be
some who are to *Obey*. Accordingly, The *Domestical Society* is of Three Sorts;
There is a *Conjugal* Society, or that between the *Husband* and the *Wife;* there
is a *Parental* Society, or that between the *Parent* and the *Child;* and there is
last, and lowest of all, an **Herile Society**, or that between the **Master** and the
Servant.

When the Providence of God, hath brought a person, into any sort of *Humane Society*, it is not the least Office of **Religion** to direct, and assist, the person, in the Discharge of the **Relation**, which he bears to that Society. The true
Religion, having a due *Impression* upon us, will vastly amend us, and improve

us, in every *Relation*, wherein the Providence of God hath placed us. It has been a *Maxime* sometimes justly used; *Be sure, that Religion cannot be right that a man is the worse for having*. And I will add *This* unto it; *Be sure, if a* Person *seem to be Religious*, but is not by *Religion*, made, a *Better* Husband or Wife, a *Better* Parent or Child, a *Better* Master or Servant, that persons *Religion is vain*.

We find therefore that the *Scriptures* of God often and largely insist on the **Duties** of men, in those **Relative** Capacities, wherein they stand obliged unto one another. But among the rest, the Duties of *Masters* and *Servants* are pressed, with a very frequent, fervent and pungent Inculcation; and this most especially in the Inspired Epistles of the *New Testament*. In the Days of *Primitive Christianity*, there were Christianized **Masters**, who had much adoe to lay aside, the fierce, harsh, bruitish and bloody Usage of their *Servants*, whereto in their *Paganism* they had been accustomed; and there were Christianized **Servants**, who on the other side had much ado to maintain a due Respect unto their *Masters*, after they were by Regeneration advanced unto the priviledges of the Gospel, and made the *Sons* and *Heirs* of God. For this cause, the Apostles, do very emphatically Demonstrate it, that *Christianity* will Teach persons to be better *Masters*, and better *Servants*, than ever they were before. . . .

'[T]is to you, **O Servants**, that the most of our Exhortations are to be directed. And although you may have your Duties, most sufficiently represented, in those Express *Edicts* from the King of Heaven, wherein you may read Him speaking of you; yet it will not be amiss to fetch out from those Heavenly *Edicts*, the particular Duties which are Incumbent on you.

There are several sorts of *Servants* now together, in this Congregation. A *Servant*, according to the Apostolical Description, in 1 Tim. 6.1. is *One that is under the Yoke*; that is, One that is under the *Domestical* and the *Despotical* Disposal of another, by *Other Bonds* besides those of *Nature*. Some of you, are under the *Yoke* of Servitude, by a perpetual *Vassalage*, to those who have by Sword or Price purchased a Dominion over you. Others of you are under the *Yoke* of Servitude, by a Temporary *Agreement*, which you have made with some, to be subject unto them for a while upon such and such Considerations. And there are of both Sexes, both *Men* and *Maids*, under both of these *Yokes*.

But, *Let as many Servants, as are under the Yoke*, now hearken, with a very great Attention, unto the counsils which the words of the Ever-living God, shall set before them. It was said, in *Psal*. 123.2. *Behold, as the Eyes of Servants Look unto the Hand of their Masters, and as the Eyes of a Maiden to the Hand of her Mistress, so our Eyes wait upon the Lord our God*. Thus, Let you that are *Servants* and *Maidens*, give a greater Attention unto the words of the *Lord* your God this Day, than ever you gave unto any *Master*, or *Mistress* whatsoever.

I. This is the first Counsil that calls for your Attention; *Servants,* In the first place, Become the **Devoted Servants**, of the Lord **Jesus Christ**, who is, *The Lord of all.* O that you might all of you, be able to say, as he in Psal. 116.16. *O Lord, Truly I am thy Servant, I am thy Servant.* It is Observable, That the *Homage* which we owe unto the Heavenly Lord, is ordinarily described by *Metaphors* drawn from the *Service,* of an Earthly Master. Among such *Metaphors,* I take a special Notice of this One; That the Lords calling of a man to *Serve him,* is expressed by His calling of that man, *unto His Feet:* In the Hebrew Original of the Old Testament, the Phrase of, *A Servant,* usually is, *One at the Feet of his Master.* At their Tables they Lay down on *Carpets,* and so the *Servants* that waited on them, stood at their *Feet* behind them. Thus among the *Roman* Writers also, *Ad Pedes,* or, *A Pedibus,* is the Phrase for a *Servant:* he was A, *Servus,* who, *Ad Pedes steterat.* Well, then; *Servants,* Do you come away unto the *Feet* of the Lord Jesus Christ; and whatever *Service* you have to do for your *Masters,* Let something analogous to that *Service* be done in the first place, unto that *Holy, Holy, Holy Lord Almighty.* It is commanded you, in Eph. 6.5, 6, 7. *Servants, Be obedient unto your Masters, as unto Christ; Not with Eye-service, but as the Servants of Christ; with good will, doing service as unto the Lord.* And it is again commanded you, in Col. 3.2, 3, 4. *Servants, whatever ye do, do it Heartily, as unto the Lord; for ye serve the Lord Christ.* So then, This is the first Thing, that is to be urged upon you; Oh! That you would become the Sincere, and Hearty *Servants* of the Lord Jesus Christ! *Then* we shall hope to see you, *Dutiful Servants* unto those Masters and Mistresses, under whom our *Common Lord* hath Stationed you.

To bring you into this Blessed *Service* of the *Lord,* there are these Directions, which in the Name of that Great Lord, *My Lord,* and *Your Lord,* I Charge you to comply withal.

First, Renounce, and, Forsake, the Service of those **Invisible Masters**, a *Slavery* of whom, is inconsistent, with the *Service* of the Lord Jesus Christ. Our Lord Jesus Christ hath said, in Math. 6.24. *Ye cannot Serve God and Mammon.* Thus, ye cannot Serve the Lord Jesus Christ, and Serve the *World,* and the *Flesh,* and the *Devil. Joshua* said unto the Idolatrous People, *Ye cannot Serve the Lord* {Josh. 24:19}. And, I say unto all, that still make sublunary *Vanities* their *Idols, Ye cannot Serve the Lord.* Hear this, All ye *Unregenerate* Servants! 'Tis possible your Service, to the Houses where you Sojourn, may for some things be Irksome Enough unto you; Oh! but you are in another Service, that would be a Million times more Irksome, if you were not stark *Dead in Trespasses & Sins.* The *Fashions* of the *World,* you must Humour, the *Cravings* of the *Flesh* you must Fulfill, the *Temptations* of the *Devil,* you cannot Resist: It may be said of you, as in

Jer. 5.19. *Ye have served strange Gods.* Wretched Servants! Oh! That you were more sensible of your horrible Captivity; When will you be *Aware*, when will you be *Weary* of it! I tell you, a Turkish, or a Spanish *Slavery*, is not a thousandth part so miserable, as the Accursed Slavery of your Souls, to the *Invisible Destroyers* of your Souls. But will you at length take a Course, for your own Deliverance, O *Wretched Servants, that you are?*

If any one should Counsel you, to **Run away**, from the Christian *Masters* in whose Houses you reside, he would be a *Wicked Counsellor*. A *Run away Servant*, is a Dishonest, and a Disgraced sort of a Creature, among all the Sober part of Mankind. It was uttered, as an Extream Reproach, upon those to whom it was offered, in 1 Sam. 25.10. *There be many Servants now adayes, that break away, Every man, from his Master.* They are not meer *Prisoners of War*, but by the Providence of God brought under further *Necessities* and *Obligations*; and yet they think of Turning *Fugitives!* The *Devil* is the *Driver* of those *Unfaithful Servants*, who *Unlawfully* Desert the Service, wherein the Good Hand of God ha's fixed them; and the Unavoidable Confusions whereunto all such *Run away Servants*, do generally *Run* themselves, would make one think, that none but the *Devil Driven* would attempt it! Wherefore, As when a Servant hardly dealt withal, was *Running away*, and *Angel* of the Lord appeared unto that Servant, and said, in Gen. 16.9. *Return to thy Mistress, and submit thy self unto her Hands*; thus if any of you are Designing or Desiring to *Run away* from your *Masters*, I do bring you a Prohibition from our Great LORD this Day, *Stay with thy Master, & submit thy self unto him, if thou wouldest not have the Plagues of God, pursue thee, wheresoever thou goest.* Hearken to me, in this thing, thou uneasy Servant; and *Poor Servant, If sinners entice thee to Run away, Consent thou not.*

But yet, for those *Invisible Masters*, I mean those *Tempters*, and those *Tempers*, which Enslave your Souls, in a Distance from God, here I will make no Scruple thus to Counsel you, O *Run away from your old Masters; as fast as you can, and as far as you can, Run away from those Hellish Taskmasters!* and I am certain, I am not your *Counsellour to your Destruction*, in thus urging of you. Draw near to the Lord Jesus Christ with such a Profession as that, in Isa. 26.13. *O Lord, other Lords besides thee, have had Dominion over us, but now we will be for thee alone.* After this manner, plead with the Glorious Lord-Redeemer; *Lord, If thou wilt make me Free, I shall be Free indeed; I can bear to be the Servant of a man, who is my Neighbour, for thy sake; but, Oh! I cannot bear to be a Servant of a Lust, and of a Devil; send me therefore, thy Free Spirit, O Lord, and let thy Spirit set me Free from the Insufferable Captivity, wherein I am sold under sin; and let me no longer be a Servant of sin, unto Death, but being made Free from sin, let me become the Servant of Righteousness for ever.* And what will be the

Effect of your thus pleading with the Lord! It will be that in Rom. 8.2. *Made Free from the Law of Sin and of Death.* Indeed you shall *Sin* still, and you shall *Dy* still; but you shall not be under the *Law* of *Sin* and of *Death.* I'l tell you, how t'will be; Among the *Romans,* there were Three states of men; there were the *Slaves,* and there were the *Free,* and there were the *Enfranchised.* The *Slaves* absolutely depended on other men; the *Free* were altogether their own men; The *Enfranchised* were such as had been *Slaves,* and were become *Free;* but yet partook of a *Middle state,* between both. Now, the old *Patrons,* of such as were afterwards *Enfranchised,* still retained some kind of Hank upon them. *Quintilian* says, *The Patron might yet lay his Hand on the Enfranchised man;*[18] he might Seize him, he might Strike him, though he might not lay him under *Chains,* much less take away his *Life.* Even so, when the Lord Jesus Christ hath once *Enfranchised* thee, *Sin* may vex thee, *Death* may smite thee, but yet thou art rescued from *Chains* forever, nor shall thy Soul *Dy* by the hands of thy old Oppressors. . . .

II. Let your Service unto the **Masters** [and *Mistresses*] of the Families, where you are *Servants,* be such, that the Lord Jesus Christ may thereby be **Glorified**.

It has been among the Wretchednesses of Mankind, that *Servants* have ordinarily been so bad, as to bring a Discredit upon the very *Names,* which were once innocently and agreeably used, for all that rank of people. Some *Names,* that formerly signified no more than *Servants,* now carry all the Dishonesties of *Knavery* and *Villany* in their signification, because that *Servants* have so often been *Dishonest.* But now may God help *you,* Our *Servants,* instead of bringing a *Blemish* upon your own poor Names, to bring a *Glory* unto the Name of that Lord, whose *Name* indeed is *Exalted far above all Blessing and Praise.* . . .

And now, *What I say unto You, I say unto All;* But I say such things as these.

I. Whatsoever *Service* you do for your *Masters* (or *Mistresses*) do it as a **Service** unto the Lord **Jesus Christ**. How urgently is this noble Principle for your *Service,* in the Book of God set before you? You have it, in Eph. 6.5, 6, 7 *Servants, Be obedient, in singleness of Heart, as unto Christ; Not with Eye service, as men pleasers, but as the Servants of Christ, Doing the Will of God from the Heart; with Good will, doing Service, as unto the Lord, and not unto men.* You have it again, in Col. 3.23, 24. *Servants, Whatever ye do, do it heartily, as unto the Lord, and not unto men; Knowing that of the Lord you shall Receive the Reward of the Inheritance; for ye Serve the Lord Christ.* Whatever *Lawful Service* you are set about, Consider this with your selves, *The Lord Jesus Christ, has put me into my Service, and the Lord Jesus Christ, has now bidden me do such a Service; Wherefore the Service which I am now set about, I'le do it out of Respect unto the Lord Jesus Christ; I'le do it, because the Lord Jesus Christ will be Dishonored, if I do it* *not.* An honest man once, Cutting of *Wood,* was ask'd, *Who are you at Work for?* And he piously answered, *I am Cutting of Wood for God.* Whatever you do in your *Service,* in the House, in the Shop, in the Field, or in the Ship, you may do it all for the *Lord Jesus Christ;* You may Sanctify all your *Servile Employments,* by doing them under this Consideration, *The Lord Jesus Christ hath Commanded me to Obey my Master and my Mistress.* It was the Speech of a Great man, *The Work of a poor Milk-Maid, if it be done with an Exercise for Grace, is more glorious than the Triumphs of a* Caesar. Truly, the meanest *Work* that you have to do, in your *Service,* though it be in the *Stable,* or the *Kitchen,* you may thus render very Glorious; Do it with such a Consideration as this, *Though it be a mean Thing that my Master, or my Mistress will have me to do, yet it is the Will of the Lord Jesus Christ, that I should now do it; & therefore I will do it cheerfully.* A Great King once Expressed this thing, in that verse.

> *Nenti fila Deus mentem Conjugit Olympo.*[19] Or,
> *The* Hand *the* Wheel *does Ply,*
> *The* Heart's *with* God *on High.*

I say, The *Favour* of the Eternal *King,* will be toward so *Wise a Servant.* And now, What a Wonderful Consolation, may this be unto you under all the Difficulties of your *Service!* The Lord Jesus Christ is your *Master;* if you cannot spend, and stoop, for a mortal man, like your selves, can't you do it for such a *Master,* as the *Lord of Hosts?* It may be, you'll have Little *Pay* from any man, for what you do. Yea, but the Lord Jesus Christ will be your *Paymaster: He* will Grant you Everlasting Recompences, in that Blisful World, where not the Least Thing that has been done for the Lord, shall ever be forgotten!

II. Yield unto your *Masters* (and *Mistresses*) that **Reverence,** which is due from a *Servant* unto a *Master.* Since by the *Ordination* of God, you are made *Servants,* don't think much of that *Inferiority,* which is to be confess'd by you, as along as you are *Servants.* It is an Apostolical Instruction, in 1 Cor. 7.21. *Art thou called, being a Servant, Care not for That. For he that is called, in the Lord, being a Servant, is the Lords Freeman. . . .* The *Proud Hearts* of many *Servants,* make them discontented, at the *Lowness* which they must Express in their Station. But I am to remind you, That this *Pride* was the Sin of the *Devils;* the *Devils* could not bear to be *Servants* in such a Station as the Almighty God had appointed from them. *Servants,* be Humble; if you would *not fall into the Condemnation of the Devil!* You are sometimes *Proudly* Enough concerned, it may be, that your *Clothes* are no finer, and you affect an unsuitable Gayety and Gallantry. But if you would have *Ornaments* indeed upon you, *Then,* as the Apostle speaks, you must be *Clothed with Humility* {1 Pet. 5:5}; that is, Wear

Humility, as a *Badge,* of your being *Servants,* unto that Blessed Lord, who once
took on Himself the Form of a Servant. . . .

III. Let your **Obedience** to your *Masters* (and *Mistresses*) while you are *Servants* be such, as will manifest that you are *Obedient Children of God.* You are
the *Animate, Separate, Active Instruments* of other men. *Servants,* your *Tongues,*
your *Hands,* your *Feet,* are your *Masters,* and they should move according to the
Will of your *Masters.* If you are those *Eye-servants,* who will Obey your *Masters*
no longer than their *Eye* is upon you, know it, the *Eye* of the All-seeing, and
Almighty God, is upon you, to Condemn you, for this *Disobedience.* . . . The
just *Commands* of your *Masters,* cannot be broken, but at the same instant you
break the *Commands* of the most High God, whose *Kingdom Ruleth over all.* As
'tis said of *Magistrates,* in Rom. 13. 2. *Whosoever Resisteth the Power, Resisteth
the Ordinance of God; and they that Resist, shall Receive to themselves Damna-
tion.* So may it be said of *Masters;* Their *Power* over you is the *Ordinance* of *God;*
When you Refuse or Forget the Doing, of what they have *Bidden* you to do, you
do so far affront the *Ordinance* of *God.* So then, the Anger of your *Masters* is
not all that you do by your *Disobedience* Expose your selves unto; you become
obnoxious to the Anger of the Dreadful God, by your *Disobedience.* Think of it,
Servants; When you have *willfully,* yea, or though but *carelessly,* transgressed,
the Commands of your *Masters,* you may thus animadvert upon your selves,
I have Sinned against God, in this Miscarriage! . . .

VII. Those things which may have a Tendency to make you **Ill Servants,** *Avoid*
them Carefully, Religiously, Eternally. Wherefore that you may not be Bad *Servants,* Abandon all *Bad Courses* whatsoever. And let all **Mispence of Time** come
under your very particular Detestation: *Divide* your Time justly between your
Masters, and your *Own Souls;* and Squander it not away, in any of those Imper-
tinences, which will at last cause you with unutterable Bitterness to utter that
Bitter Complaint, *What Fruit have I of those things whereof I am now Ashamed!*
No, But *Redeem* all the *Time,* you can do, to accomplish your selves, with such
points of *Knowledge* and of *Goodness,* as may render you Amiable to all the
World. There is one special *Mispence of Time,* whereto *Servants,* and others, are
commonly addicted; and that is, *The Reading of* **Idle Romances,** against which,
Let me become an Adviser, this Day; neither Derided nor Despised. Those *Romances* usually beget, in the unwary Readers of them, very false Notions of
Love, Honour and *Vertue;* and the Images of *Servants* occurring in them, are
usually full of *Wickedness.* Besides, The most of those *Romances,* are such Foolish Tales, that the Readers, instead of being the wiser, or the Better for them,
have their minds very Sensibly thereby Tainted with a *Frothy Vanity.* You shall
therefore find, That when you have been Reading of a *Romance,* you will have

little Heart afterwards to Read the *Bible*, the Book of *God*, and of *Life*. But indeed! Are Books of *Devotion*, or Books of True and Good History so Scarce, that like *Swine*, you have only the *Husks* or *Romances* to feed upon! I say, Distemper not your Souls, with such Venemous Papers, as will ere long leave you wishing, *Oh! that I could now Recal the Time which I spent in Reading of Silly Romances! Oh! That I had spent that Precious Time, in Reading those Things that might have helped me in the Service of God, and of my Generation.*

But all of the Pernicious Things, which do make *Ill Servants*, & are therefore to be Shunn'd by *All Servants*, there is none more Pernicious than that of **Evil-Company**! *Servants*, O Remember that *Caveat* of Wisdom, *A Companion of Fools, shall be destroyed* {Pro. 13:20}. There are *Knots*, of *Evil Companions*, in every Town; those *Knots* if once you are in them, they will hold you fast in the *Bonds of Iniquity*. 'Tis in *Bad Company*, that you will get those *Vicious Cursing, Swearing, Wanton, Lying, Scornful, Habits*, which will render you *Abhorr'd*, not only by the Holy Lord, but also by all Sober and Vertuous Men. Tis in *Bad Company*, that you'l come to be bewitched with the *Unlawful Games*, of *Cards*, and of *Dice*, which have in all Ages been Thundred against, by a *Cloud of Witnesses*, as well *Pagans*, as *Christians*, and Profane the Name of God, by *Playing* with Pure *Lots*, which are Solemn and Sacred Things. Tis in *Bad Company*, that you'l hear the Words & Wayes & People of God, Scoffed at, until you your selves have Learn't likewise to Scoff at them, and *Sit in the Seat of the Scorner*. Your *Masters* are never like to have any *Good* of you more, if you are once fallen into the Snares of *Evil Company*. Nor is this all the *Lamentation and Mourning and Wo*, which I am to produce concerning you. No, This *Evil Company* will carry thee down with them unto the *Congregation of the Damned* for ever; and the *Fiery Furnace* of Hell, will be *Seven Times the Hotter* upon thee, for thy having of thy Old, Lewd, Mad *Companions* about thee, in that hideous *Place of Torments*. How many forlorn *Servants*, have I beheld upon their Death-Beds, Looking upon their former *Companions* now visiting of them, as upon so many *Toads* of *Egypt* in their Chambers, and Crying out, with the Dimness of the Anguish, of the Second Death upon them, *Oh! These Companions have been the undoing of my Soul!* . . .

Thus have the Duties of a SERVANT been display'd before you. What can I say more but This? Consider with your selves, *Were I my self a Master, or a Mistress, what sort of a Servant would I desire?* So, *Servant*, go thy way, and be thy self *Such* a Servant. . . .

And will not the Scores of **Slaves**, the poor **Blacks**, now also in this Assembly, *Give Earnest Heed*, unto these words of God? Give Ear, ye pittied *Blacks*, Give Ear! It is allowed in the *Scriptures*, to the *Gentiles*, That they *May keep*

Slaves; although the Law of *Charity* requires your Owners, to Use you, as those that have *Reasonable Souls* within you. Yea, 'twould be against the Conscience of any Good man, to keep you for *Slaves*, if he find himself unable to use you according to that Law of *Charity*. But the most of you, have so little cause to desire your being any other than *Slaves* as you are, & where you are, that it would soon make you miserable to be otherwise. You are better *Fed*, & better *Clothed*, & better *Managed* by far, than you would be, if you were your *Own men*. All that now remains for you, is to become first the *Good Servants of the Lord Jesus Christ*, & then, of those that have purchased you. There was a Countrey of *Swarthy* People, of whom 'twas foretold, in Psal. 68.31. *Ethiopia*, [or, more truly, *Arabia*] *shall soon stretch out her Hands unto God*. Well then, poor *Ethiopians*, do you now *Stretch out your Hands* unto the Lord; even those poor Black *Hands* of yours, the Lord calleth for them. Lift those *Hands* of yours in *Petitions* to the Lord; *Pray* constantly, as well as you can, *That the Lord would make you Servants unto Himself, and Pardon you, and Accept you, and Save you, thro Jesus Christ for ever*. Set those *Hands* of yours to *Engagements* to the Lord; *Vow* solemnly as well as you can, *That you will be the Servants of the Lord, by the Help of His Grace, as long as you Live*. And be sure, that you never *Stretch forth your Hands*, unto any Evil; always *Keep your Hands from doing any Evil*; do not by Fornication, by Drunkenness, by Stealing, by Lying, by Running away, make your selves infinitely *Blacker* than you are already. No, But put yourselves into the *Hands* of the Lord Jesus Christ; be willing that the Lord Jesus Christ, should make you *His Own*. And then, for the sake of the Lord Jesus Christ, be Good *Servants*, unto those that own you; Do for your *Masters*, and your *Mistresses*, all the *Service* that you can; and be orderly in every thing.

So, though your *Skins* are of the colour of the *Night*, yet your *Souls* will be washed *White* in the *Blood of the Lamb*: and be Entitled unto an *Inheritance in Light*: Though you are in *Slavery* to men, yet you shall be the *Free-men* of the Lord, the *Children* of God: Though you are Fed among the *Dogs*, with the *Orts*[20] of our Tables, yet you shall at length, Ly down unto a *Feast* with *Abraham* himself, in the Heaven of the Blessed. Been't you Discouraged; it will be but a *Little*, a *Little*, a *Little* while, and all your pains will End in Everlasting Joyes.

But if you will not be such Orderly *Servants*, 'tis a terrible thing that I have to say unto you. All the *Sorrows* that you see in this World, are but the *Beginnings of Sorrows*, and Little *Emblems* of the *Sorrows* that remain for you in another. Do you meet with *Hunger* here? You shall there be *Tormented in a Flame* hotter than that of Brimstone for ever. Does the *Cold* afflict you here? You shall there have *Gnashing of Teeth* for ever. Do you here sometimes want your *Sleep*? There you shall *not Rest*, neither *Day nor Night*, for ever. Are you *Beaten* here? Why, the *Devil* will be your *Overseer*; and you'l be Weltring under intollerable Blows and Wounds, World without End.

Masters, These poor *Negroes* will hardly mind what I say; I pray, do you *Repeat* it unto them.

And now, may the Lord bring us all to that Bliss, where *Abraham* the Master, and *Eliezer,* or *Lazarus* the Servant, are together *With the Lord* for ever! *Amen.*

THE NEGRO CHRISTIANIZED (1706)[21]

IT is a *Golden Sentence,* that has been sometimes quoted from *Chrysostom;*[22] That *for a man to know the Art of Alms, is more than for a man to be Crowned with the Diadem of Kings: But to Convert one Soul unto God, is more than to pour out Ten Thousand Talents into the Baskets of the Poor.* Truly, to Raise a *Soul,* from a dark State of Ignorance and Wickedness, to the Knowledge of GOD, and the Belief of CHRIST, and the practice of our Holy and Lovely RELIGION; 'Tis the noblest Work, that ever was undertaken among the Children of men. An Opportunity to Endeavour the CONVERSION of a Soul, from a Life of *Sin,* which is indeed a woful *Death,* to Fear God, and Love CHRIST, and by a Religious Life to Escape the *Paths of the Destroyer;* it cannot but be Acceptable to all that have themselves had in themselves Experience of such a *Conversion.* And such an Opportunity there is in your Hands, O all you that have any **Negroes** in your Houses; an Opportunity to try, Whether you may not be the Happy *Instruments,* of Converting, the *Blackest* Instances of *Blindness* and *Baseness,* into admirable *Candidates* of Eternal Blessedness. Let not this Opportunity be Lost; if you have any concern for *Souls,* your Own or Others; but, make a Trial, Whether by your Means, the most *Bruitish* of Creatures upon Earth may not come to be disposed, in some Degree, like the *Angels* of Heaven; and the *Vassals* of Satan, become the *Children* of God. Suppose these Wretched *Negroes,* to be the Offspring of *Cham* (which yet is not so very certain,)[23] yet let us make a Trial, Whether the CHRIST who *dwelt in the Tents of Shem,* have not some of His Chosen among them; Let us make a Trial, Whether they that have been Scorched and Blacken'd by the Sun of *Africa,* may not come to have their Minds Healed by the more Benign *Beams* of the *Sun of Righteousness.*

It is come to pass by the *Providence* of God, without which there comes nothing to pass, that Poor **Negroes** are cast under your Government and Protection. You take them into your *Families;* you look on them as part of your *Possessions;* and you Expect from their Service, a Support, and perhaps an Increase, of your other *Possessions.* How agreeable would it be, if a Religious Master or Mistress thus attended, would now think with themselves! *Who can tell but that this Poor*

Creature may belong to the Election of God! Who can tell, but that God may have sent this Poor Creature into my Hands, that so One of the Elect may by my means be Called; & by my Instruction be made Wise unto Salvation! The glorious God will put an unspeakable Glory upon me, if it may be so! The Considerations that would move you, To Teach your *Negroes* the *Truths* of the Glorious Gospel, as far as you can, and bring them, if it may be, to Live according to those *Truths*, a *Sober*, and a *Righteous*, and a *Godly* Life; They are *Innumerable*; And, if you would after a *Reasonable* manner consider, the Pleas which we have to make on the behalf of *God*, and of the *Souls* which He has made, one would wonder that they should not be *Irresistible*. *Show your selves Men*, and let *Rational Arguments* have their Force upon you, to make you treat, not as *Bruits* but as *Men*, those *Rational Creatures* whom God has made your *Servants*. For,

First; The Great GOD *Commands* it, and *Requires* it of you; to do what you can that *Your Servants*, may also be *His*. It was an Admonition once given; Eph. 5.9. *Masters, Know that your Master is in Heaven.* You will confess, That the God of Heaven is your *Master*. If your *Negroes* do not comply with your *Commands*, into what Anger, what Language, Perhaps into a misbecoming *Fury*, are you transported? But you are now to attend unto the *Commands* of your more Absolute *Masters*; and they are His *Commands* concerning your *Negroes* too. What can be more Expressive, than these words of the Christian Law? Col. 4.1. *Masters, give unto your Servants, that which is Just & Equal, knowing that ye also have a Master in Heaven.* Of what *Servants* is this Injunction to be understood? Verily, of *Slaves*. For *Servants* were generally such, at the time of Writing the New Testament. Wherefore, *Masters*, As it is *Just & Equal*, that your *Servants* be not *Over-wrought*, and that while they *Work* for you, you should *Feed* them, and *Cloath* them, and afford convenient *Rest* unto them, and make their Lives comfortable; So it is *Just* and *Equal*, that you should Acquaint them, as far as you can, with the way to Salvation by JESUS CHRIST. You deny your *Master in Heaven*, if you do nothing to bring your *Servants* unto the Knowledge and Service of that glorious *Master*. One Table of the *Ten Commandments*, has this for the Sum of it; *Thou shalt Love thy Neighbour as thy self.* Man, Thy *Negro* is thy *Neighbour*. T'were an Ignorance, unworthy of a *Man*, to imagine otherwise. Yea, if thou dost grant, *That God hath made of one Blood, all Nations of men* {Acts 17:26}, he is thy *Brother* too. How canst thou *Love* thy *Negro*, and be willing to see him ly under the Rage of Sin, and the Wrath of God? Canst thou *Love* him, and yet refuse to do any thing, that his miserable Soul may be rescued from Eternal miseries? Oh! Let thy *Love* to that Poor *Soul*, appear in thy concern, to make it, if thou canst, as happy as thy own! We are Commanded, Gal. 6.10. *As we have opportunity let us Do Good unto all men, especially unto them, who are of the Houshold of Faith.* Certainly, we have *Opportunity,* to *Do Good* unto our *Servants* who are of our *own Houshold;* certainly, we may do something to *make them Good,* and bring them to be of the *Houshold of Faith.* In a word, All the Commandments in the Bible, which bespeak our *Charity* to the *Souls* of others, and our *Endeavour* that the *Souls* of others may be delivered from the Snares of Death; every one of these do oblige us, to do what we can, for the *Souls* of our *Negroes.* They are more nearly *Related* unto us, than many others are; we are more fully *capable* to do for them, than for many others. . . .

What shall we then see, but a vast company of *Christian Housholders,* filled with zealous contrivance and agony, to see their *Houses* become *Christian Temples,* and a glorious CHRIST worshipped and obeyed by all their *Housholds!* Yea, we read concerning some of the *Primitive Christians,* that with a *Prodigie* of *Charity,* they have bound themselves in the Quality of *Servants,* to Pagan *Families,* meerly that they might be in a way to *Christianize* the *Families;* And their successes were Wonderful. But what shall we say of it, When *Masters* that would be thought *Christians* already shall even refuse to have the *Servants* in their *Families* duely *Christianized?* Pray, deal faithfully; Don't mince the matter; say of it, as it is; It is a *Prodigy* of *Wickedness;* It is a prodigious Inconsistency, with true *Christianity!* Housholder, art thou a *Christian?* Then the *Glory* of a precious CHRIST is of such Account with thee, that it afflicts thee to think, that any one Person in the World should be without the Sight of it. And how can it be, that thou shouldest be negligent about bringing to a sight of the *Glory of God, in the Face of* JESUS CHRIST, *the Folks of thy own House,* upon whom thou art able to do a great deal more than upon the rest of the World? Art thou a *Christian?* Then thou dost *Pray* for thy *Servants,* that they may become the *Servants* of the Lord Jesus Christ, and the *Children* of God, and not *fall short of entering into Rest.* What! *Pray* for this; and yet never *do* any thing for it! It is impossible, or, such *Praying,* is but *Mocking* of God? Art thou a *Christian?* Then thou art apprehensive of a dreadful Danger, attending the *Souls* of them who *know not God and obey not His Gospel* {2 Thes. 1:8}: 'Tis thy perswasion, *That if our Gospel be hid, it is hid from them that are* lost {2 Cor. 4:3}; and the *Ungospelized Souls* are in danger of an Eternal *Banishment* from the *Favour* and the *City* of God. Can a *Christian* see his own *Servants* in this condition, and not be sollicitous to have them saved out of it? No; When such *Christians* appear before the Glorious LORD, it will be in vain for them to plead, that they call'd him LORD, and own'd Him for their LORD. If they did it why did they not bring their *Servants* under the Government of the LORD? *Verily,* He will say to such *Christians, I know you not?* Suppose that Language were heard from the mouth of a Master concerning a Servant; *If I can have the Labour of the Slave, that's all I care for: Let his Soul go and be damn'd for all me!* would not every Christian say, This were Language for the Mouth of a *Devil*, rather than for the Mouth of a *Christian!* Would not every Christian cry out, *Let him not be call'd a Master, but a Monster that shall speak so!* Consider, Syrs, whether *Deeds* have not a Language in them, as well as *Words*; a plainer Language than *Words*.

But we were saying; the *Condition* of the *Servants!* This invites us to say, Thirdly: The *condition* of your *Servants* does loudly sollicit your pains to *Christianize* them; and you cannot but hear the cry of it, if you have not put off all *Christian Compassion*, all Bowels of *Humanity*. When You see how laboriously, how obsequiously your *Negros* apply themselves, to serve you, to content you to enrich you, What? have you abandoned all principles of Gratitude, or of Generosity? A Generous Mind cannot but entertain such sentiments as these: *Well, what shall I do, to make this poor creature happy? What shall I do, that this poor creature may have cause, to bless God forever, for falling into my Hands!* The very *First Thought* which will arise in a Mind thus disposed, will form a Resolution, to get these poor *Negroes* well instructed in *the things of their Everlasting Peace;* It cannot be otherwise! The State of your *Negroes* in this World, must be low, and mean, and abject; a State of Servitude. No *Great Things* in this World, can be done for them. Something then, let there be done, towards their welfare in the *World to Come*. Even a Papist calls upon us; ['tis *Acosta:*] *Barbaris pro libertate erepta fidem Jesu Christi, et vitam hominibus dignam reddamus.*[24] In the mean time, tis a most horrid and cursed *Condition*, wherein your *Servants* are languishing, until *Christianity* has made saving impressions upon them. *A roaring Lion who goes about seeking whom he may devour* {1 Pet. 5:8}, hath made a seizure of them: Very many of them do with Devillish Rites actually worship *Devils*, or maintain a magical conversation with *Devils:* And all of them are more *Slaves* to *Satan* than they are to *You*, until a Faith in the *Son of God* has made them *Free indeed*. Will you do nothing to pluck them out of the Jaws of *Satan* the *Devourer?* Especially since you may justly imagine them crying to you, in terms like those of the Child whom a *Lion* was running away withal; *Help! Help! I am yet alive!* O Souls deaf to the cry of Souls, Pitty, Pitty the Souls of your *Negroes*, which cry unto you, *Have pitty on us, O our Masters, have pitty on us, whom the holy God, has justly delivered over into a woful Slavery to the Powers of Darkness: And, Oh! do something, that the light of Salvation by the glorious Lord JESUS CHRIST may arrive unto us.* A SOUL, Ignorant of God and His Christ, and vicious in all the affections of it, and that neither knows nor likes the Things that are Holy and Just and Good, and that has no illuminations from Heaven ever visiting of it, but is in *Great Folly wandering down to the Congregation of the Dead* {Pro. 21:6}; Such a Soul is a terrible sight! It can be no other than such a Soul, who does not count it so. Neighbours, you have such a sight, in all your *Negroes*, as long as they are left a *People of no understanding*. The uninstructed *Negroes* about your houses, appear like so many *Ghosts* and *Spectres*, You may, without being Fanciful, imagine that like so many Murdered *Ghosts*, they look very Ghastly upon you, and summon you to answer before the Tribunal of God, for suffering them to perish in their miserable Circumstances. Most certainly, Syrs; The *Blood* of the *Souls* of your poor *Negroes*, lies upon you, and the guilt of their Barbarous Impieties, and superstitions, and their neglect of God and their *Souls:* If you are willing to have nothing done towards the Salvation of their Souls. We read of, *People destroy'd for lack of knowledge* {Hos. 4:6}. If you withhold *Knowledge* from your *Black People*, they will be *Destroy'd*. But their *Destruction* must very much ly at *Your* doors; *You* must answer for it. It was a *Black charge* of old brought in against the *Jewish Nation*; Jer. 2.34. *In thy skirts is found the Blood of Souls*. It were to be wish'd, that in the *Skirts*, the out-borders, the Colonies and Plantations of the *English Nation*, there might be no room for such a charge. But surely, Things look very *Black* upon us. You have your selves renounced *Christianity*, if you do not receive that *Faithful saying* of it, and most *Awful* one: *Every one of us shall give account of himself to God*. But then Remember, that one Article of your *Account* will be this: *You had poor* Negroes *under you, and you expected and exacted Revenues of profit from them. Did you do any thing to save them from their Blindness and Baseness, and that the Great GOD might have Revenues of glory from them*. Alas, if you have not thought and car'd and *Watch'd for the Souls* of your *Negroes*, as *they that must give an Account*, You will give up your *Account* with *Grief*, and not with *Joy*; very *Grievous* will be the consequences. A *Prophet* of God, might without putting any *Disguise* upon the matter, thus represent it; God has brought a *Servant* unto thee, and said, *Keep that Soul, Teach it, and Help it, that it may not be lost; if thou use no means to save that Soul, thy soul shall certainly smart for it*. Vain Dreamer; canst thou suppose that the *Negroes* are made for nothing but only to serve thy Pleasures, or that they owe no Homage to their *Maker?* Do thy part, that they may become a *People of so much Understanding*, as to Understand who is their *Maker* and their *Saviour*, and what Homage they owe unto Him: Else, *He that made them will not have mercy on them* {Isa. 27:11}. Yea, but *Thy* claim to His *Mercy* will be less than *Theirs*. More *Stripes* will belong unto thee.

On the other side, Fourthly: Oh! That our Neighbours would consider the incomparable *Benefits* that would follow upon your *Endeavours* to *Christianize* your *Negroes*, and bring them to a share with your selves in the *Benefits* of the Heavenly *Inheritance*. If your care and cost about the cultivation of your *Negroes*, be laid out upon such a Stony and Barren Soil, that you can see no Fruit of it, yet it is not all thrown away. The blessed God will approve and reward what you have done; Think, *Tho' my* Negroes *will not prove a part of the Israel of God, and will not be gathered unto the Lord, yet my work is with my God, and what I do is glorious in the Eyes of the Lord.* But it is very probable, You may see some good *Success* of your Travail. And *then!* Oh! the *Consolations* that will belong unto you! *Christianity* does Marvellously befriend and enrich and advance Mankind. The greatest *Kindness* that can be done to any Man is to make a *Christian* of him. Your *Negroes* are immediately Raised unto an astonishing Felicity, when you have *Christianized* them. They are become amiable spectacles, & such as the *Angels* of God would gladly repair unto the Windows of Heaven to look upon. Tho' they remain your *Servants*, yet they are become the *Children* of God. Tho' they are to enjoy no *Earthly Goods*, but the small Allowance that your Justice and Bounty shall see proper for them, yet they are become *Heirs* of God, and *Joint-Heirs* with the Lord Jesus Christ. . . .

Yea, the pious *Masters*, that have instituted their *Servants* in Christian Piety, will even in this Life have a sensible *Recompence.* The more *Serviceable*, and Obedient and obliging Behaviour of their *Servants* unto them, will be a sensible & a notable *Recompence.* Be assured, Syrs; Your *Servants* will be the *Better Servants*, for being made *Christian Servants.* To *Christianize* them aright, will be to *fill them with all Goodness. Christianity* is nothing but a very Mass of Universal *Goodness.* Were your *Servants* well tinged with the Spirit of *Christianity*, it would render them exceeding *Dutiful* unto their *Masters*, exceeding *Patient* under their *Masters*, exceeding faithful in their Business, and afraid of speaking or doing any thing that may justly displease you. It has been observed, that those *Masters* who have used their *Negroes* with most of *Humanity*, in allowing them all the Comforts of Life, that are necessary and *Convenient* for them, (Who have remembred, that by the Law of God, even an *Ass* was to be relieved, When *Sinking under his Burden* {Exod. 23:5}, and an *Ox* might not be *Muzzled* when *Treading out the Corn* {Deut. 25:4}; and that if a *Just man will regard the Life of his Beast*, he will much more allow the comforts of life to and not hide himself *from his own Flesh:*) have been better *Serv'd*, had more work done for them, and better done, than those *Inhumane Masters*, who have used their *Negroes* worse than their *Horses.* And those *Masters* doubtless, who use their *Negroes* with most of *Christianity*, and use most pains to inform them in, and conform them in, and conform them to, *Christianity*, will find themselves no losers by it. *Onesimus* was doubtless a *Slave:*[25] but this poor *Slave*, on whose behalf a great Apostle of God was more than a little concerned; yea, one Book in our Bible was Written on his behalf! When he was *Christianized*, it was presently said unto his *Masters*, Philem. 11. *In time past he was unprofitable to thee, but now he will be profitable.* But many *Masters* whose *Negroes* have greatly vexed them, with miscarriages, may do well to examine, Whether Heaven be not chastising of them, for their failing in their Duty about their *Negroes*. Had they done more, to make their *Negroes* the knowing and willing *Servants* of God, it may be, God would have made their *Negroes* better *Servants* to them. Syrs, you may Read your *Sin* in the *Punishment*.

And now, what *Objection* can any Man Living have, to retund the force of these *Considerations?* Produce *thy cause,* O Impiety, *Bring forth thy strong reasons* {Isa. 41:21}, and let all men see what Idle and silly cavils, are thy best *Reasons* against this Work of God.

It has been cavilled, by some, that it is questionable Whether the *Negroes* have *Rational Souls,* or no. But let that *Bruitish* insinuation be never Whispered any more. Certainly, their *Discourse*, will abundantly prove, that they have *Reason*. *Reason* showes it self in the *Design* which they daily act upon. The vast improvement that *Education* has made upon *some* of them, argues that there is a *Reasonable Soul* in *all* of them. An old Roman, and Pagan, would call upon the Owner of such Servants, *Homines tamen esse memento.*[26] They are *Men,* and not *Beasts* that you have bought, and they must be used accordingly. 'Tis true; They are *Barbarous.* But so were our own *Ancestors.* The *Britons* were in many things as *Barbarous,* but a little before our Saviours Nativity, as the *Negroes* are at this day if there be any Credit in *Caesars Commentaries.*[27] *Christianity* will be the best cure for this *Barbarity.* Their *Complexion* sometimes is made an Argument, why nothing should be done for them. A *Gay* sort of argument! As if the great God went by the *Complexion* of Men, in His Favours to them! As if none but *Whites* might hope to be Favoured and Accepted with God! Whereas it is well known, That the *Whites,* are the least part of Mankind. The biggest part of Mankind, perhaps, are *Copper-Coloured*; a sort of *Tawnies.* And our *English* that inhabit some Climates, do seem growing apace to be not much unlike unto them. As if, because a people, from the long force of the African *Sun & Soyl* upon them, (improved perhaps, to further Degrees by maternal imaginations, and other accidents,) are come at length to have the small *Fibres* of their *Veins,* and the Blood in them, a little more Interspersed thro' their Skin than other People, this must render them less valuable to Heaven then the rest of Mankind? Away with such Trifles. The God who *looks on the Heart,* is not moved by the colour of the *Skin;* is not more propitious to one *Colour* than another. Say rather, with the Apostle; Acts 10.34, 35. *Of a truth I perceive, that God is no respecter of persons; but in every Nation, he that feareth Him and worketh Righteousness, is accepted with Him.* Indeed their *Stupidity* is a *Discouragement.* It may seem, unto as little purpose, to *Teach*, as to *wash an Æthiopian*. But the greater their *Stupidity*, the greater must be our *Application*. If we can't learn them so much as we *Would*, let us learn them as much as we *Can*. A little divine *Light* and *Grace* infused into them, will be of great account. And the more *Difficult* it is, to fetch such *forlorn things* up out of the perdition whereinto they are fallen, the more *Laudable* is the undertaking: There will be the more of a *Triumph*, if we prosper in the undertaking. Let us encourage our selves from that word; Mat. 3.9. *God is able of these Stones, to raise up Children unto Abraham.*

Well; But if the *Negroes* are *Christianized*, they will be *Baptised*; and their *Baptism* will presently entitle them to their *Freedom*; so our *Money* is thrown away.

Man, If this were true; that a *Slave* bought with thy *Money*, were by thy means brought unto the *Things that accompany Salvation*, and thou shouldest from this time have no more Service from him, yet thy *Money* were not thrown away. That Mans *Money will perish with him* {Acts 8:20}, who had rather the *Souls* in his Family should *Perish*, than that he should lose a little *Money*. And suppose it were so, that *Baptism* gave a legal Title to *Freedom*. Is there no guarding against this Inconvenience? You may by sufficient *Indentures*, keep off the things, which you reckon so Inconvenient. But it is all a Mistake. There is no such thing. What *Law* is it, that Sets the *Baptised Slave* at *Liberty*? Not the *Law of Christianity*: that allows of *Slavery*; Only it wonderfully Dulcifies, and Mollifies, and Moderates the Circumstances of it. *Christianity* directs a *Slave*, upon his embracing the *Law of the Redeemer*, to satisfy himself, *That he is the Lords Free-man*, tho' he continues a *Slave*. It supposes, (Col. 3.11.) That there are *Bond* as well as *Free*, among those that have been *Renewed in the Knowledge and Image of Jesus Christ*. Will the *Canon-law* do it? No; The *Canons* of Numberless *Councils*, mention, the *Slaves* of *Christians*, without any contradiction. Will the *Civil Law* do it? No: Tell, if you can, any part of *Christendom*, wherein *Slaves* are not frequently to be met withal. But is not *Freedom* to be claim'd for a *Baptised Slave*, by the *English* Constitution? The English *Laws*, about *Villians*, or, *Slaves*, will not say so; for by those *Laws*, they may be granted *for Life*, like a *Lease*, and passed over with a *Mannor*, like other *Goods or Chattels*. And by those *Laws*, the Lords may sieze the Bodies of their *Slaves* even while a Writt, *De libertate probanda*,[28] is depending. These English *Laws* were made when the *Lords* & the *Slaves*, were both of them *Christians*; and they stand still unrepealed. If there are not now such *Slaves* in *England* as formerly, it is from the *Lords*, more than from the *Laws*. The *Baptised* then are not thereby entitled unto their *Liberty*. Howbeit, if they have arrived unto such a measure of *Christianity*, that *none can forbid Water for the Baptising of them*, it is fit, that they should enjoy those *comfortable circumstances* with us, which are due to them, not only as the *Children* of *Adam*, but also as our *Brethren,* on the same level with us in the expectations of a blessed Immortality, thro' the *Second Adam.* Whatever Slaughter the Assertion may make among the pretensions which are made unto *Christianity,* yet while the *sixteenth* Chapter of *Matthew* is in the Bible, it must be asserted; the *Christian,* who cannot so far *Deny himself,* can be no *Disciple* of the Lord JESUS CHRIST. But, O Christian, thy *Slave* will not Serve thee one jot the worse for that *Self-denial.*

PURITANS AND NATIVE AMERICANS

I t would be difficult to say which were greater: the injustices that the colonizers of New England visited on Africans on both sides of the Atlantic or
those they visited on Native Americans. Each population suffered at the
hands of European settlers and their descendants in similar and distinct
ways. During the initial contact period, diseases like smallpox, yellow fever, and
tuberculosis introduced vicariously decimated America's Indigenous populations. Afterward, the English, like other Europeans, engaged in both physical
and cultural genocide, killing off the great majority of Natives through war, dis-
placement, and enslavement, while insisting that those who survived conform
to colonial hegemony. Mather was possessed of many of the conventional assumptions and attitudes of his fellow Anglo-Americans when it came to Native
Americans: they were heathens and infidels who could only improve themselves
by rejecting their ancient cultures, languages, and customs and converting to
Christianity and adopting English ways. In his writings about Natives, Mather
exhibited an ambivalence about them that was representative yet given singular
expression. On the one hand, he dominated his writings about them with depictions of wrongful violence committed by them and righteous violence visited on them, reflecting a fear and hatred of them; on the other, his descriptions
of Christianized Natives were paternalistic, with efforts to "civilize" Indigenous
peoples presented as proof of English benevolence and their cultural and spiritual superiority.[1] He also reproached his fellow New Englanders in his *Moni-*

tory, and Hortatory Letter, To those English, who debauch the Indians (1700), for selling them "*Strong Drink*" to cheat them out of their possessions.

The first selection under this topic illustrates the violent side of Mather's ambivalence toward Natives. *Humiliations Follow'd with Deliverances* was a sermon he gave in 1697 at his Boston church to celebrate the return of several individuals who had been taken captive by Natives. Taking captives was common for Natives, whether to provide potential new family members to replace ones who had died or to be held for ransom. Often, captives were English females, and the suspenseful stories of those who lived to tell their tales of abduction, forced flight, and time spent among their captors and their French allies were extremely popular among New England audiences. One such "redeemed" captive, Mary Rowlandson, along with several of her children, had been taken from her home in Lancaster, Massachusetts, during King Philip's War and spent nearly three months in captivity before being returned. She eventually published her narrative, entitled *The Soveraignty and Goodness of God*, in 1682.

Mather's sermon a decade and a half after the appearance of Rowlandson's popular account was delivered a week before an officially declared day of colony-wide fasting for the victims of Indian attacks early in the year on the northern settlements of Haverhill and Casco (the former in northeastern Massachusetts, the latter in present-day Maine). In the audience were three English individuals who had been taken in those raids, now returned. Appended to the published version of the sermon were the narratives of two redeemed women. One of them was Hannah Dustan of Haverhill, who only a week before her abduction had given birth. Separated from her husband and her other children, who escaped as the raiders approached, Dustan and the family maid were taken by their captors on a wearying trek northward, though only after Natives killed her infant and set her house ablaze. Complying with her captors at first, Dustan and her companion watched for their opportunity, and one night while the party was "in a *Dead Sleep*," they took up hatchets and killed all except a woman and a boy, who fled. Mather's alliterative and repetitive description of the murders, echoing scripture, in effect prolonged, drew out, and thereby celebrated the bloody act. He compared Dustan to the Israelite woman Jael, who, as told in

Judges 4, killed Sisera, the general of an invading army, by driving a tent spike through his head after she had lulled him to sleep with food and drink.

However, this episode for Mather was as much about conflict with Natives as it was the effect that such conflict was having on gender roles among the English. In holding up this assertive wife and mother, literary historians such as Laurel Thatcher Ulrich and Teresa Toulouse have argued that Mather was critiquing what he saw as male ineptitude to protect New England women (epitomized in Dustan's indecisive husband), which was leading to the breakdown of traditional family and gender spheres. In such an unnatural circumstance, a woman who was expected to be obedient and passive had to become ruthless. Dustan's ruthlessness extended to her intent to "bring away"—presumably to sell into slavery—the Native boy who fled. In *Magnalia Christi Americana*, Mather even noted that she brought in the scalps of her ten victims, receiving a bounty of fifty pounds from the governor of Virginia—and the hearty thanks of the Massachusetts General Assembly.[2]

The other, lengthier narrative that Mather added to *Humiliations* was that of Hannah Swarton, who had been taken at Casco in 1690 and remained a captive for five years. This text, largely a production of Mather's, was distinguished by Swarton's relation of attempts by her captors, both Native and French, to convince her to renounce her Protestantism. She also related negotiations that occurred among Natives, French, and English for possession of English captives such as herself. As for Swarton, she was sold by her Native "master" to the French and eventually redeemed either through ransom or prisoner exchange. This was not always the case, for a significant minority of English captured during the conflicts at the end of the seventeenth and beginning of the eighteenth centuries not only remained in Canada but converted to Catholicism. This posed a direct challenge to New English Protestant identity, as seen with Mather's cousin Eunice Williams, who renounced Protestantism and married a Native. Thus, Swarton's resistance to French religion and culture, her spiritual awakening during her captivity (like the Israelites of old), and her regret that she left a place that had the true worship of God in order to live in a remote settlement all were important instructive devices for Mather: "humiliations" that led to "deliverance."

In his writings on Natives, war was a constant theme because war was a formative presence in Cotton Mather's life to a degree that perhaps has not been fully appreciated. Declared and undeclared conflicts regularly punctuated his life, particularly with the French and their Native allies and, though less so, with the Spanish. The realities and lessons of wars were therefore recurrent themes in Mather's sermons and treatises. In 1699, for instance, he published *Decennium Luctuosum* ("A Sorrowful Decade"), on the War of the League of Augsburg, which in its American phase was called King William's War. The sequel, published in 1714, was entitled *Duodecennium Luctuosum* ("Two Sorrowful Decades") and related and reflected on the local fighting of the War of Spanish Succession, or Queen Anne's War, a further period of hostilities on a transatlantic scale.

Refraining and reframing earlier works such as *Humiliations*, Mather portrayed this most recent conflict as a "Long WAR With *Indian* Salvages," counterpoising his view of peaceful Christianized Natives, as in the *Monitory Letter*, with his view of violent, unconverted Natives. With peace achieved through the Treaty of Utrecht in 1713, hostilities had ended. Looking back, Mather exhorted his readers to consider the "voice" of God in all that had happened. God had punished the enemy Natives for making war on the English. To prevent further trouble from the Maine coast and interior, Mather advised "Upholding of *Religion* in the Plantations of the *East*," a theme that resonated with Hannah Swarton's regrets for going to live in a "remote place" where there were no orthodox churches, and with the *Monitory Letter*, which characterized these regions as being under the thrall of *"Frenchified"* tribes. But God's voice was also to be heard in the fire that badly damaged Boston in 1711, in the death of two ministers, in the measles epidemic of 1713, and in the many English slain and taken captive, who were subjected to torture and forced conversion. While the judgments of God could be seen in these tragedies, and in many more, the excerpt from this text concludes with Mather's litany of ways showing "HOW

Favoured" New England had been by God, as in the destruction of French ships, the shipwrecks of privateers, the fall of French posts, the assistance of other colonies—even an ability to pay off the large debts accrued during the war. Indulging in a provincialism that he otherwise shed as he matured, Mather ended by pointing out that through it all, Boston, the *"Metropolis"* of *"*the whole English *America,"* had arisen, phoenix-like, from the ashes.

HUMILIATIONS FOLLOW'D WITH DELIVERANCES (1697)

A NARRATIVE OF A NOTABLE DELIVERANCE FROM CAPTIVITY

"ON the fifteenth Day, of the Last *March* [1697], *Hannah Dustan,* of *Haver-hil,*[3] having Lain in about a Week, attended with her Nurse, *Mary Neff,*[4] a Widow, a Body of Terrible *Indians,* drew near unto the House where she lay, with Designs to carry on the bloody Devastations, which they had begun upon the Neighbourhood. Her Husband, hastened from his Employments abroad, unto the Relief of his Distressed Family; and first bidding *Seven* of his *Eight* Children (which were from Two to *Seventeen* years of age,) to get away as fast as they could, unto some Garrison in the Town, he went in, to inform his Wife, of the horrible Distress now come upon them. E're she could get up, the fierce *Indians* were got so near, that utterly despairing to do her any Service, he ran out after his Children; Resolving, that on the Horse, which he had with him, he would Ride away, with *That,* which he should in this Extremity find his Affections to pitch most upon, and leave the Rest, unto the care of the Divine Providence. He overtook his Children, about Forty Rod, from his Door; but *then,* such was the Agony of his Parental Affections, that he found it Impossible for him, to Distinguish any one of them, from the Rest; wherefore he took up a Courageous Resolution, to Live & Dy with them All. A party of *Indians* came up with him; and now, though they Fired at him, and he Fired at them, yet he manfully kept in the Reer of his *Little Army* of unarmed Children, while they March'd off, with the pace of a Child of Five years old; until, by the Singular Providence of God, he arrived safe with them all, unto a place of Safety, about a Mile or two from his House. But his House must in the mean Time, have more dismal *Tragedies* acted at it. The Nurse, trying to Escape, with the New born Infant, fell into the hands of the formidable Salvages; & those furious Tawnies, coming in to the House, bid poor *Dustan,* to Rise immediately. Full of Astonishment, she did so; and Sitting down in the Chimney, with an heart full of most fearful Expectation, she saw the Raging Dragons riffle all that they could carry away: and set the House on Fire. About Nineteen or Twenty *Indians*, now led these away, with about Half a score other, English *Captives*: but e're they had gone many Steps, they dash'd out the Brains of the *Infant*, against a Tree, and several of the other *Captives*, as they begun to Tire in their sad Journey, were soon sent unto their long Home, but the Salvages would presently bury their Hatchets in their Brains, and leave their Carcases on the ground, for Birds & Beasts, to feed upon. [Christians, A *Joshua* would have *Rent his Clothes, & fallen to the Earth on his Face* {Josh. 7:6}, and have *Humbled* himself Exceedingly upon the falling out of such doleful Ruines upon his Neighbours!] However, *Dustan* (with her Nurse,) notwithstanding her present Condition, Travelled that Night, about a Dozen Miles; and then kept up with their New Masters, in a long Travel[5] of an Hundred and fifty Miles, more or less, within a few Dayes Ensuing; without any sensible Damage, in their Health, from the Hardships, of their *Travel*, their *Lodging*, their *Diet*, and their many other Difficulties. These Two poor Women, were now in the Hands of those, *Whose Tender Mercies are Cruelty* {Pro. 12:10}: but the Good God, who hath all *Hearts in His own Hands* {Pro. 21:1}, heard the Sighs of *these Prisoners* unto Him, and gave them to find unexpected Favour, from the *Master*, who Laid claim unto them. That *Indian Family* consisted of Twelve persons, Two stout men, three women, and seven Children; and for the shame of many a *Prayerless Family* among our *English*, I must now publish what these poor women assure me; 'Tis *This*; In Obedience to the Instruction which the French have given them, they would have *Prayers* in their Family, no less than Thrice every Day; In the *Morning*, at *Noon*, and in the *Evening*; nor would they ordinarily let so much as a Child, *Eat*, or *Sleep*, without first saying their *Prayers*. Indeed, these *Idolaters*, were, like the rest of their whiter Brethren *Persecutors*, and would not Endure that these poor *Women* should Retire to their *English Prayers*, if they could hinder them. Nevertheless, the poor Women, had nothing but fervent *Prayers*, to make their Lives comfortable or tolerable; and by being daily sent out, upon Business, they had opportunities together and asunder, to do like another *Hannah*, in *pouring out their Souls before the Lord*: Nor did their Praying Friends among our selves, forbear to *pour out* Supplications for them. Now, they could not observe it, without some wonder, that their Indian Master, sometimes, when he saw them Dejected, would say unto them; *What need you Trouble your self? If your God will have you Delivered, you shall be so!* And it seems, our God, would have it so to be!

   "This Indian Family, was now Travelling with these two Captive women, (& an English Youth, taken from *Worcester*, last *September* was a Twelve-month,)[6] unto a Rendezvouze of Salvages, which they call a *Town*, somewhere beyond *Penacook*;[7] and they still told these poor women, that when they came to this

Town, they must be Stript, & Scourged, and Run the *Gantlet*, through the whole
Army of *Indians*. They said, This was the *Fashion*, when the Captives first came
to a Town; and they derided, some of the faint hearted English, which, they said,
fainted and swooned away under the *Torments* of this Discipline. [Syrs, can we
hear of these things befalling our Neighbours, & not *Humble* our selves before
our God!] But on this Day Se'night,[8] while they were yet it may be, about an
hundred and fifty miles from the Indian Town, a little before Break of Day, when
the whole Crew, was in a *Dead Sleep*, ('twill presently prove so!) One of these
women took up a Resolution, to Imitate the Action of *Jael* upon *Sisera*,[9] and being where she had not her *own Life* secured by any *Law* unto her, she thought
she was not forbidden by any *Law*, to take away the *Life*, of the *Murderers*, by
whom her *Child* had been butchered. She heartened the *Nurse*, and the *Youth*,
to assist her, in this Enterprise; & they all furnishing themselves with *Hatchets*
for the purpose, they struck such Home Blowes, upon the Heads of their *Sleeping Oppressors*, that e're they could any of them struggle into any effectual Resistance, *at the Feet* of those poor Prisoners, *They bowed, they fell, they lay down;
at their feet they bowed, they fell; where they bowed, there they fell down Dead*
{Judg. 5:27}. Onely one *Squaw* Escaped sorely wounded from them, and one *Boy*,
whom they Reserved Asleep, intending to bring him away with them, suddenly
wak'd and stole away, from this Desolation. But cutting off the Scalps of the *Ten
Wretches*, who had Enslav'd 'em, they are come off; and I perceive, that newly
arriving among us, they are in the Assembly at this Time, to give Thanks unto,
God their Saviour."

A NARRATIVE OF HANNAH SWARTON, CONTAINING WONDERFUL PASSAGES,
RELATING TO HER CAPTIVITY, AND HER DELIVERANCE[10]

I Was taken by the *Indians*, when *Casco* Fort was taken, (*May*) 1690. My Husband being slain, and Four Children taken with me. The Eldest of my Sons
they killed, about two Months after I was taken, and the rest Scattered from me.
I was now left a *Widow*, and as Bereaved of my Children; though, I had them
alive, yet it was very seldome that I could see them, and I had not Liberty to
Discourse with them, without Danger either of my own Life, or theirs; for our
Condoling each others Condition, and shewing Natural Affection, was so displeasing to our *Indian Rulers*, unto whose Share we fell, that they would threaten
to kill us, if we cryed each to other, or discoursed much together. So that my
Condition was like what the Lord threatned the *Jews*, in Ezek. 24.22, 23. We durst
not *Mourn* or *Weep*, in the sight of our Enemies, lest we lost our own *Lives*. For
the first Times while the Enemy feasted on our English Provisions, I might have

had some with them: but then I was so filled with *Sorrow* and *Tears*, that I had little *Stomach* to Eat; and when my *Stomach* was come, our English Food was spent, and the Indians wanted themselves, and we more: So that then I was pined with want. We had no Corn, or Bread, but sometimes *Groundnuts*, *Acorns*, *Purslain*, *Hogweed*, Weeds, Roots, and sometimes *Dogs Flesh*, but not sufficient to satisfy Hunger with these; having but little at a Time. We had no success at Hunting; save that one *Bear* was killed, which I had part of; and a very small part of a Turtle I had at other time, and once an Indian gave me a piece of a *Mooses* Liver, which was a sweet Morsel to me; and *Fish*, if we could catch it. Thus I continued with them, hurried up and down the Wilderness, from *May* 20, till the middle of *February*; Carrying continually, a Great *Burden* in our Travels; and I must go their pace, or else be killed presently; and yet was pinched with Cold, for want of Cloathing, being put by them into an *Indian Dress*, with a sleight Blanket, no Stockings, and but one pair of *Indian-Shoes*, and of their Leather Stockings for the Winter: My Feet were pricked with sharp Stones, and prickly Bushes sometimes; and other times Pinched with Snow, Cold, and Ice, that I travelled upon, ready to be frozen, and faint for want of Food; so that many times I thought I could go no further, but must ly down, and if they would kill me, let them kill me. Yet then, the Lord did so Renew my Strength, that I went on still further, as my Master would have me, and held out with them. Though many English were taken, and I was brought to some of them, at times, while we were about *Casco Bay* and *Kennebeck* River, yet at *Norridgawock*,[11] we were Separated, and no English were in our Company, but one *John York* and my self, who were both, almost Starved for want, and yet told, that if we could not hold up to travel with them, they would kill us. And accordingly, *John York*, growing Weak by his wants, they killed *him*, and threatened *me* with the like. One time, my Indian Mistress, and I, were left alone, while the rest went to look for *Eeles*; and they left us *no Food* from *Sabbath day* Morning, till the next *Sature-day*; save that we had a *Bladder* (of *Moose* I think) which was well filled with *Maggots*, and we boiled it, and drank the Broth; but the *Bladder* was so tough, we could not eat it. On the *Saturday*, I was sent by my Mistress, to that part of the Island, most likely to see some *Canoo*, and there to make Fire and Smoke, to invite some Indians, if I could spy any, to come to Relieve us; and I espied a *Canoo*, and by Signs invited them to come to the Shore. It proved to be some *Squaw's*; who understanding our wants, one of them gave me a Roasted *Eel*, which I eat, and it seemed unto me, the most Savoury Food, I ever tasted before. Sometimes we lived on *Wortle berries*; sometimes on a kind of *Wild Cherry*, which grew on Bushes; which I was sent to gather, once in so bitter a Cold season, that I was not able to bring my Fingers together, to hold them fast: yet under all these Hardships, the Lord kept me from any Sickness, or such Weakness as to disenable me from Travelling, when they put us upon it.

My *Indian Mistress*, was one that had been bred by the English at *Black point*,[12] and now Married to a *Canada* Indian, & turned Papist; and she would say, *That had the English been as careful to instruct her in our Religion, as the French were, to instruct her in theirs, she might have been of our Religion:* and she would say, *That God delivered us into their Hands to punish us for our Sins;* And, This I knew was true as to my self. And as I desired to consider of all my Sins, for which the Lord did punish me, so this Lay very heavy upon my Spirit, many a Time, that I had Left the Publick Worship and Ordinances of God, where I formerly Lived, (*viz.* at *Beverley*) to Remove to the North part of *Casco-Bay*, where there was no Church, or Minister of the Gospel; and this we did, for large Accommodations in the World, thereby Exposing our Children, to be bred Ignorantly like Indians, and our selves to forget what we had been formerly instructed in; and so we turned our Backs upon *Gods Ordinances* to get this *Worlds Goods*. But now, God hath stripped me of these things also; so that I must Justify the Lord, in all that has befallen me, and acknowledge that He hath punished me less than my Iniquities deserved. I was now Bereaved of Husband, Children, Friends, Neighbours, House, Estate, Bread, Cloaths, or Lodging suitable; and my very *Life did hang daily in Doubt*, being continually in danger of being killed by the Indians, or pined to Death with Famine, or tired to Death with hard Travelling, or pinched with Cold, till I dyed in the Winter season. I was so amazed with many Troubles, and hurried in my Spirit from one Exercise to another, how to preserve my self in danger, and supply my self in the want that was present; that I had not time or leisure so composedly to consider of the great Concernments of my Soul, as I should have done; neither had I any *Bible* or *Good Book* to look into, or Christian Friend to be my Counsellor in these Distresses. But I may say, The *Words of God*, which I had formerly heard or read, many of them came oft into my mind, and kept me from *perishing in my Afflictions*. As, when they threatned to Kill me many times, I often thought of the words of our Saviour to *Pilate*, Joh. 19.11. *Thou couldest have no power at all against me, except it were given thee from above.* I knew they had *no power* to kill me, but what the *Lord gave* them; and I had many times Hope, that the Lord would not suffer them to slay me, but deliver me out of their Hands, and in His Time, I hoped, return me to my Country again. When they told me, that my *Eldest Son* was killed by the Indians, I thought of that in Jer. 33.8. *I will cleanse them from all their Iniquities whereby they have sinned against me, and I will pardon all their Iniquities.* I hoped, though the Enemy had barbarously killed his *Body*, yet that the Lord had *Pardoned* his Sins, and that his *Soul* was safe. When I thought upon my many Troubles, I thought of *Jobs* complaint, chap. 14 16, 17. *Thou numbrest my steps, and watchest over my Sin; my Transgression is sealed up in a Bag, and thou sowest up my Iniquity.* This was for my Humiliation, and put me upon Prayer to God, for His *Pardoning Mercy* in Christ. . . .

I Travelled over steep and hideous *Mountains* one while, and another while over *Swamps* and Thickets of Fallen Trees, lying one, two, three foot from the ground, which I have stepped on, from one to another, nigh a thousand in a day; carrying a great Burden on my Back. Yet I dreaded going to *Canada*, to the *French*, for fear lest I should be overcome by them, to yield to their Religion; which I had *Vowed* unto God, *That I would not do*. But the Extremity of my Sufferings were such, that at length I was willing to go, to preserve my Life. And after many weary Journeys, through Frost and Snow, we came to *Canada*, about the middle of *February*, 1690, and Travelling over the River, my Master pitch'd his *Wigwam* in sight of some *French* Houses Westward of us, and then sent me to those Houses to beg Victuals for them: which I did, and found the *French* very kind to me, giving me Beef, and Pork, and *Bread*, which I had been without, near nine months before; so that now, I found a great Change as to Diet. But the Snow being knee deep, and my Legs and Hams very sore, I found it very tedious to Travel; and my sores bled, so that as I Travelled, I might be Tracked by my Blood, that I left behind me on the Snow. I asked leave to stay all Night with the *French*, when I went to beg again; which my Master consented unto, and sent me Eastward, to Houses, which were toward *Quebeck*, (though then I knew it not:) So, having begged Provisions at a French House, and it being near night, after I was Refreshed my self, and had Food to carry to the Indians, I signified, as well as I could make the French Woman understand, That I desired to stay by her Fire, that Night. Whereupon she laid a good Bed on the Floor, and good Coverings for me, and there I Lodged comfortably; and the next Morning, when I had breakfasted with the Family, and the men kind were gone abroad, as I was about to go to my Indian Master, the French Woman stept out, and left me alone in her House; and I then staid her Return, to give her thanks for her kindness; and while I waited, came in two men, and one of them spake to me in English, *I am glad to see you Country woman!* This was exceedingly Reviving, to hear the voice of an English man; and upon Enquiry, I found, he was an English man, taken at the *North West Passage;* and the other was a French *Ordinary*[13] *Keeper.* After some Discourse he asked me to go with him to *Quebeck*, which he told me, was about four miles off: I answered, my Indian Master might kill me for it, when I went back. Then, after some Discourse in *French*, with his Fellow Traveller, he said; This *French* man Engaged, that if I would go with them, he would keep me, from Returning to the *Indians*, and I should be

Ransomed: and my *French* Hostess being now Returned in a doors, perswaded me to go with 'em to *Quebeck*; which I did, and was conveyed unto the House of the Lord *Intendant*, Monsieur *Le Tonant*, who was Chief Judge, and the Second to the Governour; and I was kindly Entertained by the Lady, and had French Cloaths given me, with good Diet and Lodging, & was carried thence unto the Hospital; where I was Physicked and Blooded, and very courteously provided for. And some time after, my Indian Master and Mistress coming for me, the *Lady Intendant* paid a Ransome for me, and I became her Servant. And I must speak it to the Honour of the *French*, they were exceeding kind to me at first, even as kind as I could expect to find the *English*: so that I wanted nothing for my Bodily Comfort, which they could help me unto.

Here was a great and comfortable Change, as to my *Outward man*, in my *Freedom* from my former Hardships, and Hard hearted Oppressors. But here began a greater Snare and Trouble to my Soul and Danger to my *Inward man*. For the Lady my Mistress, the Nuns, the Priests, Friars, and the rest, set upon me, with all the strength of *Argument* they could, from *Scripture*, as they interpreted it, to perswade me to Turn *Papist*; which they pressed with very much Zeal, Love, Intreaties, and *Promises*, if I would Turn to them, and with many *Threatnings*, and sometimes Hard Usages, because I did not Turn to their Religion. Yea, sometimes the Papists, because I would not Turn to them, Threatned to send me to *France*, and there I should be *Burned*, because I would not Turn to them. . . .

I shall proceed to Relate, what Trials *I* met with, in these Things. *I* was put upon it, either to *stand* to the Religion *I* was brought up in, and believed in my Conscience to be True; or to *Turn* to another, which *I* believed was not Right. And *I* was kept from Turning, by that Scripture, Mat. 10.32, 33. *Whosoever shall confess me before men, him will I confess before my Father which is in Heaven, and whosoever denies me before men, him also will I deny before my Father which is in Heaven.* I thought that if I should *Deny* the *Truth*, and own their Religion, I should *Deny Christ.* Yet upon their perswasions, I went to see, and be present at their Worship, sometimes but never to Receive their Sacrament. And once, when I was at their *Worship*, that Scripture, 2 Cor. 6.14. to the end came into my mind: *What Communion hath Light with Darkness! What Concord hath Christ with Belial! What part hath he that believeth with an Infidel? and what Agreement hath the Temple of God with Idols? Wherefore come out from among them, and be ye Separate, and touch not the Unclean Thing, and I will Receive you, and I will be a Father to you, and you shall be my Sons and Daughters, saith the Lord Almighty.* This Scripture was so strong, upon my Spirit, that I thought I was out of my way to be present at their *Idolatrous Worship*, and I Resolved never to come unto it again. But when the time drew nigh that I was to go again, I was so Restless that Night, that I could not sleep; thinking, what I should say to them when they urged me to go again, and what I should Do. And so it was in the morning, that a French woman of my Acquaintance, told me, if I would not be of *Their* Religion, I did but *mock* at it, to go to their Worship, and therefore bid me, That if I would not be of *their* Religion, I should go no more. I answered her, *That I would not be of their Religion, and I would go no more to their Worship:* and accordingly, I never went more, and they did not force me to it.

I have had many Conflicts in my own Spirit; fearing that I was not truely *Converted* unto God in Christ, and that I had no Saving Interest in Christ. I could not be of a *False Religion,* to please men; for it was against my Conscience: And I was not fit to suffer for the *True Religion,* and for Christ; for I then feared, I had no Interest in Him. I was neither fit to *Live,* nor fit to *Dye;* and brought once to the very pit of *Despair,* about what would become of my Soul. In this Time I had gotten an *English Bible,* and other Good Books, by the Help of my Fellow Captives. I Looked over the Scripture, and settled on the Prayer of *Jonah,* and those Words, *I said, I am cast out of thy sight, yet will I Look again towards thy Holy Temple* {Jonah 2:4}. I Resolved, I would do as *Jonah* did: And in the Meditation upon this Scripture, the Lord was pleased, by His *Spirit,* to come into my Soul, and so fill me with Ravishing Comfort, that I cannot Express it. Then came to mind, the History of the Transfiguring of Christ, and *Peters* saying, Math. 17.4. *Lord, It is Good for us to be here!* I thought, it was Good for me to be here; and I was so full of Comfort and Joy, I even Wished I could be so alwayes, and never sleep; or else Dy in that Rapture of Joy, and never Live to Sin any more against the Lord. Now I thought God was my God, and my Sins were pardoned in Christ; and now I thought, I could *Suffer* for Christ, yea, *Dye* for Christ, or do any thing for Him. My Sins had been a Burden to me: I desired to see all my Sins, and to Repent of them all, with all my Heart, and of that Sin which had been especially a Burden to me, namely, *That I Left the Publick Worship and Ordinances of God, to go to Live in a Remote Place, without the Publick Ministry; depriving our selves & our Children, of so great a Benefit for our Souls, and all this, for Worldly advantages* I found an Heart to Repent of them all; and to lay hold of the *Blood of Christ,* to cleanse me from them all.

I found much Comfort, while I was among the *French,* by the Opportunities I had sometimes to *Read* the Scriptures and other Good Books, and *Pray* to the Lord in Secret; and the *Conference* that some of us Captives had together, about things of God, and *Prayer* together sometimes; especially, with one that was in the same House with me, *Margaret Stilson.*[14] Then was the Word of God precious to us, and they that *feared the LORD, spake one to another* of it, as we had Opportunity. And Colonel *Tyng,* and Mr. *Alden,*[15] as they were permitted, did speak to us, to Confirm and Strengthen us, in the wayes of the Lord. At length, the *French* debarr'd our coming together, for Religious Conference, or other Duties: And Word was sent us, by Mr. *Alden, That this was one kind of Persecution, that we must suffer for Christ.* . . .

The means of my Deliverance, were by reason of Letters that had passed between the Governments of *New-England* and of *Canada.* Mr. *Cary* was sent with a Vessel, to fetch Captives from *Quebeck,* and when he came, I among others, with my youngest Son, had our Liberty to come away: And by Gods Blessing upon us, we Arrived in Safety, at *Boston,* in *November,* 1695. our Desired Haven. And I desire to *Praise the Lord for His Goodness, and for His Wonderful Works to me.* Yet still I have left behind, Two Children, a Daughter of *Twenty* Years old, at *Mont Royal,* whom I had not seen in Two years before I came away; and a Son of *Nineteen* years old, whom *I* never saw since we parted, the next morning after we were taken. *I* earnestly Request the Prayers of my Christian Friends, that the Lord will deliver them.

What shall I render to the Lord for all His Benefits?

DUODECENNIUM LUCTUOSUM (1714)

The HISTORY of a Long WAR With *Indian* Salvages, And their
Directors and Abettors; From the Year, 1702. To the Year, 1714.

. . . ANOTHER *Long War* is now finished; A *New Peace* hath been struck up, in our Borders: And it is Time to Consider the *Voice* of our God unto us, in the *Observable Things* that have therein Passed over us. For, *O my Dear People,* While thy God has been *Striking* of thee, He has been also *Speaking* to thee; And it is of the Last Consequence, that His *Voice* be Wisely hearkened to; A Total Inadvertency to the *Voice,* will have a Consequence which we may justly tremble at;—If to be *Punished yet Ten times for our Iniquities,* or with more than *Ten Years* of Confusions repeated upon us, be a thing to be trembled at. . . .

WELL, but what Effect have the *Salvages* found of their *Perfidy?* A *Vengeance* of God has follow'd them; A *Vengeance,* that must be a *Story,* and a *Warning* to all the World.

HOW Many of them, have been Sacrificed by *Our Sword,* it is not Easy for us to say. They never *Assault,* but when they can *Surprize.* They have Quick Retreats to *Thickets* and *Mountains* that are to us inaccessible; The *Europeans,* who Wonder that all these Colonies don't Presently Swallow them up, have no *Idea* of them. When also any of them fall in *Battel,* the Survivers use more than ordinary Care to *Cover* them. However, I have been able to reckon many more than an *Hundred* of these Cursed Salvages, which have been known to be Kill'd by *Our Hands*. But, *Thy Hand*, O Lord, *has found out thine Enemies; Thy Right Hand has found out those that hate thee!* God has Plagued them with *Famine*, and *Sickness*, and many *Wasting* Miseries 'Tis affirm'd, They are so reduced, that they cannot make *Half* the Number, which they could when the *War* began. God has distress'd them Wonderfully! And so He will Some who are greater than *they*, and who have infused their Maxims into *them*.[16] There is that *Mighty Voice* from the GOD of TRUTH to *Those*, in what has befallen *These*.

AND yet, I Wish, the *Wounded Chaldeans*, may not rise up Once more to inflict *Grievous Wounds* upon *Us*. To Prevent more Desolations, I would with all *Humility*, but with all *Importunity*, most Vehemently, and with most Pressing Instances, beseech the Government, That all due Methods may be taken, for the Upholding of *Religion* in the Plantations of the *East*, as they shall be going on. Sirs, What has been done more than twice to break up our *Eastern* Plantations, has in it this *Voice* of the Glorious GOD; Yea, 'tis His *Mighty Voice*. Oh! *Let not People be any more so Foolish, as to think of taking Root, in Ungospellized Settlements; Lest I Once more do Suddenly Curse their Habitations.*

BUT then, *Thirdly*; We must be aware of this; That none of the *Particular Depredations*, which the Enemy has in this *Long War* made upon us, have been without a *Voice* from the Glorious GOD unto us in them: Yea, a *Mighty Voice*, which ought to be *heard attentively*, as the *Sound going out from His Mouth* {Job 37:2}.

HE that would Write the History of this *War*, must put upon it the Title that *Orosius* put upon his History, *De Miseria hominem*.[17]

AN Exact and Punctual Account of the several *Depredations*, with which the *Wild-beasts of the Desert* have broke in upon us, is not necessary to be Exhibited. Nor would it often afford more *Material* Passages, than those *Insipid* Ones, which the Funeral Orations on the Professors in the Universities are commonly Stuffed withal. But allow me to throw the *Murdered* and the *Captived* into the same List, as there is *too much cause* to do, and I find my self able to bring in a List of near *Seven Hundred* Persons, whom our Offended GOD has delivered up into the dreadful Hands of the Salvages. No doubt there have been more! The Boast made by One bloody Son of *Cain* among them has been generally heard of!—*Animus meminisse horret!*[18]

OFTENTIMES what the *Salvages* have done, has been upon one, or two, of theirs, at a time; done by a *Skulking* and *Wolfish* Adversary.

BUT Sometimes a Town has undergone a greater Effusion of Blood. *Haverhil* at once Loses above Thirty of it's Inhabitants; And, Poor *Deerfield!*—Never to be forgotten *Deerfield!*—An Hundred, and Perhaps twice Thirty more.[19]

HOW many *Deaths* have been Contracted and Hastened, by the *Fatigues* of Attempts against the Enemy,—there can be no Account.

ADD unto these, the Numberless *Deaths*, accelerated upon ours in their *Engagements* with the *French* at Sea, or by their *Confinements* among them:— Here our Bleeding Land would Cry out, *Oh! That my Grief were thoroughly Weigh'd! Now it would be heavy like the Sand of the Sea* {Job 6:2, Pro. 27:3}.

BUT, What I am now to note, is, There has been a *Voice* of the Glorious GOD, in every One of these Disasters.

I have reckoned up, in this *War*, near an *Hundred Times*, that *Evil Tidings* have been brought in unto us, of *Mischiefs* done to our Brethren and our Children, on the Land. *Mischief upon Mischief!*—Besides those which have come to us, on the Other Element. Among which, that on *Fishery* at one time amounting to Ten Thousand Pounds Damage, will not be forgotten! Sirs, There has been a *Voice* from the Glorious GOD Renew'd unto us, in every Stroke of such *Evil Tidings*. *A Voice from the East, a Voice from the West, a Voice from the North,* and a *Mighty Voice* coming over the *Mighty Waters* too; A *Voice from the Lord, rendring* His *Righteous Recompences* to us, by our *Enemies*. His terrible *Voice* in all these things has been, *I am displeased with you; Oh! Take up due Sentiments of my awful Displeasure at you!*

IN the midst of these Calamitous Things, could we see BOSTON in *Flames*; the very Place where I am now Standing, Perish in the Flames; the Glare whereof reached more than hundred Miles off; and not hear the *Voice* of a Provoked GOD, in these *Fiery Rebukes*?[20] Yea, our GOD Spoke to us with His *Mighty Voice* from the Midst of the *Fire*, as from another Mount *Sinai*; His *Voice* unto us was, *O Fear Me, and Receive Instruction, that so no more of your Dwellings may be cut off!* . . .

I am Sure, There has been One Article of the *Deadly Strokes*, which it will be very Proper for *Me* to be deeply affected withal. And I make no doubt, that my Brethren will be so!

THERE have been Two MINISTERS, who have Owed their *Deaths*, unto the *Sword* by which we have been so harassed.

THE Hopeful Minister of *Lancaster*, was Kill'd indeed by a most *Unhappy Mistake* of a Souldier in his own Garrison.[21] And might there not in such a thing be this *Voice* of our GOD, unto all our People, *Beware lest you Kill your faithful Ministers before you are aware: Heart-breaking Temptations multiplyed upon them will do so.*

THE Worthy Minister of *Haverhil*, was Kill'd, in a Descent of the hideous Canibals upon his Neighbourhood.[22] In this *Death*, as well as in the Other, Methinks, I hear the *Mighty Voice* of our Glorious Lord, unto the *Pastors* of His Churches; *Oh! Look into your Hearts and Lives, to see what Share you also have in the Sins of the Times! Oh! Do with your Might what your Hand finds to do; as not knowing When or How you may be taken off! Oh! Do all you can to make my People Mind what I Speak unto them, in the Things which I do among them!*

AND, O BOSTON, The *Wormwood and the Gall* of thy **Last Winter** must be remembred with thee. I am Sure, with **Thee** it must be so. A Winter wherein One *Dark Month* carried off more than One Hundred and Ten of our Inhabitants.[23] The *Voice* of it!—*Behold, I have made thee Sick in Smiting thee! Oh! Sin no more, Lest!—*

SURELY then, it the *Fourth* Place; The *Disappointments of Important Expeditions*, which in this *Long War* have humbled us, cannot but have in them a *Voice* of the Glorious GOD; A *Voice* that should *Strike us into the Dust* before Him.

I will make all the Haste I can, to See whether no *Comfortable Things* have occurr'd for our Observation. But I would ask, that you would not be out of Patience, till I have gone thro' my Enumeration, of *Afflictive* Things, yet such as have been, and should be, very *Instructive* Ones.

I must remind you; That we have made many *Salleyes* into the *Wilderness* after the Enemy, with Numerous and Courageous *Forces*, and well-Equipped Ones. And we have sometimes made our *Visits* to the *Head-Quarters* of the Enemy, big with Hopes to do something upon them there. More than *Ten Times*, have our Forces returned from their Weary Marches, without Obtaining the Ends that were aimed at. Ask not for the Full Relation of such *Expeditions*. To what Purpose, the Full Relation?—I have told you, *We went out, and we came home.*—That's the *Full Relation!*—Indeed *Much Good* was done, when there was *Nothing* done. We found the Advantage of having a *Terrified Enemy.* But still we were *Disappointed* of our Expectations. . . .

IT would be a Sad Thing, if any *Persons in Stations*, have taken Advantages from the Distresses of the Country by the *Long War*, in Unrighteous, Ungenerous, Indirect Wayes to Propose the *Enriching of themselves* on the *Miseries of their Country.* I wish that *Persons in Stations* would Examine themselves, what *Base Things* may have been done this Way, that are to be Repented of. I wish, they would now hear the *Mighty Voice of GOD* unto them, *Repent, Ye Sordid and Cruel Men, Repent of your Vile inhumanity; Lest you and yours find Sad Reserves of Sorrow for you!*

BUT, *Fifthly.* The *Case* of our *Captives*, cannot be Passed over; There is a *Voice* in their *Case*; A *Mighty Voice* of our GOD; and a very *Speaking One!*

THE Incredible *Miseries* undergone by our *Captives*; What *Labour*, and What *Hunger*, and What *Cold*, they have endured! How *Cruelly* they have been used! How *Cruelly* they have been Scourged! With what *Cruelties*, the joynts of their Fingers have been bitten off! In what insupportable *Terrors of Death*, sometimes their fierce Masters, of the true *Tygre-breed* have held them! The Hideous

Executions, with which the *Incarnate Devils* have gratified their Diabolical Rage, upon some of the Miserable Captives: Roasting them alive at Lingring Fires; Cutting and Slashing their Flesh, and Pouring hot Embers there-upon: With Slow Tortures, Putting an End unto their Lives, and with intolerable, and inconceivable Torments! There has been that *Voice* of the Glorious GOD in these things unto us all; *Oh! Be Thankful for the Comforts which you Enjoy in your Houses full of Good Things, with all your Friends about you!* But at the same Time, there has been this *Mighty Voice* of GOD unto them, who continue *Captives* to their *Lusts*, and will *Go on still in their Trespasses:—What must you Look for, O Impenitent Sinners, what must you Look for, if you Dy in your Sins, and be delivered over into the Hands of those Tormentors, which are in the tremendous Place of Torments waiting for you!*

O think of it; That some *English* Children, Yea, *Children of the Covenant*, and Children of Excellent Ministers; are now *Indianizing* in the remote and wretched Wigwams of the *Wilderness!* To think of them, That we should have still some Scores of our Men, Enchanted and Enslaved, in the Idolatries of Rome, and so held in Chains of Darkness by the Frauds, and Cheats, and Chicaneries of the French Priests, and such innumerable Circumventions, that an *Hopeless Grave-Stone* seems to be laid upon them!—Tis Lamentable. I am Sure, There is this *Voice* of our GOD unto us, in their Condition; *Oh! Be thankful for the Protestant Religion; the Precious Liberties and Instructions of your Holy Religion: Should you become a French Province, how forlorn, how rueful would be your Condition!* But is there not herein also a *Mighty Voice* of our GOD, calling upon us, to take more Pains, that we may every where be well Enlightened in the *Religion* of our Saviour; More Pains, that our *Children*, and all our *People* may be Supplyed from the *Tower of David*, with the Armour of Christianity, to defend them from the *Popish* Abominations? This *Voice* of our GOD, I am certain is very Plain unto us; *Oh! Live up to the Rules of My Holy Religion, and hold not the Truths of it in Unrighteousness, Lest I Leave you to be Entangled in strong Delusions.*

HOWEVER, At several times we have seen some Scores of our *Captives* delivered. I hope, the *Ransomed Captives*, hear the *Voice* of the Glorious GOD unto Themselves; That *Voice; O Give Thanks unto the Lord, for He is Good; for His Mercy Endureth for ever, Let the Redeemed of the Lord say so, Whom He hath Redeemed from the Hand of the Enemy!* That *Voice, O Don't remain in the Bondage to the Powers of Darkness, now thou art Redeemed from the Hand of the Enemy; Become the Servants of the Redeemer, who has Loosed thy Bonds!* That *Voice; Oh! Sin no more, Lest a worse thing do come unto thee!*

BUT if these *Redeemed* Ones, would make true and fair Collections, of their *Experiences*, t'would be a Good Work. How Strangely they have been Preserved, how Strangely they have been Supported, how Strangely they have been *Out-lived* many *Deaths*; The *Narratives* of these Things, would have in them a *Voice* of GOD unto the World: The *Power* and *Goodness* of our GOD would be Proclaimed therein most Gloriously. . . . GOD *Speaks* to us in this; *Oh! Trust Me: Oh! Love Me; Oh! See what it is to be under My Protection!*

HOW *Favoured?*—When the rich *Store-Ships* bound for *Canada*, and fill'd with Instruments of Death, have been taken by our *Fleets*; and the most Capable and Resolved Persecutors of these Colonies, have been Killed aboard them.

HOW *Favoured?*—When *Privateers* infesting our Coasts, have by Storms, [*Fulfilling thy* Word, *O our God!*] been Shipwreck'd on them. Or some of our Neighbours, Especially from One Helpful Island of our Neighbourhood, have with Sudden and Valiant Exploits, made them repent of their approaching us.

HOW *Favour'd?*—When we not only laid Waste many *French* Settlements, where the *Indians* had been Harboured and Supplyed; but anon their Citadel, with their whole Country, fell into our hands; and that *Jericho*, having been *Compassed Seven Dayes*, fell before us. I Speak *Literally* Enough in that Circumstance!

HOW *Favoured?*—In the Many and Ready Assistences, which our Brethren of the Neighbour Colonies, have Lent unto us. Our GOD *Speaks* this unto us in it, *Be Tender of One another! My Colonies, Love and Live as Brethren. I will have no unbrotherly Emulations among you.*

AND certainly the Assistences that we have given to our Neighbours,—Our Brethren in *Hampshire*, will certainly in all Things do the part of *Our Brethren*.

HOW *Favoured?*—In that altho' the Prodigious *Debts* we have Contracted, One would have thought, must have broke us, yet we find our selves able to discharge these Ponderous *Debts*; Yea, our *Debts* have rather Enriched us, by affording a *Fund* for the *Circulation of Credit*, among us.

HOW *Favoured?*—When in the midst of *Our* Charges, and Losses, and Various Troubles, we have been mov'd and help'd from Above, to Express our Charity for our Friends in the *Caribbee-Islands*, and send some Taste of our Bounty to them in *theirs*. Let not Ignorant Strangers abuse *New-England*, until they Out-do that Poor Country in the Things, that every One must Confess to be Laudable.

IN the mean time, Some Servants of God have had the *Unspeakable Satisfaction* of Expressing and Obtaining Bounties, for *Odd People*, among whom it has been a General Practice and Pleasure, to be Ignorantly and Venemously Railing at them.—*Forgive them; They know not what they do!*

AND how *Favoured?*—When under all the *Creepling Disadvantages* of the Country, We see the *Metropolis* of it, and of the whole English *America*, increase and flourish at such a rate? Yea, we see the ancient *Fable* of the *Phoenix* rising out of its *Ashes*, Moralized and Verified, O BOSTON, in thy rising out of *thine*: Things done for thee, the Report whereof will be thought a *Fable*, by them that have not seen them. . . .

MY Brethren, You hear the *Voice* of your Glorious GOD, even His *Mighty Voice*, in the Changes of His Providence that have Passed over you. A *Voice* that speaks this; *Ah! My Poor People; How shall I give thee up: As yet, I cannot do it; I will not do it! Tho' I chasten thee sore, thou shalt not yet be given over to Death!*

PIETISM AND WORLD MISSIONS

otton Mather's reformism was shaped by his emphasis on Pietism—
an emerging religious and social movement in the late seventeenth
century that was less concerned with formal assent to doctrine
than with moral reform, pastoral work, practical education, social
justice, and of course Protestant missions to teach the gospel among the "heathen."[1] Whether Mather was most informed by English models or by notable
Pietist works of such German Lutherans as Johann Arndt's *De Vero Christianismo* (1605–10, 1708), Jakob Spener's *Pia Desiderata* (1676), or the many Pietist
publications of August Hermann Francke is subject to debate. And yet, Mather
was full of praise for Francke, president of the newly founded Lutheran University of Halle (Germany), and showered him with copies of his own works and
some pieces of gold in support of Francke's famous orphanage and Pietist missions in southeastern India.[2] For Mather and his peers, the world had become a
vineyard in which to tend to education, proselytizing, and charitable works.[3]

This brave new world taught Mather that sectarian dogma and narrow de-
nominational interests stood in the way of interdenominational missions and
worldwide support of what, in time, would become the Protestant Internatio-
nale, a movement committed to spreading the gospel and social reform.[4] His
attention to ecumenical relations with other Protestant denominations can be
found in numerous works, especially in his *Nuncia Bona e Terra Longinqua*

(1715), *Menachem* (1716), *The Stone Cut out of the Mountain* (1716), *Brethren dwelling together in Unity* (1718), *India Christiana* (1721), and *The Marrow of the Gospel* (1727), among others. As Mather put it in his *Manuductio ad Ministerium,*
better known by its descriptive subtitle, *Directions For A Candidate of the Ministry* (1726), "Let the *Table* of the Lord have no *Rails* about it, that shall hinder
a Godly *Independent,* and *Presbyterian,* and *Episcopalian,* and *Antipedobaptist,*
and *Lutheran* from sitting down together there."[5] The basis of this union was
Mather's "Maxims of Piety," all dogmas of the Christian church condensed into
three essentials: worship God the Father, the Son, and the Holy Spirit; acknowledge Christ as the redeemer of immortal souls; and follow the golden rule to do
unto others as you would have them do unto yourself. These "Grand Maxims
of Piety," Mather insisted, must be accompanied by freedom of religion and separation of church and state. The mature Mather insisted on the "free *Indulgence of Civil Rights in the State,* unto all that approve themselves Faithful
Subjects and Honest *Neighbours,* and such Inoffensive Livers, that *Humane Society* cannot complain of Disturbances from them."[6] Although he still was not
accommodating to all non-reformed religions, Mather's latitude was a far cry
from the strictures of the Cambridge Platform of Faith (1649) and the stern sec-
tarianism of the Bay Colony's architects. His grandfathers, whose names Cotton Mather united in himself, would have turned over in their graves.

It is fair to argue that during the last two decades of his life, Pietism, especially when coupled with his all-consuming millennialist fervor, became the
mainspring of Mather's social and religious activism. Gesturing and signaling
toward Christ's Second Coming involved no passive waiting, even for premillen-
nialists like Mather. Quite the contrary. When he learned of the Lutheran missions and their success among the Tamils in southeastern India, he could almost
hear the prophet Joel blow his silver trumpet: "Blow ye the trumpet in Zion,
and sound an alarm in my holy mountain: let all the inhabitants of the land
tremble: for the day of the Lord commeth, for it is nigh at hand" (Joel 2:1).

Mather's exuberance seemed boundless. He celebrated the "Propagation [of]
our Holy RELIGION, in the EASTERN as well as the WESTERN, **Indies**," in
his discourse *India Christiana* (1721). He proudly included an epistolary extract

(1717) of Bartholomew Ziegenbalg (1682–1719), a pioneering Lutheran missionary in Tanquebar (southeastern India), and added his own glowing response: "You, O *Malabarian* Missionaries . . . *You have excelled them all.*" Mather drank deeply at the fountain of Ziegenbalg's missionary spirit, all the more so because they were "*Evangelizing* of the World" with Mather's own three "*Pure Maxims* of the *Everlasting Gospel.*" Like him, they were preaching to all nations "the *Weightier Matters* of the Gospel" and were triumphing over sectarian disputes by eliminating "those *Lesser Matters*" of doctrines that were adiaphora, indifferent to the "*Articles of Practical Godliness.*" To Mather, this surprising union of heart and soul reaching across the wide Atlantic and Pacific bordered on a miracle; it confirmed for him that "the *Twelve Hundred & Sixty* Years of *Antichrist* are Expired" and the prophetic spirit of piety was about to be poured out on all flesh the world over, as Joel had foretold. We are "*Joyned in our Minds, tho' parted by the Waters; One Soul, tho' not One Soyl, Uniting of us,*" Mather closed his letter to Ziegenbalg, on December 31, 1717. By the time his missive arrived in India a year later, via its circuitous route of London and Halle, Ziegenbalg, barely thirty-six, was dead. It took more than two years for an answer to arrive, in which John Ernest Gründler, Ziegenbalg's fellow missionary in Tranquebar, informed him that his esteemed colleague had passed away early in 1719. Still, Gründler included a printed copy of Ziegenbalg's translation of the New Testament in the Tamil language and printed in its own Tamil typeface on which Ziegenbalg had labored for many years. No doubt, Ziegenbalg would have appreciated his American correspondent's fervor, yet probably for reasons other than Mather indulged. Lutherans were no millenarians—but all this would have been unimportant anyway.

MANUDUCTIO AD MINISTERIUM (1726)[7]

[MAXIMS OF PIETY]

§. 18. Too Weighty are the Words of the pious *Hen. Will. Ludolf,* to be left untranscribed, when I am treating you, with the Things which I am desirous to have greatly considered with you.[8] "It [is] a great unhappiness, that the greatest part of the Clergy of all Communions, do not perceive, that GOD is upon His

Way to break down all the false Draughts and Schemes, which the Antichristian Spirit of *Sectarism* hath contrived instead of *Substantial Christianity*, which is, *The Restoring of the Image of GOD in the New Creature,* or, *The Kingdom and Life of GOD within us.*"[9] I press you to employ the *deepest Meditation* of this Important Matter. When the Lord GOD Omnipotent comes to *shake not the Earth only, but also Heaven,* it is, That those *Things that cannot be shaken may remain.*[10] What are those *Things that cannot be shaken?* But those MAX-IMS of the *Everlasting Gospel,* wherein all *Good* and *Wise* Men are *United,* and all Men become *Good* and *Wise,* when they come into that *Union* with them: The MAXIMS, which the more they are *studied,* and the *Wiser,* and the *Better,* they are who study them, the more they will be approved of: The MAXIMS which are directly calculated for the Grand Intentions of, *Glory to GOD in the Highest,* and *Peace on Earth from a Good Will in Men towards one another* {Luke 2:14}. 'Tis even the *First-born* of my Wishes for you, That you may be one of those *Angels,* that shall *fly through the midst of Heaven* {Rev. 8:13}, with this *Everlasting Gospel,* to *preach* it unto them who *dwell on the Earth,* and move all the People of GOD, tho' of *different Perswasions* in the *lesser Points,* to embrace one another upon the *Generous Maxims* of it, and keep *lesser Points* in a due *Subordination* unto the *Superiour Maxims,* and manage their *Differences* upon those *lesser Points* with another Spirit, than what the *Disputers of this World* in the several *Sects* of Christians keep commonly *Cutting* One another withal.[11]

To assist you in the Discovering and Determining of these Everlasting MAX-IMS, I will not meerly refer you to the Sentiments of a Judicious *Davenant,* in his, *Adhortatio ad Fraternam Communionem inter Evangelicas Ecclesias,*[12] or those of a Sharpsighted *Baxter,* who was a *Pen in the Hand of GOD,* when he wrote his *Catholic Unity,* and, *The True and Only Way of Concord:*[13] Much less, will I prosecute the Proposal of our celebrated *Usher,* "That if at this Day we take a Survey of the *several Professions of Christianity,* that have any large Spread in any Part of the World, and should put by the Points wherein they differ from One another, and gather into One Body the rest of the Articles, wherein they all *generally Agree;* we should find, That in those *Propositions,* which without Controversy are so *Universally received in the whole Christian World,* so much *Truth* is contained, as, being joined with *Holy Obedience,* may be sufficient to bring a Man unto Everlasting Salvation. Neither have we Cause to doubt, but that as many as do *Walk according to this Rule,* (neither overthrowing that which they have built, by superinducing any *Damnable Heresies;* thereupon, nor otherwise Vitiating their *Holy Faith* with a lewd and *wicked Conversation) Peace shall be upon them.*"[14] I will rather exhibit the MAXIMS in such a Manner, as to make the best Provision, against that *loathsome* thing, A *Lifeless Religion;* whereof an *Irreligious Life,* will be the Natural Consequence. In short, I may as with a *Burning Glass,* [Oh! That with an *Irresistible Heat* from Heaven upon you!] Contract into a little Room, *the Sum of the Matter,* and the PIETY, which will be found a *Sure Foundation* for an UNION among all Parties of true CHRISTIANS, however they may be Denominated or Distinguished. As our SAVIOUR, whom His FATHER *heareth always,* has prayed, for His People, that they *all may be ONE,* so, it is impossible, that all the Genuine People of GOD should not *Unite* with one another in much greater Things, than those in which it is possible for them to *Dissent* from one another. Such Things are those *Graviora Evangelii,*[15] which to *cut short the Work in Righteousness,* I shall in these Three MAXIMS compendiously set before you.

"I. The ONE most High GOD, who is the FATHER, and the SON, and the Holy SPIRIT, must be my GOD: And I must make it the *main Intention* of my Life to *Serve* and *Please* Him, in all Holy *Obedience* and *Submission* to Him, Remembring that His Eye is always upon me; and be afraid of *every Thing,* which His *Light* in my Soul shall condemn as an *Evil Thing.*

"II. A Glorious CHRIST who is the Eternal SON of GOD, Incarnate and Enthroned in the Blessed JESUS, is the REDEEMER, on whose great *Sacrifice* I must Rely for my *Reconciliation* to GOD, looking to Him, at the same time, that I may live unto GOD by Him *Living in me:* And under His Conduct I am now to expect a Blessedness in a *Future State,* for my *Immortal Soul;* to which He will restore my *Body,* when He shall come to *Judge the World.*

"III. Out of Respect unto GOD and His CHRIST, I must heartily *Love my Neighbour,* and forever do unto *Other Men,* as I must own it Reasonable for them to do unto *myself.*"

The *Foundation of GOD* is in these *Holy Mountains.* While these Glorious MAXIMS are [as, why should they not be? I am sure much more Questionable Ones, are daily required for to be] subscrib'd unto, it is to be wished, that these *Two* [I can scarce call them, *Two more*] may in Subserviency to the *First Three,* be also brought into the Subscription.

"I adhere to the Sacred SCRIPTURES, as the *sufficient Rule,* for *Belief,* and *Worship,* and *Manners,* among the People of GOD, and I would maintain a *Brotherly Fellowship* with all Good Men, in the Things wherein I apprehend them to follow these *Divine Directions.*

And,

"I Declare for the just Liberties of *Mankind,* and of our Nations: And for a Christian Encouragement in the *Church* for all that observe the Grand

MAXIMS of PIETY, accompanied with a free *Indulgence* of *Civil Rights* in the *State*, unto all that approve themselves Faithful *Subjects* and Honest *Neighbours*, and such Inoffensive Livers, that *Humane Society* cannot complain of Disturbances from them."

I will not now suppose a *Quinquarticular Controversy*,[16] but rather propose a *Ternarticular Period of all Controversies*.[17] And the very first Thing, that I offer upon it, is, That in these MAXIMS, *of Godliness*, which are all *without Controversy*, you behold all *Controversies* of Religion, as coming to an Amicable and a Comfortable Period. My Advice to you, is; That when you make some Figure in the Field of the *Church-Militant*, you be drawn as little as may be, into an *Eristic Writings*;[18] wherein you shall be surprised unawares into the Errors of *Passion*, and into the *Follies* of taking Pains to convince a few Readers that you have more *Wit* than your Antagonist. Every Man who pulls at the *Polemic Saw*, and manages any *Controversy* in Religion, always pretends a *Zeal* to uphold in the *Issue* of the Disputation, some certain Point of *Practical* PIETY, which is in these Indisputable MAXIMS declared for. If it were not from a *zealous Concern* which the Contenders have that the *Practice of Piety*, may not suffer in such a Point, they profess, that they would not *contend so earnestly for the Faith*. If they can't sincerely make this Profession, they are but *Litigious*, and *Vexatious*, and the *Gladiators* are to be hiss'd off the *Theatre*, by all that wish well to Christianity. Now, how commonly are *both Parties* well agreed, in the Point of PIETY, which the One says, can't be preserved but upon *his Positions*; and the other says, can't be preserved if *his* be denied? Be sure, All the *Truly Pious* are so! But, if *both Parties* are agreed for that PIETY, which is the Main, and the Scope of all, how much Good may you do, if you can so Syringe the *Odoriferous Water* of the confessed MAXIMS upon them, that the *Quarrelling Hives* in the Loss of their Distinction may give over their Quarrels, and the Children of *Jacob* not *fall out by the Way*, or be so angry about the Way, *seeing they are Brethren*? Or, if the *Brethren* will yet *fall out*, and the *Controversies* must *go on*, and you are called forth to bear a Part in them, yet, *My Son*, continue to play these *Engines*, for the extinguishing of the *Fires*; Govern your *Mind*, and your *Pen*, by the MAXIMS of PIETY; perswade others what you can to do so too; and carry not on any but the *Wars of the Lamb* in your Contestations. What I could most of all wish for is, That for your *Defence* of the *Truth*, which is always for PIETY, you do what you have to do, mostly in that *Positive Way*, of asserting, and evincing, and advancing the PIETY, which the *Truth* you would have to be defended, is to animate. *Conscience* will quickly come in, with a Testimony on the behalf of that PIETY; and the Truth which appears necessary to support that PIETY, will easily be taken in, and not easily parted with. This is for the most part better than the *Elenctic Way*[19] of sheltering the Truth from the Assaults which they that *corrupt the Earth* would make upon it: Instead of *Swords*, it is to employ *Pruning-Hooks*; and the State and Work of *Paradise* is a little emulated and anticipated.

But, if the *Elenctic Way* become necessary to be taken, and if you must *go down into the Battel*, and smite the Enemies in the *Valley of Salt*, I again, and again say, *Take heed unto your Spirit:* Let the Designs of PIETY Regulate your whole Proceeding. Furnish no new Matter for the old Complaint of,—*Sibi ferales plerique Christiani;*[20] and add nothing to the Instances of such Outrages, as the *Jesuites* have with Derision censured in the *Controversial Writings* of the mutual Firings between the *Lutherans* and the *Calvinists*.

Lutherans, and *Calvinists!*—Inasmuch as I have thus unawares mentioned These, I will upon these make the *Experiment*, [whether with any better Success, than my dear *Pitiscus*[21] did, I know not!] how far a *Syncretism* of PIETY will *Unite* the People of GOD, or *Abate* their *Cursed Anger*, and *Cruel Wrath* against One another in pursuing of *Religious Controversies*. The Sagacious Baron *Puffendorf*,[22] while he despairs not of breaking down the *Partition Wall* between those two mighty Parties of *Protestants*, in other Parts of it, yet it appears unto him little short of Desperate, when the Sublime and Obscure Doctrines of *Predestination* (wherein *Luther* and *Calvin* themselves, were better agreed than their Followers,) come to be considered. However, even here also at last he takes Courage, and says, *If ever there is to be a Better Condition of Mankind, and an Happier State of the World, it is not to be Expected, but from a serious and universal Practice of Christian PIETY.* Let us then with a little Patience hear both Parties declare themselves.

Say, Master *Lutheran*, What is the PIETY, for the maintaining whereof you so eagerly advance your *Principles?* His Answer is; "I would not have the most *Holy* and *Sin-hating* Lord, Reproached as the *Impeller* of the *Sin* whereof he is the *Revenger*. I would not have our *Merciful* Father blasphemed, as dealing *after an Illusory Manner* with Men, when He invites them to His *Mercy*. I would not have any among the fallen Race of the *First Adam*, shut out from the just Hopes of *Life* in the *Death* of the *Second Adam*. I would not have *Impenitent Unbelievers* cast upon GOD the *Blame* of their *Impenitency*; but the Wicked lay wholly *on themselves* the Fault of their own Destruction. I would have Men *Work about their own Salvation*, with as much Diligence and Vigilance, as if all turned upon their own *Will* and *Care* whether they shall be Saved or no." The pious *Calvinist* hears all this with Pleasure; and can say, *My Brother, In all these Things my Heart is with you.*

But now, Master *Calvinist*, it is your Turn. Say, What is the PIETY, for the maintaining whereof you so eagerly Prefer your *Principles?* His Answer is; "I would have our GOD, forever adored, as the *Original* of all the *Good*, that we *Have*, or that we *Do*. If Men arrive to any Good *Spiritual* as well as *Temporal*, I would have our GOD praised for it; and I would have His *Favours* confessed as most *Unmerited* by us in all our *Praises*. I would not admit the least Insinuation, as if the *King Eternal*, who is the *Only Wise GOD*, had not an Infallible *Fore-knowledge* from all Eternity of whatever comes to pass in Time. I would have all that come unto *Everlasting Life*, to admire the *Everlasting Love* of GOD unto them; and with Endless Admiration own, *That their SAVIOUR has done more for them, than for others.* I would have Men look up to GOD, with ardent *Prayers* for His Gracious, and Enlightening, and Sanctifying Influences, and *Pray* unto Him as the *GOD of all Grace*, and the GOD who *gives Repentance*, and Re-member that *Faith* is the *Gift of GOD*. I would have Man to be very Humble, and humbly to Annihilate himself before the Glorious GOD, *with whom there is terrible Majesty.*" The pious *Lutheran* hears all this with Delight; and can say, *My Brother, My Heart cannot but concur with you, in such Things as these.*

At the same time, they both find that the several *Schemes*, with which they would have this PIETY served, are encumbered with *Insuperable Difficulties;* and the *Lutheran* may have retorted upon him those very *Difficulties* which he thinks he sees the *Calvinist* overwhelmed withal. The old Law, *Qui non vetat cum potest Jubet*,[23] Encumbers *Arminius* with as *hard Consequences* as he charges on *Gomarus*.[24] *Maimonides* will tell you, how much the *Jewish* World, and *Cicero* how much the *Pagan* has been divided, in their Opinions, *De Fato*.[25] Among the *Papists*, how do the *Dominicans*, and after these, the *Jansenists*, and their Opposites, keep *in the dark, buffeting* one another upon them? So that after all, Tis PIETY that must bring all to rights: and *Melancthons* Resolution; *Officium agamus, et Disputationes de Predestinatione seponamus*.[26]

The Experiment may be made on many other Doctrines, [Among which, I pray take notice, you'l never find me mentioning the *Damnable Heresies*, of the *Arian*, and the *Socinian!*][27] wherein they that have the true *Fear* of GOD, and *Love* of CHRIST, may have their *Differing Sentiments;—Incolumi semper Amicitia*.[28]

Instead of my going on to do That, I rather pass now to say, That I would have you lay aside all Thoughts, of any *Foundation* for an *Union* among the Profes-sors of Christianity, but what shall be in the *Unity of Spirit*; or that Work of the Holy SPIRIT on the Hearts of Men, that inclines them to Glorify GOD with an *Obedience* to His Will revealed in His Word, and Glorify CHRIST with a *Dependence* on Him for all their Happiness; and *Love their Neighbour as them-*

selves. Other Foundation can no Man lay! All Attempts to build the *Tower of Zion* on any other Foundation, will come to nothing; You'l prosper no better in them, than they who go to build a *Tower of Babel.* But then, Let ALL that are by Visible PIETY qualified for it, find a due and a kind Reception with you. Let your *Feet stand in a large Place,* and, *Add unto your Faith, Godliness, and Brotherly-kindness, and unto your Brotherly-kindness, Charity:* {2 Pet. 1:7} And, Pay the Regards of *Brethren in CHRIST,* unto all those, who by owning and living the Everlasting MAXIMS of PIETY, may claim what the true Citizen of *Zion* will yield unto *them that Fear the Lord.* Allow to, yea, Challenge for, this People, the *Rights* which belong unto them, and the *Liberties* with which the SON of GOD has *made them free.* The People, *who Worship GOD in the Spirit,* and *who Rejoyce in CHRIST JESUS,* and who *have no Confidence in the Flesh,* or, value not themselves upon a *Religion* which is nothing but *Flesh,* and exteriour; THESE are the true *People of GOD:* The PEOPLE, which have the *Promise* in the Covenant of GOD pertaining to them; and whereto the *Kindnesses,* or the *Injuries* that are done, are done unto their Glorious *Head,* in the Heavens. Be not such a *Donatist,*[29] as to dream, that the *People of GOD* are no where to be found, but in *One Party,* which you have your greatest Esteem for. But, look for them, as to be found under various *Forms;* and let your Judgment, how it fares *Well* or *Ill* with the *People of God* in the World, fetch its Measures not from the *Good* or *Bad* Circumstances of *One Party* only, but from the Prevailing or the Suppressing of true PIETY, and what has a Tendency to That, wherever it is to be met withal.

Challenge for this *People,* a Power to *Associate,* or form *Assemblies* for the Worship of GOD our SAVIOUR, according to the *Directions* which they apprehend his Gospel has given them. Challenge for the *Societies* of this People, the Power to elect their own *Pastors;* which was one of the *Last Things* lost in the Robberies which the *Man of Sin* committed on the *Temple* of GOD. Challenge for these *particular Churches,* the Rights of Sacred *Corporations,* that have all the Needful Power of *Self-Preservation,* and *Self-Reformation:* Yet obliged in Things of *common Concern,* so far to act in Conjunction with other Churches *Walking in the Faith and Order of the Gospel,* as to Consult them, and be Directed and Restrained by them, on just Occasions.

For *Communion* in these Churches, and *Admission* to all the Priviledges and Advantages of the *Evangelical Church-State,* I would have you insist upon it, That no *Terms* be imposed, but such *Necessary Things,* as Heaven will require of all, who shall *Ascend into the Hill of the Lord, and stand in His Holy Place* {Ps. 24:3}. Be sure to stand by that *Golden Rule, Receive ye one another, as CHRIST has received us unto the Glory of GOD* {Rom. 15:7}; That is to say, Those of whom it is our Duty to *Judge*, that our SAVIOUR will *Receive them to His Glory* in the Heavenly World, we ought now to *Receive* unto all the Enjoyments of our *Christian Fellowship*: And let the *Table* of the Lord have no *Rails* about it, that shall hinder a Godly *Independent*, and *Presbyterian*, and *Episcopalian*, and *Antipedobaptist*, and *Lutheran* from sitting down together there. *Corinthian Brass*[30] would not be so bright a *Composition*, as the People of GOD in such a *Coalition*, feasting together on His *Holy Mountain*. I wish, they do not see the Fate of *Corinth*, to compel them to it!—Tho' in the Church that I serve, I have seen the grateful Spectacle!— This I must say; A *Church* that shall banish the *Children of GOD* from His *Holy Table*, and shall exclude from its *Communion* those *that shall be Saved*, meerly for such Things as are Consistent with the Maxims of PIETY, does not exhibit, *The Kingdom of GOD*, unto the World, as a *Church* ought to do. Churches that will keep up *Instruments of Separation*, which will keep out those that have the Evident *Marks* and *Claims* of them that are *One with CHRIST* upon them, are in Reality but *Combinations* of Men, who under Pretence of *Religion*, are pursuing some *Carnal Interests*. Their *Diana* is very *Visible!*[31] Tis a Complicated *Profanity* and *Hypocrisy*, that these *Churches* are to stand indicted for. It is to be lamented, That more *Churches* than *One* have the Guilt of a very sinful *Schism* to be charged upon them, for their Chasing from their *Communion*, and the annexed *Encouragements* and *Emoluments*, many of the *Righteous Nation*, which have the *Gates of Heaven* standing *open* for them: and yet such is the *Mystery of Iniquity* {2 Thess. 2:7}, that at the same time they make Outcries of *Schism*, against the Consciencious People, for keeping out, while they violently shut the Doors upon them. Yea, There has been *One Church* [Tho' *I have never heard of but One!*] which has punished and even destroyed Multitudes of Godly Men, for not Conforming to things which the *Imposers* themselves have confessed *Indifferent*.

I hope, I have said enough, to disengage you from all *Schismatical Combinations*, and Intimate the *Catholic Spirit*, which I would have to be exercised, in the whole Progress of your Ministry. *Catholicism without Popery*, is the Title of an Essay, which therefore I particularly commend unto a Perusal with you.[32]

Finally. As it must be the Grand Aim of your Ministry, to propagate the PIETY of the *Everlasting Gospel*; And tho' vain Men may boast what they will of this or that being the *Best constituted Church in the World*, and celebrate their own *Admirable Constitution*,[33] yet that should be esteemed by you the *Best constituted Church*, in which the PIETY of the Grand *Evangelical Maxims*, is most Animated and Exhibited; and *That the Best Constitution*, which is most calculated for the *Cultivation* of this Indisputable PIETY: So, I would have you go forth to it, under a strong Tincture of this Apprehension, *That a Church which makes the Terms of Communion very different from the Terms of Salvation, and*

excludes from any Means of Salvation, or from any due Expressions of Brotherly-
kindness, those whom it is a Duty to acknowledge as Brethren in CHRIST, is guilty
of an Iniquity, against which all Good Men ought to bear a Testimony.

There are Concurring with you, Hundreds of Thousands of Generous Minds,
in which this Apprehension lies now shut up as an *Aurum Fulminans:*[34] But it
will break forth more and more, *As the Day approaches,* and as Men improve in
Manly Religion, in Explosions that will carry all before it: And the Mean, Little,
Narrow Souls, that know no *Religion,* but that of a *Party,* and their *Secular In-*
terest, will become deserted Objects for the *Disdain* and *Pity,* of them who have
taken the *Way that is above them.* I hope, You will do all you can, to *strengthen*
your Brethren, as GOD shall give you, [*And may He give you!*] Opportunities. . . .

INDIA CHRISTIANA (1721)

III. UNIO FIDELIUM.[35] COMMUNICATIONS BETWEEN
THE WESTERN AND EASTERN INDIA

¶ Unto many of the Faithful, the Matters now to be related, will be *Good News*
from a far Country. It will be a pleasure unto them who are *Waiting for the King-*
dom of GOD, when they see some opening of it in the *Eastern* as well as the
Western INDIES. It will be an Addition unto the pleasure, to see the *Harmony*
which True, Right, Genuine PIETY will produce, in Persons that are in many
Sentiments as well as *Regions,* distant from one another. And if that Article of
our Creed, *The Communion of Saints,* be illustrated in this Correspondence,
Of *this* also we will say, *How Good and how pleasant is it?* {Ps. 133:1}

In the Latter End of the Year, 1714. the Illustrious Dr. *Franckius,* did me the
Honour of writing to me, from *Hall* in the Lower *Saxony,* a very large Letter,
which has been since Translated and Published (by that *Man of an Excellent*
Spirit, Mr. Boehm) in *London.*[36] And from that Letter, I will now transcribe one
Historical passage, which will Introduce those that are now going to be divulged.

"I can't but Entertain you on this occasion with another Charitable work, but
of a very Singular Nature, and Extending it self as far as the Coast of *Coroman-*
del in the *East-Indies.* In the Year 1705. Two Young Candidates of Divinity, *Bar-*
tholomew Ziegenbalgh, and *Henry Plutscho,* Natives of *Germany,* were sent by
Frederick IV. the present King of *Denmark,* to the *East-Indies,* to attempt the
Conversion of the *Malabar*-Heathens there.[37] They arrived safely at *Tranquebar,*
in the Month of *June,* 1706. and immediately applied themselves to Learn the
Portuguese and *Malabar* Tongues. The Latter of these Languages, tho' exceeding Hard and Intricate, was, within Eight Months time, so far Mastered by

Mr. *Ziegenbalgh*, that he began to Preach to the *Malabar* Heathen in it, and by this Means, to Explain unto them the *Method of Salvation.*

"In Effect, GOD left not their Endeavours without a Blessing: For, soon after, some of these Heathens being wrought upon by the Word of Salvation, did shake off their Pagan Idolatry, and readily came over to Christianity. And this hopeful Beginning proved a New Encouragement unto these Labourers, to go on with the work so happily set on foot, tho' not without Toil and Difficulty. However, after a Little while, they found so many *Lets* and *Impediments* in their way, raised by Heathens & Christians, as seemed to break the very first Efforts tending to the Conversion of the Heathen, to the Church of CHRIST.

"The Pagans were generally possessed with an utter Aversion to the Christian Religion; and this for no other Reason, but because they saw so much Impiety and Profaneness abounding among those that Call themselves by This Name. This was attended with many Consequences. For no sooner did an Heathen Embrace the Christian Faith, but he was for ever banished from all his former Goods and Possessions, and left to the wide World, to shift for himself. However, there were some other Impediments thrown in their way, far more Obstructive to the Propagation of the Gospel, than all what the Heathens could do to Oppose it. Those Impediments were started on the part of the *Christians* themselves, whose Duty it had been to aid and support so laudable an Undertaking.

"But in the midst of these Various obstacles, raised Originally by the Common Enemy of Souls, GOD was pleased to Excite many persons in *Germany*, to favour the Labours of the Missionaries; Especially after they were Convinced, with what Candour and Diligence they endeavoured to manage the work Committed unto their Trust. And truly, Considerable Sums of Money were required, for Settling and improving, the several Branches of this Constitution. It was necessary, that a Church should be built, and Charity-Schools should be set up, and all manner of *Malabarian* and Christian Books transcribed, for the Improvement of the whole Design.

"About the Latter End of the Year, 1708, when the work increased under their hands, Three Persons more, were sent over on the same Errand.—They were supplied with a Printing-Press, a Font of Latin Types, and other Necessaries, at the Expence of the English Nation; the whole being accompanied with a present of Fifty Pounds in Money, for carrying on the better the Design in hand.— And we in *Germany* did what we could, to prepare a Font of *Malabar* Types, in order to Print off, such Books as were thought necessary for the Church and Schools gathered on the Coast of *Coromandel.*[38]—A Printer come from *Leipsick* freely offered himself to go over to the *East-Indies*, to manage the Printing part for the use of the Mission. We readily Embraced this offer, and looked upon it, as a Finger of Providence, thereby to settle this work on a Good and Promising Foundation; since this Person was not only acquainted with the Art of Printing, but had also a sufficient skill in Graving and Casting of the necessary Letters.— Having put themselves on board the *English* Fleet, they pursued their Voyage to India; where they happily landed the *June* Ensuing."

The Methods & the Effects of the Mission, whereof this Great Man has given this brief Account, have been wonderful.

It pleased the Excellent *Ziegenbalgh* to address his Letters unto a Mean *American:* who happened (I scarce know, how) to be known unto him, under an Undeserved Character;[39] Expressing his Desires of an Epistolary Correspondence; and that he might have our Sentiments upon the ways of advancing the Kingdom of GOD.

In answer to his Desires, there went from New England, the following Letter to him. . . .

TO THE REVEREND . . . MR. BARTHOLOMEW ZIEGENBALGH

To the Reverend,
and every where known and honour'd
Minister of the Gospel,
Mr. Bartholomew Ziegenbalgh,
Pastor of the Indian Church,
And an Indefatigable Missionary, and most
faithful and famous Servant of CHRIST,
among the *Malabarians* in the *East Indies;*
Much Happiness in the Lord.

That *Evangelical* and indeed *Angelical* work, in which (*Reverend* Sirs, You and your Colleagues) We with a Joyful & Grateful Mind, see you Engaged with such a toylsome Labour; 'Tis truly, the most Noble of all that are or ever can be undertaken among the Children of Men. Than this most *Holy Work*, there can be Invented, Nothing more Heavenly, Nothing more Gracious, Nothing more Agreeable & Subservient unto the First and Main End, and Chief Good, of Men; There can be nothing more Profitable to Mankind; or more worthy of Emulation even among the very *Angels* of GOD.

It is a GOD full of Mercy, for ever darting out the Beams of His Love to Mankind, who has first Excited you, and thereupon Assisted you, for the *Propagation* of His *Religion*; which wherever it is Preach'd & own'd, it fetches out of the Grave, a World buried in its truly Miserable Corruption and Perdition, and Restores it unto that Life Eternal, which we have lost by the Apostasy of our First Parents, and our own.

'Tis the *Religion* which brings the chosen of GOD into the Blessedness unto which He has Chosen them; and opens & sets up the Kingdom of GOD among the Nations. 'Tis the *Religion* that brings in Faithful Subjects and Souldiers for the Lord of Hosts, and builds up *Living Tempels* for GOD, which are far more precious than any that are but Artificial and Inanimate. This *Religion* it is, that Invites and fetches down *Heaven* to the *Earth*, and prepares the Inhabitants of the *Earth* to be received into the most Blessed Mansions of *Heaven*.

A Work, How Illustrious! How Celestial! How Sublime! Oh! Thrice and four times Happy they, who are Ministers of GOD in such a Work! Happy, tho' never so much harass'd with Labours, and Watchings, and Perpetual Troubles! *Happy beyond all Expression, did they but know their own Happiness!*

This Ministry, Suppose it a Load which even the *Backs of Angels* may tremble at; yet it is a work, which the *Wings of Angels* would be with the highest Flights and Joys applied unto: Yea, and a work, in which the Ministers who Execute the Pleasure & Command of GOD, with Essays to have *His Kingdom ruling over all*; These not only are a sort of Competitors with the *Angels*, but also in these Essays Enjoy them for their Companions and Coadjutors.

Great and Grievous and never enough to be bewailed, has been the Scandal given in the Churches of the Reformation; in that so very little, yea, next to nothing, has been done in them, for the Propagation of a *Faith*, which breathes nothing but the most unexceptionable Wisdom and Goodness; and by which the Kingdom of GOD comes down into a World, which Satan Reigning every where in it, Possesses and Oppresses, with how direful Chains of his upon it! While at the same time, the Church of *Rome*, strives with an Unwearied and Extravagant Labour, to Propagate the Idolatry and Superstition of *Antichrist*, and advance the Empire of Satan. And the Missionaries and Brokers of that Harlot, are indeed more than can be numbred. The Zeal of those Panders, how Ardent is it! Their Attempts, how never tired! Their Travels how very tedious! And with what an Ardour are they Ambitious of a *Crown*, which appears to them a True Martyrdom, & for the Truth.

But Blessed be the Name of our GOD, in that He hath inclined the Minds of some Eminent Persons, to take away such a Scandal, and instigated them to roll off this Reproach from us. And among these, if any *have done vertuously,* You, O *Malabarian* Missionaries, (which I would Speak, not for the Flattering of you, but as Admiring the Divine Grace which has assisted you!) *You have excelled them all.*

The Report of your Mission and of your Diligence, hath reached from the Eastern even to the Western *Indies.* And what the Grace of Heaven has helped you to do, towards the producing of a Christian People among the *Indians,* is heard among the *American* Christians, with the highest Praises offered up to GOD on the occasion, and *as cool waters to our Thirsty Souls is the Good News from a far Country* {Prov. 25:25}.

Being Invited by your most Courteous and Christian Letters to me, and being a most hearty well-wisher to your Enterprizes for the Enlargement of the Church, I am willing to declare, in a few words, and with the Modesty which becomes me, what my Apprehensions are concerning the *Glorious* and *Weighty* Affair which you have upon your hands.

And in the *First* Place, this is the very *First-born* of my Wishes; nor is there any thing that I more wish, or have more Earnest desires for, than this: That all the Servants of GOD, who *Do and Endure* many Things for the *Evangelizing* of the World may Exhibit unto the whole World the *Pure Maxims* of the *Everlasting Gospel,* and would Preach unto the Nations, the *Weightier Matters* of the Gospel, and the *Wheat* well cleansed from the *Chaff,* and from those *Lesser Matters,* whereabout Good Men, may and often do, carry on their Disputations.

'Tis most certain, That the *Christian Religion* is no other than the Doctrine of Living to GOD by CHRIST; and is a *Practical Thing* rather than a meer *Theory;* the Intention whereof is, to animate a Real, Solid, Vital PIETY, and Call forth such as ly *dead* in their Sins, unto a *Godly,* & a *Sober,* & a *Righteous* Life.

'Tis most certain, That in the *Christian Religion,* which is indeed a Doctrine of PIETY, there are sundry Practical Articles, in which all the *Children of GOD* are United; and they who seriously and sincerely Coalesce in this *Union* are to be reckoned among the *Children of GOD.*

It is very certain, That these few Articles of *Practical Piety,* being first offered and well Received, the *Mind* thus *Healed,* will now make a Righter and Fuller Judgment, of those *Lesser Matters,* upon which Good Men have many, mischievous and marvellous Controversies. *The love of GOD will Enlighten the Mind that has it;* And indeed they that manage Controversies, do on both sides make a profession of Zeal to maintain these *Articles of Practical Godliness.*

This therefore is the One Thing, which I earnestly Request of you; That you first of all propound unto the Nations among whom you *abound in the work of the Lord,* these *Articles of the First Magnitude,* wherein *True Christianity* does Firstly and Chiefly consist.

In the *First Place;* The One GOD, who Subsisteth in *Three Persons,* the *Father,* and the *Son,* and the *Holy Spirit;* and who in the Beginning did *Create* the World; is to be Embraced and Adored for OUR GOD. It must be the *Principal Aim* of our Life, in all things to yield *Obedience* unto Him. And it must be our most hearty Care, to Avoid every Thing which His Light shining in our Soul shall condemn as an Evil Thing.

In the Next Place; The CHRIST, who is the Eternal SON of GOD Incarnate in our Blessed JESUS, is our only *Redeemer;* who Dying for us, has offered a most Acceptable *Sacrifice* to the Divine Justice, on which relying by *Faith* we become Reconciled unto GOD; and under the Conduct of Him who being received up into the Heavens, now Reigns on the Throne of GOD, we are to expect a wonderful and unspeakable Blessedness for our *Immortal Soul,* whereto our Body shall be Re-united in a Glorious *Resurrection,* when He shall *Return* unto us to *Judge the World.*

Lastly; Being filled with the Love of GOD and of CHRIST, we must most Heartily Love our *Neighbours;* and for ever go by that Golden Rule, *Whatsoever you would have Men do unto you, do you even the same unto them* {Math. 7:12}.

THIS is that PURE CHRISTIANITY, which when it shall be by the Trumpets of GOD purely and plainly Preached unto the Nations, the Preachers will doubtless have GOD smiling upon them; *The Hand of the Lord will be with them; and many will Believe, and be turned unto the Lord* {Acts 11:21}.

But, *The Hand of the Lord!* What is it, but that SPIRIT of GOD, without whose Aids, they that would *Build the House of the Lord,* will but *Labour in Vain?*

'Tis indeed with a very Trembling Heart, and not without the most profound Submission, that I would now hint a matter to you, or at least insinuate it with a whisper hardly to be uttered. Some eminently Learned Men, Persons of the most finished Erudition, and the farthest in the World from all Fanaticism, are of this Perswasion; That the *Reformation* and *Propagation* of *Religion,* will be accomplished, by Granting over again, those *Extraordinary Gifts of the Prophetic Spirit,* by which the Holy Spirit watered the Primitive Church, and at first spread and confirmed the *Christian Religion* in the World.[40]

The most Holy SPIRIT of GOD has used this Method from the very beginning of the World; that so He might communicate the Light, with which He would lead His People travelling on the *Earth,* to the Rest which the Saints have in the Heavens reserved for them. It hath seemed Good unto Him, to send down from on High, into the Children of Men, those *Good Angels,* who have always been the most proper and ready Instruments of the *Eternal Spirit* for such a Purpose; and the Favourites of GOD, who have been so managed and inspired by *Angels,* have been the Messengers and Proclaimers, by whom He has revealed

His Will both in Word and Writing, to the Children of Men. Various and Wondrous have been the Operations of the *Angels* in these Ministers of GOD; but *all these things worketh that one and self-same Spirit, who divides to every Man severally as He pleases* {1 Cor. 12:11}.

This *Angelical* Possession and *Energy* of the *Prophetic Spirit*, has ever been to the People of GOD as a *Light shining in a dark place*; A Place, alas, how *Dark*, how buried in *Darkness*, would it have been, if it had not been allowed unto this our World; for to Rejoyce in the Consolation of such a Light! The Immense *Treasures of Truth*, which we have treasured up for us in the Sacred Scriptures, we confess to be owing unto this *Prophetic Spirit*; yea, 'tis owing to the Afflations thereof, that the Church is continued against all the Hazards and Horrors of Extinction, tho' it be like a little spark in the midst of a Tempestuous Ocean.

For Four Hundred Years before the Incarnation of our SAVIOUR, there was a Ceasing and Silence of this *Prophetic Spirit*. But when that Great KING Ascending on High, *Sat down on the Right Hand of the most High* GOD, He received *Gifts*, which He gave unto Men, and He sent down into the *Preachers of the Everlasting Gospel*, the Angels, who were all *made Subject* unto Him; and He Distilled a most *Plentiful Shower* of the Heavenly Gifts, with which *He Refreshed His weary Heritage*.

For more than Two Hundred Years after this, the Church was Enlarged and Governed by these Gifts of the *Prophetic Spirit*; and the Church enjoy'd a sensible presence of her *Beloved* with her. But when the *Carnal Spirit of this World*, fermented with the Venom of the *Epicurean Philosophy*, entred into the Church, and she would no more acknowledge her SAVIOUR as her Governour, the Grieved *Paraclet* withdrew, and there Succeeded a Kingdom animated with the Unclean Spirit of Antichrist; and *for Three Years and Six Months* {Luke 4:25; Dan. 7:25, 12:7}, the *Rain* is witheld, from a Land Languishing under the *Indignation of* GOD.

But now at last; what if after the *Twelve Hundred & Sixty* Years of *Antichrist* are Expired {Rev. 11:2–3}, there should be heard the *Sound of Abundance of Rain!* {1 Kings 18:41}[41] What if the *Dove* sent forth *Twice* and Returning again, should go forth a *Third Time*, never to Return any more; and Abide with us, until the *Flood* of Ignorance and Wickedness in which the whole World at this day lies in a manner drowned, shall go off wholly from the face of the Earth? What if the *Kingdom of* GOD should come, with the Joy of the Holy SPIRIT, working with such *Gifts* and in such *Ways*, as He has promised, for both the *Internal & External* Propagation of His Gospel? Whether it shall be so or no;—*I know not,* GOD *knows!*

It is very sure, That the Prophecy in *Joel, I will pour out my SPIRIT upon all Flesh* {Joel 2}, yet remains to be accomplished. And it is not unlikely, That the *Effusion of the SPIRIT,* by which the *Primitive Church* flourished, might be but as *Drops,* which will be follow'd with *Mighty Showers,* for the Accomplishment of this Prophecy still to be Expected *in the Latter Days.*

The Lord will *Consume* the most wicked *Antichrist,* by the *Breath of His Mouth,* and will *Destroy* him with the *Brightness of His Coming* {2 Thess. 2:8}. What if by the *Breath of His Mouth,* we should understand such *Gifts* of the Holy SPIRIT, as He signified unto His Disciples, when with His *Mouth* He *breathed* on them, and said, *Receive an Holy Spirit?*

I Confess. That the *Extraordinary Gifts* of the Holy SPIRIT are to be less esteemed of, than that *Quickening Grace,* by which all that have their Names written in the Book of Life, are *Ordinarily* Sanctified, and Live unto their GOD. I most willingly Confess, That a Soul Sanctified with the *Love* of GOD and of CHRIST, and of our Neighbour, is altogether to be preferred before all the Extraordinary Gifts of the Holy SPIRIT. I most readily Confess, That the *Extraordinary Gifts* of the Holy SPIRIT bestowed upon Men are to be Examined by the *Rules of PIETY,* and if the *Operations* that look *Miraculous* do lead us unto any thing that is contrary to PIETY, they are to be rejected, among the *Wiles* of the *Prince of Darkness transforming himself into an Angel of Light* {2 Cor. 11:14}. I also Grant, and always Think, that there can be nothing more wholesome to be inculcated, than that Advice of our *Franckius, It is not safe to affect Extraordinary Gifts: For they may be at least accidentially, attended with Mighty Dangers to them that are not very deeply rooted in Humility. But who dare engage for himself his being so?*

Nevertheless, What is there to hinder, but that our *Heavenly Father, who gives His Holy Spirit unto them that ask Him,* can grant your Petition, when you shall ask it of Him, that in His work you may have His Angels for your Assistents and Associates? Truly, 'Tis not utterly to be despaired of as a Thing Impossible. But if by the Extraordinary Prayer with Fasting that shall be Necessary, and *beseeching the Lord Thrice,* and oftener, you shall ask it of the Lord, Behold, You may be sensible of His Holy Spirits descending on you, who perhaps will supply you with such *Gifts* and *Helps,* as were conferred of old, and are to be Renewed in the Age that is coming on, and will procure for you an easy and speedy Progress in the Work before you.

Whether the Time appointed by GOD for such an Effusion of the Holy Spirit may quickly come on, *& the Kingdom of GOD be suddenly to appear?* {1 Thess. 5:2} For my part, I do not Know.[42] But that it is not very far off, I do Believe. Whether *You,* who are such Devout Worshippers of GOD, and who with so much of Charity and Self-denial, industriously prosecute the work of the Gospel, may Enjoy (what I wish for you) the *First Fruits* of this Effusion; I confess,' tis what I know not. But that GOD may favour you with Plentiful Successes, This is what I constantly & fervently Pray for, and what upon some good Grounds I hope for.

But its time to have done. My design was to Write a *Letter* & not a *Volumn*; 'Tis enough to Point at these things, without Amplifications upon them. Reverend Sir, You plainly see, What we are; *Joyned in our Minds, tho' parted by the Waters; One Soul, tho' not One Soyl, Uniting of us* {1 Cor. 6:17}. What remains is, that by Mutual Prayers to our most Merciful GOD and Father, we be helpful to one another.

Live and Prosper; Always what you are, and what you would be; always Living to your SAVIOUR; and not only very dear unto me, but also unto the whole Christian World, yea, unto the *Angels* of GOD, unto whom you are a Spectacle. I am,

Yours in the Lord,

Boston, New-England,   most Heartily;

Dec. 31. 1717.   *Cotton Mather.*

The Second Coming and Millennialism

ead closely, Mather's *Wonders of the Invisible World* (1693) linked the devil's descent in Massachusetts with end-time visions of the apocalypse. In fact, millennialism, or belief in the thousand-year reign of Christ, was a commonplace among clergy and parishioners alike. Even Judge Samuel Sewall, Lieutenant Governor William Stoughton, and Boston's famed Latin School teacher Ezekiel Cheever were no exceptions. Both Mathers were avid students of the Bible's prophecies, invoked telltale signs of the end from their pulpits, and hashed out their conjectures in regular meetings of fellow millenarians. A case in point, Reverend Michael Wigglesworth's *The Day of Doom; or, A Poetical Description of the Great and Last Judgment* (1662), a doggerel poem of 224 stanzas in galloping fourteeners (heroic alexandrines), was the first colonial American bestseller. No copies of the first edition have survived; his poetic visions of Judgment Day were read to pieces by popular demand, and children learned the stanzas by heart.

Cotton Mather too was a lifelong student of the Bible's prophecies of the end-times. In fact, there are hardly any of his published sermons that do not somehow allude to the pending *annus mirabilis*, or promised "Halcyon Days" of Christ's reign on earth. Millennialists of all stripes were given to devising elaborate chronologies to calculate when the Lord might come as a thief in the night, accompanied or followed by the great conflagration of the earth. Mather's understanding of the Salem crisis was carefully informed by his calculations for the years 1697, 1716, 1736—all projected dates when the six thousand years of human history from the creation of Adam to the Second Coming might run their course.

The selections on the Second Coming and millennialism are taken from Mather's last word on the subject: *Triparadisus* ("Threefold Paradise"), a manuscript of nearly four hundred pages, only recently edited and published as *The Threefold Paradise of Cotton Mather* (1995). Its title signifies a trio of paradises: the first, the Garden of Eden; the second, the abode of the departed souls *before* their resurrection; the third, the post-conflagration new earth during the millennium. He worked on this tome for nearly thirty years, and during this time considerably revised his insights on such mainstays as the national conversion of the Jews, the conflagration, the rapture, the resurrection, and the raised saints governing with Christ from above. He sent the manuscript of his final version to a London publisher sometime in 1727, but unbeknownst to Mather, the publisher had died and the clean copy of *Triparadisus* was lost—but a handwritten copy with his final revisions was found among the Mather Papers in Boston. The selection included from this text illustrates his tightly reasoned views on what the new earth would look like *during* Christ's thousand-year reign *between* the conflagration of the old earth at the *beginning* and judgment day at the *end* of the millennium (premillennialism).

What, for Mather, did this post-conflagration earth look like, and who were the people who would live there during the thousand years? Briefly, Mather distinguished between two groups or classes of saints in this New World: the "*Saved Nations*," whom he also called the "CHANGED Ones," and the "*Raised Saints*," those ruling with Christ in heaven. The former were those alive on earth at the Second Coming; the latter the ones raised from their graves. So far, Mather was on safe hermeneutical grounds with most of his fellow millenarians, who assigned different functions to these two classes of saints. In Mather's reading of the prophecies, these changed ones would be caught up in the clouds of heaven (rapture) while the flames of the conflagration incinerated the old earth. These raptured, changed saints would have their immortality miraculously restored but be returned to the post-conflagration earth. There they would beget millions of immortal offspring (saved nations) and with their help turn the cleansed earth into a paradise restored—like that of Eden before the wily serpent wriggled himself into Eve's confidence. *"Ah, Lord, He speaketh Parables!"* Mather facetiously interjected, knowing how his fellow millenarians might wince at his conjectures.

The second group, the raised saints, are particularly privileged in Mather's view. They are the worthy saints whom Christ would raise from their graves. They too would have their immortal bodies restored (like that of the prelapsarian Adam) and be made *"Equal to the Angels."* However, they would join Christ in the celestial New Jerusalem and "do the Part of *Angels* to the *Holy People* on the *New Earth.*" They would fly like angels down to Earth to instruct the saved nations as occasions would warrant. The saved nations in this new earth and their immortal offspring would write learned books and found universities. "The Learning of the World will not then be the Jargon of a fumivendutous *Aristotle,* and such Trash as the Colledges in our days have sometimes valued themselves upon," Mather wrote, and his eyes widened at the mere thought of it. "But the World will be filled with the most Noble & Useful Knowledge, and all the *Sciences* will terminate in *Living unto GOD:* Every Part of the World, superior even to a *Frederician* University" of Halle. No doubt, "Here will be a True *Eutopia!*"

Mather anticipated his readers' stares of disbelief about his seemingly novel ideas: "We must not be surprised at it, if they who are *Swifter* to *Speak* than to *Hear,* tell us at once, *Our Milk boils over;* and refuse to give us a Patient Hearing," he preempted his readers' objections. No doubt, some such comments would be made by his critics, especially once they had read his ideas about the nature of the New Jerusalem above. Most intriguing was Mather's vision of this celestial city: a gigantic, four-square cube measuring fifteen hundred miles in all directions, a material city, the abode of Christ and his raised saints. In Mather's eschatology, the New Jerusalem, with its twelve towers, walls, and gates all made from precious stones (Rev. 21) was no metaphor for the harmony between the new heaven and new earth, as it was for his father,[1] but a literal city visibly hovering above this new earth—like some spherical spaceship or (closer to Mather's own time) like Jonathan Swift's flying island of Laputa in *Gulliver's Travels.*[2]

What about Satan and his minions *during* the millennium? Would they be destroyed? Not yet. "SATAN, with his *Apostate Legions*" would be confined "unto the *Prison*, which will be a *Place of Torment* unto them," Mather argued. They would be kept in this abyss of hell until the new earth's halcyon days had run their course. And yet, toward the end of that period, just before the last judgment, the devil, his demons, and the souls of the wicked (Gog and Magog) would be released from their chains and be allowed—one final time—to assail the immortalized offspring of the saved nations on Earth in the battle of Armageddon.

TRIPARADISUS (1727)

THE THIRD PARADISE: AN INTRODUCTION[3]

PARADISE, is what we have under our Cultivation. The Miserable *Earth* whereon we now see the dismal Ruines of a *Paradise*, we have considered as what *once it was*; in the day when GOD created Man, and Man took delight in, *Seeing & Serving* His Creator, and *out of the Ground, the Lord GOD made every thing to grow* {Gen. 2:9}, that might be grateful and useful unto him.

And that we might releeve the *Sorrow*, of the Reflection with which our Sinful Parents have obliged us to behold the *Cursed Ground* in which we see the *Reverse* of it *all the Days of our Life* {Ps. 23:6}, we have considered the *Heavenly Paradise* provided by the *Second Adam* for our *Spirits*, in the *Day* when our *Breath goeth forth*; and our *Thoughts* of what is to be *done* and *had* here, shall perish. But *Lett the Heavens rejoice, & Lett the Earth be glad* {Ps. 96:11}; For, Behold, There must be a *Restitution of all Things* {Acts 3:21}; even the *Earth* must again become a *Paradise*; Yea, a *Paradise* which will so much exceed what was exhibited near Six thousand Years go, That, *Behold, I create New Heavens & a New Earth*, saith our GOD, and the *Former shall not be Remembred, nor Come into Mind* {Isa. 65:17}. It is a Matter of deep Contemplation, That the Great Works of the Sovereign GOD, have usually *Two Editions*. The *First* is glorious. But for Ends unknown to us, [*Thou shalt know hereafter!*] He suffers, as one may say, the *Work to be marred in the hand of the Potter* {Jer. 18:4}. Anon, a *Second* comes forth; when *that which was made glorious, has no Glory, in this Respect, by reason of the Glory that excelleth*, in that which *remaineth, & is more glorious* {2 Cor. 3:10}. Thus, *The New Things which I make, shall remain before me, saith the Lord* {Isa. 66:22}. In a *Paradise* to come, it will be wondrously exemplified. And this is the PARADISE, that we proceed now to take into our Consideration. . . .

X: THE NEW EARTH SURVEY'D

Be Joyful, O Earth; and break forth into Singing, O Mountains! {Isa. 49:13} Our GOD is going to *Renew the Face of the Earth* {Ps. 104:30}; and we are going to see an *Earth full of His Mercy; An Earth,* No longer a Nest of *Serpents,* no longer a Den of *Dragons,* no longer a *Land that Eats up the Inhabitants thereof* {Num. 13:32}, and that affords not unto the Children of GOD, a *Quiet Habitation:* But a *Mountain of Holiness, & a Dwelling of Righteousness:* The *Blessed* of the Lord!

We left the *Earth* all on *Fire:* Every where covered and perishing in the *Flames,* whereto a GOD, who *Judges in the Earth,* and is of *Purer Eyes than to behold the Evil, & look on the Iniquity* {Hab. 1:13}, which the *Earth* is every where filled withal, has condemned it. How long the *Fire* will persist, and how far it will proceed in its all-devouring Rage, we know not. But in a little while, there will be seen an *Earth,* in all the Beauties of a PARADISE; praepared for an *Holy People,* that shall have no *Satan* to annoy them there. In this *Paradise* they shall continue At Least a *Thousand Years* {Rev. 20:2}. If I say, *At Least,* it is because the Reception of the Term, A *Thousand Years,* no less than *Six times* over in the Prophecy that has informed us & assured us of it, has invited some to think, It may be *Six Thousand* Years, and as long as the Duration of this World has been before the Arrival of it. So *we shall be made Glad according to the Years wherein we have seen Evil* {Ps. 90:15}. Yea, from the constant Usage of the Book, in which This Prophecy occurs, & indeed of all Sacred Prophecy, which putts a *Day* for a *Year,* some very considerable Writers, urge that the Space may be prolonged unto *Three Hundred & Sixty Five Thousand Years:* if not *Cubically* to a *Thousand Thousand.*

Can any one tell, how much the *Shape* of the *Earth* shall be changed from what it was, by the *Conflagration* doing the *Strange Work* of GOD upon it? Shall we imagine, that the *Fire* which is to take Vengeance on the *Wickedness* of the World, will have a Commission to make no Impression any where, but on the *Wicked Part* of it: and like the *Fire* which once did not consume the Innocent *Bush* {Exod. 3:2} from which the ancient Lawgiver, heard GOD speaking to him, it shall not prey upon Objects that have not been rendred *Combustible,* by *Sin* defiling of them? Or, shall we imagine, that the World will undergo little more than a *Singeing* from the *Fire,* that is to fall upon it; and the *Fire* prove not much more Destructive, than the *Water* that once *Washed* it, when the *Foundation of the Ungodly was overflown with a Flood* {Job 22:16}: Some have imagined, that the *Old Seats* of the *Earth,* will not be so much altered by the *Conflagration,* but that there may in the Ruines be left some *Remembrances* of them. Some have particularly apprehended, that the Spott of the *Earth*, which was the *Land of Promise*, whereof the Blessed GOD promised unto *Abraham*, *The Land which thou seest, unto Thee will I give it, and unto thy Seed forever* {Gen. 13:15}: will be the Distinguished *Midst of the Earth*, when the New *Earth* is to be brought on. And when the Apostle proves, That the *Patriarchs desired an Heavenly Countrey* {Heb. 11:16}, Because they might have had *Opportunity to return unto the Countrey from which they came out, and made no Use of it* {Heb. 11:15}; Such Writers as honest *Maton*, think, it looks as if the *Heavenly Countrey* which they *desired*, were the Land of *Canaan*, to be possess'd by them, when it should be Restored unto an *Heavenly* Condition.[4] And others, improving on that Notion, consider the *Holy City* of the *Raised*, in the *Clouds* of the *New Heavens*, as being more peculiarly over *That Land*, at the Time of the *Restitution*, and *That Land* as having a peculiar share above other Countreys, in the Visits which the *Raised Saints* from time to time shall give unto the Lower World.[5] Had *Heaven* in general been the *Heavenly Countrey* here spoken of, it might be argued, that they might as well have obtained *That*, or have expressed their Affection to it, *in their own Countrey from which they came;* They might have returned unto *That*, and have *Lived as Pilgrims* There. But they would *this Way* express their *Faith*, of what GOD had promised One Day to do for them & theirs in *This Land*, when He should *Raise the Dead*, and be *Their GOD*. Indeed, *This Land*, as it should seem, shall then after a Singular Manner be an *Heavenly Countrey*; And it seems to be foretold in *Ezekiel*, That it shall become *Like the Garden of Eden* {Ezek. 36:35}; in which *Garden*, the SON of GOD in the *Shechinah*, with His *Angels*, was visibly & familiarly conversant. This also, they suppose, maybe to the Intention of *Joseph*, in ordering his *Bones* {Josh. 24:32}, without any regard unto the Whimsey of, *The rolling of the Caverns*,[6] to be transported into the *Land of Canaan*. . . .

The Thing whereof We are assured, is, [Act. III.21.] That when our Blessed JESUS does Return from the *Heavens*, which have *received Him*, there will be a *RESTITUTION OF ALL THINGS*. Now, we will not go to any *Pagans* or *Gnosticks* for the Meaning of this, ΑΠΟΚΑΤΑΣΤΑΣΙΣ:[7] but according to the Scriptures, understand it, for the *Restauration* of the Earth, to the State of a PARADISE, or the Putting of the World into the Condition, in which it was, before the *Apostasy* of Man from the GOD that formed Him; which is the Thing to be understood, by what GOD hath under Various Ways of expressing it, *Spoken by the Mouth of all His holy Prophets that have been since the Beginning of the World* {Acts 3:21}. Calovius well notes, [and proves it from what we call, The LXX,] That the Term is to be taken, *De Restitutione in pristinum statum, vel meliorem*.[8] To take it for the Destruction of the *Jews*, & the Vocation of the *Gentiles*;—Away with such Excessive and Exalted *Folly!* Unworthy of a Refutation!—This, *Restitution of all things*, is in the Gospel [Matth. XIX.28.] called, ΠΑΛΙΓΓΕΝΕΣΙΑ,[9] The *Regeneration*: which indeed carried, *The First Chapter of GENESIS over again*, in the Signification of it. The Term used for it by the Ancients, & particularly by *Justin Martyr*, [A *Man*, one who quotes him says, *of profounder Learning than any of our Modern & Modish Infidels.*] was that of an ΑΝΑΚΤΙΣΙΣ, or, *The Creation done over again.*[10] They explained it, by, *The Creature purged from the Irregularity and Imperfection, which the Sin of Man has brought upon it.* Briefly, The *Earth* is to be CREATED over again, into an entire PARADISE; and, no doubt, the *Second Edition* will be, *Auctior et Emendatior*,[11] and the World will be *Recovered* into a Better Condition, than it had before, *Sin did by one Man enter into the World, & Death by Sin, and so Death has passed upon all Men, for that all have sinned* {Rom. 5:12}. The Earth will be *Refined* into a Noble, Holy, *Heavenly Seat*; in which GOD *will govern the Nations upon the Earth; All the People shall Praise Him; and GOD, even their own GOD, will Bless them* wonderfully {Ps. 67:4–6}. . . .

We see a NEW EARTH CREATED. But shall it remain empty of *Inhabitants?* GOD forbid! Some have apprehended Ground enough, to replenish all the *Planets* with *Inhabitants*, from that Word, [Isa. XLV.18.] GOD *that formed the Earth, He created it not in Vain, He formed it to be Inhabited.* Be sure, This Word may be *Applied* to the *New Earth*, and was indeed *Intended* for it. We find those Things done in the *New Earth*, which cannot be done without *Inhabitants*. Yea, Tis expressly called, OIKOYMENH· *An Inhabited World.*[12]

But I again enquire, By whom *Inhabited?* Most certainly, The *Wicked* shall not *Inhabit* it. The *Conflagration* has dispatch'd all of them. *The Day shall burn them up, & leave them neither Root nor Branch* {Mal. 4:1}. We are assured, That GOD will then *Destroy them who Corrupt the Earth* {Rev. 11:18}. In the Prospect of it, *That Sinners will be consumed out of the Earth, & the Wicked be no more* {Ps. 104:35}, we have the first *Hallelujah* that occurs in the Bible: and it calls for one! The *Raised* shall not *Inhabit* it. They are *Elsewhere* provided for. And, of them that are found here after the *Conflagration*, it is expressly said, They shall not only *Build Houses*, and *Plant Vineyards*, but also have an *Offspring*. Whereas, for them that obtain *the Resurrection from the Dead*, our Lord has, as one may say, *Forbidden their Bannes*, and has declared, *They neither Marry, nor are given in Marriage* {Luke 20:35}. From whence then, I beseech you, shall the *New Earth* be stocked with Suitable *Inhabitants?*—

The *New Earth* must be mightily, filled with *Inhabitants*; yea, and speedily too: There must be mighty *Nations* of them. And inasmuch as there must be *no Curse* in the *New Earth*, and in what the REDEEMER will do for the Rescue of it, *His Work is perfect;* Hence the *New Earth* must have no *Dying,* and by Consequence, no *Sinning,* in it: The Inhabitants of it must be a *Deathless,* and by Consequence, a *Sinless* People. I beseech you again, Tell me, From whence will you supply the *New Earth,* with a People proper for it? Or, If I now tell you, O *Ye Sober Enquirers,* Will you receive it? Or, Shall it be hastily rejected, with an *Ah, Lord, He speaketh Parables!* {Ezek. 20:49}——

I say then, It will be Impossible for you to find any where, a People for these Lovely Regions, but the *Saved Nations,* that shall not be *utterly consumed in the Terrors* of the *Conflagration* {Ps. 73:19}; Even those that are *Caught up to meet the Lord* at His Coming {1 Thess. 4:17}, to Judge the World.

When the *New Earth* is by the Almighty *Will & Word* of our GOD, [And, *Job* {42:2} upon his *Restoration,* must say, O *Lord, I know that thou canst do every thing!*] brought into the Condition of a PARADISE, the Faithful, who were by the *Angelical* Ministry, *Caught up* to the Place, where the LORD will have His *Holy Ones* with Him, at such a Distance from the *Earth* as to *Deliver* them *from the Wrath to Come* {1 Thess. 1:10}, and from the Flames of a World on Fire; They will be then again Returned unto the *Field* praepared for them, and be on the *New Earth,* as ADAM and EVE was in the *Terrestrial Paradise,* before they Rebelled against their *Maker,* and before they Sinned away those *Garments of Light,* the Loss of which *Defence & Beauty* made them *Ashamed* of Appearing before their *Judge;* and before their *Sin* opened the *Floodgates* for all *Miseries* to break in upon the World: And they shall here *long enjoy the Work of their Hands* {Isa. 65:22}. They shall be Persons of *Heavenly* Tempers tuned unto *Unison* with what is Above: They shall Abound in *Heavenly* Exercises of Devotion: They shall have a Variety of most Suitable *Employments:* They shall serve and please the Holy GOD with a perpetual Homage paid unto Him in all they do; and be *Holy in all Manner of Conversation* {1 Pet. 1:16}: They shall *Taste* the Goodness of GOD in the Fruits of His Bounty plentifully allow'd unto them: They shall in a most Virtuous, and Rational and Regular Manner make Use of those *Oblectations,* with which their *Senses* will be gratified: They shall perfectly & practically understand how, *Frui Deo,* and, *Uti Creaturis;*[13] They shall be Visited, & Instructed & Ordered, by the *Citizens* of the *Holy City* coming down as there may be Occasion to them: And while they *Walk with GOD* at an High Rate of *Sanctity* and *Purity,* they shall *Begett Sons and Daughters:* & have them *Translated,* either *Successively* one after another as they may Ripen for it, or, anon, *all at once* in His Time for it, into the Superiour Circumstances of the *Holy City.*

These CHANGED Ones will in many Points be Sharers with the RAISED Ones in their *Faelicity.* While the Flames of a perishing World are doing their Execution, and the Formation of the *New Earth* is going on, they be *Both* of

Them together with the LORD in the *Ærial* Place of Safety. They shall be *Both* of them rid of all Sinful *Pollution; of Corruption* and of *Mortality.* They shall *Both* of them have *all Tears wiped from their Eyes* {Rev. 21:4}, and see *Rest from Adversity.* Yett, in Sundry Points there will be a *Difference* between them: And if when we read, *He tells the Number of the Stars, He calls them all by Names* {Ps. 147:4}, not only *Kimchi* but also *Arnobius*[14] expound it right concerning, *The Just of the World to come,* we may here apply the Passage, *One Star differeth from another Star in Glory* {1 Cor. 15:41}. The *Changed* Ones have not had their *Bodies* passing thro' the Rotting Alterations of *Death feeding on them* {Ps. 49:14} in the Grave. But the *Raised* Ones may from thence have their *Bodies* on some Accounts in more *Ethereal Aptitudes* for the *Holy City.* And it is most particularly declared in the Divine Oracles, That the *Changed* Ones will on the *New Earth* have some Circumstances of the *Animal Œconomy,* which the *Raised* Ones will forever have done withal.

Upon the Mention of an *Earth,* inhabited by a People who shall have no *Death* nor *Sin* among them, and who shall maintain a most Intimate Fellowship with such as will be *Equal to the Angels;* and yett shall *Build Houses and Inhabit them,* and shall *Plant Vineyards & Eat The Fruit of them* {Isa. 65:21}, and be *The Seed of the Blessed Lord, and their OFFSPRING with them* {Isa. 61:9}; we must not wonder if some angry and froward *Jerom* come in and *Push* with his Invectives, and cry out, *Carnal! Carnal!*—it may be, *Cerinthian!* It may be, *Mahometan!*[15] And rail against such *Sensuality,* as hee'l call it, with Vociferations as Impertinent and Ridiculous as those with which that *Furious Man* entertained his Lady *Hedibia.*[16] Or, if we should express the Matter as *Lactantius* has done it; "That those who shall be at that time alive in their Bodies, will never Die, but shall *begett an Infinite Multitude,* & have an *Offspring,* during that Space of a *Thousand Years,* and their Offspring shall be Holy and Beloved of GOD: But, they who shall be *Raised* from the Graves, will praeside as Judges or Princes over the rest."[17] We must not be surprised at it, if they who are *Swifter* to *Speak* than to *Hear,* tell us at once, *Our Milk boils over;* and refuse to give us a Patient Hearing. But, O *Vain Man, Born like the Wild Asses Colt* {Job 11:12}; Wilt thou be Wiser than the Glorious GOD, who has in His *Promise* expressly bidden us to *Look for such things?* Or, if we don't *Look for such things,* what *Signification* can we putt upon His *Promise,* but what will render it utterly *Insignificant?* Will the *Changed Bodies* of them that are saved out of the *Fire* which will purify the World, have their *Senses* left unto them; and must their *Senses* be used no more in Conversing with the Proper *Objects* of them? Or shall the World that Survives & Succeeds the *Fire* be filled with such Things as are made for the *Use* of *Man,* & are Proper *Objects* for the *Senses* of the *Changed Bodies;* and shall they have nothing more to do with them? Shall Man be restored unto the Condition, wherein our *Protoplast* shone before he was chased out of *Paradise,* and must there be a *Turpitude* in his doing those things which were to be done in *Paradise,* and which his Creator had in the Tendencies of His *Plasmation* an Eye unto! The Vile *Marcionites,* who ΑΓΑΜΙΑΝ ΕΚΗΡΥΞΑΝ, were not such a Sect as we should be ambitious to *Herd* withal![18] . . . .

This *Holy People,* shall for their Vast Multitude, soon be, *as the Flock of Holy Things, as the Flock of* Jerusalem *in her Solemn Festivals* {Ezek. 36:38}: The *Waste World* shall be *filled with the Flocks of Men.* Our Glorious GOD, will fulfill that Word among them, *They shall be my People, and I will be their GOD; They shall walk in my Judgments, and they shall dwell in the Land that I have given unto my Servants; Even THEY and their CHILDREN, and their CHILDRENS CHILDREN forever* {Ezek. 37:24–25}. Thus it will be, when that Word shall be fulfill'd, *My Tabernacle shall be with them* {Ezek. 37:27}: which is the Character of the *New Earth,* and of the Time, when GOD *shall dwell with Men, and they shall be His People, and GOD Himself shall be with them, & be their GOD; and there shall be no more Death, neither shall there be any more Pain; for the former Things are passed away* {Rev. 21:3–4}. Yea, Now, O Ye Mountains of Israel, says our GOD, *Behold, I am for you, and I will turn to you, and Ye shall be till'd and sown, and I will MULTIPLY MEN upon you* {Ezek. 36:9–10}. Doubtless, the Inhabitants of the *New Earth* will be greatly & quickly *Multiplied;* and within a very little while, almost as if a *Nation were born at once,* here will soon be mighty *Nations,* and People enough to afford *Subjects* for the *Raised Saints* to find Work among. . . .

Of THIS MATTER, there appears to be an Admirable Representation in the VII Chapter of the *Apocalypse:* and when I have told *how* I apply what I Read there, I will tell *why* I do so.

We find a Provision made for the *Sealing of One Hundred & fourty four Thousand,* from the *Tribes of Israel* {Rev. 7:4}, that by the *Mark* of GOD & His CHRIST upon them, they may be praeserved from the *Hurt* which is to be done by the *Angels* of GOD unto the *Earth* and the *Sea.* If we take this *Hurt* ultimately to intend the *Conflagration,* we shall not be alone in the Exposition. And if we look for the *Tribes of Israel,* in the *Surrogate Israel,* and among the *Gentiles,* among whom the Children of GOD are the Genuine *Israel,* we shall do but as it becomes *Christians* to do. We have here then at Least *One Hundred & fourty four Thousand* that are saved out of the *Conflagration.* They are elsewhere called, *The Redeemed from the Earth* {Rev. 14:3}, on the Score of their being so. Well; *After this,* and it won't be long first, we shall *Behold,* and, *Lo, There will be a great Multitude which no Man can number,* that will have the *White Robes* of a *Priesthood* {Rev. 7:9} upon them, obtained by *the Blood of the Lamb* {Rev. 12:11}, which is applied unto them, & is the *Sacrifice* which they plead before GOD continually. And why may not these be the *Offspring* of the *One Hundred & fourty four Thousand*, Saved Ones? It is Evidently the *Blessedness* of the *World to Come*, which is here assigned unto them. We read, *He that sits on the Throne shall dwell among them; They shall hunger no more, neither thirst any more; neither shall the Sun light on them, nor any Heat. For the Lamb who is in the Midst of the Throne, shall feed them, and shall lead them unto Living Fountains of Waters; and GOD shall wipe away all Tears from their Eyes* {Rev. 7:16–17}. Every Word calculated for the *Blessedness* of the *World to Come*! And yett it seems as if they were the *Holy People*, of the *New Earth*, which this *Blessedness* is intended for.—I am now to answer my Engagement, plainly to confess, wherefore I suspect THIS MATTER to be represented here; Why, we read of these *Marked*, and *Saved* Ones, and of the *Great Multitude* following, *They are before the Throne of GOD, and they serve Him DAY and NIGHT in His TEMPLE* {Rev. 7:15}. Now, in the *Holy City* the *New Heavens* we read, It is all DAY, there is no NIGHT there {Rev. 22:5}; and one who saw it, says, *I saw no TEMPLE therein* {Rev. 21:22}. So then, it looks as if the Condition of the *New Earth*, may be what this Prophecy may at least ultimately, refer unto. However *This* I will not insist upon.—*Valeat quantum valere potest.*[19]

What I must and shall insist upon is, That they who have been *Redeemed from the Earth*, and whom the LORD sends down to the *Earth*, which *He gives to the Children of Men*, whom He will *Bless, and Increase more & more, them & their Children* {Ps. 115:14–15}, shall then be entirely *delivered* from the Worst of all their *Enemies*, even from SIN, and *Serve Him without* any of the *Fear* that SIN forever brings with it, in a Sinless *Holiness and Righteousness before Him all the Days of their Life* {Luke 1:75}: They shall be a *Sinless People*. Whatever *Sin* they had before their being fetch'd up from the *Conflagration*, in which GOD will fulfill that Word unto them; *When thou walked thro' the Fire, thou shalt not be Burnt, neither shall the Flame kindle upon thee* {Isa. 43:2}, they shall be cleared of it and they shall have nothing of it left in them, to disqualify them for the Favours of the LORD: No *Leven* left in them, to disqualify them for the *Feat* of GOD in the *Holy Mountain*. Certainly, This *Old Leven* was thoroughly *Purged* out of *Enoch*, while the GOD who *Took him* up, was *Translating* of him! When the Lord, in the *Day of His Coming*, shall *Appear*, as *a Refiners Fire*, He will *Sitt as a Purifier of Silver, that they may offer to the Lord an Offering of Righteousness* {Mal. 3:3}. What shall be done for them, in their Deliverance from the *Terrors* of that formidable *Fire*, will be the True *Purgatory*, of which the *Seducing Spirits* of the *Latter Times*, have made an Handle to trump up the *Fic-*

tion, which the *Priestcraft* of *Rome* lives upon. The Holy SPIRIT of the REDEEMER, will with a marvellous Efficacy fall upon them, & come into them; and so, tho' the *Brands pluckt out of the Fire,* have been *clothed with Filthy Garments,* GOD will say of them, *Take away the Filthy Garments from them;* and say to them, *Lo, I have caused thy Iniquity to pass from thee, and I will clothe thee with Change of Raiment* {Zech. 3:2, 4}. . . .

A Concomitant of the Deliverance from SIN, wherein the *Holy People* will be *cleansed according to the Purification of the Sanctuary* {2 Chron. 30:19}, and what will inexpressibly contribute unto the *Tranquillity* of the *New Earth,* will be the, *Legatio Satanae,*[20] or, the Confinement of SATAN, with his *Apostate Legions,* unto the *Prison,* which will be a *Place of Torment* unto them; and which will forbid their being such *Prisoners at large* as now they are. *Satan* will no longer be able to pretend unto, *Going to & fro in the Earth, & Walking up & down in it* {Job 1:7}. The *New Earth* will not be, A *Whole World lying in the Wicked One* {1 John 5:19}; There shall be *no Part* of it left in his Bloody Hands. Who of us can say, how far may extend the Sense of that awful Word; *He that has had the Power of Death, that is, the Devil!* {Heb. 2:14} This we can say, *The Wicked Spirits are the Rulers of the Darkness of this World* {Eph. 6:12}; a *World,* which they *Rule* very much by keeping it in *Darkness.* And this we can say very much of the *Wickedness done* in the World by the Men who have *not the Fear of GOD,* is done by *Men moved by the Instigation of the Devil.* . . . When *Satan* is *Bound,* and *Seal'd up in the Abyss* {Rev. 20:3}, it will be another Sort of a *Time,* than any *History* can yett show unto us. The NEW EARTH shall see the *Time,* THEN will the *Oppressor cease;* THEN will the *Whole Earth be at Rest, and be quiet, & break forth into Singing;* and say, *Since thou art laid down, there is no Fetter come up against us. How art thou cutt down, to the Ground, which didst weaken the Nations! Thou hast said in thine Heart, I will exalt my Throne above the Stars of GOD: I will ascend above the Heights of the Clouds; I will be like the Most High; Yett thou shalt be brought down to Hell, to the sides of the Pitt!* {Isa. 14:7–8, 12–15} Yea; So far will the *Holy People* of the *New Earth* be, from the Infestations of the *Wicked Spirits,* that they may rather have some share in what their Bretheren, the *Holy People* of the *New Heavens,* will then be concerned in doing upon these their ancient Adversaries. This will be one admirable *Recompence* of the *Resistence,* with which their *Steadfast Faith* in the Days of their *Trial, they stood against the Wiles of the Devil* {Eph. 6:11}; and *withstood the Wicked Spirits in the Evil Day* {Prov. 16:4}. Of old, even while the *Old Heavens* and the *Old Earth* were yett in Being, there have been *Saints* that have had *Power* over the *Wicked Spirits, to cast them out* of their Strong Holds. Much more, the Saints of the *New Heavens,* having those of the *New Earth* in some Degree associated

with them, will exert a *Power* over these *Fiends of Darkness*. As they have been
once *Cast into Prison* by these *Wicked Spirits*, they shall now *Cast* these into
*Prison; They shall take them Captives, whose Captives they have been, and rule
over their Oppressors* {Isa. 14:2}: and, *Bind* those which are at this day, *By the
Wrath of GOD, the Kings* of this World, *in Chains, and these Nobles of Babylon,
in fetters of Iron. This Honour have all the Saints!* {Ps. 149:8–9} Thus, they *shall
Judge the Angels* {1 Cor. 6:3}: They shall do it, in the Acclamations, with which
they shall accompany the Act of our Descending REDEEMER, that will in the
Judgment of the Great Day, lay *Everlasting Chains of Darkness* {Jude 1:6} upon
them. . . .

    Such an *Holy People* will be Able to *bear*, such Easy and Wealthy and Plenti-
ful Circumstances, as the *Church upon Earth* could never yett see any Thing
so much as *Tending* to them, without *Swift Apostasies*, and without Occasions
for that Cry; *Venenum effusum in Ecclesiam!*[21] To imagine, that without and before such a *Change* upon the Children of Men, as can be produced by nothing
but the *Coming of the Lord*, the *Church upon Earth* can enjoy an *Undisturbed
Condition*, or a Freedom from the Discipline of the *Cross*, for a *Thousand Years*
together, or one *Twentieth* Part of the Time, without falling into a fearful *Decay
of Piety*; tis to imagine something much more *Improbable*, and *Miraculous*, than
any thing that has been offered in our *Scheme*, whereof a *Nicodemus* cries out,
How can these things be! {John 3:9}[22] And it is infinitely *Unscriptural*: The *Scriptures* having every where taught us, *That thro' much Tribulation we must enter
into the Kingdome of GOD* {Acts 14:22}. But a People so *Changed*, and under
the Influences of the *New Heavens*, as the *Holy People* of the *New Earth* will
be, will find a *Well-accommodated* World, no Praejudice unto their *Holiness*. Accordingly, we every where find the, *New Earth* described as, *A Good Land*; and
much more worthy than that which the Five *Danites* brought such a Report of,
to be so esteemed, *Behold, It is a very Good Land, and a Place where there is no
Want of any thing that is in the Earth* {Judg. 18:9–10}. . . . Or, Give me Leave to
carry you, unto a more Surprising Expositor upon the *Prophecies*. Be n't sur-
pized, when I tell you; *Virgil* is the Man. Read *Virgil*, I pray. And what says he?
"He speaks of an *Age to Come*, which he calls, *The Last Age*: [And so, as Dr. *Chandler*[23] observes, it must be, the *Fifth*,—succeeding to the *Iron Age*, which the
Poets counted the *Fourth*;] when the *Grand Revolution* of the Former Times,
and a *New Birth* of the *Old World* shall begin, and *Nature* shall resume its Pristine Vigour. When the Simplicity, and Probity and Equity of the *Paradisical State*
shall be restored; which was called *Golden*, in respect unto the following Times;
And *Manners* would be so Reformed, as if a *New Race* of Men were drop'd from
Heaven. In this *New Kingdom*, the Poet promises an End of all *War*; and *Uni-*

versal Peace throughout the World; a benign *Concord* between the most fierce & voracious Animals, and the weakest, & such as are least able to defend themselves: And no Poisonous *Reptile* or *Vegetable* remain in the World. For the *Plenty* and *Security* of that Age, the Poet says, *The Flocks* will need no *Shepherds* to look after them: they shall of their own Accord bring home their *Milk*, unto their Owners: The *Earth* shall not want the Rake, nor the *Corn* the Plow, nor the *Vine* the Knife: nor shall the Merchants bring in *foreign Commodities*, but *Every Countrey* shall produce every thing that is Desireable: Ripe *Grapes* hang on the *Bramble*: *Honey* drop from the *Oaks*; and *Spiknard* be as common as *Ivy*." All this appears to be fetch'd out of our *Bible*. And I affirm *Virgil* to be in his *Fourth Eclog*,[24] a better Commentator on the *Prophecies* there, than some that have written professed Commentaries.

NOW, and never until NOW, will that Word be fulfilled, [2. Sam. VII.10.] I *will appoint a Place for my People Israel, and will plant them, that they may dwell in a Place of their own, and move no more; neither shall the Children of Wickedness afflict them any more as in former times.* Here will be a True *Eutopia*!

A very Natural Consequence will be, *The Inhabitants shall not say, I am sick* {Isa. 33:24}. For to taste such Blessings, *Valeat possessor oportet.*[25] There will be no *Physicians* on the *New Earth*: *The Whole need them not!* {Matt. 9:12} Tho,' doubtless, notwithstanding the Hard *Jewish Sentence* upon them, there will in the *New Heavens* be many, besides our *Evangelist*, that have been of their Profession; and will in their *Own Bodies* receive the Reward of what they once did upon a Pious Intention for the *Bodies* of others. The *New Earth* will have in it the *Tree*, the *Leaves* whereof will be *for the Health of the Nations* {Rev. 22:2}.

But that which will be of the Last Importance, to the Welfare of the *Nations*, will be their *Walking in the Light of the Holy City* {Rev. 21:24}. The *Raised Saints* of the *Holy City*, I again insist upon it, will do the Part of *Angels* to the *Holy People* on the *New Earth*: and be continually doing them all the Good that can be imagined; *Good surpassing all Imagination!* It is expressly said, *They shall REIGN*: and, [Dan. VII.27.] *The Kingdom, & the Dominion, and the Greatness of the Kingdom UNDER THE WHOLE HEAVEN, shall be given to the People of the Saints of the Most High.* Happy Revolution! . . . So, the Love of GOD unto *Mankind*, inclined Him to sett *Angels* over Men. But, behold, the Love of GOD unto His *Holy People* in the *New Earth*, setting *Men Equal to Angels* {Luke 20:36} over them: and fulfilling that Word unto them; *I will make thy Officers Peace; Violence shall no more be heard in thy Land; Thy People also shall be all Righteous; They shall inherit the Earth forever* {Isa. 60:17, 18, 21}. The *Officers*, whether Greater or Smaller, coming down from the *New Heavens* to discharge Various Offices among them, will be the fulfilling of that Word unto them: [Psal.

LXXII.3.] *The Mountains to thy People shall bring forth a Prosp'rous Peace; and so the Little Hills shall do, because of Righteousness* {Ps. 72:3}. What a *Blessed People* will they be, that shall have *Shepherds* of such *Upright Hearts* and *Skilful Hands*, to *Teach* them and *Lead* them; and be under the Conduct of such *Angelical* Ones, who will be *wise like Angels of GOD*, and like the *Good Angels* forever *full of Goodness!* Under Conductors who will be True *Benefactors*, and whom they will most heartily, & with Cause enough, pay the Salutation of an, *Abrek*, to![26] Under *Commissioners* coming down unto them, with Directions, from a Glorious REDEEMER, who has *loved them, & washed away their Sins in His own Blood* {Rev. 1:5}, and will make them sensible in astonishing Ways, that He *Delights* in shewing *Mercy* to them! And as, no doubt, the *Dwellers* on the *New Earth*, will be very much employ'd in Studying the *Works* of GOD, with what marvellous *Illuminations* may their Studies be assisted from Coelestial *Tutors!* Perhaps, no *Solomon* ever so Illuminated, as *the Least in the Kingdom of GOD!* {Matt. 5:19} A very Ordinary Scholar *there*, will much more truly have it allow'd for him, than it was to that *Voluminous* Writer here, of whom it was pretended,—*Scibile discunt omne:*[27]—much more truly be celebrated, as a well-known *Literator* once was by another, in those Terms; *There was nothing that any Man could desire to Learn, but what He was able to Teach.* The Learning of the World will not then be the Jargon of a fumivendutous *Aristotle*, and such Trash as the Colledges in our days have sometimes valued themselves upon.[28] But the World will be filled with the most Noble & Useful Knowledge, and all the *Sciences* will terminate in *Living unto GOD*: Every Part of the World, superior even to a *Frederician* University.[29] Tho Dr. *More* had not risen to such Sentiments of a *New Earth* So *Deathless* and *Sinless* as ours, yett he could not but say: "In the *Seventh Thousand* Year, I do verily Beleeve, that there will be so great *Union* between GOD and Man, that they shall not only partake of His *Spirit*, but that the Inhabitants of the *Æthereal Regions*, will openly converse with those of the *Terrestrial*. And such frequent Conversation and ordinary Visits of our *Cordial Friends* in that *Other World*, will take away all the Toil of *Life* and *Fear* of *Death*, among Men.—*Heaven* and *Earth* shall then Shake Hands together, or become as *One House*; and to *Die* shall be accounted, but to ascend into the Higher Room:—tho' this Dispensation for the Present, be but very sparingly sett on foot."[30] And tho' Dr. *Willet* had not so distinct *Idaeas* of this affair, as there are in our *Scheme*, yett his *Expressions* are such, That we may clothe *Ours* in them; "There shall be an *Intercourse* between *Heaven* and *Earth*, as the *Angels* sometimes came from *Heaven*, & appeared in Humane Bodies; and *Moses* and *Elias* talked with CHRIST in the Mount: And our SAVIOUR Himself, after He was *Risen again*, was conversant forty Days with the Apostles on *Earth*. All which are Good Probabilities that the Saints shall pass to & fro, from *Heaven* to *Earth*, & shall *follow the Lamb withersoever He goeth*" {Rev. 14:4}.[31] But, I hope, we have settled the Matter more to Satisfaction.

There will be no *Carcases of Kings* in the *New Earth*: nor Princes, who, tho' basely flattered with *Blessed Memory*, deserve that their *Memory* should *Rott*. The *Raised Saints* of the *New Heavens*, will be the *Kings* of that *Earth*. And these *Kings of the Earth*, Returning from the Execution of their *Commission*, and with the *Glory* and *Honour* of the *Services*, which the LORD has given them to do in it, they shall *bring their Glory and Honour* into the *Holy City* {Rev. 21:24}, [In a much more Illustrious Manner, than the Old Conquerors did *Theirs* into the *Capitol!*][32] and render it all unto their Great REDEEMER on the Throne; And *they shall bring the Glory and Honour of the Nations* thither, in the Reports of what has been done among the Obedient *Nations*.

—Yea, what raises the Faelicity of the *Holy People* on the *New Earth*, to the highest Pitch of Astonishment!—It appears, that not only the *Raised Saints* of the *New Heavens*, will do so, but even the Glorious LORD of the *Holy City* Himself will in *His Times* for it, make His *Visits* to the *Earth*, and show Himself in His Radiant Glory to His *Holy People* here, and receive their most affectuous Adorations.[33] But, O! the *Times of Refreshment*, that shall *come from the Presence of the LORD!* {Acts 3:19} An Apostle of His, has intimated, that such *Times of Refreshment* would be granted unto others besides the *Raised* from the *Dead*. They that *Behold & Possess* the Land that was *very far off*, Twenty four Hundred Years ago, [but now *the Salvation is near to come*, & the *Righteousness to be reveled!*] shall have their Opportunities, for their *Eyes to see the King in His Beauty*. Who can comprehend the Consequences of these Wonderful *Appearances!* What *Glad Shouts* as of a *Jubilee*, will be made *unto the Lord in all the Earth!* With what a *Shining Joy* will they *Serve the Lord*, and with what *Joyful Acclamations* will they *come into His Presence!* What Confirmations in *Holiness*, will His Reviving and Comforting Rays give unto them; and what *Gifts* will He with a Munificence & Magnificence infinitely more than Royal scatter among them!

They that were *caught up to meet the Lord* {1 Thess. 4:17}, may notwithstanding their having that Part of the *Kingdom* which is to be transacted on the *New Earth* allotted for a while unto them, still very well be comprehended in that Word, *So we shall be forever with the Lord* {1 Thess. 4:17}. For the *New Heavens*, wherein the Lord will be enthroned, will now be *forever* nigh unto them: His *Pavilion* will be *forever* in their View. The Messengers of the Lord will be *forever* conveying of Messages from *Him* down unto them. Yea, the LORD Himself will *Visibly* exhibit Himself unto them, in the proper Season for it. And by being SO *caught up again*, with a Translation to the *Holy City*, when their Work on the *Earth* is all finished, SO shall they be with a yett nearer Access *forever with the Lord.*

Finally; That the Faelicity of the *New Earth* may in a more *Summary Way* be declared unto us, We will in One Word say, Tis the State which the WHOLE CREATION is GROANING for. There is a famous Passage of our Apostle *Paul* concerning this Matter; [Rom. VIII.19–23.] *The Earnest Expectation of the Crea-ture, waiteth for the Manifestation of the Sons of GOD; For the Creature was made Subject unto Vanity, not willingly, but by reason of him who hath subjected the Same, in Hope; Because the Creature itself also shall be delivered from the Bondage of Corruption, into the Glorious Liberty of the Children of GOD; For we know that the whole Creation groneth and Travaileth in Pain together until Now: And not only they, but we ourselves also, who have the First-fruits of the Spirit, even we ourselves grone within ourselves, waiting for Adoption, The Redemption of our Body.*

APPENDIX: TEXTS AND SOURCES

Sources for the selections in this *Cotton Mather Reader* are taken from the first printed editions, where available, largely from the online Evans Bibliography of Early American Imprints, or from manuscripts found in the Mather Family Papers, located at the Massachusetts Historical Society, Boston, and the American Antiquarian Society, Worcester, Massachusetts. We have attempted to retain the original appearance of the text as much as possible, with only light editing, such as rendering ligatures as "ae." Biblical references supplied by the editors are in braces { }. The sources for the selections, by topics, are as follows:

AUTOBIOGRAPHY AND MEDITATIONS

"Paterna" (MSS 3860), Special Collections, Tracy W. McGregor Library of American History, Albert and Shirley Small Special Collections Library, University of Virginia, Charlottesville. MS pp. 1–2, 3–9, 20–22, 45–46, 61–63, 100–101, 128–32, 134, 172, 186–87, 191, 212–13, 223–24, 235–38, 271, 352, 353–54. These MS pages correspond to those in the published edition: *Paterna: The Autobiography of Cotton Mather.* Edited by Ronald A. Bosco. Delmar, N.Y.: Scholars' Facsimiles and Reprints, 1976. Pp. 4–10, 19–21, 41–42, 54–56, 86–88, 109–13, 114–15, 145, 157–59, 161–62, 180–81, 189–90, 198–201, 229, 296, 297–98.

The Diary of Cotton Mather. 2 vols. Edited by Worthington C. Ford. *Collections of the Massachusetts Historical Society,* 7th series, 7–8 (1911–12). Vol. 1, p. 2 (entry for March 1680—81). Hereafter cited as Mather, *Diary.*

Samuel Mather. *The Life of the Very Reverend and Learned Cotton Mather.* Boston, 1729. Ch. 2, pp. 26–27.

Christianus per Ignem. Or, A Disciple Warming of himself and Owning of his Lord: With Devout and Useful Meditations, Fetch'd out of the Fire. Boston, 1702. Pp. 7–8, 13–15, 43–47, 53–54, 58–60, 71–73, 79–80, 88–89, 120–27, 161–62, 165–67, 171–72, 181–82, 183–87, 190–95.

NEW ENGLAND HISTORY AND THE GLORIOUS REVOLUTION

Magnalia Christi Americana; or, The Ecclesiastical History of New-England. London, 1702.
"A General Introduction." Pp. C1r–D1v.
"Nehemias Americanus: The Life of John Winthrop, Esq." Bk. 2, ch. 4, fols. 8–15, pp. 8–12,
14–15.
*The Declaration, of the Gentlemen, Merchants, and Inhabitants of Boston, and the Coun-
trey Adjacent. April 18th, 1689.* Boston, 1689. Pp. 1–3.

GENDER, CHILDREARING, AND EDUCATION

*Ornaments for the Daughters of Zion. Or The Character and Happiness of a Vertuous
Woman: in a Discourse Which Directs The Female-Sex how to Express, The Fear of God,
in every Age and State of their Life; and Obtain both Temporal and Eternal Blessedness.*
Boston, 1692. Pp. 72–90, 92–104.
*Bonifacius. An Essay Upon the Good, that is to be Devised and Designed, by those Who
Desire to Answer the Great End of Life, and to Do Good While they Live.* Boston, 1710.
§ 11. Pp. 50–67.

NATURAL PHILOSOPHY (SCIENCE)

*The Christian Philosopher: A Collection of the Best Discoveries in Nature, with Religious
Improvements.* London, 1721. Pp. 7–8.
Essay I. *Of the* LIGHT. Pp. 8–16.
Essay XXI. *Of* GRAVITY. Pp. 81–88.
Conclusion. Pp. 294–95.

MEDICINE AND THE CURE OF DISEASES

"The Angel of Bethesda." Massachusetts Historical Society, Mather Family Papers, MS
(microfilm), pp. 43–48.
An Account of the Method and Success of Inoculating the Small-Pox. London, 1722. Pp. 1–11,
13–27.
Diary of Cotton Mather. Vol. 2, pp. 657–58 (entry for November 14, 1721).

MERCANTILISM AND PAPER MONEY

Some Considerations on the Bills of Credit. Boston, 1691. Pp. 1–5, 6–7, 8–9.
Theopolis Americana. An Essay on the Golden Street Of the Holy City. Boston, 1710. Pp. 1–2,
4–7, 10–11, 12–26, 42–44.

BIBLICAL HERMENEUTICS

*Psalterium Americanum. The Book of Psalms, In a Translation Exactly conformed unto the
Original; but all in Blank Verse, Fitted unto the Tunes commonly used in our Churches.*
Boston, 1718. Pp. i, vii–viii, ix, x–xii, xxi, xxiii–xxiv, xxxv–xxxvi, 50, 375–76.

Manuductio ad Ministerium. Directions for a Candidate of the Ministry. Boston, 1726.
§ 14, pp. 80–81, 82.

Biblia Americana: America's First Bible Commentary. A Synoptic Commentary on the Old and New Testaments. Vol. 1, *Genesis.* Edited by Reiner Smolinski. Tübingen, Germany: Mohr Siebeck and Baker Academic, 2010. Pp. 357–58, 357–76, 380.

Biblia Americana: America's First Bible Commentary. A Synoptic Commentary on the Old and New Testaments. Vol. 2, *Exodus–Deuteronomy.* Edited by Reiner Smolinski. Tübingen, Germany: Mohr Siebeck, 2019. Pp. 248–51.

Biblia Americana: America's First Bible Commentary. A Synoptic Commentary on the Old and New Testaments. Vol. 3, *Joshua–2 Chronicles.* Edited by Kenneth P. Minkema. Tübingen, Germany: Mohr Siebeck and Baker Academic, 2013. Pp. 112–13, 191–92, 736–37.

Biblia Americana: America's First Bible Commentary. A Synoptic Commentary on the Old and New Testaments. Vol. 4, *Ezra–Psalms.* Edited by Harry Clark Maddux. Tübingen, Germany: Mohr Siebeck and Baker Academic, 2014. Pp. 339–41.

Biblia Americana: America's First Bible Commentary. A Synoptic Commentary on the Old and New Testaments. Vol. 5, *Proverbs–Jeremiah.* Edited by Jan Stievermann. Tübingen, Germany: Mohr Siebeck, 2015. Pp. 610–14.

Biblia Americana: America's First Bible Commentary. A Synoptic Commentary on the Old and New Testaments. Vol. 9, *Romans–Philemon.* Edited by Robert E. Brown. Tübingen, Germany: Mohr Siebeck, 2018. Pp. 98–100, 490–92.

THE INVISIBLE WORLD AND SALEM WITCHCRAFT

Memorable Providences, Relating to Witchcrafts and Possessions. Boston: R. P., 1689. Pp. 1, 2–5, 6–15, 17–23, 27–29, 30–34, 37–41.

"The Return of Several Ministers Consulted by his Excellency, and the Honourable Council, upon the Present Witchcrafts in Salem Village" (June 15, 1692). In Increase Mather, *Cases of Conscience* (Boston, 1693). "Postscript," G4r–v.

Diary of Cotton Mather. Vol. 1, pp. 150–57 (entries for May–December 1692).

"Letter of Cotton Mather to John Foster (17th 6m [August], 1692)." *Transactions of the Literary Society of Quebec* 2 (1831): 313–16.

The Wonders of the Invisible World. Boston, 1693. Pp. xi–xx, xi–xxiv, 94–104, 114–26.

RACE, SLAVERY, AND SERVITUDE

Biblia Americana: America's First Bible Commentary. . . . Vol. 1, *Genesis.* P. 672 (entry on Gen. 9:27).

Biblia Americana: America's First Bible Commentary. . . . Vol. 1, *Genesis.* Pp. 673–77 (entry on Gen. 9:20–27).

Biblia Americana: America's First Bible Commentary. . . . Vol. 1, *Genesis.* Pp. 698–99 (entry on Gen. 10:20).

Diary of Cotton Mather. Vol. 1, p. 176 (entry for October–December 1693).

Rules for the Society of Negroes. 1693. Boston, c. 1706–13. Broadside.

A Good Master Well Served. A Brief Discourse On the Necessary Properties & Practices Of a Good Servant In every-kind of Servitude: And of the Methods that should be taken by the Heads of a Family, to Obtain such a Servant. Boston, 1696. Pp. 4–6, 20–26, 30–31, 33–36, 38–39, 48–55.

The Negro Christianized. An essay to excite and assist the good work, the instruction of Negro-servants in Christianity. Boston, 1706. Pp. 1–6, 11–28.

PURITANS AND NATIVE AMERICANS

Humiliations follow'd with Deliverances. A Brief Discourse on the Matter and Method, Of that Humiliation which would be an Hopeful Symptom of our Deliverance from Calamity. Boston, 1697. Pp. 40–47, 51–69, 71–72.

Duodecennium Luctuosum. The History of a Long War with Indian Salvages, And their Directors and Abettors; From the Year, 1702. To the Year, 1714. Boston, 1714. Pp. 5, 11–17, 19–21, 23–26.

PIETISM AND WORLD MISSIONS

Manuductio ad Ministerium. § 18. Pp. 115–29.

India Christiana. A Discourse, Delivered unto the Commissioners, for the Propagation of the Gospel among the American Indians which is Accompanied with several Instruments relating to the Glorious Design of Propagating our Holy Religion, in the Eastern as well as the Western, Indies. Boston, 1721. Pp. 56–61.

THE SECOND COMING AND MILLENNIALISM

The Threefold Paradise of Cotton Mather. An Edition of "Triparadisus." Edited by Reiner Smolinski. Athens: University of Georgia Press, 1995. Pp. 153–54, 268–69, 271, 272–74, 275, 276–78, 279, 280–81, 282, 284–85, 286–88.

CHRONOLOGY

1662/63	February 12, 1662 (Old Style), born at Boston; eldest child of Reverend Increase Mather and Maria (Cotton) Mather, grandson of Richard Mather and John Cotton
1674–78	Admitted to Harvard at age eleven; baccalaureate degree at fifteen; develops stammer
1678–79	Admitted to church membership in his father's North Church (Second Congregational); studies medicine as alternative vocation
1680	Delivers his first public sermon in Dorchester at his grandfather's church
1681	M.A. at eighteen; declines a call to the church of New Haven
1683–85	Chosen pastor of the North Church (ordained in 1685) to assist his father; ministers for more than forty-two years
1684	Revocation of the Old Charter
1685	Appointed overseer at Harvard; experiences an angelic vision; Increase Mather assumes presidency of Harvard (resigns in 1701)
1686	Publishes his first sermon, *The Call of the Gospel*; marries Abigail Phillips of Charlestown; arrival in Boston of Governor Edmund Andros
1688	Increase Mather sent to London to secure a new charter; Glorious Revolution in England; accession of William and Mary
1689	April 18, 1689, Glorious Revolution in New England; Mather delivers *The Declaration of the Gentlemen, Merchants, and Inhabitants of Boston*; ouster of Edmund Andros; publishes *Memorable Providences, Relating to Witchcrafts and Possessions*
1690	Baptizes Sir William Phips; elected fellow at Harvard
1691	Witchcraft hysteria begins to spread; publishes (anonymously) *Some Considerations on the Bills of Credit*
1692	Increase Mather returns from England with the Second Charter (1691); William Phips appointed governor of New England; June 10, 1692, Bridget Bishop executed for witchcraft in Salem; June 15, 1692, publishes

"The Return of Several Ministers Consulted," warning against the use of spectral evidence to convict the accused; publishes *Ornaments for the Daughters of Zion*, which runs through four editions

1693 Begins work on *Magnalia Christi Americana* (published London, 1702); begins medical handbook *Angel of Bethesda* (published 1972); begins *Biblia Americana*; publishes *Wonders of the Invisible World*; and writes *Rules for the Society of Negroes*

1695 Death of William Phips in London

1697 Publishes *Humiliations follow'd with Deliverances*; completes manuscript of *Magnalia Christi Americana* (sent to London in 1699); publishes *Pietas in Patriam: The Life of His Excellency Sir William Phips* in London

1698 Appointed commissioner of the Society for the Propagation of the Gospel in New England

1699 July 9, 1699, birth of son Increase Mather ("Creasy"); Brattle Street Church ("Manifesto Church") established; publishes *Decennium Luctuosum*; begins autobiography "Paterna"

1700 Publishes *Indian Primer*; Robert Calef's *More Wonders of the Invisible World* blames the Mathers and their fellow ministers for instigating the witchcraft hysteria; publishes *Reasonable Religion*

1701 Increase Mather steps down from the presidency of Harvard

1702 Publishes *Christianus per Ignem*; *Magnalia Christi Americana* published in London; death of Abigail, Mather's first wife; Joseph Dudley appointed royal governor

1703 August 18, 1703, marries widow Elizabeth Clark Hubbard; resigns from his position of overseer at Harvard; begins "Problema Theologicum"

1705 Publishes *Family Religion, Excited and Assisted* and *Lex Mercatoria*

1706 Publishes *The Negro Christianized* and *Private Meetings Animated & Regulated*; birth of son Samuel Mather

1708 Publishes *Corderius Americanaus. An Essay upon The Good Education of Children*

1710 Publishes *Bonifacius*; begins *The Christian Philosopher*; publishes *Theopolis Americana*

1712 Begins "Curiosa Americana"

1713 Elected fellow of the Royal Society of London; November 9, 1713, death of Elizabeth, Mather's second wife, during a measles epidemic; publishes *A Letter about a Good Management under the Distemper of the Measles*

1714 Publishes *A New Offer to the Lovers of Religion and Learning* (advertisement for *Biblia Americana*) and *Duodecennium Luctuosum*

1715 Marries third wife, widow Lydia Lee George; death of Governor Joseph Dudley

1716 Publishes *The Stone Cut out of the Mountain*

1717 Persuades Elihu Yale to endow a new college in New Haven; son "Creasy" charged with paternity suit; publishes *Malachi*, calling for union on the basis of his "Maxims of Piety"

1718	Bankruptcy over Lydia's inherited estate; nearly loses his prized library; publishes *Psalterium Americanum*
1720/21	Publishes *The Christian Philosopher* (London); begins *Triparadisus*
1721	Publishes *India Christiana*; smallpox epidemic in New England; with Zabdiel Boylston, a Boston physician, introduces smallpox inoculation (vaccination); publishes *Sentiments On the Small Pox Inoculated* and (with Boylston) *Some Account of . . . Inoculating or Transplanting the Small Pox*
1722	Publishes *An Account of the Method and Success of Inoculating the Small-Pox* (London); *Account of Inoculating the Small Pox Vindicated*; and *Vindication of the Ministers of Boston*
1723	August 23, 1723, death of Increase Mather; publishes *Coelestinus* and *A Father Departing*
1724	Publishes *Parentator*, a biography of Increase Mather; death of son "Creasy," lost at sea
1726	Publishes *Ratio Disciplinae Fratrum Nov-Anglorum* and *Manuductio ad Ministerium*
1727	Earthquakes in New England; publishes *Boanerges* and *The Terror of the Lord*
1728	Dies February 13, 1728; burial in Copp's Hill Burial Ground in Boston (North End); publishes *The Comfortable Chambers* and *Mystical Union*
1729	Samuel Mather, Cotton Mather's son, publishes *The Life of the Very Reverend and Learned Cotton Mather*

NOTES

Translations are the editors' unless otherwise identified.

EDITORS' INTRODUCTION

1. See Bailyn, *The New England Merchants*; Peterson, *The City-State of Boston*; and Valeri, *Heavenly Merchandise*.
2. Samuel Mather, *Life*, 5. See also Horace E. Mather, *Lineage of Rev. Richard Mather*, 11–13.
3. See Holmes, *Cotton Mather*, 1:ix, and Amory, "A Note on Statistics."
4. See Silverman, *Selected Letters*.
5. Samuel Mather, *Life*, 15, 16, 17.
6. Prince, *Departure*, 19, 20, 21; "The Preface," 4.
7. Colman, *Holy Walk*, 23–24.
8. Prince, *Departure*, 21.
9. Mather, *Diary*, 1:272–73, 363, 401.
10. See Miller, *New England Mind*, and Morison, *Intellectual Life*.
11. See Lovejoy, *Glorious Revolution*; Hall, *Worlds of Wonder*; and Peterson, *The City-State of Boston*.
12. Samuel Mather, *Life* 42; Calef, *More Wonders*, 149; Hutchinson, *History*, 1:381.
13. Mather, *Magnalia Christi Americana*, 2.45. Unless otherwise indicated, all references to Cotton Mather's *Magnalia Christi Americana* are to the first edition, London, 1702, published by Thomas Parkhurst.
14. Mather, *Pietas in Patriam*, § 16, pp. 79, 80.
15. See Pope, *The Half-Way Covenant*.
16. "Cotton Mather to John Richards" (February 13, 1692).
17. See Pope, *The Half-Way Covenant*; and Harper, *A People So Favored of God*.
18. See Lovelace, *American Pietism*.

19. Mather, *Diary*, 1:520.
20. See Silver, "Financing the Publication of Early New England Sermons."
21. Mather, *Parentator*, 198.
22. "Cotton Mather to Zabdiel Boylstone" (June 24, 1721). See also Kittredge, "Some Lost Works."
23. The history of Boston's smallpox epidemic of 1721–22 has engaged numerous schol-ars, including Beall and Shryock, *Cotton Mather*; Blake, *Public Health*; Coss, *The Fever of 1721*; Duffy, *Epidemics*; Kass, "Boston's Historic Smallpox Epidemic"; Silva, *Miraculous Plagues*; Stearns, *Science in the British Colonies of America*; G. Williams, *Angel of Death*; T. Williams, *The Pox*; and Winslow, *A Destroying Angel*.
24. See Cotton Mather, "An Original Letter from Dr. C. Mather, to Governour Dudley," and Increase Mather, "An Original Letter from Dr. Increase Mather, to Governour Dudley." See also Joseph Dudley's response to the Mathers, Dudley, "An Original Let-ter from Governor Dudley, to Dr. Increase and Cotton Mather."
25. See Minkema, "Reforming Harvard."
26. See Haffenden, *New England*; Peterson, *The City-State of Boston*; Sossin, *English America*; and Valeri, *Heavenly Merchandise*.
27. See Gildrie, *The Profane, the Civil, and the Godly*.
28. Mather, *Diary*, 2:442, 500, 54.
29. Carnegie, *The Gospel of Wealth*, 22.
30. Mather, *Bonifacius*, 136, 137.
31. "Cotton Mather to Elihu Yale" (January 14, 1718).
32. Samuel Mather, *Life*, 153, 159.
33. Colman, *Holy Walk*, 23–24.
34. See Mages, *Magnalia Christi Americana*.
35. Franklin, "Letter to Samuel Mather, 12 May, 1784."
36. See Broyles, "*Music of the Highest Class*"; McKay, "Cotton Mather's Unpublished Singing Sermon"; and Music, "Cotton Mather."
37. Mather, *Psalterium Americanum*, xxxiv, vii.
38. Mather, *Psalterium Americanum*, ii, xiv–xv.
39. See Mather, *Magnalia Christi Americana*, bk. 3, chap. 12, fol. 100.
40. Mather, *Christian Philosopher* (1721), 1.
41. Stearns, "Colonial Fellows." Benjamin Franklin was the twenty-ninth elected colonial American.
42. Stearns, *Science in the British Colonies of America*, 152–53.
43. See Beall and Shryock, *Cotton Mather*; Warner, "Vindicating the Minister's Medi-cal Role"; and Watson, *The Angelical Conjunction*.
44. Jones, "Introduction," xxxvi.
45. Mather, *Manuductio*, § 18, p. 118.
46. Galileo, "Letter to the Grand Duchess Christina," 96.
47. Currently available in microfilm (19 reels), Massachusetts Historical Society.
48. Samuel Mather, *The Departure and Character of Elijah Considered and Improved* (Boston, 1728), 24.
49. Silverman, *Life and Times*, 425; Holifield, "The Abridging of Cotton Mather," 95.

AUTOBIOGRAPHY AND MEDITATIONS

1. See Bosco, "Introduction," and Post, *Signs of the Times*.
2. Mather, *Diary*, 2:267.
3. Mather, "Paterna," 218–19, 172. See also Mather, *Diary*, 1:195.
4. Mather, "Paterna," 34.
5. Mather, *Christianus per Ignem*, 7.
6. Mather refers to his extant diaries.
7. Rev. Increase Mather, D.D. (1639–1723).
8. Ezekiel Cheever (1614–1708), headmaster of Boston Latin School.
9. "Your diligence is praiseworthy!"
10. Not quite twelve, Mather was admitted to Harvard College in 1674.
11. See Mather's medical essay "De Tristibus, or the Cure of MELANCHOLY," in *The Angel of Bethesda*, 132–37.
12. The following two excerpts from Cotton Mather's *Diary*, 1:2, and from Samuel Mather's *Life* (1729), 26–27, are here interpolated to describe the nature of Cotton Mather's speech impediment.
13. Elijah Corlet, M.A. (1610–1687), headmaster of Cambridge Grammar School.
14. Years later, when writing one of the first medical treatises on stuttering, Cotton Mather confessed, "I know one, who had been very much a *Stammerer*; and no words can tell, how much his Infirmity did Encumber and Embitter the first years of his Pilgrimage." Mather, *The Angel of Bethesda*, 230.
15. Mather married Abigail Philips (1670–1702) on May 4, 1686. She bore him nine children, of whom only four survived her.
16. See also Increase Mather's *Angelographia*.
17. "A strange and memorable thing. After outpourings of prayer, with the utmost fervour and fasting, there appeared an Angel, whose face shone like the noonday sun. His features were as those of a man, and beardless; his head was encircled by a splendid tiara; on his shoulders were wings; his garments were white and shining; his robe reached to his ankles; and about his loins was a belt not unlike the girdles of the peoples of the East. / And this Angel said that he was sent by the Lord Jesus to bear a clear answer to the prayers of a certain youth, and to bear back his words in reply. / Many things this Angel said which it is not fit to set down here. But among other things not to be forgotten he declared that the fate of this youth should be to find full expression for what in him was best: and this he said in the words of the prophet Ezekiel." Translated in Wendell, *Cotton Mather*, 64.
18. This and the following passage in brackets appear in his *Diary*, 1:87.
19. "And in particular this Angel spoke of the influence his branches should have, and of the books this youth should write and publish, not only in America, but in Europe. And he added certain special prophecies of the great works this youth should do for the Church of Christ in the revolutions that are now at hand. / Lord Jesus! What is the meaning of this marvel? From the wiles of the Devil, I beseech you, deliver and defend Thy most unworthy servant." Translated in Wendell, *Cotton Mather*, 64. See also Mather, *Diary*, 1:86–87.

20. Katherine Mather (c. 1693–1716).
21. In April 1696, Mather was chosen to deliver the election sermon for the year. Mather, *Diary*, 1:191–92.
22. This text was a record of his own vileness to serve his ritualistic abnegation in his quest for spiritual reassurance. Mather, *Diary*, 1:195.
23. A "lustre" is a period of five years.
24. Increase ("Creasy") Mather (1699–1724), lost at sea.
25. Rev. Samuel Mather (1706–1785).
26. Sparse English coin in the colonies was frequently supplemented with widely available Spanish currency. Spanish silver dollars, aka "pieces of eight," were cut into halves, quarters, and even eighths to make up for a lack of English money.
27. See his specific recommendations in *Bonifacius*, 96–100.
28. Similarly, he complained, "Men will sooner Forgive Great *Injuries*, than Great *Services*." Mather, *Bonifacius*, x.
29. See also Mather, *Manuductio*, 33.
30. See also Mather, *Manuductio*, 23–24, and *Christian Philosopher* (1721), 282–83.
31. Mather discusses the utility of this occasional meditation in his *Diary*, 1:381–82. The publication of this document was subventioned by one of his neighbors.
32. "Cogito ergo sum," the famous conclusion of René Descartes (1596–1650), French philosopher, scientist, and mathematician.
33. "Accept, Return, Avoid." Hugh of Saint-Victor (1096–1141) was a French scholastic theologian and Augustinian monastic in Germany. See also Mather, *Christian Philosopher* (1721), 13.
34. "Who would be so foolish as to touch fire."
35. "The multitude of activities endangers devotion."
36. "Let us go [into hell] while we are alive, that we may not go into it when we are dead." John Chrysostom (c. 347–407), archbishop of Constantinople.
37. Fernando Alvarez de Toledo, Grand Duke of Alba (1507–1582), who sent Dutch insurgents to their death; Edmund Bonner (c. 1500–1569), Roman Catholic bishop of London who burned dissenters at the stake in Smithfield. Foxe, *Actes and Monuments* (better known as *The Book of Martyrs*).
38. François Ravaillac (1578–1610), French Catholic assassin of King Henry IV of France.
39. The Venetian Luigi Cornaro (c. 1467–1566) published his oft-reprinted *Discorsi Della Vita Sobria* (Padova, 1591) on the art of healthy living.
40. See Mather, *Methods and Motives for Societies*, and *Private Meetings Animated & Regulated*.
41. Boyle, *New Experiments Physico-Mechanicall*.
42. Roger Bacon (c. 1220–1292), English Franciscan friar and philosopher who developed gunpowder in Europe.
43. A naturally occurring mineral, ammonium chloride.
44. Joseph du Chesne, aka Josephus Quercetanus (c. 1544–1609), French Paracelsian alchemist and physician.
45. "The resurrection of the dead is the Christian's trust." Tertullian, *On the Resurrection of the Flesh*, chap. 1, transl. Rev. Peter Holmes, in *Ante-Nicene Fathers*, ed. Alexander Roberts and James Donaldson (Peabody, Mass.: Hendrickson, 1999), 3:545.

46. Midrash Coheleth mentions a poor, naked, and famished beggar by the name of Diglus Petargus, whom Mather here compares to wise Solomon; the Lydian King Croesus (fl. 560–546 BCE), fabled for his riches; and Irus (aka Arnaeus), messenger of Penelope's suitors. Homer, *Odyssey*, transl. A. T. Murray, ed. George E. Dimock, 2 vols. (Cambridge, Mass.: Harvard University Press, 1995), 2:18.1–49.

47. From George Herbert, "Content," in *The Temple: Sacred Poems and Private Ejaculations* (Cambridge, 1633), 60.

48. "Remember, man, that you are dust."

49. "Cover your fire," referencing the ancient custom of requiring that all hearths be extinguished before the household went to bed to prevent accidental fires, especially in cities.

50. The infamous "Donatio Constantini" of Roman emperor Constantine the Great (272–337), a medieval forgery that granted Pope Silvester I (314–335) power over the Western Roman Empire.

51. Adapted from Augustine, *Confessions*, 8.8: "The unlearned men rise up, and take heaven, but we, with our learning, plunge into Hell."

NEW ENGLAND HISTORY AND THE GLORIOUS REVOLUTION

1. See Miller, *The New England Mind*, 189–91; Bercovitch, *American Jeremiad*, 86–88; Halttunen, "Cotton Mather and the Memory of Suffering," 311–29; and Stievermann, "General Introduction," 24–25.

2. Bercovitch, *American Jeremiad*, 89.

3. See Hutchins, *Inventing Eden*.

4. See Stievermann, "Writing 'to Conquer All Things,'" 265.

5. Mather, *Magnalia Christi Americana*, bk. 2, p. 8, sec. 3.

6. For the charges against the abuse of the royal prerogative under the Old Charter, see Randolph, "Articles."

7. For New England's grievances against Sir Edmund Andros (1637–1714), see the anonymous pamphlet *The Revolution in New England Justified*. Mather also presents some of the same charges in his *Pietas in Patriam*, § 8, pp. 19–26.

8. Silverman, *Life and Times*, 70.

9. Mather adapts two lines from "The Church Militant," in Herbert, *The Temple*, 190, lines 235–36: "Religion stands on tip-toe in our land, / Readie to passe to the *American* strand."

10. Harvard, founded in 1636.

11. I.e., Creoles, or people of mixed descent, usually Spanish–Native American, though here Mather seems to use the term to apply to any non-Native person born in the Americas.

12. Adapted from Virgil's *Aeneid*, 1:1.9–10: "Drove men, of goodness so wondrous, to traverse so many perils, to face so many toils."

13. The citation is from *Antiquities of the Jews*, 6.7.4, by the Roman-Jewish historian Flavius Josephus (c. 37–100).

14. John Foxe (1516–1587), English martyrologist and author of the hugely popular and frequently reprinted *Actes and Monuments*.

15. I.e., decried, or denounced.

16. John Wycliffe (c. 1330–1384), English theologian and reformer who translated the Bible into English.

17. Thomas Cranmer (1489–1556), English reformer and archbishop of Canterbury; Martin Bucer (1491–1551), German Protestant reformer and author of *Scripta Anglicana* (Basel, 1577).

18. Peter Heylyn (1599–1662), English theologian and cosmographer.

19. John Owen (1616–1683), English Puritan theologian and author of *An Enquiry Into the Original, Nature, Institution, Power, Order and Communion of Evangelical Churches* (London, 1681).

20. "That they acknowledge their own imperfections."

21. Constantinus Northmannus of Rouen (d. 1542), Norman martyr.

22. *Cyropaedia*, 8.7.24, lines 2–3, a fictional biography of Cyrus the Great of Persia (c. 590–c. 529 BCE), by the Greek historian Xenophon of Athens (c. 431–354 BCE).

23. *Sermones in Cantica*, Sermo 38, by the French Benedictine abbot St. Bernard of Clairvaux (1090–1153): "He [Solomon] calls her fair, not in a universal sense, but fair among women, yet with the distinction that his praise is qualified, and that she may know her own shortcomings." "Canticles" is an alternate title for the biblical book the Song of Songs.

24. "The outer regions" and "outer darkness."

25. Herodotus (c. 484–c. 420 BCE), Greek historian and geographer whose *Histories* earned him the title "The Father of History"; William Howell (1631–1683), English lawyer and historian, author of *An Institution of General History* (1661). A polyanthea is an anthology.

26. See also Mather, *Manuductio*, § 11, pp. 64–69.

27. Original reads "implies." Mather provided a list of errata to the Boston booksellers; his corrections are silently incorporated here.

28. Publius Cornelius Tacitus, second-century CE Roman historian and politician, *Annals*, 4.32: "Big wars, dramatic sieges of cities, defeated and captured kings."

29. Didymus the Blind (c. 313–c. 398), an Alexandrian theologian and grammarian touted to be a voluminous author of unremarkable books.

30. In the original (fol. C2v), the last word of the quotation reads, "Lymei." It translates, "Read historians with moderation & indulgence, & remember that it is not possible for them to be like Lynceus in all circumstances."

31. Polybius (c. 200–c. 118 BCE) was a Greek historian who commented, "Philinus will have it that the Carthaginians in every case acted wisely, well, and bravely, and the Romans otherwise, whilst Fabius takes the precisely opposite view." Polybius, *The Histories of Polybius*, 2 vols., transl. Evelyn Shirtley Shuckburgh (New York: Macmillan, 1889), 1:14.

32. Lucian of Samosata was an Assyrian satirical writer of the second century CE. In the mythology of the Trojan War, Achilles was the great admired hero, while Thersites was the deformed ignoble critic.

33. "Honest Truthful," the pseudonym of Claudius Salmasius, or Claude de Saumaise (1588–1653), French Huguenot and classical scholar.

34. St. Zacharias (679–752), last of the Greek popes in Rome.

35. Conrad Schlüsselberg (1543–1619), German Lutheran clergyman, author of a catalogue on heretics.

36. Adapted from the Greek historian Polybius: "It is history's most important province
to praise good deeds." Polybius, *Histories*, 2:61.

37. I.e., it is better to be forthright than charming.

38. See Polybius, *Histories*, 1:14.

39. See Polybius, *Histories*, 2:61.

40. Daniel Chamier (1565–1621) and André Rivet (1572–1651), French reformed theologians
and academics.

41. Pope Sixtus V (1585–1590) pokes fun (*pasquil*) at his short-lived predecessor, Pope
Urban VII (d. 1590).

42. "The simplest style of writing."

43. Eusebius of Caesarea (c. 260–c. 340), father of church history, refers to Hegesippus
the Nazarene (second century CE), Christian writer and author of *Hypomnemata*,
or *Memoirs*. The Greek passage reads, "Memoirs of Ecclesiastical Transactions."

44. "Just as a little salt seasons food and increases its flavor, so a modicum of antiquity
elevates the charm of style."

45. Marcus Tullius Cicero (106–43 BCE), the Roman statesman and lawyer, cautions his
interlocutor, "But before we come to the subject, let me say a few words about myself." *On the Nature of the Gods*, transl. H. Rackham (Cambridge, Mass.: Harvard
University Press, 1933), 3.2.5.

46. Greek mythological monsters: hundred-headed Typhoeus (Typhon); hundred-eyed,
all-seeing giant Argos; hundred-armed and fifty-headed Briareus (Aegaeon).

47. "Deliver me from the man of single business."

48. Diodorus of Sicily, a first-century BCE Greek historian, author of the *Bibliotheca historica*; Jean Bodin (1540–1596), French historian and political philosopher; Carlo
Sigonio (c. 1524–1584), Italian humanist and complainer about "errors."

49. Thomas Coryat (c. 1577–1617), English traveler whose *Crudities* (London, 1611) is an
account of his journeys through Continental Europe.

50. Protogenes and Apelles (fourth century BCE) were ancient Greek artists who were
contemporaries and rivals.

51. Another reference to John Foxe, author of *Actes and Monuments*.

52. Nightly labors.

53. Hermes Mercurius Trismegistus, long thought to be a wise pagan prophet to whom a
large collection of esoteric writings called the *Hermetic Corpus* was attributed.

54. Jean Claude (1619–1687), French Huguenot minister.

55. Richard Baxter (1615–1691), English Puritan clergyman and friend of the Mathers.

56. Like Baxter, Increase and Cotton Mather strove for decades to bring about a union
among Congregationalists, Independents, and Presbyterians.

57. Straton of Lamsacus (c. 335–c. 269 BCE), Athenian peripatetic philosopher, was rewarded by Ptolemy I Soter of Egypt (c. 367–282 BCE) for his help in establishing the
famous library of Alexandria.

58. Athanaeus of Naucratis, a third-century CE Greek writer, recounts that Hiero II, king
of Syracuse (c. 270–c. 216 BCE), sent a large reward of wheat to the Greek poet Archimelus (third century BCE) for an epigram written about his flagship; Saleius Bas-

sus was a first-century CE Roman epic poet who, impoverished but highly regarded, was given 12,500 Philippics (gold coins of Philip of Macedonia) by Roman Emperor Vespasian (9–79 CE); Oppian was a second-century CE Greco-Roman poet, most known for his epic on fishing, *Halieutica*, and favored by Roman Emperor Caracalla (r. 211–217 CE).

59. Lycurgus was, according to legend, the ninth-century BCE lawgiver of Sparta; Numa Pompilius was the seventh-century BCE king and lawgiver of Rome.

60. John Winthrop (1587–1649), first governor of the Massachusetts Bay Colony.

61. Plutarch (46–c. 120 CE) was a Greek Platonist philosopher famous for his *Lives*, biographies of prominent Greeks and Romans.

62. John Philpot (1516–1555), archdeacon of Winchester, was martyred in Smithfield. His martyrdom is recorded in John Foxe, *Actes and Monuments*, 2nd ed. (London, 1583), 1717–20.

63. Sir Edward Coke (1552–1634), British jurist, politician, and author of *Institutes of the Lawes of England* (London, 1628–44).

64. I.e., face worship.

65. Grammar, rhetoric, logic, arithmetic, music, geometry, and astronomy.

66. "A commission authorizing a British judge to hear and determine a criminal case at the assizes." *Merriam-Webster Dictionary* (online).

67. 18.6 years.

68. Meaning he did not take notes as he was hearing sermons, as others of the time commonly did.

69. An early settler of Massachusetts, Thomas Morton (c. 1579–1647) caricaturized Winthrop as "John Temperwell," in *New English Canaan* (London, 1637), bk. 3, chap. 23, p. 162.

70. George Cleaves (c. 1586–c. 1659), founder of Portland, Maine, and deputy president of the province of Lygonia.

71. "Slowly."

72. Winthrop, entry for January 18, 1636, in Winthrop, *Journal of John Winthrop*, 167.

73. Winthrop, entry for December 4, 1639, in Winthrop, *Journal of John Winthrop*, 167, 168.

74. As described in the book of Nehemiah (chaps. 2, 4, 6), Sanballat the Horonite and Tobiah the Ammonite, his servant, opposed the rebuilding of the walls of Jerusalem after the Jews were returned from their Babylonian captivity.

75. Martin Luther, as quoted in Johann Gerhard (1582–1637), *Loci Theologici*, 3 vols. (Steinmann, 1610–13; reprint, 8 vols., Berlin, 1863–70), 5:294: "Every ruler is like a target for Satan and the World to aim their darts."

76. Rev. Francis Higginson migrated to New England in 1629 and became a minister at Salem, Mass., but died the following year; his son Rev. John Higginson became the minister of that town as well, dying in 1708.

77. Plato, *Republic*, 361c, line 6.

78. Rev. Ezekiel Rogers (1590–1661), pastor at Rowley, Mass. Winthrop recorded the incident (May 10, 1643) in his *Journal*. Winthrop, entry for May 10, 1643, in Winthrop, *Journal of John Winthrop*, 219.

79. The noble Florentine family of the Piazzi engaged in a failed assassination attempt against the Italian statesman Lorenzo de Medici (1449–1492).
80. "The prudent man is patient," the motto of Sir Edward Coke.
81. Gulielmus Parisiensis, aka William of Auvergne, bishop of Paris (1180–1249).
82. Emperor of the Eastern Roman Empire during the fourth century CE.
83. Referring to the Free Grace Controversy of the 1630s, which resulted in the banishment of Anne Hutchinson and her Antinomian followers.
84. "Would surely bear off with them in wild flight seas and lands and the vault of heaven, sweeping them through space." Virgil, *Aeneid*, 1:1.58–60.
85. The following extract is from Winthrop's speech (November–December 1637). Winthrop, entry for October 13, 1643, in Winthrop, *Journal of John Winthrop*, 242–43.
86. Virgil, *Aeneid*, 1:1.154: "Even so, all the roar of ocean sank."
87. Pliny the Elder, *Naturalis Historia*, transl. Jeffrey Henderson (Cambridge, Mass.: Harvard University Press, 1949), bk. 8, chap. 43, p. 104. The story of the Pied Piper of Hamlin (Hameln, Germany) may account for Mather's following allusion.
88. Referring to Capt. Robert Keayne (1595–1656), cofounder of the Ancient and Honorable Artillery Company of Massachusetts, wealthy merchant, and speaker of the General Court, who feuded with Elizabeth Sherman, his neighbor, over her pig gone astray into his yard. Winthrop, entries for June 22, 1642, and June 12, 1643, in Winthrop, *Journal of John Winthrop*, 204–5, 229–32. See also *The Apologia of Robert Keayne: The Last Will and Testament* (1653), ed. Bernard Bailyn (Gloucester, Mass.: Peter Smith, 1970).
89. The following citation is from Winthrop's entry for May 10, 1643, in Winthrop, *Journal of John Winthrop*, 219–23.
90. Virgil, *Aeneid*, 1:1.142–43: "Thus he speaks, and swifter than his word he calms the swollen seas, puts to flight the gathered clouds, and brings back the sun."
91. Macarius the Great (300–390), an Egyptian monk, one of the Desert Fathers.
92. Thus, Winthrop was fifty-five at the time. He died in his sixty-second year.
93. Maximianus, sixth-century CE Latin poet: "I am not what I was in form or face, / In healthful colour or in vigorous pace." Maximianus, *Elegy*, 1.1.211–12, transl. Lucius F. Robinson, in Mather, *Magnalia Christi Americana* (Hartford, Conn., 1853), 1:130.
94. "To think that I who have judged others, am now going to be judged myself." Cited by Bishop Lewis Bayly (d. 1631), "Meditations Directing a Christian How He May Walk All the Day with God, Like Enoch," in *The Practice of Piety* (London, 1619), sec. 9, p. 309.
95. John Cotton (1585–1652), pastor of the first church of Boston.
96. John Cotton's funeral sermon of John Winthrop appears to be lost.
97. Flavius Josephus, *Antiquities of the Jews*, 11.5.8: "He was a man honest and just by nature, and most zealous for the honor of his countrymen, and to them he left an eternal monument—the walls of Jerusalem [New England]."
98. The fabricated conspiracy of Titus Oates (1649–1705), an Anglican clergyman who alleged that the Jesuits were plotting against King Charles II in 1678 to set up Roman Catholicism in England.

99. Mary Stuart, queen of Scots (1542–1587), executed for plotting the assassination of Queen Elizabeth I.
100. King James II of England (1633–1701) was overthrown in 1688 by the Dutch Stadholder William III (1650–1702) of Orange and his wife, Princess Mary (1662–1694), eldest daughter of James II (1633–1701).
101. Referring to the Second Indian War, beginning in 1688, the North American version of the Nine Years' War (1688–1697).
102. In 1688, William and Mary were invited by Parliament to assume the English throne in what was called "The Glorious Revolution."

GENDER, CHILDREARING, AND EDUCATION

1. See Gelinas, "Regaining Paradise," 463.
2. See Bernhard, "Cotton Mather's 'Most Unhappy Wife.'"
3. An expanded version of Mather's *Bonifacius*, § 11, was published separately as *A Family Well-Ordered*.
4. Mather, *Bonifacius*, 52–66.
5. See Greven, *Spare the Child*; Marten, *Children in Colonial America*; and Monaghan, *Learning to Read and Write in Colonial America*.
6. In the congregational churches of colonial New England, candidates for full membership, which included access to the sacraments, would be "addressed" or presented to the congregation, which would vote for approval or disapproval.
7. "Peace."
8. An aromatic Asian tree or shrub. Here, a sweet-tempered person.
9. Prince Edward (1239–1307), later King Edward I of England, and his spouse, Eleanor of Castile (d. 1290). According to legend, Eleanor sucked the poison out of her husband's arm when Edward was injured at Acre (northern Israel) in a battle with Saladin's Ottoman Army near the end of the Great Crusade.
10. In 1140, King Conrad III of Germany (1093–1152) defeated Welf VI, Duke of Bavaria (1115–1191), and besieged Weinsberg, in what is now southwestern Germany, after which the women of the city negotiated this deal with the amused Conrad.
11. Tigranes II, king of Armenia during the second and first centuries BCE; his wife was Cleopatra, daughter of Mithridates VI, king of Pontus.
12. John Chrysostom, fourth-century CE Christian theologian and archbishop of Constantinople. Chrysostom, *Homilies on First Corinthians*, Homily 26, treating 1 Corinthians 11:16. See *Nicene and Post-Nicene Fathers*, 1st series, 14 vols., ed. Philip Schaff, transl. J. G. Cunningham (Peabody, Mass.: Hendrickson, 1999), 12:269–71.
13. I.e., travailing, or laboring.
14. Monica (c. 332–387) was the mother of the famed early church father Augustine, sometimes called "Austin."
15. Daughter of a Roman general and wife of a Roman consul, Cornelia (second century BCE) devoted herself to the education of her two sons, Tiberius Sempronius Grac-

chus the younger (d. 133 BCE) and Caius Sempronius Gracchi (d. 121 BCE), who became an influential statesman and social reformer.

16. Jerome of Stridon, who lived from the fourth to the fifth centuries CE, was a Latin theologian and historian whose translations of the Bible became the basis for the Vulgate edition.

17. Johannes Buxtorf the Elder (1564–1629), professor of Hebrew and student of rabbinic learning. *Lexicon Chaldaicum, Talmudicum et Rabbinicum* (Basel, 1639).

18. I.e., false accusers.

19. A fuller version of this selection can be found in Mather's *A Family Well-Ordered*.

20. Gervase Disney (1641–1691), English philanthropist of Southwark (London). See his memoir, *Some Remarkable Passages in the Holy Life and Death of Gervase Disney, Esq; To which are added Several Letters and Poems* (London, 1692), 113.

21. The early Latin church father Tertullian of Carthage (c. 150–225) praises holy marriage founded on the love of Christ in his essay "To His Wife": "Whence are we to find [words] enough fully to tell the happiness of that marriage." Tertullian, *Ad uxorem*, transl. Rev. S. Thelwall, in Roberts and Donaldson, eds., *Ante-Nicene Fathers*, 4:39–49; 48 (quotation).

22. The Gallo-Roman orator, poet, panegyrist, and proconsul of Africa Pacatus Drepanius (fl. fourth century CE) honored Roman Emperor Theodisus I (347–395) with the following praise: "Guided by nature, we almost always love our sons more than ourselves." Depranius, *Panegyrici Latini*, in *In Praise of Later Roman Emperors: The Panegyrici Latini*, transl. C. E. V. Nixon and Barbara S. Rodgers (Berkeley: University of California Press, 1994), 2.17.2.

23. Buxtorf the Elder, *Lexicon Chaldaicum, Talmudicum et Rabbinicum*, vol. 1, fol. 65. Rabbi Judah explains, "Whoever does not teach his son a handicraft, it is just as if he harms him and also teaches him larceny." Babylonian Talmud, tractate Kiddushin 29a, *The Babylonian Talmud* (Soncino) (Brooklyn, N.Y.: Judaica Press, 1975).

NATURAL PHILOSOPHY (SCIENCE)

1. Sewall, *Diary*, 3:31.

2. Mather, *Christian Philosopher* (1721), 164.

3. See Solberg, "Introduction," and Winship, *Seers of God*.

4. Theophilus, patriarch of Antioch (d. c. 180), addresses his friend in *Ad Autolycum*. R. M. Grant, *Theophilus of Antioch: Ad Autolycum* (Oxford: Clarendon Press, 1970), bk. 2, chap. 12, lines 5–6. Mather provides his own translation.

5. John Chrysostom in his polemic *Ad populum Antiochenum*. J. P. Migne, *Patrologia cursus completes (series Graecae)* (Paris: Migne, 1855–66), Homily 9, line 25.

6. "The whole universe of natural things." See Simone Brosserio, *Totius philosophiae naturalis epitome, seu Enchiridion, ex universis Physicis Aristotelis nunc primum decerptum* (Paris, 1546). Mather probably refers to Aristotle.

7. "This can be read easily by all, and even if they have not learned to read, it is common to all and open to the eyes of all." The Latin passage is from ΓΝΩΘΙ ΣΕΑΥΤΟΝ

Sive. Tractatus Utilissimus De vera Microcosmi Cognitione Tum Naturali, Tum Super-
naturali, Vel. De Scientia Illa Divina (Hamburg, 1621), 15, by the German Lutheran
pastor Paulus Egardus, aka Paul Eggers (1570–1655). See also Mather, *Diary*, 2:395–96.

8. George Cheyne (1671–1743), English physico-theologian, mathematician, and
physician.

9. Sir Isaac Newton's laws of motion, in *Philosophiae Naturalis Principia Mathematica*
(London, 1687), Axiomata, pp. 12–13.

10. "Here it begins to know god," by Lucius Annaeus Seneca the Younger (c. BCE 4–65
CE), Roman philosopher and dramatist. Seneca, *Natural Questions*, 2 vols., transl.
Thomas H. Corcoran (Cambridge, Mass.: Harvard University Press, 1971), 1:13.

11. Johann Arndt (1555–1621), a German Lutheran Pietist. Mather refers to Anthony Wilhelm Boehm's Latin translation *De Vero Christianismo libri quatuor* (London, 1708).

12. Adapted from Aristotle's *De anima*, in W. D. Ross, *Aristotle: De anima* (Oxford: Clarendon Press, 1961), 2.7.418b, lines 9–10.

13. Robert Hooke (1635–1702), English physico-theologian. Hooke, *Posthumous Works*
(London, 1705), 75–76.

14. William Molyneux (1656–1698), English natural philosopher and author of *Dioptrica*
Nova (London, 1692).

15. Sir Isaac Newton (1642–1727), renowned English natural philosopher, physicist, and
astronomer.

16. Ole Christensen Rømer (1644–1710), Danish astronomer; Christiaan Huygens (1629–
1695), distinguished Dutch physicist and astronomer.

17. John Dee (1527–1609), a Welsh astrologer, mathematician, and occultist; Girolamo
Cardano (1501–1576), an Italian polymath and professor at the University of Pavia.

18. Simon Stevin (1548–1620), a Flemish physicist and engineer.

19. Marin Mersenne (1588–1648), French natural philosopher and theologian.

20. Girolamo Cardano, *De Rerum Varietate* (Vincentium, 1558), lib. 9, chap. 47, p. 474:
"Very slow movements have intermissions by necessity."

21. "The creation's external works comprise within themselves the image of the internal
creation."

22. "Accept, Return, Avoid." Hugh of Saint-Victor (1096–1141), French scholastic theologian and Augustinian monastic in Germany.

23. Methods of meditation.

24. "Accept the good."

25. "Return the service."

26. "Steer clear of suffering."

27. Lucius Mestrius Plutarchus (46–110), Greco-Roman Platonist philosopher and biographer.

28. Adapted from Marcus Tullius Cicero, *Tusculanarum Disputationum*, transl. J. E. King
(Cambridge, Mass.: Harvard University Press, 1954), 1.28.70: "We recognize God from
His works."

29. Bernard of Clairvaux (c. 1090–1153), French Cistercian abbot, reminds us, "The true
lover of God, whichever way he turns, has a familiar admonition of his God."

30. The early Christian theologian Clement of Alexandria (150–c. 215): the world as a "Natural Preacher" (*Concionatores Reales*).

31. The secondhand citation from an elegy on Johannes Stigelius (1515–1562), German poet and rhetorician, appears in a slightly different form in *Calendarium Historicum conscriptum* (Vitebergae, 1571), signature B, by the German Lutheran hymnodist Paul Eber (1511–1569): "While I scan the bright wonders of the world, / While I admire Nature giving birth to her works, / Divine power springs forth from the things themselves; / And it is the plain sod that attests that God exists."

32. William Derham (1657–1735), English physico-theologian and natural philosopher. Mather refers to Derham's *Physico-Theology; or, A Demonstration of the Being and Attributes of God* (London, 1714), bk. 2, chap. 5, pp. 31–34.

33. Centripetal force moving toward the center.

34. "Furrowed or grooved particles" of the great vortex of René Descartes.

35. John Keill (1671–1721), Scottish natural philosopher and mathematician.

36. Robert Hooke, English natural philosopher and polymath who theorized that heat was a caloric (atomic) fluid.

37. Edmond Halley's A *Discourse concerning Gravity*, in *Miscellanea Curiosa*, 2 vols., (London, 1705), 1:304–25.

38. M. Sedileau (d. 1693), French natural philosopher and author of *Observations sur la quantité de l'Eau de Pluye tombée à Paris . . . & de la quantité de l'évaporation* (Paris[?], 1692).

39. Impulse.

40. David Gregory (1659–1708), Scottish astronomer and mathematician.

41. Cicero, *De Natura Deorum*: "This [gravitational] function [of Nature] is fulfilled by that rational and intelligent substance which pervades the whole world as the efficient cause of all things." *On the Nature of the Gods*, transl. H. Rackham (Cambridge, Mass.: Harvard University Press, 1933), 2.45.115.

42. Samuel Clarke (1675–1729), English Newtonian physico-theologian.

43. Samuel Clarke, *Discourse Concerning the Unalterable Obligations of Natural Religion* (London, 1706), 22.

44. Plato (c. 428–347 BCE) posited that the world is permeated by an all-encompassing and governing world soul (*Timaeus*).

45. Likewise, Plato's disciple Aristotle (384–322 BCE) argues that primal matter (hyle) is organized by substantial forms according to their properties (shape, size, quantity, density, etc.).

46. The father of medicine, Hippocrates of Kos (c. 460–c. 375 BCE), theorized that all animate beings are pervaded by an "innate heat."

47. Julius Caesar Scaliger (1484–1558), French-Italian scholar and polymath, rejected philosophical materialism by arguing that spirit and matter interact (plastic nature).

48. Rejecting Descartes's claim that formless spirit cannot interact with physical matter, the Cambridge Platonist philosopher Henry More (1614–1687) insisted that all matter is ruled by an innate spiritual power.

49. George Cheyne.

50. "Inert force."
51. A proverb attributed to the Dutch philosopher Desiderius Erasmus of Rotterdam (1466–1536).

MEDICINE AND THE CURE OF DISEASES

1. See Watson, *The Angelical Conjunction.*
2. Mather, *The Angel of Bethesda*, 231.
3. Mather, *The Angel of Bethesda*, 343–44; Silverman, *Life and Times*, 344.
4. See Morens, "The Past Is Never Dead."
5. Mather, *Diary*, 2:620–21.
6. Virgil, *Georgics*, 1:2.490: "Blessed is he who has been able to win knowledge of the causes of things."
7. Mather's subsequent paragraph is a pastiche of quotes and paraphrases from *A New Theory of Consumptions* (London, 1720), chap. 2, by London physician Benjamin Marten (c. 1690–1752).
8. "Murrains" is an archaic term for any number of infectious diseases that affect livestock. Mather draws on English chemist Frederick Slare (c. 1647–1727), who published articles on insect-borne diseases in the *Philosophical Transactions of the Royal Society of London.*
9. Athanasius Kircher (1602–1680), German Jesuit polymath at the Collegium Romanum, whose *Scrutinium Physico-Medicum Contagiosae Luis, quae dicitur Pestis* (Leipzig, 1659), sec. 1, explores the causes of diseases attributed to animalcular vermin multiplying in the body; German physician and chemist August Hauptmann (1607–1674), who posited that microscopic worms (parasites) cause diseases; Dutch physician and entomologist Steven Blankaart, or Blancard (1650–1702), author of the oft-reprinted *The Physical Dictionary; In which, all the Terms Relating either to Anatomy, Chirurgery, Pharmacy, or Chymistry are accurately explained* (London, 1684).
10. German physician Michael Ettmüller (1644–1683), a professor of medicine at Leipzig, published numerous tracts on medicine and chemistry collected in his *Chimia Rationalis ac Experimentalis Curiosa* (Leiden, 1684).
11. A common venereal disease associated with syphilis, which was believed to be endemic among Native Americans. Deadly smallpox epidemics, thought to have originated in Africa and Asia Minor, ravaged the lives of tens of thousands of Native Americans who had no immunity to this prevalent Old World pestilence.
12. Martin Lister, M.D. (c. 1638–1712), an English physician, naturalist, and member of the Royal Society whose discussion of smallpox appears in his *Octo Exercitationes Medicinales* (London, 1697); English physician William Oliver (1659–1716) published *A Practical Essay on Fevers, Containing Remarks on the Hot and Cold Methods of their Cure* (London, 1704).
13. Dutch physician Nicolaas Hartsoeker (1656–1725), in a letter to the French physician Nicholas Andry (1658–1742) published in Andry's *An Account of the Breeding of Worms*

in *Human Bodies* (London, 1701), speculated that nearly invisible worms, springing from insect eggs, breed an infinite number of disease-causing vermin.

14. Italian physician Giovanni Alfonso Borelli (1608–1679), one of Europe's most outstanding contemporary physicians, whose *De Motu Animalium* was posthumously published (Leiden, 1685).

15. Sir Théodore Turquet de Mayerne (1573–1655), a celebrated Swiss Huguenot, Paracelsian physician, and anatomist who advocated pharmaceutical remedies to combat diseases. Mather probably refers to Mayerne's treatise on insects and parasites, *Insectorum, sive Minimorum Animalium Theatrum* (London, 1634), a collection of medical tracts composed by his peers.

16. A reference to Andry's *An Account of the Breeding of Worms in Human Bodies.*

17. English botanist and horticulturalist Richard Bradley (1688–1732), author of the popular *New Improvements of Planting and Gardening, both Philosophical and Practical*, 2 vols. (London, 1718).

18. Dutch scientist Antonie Philips van Leeuwenhoek (1632–1723), a pioneering microbiologist whose publications on bacteriological animalcula ("little animals") were among his most important achievements. Mather may well have in mind *Observationes Microscopicae*, published in *Acta Eruditorum* (1682), a scientific journal published in Germany.

19. Probably a reference to the English physician Peter Ball (c. 1638–1675).

20. Bacteria likened to "velites," armed Roman soldiers.

21. A cathartic medicine that removes obstructions from bodily ducts.

22. The French physician and Paracelsian chemist Pierre de la Poterie (b. 1581) authored *Pharmacopea Spagyria* (Bogna, 1622). He employed oxide of antimony as an emetic to treat fever.

23. English physician and epidemiologist Richard Mead (1673–1754), whose publications include *A Mechanical Account of Poisons In Several Essays* (London, 1702) and his oft-reprinted *Short Discourse concerning Pestilential Contagion, and the Method To be used to Prevent it* (London, 1720); Thomas Morgan (fl. early eighteenth century), English Deist, moral philosopher, medical writer, and author of *Philosophical Principles of Medicine* (London, 1725) and *The Mechanical Practice of Physick* (London, 1735).

24. Addressed to Jeremiah Dummer.

25. Cotton Mather.

26. A North African Berber people who lived in what is the southern part of modern Libya. Mather refers to his slave Onesimus.

27. Coastal region of west Africa.

28. *Philosophical Transactions of the Royal Society of London* (1665–), the oldest and longest running journal on natural science, was begun by Henry Oldenburg (c. 1619–1677).

29. Emanuel Timonius, aka Timoni (1669–1718), a Greek physician and elected member of the Royal Society of London.

30. Timonius, "An Account of history, of the procuring the Small-Pox by Incision, or Inoculation," dated at Constantinople, December 1713, in *Philosophical Transactions of the Royal Society* 29, no. 339 (1714): 72–82.

31. *Apostem*: abscess; "Suppuration": discharge of pus.

32. Jacobus Pylarinus, aka Giacomo Pilarino (1659–1718), a Greek physician, citizen of the Venetian Republic, and author of *Nova et Tuta Variolas excitandi per Transplantationem Methodus* (Venice, 1715), reprinted the following year in the *Philosophical Transactions of the Royal Society of London* 29, no. 347 (1716): 393–99, from which Mather quotes in the next paragraph. The Latin title can be rendered "A New and Safe Method of Beginning Smallpox by Transplantation." See also George W. Jones, "Notes to Introduction," in Mather, *The Angel of Bethesda*, 350.

33. English physician William Harvey (1578–1657) described his discovery of the bodily circulation of blood in *Exercitatio Anatomica De Motu Cordis et Sanguinis in Animalibus* (Frankfurt, 1628).

34. Zabdiel Boylston and Cotton Mather, *Some Account Of what is said of Inoculating or Transplanting the Small-Pox*; Mather, *The Angel of Bethesda*, 109–12.

35. English astronomer Edmond Halley (1656–1742), discoverer of Halley's Comet.

36. Boston physician Zabdiel Boylston (1679–1766) was the sole person to heed Mather's call for inoculation.

37. A likely reference to the anonymously published *Friendly Debate; or, A Dialogue, Between Academicus* [Dr. Boylston]; *and Sawny* [Dr. William Douglass] *& Mundungus* [John Williams], *Two Eminent Physicians, About some of their Later Performances* (Boston, 1721); and *A Friendly Debate; or, A Dialogue Between Rusticus and Academicus About the late Performance of Academicus* (Boston, 1722).

38. Any organ of the body.

39. Mather refers to Samuel Granger's anonymous antivaccination pamphlet *The Imposition of Inoculation As a Duty Religiously Considered. In a Letter to a Gentleman in the Country, Inclin'd to admit it* (Boston, 1721).

40. "Swiftly, safely, and pleasantly."

41. Hieronymous Rorarius (Girolamo Rorario; 1485–1556), emissary of Emperor Charles V of Habsburg, who in *Quod Animalia bruta ratione utantur melius Homine* (Amsterdam, 1654) rejected Descartes's assertion that animals are mere machines without souls and argued to the contrary that animals use reason better than men do. *Oxford Dictionary of Philosophy*, 3rd edition, ed Simon Blackburn (Oxford: Oxford University Press, 2016).

42. Granger, *The Imposition of Inoculation*.

43. Discharge.

44. *Venice Theriaca*, an antidote to various poisons, including the bite of a poisonous animal. *Medical Dictionary* (online), s.v. "Theriaca."

45. A panacea against all poisons and disease.

46. Ovid, *Metamorphoses*, 1.759: "It is shameful that such reproaches should be cast [upon us]."

MERCANTILISM AND PAPER MONEY

1. See Bailyn, *The New England Merchants*; Peterson, *The City-State of Boston*; and Valeri, *Heavenly Merchandise*.

2. Mather, *Pietas in Patriam*, § 12, p. 43.

3. Mather, *Pietas in Patriam*, § 12, pp. 43, 44.

4. See Goldberg, "Massachusetts Paper Money."

5. Mather, *Pietas in Patriam*, § 12, p. 45.

6. Mather, *Diary*, 2:19.

7. Sewall, *Diary*, 2:269.

8. See Smolinski, *"Israel Redivivus."*

9. Cotton Mather addresses this tract to "John Philips, Esq.," i.e., Colonel John Phillips, a wealthy Charlestown merchant, magistrate, and treasurer of Massachusetts— and Mather's father-in-law.

10. I.e., one thousand English pounds. £1 = 20s (shillings), 1s = 12d (pence).

11. In his famous *Leviathan; or, The Matter, Forme & Power of a Common-Wealth Ecclesiasticall and Civill* (London, 1651), part 1, chaps. 12–13, the English philosopher Thomas Hobbes (1588–1679) argues that in the state of nature, in which no civil laws or mutual contracts govern the relations between people, man is in a state of perpetual war "of every man against every man." There is no right or wrong, no virtue or vice, neither justice nor injustice, for brute force determines all.

12. See also Mather's *Lex Mercatoria; or, The Just Rules of Commerce Declared* (Boston, 1725).

13. "The earth shall be."

14. Pseudonym of the German Hebraist and Christian Cabbalist and mystic Freiherr Johann Christian Knorr von Rosenroth (1636–1689), best known for his *Kabbala denudata* (Sulzbaci, 1677).

15. Literally, "a field of blood," a reference to the Potter's Field purchased with Judas's blood money.

16. King David's nephew and his military commander murdered by Joab, Amasa's cousin (2 Sam. 19:14; 20:10, 12).

17. Richard Baxter, *A Christian Directory; or, A Summ of Practical Theologie, and Cases of Conscience* (London, 1673), tome 3, chap. 14, quest. 2.5, p. 559.

18. Baxter, *A Christian Directory*, tome 3, chap. 14, title 2, direction 2, p. 557. "Titles" and "directions" were discrete subsections of sermons.

19. See Mather's *A Monitory, and Hortatory Letter, To those English, who debauch the Indians, By Selling Strong Drink unto them* (Boston, 1700).

20. See Mather's *Fair Dealing between Debtor and Creditor* (Boston, 1716).

21. Claudius Aelianus (c. 175–c. 235), a Roman rhetorician and historian who wrote in Greek. Mather refers to the discourse between Midas and Silenus, according to whom the city of "Eusebes" ("Pious") was located on this lost continent and occupied by prosperous and happy people whose laws maintained peace throughout. Mather's likely source is *Claudius Aelianus His Various History* (London, 1666), bk. 3, chap. 18, pp. 77–78.

22. Mather alludes to Joseph Mede's conjecture ("De Gogo & Magogo Conjectura," appended to *Clavis Apocalyptica* [Cambridge, 1649], separate pagination, 6–7) that the American hemisphere is the place of outer darkness, the abode of the apocalyptic Gog of Magog, which would attack God's elect in Europe in the Battle of Armageddon. See Smolinski, *"Israel Redivivus."*

BIBLICAL HERMENEUTICS

1. Eames, "Introduction," ix.
2. *The Whole Booke of Psalmes* (1640), "The Preface," signature **3ᵛ.
3. See Music, "Cotton Mather," and Silverman, "Reform."
4. Mather, *Diary*, 2:437, 560.
5. Walter, *The Grounds and Rules of Music*, 3.
6. Mather, *Psalterium Americanum*, xxxiv.
7. Mather, *Biblia Americana*, 1:365.
8. Morison, *Harvard College*, 1:216; Stearns, *Science in the British Colonies of America*, 152, 159.
9. Maimonides, *Guide for the Perplexed*, part 2, chap. 35, pp. 224–25.
10. See Gale, *The Court of the Gentiles*. Gale gifted a copy of this work to Increase Mather.
11. A fuller version of Mather's introduction appears in his *The Accomplished Singer* (Boston, 1721), in which he engaged his colleagues in a needful reform of Psalm singing in church and at home.
12. By the time Mather published his *Accomplished Singer*, he had seen "about Three Times seven Translations of the *Psalms* . . . fitted for the Tunes of our *Sacred Songs*." Mather, *The Accomplished Singer*, 7.
13. The German Calvinist polymath and encyclopedist Johann Heinrich Alsted (1588–1638) is renowned for his *Encyclopaedia septem tomis distincta* (Herborn, 1630). Mather shared a deep affection for Alsted's vast learning, especially for his millenarian *The Beloved City; or, The Saints Reign on Earth a Thousand Yeares* (London, 1643). The Latin quotation is from Alsted's discussion of Hebrew poetics in *Encyclopaedia*, lib. 10, sect. 2, cap. 2, fol. 529, and reads, "No song is burdened with heavy metrical laws, but they are merely poetic characters animated by prayer."
14. Alternating lines of eight and six syllables.
15. I.e., iambic tetrameter and trimeter.
16. "A good handler of the text," or "until you know your text (and context) well."
17. "Porismatic," suggesting "inferential" or "by way of inferences."
18. St. Augustine of Hippo (354–430) in his 412 CE letter to Volusianus, a Roman nobleman, exhorts his correspondent "to devote attention to the study of the Writings which are truly and unquestionably holy." Schaff, ed., *Nicene and Post-Nicene Fathers*, letter 132, 1:470.
19. "Turn them over, and turn them over, for all things are in it."
20. *A New Theory of the Earth* (London, 1696), by William Whiston (1667–1752), English physico-theologian, Lucasian Professor of Mathematics at Cambridge, and anti-Trinitarian.
21. Edmund Dickinson, M.D. (1624–1707), an English alchemist and physician in ordinary to King Charles II and James II, published *Physica Vetus & Vera* (London, 1702), an arcane atomist defense of Genesis. Dickinson's earlier work to which Mather alludes is *Delphi Phoenicizantes*.
22. "In the history of creation, at one time the method and manner of every generation, at another time the principles of the true philosophy, are precisely and concisely taught by Moses."

23. "Six days of creation."
24. The theory that atoms adhere to one another because of their different shapes: "little pills," "globules," and "leaflike parts arising from the axis of a floral stem."
25. The hemisphere from which God and Sophia (Christ) created the universe.
26. "Æther," a pure airy substance, the terrain of the gods above the terrestrial sphere.
27. "Out-flowing fire."
28. "The sun, the first principle [archetype] of all things," the Greek original appearing in a fragment of the Greek philosopher Empedocles (c. 493–c. 433 BCE), who taught that the universe consists of four intermingled elements—fire, air, water, and earth.
29. The controversial idea posited in *Prae-Adamitae* (Leyden, 1655), by the French Marrano of Bordeaux Isaac La Peyrère (1596–1676), that God created a set of human beings, or pre-Adamites (Gen. 1:25–27), before he created Adam and Eve (Gen. 2:7, 21–24). The former were the protoplasts of the Gentiles, the latter of the Jewish people.
30. Fringes or outer edge.
31. "To whom the abbreviations always please."
32. "Impulse to expand."
33. "Nutritious sap."
34. "Sunspots."
35. The Roman natural philosopher Gaius Plinius Secundus, aka Pliny the Elder (23–79 CE), mentions that at Caesar's murder (44 BCE), a solar eclipse "caused almost a whole year's continuous gloom." *Naturalis Historia*, bk. 2, chap. 30, p. 99.
36. "Fundamental moisture."
37. "Ur-egg" or "First Egg" at the mouth of Kneph, an ancient Egyptian deity.
38. The Greek philosopher Archelaus (fl. fifth century BCE) explains that through spontaneous generation, "the animals had been brought forth through the warmth of the earth, liquefying mud [serving] as nourishment similar to milk."
39. *Neshamah*, "a puff" (of wind), "vital breath" (Gen. 2:7); *Shemayim*, "heavens" or "aether," the abode of the celestial bodies (Gen. 1:2).
40. "Bullula," a watery vesicle (bubble); Mather's Greek term Χόριον, i.e., Chorion (Korion), a "sac enclosing the fetus" (placenta).
41. "Genesiourgos," the great "maker."
42. William Harvey describes mammalian generation and embryonic development in his *Exercitationes de Generatione Animalium* (1651).
43. Plato speaks of "the place beyond heaven." *Phaedrus*, 247c.
44. The Greek philosopher Pythagoras (fl. sixth century BCE) calls this heavenly country "unrestricted heaven," where the heroic souls remained "immortal and incorruptible." *Carmen aureum*, 70, 71.
45. Aristotle argues for a natural principle, or breath, akin "to the element of the stars." *De generatione animalium*, transl. A. L. Peck (Cambridge, Mass.: Harvard University Press, 1942), 2.3.737a, 1.
46. Probably "No-Amon" (Diospolis Magna), in Upper Egypt on the Nile.
47. Mather rejects the ancient concept of spontaneous generation (abiogenesis) from the mud of the earth.

48. Richard Bentley (1662–1742), an English theologian and classical scholar, in his fourth Boylean lecture, *The Folly and Unreasonableness of Atheism* (London, 1699), 27.

49. Francesco Redi (1626–1697), a celebrated Italian physician, naturalist, and author of *Experimenta circa Generationem Insectorum* (Amsterdam, 1671).

50. "Lawn," A fine linen or silk fabric of high thread count often used in dress making; "a fine sieve, generally of silk" to strain liquids uniformly. *Oxford English Dictionary*, 2nd ed. (New York: Oxford University Press, 1989).

51. Marcello Malpighi (1628–1694), renowned Italian physician and biologist, founder of microcosmic anatomy. His major work is *Anatomus Plantarum pars altera*, published in *Opera Omnia Figuris* (London, 1686–97).

52. Phthiriasis is a skin infection caused by pubic lice (*Phthirus pubis*). *Oxford English Dictionary*. Acts 12:23 relates how King Herod Agrippa (10 BCE–44 CE) was "eaten by worms."

53. Antonie Philips van Leeuwenhoek, *Continuatio Epistolarum* (Leyden, 1696).

54. The Dutch biologist and anatomist Jan Swammerdam (1637–1680) demonstrated in his *Historia Insectorum Generalis* (1669) that all insects pass through several stages in their life, from egg to larva, pupa, and adult.

55. Sheathed coverings.

56. Bentley, *Confutation of Atheism*.

57. "Let it be spoken with the rabble."

58. Disciples of the French philosopher René Descartes.

59. Daughter of King Agamemnon and Clytemnestra of Mycenae. Euripides, *Iphigenia at Aulis*.

60. Dio Chrysostom (c. 40–c. 115), Greek orator and historian of the Roman Empire, in his *Eleventh Discourse*.

61. Trojan War (thirteenth–twelfth century BCE); Jephthah (c. 1118–1094 BCE).

62. Artemis, the Greek-Roman goddess of the hunt and protectress of childbirth.

63. Aurelius Ambrosius (c. 338–397), bishop of Milan; John Chrysostom; Jan Laski (1499–1560), Polish Protestant reformer; John George I, prince of Anhalt-Dessau (1567–1618), German prince who established Protestantism in his state.

64. Sixtinus Amama (1593–1629), reformed professor of Oriental languages at Franeker and author of *Anti-Barbarus Biblicus* (Franeker, 1656).

65. "I possess a Psalter which was edited in Sabbioneta [northern Italy] in 1556. A small book is added to its end called *Uses of the Psalms*. In it a use is assigned to each Psalm. I shall give you a taste."

66. "In order to be freed from the tempest of the sea, recite this Psalm, and write it on a shard, and throw that into the sea, and it will become calm." / "If one has a headache, write out this Psalm to these words 'Destroy them with an iron rod,' and suspend that paper from his head."

67. "If someone has shoulder and head pain, let him recite this Psalm over olive oil and then anoint the affected parts with it."

68. "This Psalm is useful for preventing men from hurting you and for putting to flight your enemy who is pursuing you." / "Take some dust from the earth and recite over it this Psalm and sprinkle the dust before your enemy who is pursuing you and he will yield." / "Furthermore if anyone has an enemy, let him take a new bronze vase and fill

it from a fountain of water and let him recite this Psalm four times from" / "Arise, O Lord" / "to the end. Pour that water in the place of your enemy, and you shall prevail over him."

69. "When you see a serpent or a scorpion, recite it seven times."

70. "[To be used] against a fugitive slave. Write in a tin plate those two names, *Master*, and *Slave*, and he will return [or will be returned]."

71. "It is useful to a woman whose children are dying. Write it on a parchment, and write beneath it the following: / שׁנוי סנסנוי סמנגלף / [the name of three angels] Place it in the four corners of your house."

72. "When guards are surrounding the city, if you want to pass before them without being seen, murmur this to the four quarters of the world, and sleep will overcome them. It pains me to write these many things."

73. Nicolaus Hemmingius, aka Niels Hemmingsen (1513–1600), Danish Lutheran theologian and professor of Hebrew at Copenhagen.

74. John Green (d. 1774), curate of Thurnscoe, in *Letters to the Author of the Discourse of the Grounds and Reasons of the Christian Religion* (London, 1726).

75. Diglat-Pileser III, king of Assyria (eighth century BCE).

76. Green, *Letters to the Author*, 80–81.

77. Nicholas Clagett, D.D. (1654–1727), Anglican preacher at St. Mary's Church, Bury St. Edmunds, in *Truth defended, and Boldness in Error rebuk'd* (London, 1710), esp. pp. 78–87; William Whiston, whose *Accomplishment of Scripture-Prophecy* (Cambridge, 1708) aroused the ire of Clagett and his peers.

78. Whiston.

79. Clagett.

80. Isaac Watts (1674–1748), English nonconformist minister and famous hymnodist.

81. Isaac Watts, *An Essay Against Uncharitableness* (1707), 11–12.

82. Jacques Basnage (1653–1723), French reformed pastor who settled in Holland after the Edict of Nantes (1685). He is best known for his *L'histoire et la religion des juifs* (4 vols., Rotterdam, 1706–7), translated into English as *History and Religion of the Jews* (London, 1708).

83. Clemens Romanus (c. 35–99), aka Pope Clement (88–99).

84. Cotton Mather, *Adversus libertinos* (Boston, 1713).

85. Pierre Allix (1641–1717), a French Huguenot minister who was ordained an Anglican priest after his escape to England following the Revocation of the Edict of Nantes (1685). Mather refers to Allix's *The Judgment of the Ancient Jewish Church Against the Unitarians* (London, 1699), chap. 21, p. 336.

86. Joseph de Voisin (c. 1610–1685), learned French Roman Catholic Orientalist and author of *Theologia Iudaeorum* (Paris, 1647).

87. Sebastian Münster (1488–1552), German Christian Hebraist and cosmographer.

88. "Visible things are imitations of thoughts."

89. Mather's extracts the following paragraphs from Ralph Cudworth's *The Union of Christ and the Church in a Shadow* (London, 1642), 3–7, 29, 33–34.

90. Johann Reuchlin (1455–1522), German humanist, classical scholar, and Cabbalist, best known for his *De Arte Cabbalistica* (Hagenau, 1517). The Latin quote reads, "That God is accustomed to symbolize diverse things with one sign."

91. Francis Bacon (1561–1626), first Baron Verulam (1618), English philosopher and states-man: "One and the same mark of nature, impressed upon various materials and subjects."

92. "Archetypal husband and wife."

93. "Ectypal husband and wife."

94. "He introduces the groom Tipheret and the bride Malcuth speaking in turns." Tife-ret is the sixth emanation of God in the Kabbalah, associated with both maleness and beauty or spirituality. It is the counterpart to Malkuth (literally "kingdom," but also understood as the Shekinah), the tenth emanation of God, associated with fe-maleness and with the earthly creation. In Christian Kabbalism these two figures are identified as Jesus Christ and the Kingdom of God (i.e., the Church), bridegroom and bride. See *EJ*, 11:631–35, 671–37.

95. St. Jerome, *Contra Ioannem Hiersolymitanum Episcopum ad Pammachium*, 22: "Eve, an image of the Church, is made out of the rib of a man."

96. St. Thomas Aquinas (1225–1274), Italian Dominican monk and philosopher: "The Church is made from the side of Christ, dying on the cross." *St. Thomas Aquinas Summa Theologica*, 5 vols., transl. Fathers of the English Dominican Province (New York: Benziger, 1948), 1:468 (question 92, article 3, argument 3).

THE INVISIBLE WORLD AND SALEM WITCHCRAFT

1. The legal process of the pretrial hearings and the nature of the trials are described by Powers, *Crime and Punishment in Early Massachusetts*, 438–39, 469, 477; Weis-man, *Witchcraft, Magic, and Religion in 17th-Century Massachusetts*, 14–15, 132–59; and Friedman, *Crime and Punishment in American History*, 24–30.

2. Calef, *More Wonders*, 152.

3. Calef, *More Wonders*, 103–4. Tellingly, the investigation of Rev. William Bentley (1759–1819), Unitarian pastor of Salem's East Church, refuted Calef's charge that George Burroughs was impiously buried in a hole "about two Foot deep" (104). Ac-cording to Bentley, "It was said, that the bodies were not properly buried; but upon examination of the ground, the graves were found of usual depth, and remains of the bodies, and of the wood, in which they were interred." Bentley, "Description of the History of Salem," 268. See also Poole, "Cotton Mather and Salem Witchcraft," 384–85. Salem's own Reverend Charles W. Upham (1802–1875), a Unitarian minister turned local historian before running for high office in state and federal government, un-critically rehearsed Calef's version in *Lectures on Witchcraft* (Boston, 1831, 1832), 101–4, and repeated the same verbatim in his popular two-volume *Salem Witchcraft* (Bos-ton, 1867), 2:300–301. From here, the story of Cotton Mather on horseback harangu-ing the crowd at Burroughs's execution was didactically rehearsed in the popular schoolbook histories, such as educator Emma Willard's *Abridged History of the United States* (New York, 1844, 1871), 130–31, and school principal George P. Quack-enbos's *Illustrated School History of the United States* (New York, 1857, 1877), 138–50, and taught to whole generations of students across the nation. The rest is history.

4. Calef, *More Wonders*, 103–4.

5. Sewall, *Diary,* 1:363.

6. Brattle, "Letter," 68–69.

7. Levin, *Forms of Uncertainty,* 161. The issue of Mather's reputation will be covered in Smolinski's forthcoming biography, *Cotton Mather: A Life.*

8. See Hansen, *Witchcraft at Salem.*

9. See Perkins, *A Discourse of the Damned Art of Witchcraft.*

10. Mather, *Diary,* 1:150.

11. Mather, *Diary,* 1:151–52, 216; Mather, *Pietas in Patriam,* § 16, p. 76.

12. Sewall, *Diary,* 1:445. See also Francis, *Judge Sewall's Apology.*

13. For the approximate publication date of Cotton Mather's *Wonders of the Invisible World* (c. October 11–20, 1692), see *Wonders,* 147, and "Cotton Mather to John Cotton" (October 20, 1692). Mather sent a printed copy to Cotton. For the publication of Increase Mather's *Cases of Conscience* (c. early November 1692), see Holmes, *Increase Mather,* 1:106, 123.

14. See Levin, *Forms of Uncertainty,* 67–83.

15. "Cotton Mather to John Cotton" (October 20, 1692).

16. "Cotton Mather to William Stoughton" (September 2, 1692).

17. Stoughton, in Mather, *Wonders,* A3v–4r.

18. Mather provides his conjectural timeline in "Corollary V" and in "The First" and "Second Conjecture," in *Wonders,* 36–41; See also *Threefold Paradise,* 60–78.

19. Mather, "The Authors Defence," in *Wonders,* A3r.

20. See Hall, *Worlds of Wonder.*

21. Nearly a decade and a half after the Salem debacle had run its course, Mather called on the General Assembly of Massachusetts on November 3, 1709, to argue that "the General Day of *Humiliation*" was not enough unless repentance for "the Errors of our Dark Time, some years ago" was accompanied by "*Reparation.*" Mather, *Theopolis Americana,* 29–30.

22. Mather included a slightly shorter version of this text in his *Magnalia Christi Americana,* bk. 6, chap. 7, fols. 71–75.

23. Ann Glover (d. 1688), aka Goody Glover, an Irish Roman Catholic immigrant.

24. Thomas Oakes (1644–1719), Boston physician and speaker of the Massachusetts House of Representatives.

25. Spirits.

26. Sound mind.

27. Rev. Moses Fiske (1642–1708) of Wenham, Mass.; Rev. Peter Thacher (1651–1727) of Milton, Mass.

28. The Sadducees, an ancient Jewish sect in the intertestamental period, were believed to have denied the immortality of the soul. The Anglican clergyman Joseph Glanvill (1636–1680) collected ghost stories to evince life after death and the existence of devils and witches, in his popular *Saducismus Triumphatus* (London, 1681).

29. Martha Goodwin (1674–1701), who was about thirteen at the time.

30. Probably *The Displaying of Supposed Witchcraft* (London, 1677) by John Webster (1610–1682), an Anglican clergyman, physician, alchemist, and skeptic.

31. Probably Joseph Glanvill's *Saducismus Triumphatus.*

32. Increase Mather's *An Essay for the Recording of Illustrious Providences* (Boston, 1684), 135–39, tells the story of Ann Cole of Hartford, who accused neighbors of having bewitched her in 1662–63.

33. *A Guide to Heaven, from the Word* (London, 1664) by Samuel Hardy (1636–1691), an English nonconformist minister.

34. *A Brief Discourse of Justification* (Boston, 1686) by Samuel Willard (1640–1707), a Puritan clergyman at Boston's First Church.

35. *The Mystery of Christ Opened and Applyed* (Boston, 1686); *The Day of Trouble is near* (Boston, 1674).

36. *Milk for Boston Babes* (London, 1646) by John Cotton, Cotton Mather's maternal grandfather. Collaborating with Richard Mather, John Cotton composed *The Cambridge Platform of Church Discipline* (Cambridge, Mass., 1648).

37. Cotton Mather's study.

38. Mather was twenty-five at the time.

39. Charles Morton (1627–1698); James Allen (1632–1710); Joshua Moody (1633–1697); Samuel Willard (1640–1707).

40. In his *Magnalia Christi Americana*, bk. 3, chap. 3, fol. 193, Mather identifies it as "this *Indian* Language," i.e., the Algonquian language of New England's Native Americans.

41. Christmas was not observed in Puritan New England.

42. The spirit world.

43. Appended to Increase Mather's *Cases of Conscience*, "Postscript," G4r–v. In his *Diary*, 1:150–51, Cotton Mather explains that from the start he did not want to "convict and condemn any Person, as a *Confoederate* with afflicting Daemons, upon so feeble an Evidence, as a *spectral Representation*. Accordingly, I ever testified against it, both publickly and privately; and in my *Letters to the Judges*, I particularly, besought them, that they would by no means admit it; and when a considerable *Assembly* of *Ministers* gave in their *Advice* [Mather, "The Return of Several Ministers"] about that Matter, I not only concurred with their Advice, but it was *I* who drew it up."

44. William Perkins (1558–1602), a highly influential English Reformed theologian, whose *Discourse of the Damned Art of Witchcraft* (London, 1608) served as a guide to the Salem judges, along with *A Guide to Grand-Jury Men* (London, 1627) by Richard Bernard of Batcombe (1568–1641), an English Puritan divine.

45. Sleight of hand, trick.

46. *An Act against Conjuration, Witchcraft and dealing with evil and wicked Spirits* (Witchcraft Act of 1604), instituted by King James I (1 Ja. I. c. 12), made the practice a capital crime. This law was applicable in the English-speaking world until its revocation via the Witchcraft Act of 1735 by King George II (9 Geo. 2 c. 5). The Statutes Project, https://statutes.org.uk/site/the-statutes/eighteenth-century/1735-9-george-2-c-5-the-witchcraft-act/. Nonetheless, persons engaging in any forms of witchcraft continued to be subject to fines and imprisonment.

47. Sighting of a spirit in the shape of the accused.

48. See "Cotton Mather to John Richards," [May] 31, 1692, and "Letter of Cotton Mather to John Foster (17th 6m [August], 1692)."

49. See Mather, "The Return of Several Ministers."

50. A person possessed by an evil spirit.

51. As he had done with Martha Goodwin in 1688, in *Memorable Providences*.

52. Boston, 1693.

53. Increase Mather, *Cases of Conscience*. It appeared just a week or two after his son's *Wonders of the Invisible World*.

54. Increase Mather, *Cases of Conscience*, "Postscript," G4r–v.

55. William Stoughton (1631–1701), lieutenant governor of Massachusetts, who served as chief justice during the trials and wrote a letter of endorsement, published in Mather, *Wonders*, vi–vii.

56. Mather added this reflection at a later time. Years later (c. 1727), he still felt that "the foolish, and flouting, & bruitish, & short-winded Way of passing a Sentence upon *Extraordinary Descents from the Invisible World*, which we have seen in our Days, is sufficient Indication, how much the most Shocking *Signs of the Times* are lost upon us." Mather, *Threefold Paradise*, 342.

57. In *Unum Necessarium* (1693).

58. See also Mather, *Magnalia Christi Americana*, bk. 2, chap. 16, fol. 60.

59. John Foster (1648–1711), an important member of Mather's Second Church and one of the leaders in the arrest of Governor Sir Edmund Andros during the Glorious Revolution in Boston on April 18, 1689. The transcript of the lost original is taken from the published copy in the *Transactions of the Literary Society of Quebec* 2 (1831): 313–16.

60. Samuel Fairclough (1594–1677), an English nonconformist minister and member of the commission at the witch trials at Bury St. Edmunds, Suffolk, England. *Oxford Dictionary of National Biography* (online). Mather refers to the records of the trial in *A True Relation Of the Araignment Of eighteene Witches* (London, 1645).

61. According to Beverly's pastor John Hale (1636–1700), "W.B." (i.e., William Barker Sr. of Andover), "a man of Forty years of Age," confessed that the devil and his covenanted witches "*design[ed] to destroy* Salem *Village, and to begin at the Ministers House, and to destroy the Church of God, and to set up Satan's Kingdom, and then all will be well.*" Much the same is attributed to George Burroughs, whom "confessing witches" accused of "exhort[ing] the Company [of gathered witches] to pull down the Kingdom of God, and set up the Kingdom of the Devil." Hale, *A Modest Enquiry Into the Nature of Witchcraft*, 33–34, 35. The same is related by Mary Toothaker, one of the confessed witches, in "Examination of Mary Toothaker," in *Records of the Salem Witch-Hunt*, ed. Bernard Rosenthal (Cambridge: Cambridge University Press, 2009), 492 (hereafter *Records*).

62. See also *Magnalia Christi Americana*, bk. 2, chap. 16, fol. 60.

63. See Anthony Horneck, D.D., *An Account Of what happen'd in the Kingdom of Sweden In the Years 1669, and 1670 and upwards* (N.p., 1682).

64. Duchy of Jülich, in northwestern Germany.

65. The italicized text is identical with those of the minutes of the August 1, 1692, meeting of ministers held at Cambridge. The assembly included Cotton and Increase Mather, Morton, Allen, Wigglesworth, Willard, Gookin, Walter, Pierpont—Cotton

Mather served as moderator, and his father Increase as recorder of minutes. *Records of the Cambridge Association of Ministers, Proceedings of the Massachusetts Historical Society* 17 (1879–80): 268.

66. Inquiry.

67. See Joseph Glanvill's response to "Some Considerations About Witchcraft: In a Letter to Robert Hunt, Esquire," in *A Blow at Modern Sadducism In some Philosophical Considerations About Witchcraft* (London, 1668), 1ff., esp. 11–12.

68. Palmistry.

69. Sir William Phips (1651–1695), governor of Massachusetts (1691–95) and member of Cotton Mather's North Church congregation.

70. Lieutenant Governor William Stoughton.

71. St. Augustine of Hippo warns St. Jerome that if a breach of friendship were to occur between Jerome and Rufinus of Aquileia (344–411), a Greco-Roman theologian and translator of Greek patristics, our "portion" would be "sad and piteous." Schaff, ed., *Nicene and Post-Nicene Fathers*, letter 73, 1:331.

72. St. Gregory Nazianzen (c. 330–390), archbishop of Constantinople and Cappadocian father of the Greek church.

73. Quoted from Mather, "The Return of Several Ministers," arts. 6, 8.

74. The judges at the Court of Oyer and Terminer (May–October 1692): William Stoughton (chief justice), Jonathan Corwin, Bartholomew Gedney, John Hathorne, John Richards, Samuel Sewall, Nathaniel Saltonstall, Peter Sergeant, and Waitstill Winthrop.

75. This old chestnut is retold in many places, including in Alexander Clogie, "To the Christian Reader," in *Vox Corvi; or, The Voice of a Raven. That Thrice spoke these Words distinctly* (London, 1694), A3r–A6v.

76. George Burroughs (c. 1650–1692), sometime minister at Salem Village prior to Samuel Parris's arrival, accused as the ringleader.

77. John Gaule (c. 1603–1687), English nonconformist clergyman at Great Stoughton (Huntington), wrote *Select Cases*.

78. Perkins, *Discourse on the Damned Art of Witchcraft*, sec. 2, pp. 199–218. Mather abstracts Perkins's guidelines in his *Wonders*, § 7, B6r–B7r.

79. Statement of Elizabeth Hubbard (May 9, 1692) and Deposition of Mary Walcott (May 9, 1692), in *Records*, 243, 248.

80. Deposition of Mercy Lewis (May 9, 1692), in *Records*, 245.

81. Deposition of Ann Putnam Jr., in *Records*, 245–46.

82. Depositions of Mercy Lewis, Ann Putnam, John Putnam, Mary Walcott, in *Records*, 245, 246, 247, 248, 505.

83. Thomas Potts (court clerk), *The Wonderfull Discoverie of Witches in the Countie of Lancaster* (London, 1613), records the trial and hanging of ten people for witchcraft in 1612. The lengthy report provides the accounts of interrogation, indictment, and executions of the accused—along with pious improvements.

84. The italicized passage is extracted from Gaule, *Select Cases*, 82–83.

85. Depositions and Testimonies of Simon Willard and William Wormall v. George Burroughs, in *Records*, 249, 497.

86. Deposition of Simon Willard and Testimony of Samuel Webber v. George Burroughs, in *Records*, 249, 497.
87. Testimony of Thomas Ruck v. George Burroughs, in *Records*, 531–32, 647.
88. Testimony of Thomas Ruck v. George Burroughs, in *Records*, 532, 647.
89. Extract from Gaule, *Select Cases*, 80–81.
90. Adapted from Thomas Ady, M.A. (fl. seventeenth century), English humanist and skeptic accused of denying the existence of witches, in *A Candle in the Dark* (London, 1656), 96, 162, and *A Perfect Discovery of Witches* (London, 1661), 79.
91. Examination of Susannah Martin, in *Records*, 228–29.
92. Examination of Susannah Martin, in *Records*, 229, 231.
93. Deposition of John Allen v. Susannah Martin, in *Records*, 392–93.
94. Testimony of John Atkinson v. Susannah Martin, in *Records*, 425.
95. Deposition of Bernard Peach v. Susannah Martin, in *Records*, 256–57, 303.
96. Deposition of Robert Downer, Mary Andrews, and Moses Pike v. Susannah Martin, in *Records*, 436.
97. Deposition of John Kimball v. Susannah Martin, in *Records*, 275–77.
98. Goodman Blezdell, in Deposition of John Kimball v. Susannah Martin, in *Records*, 276.
99. Kimball, in *Records*, 276.
100. Deposition of William Brown v. Susannah Martin, in *Records*, 257–58.
101. Elizabeth Brown, in Deposition of William Brown, in *Records*, 257–58.
102. Testimony of Sarah Atkinson v. Susannah Martin, in *Records*, 426.
103. Testimony of John Pressy v. Susannah Martin, in *Records*, 258–59.
104. Deposition of John Pressy and Mary Pressy v. Susannah Martin, in *Records*, 260.
105. Deposition of Jarvis Ring v. Susannah Martin, and Deposition of Joseph Ring v. Susannah Martin and Thomas Hardy, in *Records*, 265–66.
106. Deposition of Joseph Ring v. Susannah Martin, and Thomas Hardy, in *Records*, 266–67.
107. "T.H.," i.e., Thomas Hardy, in Deposition of Joseph Ring v. Susannah Martin and Thomas Hardy, in *Records*, 266–67.

RACE, SLAVERY, AND SERVITUDE

1. Mather, *Biblia Americana*, 1:1111–13.
2. The English biblical scholar Joseph Mede (1586–1639), adapting the conqueror Hannibal's contrite acknowledgment about Carthage from Roman historian Livy (*Ad Urbe Condita*, 27.51.13).
3. Augustine, *City of God*, 18.38: "a prophecy of our times." Schaff, ed., *Nicene and Post-Nicene Fathers*, 2:383.
4. Noah "through ignorance of the proper amount [of wine] to drink fell into a drunken stupor." Chrysostom, *Homilies on Genesis*, in *Saint John Chrysostom Homilies on Genesis 18–45*, transl. Robert C. Hill (Washington, D.C.: Catholic University of America Press, 1990), Homily 29, 202–203. All of Mather's references to Chrysostom in this document are to this Homily.

5. Johann Heinrich Heidegger, seventeenth-century Swiss theologian, author of *De Historia Sacra Patriarcharum* (Amsterdam, 1667–71).

6. "The arts pertaining to life," that is, "agriculture."

7. Onkelos and Jonathan Ben Uziel are authors of targums, which are ancient Aramaic paraphrases of the Hebrew Bible: "and he devoted [himself]." John Calvin, sixteenth-century French Protestant reformer, commentary on Genesis 9:20: "Leaving this question undetermined, I rather suppose, that we are to learn from the drunkenness of Noah, what a filthy and detestable crime drunkenness is." *The Commentaries of John Calvin*, transl. John King, 22 vols. (Grand Rapids, Mich.: Baker, 2005), 1:300.

8. Theodoret of Cyrus and Procopius of Gaza, fifth-century CE Christian leaders and biblical commentators; Nicholas of Lyra, a fourteenth-century French Franciscan teacher and biblical exegete; Alfonso Tostado of Avila, aka Abulensis, a fifteenth-century Spanish theologian.

9. Chrysostom, *Homilies on Genesis*, Homily 29, p. 212: "for some hidden reason." Augustine's commentary on Genesis 9:25: "It is asked, for what other reason is Ham, when sinning against his father, cursed not in himself, but in his son Canaan, other than because it was prophesied that the Canaanites would be subdued and cast out from the land of Canaan, and that the children of Israel, who would come from the seed of Shem, would take it."

10. Theodoret of Cyrus, *Quaestiones in Octateuchum*, question 58: "but [should also] deter future generations from sinning against their parents." Theodoret, *Questions on the Octateuch*, transl. Robert C. Hill, 2 vols. (Washington, D.C.: Catholic University of America, 2007), 1:120, 121.

11. Seventeenth-century Dutch classical scholar and royal tutor Isaac Vossius (1618–1689), author of *Observationes ad Pomponium Melam* (The Hague, 1658): "Art was afterwards turned into nature."

12. First-century CE Hellenistic Jewish philosopher Philo Judaeus, *Quaestiones et solutiones in Genesin II*, 2.76.

13. Nicholas Fuller (c. 1557–1626), English Hebraist and author of *Miscellaneorum Theologicorum* (Oxford, 1616).

14. "The canon of prophecy, and the epitome of almost all subsequent prophecies."

15. "Shines out much more widely and successfully, by the grace of God, among the descendants of Japheth, than it ever blossomed among the descendants of Shem and Ham."

16. The identity of this location—probably a homonymic spelling of a South or Central American place name—remains unidentified.

17. English physician and plant anatomist Nehemiah Grew (1641–1712), *Cosmologia Sacra* (London, 1701), bk. 4, chap. 4.

18. Marcus Fabius Quintilianus of Hispania (c. 35–c. 100) was a Roman teacher and rhetorician.

19. "God's mind spins the thread on Mt. Olympus." Attributed to Charlemagne, Holy Roman Empire during the early ninth century.

20. I.e., scraps.

21. In his *Diary*, 1:564, Mather confesses, "I wrote as well contrived an Essay as I could, for the animating and facilitating of that Work, the Christianizing of the *Negroes*. It

is entitutled THE NEGRO CHRISTIANIZED. *An Essay, to excite and assist that Good Work; the Information of the Negroes in Christianity.* And my Design is; not only to lodge one of the Books, in every Family of *New England*, which has a *Negro* in it, but also to send Numbers of them into the *Indies*; and write such Letters to the principal Inhabitants of the Islands, as may be proper to accompany them."

22. John Chrysostom.

23. See Mather's entry on this question in his *Biblia Americana*, 1:672, and our [Entry on Genesis 9:27 (The Curse of Cham)] at the beginning of our selection on Race, Slavery, and Servitude.

24. José Acosta, sixteenth-century Spanish Jesuit missionary: "The barbarian whose freedom is taken receives in return the religion of Jesus Christ and a dignified life as a human being."

25. For the biblical Onesimus, see Philemon 1. For Mather's own slave of that name, see *Diary*, 1:579, 2:271, 363, 446, 456, and "Medicines and Cures," below, for Onesimus's role in inoculation therapy. See also Koo, "Strangers in the House of God," and Tindol, "Getting the Pox Off All Their Houses."

26. Dionysius Cato, a Latin author of the third or fourth century CE: "*Cum servos fueris proprios mercatus in usus / Et famulos dicas, homines tamen esse memento.*" Mather only quotes the last line of Cato's *Distich*, 4.44: "When servants thou hast bought, remember then, / Altho' thou term'st them slaves, they still are men." *The Distichs of Cato*, 43.

27. Julius Caesar, first-century BCE Roman general and emperor, wrote commentaries on his campaigns in Western Europe and on the Roman Civil War.

28. "Of certified freedom," or manumission.

PURITANS AND NATIVE AMERICANS

1. See, for example, Mather, *A Letter, about the Present State of Christianity.*

2. Mather, *Magnalia Christi Americana*, bk. 7, chap. 25, fol. 91.

3. Hannah Emerson Dustan (1657–1736).

4. Mary Corliss Neff (1646–1722).

5. This can be taken to mean "travail," labor, or hardship.

6. Samuel Leonardson (1683–1718), then fourteen years old.

7. A location in current-day south-central New Hampshire, near the city of Concord, along the Contoocook River, territory of the Penacook tribe.

8. That is, "seven nights," or a week, later.

9. The story of a Hebrew woman, Jael, slaying the invading general Sisera by driving a tent spike through his head while he slept is told in Judges 4.

10. Mather reprints this story in his *Magnalia Christi Americana*, bk. 6, chap. 2, fols. 10–14.

11. Or Norridgewock, in present-day southwestern Maine on the Kennebec River, the territory of the Abenakis.

12. Possibly referring to a location within the territory of the Mikmaq, on current-day Cape Breton Island at the eastern end of Nova Scotia, which in the early seventeenth century was taken from the French by the English. Although the Maritime Islands

were returned to France in the 1630s, some English remained there, and the English would reclaim the islands again through the Treaty of Utrecht (1713).

13. I.e., tavern.

14. Possibly Margaret Stilson, born in 1679 in Marblehead, Mass., who would marry William Hilton in 1699 and John Allen in 1727, dying in 1763.

15. Probably Colonel Jonathan Tyng (1642–1724), born in Boston, who was a militia officer, judge, and member of the governor's council; and possibly Capt. John Alden, Jr. (1626–1702), who had been accused of witchcraft during the Essex County hysteria. These men were most likely in New France negotiating for the release of hostages.

16. I.e., the French.

17. "Of human wretchedness." From *Historiae Adversum Paganos*, by the late fourth-century Spanish historian and theologian Paulus Orosius.

18. Virgil, *Aeneid*, 1:2.12: "My mind shudders to remember."

19. Referring to raids by the French and their Native allies on these towns, respectively, in 1697 and 1704.

20. The Great Fire of Boston (October 1711), which destroyed the first Old State House along with the First Church.

21. Andrew Gardner, b. 1674, minister of Lancaster, Mass., from 1701 until accidentally shot while on sentry duty in 1704.

22. Benjamin Rolfe, b. 1662, minister of Haverhill, Mass., from 1698 until his death in 1708, when he was killed by Indians.

23. Referring to a measles epidemic in 1713, which took hundreds of lives, including five in Mather's household. See Mather, *A Letter About a Good Management under the Distemper of the Measles* (Boston, 1713).

PIETISM AND WORLD MISSIONS

1. See Gildrie, *The Profane, the Civil, and the Godly*; Rooy, *Theology of Missions*; and Winn et al., *Pietist Impulse*.

2. Interest in Mather's communications with his Pietist colleagues in Germany has received much attention in the past two decades. See Benz, "Pietist and Puritan Sources"; Corrigan, *Prism of Pietism*; Francke, "Beginning of Cotton Mather's Correspondence," "Cotton Mather and August Hermann Francke," and "Further Documents"; Lindberg, *Pietist Theologians*; Lovelace, *American Pietism*; Splitter, "Fact and Fiction"; Strom et al., *Pietism in Germany and North America*; and Ward, *Early Evangelicalism*.

3. See Scheiding, "The World as Parish."

4. See Green and Viaene, *Religious Internationals*; Haykin and Stewart, *Advent of Evangelicalism*; Kennedy, *Cotton Mather*; Noll, *Rise of Evangelicalism*; and Stievermann, *Prophecy, Piety, and the Problems of Historicity*.

5. Mather, *Manuductio*, 127.

6. Mather, *Manuductio*, 118, 119.

7. Woody, "Biographical Notes to Cotton Mather's 'Manuductio ad Ministerium,'" is exemplary for painstaking historical scholarship on this text.

8. The German Pietist Heinrich Wilhelm Ludolf (1655–1712) served as secretary to Queen Anne's consort, Prince George of Denmark, and as corresponding member of the Society for Promoting Christian Knowledge. With his famous German Lutheran Pietist colleagues August Hermann Francke (1663–1727) of the Lutheran University of Halle (Saxony) and Anthony Wilhelm Boehm (1673–1722), court preacher at St. James, London (1705), Ludolf promoted an "ecclesia universalis" as a means to spread the Protestant Reformation far and wide.

9. Mather's quote is from Ludolf's second edition of "Reflexions on the Present State of the Christian Church," appended to Ludolf's *Reliquiae Ludolfianae* (London, 1712), 156–57. See also Mather, *Malachi* (Boston, 1717), 55.

10. For Mather's expectations of the Second Coming, see Mather, *Threefold Paradise*.

11. See also Mather's bilingual *Stone Cut out of the Mountain. And the Kingdom of God, in Those Maxims of it, that cannot be shaken* (1716) and *Malachi*.

12. John Davenant (c. 1572–1641), Anglican bishop of Salisbury, *Ad Fraternam Communionem inter Evangelicas Ecclesias Restaurandam Adhortatio, in eo fundata, quod non dissentiant in ullo fundamentali Catholicae* (Cambridge, 1640). An English translation of Davenant's essay was published as *An Exhortation to Brotherly Communion betwixt the Protestant Churches* (Oxford, 1641).

13. Richard Baxter, Reformed pastor at Kidderminster (Worcestershire), was a friend and correspondent of both Mathers. Baxter's *Catholick Unity; or, The Only Way to bring us all to be of one Religion* (London, 1660) and his huge *The True and Only Way of Concord Of all the Christian Churches* (London, 1680) are part of the same effort to unite the Protestant churches on a set of doctrines similar to those of Mather's "Maxims of Piety." Mather's *"Damnable Heresies"* is directed against the rise of anti-Trinitarian Arianism, the denial of Christ's Godhead.

14. The quote is adapted from *A Briefe Declaration of the Universalitie of the Church of Christ, and the Unitie of the Catholike Faith Professed* (London, 1624), 44, by the learned Anglican divine James Ussher (1581–1656), bishop of Meath and later archbishop of Canterbury.

15. "The important points of the Gospel."

16. The controversy between Calvinists and Arminians at the Synod of Dort (1618).

17. A likely wordplay on the five (Lat. *quinque* + articulus) articles of Calvinism and the three (Lat. *ternarius*) points of his Three Maxims of Piety—one of Mather's own devising and not to be found in any *Oxford English Dictionary*.

18. Argumentative or controversial writings.

19. Arguments to refute an opponent's position.

20. The secondhand quotation is from Roman historian Ammianus Marcellinus (c. 330–395), *Roman History*, 22.5.4, who likens sectarian hatred among Christians to that of wild beasts: "such deadly hatred among Christians for one another." *Ammianus Marcellinus: History*, transl. J. C. Rolfe, 3 vols. (Cambridge, Mass.: Harvard University Press, 1950), 2:203.

21. The German astronomer and court chaplain to Frederick IV, elector of the Palatinate, Bartholomew Pitiscus (1561–1613), is credited with having coined the word "trigonometry" and for devising trigonometric tables. He was a disputatious and uncompromising Calvinist.

22. The German jurist, political philosopher, and historian Samuel von Pufendorf (1632–1694) is renowned for his contributions to natural law theory. His *De Jure Naturae et Gentium* (London, 1672) is among his most important works.

23. Adapted from Seneca's *Trojan Women*: "qui non vetat [peccare], cum possit, iubet," or "one who does not forbid [wrongdoing], when he has the power, commands it." Seneca, *Tragedies, Volume I*, transl. John G. Fitch (Cambridge, Mass.: Harvard University Press, 2018), 291.

24. Mather describes the acrimonious debate at the Synod of Dort (1618–19) between the followers of Jacobus Arminius (1560–1609) and those of Franciscus Gomarus (1563–1641), a conservative Dutch Calvinist, leading to the definition of the Five Points of Calvinism.

25. The great Jewish philosopher Moses ben Maimon (1135–1204) is renowned for his explication of Halakha, the Jewish religious code, in his *Mishneh Torah*. Mather cites Maimonides's popular *Guide for the Perplexed* throughout the volumes of *Biblia Americana*. Marcus Tullius Cicero debated the question of free will versus implacable fate in his *De Fato* ("Of Fate"), which was appended to his *De Natura Deorum* (44 BCE).

26. The German Lutheran reformer Philipp Melanchthon (1497–1560) was one of the earliest systematic theologians in the Protestant Reformation. His advice: "It is our duty to disregard the disputations on predestination."

27. Mather is prepared to go along with Melanchthon's recommendation but draws the line at the Arian and Socinian heresy of denying the Trinity, the Godhead and divinity of Christ, and original sin.

28. Yet Mather recommends to maintain "always unimpaired friendship."

29. An early medieval Christian sect in North Africa espousing asceticism and holiness of the priesthood to the point of martyrdom.

30. Corinthian brass—a high-grade, shiny bronze—was the most valuable alloy in classical antiquity.

31. Diana (Artemis) of Ephesus, the ancient Greek goddess of the hunt, was revered by her devotees in Asia Minor.

32. Mather refers to *Catholicism without Popery, An Essay to render the Church of England a Means and a Pattern of Union to Christian World* (London, 1669) by John Hooke (1655–1712), a distinguished member of the Royal Society of London and natural philosopher. Mather quotes him at great length in his *Christian Philosopher*.

33. By the end of his life, Mather has moved a far cry away from his myth-making proclamation, "The *First Age* was the *Golden Age*: To return unto *That*, will make a Man a *Protestant*, and I may add, a *Puritan*." "General Introduction," in *Magnalia Christi Americana*, § 3, fol. Cv.

34. "Shining gold."

35. "Union of Faith."

36. August Hermann Francke of the University of Halle sent Mather copies of his *Pietas Hallensis, or A Publick Demonstration of the Footsteps of a Divine Being yet in the World* (London, 1705), a German publication translated into English and published in London, by Anthony Wilhelm Boehm. See Benz, "Ecumenical Relations."

37. The German Lutheran Bartholomew Ziegenbalg (1682–1719) and Heinrich Plütschau (1676–1752), graduates of August Hermann Francke's Pietist seminary at the University of Halle (Saxony), were pioneering missionaries sent to the Danish trading mission at Tranquebar (Tharangambadi, South-Eastern India) by King Frederick IV of Denmark (1671–1730). They translated and published the New Testament into the Tamil language and communicated with their Lutheran headquarters in Halle, Copenhagen, and London. Mather's epistolary communications with Ziegenbalg and his successors in Tranquebar were channeled through Anthony Wilhelm Boehm in London. Mather's exuberance is informed by his millenarian visions of Christ's worldwide kingdom on earth and the pouring out of the Holy Spirit (Joel, chap. 2).
38. A coastal region south of the Bay of Bengal.
39. Cotton Mather's humble self.
40. Joel, chap. 2.
41. For Cotton Mather's eschatological timetables, see Mather, *Threefold Paradise*, 60–78, 319–47.
42. At this time, Mather's eschatological calculations for the Second Coming centered on the periods between 1716 and 1736.

THE SECOND COMING AND MILLENNIALISM

1. Increase Mather, "A Discourse Concerning the Glorious State of the Church on Earth," 364.
2. Mather, *Threefold Paradise*, 244–48.
3. "The Third Paradise" is part of Mather's book-length holograph manuscript "Triparadisus" (1720–27), his last word on his lifelong millenarian speculations about the Second Coming of Christ.
4. Robert Maton (1607–c. 1653), an English millenarian and author of several chiliastic tracts, including *Israels Redemption* (London, 1642) and *Christs Personal Reigne on Earth, One Thousand Years with the Saints* (London, 1652)—both about the national conversion of the Jews and Christ's millennial reign on earth.
5. Mather alludes to the position of New England's own Samuel Hutchinson (1618–1667), *A Declaration of a Future Glorious Estate of the Church to be here upon Earth at Christ's Personal Appearance* (London, 1667).
6. See Babylonian Talmud, Tractate Kethuboth, 111a—subterraneous caverns linking Egypt with Israel.
7. *Apokatastasis*, i.e., restoration, restitution.
8. Abraham Calovius (1612–1686), an orthodox Lutheran theologian, professor at Wittenberg (Germany), and distinguished Orientalist: "Concerning the restitution to the former, or better, state."
9. "Palingenesis."
10. Mather's secondhand quote "Anaktisis" (via Calovius) suggests "re-creation" and "re-construction," and appears in Pseudo-Justinus Martyr, *Quaestiones gentilium ad Christianos* (210), attributed to the early Christian apologist Justin Martyr (100–165).
11. "Larger and more flawless."

12. *Eukoumene*, i.e., "Inhabited." See Acts 24:5.

13. "To enjoy God" and "to make use of his creatures."

14. R. David Kimchi, aka Kimḥi (1160–1235), a French medieval biblical scholar, Hebrew grammarian, and philosopher, who wrote *Rabbi Davidis Kimhhi Commentarii In Psalmos Davidis* (Paris, 1666); Arnobius (fl. 284–305), a Christian apologist and rhetorician at Sicca Veneria (North Africa) who authored *Adversus Nationes* (303).

15. Cerinthius (fl. 100 CE), a Gnostic, taught that Christ was merely human at birth but became divine through baptism, when a divine power descended on him, although this power left him at the crucifixion. In objecting to the immoderate carnal banquets that Islam was alleged to promise the just in a paradisiac Lubberland, Mather adopts the Augustinian position and pleads for moderation. Augustine, *City of God*, 20.7. According to Al-Qur'an (sura 16:97), the faithful who do good works will be rewarded "in accordance with the best of what they have done." Transl. Ahmed Ali (Princeton, N.J.: Princeton University Press, 1994).

16. Lady Hedibia of Gaul (fl. fourth–fifth century CE), a Druidic priestess, was the learned woman to whom St. Jerome, aka Eusebius Hieronymus (c. 347–420), addressed his Epistola 120, in *De Poenitentia*.

17. Lucius Caecilius Firmianus Lactantius (c. 250–c. 325), a North African Christian apologist. Mather translates a passage from Lactantius's *Divine Institutes*, 7.24.

18. Disciples of the Pontian Gnostic Marcion (c. 110–c. 160), the Marcionites taught that Christ was the son of the loving God—not the one of the punishing Jehovah of the Old Testament. They also "preached celibacy," as suggested in Irenaeus, *Adversus Haereses*, 1.26.1, line 2, and Eusebius, *Historia Ecclesiastica*, 4.29.2, line 2. See also Tertullian, *Against Marcion*, transl. by Rev. Peter Holmes, 5.9–10, in Roberts and Donaldson, eds., *Ante-Nicene Fathers*, 3:447–52.

19. Mather asserts a double Jerusalem here: The celestial New Jerusalem, a literal, corporeal, cubic city where the raised saints obtain their beatific vison, is without a temple because God is there. Its earthly counterpart, the restored Judean capital, however, will maintain its temple. Yet Mather does not wish to press the point too much, as is evident from his dictum: "Let it be of as much value as it can."

20. "Satan's minions."

21. According to a medieval legend, an angel is to have cried out, "Poison [has been] poured out into the Church," when the Roman Emperor Constantine the Great (c. 272–337), after his conversion to Christianity, allegedly transferred his power over the Western Roman Empire to the papal See of Rome (Donation of Constantine).

22. Nicodemus, the Pharisee and member of the Sanhedrin who believed in Christ but was afraid to acknowledge him publicly.

23. Edward Chandler (c. 1668–1750), bishop of Coventry and Lichfield. Mather relies on Chandler's *Defence of Christianity from the Prophecies of the Old Testament* (London, 1725), chap. 1, sec. 1, pp. 16, 17, 18, who paraphrastically translates Virgil's *Fourth Eclogue*, 1:4.53ff, and pairs it with Old Testament biblical prophecies.

24. Always looking for non-Christian sources to corroborate the prophecies, Mather draws on Virgil's *Fourth Eclogue*, 1:4.37ff, in which the poet-seer prophesies the birth of a child attended by the coming of the Golden Age.

25. Horace, *Epistles*, 1.49: "The one who possesses it ought to be healthy."

26. Also *Abrech*, from Heb. אברך (Gen. 41:43), probably a title, but neither its etymology nor its precise meaning is known.

27. The Latin passage reads, "They learn everything that can be known," and alludes to the dicta of St. Thomas Aquinas.

28. Mather's less-than-flattering epithet for the "smoking" or "babbling" Aristotle comes as no surprise. With the rise of the natural sciences in the late seventeenth century, the Greek philosopher fell on hard times in college curriculums. Mather's own recommendations for improving Harvard's curriculum can be found in *Manuductio*, 35–36, and for his donations of Pietist books to Harvard, see *Diary*, 2:192, 194, 348, 380–81, 405–6, 723–24.

29. Founded in 1694 by Frederic I (1657–1713), first king of Prussia, the University of Halle in Saxony was renowned for its school of Protestant theology, at which Mather's correspondent August Hermann Francke was teaching.

30. Henry More, D.D. (1614–1687), Anglican theologian and Cambridge Platonist. Mather cites from *Conjectura Cabbalistica* (London, 1662), "Defence of the Moral Cabbala," chap. 2, in *A Collection Of Several Philosophical Writings* (London, 1662), 165.

31. Andrew Willet, D.D. (1562–1621), rector of Childerley, Cambridgeshire; staunch opponent of Roman Catholicism; and author of several commentaries on the Old Testament.

32. The "Old Conquerors" placed their trophies in the Capitolium in ancient Rome, consisting of three temples dedicated to Jupiter Optimus Maximus, Minerva, and Juno.

33. For parallel ideas, see Increase Mather, "A Discourse Concerning the Glorious State of the Church on Earth," and *Dissertation Concerning the Future Conversion of the Jewish Nation*, 34.

BIBLIOGRAPHY

A PARTIAL LIST OF PUBLISHED AND UNPUBLISHED
WRITINGS BY COTTON MATHER

The titles below are those consulted for this *Reader*. For a nearly complete, annotated list of Mather's publications, see Thomas J. Holmes, *Cotton Mather: A Bibliography of His Works*, 3 vols., 1940; reprint, Newton, Mass.: Crofton, 1974.

The Accomplished Singer. Instructions How the Piety of Singing with a True Devotion, may be obtained and expressed. Boston, 1721.
An Account of the Method and Success of Inoculating the Small-Pox in Boston in New-England. London, 1722.
Address to the Physicians (June 6, 1721). In Isaac Greenwood, *A Friendly Debate; or, A Dialogue between Rusticus and Academicus*. Boston, 1722.
"Angel of Bethesda." Mather Family Papers. American Antiquarian Society, Worcester, Mass.
The Angel of Bethesda. An Essay Upon the Common Maladies of Mankind. Edited by Gordon W. Jones. Barre, Mass.: American Antiquarian Society and Barre Publishers, 1972.
Biblia Americana: America's First Bible Commentary. A Synoptic Commentary on the Old and New Testaments. Vol. 1, *Genesis*. Edited by Reiner Smolinski. Tübingen, Germany: Mohr Siebeck and Baker Academic, 2010.
Biblia Americana: America's First Bible Commentary. A Synoptic Commentary on the Old and New Testaments. Vol. 2, *Exodus–Deuteronomy*. Edited by Reiner Smolinski. Tübingen, Germany: Mohr Siebeck, 2019.
Biblia Americana: America's First Bible Commentary. A Synoptic Commentary on the Old and New Testaments. Vol. 3, *Joshua–2 Chronicles*. Edited by Kenneth P. Minkema. Tübingen, Germany: Mohr Siebeck, 2013.
Biblia Americana: America's First Bible Commentary. A Synoptic Commentary on the Old and New Testaments. Vol. 4, *Ezra–Psalms*. Edited by Harry Clark Maddux. Tübingen, Germany: Mohr Siebeck, 2014.

Biblia Americana: America's First Bible Commentary. A Synoptic Commentary on the Old and New Testaments. Vol. 5, *Proverbs–Jeremiah.* Edited by Jan Stievermann. Tübingen, Germany: Mohr Siebeck, 2015.

Biblia Americana: America's First Bible Commentary. A Synoptic Commentary on the Old and New Testaments. Vol. 9, *Romans–Philemon.* Edited by Robert E. Brown. Tübingen, Germany: Mohr Siebeck, 2018.

Bonifacius. An Essay Upon the Good, that is to be Devised and Designed. Boston, 1710.

Brethren dwelling together in Unity: The True Basis for an Union Among the People of God. Boston, 1718.

The Christian Philosopher. Edited by Winton U. Solberg. Urbana: University of Illinois Press, 1994.

The Christian Philosopher: A Collection of the Best Discoveries in Nature, with Religious Improvements. London, 1721.

Christianus per Ignem; or, A Disciple Warming of himself and Owning of his Lord: With Devout and Useful Meditations, Fetch'd out of the Fire. Boston, 1702.

A Comforter of the Mourners. An Essay For the Undoing of Heavy Burdens In an Offer of such Good Words As have a Tendency to cause Glad Hearts, in those that are Stouping Under Various Matters of Heaviness. Boston, 1704.

Companion for Communicants. Discourses Upon the Nature, the Design, and the Subject of the Lords Supper. Boston, 1690.

"Cotton Mather to Elihu Yale" (January 14, 1718). In Josiah Quincy, *The History of Harvard University.* 2 vols. Boston: Crosby, Nichols, Lee, 1860. 1:524–26.

"Cotton Mather to James Jurin" (May 21, 1723). In *The Correspondence of James Jurin (1684–1750).* Edited by Andrea Rusnock. Amsterdam: Radopi, 1996. 150–63.

"Cotton Mather to John Cotton" (October 20, 1692). In John Cotton Jr., *The Correspondence of John Cotton Junior.* Edited by Sheila McIntyre and Len Travers. Boston: Colonial Society of Massachusetts, 2009. 424–25.

"Cotton Mather to John Richards" (13d 12m 1691[–2]; [February] 13, 1692). In *The Mather Papers, Collections of the Massachusetts Historical Society,* 4th series, 8 (1868): 390–91.

"Cotton Mather to John Richards" (31d 3m [May] 31, 1692). In *The Mather Papers, Collections of the Massachusetts Historical Society,* 4th series, 8 (1968): 391–97.

"Cotton Mather to William Stoughton" (September 2, 1692). In *Selected Letters of Cotton Mather.* Edited by Kenneth Silverman. Baton Rouge: Louisiana University Press, 1971. 43–44.

"Cotton Mather to Zabdiel Boylstone [sic]" (June 24, 1721) ("Circular Letter"). In *The Massachusetts Magazine; or, Monthly Museum of Knowledge and Rational Entertainment,* December 1789, 778.

"Curiosa Americana." Massachusetts Historical Society, Boston, and Royal Society of London.

Death Approaching. A very brief Essay on A Life drawing nigh unto the Grave. Boston, 1714.

Death made Easie & Happy. Two Brief Discourses on the Prudent Apprehensions of Death. London, 1701.

The Declaration, Of the Gentlemen, Merchants, and Inhabitants of Boston, and the Countrey Adjacent. April 18th, 1689. Boston, 1689.

The Deplorable State of New-England, By Reason of a Covetous and Treacherous Governour. London, 1708.

The Diary of Cotton Mather. 2 vols. Edited by Worthington C. Ford. *Collections of the Massachusetts Historical Society,* 7th series, 7–8 (1911–12).

The Diary of Cotton Mather . . . for the Year 1712. Edited by William R. Manierre III. Charlottesville: University Press of Virginia, 1964.

Duodecennium Luctuosum. The History of a Long War with Indian Salvages, And their Directors and Abettors; From the Year, 1702. To the Year, 1714. Boston, 1714.

The Duty of Children, Whose Parents have Pray'd for them. Boston, 1703.

Early Piety, Exemplified in the Life and Death of Mr. Nathanael Mather. London, 1689.

Early Religion, Urged in a Sermon, Upon The Duties Wherein, And the Reasons Wherefore, Young People Should Become Religious. Boston, 1694.

Elizabeth in her Holy Retirement. An Essay To Prepare a Pious Woman for her Lying in. Boston, 1710.

Family-Religion, Excited and Assisted. Boston, 1705.

A Family Well-Ordered; or, An Essay To Render Parents and Children Happy in one another. Boston, 1699.

Good Lessons for Children; or, Instructions, Provided for a Little Son to Learn at School, when Learning to Read. Boston, 1706.

A Good Master well Served. A Brief Discourse On the Necessary Properties & Practices of a Good Servant In every kind of Servitude. Boston, 1696.

Help for Distressed Parents; or, Counsels & Comforts for Godly Parents Afflicted with Ungodly Children. Boston, 1695.

Humiliations follow'd with Deliverances. A Brief Discourse On the Matter and Method, Of that Humiliation . . . with A Narrative, Of a Notable Deliverance lately Received by some English Captives. Boston, 1697.

India Christiana. A Discourse, Delivered unto the Commissioners, for the Propagation of the Gospel among the American Indians which is Accompanied with several Instruments relating to the Glorious Design of Propagating our Holy Religion, in the Eastern as well as the Western, Indies. Boston, 1721.

A Letter About a Good Management under the Distemper of the Measles. Boston, 1713.

A Letter, About the Present State of Christianity, Among the Christianized Indians of New-England. Boston, 1705.

"Letter of Cotton Mather to John Foster (17th 6m [August], 1692)." In *Transactions of the Literary Society of Quebec* 2 (1831): 313–16.

Magnalia Christi Americana. Books I and II. Edited by Kenneth B. Murdock. Cambridge, Mass.: Belknap Press of Harvard University Press, 1977.

Magnalia Christi Americana; or, The Ecclesiastical History of New-England. London, 1702.

Magnalia Christi Americana; or, The Ecclesiastical History of New-England. Introduction and notes by Thomas Robbins. 2 vols. Hartford, Conn.: Silas Andrus and Sons, 1853.

Manuductio ad Ministerium. Directions for a Candidate of the Ministry. Boston, 1726.

Marah spoken to. A brief Essay To do Good unto the Widow. Boston, 1718.

The Marrow of the Gospel. A very brief Essay on the Union Between the Redeemer And the Beleever. Boston, 1727.

The Mather Papers. In *Collections of the Massachusetts Historical Society*, 4th series, 8 (1868).

Memorable Providences, Relating to Witchcrafts and Possessions. Boston, 1689.

A Memorial Of the Present Deplorable State of New-England, With the many Disadvantages it lyes under, by the Male-Administration of their Present Governour, Joseph Dudley, Esq. Boston, 1707.

Menachem. A very brief Essay, on Tokens for Good. Boston: Benjamin Gay, 1716.

Methods and Motives for Societies to Suppress Disorders. Boston, 1703.

The Negro Christianized. An Essay to Excite and Assist that Good Work, The Instruction of Negro-Servants in Christianity. Boston, 1706.

"An Original Letter from Dr. C. Mather, to Governour Dudley" (January 20, 1707/8). In *Collections of the Massachusetts Historical Society*, 1st series, 3 (1794): 128–34. Reprint, *Collections*, vol. 3, Boston: Munroe and Francis, 1810.

Ornaments for the Daughters of Zion. Cambridge, Mass., 1692.

Parentator. Memoirs of Remarkables in the Life and the Death of the Ever-Memorable Dr. Increase Mather. Boston, 1724.

A Pastoral Letter, to Families Visited with Sickness. Boston, 1721.

"Paterna." MSS 3860. Special Collections, Tracy W. McGregor Library of American History, Albert Shirley Small Special Collections Library, University of Virginia, Charlottesville.

Paterna: The Autobiography of Cotton Mather. Edited by Ronald A. Bosco. Delmar, N.Y.: Scholars' Facsimiles and Reprints, 1976.

"Pietas In Patriam: The Life of his Excellency Sir William Phips." In *Magnalia Christi Americana*. London, 1702. Bk. 2, fols. 35–75.

Pietas in Patriam: The Life of his Excellency Sir William Phips, Knt. Late Captain General, and Governour in Chief of the Province of the Massachuset-Bay, New England. London, 1697.

Private Meetings Animated & Regulated. Boston, 1706.

Psalterium Americanum. The Book of Psalms, In a Translation Exactly conformed unto the Original; but all in Blank Verse, Fitted unto the Tunes commonly used in our Churches. Boston, 1718.

"Quotidiana." American Antiquarian Society, Worcester, Mass.

The Religious Marriner. A Discourse Tending to Direct the Course of Sea-men, In those Points of Religion, Which may bring them to the Port, of Eternal Happiness. Boston, 1700.

"Retired Elizabeth. A Long, tho' no very Hard Chapter For, a Woman Whose Travail Approaches With Remedies to Abate the Sorrows of Child-bearing." In *Angel of Bethesda: An Essay upon the Common Maladies of Mankind*. Edited by Gordon W. Jones. Barre, Mass.: American Antiquarian Society, 1972. 235–48.

"The Return of Several Ministers Consulted by his Excellency and the Honourable Council, Upon the Present Witchcrafts in Salem-Village" (June 15, 1692). In Increase Mather, *Cases of Conscience*. Boston, 1693. G4r–v.

Rules for the Society of Negroes. 1693. 2nd edition. Boston, c. 1706–13.

The Sailours Companion and Counsellour. An Offer of Considerations for the Tribe of Ze-bulun; Awakening the Mariner, To Think and to Do, Those things that may render his Voyage Prosperous. Boston, 1709.

Selected Letters of Cotton Mather. Edited by Kenneth Silverman. Baton Rouge: Louisiana State University Press, 1971.

Some Considerations on the Bills of Credit Now Passing in New-England. Addressed unto the Worshipful, John Philips Esq. Published for the Information of the Inhabitants. Boston, 1690.

"Special Points on Education of Children." In *Bonifacius*, 150–57.

The Stone Cut out of the Mountain. And the Kingdom of God, in Those Maxims of it, that cannot be shaken. Lapis e Monte Excisus. Boston, 1716.

Theopolis Americana. An Essay on the Golden Street Of the Holy City: Publishing, A Testimony against the Corruptions of the Market-Place. Boston, 1710.

Things that Young People should Think upon. Boston, 1700.

The Threefold Paradise of Cotton Mather. An Edition of "Triparadisus." Edited by Reiner Smolinski. Athens: University of Georgia Press, 1995.

"Triparadisus." American Antiquarian Society, Worcester, Mass.

Unum Necessarium Awakenings for the Unregenerate. Or, The Nature and Necessity of Regeneration. Boston, 1693.

Wholesome Words, To Families Visited with Sickness. Boston, 1713.

Winter-Meditations. Directions How to employ the Liesure of the Winter For the Glory of God. Boston, 1693.

Wonderful Works of God Commemorated. Praises Bespoke for the God of Heaven, In a Thanksgiving Sermon. Boston, 1690.

Wonders of the Invisible World. Boston, 1693.

The Young Man Spoken to. Another Essay to Recommend & Inculcate the Maxims of Early Religion, unto Young Persons. Boston, 1712.

Youth Advised. An Essay on the Sins of Youth. Boston, 1719.

REFERENCES

American Antiquarian Society, Worcester, Mass.
    Mather Family Library.
    Mather Family Papers, 1613–1819.
Holmes, Thomas J. *Cotton Mather: A Bibliography of His Works.* 3 vols. 1940. Reprint, Newton, Mass.: Crofton, 1974.
———. *Increase Mather: A Bibliography of His Works.* 2 vols. 1931. Reprint, Mansfield Centre, Conn.: Martino, 2003.
Massachusetts Historical Society, Boston
    Cotton Mather Papers, 1636–1724. MS N-527.
    Mather Family Papers in the Prince Collection, 1635–89. MS N-531.
The Mather Project. matherproject.org.

Tuttle, Julius H. "The Libraries of the Mathers." *Proceedings of the American Antiquarian Society* 20 (1910): 269–356. Reprint, Worcester, Mass.: Davis Press, 1910.

OTHER PRIMARY SOURCES

Anonymous. *The Revolution in New England Justified. And the People there Vindicated From the Aspersions cast upon them By Mr. John Palmer.* Boston, 1691.

Arndt, Johann. *De Vero Christianismo libri quatuor* (1605–10). London, 1708.

Bentley, Richard. *A Confutation of Atheism from the Origin and Frame of the World.* London, 1692, 1693.

———. *The Folly and Unreasonableness of Atheism.* London, 1692.

Bernard, Richard (of Batcombe). *A Guide to Grand-Jury Men.* London, 1627.

St. Bernard of Clairvaux (Bernardus Claraevallensis Abbas). *Sermones in Cantica*, Sermo 38. In *Patrologiae Cursus Complectus: Series Latina.* Vol. 183. Edited by Jacques Paul Migne. Paris: Apud Garnier Fratres, 1879. PL 183. 0974–0977.

Boyle, Robert. *New Experiments Physico-Mechanicall, Touching the Spring of the Air, and its Effects.* Oxford, 1660.

Boylston, Zabdiel, and Cotton Mather. *Some Account Of what is said of Inoculating or Transplanting the Small-Pox.* Boston, 1721.

Brattle, Thomas. "Copy of MS. Letter, [October, 8, 1692] Giving a full and candid Account of the Delusion called Witchcraft, which prevailed in New-England; and of the Judicial Trials and Executions at Salem, in the County of Essex, for that pretended Crime, in 1692. written by Thomas Brattle, F.R.S. and communicated to the Society by Thomas Brattle, Esq. of Cambridge." In *Collections of the Massachusetts Historical Society*, 1st series, 5 (1798): 61–79. Reprint, *Collections*, vol. 5, Boston: John H. Eastburn, 1835.

Brigden, Zechariah. "A breif Explication and proof of the Philolaick Systeme." In *An Almanack of the Coelestial Motions.* Cambridge, Mass., 1659. N.p.

Calef, Robert. *More Wonders of the Invisible World.* N.p., 1700.

Cheyne, George. *Philosophical Principles of Natural and Revealed Religion: In Two Parts.* London, 1705.

Collins, Anthony. *A Discourse of the Grounds and Reason of the Christian Religion.* London, 1724.

Colman, Benjamin. *The Holy Walk and Glorious Translation of Blessed Enoch.* Boston, 1728.

Cotton, John, Jr. *The Correspondence of John Cotton Junior.* Edited by Sheila McIntyre and Len Travers. Boston: Colonial Society of Massachusetts, 2009.

Dickinson, Edmund. *Delphi Phoenicizantes.* Oxford, 1655.

———. *Physica Vetus & Vera: Sive Tractatus de Naturali veritate hexaëmeri Mosaici.* London, 1702.

The Distichs of Cato: A Famous Medieval Textbook. Translated by Wayland Johnson Chase. *University of Wisconsin Studies in the Social Sciences and History* 7 (April 1922): 1–43.

Du Bartas, Guillaume. *Divine Weekes and Workes.* Translated by Josuah Sylvester. London, 1641.

Dudley, Joseph. "An Original Letter from Governor Dudley, to Dr. Increase and Cotton Mather" (February 3, 1707/8). In *Collections of the Massachusetts Historical Society,* 1st series, 3 (1794): 135–37. Reprint, *Collections,* vol. 3, Boston: Munroe and Francis, 1810.

Dustan, Hannah. *A Narrative of a Notable Deliverance from Captivity.* In Cotton Mather, *Humiliations follow'd with Deliverances.* Boston, 1697. 41–50.

Eliot, John, et al. *The Glorious Progress of the Gospel amongst the Indians in New England.* Boston, 1649.

Experience Mayhew's Indian Converts: A Cultural Edition. Edited by Laura Arnold Leibman. Amherst: University of Massachusetts Press, 2008.

Foxe, John. *Actes and Monuments.* London, 1563.

Franklin, Benjamin. *The Autobiography of Benjamin Franklin.* New York: Norton, 2012.

———. "Letter from Benjamin Franklin to Samuel Mather, 12 May 1784." In Miscellaneous Bound Manuscripts, Massachusetts Historical Society, https://www.masshist.org/database/533.

Gale, Theophilus. *The Court of the Gentiles.* 4 vols. London, 1669–78.

Galileo Galilei. "Letter to the Grand Duchess Christina" (1615). In *The Galileo Affair: A Documentary History.* Edited and translated by Maurice A. Finocchiaro. Berkeley: University of California Press, 1989. 87–118.

Gaule, John. *Select Cases of Conscience Touching Witches and Witchcrafts.* London, 1646.

Hale, John. *Modest Enquiry Into the Nature of Witchcraft.* Boston, 1702.

Harvey, William. *Exercitatio Anatomica De Motu Cordis et Sanguinis in Animalibus.* Frankfurt, 1628.

———. *Exercitationes de Generatione Animalium.* London, 1651.

Hutchinson, Thomas. *The History of the Colony of Massachusetts Bay.* Vol. 1. London, 1765.

Josephus, Flavius. *Antiquities of the Jews.* In *The Complete Works of Josephus.* Translated by William Whiston. Grand Rapids, Mich.: Kregel, 1960. 22–426.

Marten, Benjamin. *A New Theory of Consumptions: More especially of Phthisis, or Consumption of the Lungs.* London, 1720.

Mather, Increase. *Angelographia; or, A Discourse Concerning the Nature and Power of the Holy Angels.* Boston, 1696.

———. *Cases of Conscience Concerning evil Spirits Personating Men, Witchcrafts, infallible Proofs of Guilt in such as are accused with that Crime.* Boston, 1693.

———. "A Discourse Concerning the Glorious State of the Church on Earth under the New Jerusalem." In "Increase Mather's 'New Jerusalem': Millennialism in Late Seventeenth-Century New England." Edited by Mason I. Lowance Jr. and David Watters. *Proceedings of the American Antiquarian Society* 87, no. 2 (1977): 343–408.

———. *Dissertation Concerning the Future Conversion of the Jewish Nation.* London, 1709.

———. *An Essay for the Recording of Illustrious Providences.* Boston, 1684.

———. *ΚΟΜΗΤΟΓΡΑΦΙΑ* [*Kometographia*]; *or, A Discourse Concerning Comets; wherein the Nature of Blazing Stars is Enquired into.* Boston, 1683.

———. "An Original Letter from Dr. Increase Mather, to Governour Dudley" (January 20, 1707/8). In *Collections of the Massachusetts Historical Society*, 1st series, 3 (1794): 126–28. Reprint, *Collections*, vol. 3, Boston: Munroe and Francis, 1810.

Mather, Samuel (son). *The Life of the Very Reverend and Learned Cotton Mather D.D. & F.R.S. Late Pastor of the North Church in Boston. Who Died, Feb. 13. 1727/8.* Boston, 1729.

Mather, Samuel (uncle). *The Figures or Types of the Old Testament.* Dublin, 1683. Reprint, London, 1705.

Maimonides, Moses. *The Guide for the Perplexed.* Translated by M. Friedländer. 2nd revised edition. New York: Dover, 1956.

Morton, Charles. *Compendium Physicae ex authoribus extractum* (1687). Boston: D. B. Updike and the Merrymount Press, 1940.

Perkins, William. *A Discourse of the Damned Art of Witchcraft.* Cambridge, Mass., 1608.

Prince, Thomas. *The Departure of Elijah lamented. A Sermon Occasioned By the Great & Publick Loss In the Decease Of the very Reverend & Learned Cotton Mather, D.D. F.R.S.* Boston, 1728.

———. "The Preface." In Samuel Mather, *The Life*. Boston, 1729. 1–6.

Quincy, Josiah. *The History of Harvard University.* 2 vols. Boston: Crosby, Nichols, Lee, 1860.

Randolph, Edward. "Articles Agt Ye Gomt & Company of Ye Mass Bay in New Engn." In *Edward Randolph; Including His Letters and Official Papers.* 5 vols. Boston: Prince Society, 1899. 3:229–30.

Records of the Salem Witch-Hunt. Edited by Bernard Rosenthal. New York: Cambridge University Press, 2009.

Records of the Cambridge Association of Ministers. Proceedings of the Massachusetts Historical Society 17 (1879–80): 262–81.

Rowlandson, Mary. *The Soveraignty and Goodness of God, Together With the Faithfulness of His Promises Displayed; Being a Narrative Of the Captivity and Restoration of Mrs. Mary Rowlandson.* Cambridge, Mass., 1682.

Sewall, Samuel. *Diary of Samuel Sewall, 1674–1729.* 3 vols. *Collections of the Massachusetts Historical Society*, 5th series, 5–7 (1878–82).

Spener, Philipp Jacob. *Pia Desideria: Oder Hertzliches Verlangen.* Franckfurt am Mayn, 1676.

Swarton, Hannah. *A Narrative of Hannah Swarton, Containing Wonderful Passages, relating to her Captivity, and her Deliverance.* In Cotton Mather, *Humiliations follow'd with Deliverances.* Boston, 1697. 51–72.

Virgil. *Eclogues, Georgics, Aeneid.* 2 vols. Translated by H. R. Fairclough. Cambridge, Mass.: Harvard University Press, 1935.

Walter, Thomas. *The Grounds and Rules of Music.* Boston, 1721.

Whiston, William. *The Accomplishment of Scripture Prophecies. Being Eight Sermons Preach'd at the Cathedral Church of St. Paul, In the Year 1707.* Cambridge, 1708.

———. *An Essay Toward Restoring the True Text of the Old Testament.* London, 1722.

Wigglesworth, Michael. *The Day of Doom; or, A Poetical Description of the Great and Last Judgment.* Boston, 1662.

Winthrop, John. *The Journal of John Winthrop, 1630–1649.* Edited by R. S. Dunn, J. Savage, and L. Yeandle. Cambridge, Mass.: Belknap Press of Harvard University Press, 1996.

SECONDARY SOURCES AND FURTHER READING

Amory, Hugh. "A Note on Statistics." In *A History of the Book in America*, vol. 1, *The Colonial Book in the Atlantic World.* Chapel Hill: University of North Carolina Press, 2007. 504–18.

Bailyn, Bernard. *The New England Merchants in the Seventeenth Century.* 1955. Reprint, Cambridge, Mass.: Harvard University Press, 1979.

Beall, Otho T., and Richard H. Shryock. *Cotton Mather: First Significant Figure in American Medicine.* Baltimore: Johns Hopkins University Press, 1954.

Bentley, William. "Description of the History of Salem." *Collections of the Massachusetts Historical Society for the Year 1798*, 1st series, 6 (1800): 212–77.

Benz, Ernst. "Ecumenical Relations Between Boston Puritanism and German Pietism: Cotton Mather and August Hermann Francke." *Harvard Theological Review* 54, no. 4 (1961): 159–63.

——. "Pietist and Puritan Sources of Early Protestant World Missions." *Church History* 20, no. 2 (1951): 28–55.

Bercovitch, Sacvan. *The American Jeremiad.* Madison: University of Wisconsin Press, 1978.

Bernhard, Virginia. "Cotton Mather's 'Most Unhappy Wife.'" *New England Quarterly* 60, no. 3 (1987): 341–62.

Blake, John H. *Public Health in the Town of Boston, 1630–1822.* Cambridge, Mass.: Harvard University Press, 1959.

Bosco, Ronald A. "Introduction." In *Paterna. The Autobiography of Cotton Mather.* Edited by Ronald A. Bosco. Delmar, N.Y.: Scholars' Facsimiles and Reprints, 1976. iii–lxvii.

Boylston, Arthur. "The Origins of Inoculation." *Journal of the Royal Society of Medicine* 105, no. 7 (July 2012): 309–13.

Breitwieser, Mitchell R. *Cotton Mather and Benjamin Franklin: The Price of Representative Personality.* Cambridge: Cambridge University Press, 1984.

Bremer, Francis. *John Winthrop: America's Forgotten Founding Father.* New York: Oxford University Press, 2005.

Brown, Thomas H. "The African Connection: Cotton Mather and the Smallpox Epidemic of 1721–22." *Journal of the American Medical Association* 260, no. 15 (1988): 2247–49.

Broyles, Michael. *"Music of the Highest Class": Elitism and Populism in Antebellum Boston.* New Haven, Conn.: Yale University Press, 1992.

Carnegie, Andrew. *The Gospel of Wealth.* Edited by Edward C. Kirkland. Cambridge, Mass.: Belknap Press of Harvard University Press, 1965.

Cogley, Rick W. *John Eliot's Mission to the Indians Before King Philip's War.* Cambridge, Mass.: Harvard University Press, 1999.

Corrigan, John. *The Prism of Pietism: Catholic Congregational Clergy at the Beginnings of the Enlightenment.* New York: Oxford University Press, 1991.

Coss, Stephen. *The Fever of 1721: The Epidemic That Revolutionized Medicine and American Politics.* New York: Simon and Schuster, 2016.

"Cotton Mather Papers. 1636–1724. Guide to the Microfilm Edition." P-207 (part 1). Massachusetts Historical Society, Boston.

Duffy, John. *Epidemics in Colonial America.* Baton Rouge: Louisiana State University Press, 1971.

Eames, Wilberforce. "Introduction." In *The Bay Psalm Book Being a Facsimile Reprint of the First Edition, Printed by Stephen Daye At Cambridge, in New England in 1640.* New York: Dodd, Mead, 1903. v–xvii.

EJ: Encyclopedia Judaica. 26 vols. Jerusalem: Keter, 1971–72.

Forde, Georgiana M. *Missionary Adventures: A Simple History of the Society for Propagating the Gospel.* London: Skeffington and Son, 1911.

Francis, Richard. *Judge Sewall's Apology: The Salem Witch Trials and the Forming of an American Conscience.* New York: HarperCollins, 2005.

Francke, Kuno. "The Beginning of Cotton Mather's Correspondence with August Hermann Francke." *Philological Quarterly* 5, no. 3 (1926): 193–95.

——. "Cotton Mather and August Hermann Francke." *Harvard Studies and Notes in Philosophy and Literature* 5 (1896): 57–67.

——. "Further Documents Concerning Cotton Mather and August Hermann Francke." *Americana Germanica* 1 (1897): 31–66.

Friedman, Lawrence M. *Crime and Punishment in American History.* New York: Basic Books, 1993.

Gelinas, Helen K. "Regaining Paradise: Cotton Mather's 'Biblia Americana' and the Daughters of Eve." In *Cotton Mather and Biblia Americana—America's First Bible Commentary: Essays in Reappraisal.* Edited by Reiner Smolinski and Jan Stievermann. Tübingen, Germany: Mohr Siebeck, 2010. 463–94.

Gildrie, Richard P. *The Profane, the Civil, and the Godly: The Reformation of Manners in Orthodox New England, 1679–1749.* University Park: Pennsylvania State University Press, 1994.

Glasson, Travis. "The Society for the Propagation of the Gospel in Foreign Parts." *Oxford Bibliographies Online.* oxforddnb.com.

Goldberg, Dror. "The Massachusetts Paper Money of 1690." *Journal of Economic History* 69, no. 4 (2009): 1092–1106.

Green, A., and V. Viaene, eds. *Religious Internationals in the Modern World.* New York: Palgrave Macmillan, 2012.

Greven, Philip. *Spare the Child: The Religious Roots of Punishment and the Psychological Impact of Physical Abuse.* New York: Knopf, 1991.

Haffenden, Philip S. *New England in the English Nation, 1689–1713.* Oxford: Clarendon Press, 1974.

Hall, David D. *Worlds of Wonder, Days of Judgment: Popular Religious Belief in Early New England.* New York: Knopf, 1989.

Hall, Michael G. *Edward Randolph and the American Colonies, 1676–1703*. 1960. Reprint, New York: Norton, 1969.

——. *The Last American Puritan: The Life of Increase Mather*. Middletown, Conn.: Wesleyan University Press, 1988.

Halttunen, Karen. "Cotton Mather and the Meaning of Suffering in the *Magnalia Christi Americana*." *Journal of American Studies* 12, no. 3 (December 1978): 311–29.

Hansen, Chadwick. *Witchcraft at Salem*. 1969. Reprint, New York: New American Library, 1970.

Harper, George W. *A People So Favored of God: Boston's Congregational Churches and Their Pastors, 1710–1760*. 2nd edition. Eugene, Ore.: Wipf and Stock, 2007.

Haykin, Michael A. G. and Kenneth J. Stewart. *The Advent of Evangelicalism: Exploring Historical Continuities*. Nashville, Tenn.: B and H Academic, 2008.

Holifield, E. Brooks. "The Abridging of Cotton Mather." In *Cotton Mather and Biblia Americana—America's First Bible Commentary: Essays in Reappraisal*. Edited by Reiner Smolinski and Jan Stievermann. Tübingen, Germany: Mohr Siebeck, 2010. 83–109.

Hutchins, Zachary McLeod. *Inventing Eden: Primitivism, Millennialism, and the Making of New England*. New York: Oxford University Press, 2014.

Jones, Gordon W. "Introduction." In *The Angel of Bethesda: An Essay upon the Common Maladies of Mankind*. Edited by Gordon W. Jones. Barre, Mass.: American Antiquarian Society, 1972. xi–xl.

Kass, Amalie M. "Boston's Historic Smallpox Epidemic." *Massachusetts Historical Review* 14 (2012): 1–51.

Kennedy, Rick. *Cotton Mather, The First American Evangelical*. Grand Rapids, Mich.: Eerdmans, 2015.

Kittredge, George Lyman. "Cotton Mather's Scientific Communications to the Royal Society." *Proceedings of the American Antiquarian Society*, new series, 26 (1916): 18–57.

——. "Some Lost Works of Cotton Mather." *Proceedings of the Massachusetts Historical Society* 45 (1912): 418–79.

Koo, Kathryn S. "Strangers in the House of God: Cotton Mather, Onesimus, and an Experiment in Christian Slaveholding." *Proceedings of the American Antiquarian Society* 117 (2007): 143–76.

Levin, David. *Cotton Mather: The Young Life of the Lord's Remembrancer, 1663–1703*. Cambridge, Mass.: Harvard University Press, 1978.

——. *Forms of Uncertainty: Essays in Historical Criticism*. Charlottesville: University Press of Virginia, 1992.

Lindberg, Carter, ed. *The Pietist Theologians*. Malden, Mass.: Blackwell, 2005.

Lovejoy, David S. *The Glorious Revolution in America*. Middletown, Conn.: Wesleyan University Press, 1986.

Lovelace, Richard F. *The American Pietism of Cotton Mather: Origins of American Evangelicalism*. Grand Rapids, Mich.: Eerdmans, 1979.

Mages, Michael J. *Magnalia Christi Americana: America's Literary Old Testament*. Bethesda, Md.: International Scholars, 1999.

Marten, James. *Children in Colonial America*. New York: New York University Press, 2007.

Mather, Horace E. *Lineage of Rev. Richard Mather.* Hartford, Conn.: Case, Lockwood and Brainard, 1890.

McKay, David P. "Cotton Mather's Unpublished Singing Sermon." *New England Quarterly* 48, no. 3 (1975): 410–22.

Middlekauff, Robert. *The Mathers: Three Generations of Puritan Intellectuals, 1596–1728.* New York: Oxford University Press, 1971.

Miller, Perry. *The New England Mind: From Colony to Province.* Cambridge, Mass.: Harvard University Press, 1952.

———. "A Note on the *Manuductio ad Ministerium.*" In Thomas J. Holmes, *Cotton Mather: A Bibliography of His Works.* 3 vols. 1940; reprint, Newton, Mass.: Crofton, 1974. 2:630–36.

Minardi, Margot. "The Boston Inoculation Controversy of 1721–1722: An Incident in the History of Race." *William and Mary Quarterly,* 3rd series, 61, no. 1 (2004): 47–76.

Minkema, Kenneth P. "Reforming Harvard: Cotton Mather on Education at Cambridge." *New England Quarterly* 87, no. 2 (June 2014): 319–40.

Monaghan, E. Jennifer. *Learning to Read and Write in Colonial America.* Amherst: University of Massachusetts Press, 2005.

Morens, David M. "The Past Is Never Dead—Measles Epidemic, Boston, Massachusetts, 1713." *Emerging Infectious Diseases Journal* 21, no. 7 (2015): 1257–60.

Morgan, Edmund S. *The Puritan Dilemma: The Story of John Winthrop.* Boston: Little, Brown, 1958.

Morison, Samuel Eliot. *Harvard College in the Seventeenth Century.* 2 vols. Cambridge, Mass.: Harvard University Press, 1936.

———. *The Intellectual Life of Colonial New England.* 1936. Reprint, Ithaca, N.Y.: Cornell University Press, 1960.

Music, David W. "Cotton Mather and Congregational Singing in Puritan New England." *Studies in Puritan American Spirituality* 2, no. 2 (1992): 1–30.

Noll, Mark A. *The Rise of Evangelicalism.* Downer's Grove, Ill.: InterVarsity, 2003.

Peterson, Mark. *The City-State of Boston: The Rise and Fall of an Atlantic Power, 1630–1865.* Princeton, N.J.: Princeton University Press, 2019.

Poole, William Frederick. "Cotton Mather and Salem Witchcraft." *North American Review* 223 (April 1869): 337–97.

Pope, Robert G. *The Half-Way Covenant: Church Membership in Puritan New England.* Princeton, N.J.: Princeton University Press, 1969.

Post, Constance J. *Signs of the Times in Cotton Mather's* Paterna: *A Study of Puritan Autobiography.* New York: AMS Press, 2000.

Powers, Edwin. *Crime and Punishment in Early Massachusetts, 1620–1692: A Documentary History.* Boston: Beacon Press, 1966.

Quackenbos, George P. *Illustrated School History of the United States.* 1857; reprint, New York: D. Appleton and Co., 1877.

A Report of the Record Commissioners of the City of Boston, Containing the Boston Records from 1700–1728. Boston: Rockwell and Churchill, 1883.

Rivett, Sarah. *The Science of the Soul in Colonial New England.* Chapel Hill: University of North Carolina Press, 2011.

Robbins, Chandler. *A History of the Second Church, or Old North, in Boston*. Boston, 1852.

Robbins, R. D. C. "Cotton Mather and the Witchcraft Delusion: The Views of Cotton Mather and His Age Concerning Unseen and Spiritual Agency." In *Bibliotheca Sacra* 34, no. 135 (1877): 473–513.

Rooy, Sidney H. *The Theology of Missions in the Puritan Traditions. A Study of Representative Puritans: Richard Sibbes, Richard Baxter, John Eliot, Cotton Mather and Jonathan Edwards*. Grand Rapids, Mich.: Eerdman's, 1965.

Scheiding, Oliver. "The World as Parish: Cotton Mather, August Hermann Francke, and Transatlantic Religious Networks." In *Cotton Mather and Biblia Americana—America's First Bible Commentary: Essays in Reappraisal*. Edited by Reiner Smolinski and Jan Stievermann. Tübingen, Germany: Mohr Siebeck, 2010. 131–66.

Silva, Cristobal. *Miraculous Plagues: An Epidemiology of Early New England Narrative*. New York: Oxford University Press, 2011.

Silver, Rollo G. "Financing the Publication of Early New England Sermons." *Studies in Bibliography* 11 (1958): 163–79.

Silverman, Kenneth. "Cotton Mather and the Reform of Puritan Psalmody." *Seventeenth-Century News* 34 (Summer–Fall 1976): 53–57.

———. "Cotton Mather's Foreign Correspondence." *Early American Literature* 3, no. 3 (Winter 1968–69): 172–85.

———. *The Life and Times of Cotton Mather*. New York: Harper and Row, 1984.

Smolinski, Reiner. "Cotton Mather." *Oxford Bibliographies Online*. Edited by Jackson Bryer and Paul Lauter. New York: Oxford University Press, 2012. www.oxfordbibliographies .com.

———. *Cotton Mather: A Life*. New Haven, Conn.: Yale University Press, forthcoming.

———. "*Israel Redivivus*: The Eschatological Limits of Puritan Typology." *New England Quarterly* 63 (September 1990): 357–95.

Smolinski, Reiner, and Jan Stievermann, eds. *Cotton Mather and Biblia Americana—America's First Bible Commentary: Essays in Reappraisal*. Tübingen, Germany: Mohr Siebeck, 2010.

Solberg, Winton U. "Introduction." In *Cotton Mather: The Christian Philosopher*. Urbana: University of Illinois Press, 1994. xix–cxxxix.

Sossin, Jack M. *English America and the Restoration Monarchy of Charles II: Transatlantic Politics, Commerce, and Kinship*. Lincoln: University of Nebraska Press, 1980.

———. *English America and the Revolution of 1688: Royal Administration and the Structure of Provincial Government*. Lincoln: University of Nebraska Press, 1982.

Splitter, Wolfgang. "The Fact and Fiction of Cotton Mather's Correspondence with German Pietist August Hermann Francke." *New England Quarterly* 2010, no. 1 (2010): 102–22.

Stearns, Raymond Phineas. "Colonial Fellows of the Royal Society of London, 1661–1788." *Osiris* 8 (1948): 73–121.

———. *Science in the British Colonies of America*. Urbana: University of Illinois Press, 1970.

Stievermann, Jan. "The Genealogy of Races and the Problem of Slavery in Cotton Mather's 'Biblica Americana.'" In *Cotton Mather and Biblia Americana—America's First Bible*

Commentary: Essays in Reappraisal. Edited by Reiner Smolinski and Jan Stievermann. Tübingen, German: Mohr Siebeck, 2010. 515–76.

———. "General Introduction." In *Cotton Mather and Biblia Americana—America's First Bible Commentary: Essays in Reappraisal.* Edited by Reiner Smolinski and Jan Stievermann. Tübingen, Germany: Mohr Siebeck, 2010. 1–58.

———. *Prophecy, Piety, and the Problems of Historicity: Interpreting the Hebrew Scriptures in Cotton Mather's Biblia Americana.* Tübingen, Germany: Mohr Siebeck, 2016.

———. "Writing 'to Conquer All Things': Cotton Mather's *Magnalia Christi Americana* and the Quandary of *Copia*." *Early American Literature* 39, no. 2 (2004): 263–97.

Strom, Jonathan, et al., eds. *Pietism in Germany and North America, 1680–1820.* Farnham, U.K.: Ashgate, 2009.

Szasz, Margaret C. *Indian Education in the American Colonies, 1607–1783.* Lincoln: University of Nebraska Press, 1988.

Tindol, Robert. "Getting the Pox Off All Their Houses: Cotton Mather and the Rhetoric of Puritan Science." *Early American Literature* 46, no. 1 (2011): 1–23.

Toulouse, Teresa. *The Captive's Position: Female Narrative, Male Identity, and Royal Authority in Colonial New England.* Philadelphia: University of Pennsylvania Press, 2006.

Tuttle, Julius Herbert. "The Libraries of the Mathers." *Proceedings of the American Antiquarian Society* 20, no. 2 (April 1910): 269–356.

Ulrich, Laurel Thatcher. *Good Wives: Image and Reality in the Lives of Women in Northern New England, 1650–1750.* New York: Vintage, 1982.

Upham, Charles W. *Lectures on Witchcraft, Comprising a History of the Delusion in Salem, in 1692.* 2nd edition. Boston: Carter, Hendee, and Babcock, 1831.

———. *Salem Witchcraft; with an Account of Salem Village, and a History of Opinions on Witchcraft and Kindred Subjects.* 2 vols. Boston: Wiggin and Lunt, 1867.

Valeri, Mark. *Heavenly Merchandise: How Religion Shaped Commerce in Puritan America.* Princeton, N.J.: Princeton University Press, 2010.

Ward, W. R. *Early Evangelicalism: A Global Intellectual History, 1670–1789.* Cambridge: Cambridge University Press, 2006.

Warner, Margaret H. "Vindicating the Minister's Medical Role: Cotton Mather's Concept of the *Nishmath-Chajim* and the Spiritualization of Medicine." *Journal of the History of Medicine and Allied Science* 36, no. 3 (1981): 278–95.

Watson, Patricia Ann. *The Angelical Conjunction: The Preacher-Physician of Colonial New England.* Knoxville: University of Tennessee Press, 1991.

Weisman, Richard. *Witchcraft, Magic, and Religion in 17th-Century Massachusetts.* Amherst: University of Massachusetts Press, 1984.

Wendell, Barret. *Cotton Mather.* Introduction by Professor David Levin. 1891. Reprint, New York: Chelsea House, 1980.

Willard, Emma. *History of the United States.* 1826. New and enlarged edition. New York: A. S. Barnes, 1868.

Williams, Gareth. *Angel of Death: The Story of Smallpox.* New York: Palgrave MacMillan, 2010.

Williams, Tony. *The Pox and the Covenant: Mather, Franklin, and the Epidemic That Changed America's Destiny.* Naperville, Ill.: Sourcebooks, 2010.

Winn, Christian, et al., eds. *The Pietist Impulse in Christianity.* Eugene, Ore.: Pickwick, 2011.

Winship, Michael P. *Seers of God: Puritan Providentialism in the Restoration and Early Enlightenment.* Baltimore: Johns Hopkins University Press, 1996.

Winslow, Ola E. *A Destroying Angel: The Conquest of the Smallpox in Colonial Boston.* Boston: Houghton Mifflin, 1974.

Wisecup, Kelly. "African Medical Knowledge, the Plain Style, and Satire in the 1721 Boston Inoculation Controversy." *Early American Literature* 46, no. 1 (2011): 25–50.

Woody, Kennerly M. "Biographical Notes to Cotton Mather's 'Manuductio ad Ministerium.'" *Early American Literature* 6, no. 1, Supplement (Spring 1971): 1–98.

GENERAL INDEX

INDEX OF NAMES